Wales

Anglesey & the
North Coast
(p270)

Snowdonia &
the Llŷn
(p226)

Aberystwyth &
Mid-Wales
(p190)

St Davids &
Pembrokeshire
(p152)

Swansea,
Gower &
Carmarthenshire
(p126)

Brecon Beacons &
Southeast Wales
(p82)

Cardiff ★
(p50)

Kerry Walker, Peter Dragicevich, Anna Kaminski, Luke Waterson

PLAN YOUR TRIP

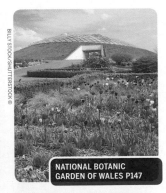

NATIONAL BOTANIC
GARDEN OF WALES P147

WALES MILLENNIUM
CENTRE P62

ON THE ROAD

Contents

COVID-19

We have re-checked every business in this book before publication to ensure that it is still open after the COVID-19 outbreak. However, the economic and social impacts of COVID-19 will continue to be felt long after the outbreak has been contained, and many businesses, services and events referenced in this guide may experience ongoing restrictions. Some businesses may be temporarily closed, have changed their opening hours and services, or require bookings; some unfortunately could have closed permanently. We suggest you check with venues before visiting for the latest information.

Right: Tryfan,
Ogwen Valley
(p251)

Why I Love Wales

Wales stole my heart for good four years ago when I moved to a lonely valley north of the Brecon Beacons, where the moors meet the mountains and the meadows glisten green. The screech of red kites are my wake-up call, a hundred bleating sheep lull me to sleep and the skies are some of the country's starriest. Wales is so darned beautiful that you can forgive it the relentless rain. For such a small country, it has an almost obscene amount of wilderness, not to mention ravishing beaches, a one-of-a-kind culture and epoch-defining history.

By Kerry Walker, Writer
🐦 @kerryawalker 📷 undiscoveredwal
For more about our writers, see p352

JOE DANIEL PRICE/GETTY IMAGES ©

Wales

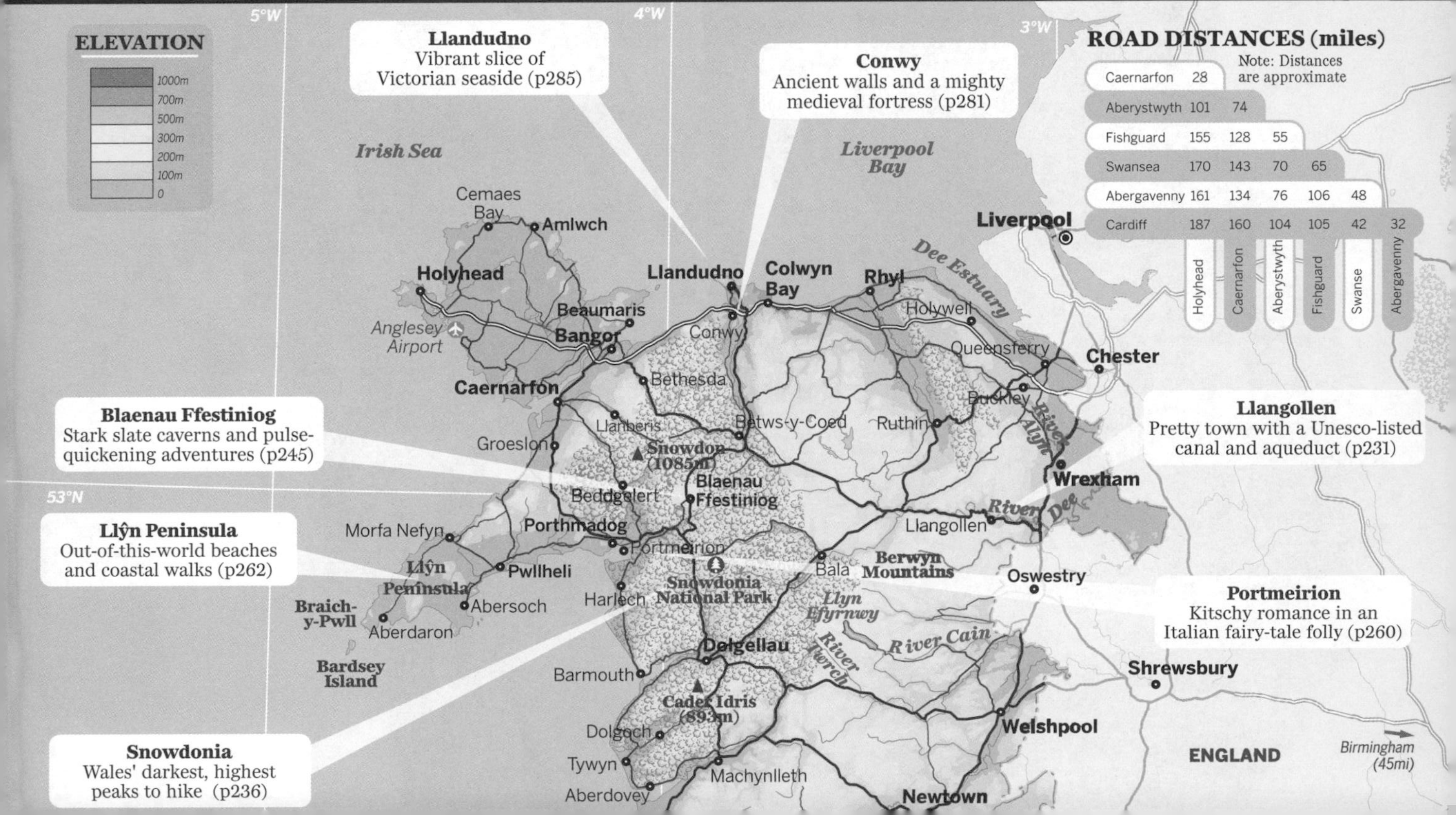

ROAD DISTANCES (miles)

Note: Distances are approximate

	Holyhead	Caernarfon	Aberystwyth	Fishguard	Swansea	Abergavenny
Caernarfon	28					
Aberystwyth	101	74				
Fishguard	155	128	55			
Swansea	170	143	70	65		
Abergavenny	161	134	76	106	48	
Cardiff	187	160	104	105	42	32

Llandudno
Vibrant slice of Victorian seaside (p285)

Conwy
Ancient walls and a mighty medieval fortress (p281)

Llangollen
Pretty town with a Unesco-listed canal and aqueduct (p231)

Portmeirion
Kitschy romance in an Italian fairy-tale folly (p260)

Blaenau Ffestiniog
Stark slate caverns and pulse-quickening adventures (p245)

Llŷn Peninsula
Out-of-this-world beaches and coastal walks (p262)

Snowdonia
Wales' darkest, highest peaks to hike (p236)

ENGLAND

Irish Sea

Liverpool Bay

Dee Estuary

Birmingham
(45mi)

50 km
25 miles

N

5°W
4°W
3°W
53°N

Liverpool
Chester
Queensferry
Holywell
Rhyl
Ruthin
Wrexham
Oswestry
Shrewsbury
Welshpool
Newtown
Machynlleth
Llangollen
Berwyn Mountains
Bala
Llyn Efyrnwy
Dolgellau
Cadair Idris
(893m)
Barmouth
Dolgoch
Tywyn
Aberdovey
Harlech
Snowdonia National Park
Snowdon
(1085m)
Betws-y-Coed
Blaenau Ffestiniog
Colwyn Bay
Llandudno
Conwy
Bethesda
Bangor
Beaumaris
Amlwch
Cemaes Bay
Holyhead
Anglesey Airport
Caernarfon
Llanberis
Groeslon
Beddgelert
Porthmadog
Pwllheli
Abersoch
Morfa Nefyn
Llŷn Peninsula
Braich-y-Pwll
Aberdaron
Bardsey Island
River Alyn
River Dee
River Ceiriog
River Cain
River Efyrnwy
River Twrch

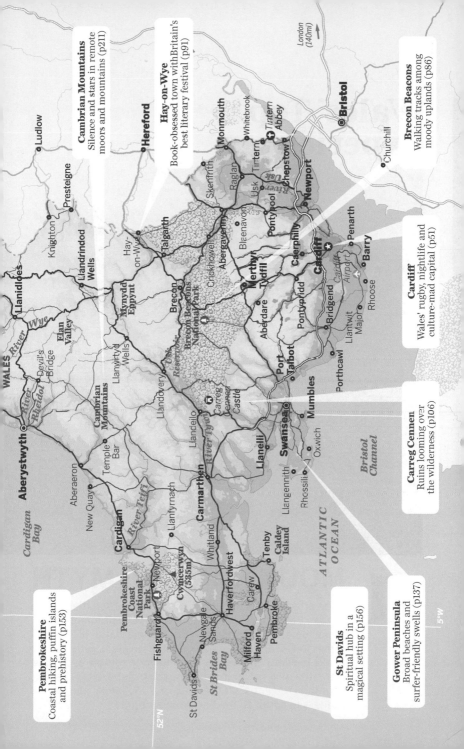

Cambrian Mountains
Silence and stars in remote moors and mountains (p211)

Hay-on-Wye
Book-obsessed town with Britain's best literary festival (p91)

Brecon Beacons
Walking tracks among moody uplands (p86)

Cardiff
Wales' rugby, nightlife and culture-mad capital (p51)

Carreg Cennen
Ruins looming over the wilderness (p106)

Gower Peninsula
Broad beaches and surfer-friendly swells (p137)

St Davids
Spiritual hub in a magical setting (p156)

Pembrokeshire
Coastal hiking, puffin islands and prehistory (p153)

London (140mi)

Ludlow
Presteigne
Knighton
Hereford
Llandrindod Wells
Hay-on-Wye
Talgarth
Monmouth
Whitebrook
Tintern Abbey
Raglan
Skenfrith
Usk
Tintern
Chepstow
Bristol
Churchill
Crickhowell
Abergavenny
Bleenavon
Pontypool
Newport
WALES
River Wye
Llanidloes
Elan Valley
Devil's Bridge
River Rheidol
Mynydd Epynt
Brecon
Usk Reservoir
Brecon Beacons National Park
Merthyr Tydfil
Aberdare
Caerphilly
Cardiff
Penarth
Barry
Cardiff Airport
Rhoose
Aberystwyth
Llanwrtyd Wells
Llandovery
Carreg Cennen Castle
River Tywi
Pontypridd
Bridgend
Llantwit Major
Port Talbot
Porthcawl
Cardigan Bay
Temple Bar
Aberaeron
New Quay
Cardigan
River Teifi
Llanfynach
Carmarthen
Llandeilo
Llanelli
Swansea
Mumbles
Oxwich
Bristol Channel
ATLANTIC OCEAN
Llangennith
Rhossili
Pembrokeshire Coast National Park
Newport
Cwmcerwyn (535m)
Whitland
Haverfordwest
Carew
Tenby
Caldey Island
Fishguard
Newgale Sands
Milford Haven
Pembroke
St Davids
St Brides Bay
52°N
5°W

Wales' Top Experiences

JOE DANIEL PRICE/GETTY IMAGES ©

1 MOUNTAINS OF MYTH

Soon after crossing the English–Welsh border, the Brecon Beacons (pictured above) raise their mighty fins in welcome. Further north in Snowdonia National Park things get wilder and more mountainous still, with gnarly peaks to climb. Choose a clear day for a ramble and enjoy views that will set your spirits soaring higher than the country's red kites. Or for more of a challenge, join fell runners to sprint to the Snowdon summit.

Snowdon

You won't hike alone, but don't let that deter you from clambering up Snowdon, Wales' loftiest peak at 1085m. On cloud-free days you'll be flabbergasted by out-of-this-world views, which reach over ridge and shimmering lake to Ireland's shores. p255

Pen-y-Fan

Lifting above the Brecon Beacons like a mighty sail, this bald, dramatic, 886m-high mountain sends out a siren call to peak baggers. Puff to the top or, even better, hook onto the horseshoe walk to tick off four summits. p106

Cader Idris

Crowning the horizon in the south of Snowdonia, this incredible hulk of a mountain takes its name from Idris (a legendary giant). The views from the rocky summit are top-of-the-beanstalk stuff, with glacial lake Llyn Cau glimmering far below. p241

2 COASTAL PATHS

Over stile and through kissing gate, past ivy-draped wood and waterfall, through fishing village and seaside town – the coastal footpath rimming western Wales is spirit-liftingly beautiful. Taking in the entire swoop of the country's coastline, the 870-mile Wales Coast Path rambles from hidden bays to countless miles of dune-backed sands. In spring and summer, everything bursts into flower and wildlife peaks.

Pembrokeshire Coast Path

This 186-mile coastal path is an absolute beauty, revealing the coast's most off-the-radar nooks and crannies, from secluded coves to seal-basked rocks, surf-lashed beaches and stone circles. p173

Anglesey Coast Path

Little is more satisfying than hiking around an entire island. This 140-mile circular walk (pictured above left) takes in brooding sea views, lighthouses, medieval castles, puffins, beaches and more. p300

Llŷn Coastal Path

Where Wales slings its northwestern hook into the wild Irish Sea, the Llŷn Peninsula makes for profound walking. This 110-mile trail (pictured above right) opens up surreally lovely coastscapes. p263

3 CASTLE COUNTRY

No country on Earth has more castles than Wales. From romantic, crumbling, ivy-strangled ruins astride lonely hilltops to World Heritage medieval fortresses, you are never far from the next *castell*. Wherever you are heading, these fortifications lift the gaze and their turbulent histories fire the imagination.

Caerphilly

High, mighty, moated and medieval, this whopping great castle looks freshly minted for a fairy tale with its riot of turrets and towers. p125

Caernarfon

Part of Edward I's 'iron ring' of castles – now forming a Unesco World Heritage Site – this formidable medieval fortress is possibly the fairest of them all. p274

Carreg Cennen

'Wow' is the word that leaps to the lips when you first clock this dramatically positioned fortress, guarding a lonely stretch of Brecon Beacons National Park. p106

4 FOOD AT THE SOURCE

HANS GEEL/SHUTTERSTOCK ©

One of the true joys of Wales is tasting sensational local produce at the source. Snowdonia's pungent cheddars, sublimely fresh Pembrokeshire seafood and Brecon's venison is just tip-of-the-iceberg stuff. Nowadays you'll find everything from craft breweries and small-scale gin and whisky distilleries to coffee roasteries in former coal-mining towns and wine in vineyards oblivious to a bit of rain in this food- and drink-mad land.

Coaltown Coffee

Paying tribute to South Wales' coal mining past, this small-batch, sustainability-focused roastery and cafe has given Ammanford seriously good coffee and an air of newfound cool. p147

Lobster and Môr

Picnic on the beach in Little Haven? Stop by this Pembrokeshire deli-cafe for a brioche stuffed with boat-fresh lobster, crab sandwiches, seaweed-infused ales and local cheeses. p188

Black Mountains Smokery

In the foothills of the Black Mountains, this place gently smokes salmon, chicken, duck, quail, trout and haddock over Welsh oak. For more insight, join a smokery tour. p99

5

INDUSTRIAL HERITAGE

To tap into Wales' soul, dig deep into its enthralling industrial heritage. Many former coal and slate mines and ironworks, once the backbone of the country's industry, have been born again as insightful attractions and pulse-racing activities. These skip from underground tours in mining shafts to heritage parks, museums, and even subterranean trampolines.

INTREEGUE PHOTOGRAPHY/SHUTTERSTOCK ©

CROWN COPYRIGHT (2021) VISIT WALES ©

GAIL JOHNSON/SHUTTERSTOCK ©

Blaenavon

Get a taster of what coal-mining life was really like with guides who once worked the black seam at Big Pit (pictured top left) and explore the well-preserved ironworks of this Unesco World Heritage Site. p123

National Slate Museum

At the foot of Snowdon, the austere cliffs of Llanberis' former slate quarry set the scene for this engrossing museum (pictured above left), zooming in on slate mining in Victorian times. p253

Blaenau Ffestiniog

Blaenau once put a roof over Britain's head with its booming 19th-century slate industry. Now you can visit a slate mine and bounce on giant trampolines in cathedral-sized caverns. p245 Above: Zip World Slate Caverns (p246)

6

EPIC ROAD TRIPS

Where will that lonely single-track lane take you? Wales is braided with narrow back lanes that thrust you straight into the heart of the most phenomenal mountain, moorland or coastal scenery. Get behind the wheel for a gear-crunching, sheep-dodging, stop-the-car-and-grab-the-camera road trip to remember.

Coastal Way

One of three national driving routes, the 180-mile Coastal Way loops around Cardigan Bay to sublime beaches, wildlife-rich islands, prehistoric hill forts and wave-hammered headlands. p159

Gospel Pass

Crunch gears as you drive through the off-the-radar Vale of Ewyas in the Black Mountains (pictured top left), over brutally wild, windswept moorland to the 549m Gospel Pass, Wales' highest road. p91

Abergwesyn Pass

Twenty miles seems like nothing on paper, but you'll want to go slowly on this drive from Llanwrtyd Wells to Tregaron, which thrusts you into some of the starkest moors and mountains in the Cambrian Mountains. p213 Left: River Irfon, Abergwesyn Pass

7 BEACH-HOPPING

Cornwall gets the hype when it comes to Britain's best beaches, but – trust us – Wales is every bit as ravishing, albeit with just a trickle of the visitors. We're talking childhood fantasy stuff: from deliciously hidden, cliff-rimmed coves and surf-battered bays in Pembrokeshire and Ceredigion, to Snowdonia's wild, broad beaches of butterscotch sand and the Gower's rolling dunes and soul-stirring views.

Porthor

Remote and gorgeous, this arc of pale sand on the north coast (pictured below right) of the Llŷn Peninsula has sands that 'whistle' underfoot. Keep a close lookout for seals, dolphins and porpoises offshore. p267

JOHNNY GREIG/GETTY IMAGES ©

FULCANELLI/SHUTTERSTOCK ©

Rhossili

So precious it is guarded by a dragon, this three-mile curve of golden sand on the Gower is ravishing. Tiptoe across dunes to the shipwrecked remains of the *Helvetica*. p140

Barafundle Bay

Like all of the most enchanting beaches, Pembrokeshire's Barafundle (pictured bottom right) can only be reached on foot. Head over the clifftop and down steps to this crescent of cliff-backed, straw-coloured sand. p179

8 RURAL PUBS

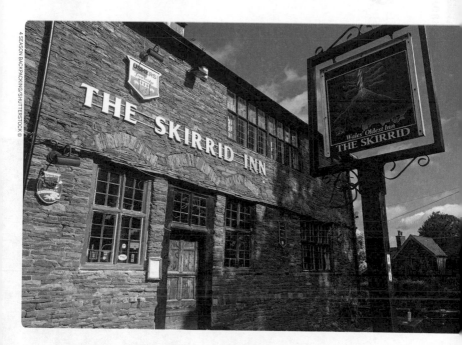

Cornerstones of the community, Wales' pubs charm with history creaking from timber beams, real ales, hearty grub and stories aplenty. From the boozers that inspired poet Dylan Thomas' pen in Swansea; to old coaching inns in the Brecons, where thirsty drovers once hung out; and Snowdonia's stone-walled taverns, which round out a bracing hike perfectly – there's a pint with your name on it.

Skirrid Mountain Inn

With its sagging beams and inglenook fireplace, this medieval dream of a 900-year-old tavern in the Black Mountains claims to be Wales' oldest and most haunted boozer. p91

Sloop Inn

A salty seadog of a Pembrokeshire tavern full of timber beams, nautical knick-knacks and coastal character. Going strong since 1743, it's a cracking spot for a pint and fish supper. p164

Pen-y-Gwryd

The stuff of mountain legend as the 1953 Everest training base, this pretty Georgian coaching inn at Snowdon's foot is a cracking choice for Welsh ales, hearty food and banter. p257

9 NATURAL WONDERS

Vast, lonely moors; great rivers and forests; peaks and valleys; and lakes, beaches and islands are all wrapped up in this one tiny country. In amongst them are natural wonders that enchant: from gorges, waterfalls, lagoons and rock stacks to moss-draped woodlands of sprite-like fantasy.

RICHARD WHITCOMBE/SHUTTERSTOCK ©

PANDA296/SHUTTERSTOCK ©

HELEN HOTSON/SHUTTERSTOCK ©

Ystradfellte

Wander through ivy-draped, fern-brushed forest that looks like a figment of Tolkien's imagination to four waterfalls, including the wispy Sgwd-yr-Eira (Waterfall of the Snow), which you can walk behind. p107

Blue Lagoon

Wild swimmers and cliff divers are in their element at this surreally turquoise blue lagoon in a sheer-sided flooded quarry in Abereiddi, just north of St Davids. p162

Fairy Glen

Sprites are said to inhabit the Fairy Glen, deep in Snowdonia's rugged heart. The River Conwy tumbles in rapids and falls through this narrow, sheer, thickly wooded dingle on the fringes of Betws-y-Coed. p247

10 ROMANCING THE STONES

CHARLES BOWMAN/SHUTTERSTOCK ©

Tintern Abbey

Rising romantically above the River Wye, the evocative ruins of this former Cistercian abbey (pictured top left), exposed to the sky, inspired poet Wordsworth's pen and artist Turner's paintbrush. p113

STUARTH/SHUTTERSTOCK ©

Pentre Ifan

Tucked away in the silent Pembrokeshire hinterland, this is Wales' largest megalithic tomb (pictured below left), made of the same bluestone that was used for the menhirs of Stonehenge. p170

Preseli Hills

Pembrokeshire's brooding Preseli Hills hide Wales' greatest stash of hill forts, standing stones, cairns and burial chambers. Hike the Golden Road track to get well and truly stoned... p170

Wales lives and breathes history. Exploring the hills and coast, Iron Age hill forts cresting summits are two a penny. Head off on a hike across a lonely moor and you'll find stone circles, standing stones and dolmens that bear silent witness to the mysteries of the past. Upping the romance are abbey ruins that have captivated poets and painters for centuries.

Need to Know

For more information, see Survival Guide (p327)

Currency
Pound, also called 'pound sterling' (£)

Language
English, Welsh

Visas
Not required for most citizens of Europe, Australia, New Zealand, Canada and the USA.

Money
ATMs are widely available. Major credit cards such as Visa and MasterCard are accepted in most but not all hotels and restaurants.

Mobile Phones
The UK uses the GSM 900/1800 network, which is compatible with most of the world except the Americas. However many new phones have a multiband function that will allow them to work anywhere; check before leaving home.

Time
Greenwich Mean Time (GMT)

When to Go

 Mild to warm summers, cold winters

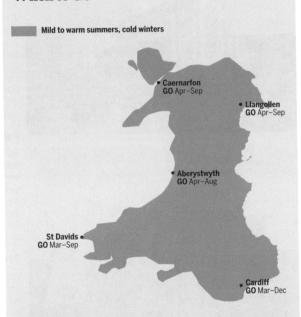

High Season
(Jul & Aug)

➡ Weather is at its warmest; lots of festivals and events.

➡ Accommodation prices increase in coastal areas and national parks, but not in cities.

➡ The absolute peak is the August school holidays.

Shoulder
(Apr–Jun, Sep & Oct)

➡ The season doesn't kick off until Easter, which can be in March or April.

➡ Prices rise to peak levels on bank holidays.

➡ April to June are the driest months; October is one of the wettest.

Low Season
(Nov–Mar)

➡ Prices rise to peak levels over Christmas and New Year.

➡ Snow can close roads, particularly in the mountains.

➡ January and February are the coldest months.

Useful Websites

Visit Wales (www.visitwales.com) Official resource for tourist information.

BBC Wales (www.bbc.co.uk/wales) The national broadcaster's portal on Wales.

WalesOnline (www.walesonline.co.uk) News and views concerning Welsh life.

Traveline Cymru (www.traveline.cymru) Essential public transport information.

Lonely Planet (www.lonelyplanet.com/wales) Destination information, hotel bookings and more.

Important Numbers

Emergency	☏999
Wales (& UK) country code	☏44
International access code	☏00
Traveline Cymru (public transport)	☏0800 464 00 00
Visit Wales (tourist information)	☏0333 006 3001

Exchange Rates

Australia	A$1	£0.55
Canada	C$1	£0.59
Europe	€1	£0.91
Japan	¥100	£0.73
New Zealand	NZ$1	£0.51
USA	US$1	£0.77

For current exchange rates, see www.xe.com.

Daily Costs
Budget: Less than £50

➡ Dorm bed: £14–23

➡ Cheap meal in a cafe or pub: £3–10

➡ Bus ticket (less than 100 miles): up to £18

Midrange: £50–120

➡ Double room in a hotel/B&B: £65–130

➡ Main course in a midrange restaurant: £10–20

➡ Castle admission: £4–11

➡ Car rental: per day from £30

Top end: More than £120

➡ Luxury hotel or boutique B&B room: from £130

➡ Three-course meal in a top restaurant: £20–50

➡ Theatre ticket: £10–50

Opening Hours

Opening hours tend to be fairly standard throughout the year, except at venues with an outdoor component (castles, gardens, beach cafes etc), which close earlier in winter.

Banks 9.30am–5pm Monday to Friday, 9.30am–1pm Saturday

Post offices 9am–5pm Monday to Friday, 9am–12.30pm Saturday

Cafes 9am–5pm Monday to Saturday, 11am–4pm Sunday

Restaurants noon–2pm and 6–10pm; often closed Sunday evening and Monday

Pubs 11am–11pm

Shops 9am–6pm Monday to Saturday, 11am–4pm Sunday

Arriving in Wales

London Heathrow Airport Has National Express coaches to Newport (from £26, three hours), Cardiff (from £14, 3½ hours) and Swansea (from £21, 5½ hours). For train connections, catch the Heathrow Express to Paddington Station.

Cardiff Airport The T9 Cardiff Airport Express bus (£5, 44 minutes, every 20 minutes) heads between the airport and Cardiff Bay via the city centre, although this was currently suspended due to Covid-19. The 304 Cardiff–Llantwit Major service (£2.65, one hour, hourly) stops at the airport too.

Holyhead Ferry Terminal Trains head to Rhosneigr (£4.40, 10 minutes), Bangor (£9.50, 30 minutes) and Conwy (£15, one to 1¼ hours).

Fishguard Harbour Trains head to Swansea (£17.30, two hours) and Cardiff (£28.20, 2½ hours).

Getting Around

Car Driving will get you to remote corners of Wales not connected to public transport. Cars can be hired from the main cities and the airports.

Bus The most useful form of public transport, with routes connecting most towns and villages. Many services don't run on Sunday. National Express coaches only stop in major destinations.

Train The network isn't extensive, but it's handy for those towns connected to it. Trains are comfortable and reliable, but more expensive than the buses.

For much more on **getting around**, see p334

PLAN YOUR TRIP NEED TO KNOW

Accommodation

Find more accommodation reviews throughout the On the Road chapters (from p49)

Accommodation Types

B&Bs These swing from humble doubles to chic boutique options with incredible views.

Campsites Dotted all over the country – often in the most beautiful locations – from seaside resorts to silent spots to pitch up in the hills.

Glamping A step-up from camping, with one-off experiences from tepees to tree houses and cool shepherd's hut conversions.

Hostels Often in lovely settings, YHA and independent hostels are liberally sprinkled across Wales.

Hotels The whole shebang: from small, family-friendly affairs to castle stays and manor houses in lavish grounds.

Best Places to Stay

Best on a Budget

Campgrounds and hostels are always competitively priced. If you're travelling as a couple, you can get reasonably priced B&Bs

PRICE RANGES

The following price ranges refer to the cheapest double on offer in high (but not necessarily peak) season. Unless otherwise stated, prices include private bathrooms and breakfast.

Category	Cost
£	less than £65
££	£65–130
£££	more than £130

(especially if you avoid high season), while self-catering accommodation tends to work out the best deal for groups and families.

➡ Old School Hostel (p164), Trefin

➡ Bryn Elltyd Eco Guesthouse (p246), Blaenau Ffestiniog

➡ Plas Curig Hostel (p251), Capel Curig

➡ Sleeperz (p67), Cardiff

➡ Hill Fort Tipis (p166), Fishguard

➡ Nicholaston Farm (p138), Parkmill

Best for Families

Kids love a bit of quirk factor and space to play. Campgrounds are a great option, as are self-catering picks on the coast and in the hills, which range from glamping pods to tree houses and farmstays. Many B&Bs and hotels offer competitive rates, with family discounts and free cots.

➡ Manor Town House (p166), Fishguard

➡ Fforest Farm (p172), Cilgerran

➡ Mandinam (p108), Llangadog

➡ Porth Tocyn (p265), Abersoch

➡ Llama Lodge (p170), Preseli Hills

➡ Living Room Treehouses (p209), Machynlleth

Best for Solo Travellers

Many B&Bs and hotels only have double rooms and give just a tiny discount to solo travellers. So if budget is an issue – and you fancy a bit of wilderness – you might be better off camping (or glamping) or bedding down in one of the country's terrific hostels.

➡ Priory Mill Farm (p105), Brecon

➡ Bethsaida (p172), St Dogmaels

➡ Lighthouse (p288), Llandudno

➡ Tyddyn Mawr Farmhouse (p239), Dolgellau

ANDREW KEARTON/ALAMY STOCK PHOTO ©

Lighthouse at the Great Orme (p288), Llandudno

Best Rural Escapes

One of the true joys of travelling in Wales is going off-grid and back to nature for a night or two. Dreamy escapes abound all over the country: from tucked-away castles near the coast to stately manors in their own botanical gardens. And some are more affordable than you might think.

➡ By the Wye (p92), Hay-on-Wye
➡ Gliffaes (p98), Crickhowell
➡ Slebech Park Estate (p185), Haverfordwest
➡ Plas Dinas Country House (p276), Caernarfon
➡ Nanteos Mansion (p204), Aberystwyth
➡ Bodysgallen Hall (p288), Llandudno

Booking

Book ahead for Easter, Christmas and summer peak season (July and August), and year-round at weekends. High season runs from mid-May to mid-September. Outside the high season, rates plummet and special deals may be available. Some places, especially hostels and campgrounds, shut completely from November until Easter.

Lonely Planet (lonelyplanet.com/hotels) Find independent reviews, as well as recommendations on the best places to stay – and then book them online.

Boltholes & Hideaways (www.boltholesandhide aways.co.uk) The definitive booking site for holiday cottages on Anglesey, with some one-of-a-kind picks – from converted dairies to windmills – in the mix.

Quality Cottages (www.qualitycottages.co.uk) Search by region for 435 hand-picked cottages across Wales. The same folk run Quality Unearthed (www.qualityunearthed.co.uk), with a specific focus on quirky glamping holidays.

Sugar & Loaf (www.sugarandloaf.com) An enticing selection of luxe self-catering picks across the country, from shepherd's huts to coach houses.

Undiscovered Wales (www.undiscovered-wales.co.uk) In-depth reviews of unusual accommodation options, plus other offbeat travel across Wales.

Wales Cottages (www.walescottageholidays.co.uk) Self-catering cottages galore.

Welsh Rarebits (www.rarebits.co.uk) Great site with a clickable map taking you to luxury retreats and boutique boltholes across Wales.

Month by Month

looks glorious in its gleaming white coat. The Six Nations rugby starts to heat things up sports-wise.

🏃 Six Nations

The highlight of the Welsh rugby calendar, with home matches played at Cardiff's Principality Stadium in February and March, enthusiastically viewed in pubs all over the country. (p66)

two-digit mark throughout the country. April's also the driest month in Mid-Wales and much of the north.

☆ Laugharne Weekend

Musicians, comedians and writers take to various small stages in Dylan Thomas' old stomping ground for the Laugharne Weekend, held over a long weekend in April. (p146)

January

Rug up warm for one of Wales' coldest months, with temperatures in single digits (Celsius) throughout the country. Spare a thought for the hardcore surfers braving the swells in Pembrokeshire.

🍷 Saturnalia

Roman-themed beer-drinking, bull-testicle-eating and mountain-bike-chariot-racing festival warms spirits in mid-January in the Welsh home of all things weird and wacky, Llanwrtyd Wells. (p213)

February

The cold and drizzle don't let up in February. In fact, it can even be slightly worse than January. Snowdonia

March

Temperatures rise slightly, maybe even scraping into double digits in Cardiff. Daffodils pop up in time for their name-saint's feast day. On fine days, March is a cracking month for hiking and biking.

🎆 St David's Day Celebrations

Wales honours its patron saint on 1 March, with black-and-gold St David's Cross flags draped throughout the country.

April

Spring finally starts to kick in properly, with temperatures breaking the

May

Head to the north coast, where May is both the driest and the sunniest month. There might still be snow on the paths heading up Snowdon though.

🎆 Victorian Extravaganza

Hitch up your skirts and stitch up your corset for this dress-up-for-grown-ups festival in Llandudno, held over the early May bank holiday weekend. (p287)

☆ Urdd National Eisteddfod

One of Europe's biggest youth events, this performing arts competition alternates between North and South Wales in May/June. (p314)

✿ Hay Festival

Arguably Britain's most important cultural event, this ever-expanding festival of literature and the arts is held over 10 days in late May, bringing an intellectual influx to book-town Hay-on-Wye. (p92)

☆ Fishguard Folk Festival

Folk bands from Wales, Ireland and beyond get pubs and stages swinging with shanties, Welsh songs, jigs and reels at this family-friendly festival in Fishguard. (p165)

June

Early summer is the prime time to head out walking, with a winning combination of higher temperatures, lower rainfall and lower winds. Cardiff celebrates its driest month.

☆ Gŵyl Gregynog Festival

This classical music festival brings live music to various historic buildings in northern Powys, with the main action centred on the University of Wales' Gregynog Hall. (p221)

🏃 Three Peaks Yacht Race

Departing from Barmouth in late June, this gruelling yachting, cycling and fell running race tackles Snowdon before hitting the highest peaks in Scotland and England. (p242)

🏃 Man vs Horse Marathon

Competitors full of brawn and bravado pit themselves against horses in this wacky race over mountainous terrain in Llanwrtyd Wells. (p214)

✕ Pembrokeshire Fish Week

Kicking off with a launch event on Nelson Quay in Milford in late June, this cracking fish fest dishes up cookery demos and workshops, foraging sessions, fishing tasters, tasting menus, barbecues and more.

July

The best bet for beach weather. July is one of the warmest and driest months for most of the country – although in Wales there are no guarantees.

✿ Royal Welsh Show

Prize bullocks and local produce are proudly displayed at Wales' biggest farm and livestock show at Builth Wells' Royal Welsh Showground. (p215)

✿ Underneath the Arches

The Pontcysyllte Aqueduct provides a dramatic backdrop for this family-friendly festival (www.facebook.com/underneaththearches), lighting up midsummer with music, picnics and fireworks.

☆ International Musical Eisteddfod

A week-long festival of music, including big-name evening concerts, held at Llangollen's Royal International Pavilion during the second week of July. (p234)

✕ Cardiff International Food & Drink Festival

Eat and drink your way around street food stalls and farmers markets at this food-loving fest on Roald Dahl Plass. (p67)

August

The good weather continues into August, which is officially the warmest month in Cardiff. It couldn't be described as tropical though; average temperatures only just sneak into the 20s.

☆ National Eisteddfod of Wales

Held alternately in North and South Wales in the first week of August, this is the largest celebration of Welsh culture, music and poetry (www.eisteddfod.wales), steeped in history, pageantry and pomp. (p314)

☆ Brecon Fringe Festival

The Fringe brings a feast of live music to country pubs scattered all around Brecon. (p105)

☆ Green Man Festival

A firm favourite on the UK's summer music festival circuit, Green Man offers four days of alternative folk and rock music in a verdant Brecon Beacons setting. (p98)

🏃 World Bog Snorkelling Championships

Does diving into a cold, murky bog wearing a snorkel sound like fun to you? If so, join the crazy folk in flippers at this bonkers event in Llanwrtyd Wells. (p214)

🏃 Welsh Open Stone Skimming

Another crazy one courtesy of Llanwrtyd Wells, this mid-August event invites 'tossers' to compete in 'stoned' and 'stoneless' categories. Bring your own stone or use one provided and skim away! (p214)

September

Summer comes to an end with more of a fizzle than a jolt, but temperatures start to creep down. Grab your surfboard and head to Pembrokeshire before the chill really sets in.

🍴 Abergavenny Food Festival

Held on the third weekend in September, this is the mother of all Welsh food festivals and the champion of the burgeoning local produce scene. (p88)

Llandovery Sheep Festival

Flock to this sheep-mad weekend in the former drovers' town of Llandovery. The fun ranges from sheepdog trials to a bucking sheep challenge, shearing demos, rare breed sheep, and oodles of food and rural crafts. (p150)

☆ Tenby Arts Festival

A week-long festival of autumnal music, literary and theatre events, and sandcastle competitions in the seaside town of Tenby in late September. (p177)

☆ Escape Festival

Get your groove on at Wales' biggest dance music event, with DJs working the decks in Swansea's Singleton Park. (p130)

October

Here comes the rain again: October is Aberystwyth's wettest month. The mountains of Snowdonia set about living up to their name, with the earliest falls on the higher peaks.

☆ Sŵn

Cardiff gets its groove on at this festival of music from Wales and beyond, staged at a number of venues across the city in October. (p67)

🍴 Gwledd Conwy Feast

Feast on fine food, music and digital art projections at this festival held over a weekend in late October in the historic walled town. (p283)

November

It's the rest of the country's turn to get properly soggy, with the wettest month on both the north and south coasts. It's back to single digits temperature-wise, too.

🍷 Mid-Wales Beer Festival

Held in Llanwrtyd Wells (where else), this 10-day festival includes the Real Ale Wobble & Ramble cycling, walking and beer-guzzling event. (p214)

December

There's no point dreaming of a white Christmas – for many people in Wales it's pretty much a given. Christmas cheer helps combat the gloomiest month, sunshine-wise.

🏃 Cardiff Christmas Market

The Welsh capital is full of festive sparkle at this market, with more than 200 stalls providing plenty of stocking-filler inspiration. (p67)

Cardiff Christmas Market (p67)

Plan Your Trip
Itineraries

 Full Welsh Circuit

This three-week road trip is the big one: a grand tour of the entire country, whisking you from the south coast to the high, brooding peaks of Snowdonia.

Kick off in **Cardiff** then swing north to the fairy-tale **Caerphilly** castle, topped with a riot of turrets and towers, before cutting west to **Swansea**. Head along the Gower Peninsula to ravishing **Rhossili Bay**, before continuing north to remote **Carreg Cennen** in the wild Brecon Beacons. Base yourself in **Llandeilo** for a day of botanical gardens and manor houses.

Go west to the cheerful seaside town of **Tenby** in Pembrokeshire, ticking off hidden bays en route to the medieval pilgrimage magnet of **St Davids**. Head up the coast to pretty **Newport** for local galleries, good food and clifftop rambles at nearby Dinas Island. Get a history fix at neolithic Pentre Ifan and Iron Age Castell Henllys on the cruise through the Preseli Hills and along the coast to cool, cultured **Aberystwyth**.

Continue on to ecofriendly **Machynlleth** and dark-stone **Dolgellau**, a fine base for hiking Snowdonia peaks like Cadair Idris. Visit **Harlech** and its coastal castle, before popping into the trippy Italianate village of

Tenby (p175)

Portmeirion and continuing on to nearby **Porthmadog**. Take a ride on the narrow-gauge railway to **Blaenau Ffestiniog**, pausing for a tour of the slate caverns. Linger on the lovely Llŷn Peninsula: in **Aberdaron**, say, for surf-battered views over Bardsey Island from Braich-y-Pwll.

Follow the coast to fortress-topped **Caernarfon**, then hit **Llanberis**, where you can stop by the National Slate Museum and brace yourself to tackle Snowdon. Double back to the Menai Strait and hop across to Anglesey to visit romantic **Beaumaris**, surf-hammered **Rhosneigr** and lavish neo-Gothic **Plas Newydd**.

Follow the north coast to impressively walled **Conwy** and Victorian-era **Llandudno** before turning south to forest-dwelling **Betws-y-Coed**. Head to riverside **Llangollen**, stop at Powis Castle in **Welshpool**, then pootle south to **Llanwrtyd Wells** of wacky event fame and on to the market town of **Llandovery**. Head east to **Brecon**, a good base for climbing Pen-y-Fan, then pop up to book-obsessed **Hay-on-Wye**. Cut down through **Crickhowell** to food-focused **Abergavenny**. Visit former mining town **Blaenavon**, skirt Monmouth and follow the peaceful Wye Valley to **Tintern Abbey** and on to the border town of **Chepstow**.

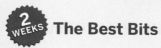
The Best Bits

2 WEEKS

This itinerary gives you a taster of all Wales has to offer at a breakneck pace. It includes the two major cities, all three of the national parks and some of the most enticing small towns, beaches, mountains and castles. You can just about pack the lot into two weeks.

Launch your tour in the literary honeypot of **Hay-on-Wye**, a handsome little town with a book fetish and one of the country's most important literature and arts festivals. Pause in Talgarth to explore woods, waterfalls and a working 17th-century water mill, before driving in silent exhilaration through the heather-flecked moors and brooding, fin-shaped mountains of the Brecon Beacons National Park.

Choose a good old-fashioned coaching inn for a night's stay in the cute-as-a-button Georgian town of **Crickhowell,** which scoops awards for its pristine high street. The brooding peaks of the Black Mountains pucker up as you drive east to the neighbouring market town of **Abergavenny**, a fine base for a stomp up the Skirrid. The following day detour east to Monmouth and trace the Wye Valley down past **Tintern Abbey**, a medieval monastic ruin that captured the imagination of that old romantic Turner.

Cruise south past wood, hill and meadow to the appealing market town of **Chepstow** and its Norman castle, before blazing west to **Cardiff**. Base yourself in the enthralling Welsh capital for a couple of days, exploring its revamped Bay, food scene and clutch of high-calibre museums.

Blast along the M4 motorway to **Swansea** next, using Wales' second city (and former stomping ground of poet Dylan Thomas) as a base to explore the beautiful bays of the **Gower Peninsula**. Detour to the remote, crag-topped ruins of **Carreg Cennen** before factoring in some seaside fun in **Tenby** and coastal walking in **St Davids** in the Pembrokeshire Coast National Park.

Allow time for discovering hidden bays and headlands en route north to **Aberystwyth** in Ceredigion, then veer inland to mountain-rimmed **Machynlleth**. Dip into the rugged heart of Snowdonia National Park to Dolgellau and onto **Llanberis** to get up close and personal with Snowdon, Wales' highest peak.

Explore the castle towns of **Caernarfon** and **Conwy** before washing up on the Victorian seaside promenade of **Llandudno**.

Top: Chepstow Castle (p110)
Bottom: Hay-on-Wye (p91)

South Wales Circuit

9 DAYS

This South Wales circuit takes in its stride the capital, two national parks, a liberal sprinkling of castles and glorious beaches, post-industrial sites, and cities associated with Dylan Thomas, St David and Merlin the Magician. Factor in sufficient time for coastal walks and lazy beach days on the Gower Peninsula and in Pembrokeshire as well as a hike or two in the Brecon Beacons.

Start by thoroughly exploring **Cardiff** and its surrounds before heading west to **Swansea** for a Dylan Thomas fix. Spend a day on the beach-lined **Gower Peninsula** before proceeding to **Carmarthen**, Merlin's town. Settle in to the seaside vibe at candy-striped **Tenby**, Wales' most appealing resort town and the gateway to the insanely lovely Pembrokeshire Coast National Park. Check out the mighty castle at **Pembroke** and head on through **Haverfordwest** and the pretty fishing harbour of **Solva** to **St Davids**, the UK's smallest city, with its pilgrim's fantasy of a medieval cathedral and dreamy setting. Visit **Fishguard** on your way to food- and beach-loving **Newport**, where neolithic and Iron Age sites hide in the surrounding hills.

From **Cardigan**, follow the lush Teifi Valley along the border of Ceredigion, stopping at the cute village of Cenarth and the National Wool Museum. The Cambrian Mountains pucker up between here and **Llandeilo**, so cut south towards Carmarthen before heading east. Factor in time for the botanical gardens, manor houses and castles in this neck of the Carmarthenshire countryside. Head on to the market town of **Llandovery**, with its rich drovers' heritage, and then skirt the northern edge of Brecon Beacons National Park en route to **Brecon**.

The Beacons ripple south of here, offering boundless opportunities for hiking, mountain biking, rafting, horse riding and canal trips. Pretty **Crickhowell** is another cracking base for hill walking. Cross the River Usk and cut down towards **Blaenavon**, a small town that wears its coal-mining and iron-smelting history on its sleeve, and has been inscribed on the World Heritage list. Backtrack towards **Abergavenny**, home to some of Wales' best country restaurants and gastropubs. Finish with a saunter down the Wye Valley, past romantically ruined **Tintern Abbey**, to **Chepstow**.

Top: Solva (p161)
Bottom: Big Pit National Coal Museum (p123), Blaenavon

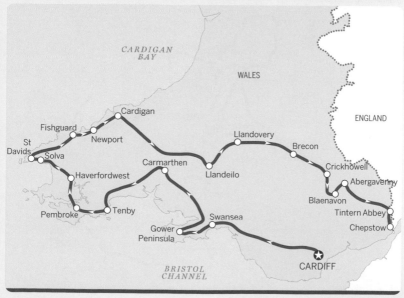

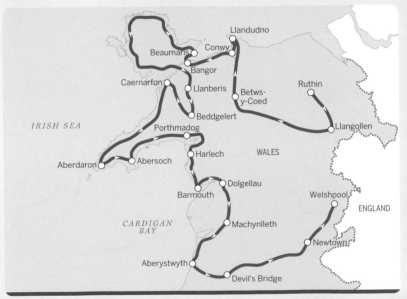

Llandudno

Beaumaris
Conwy

Bangor

Caernarfon
Llanberis

Betws-
y-Coed

Ruthin

Beddgelert

Llangollen

Porthmadog

IRISH SEA

WALES

Aberdaron
Abersoch

Harlech

Dolgellau

Welshpool

Barmouth

ENGLAND

CARDIGAN
BAY

Machynlleth

Newtown

Aberystwyth

Devil's Bridge

10 DAYS North & Mid-Wales

Mid-Wales is the Welsh wilderness proper, with wide open moors, river valleys and a cliff-backed coastline. The further north you venture, the higher and darker the peaks become as you hit Snowdonia. This itinerary cuts a broad arc through the Welsh-speaking heartland, presenting a feast of magnificent castles, cultural sites and beaches.

Start in historic **Ruthin** and take the beautiful back road that cuts through the bottom of the Clwydian Range to **Llangollen**, a small riverside town famous for outdoor pursuits and its World Heritage–listed canal and aqueduct. From here head west on the A5, swapping Denbighshire for the eastern reaches of Snowdonia National Park. **Betws-y-Coed** makes an enticing base for forest and river rambles, and mountain biking.

Put Snowdonia behind you for a few days as you head north on the A470, shadowing the River Conwy. Stop along the way at Bodnant Estate before heading north to the genteel Victorian beach resort town of **Llandudno**. Hop down to **Conwy** to immerse yourself in the medieval world between its town walls and tick off castle number one of the 'Castles of Edward I in Gwynedd' World Heritage Site. The A55 hugs the coast as it heads southwest towards **Bangor**. Stop for a quick look at the pier and the cathedral before crossing the Menai Strait to the Isle of Anglesey. Base yourself at **Beaumaris** (where you'll find castle number two) and circle the sacred island of the druids.

Cross the Menai Strait again and head to **Llanberis**, where you can plan your assault on Snowdon, either on foot or by train. Circle the mighty mountain, stopping at **Beddgelert**, before heading back to the coast at **Caernarfon** for castle number three. Circle the remote, sublimely beautiful Llŷn Peninsula, hopping between beaches and pubs in **Aberdaron**, **Abersoch** and beyond. Continue through **Porthmadog**, **Harlech** (castle number four) and beachy **Barmouth** before following the Mawddach Estuary to stony-faced, heritage-filled **Dolgellau**. Head south to eco trailblazer **Machynlleth** before rejoining the coast at the buzzy coastal student town of **Aberystwyth**. Gawp at the **Devil's Bridge** waterfalls and the gallery at **Newtown**, before finishing at **Welshpool** with a visit to opulent Powis Castle.

Top: Llangollen (p231)
Bottom: Beaumaris Castle (p294)

Walking the Pembrokeshire Coast Path (p17

Plan Your Trip
The Great Outdoors

Rain? You call that rain? A mere drizzle can't halt the hardy Welsh in their pursuit of outdoor thrills in the hills, moors, mountains and on the coast. From long-distance hikes in Snowdonia's wild heights to mountain biking and rafting in the Brecon Beacons and coasteering in Pembrokeshire, this country pulses with adventure.

Best Experiences

Dark Sky Gazing

Feel like a speck on the surface of the Earth while gazing up at the Milky Way in the Brecon Beacons Dark Sky Reserve.

Peak Bagging

Snowdon is grand, for sure, but don't go for height alone. Cadair Idris is an equally memorable climb – all the lovelier for being less crowded.

Wildlife Watching

Take a bumpy early morning boat ride to cliff-rimmed Skomer for breathtakingly close encounters with puffins.

Ancient Stones

Ponder the force of prehistory admiring standing stones, dolmens and Iron Age hill forts in Pembrokeshire's mythology-rich Preseli Hills.

Sheep Trekking

Yep, you read that correctly. An organic farm in the Brecon Beacons now lets you go for a stroll with a woolly friend – perfect for motivating kids to walk!

Poetic Footsteps

Go for a coastal ramble where the sea meets the sky along the Taf Estuary around Laugharne, the 'heron-priested shore' that inspired Dylan Thomas.

Walking

Over bare mountain and heather-flecked moor, over stile and through kissing gate, Wales is a walker's dream – whether you're an ambler, hardcore hill rambler, peak-bagger or fell runner. There are some 25,500 miles of footpaths, bridleways and byways – all public rights of way – tempting you to don waterproofs, whack on walking boots and get out and stride.

For the most challenging walks, head for Snowdonia National Park, capped off by the highest mountain in England and Wales (1085m Snowdon) and a ripple of dark, ragged peaks grazing the 1000m mark. Or instead hike the fin-shaped mountains, glacial valleys and wild moors of the Brecon Beacons – in the western end of the park, you can walk in almost total isolation. And, for the ultimate experience, connecting the sensational Wales Coast Path with the borderland Offa's Dyke Path lets you circumnavigate the entire country.

But with just a week or two on your hands, steer your focus towards the likes of the upliftingly beautiful Pembrokeshire Coast Path, the national park–traversing Beacons Way, or the recently launched Heart of Wales Line Trail, dipping into some properly remote terrain.

Walking can be enjoyed year-round, but be prepared for crowds in July and August, short days in winter and spontaneous downpours at any time. Make sure you're kitted out with decent, warm clothing, sturdy footwear and waterproofs. A map, compass, first-aid kit, food and water are recommended for more adventurous hikes. It's advisable to let someone know your intended route and planned return time and to check the weather forecast with the local tourist office before setting off.

For more details on everything from long-distance hikes to summit ascents, family-friendly rambles and walking festivals, visit www.visitwales.com.

Top Walks

The first three of these walks are national trails, open to walkers and horse riders and waymarked with an acorn symbol:

Glyndŵr's Way (www.nationaltrail.co.uk/glyndwrsway; 132 miles) Connecting sites associated with the rebellion led by Owain Glyndŵr in the early 15th century.

Offa's Dyke Path (www.offas-dyke.co.uk; 177 miles) Skirting the Wales–England border through an astonishing range of scenery and vegetation.

Pembrokeshire Coast Path (PCP; www.visitpembrokeshire.com; 186 miles) Hugging the sea cliffs of the Pembrokeshire Coast National Park, this is one of the UK's most beautiful coastal walks.

Beacons Way (www.breconbeacons.org; 99 miles) Strap on a backpack to cross the entire Brecon Beacons National Park on this eight-day trek.

Heart of Wales Line Trail (www.heart-of-wales.co.uk; 122 miles) This recently launched trail

Mountain biking in Brecon Beacons National Park (p100)

BEST COASTAL PATHS

Rambling its way along the country's entire, craggy, glorious coastline, the 870-mile Wales Coast Path (www.walescoastpath.gov.uk) takes around two months on average to complete. These are our favourite bits:

Pembrokeshire Coast Path (p173) 186 miles; Poppit Sands to Amroth

Ceredigion Coast Path (p196) 63 miles; Ynyslas to Cardigan

Llŷn Coastal Path (p263) 110 miles; Bangor to Porthmadog

Isle of Anglesey Coastal Path (p300) 140 miles; circular walk beginning in Holyhead

traces a scenic railway through some dreamy countryside from Shrewsbury to Swansea.

National Parks

The wonderfully varied landscapes of Wales' three national parks offer dramatic hikes, from coastal cliffs to knife-edge peaks and lonesome moors where you'll have only the odd sheep for company.

Snowdonia (www.eryri-npa.gov.uk) Designated in 1951, this North Wales stalwart is also home to the highest mountain in England and Wales and is great for off-season walking.

Pembrokeshire Coast (www.visitpembrokeshire.com) Coastscapes to make the heart sing, trails to hidden beaches and boat trips to a scattering of wildlife-rich islands. Designated in 1952.

Brecon Beacons (www.breconbeacons.org) Ice Age–carved valleys, remote moors and wind-battered summits that blow you away in every sense of the word. A haven to the red kite. Designated in 1957.

Cycling

Wales is quite the two-wheel dream, whether you're into slow touring along hedgerowed back lanes, road cycling deep in forested valleys or tearing down old slate tracks in former mining towns on a mountain bike.

Around 1400 miles of National Cycle Network routes wrap themselves around the country, with 331 miles of traffic-free rides. Local cycling operators can advise on regional routes, while a handful also offer pan-Wales packages for a countrywide adventure. Look out, too, for local cycling events and festivals.

The traffic-free section of the **National Cycle Network** North Wales Coastal Route, running along the seaside promenade from Colwyn Bay to Prestatyn, is one of the best in the UK for cyclists of all abilities.

Take your own bike or rent one from many outlets across the country. Be aware it's best to stick to tracks marked as bridleways on Ordnance Survey (OS) maps and cycling lanes. Avoid footpaths that haven't been split to incorporate cycling lanes. With the exception of July and August when tourism peaks, the unnumbered roads and lanes are quiet and cyclist friendly.

For mountain biking, Wales is second to none, with eight bike centres ramping up downhill thrills and testing skill and stamina. All have networks of bike routes, including at least one designed for families. Coed y Brenin Forest near Dolgellau in

Kayaking on the River Dee (p234)

Snowdonia National Park stands out with its thrillingly rocky, technically advanced routes and dual slalom course.

For more information, check out the cycling pages at www.visitwales.co.uk and www.mbwales.com.

Watersports

Wales is a country shaped and defined by the rough waves of the Atlantic, the steel-blue lakes that bejewel the hills, and the mountain rivers and streams that carve up its valleys.

For canoeing and sea-kayaking, swing over to Pembrokeshire or Anglesey to paddle in exhilaration below cliffs that have been around since dinosaurs roamed the Earth. Powerful tidal currents create huge standing waves between the Pembrokeshire coast and offshore islands, making the national park here one of the UK's hottest sea-kayaking destinations. Freshwater and Newgale Sands are favourite kayaking spots. **Canoe Wales** (www.canoewales.com) lists the waterways that permit kayaking and canoeing.

Inland, Llyn Tegid (Bala Lake) and Llyn Gwynant in North Wales beckon kayakers and canoeists, while slow-moving rivers include River Teifi, near Cardigan, and North Wales' River Dee.

Prolific sea life and a seabed littered with shipwrecks make diving in Wales an enticing prospect. Pembrokeshire, again, is diving central, and is the access point for the Smalls, a group of rocks famous for marine life, including a large colony of seals and pods of dolphins. Visibility here can reach up to 25m, although diving is restricted by the weather and tides. In North Wales, plump for Bardsey Island, the Skerries or the Menai Strait. Be aware that tidal currents rage dangerously at many of Wales' best dive sites, so seek advice locally before taking the plunge.

Surrounded by sea on three sides and netting some of the highest tidal ranges in the world – the Severn Estuary has the second-biggest tidal range anywhere – Wales has no shortage of surfing opportunities. Popular beaches get more crowded between April and September but with a little effort, you can easily give the crowds the slip. Sea temperatures are often

Surfers at Manorbier (p178)

and Llangennith. The best breaks in Pembrokeshire are to be found at Manorbier, Freshwater West and West Dale. St Davids' immense Whitesands Bay is good for beginners, although it's often busy. You'll find surf schools at most surf beaches. For more information, click onto the website of the **Welsh Surfing Federation Surf School** (www.surfschool.wsf.wales).

There's great potential for windsurfing all around Wales' coast and on many inland lakes. Many surf beaches also target windsurfers, with gear hire and lessons available. Rhosneigr, on the Isle of Anglesey, is growing as a centre for windsurfing and other watersports. Check out www.ukwindsurfing.com.

Opportunities for white-water rafting are limited. One of the few Welsh rivers with big and fairly predictable summertime white water (grades III to IV) is the dam-released Tryweryn near Bala. Moderate rapids (grades II to IV) are found on the River Usk and between Corwen and Llangollen on the River Dee.

For more information about watersports, visit www.watersportswales.co.uk.

warmer than you might imagine, thanks to the North Atlantic Drift, but you'll always need a wetsuit, and possibly boots, a hood and gloves in winter.

The wave-lashed Gower Peninsula is beloved of surfers, cramming in a wide choice of breaks and plenty of post-surf activity. Hot spots include Caswell Bay, the Mumbles, Langland Bay, Oxwich Bay

Wildlife Watching

With an abundance of wide-open, rugged, sparsely populated spaces, Wales is hands-down one of Britain's best places for spotting wildlife and birdlife. National parks are naturally ideal for this because of their remoteness and minimal human

LONG-DISTANCE CYCLE RIDES

Two of Wales' most popular long-distance rides come under the auspices of the **National Cycle Network**. End points are linked with the rail network so you can make your way back to the start by train.

Lôn Las Cymru (Greenways of Wales/Welsh National Route; NCN Routes 8 & 42) This 254-mile route runs from Holyhead, through to Hay-on-Wye, then on to Cardiff via Brecon or Chepstow via Abergavenny. Encompassing three mountain ranges – Snowdonia, the Brecon Beacons and the Cambrian Mountains – there's a fair amount of uphill, low-gear huffing and puffing to endure along the way. But each peak promises fantastic views and plenty of downhill, free-wheeling delights.

Lôn Geltaidd (Celtic Trail; NCN Routes 4 & 47) A 337-mile route snaking from Fishguard through the West Wales hills, the Pembrokeshire Coast, the former coalfields of South Wales and ending at Chepstow Castle. The glorious, ever-changing landscape provides a superb backdrop.

Top: Puffins on Skomer (p187)

Bottom: Dolphin in Cardigan Bay (p198)

TOP PLACES TO SPOT WILDLIFE

Skomer This tiny isle's ragged, lush green cliffs of ancient volcanic rock attract 10,000 breeding pairs of puffins, not to mention the world's largest population of Manx shearwaters (350,000 pairs).

Cardigan Bay Get close to grey seals, porpoises and dolphins on boat trips in Cardigan Bay.

Gower Peninsula A feast of seabirds and sightings of dolphins, harbour porpoises and Atlantic grey seals.

Ynyslas Dunes Part of the Dyfi Unesco Biosphere Reserve, these spectacular dunes offer sightings of ringed plovers and shelducks, plus ospreys and red kites, dolphins, porpoises and otters.

South Stack, Holyhead, Anglesey Dramatic cliffs attracting guillemots, razorbills, puffins and choughs.

Horse riding on Anglesey

intervention, as are the numerous reserves that sprinkle the country, many of which are operated by the likes of the **RSPB** (www.rspb.org.uk), the **National Trust** (www.nationaltrust.org.uk) and **Wildlife Trusts Wales** (www.wtwales.org).

In the Brecons and Cambrian Mountains, red kites are readily spotted wheeling overhead, skylarks sing their hearts out above moors and meadows, and more elusive otters, kingfishers and little ringed plovers can be, with luck and patience, sighted along waterways. Red squirrels scamper around woods in Mid and North Wales, and Carmarthenshire is reintroducing beavers to its rivers with some success.

The sea cliffs, rock stacks and dunes hemming the Welsh coast, and the uninhabited islands off the coast, attract a profusion of birdlife (some of it migratory), from stonechats, linnets and larks, to waders like lapwings, golden plovers and curlews, and seabirds like Manx shearwaters, puffins, razorbills, gannets, kittiwakes, rare choughs, red-billed oystercatchers and fulmars. Dolphins, harbour porpoises and Atlantic grey seals also splash around off shore.

Horse Riding

Saddling up in Wales is a joy thanks to the country's fabulous mix of sandy beaches, rolling hills and dense forest. Mid-Wales and the Cambrian Mountains, the forests, trails and uplands around Betws-y-Coed, and the gentle Clwydian Range are prime horsey territory to be explored. Riding schools catering for all levels of proficiency are found throughout the country. You can hire a horse or bring your own steed (guests' horses are offered stabling at some riding centres); check out www.riding wales.com.

Caving

South Wales is holed out like a Swiss cheese, with caves reaching from Crickhowell to Carreg Cennen Castle in the Brecons. Caves are also found in North Wales, on the Gower Peninsula and in Pembrokeshire. Highlights for the more experienced caver include the UK's second-longest cave, **Ogof Draenen**, and the deepest, **Ogof Ffynnon Ddu**.

Climbers on Crib Goch, Mount Snowdon (p256)

Porth-yr-Ogof in the Brecon Beacons and **Paviland Cave** on the Gower Peninsula are better suited to beginners. For more information, contact the British Caving Association (www.british-caving.org.uk).

Climbing

Wales is a cracking country for pitting yourself against rocks, mountains and sheer cliff faces, with some of the UK's best climbing: Cader Idris and the slopes between Llanberis and Pen-y-Pass are just two sites of particular renown. It's hardest to get a foothold during summer when rock faces are particularly crowded. In winter, ice-climbing is popular in Snowdonia. Equip yourself for emergencies, check the Met Office weather forecast and seek advice from local climbing shops, climbers' cafes and tourist-information points before making your ascent.

To get a feel for the rock face, get in touch with Safe & Sound Outdoors (p234) or Ty Nant Outdoors (p234) in Llangollen, or take a course at the Plas y Brenin National Mountain Sports Centre (p250) in Capel Curig. For more information, contact the British Mountaineering Council (www.thebmc.co.uk).

Canyoning

Like white-water rafting without the burden of a raft, canyoning is a thrill a minute. Having found a suitably terrifying set of rock-bound rapids, you'll climb, slide, shimmy and swim down any which way you can, protected only by a helmet, wetsuit and life-vest. The Brecon Beacons and Llangollen are just two of the many areas with companies offering this sport.

Plan Your Trip
Family Travel

With boundless space for free play, miles of gorgeous beaches, and back-to-nature stays with farm animals to pet and night skies to gaze at, Wales is a surefire kid-pleaser. Fantasy castles, caves and rock pools fire little imaginations, and outdoor activities keep kids as active as can be in this child-friendly land.

Keeping Costs Down

Sleeping

Self-catering is often the best way to save, especially if you avoid peak periods (Easter and summer holidays). Besides campgrounds and holiday cottages, there are plenty of quirkier options: from farmstays to shepherd's huts and tree houses to tepees.

Eating Out

Wales is a shade cheaper than elsewhere in the UK when it comes to eating out. To cut costs, consider packing up a picnic for a ramble in the hills or grabbing a fish-and-chip supper by the coast.

Sightseeing

Some of the best sights in Wales are free: from castle ruins to nature reserves and coastal trails, not to mention some major museums (most notably the National Museum Cardiff with its terrific natural history exhibition).

Transport

Look out for advance and off-peak tickets that yield substantial discounts. On Transport for Wales services, up to two children aged 10 and younger enjoy free travel when accompanied by a fare-paying adult.

Children Will Love

Family-Friendly Beaches

Whitesands Bay, St Davids (p157) A broad arc of golden sand, ideal for swimming, surfing and rock pooling.

Barafundle Bay, Stackpole (p179) A cliff path leads over dunes and through stone archways to this dreamy hidden bay.

Mwnt, Cardigan (p194) A stream cascades down to this deliciously secluded cliff-backed cove, with visits from dolphins, porpoises and seals if you're lucky.

Oxwich Bay, Gower Peninsula (p139) Miles of dune-backed golden sand, salt marshes and woodland.

Castle Beach, Tenby (p176) A velvety-soft beach perfect for sandcastles, ball games and kite flying.

Rainy-day Fun

Techniquest, Cardiff (p62) Whizz-pop science adventures for all.

Centre for Alternative Technology, Machynlleth (p207) Interactive displays and a great adventure playground for curious kids.

Zip World Slate Caverns, Blaenau Ffestiniog (p246) Go underground to trampoline on giant nets, slide and explore caves.

Dan-yr-Ogof, Fforest Fawr (p107) Eerie caves, dinosaurs, shire horses and a petting farm entertain.

National Museum, Cardiff (p55) Big bangs, volcanoes and dinosaurs galore.

Outdoor Thrills

Zip World Slate Caverns, Blaenau Ffestiniog (p246) Strap the kids in, and watch them zip line at breathtaking speeds over mountainsides and quarries.

Talyllyn Railway, Tywyn (p241) What kid wouldn't love getting to ride the inspiration behind Thomas the Tank Engine?

Zip World Fforest, Betws-y-Coed (p249) Plunge through a trap door and freefall 100 feet in 'Plummet'.

Gwydyr Stables, Penmachno (p247) Explore Snowdonia's hills and forests on horseback.

Thousand Islands Expeditions, St Davids (p159) Head to the edge of the Celtic Deep to spot whales, porpoises and dolphins.

Castles Galore

Beaumaris Castle, Beaumaris (p294) Act out fairytale fantasies at Edward I's greatest castle.

Conwy Castle, Conwy (p281) A stunning fortress looming over the complete medieval walls of Conwy.

Pembroke Castle, Pembroke (p182) Ramble along walls, passages and from tower to tower at this forbidding castle.

Carreg Cennen, Trapp (p106) Atmospheric 13th-century ruins with a clifftop passage down to a spooky cave.

Caernarfon Castle, Caernarfon (p274) The castle of childhood dreams, with excellent exhibitions pitched at families.

Region by Region

Cardiff

A castle and park to romp around, dinosaurs at the National Museum (p55), science wizardry at Techniquest (p62) in Cardiff Bay, and a shot of open-air history at St Fagans (p63).

Mid-Wales

Kayaking with dolphins in Cardigan Bay, seaside fun in Aberystwyth (p200), mighty dams in the Elan Valley (p212), mountain-

Punch and Judy show, Llandudno (p285)

bike and walking trails in the hills, and medieval Powis Castle (p224).

Snowdonia & the Llŷn

Adventure thrills from zip lines to trampolines in old slate mines (p246), narrow-gauge railways, Harlech Castle (p244), the fabulous beaches of the Llŷn Peninsula (p262) and mountains all the way.

Anglesey & the North Coast

A trio of World Heritage castles (p274), the world's fastest zip line (p279) in Bangor, Punch and Judy in Llandudno (p285) and ecofriendly thrills at GreenWood Forest Park (p276).

Brecon Beacons & Southeast Wales

Ruined castles to climb, Big Pit National Coal Museum (p123) and National Showcaves (p107) to explore, and mountains where you can walk, cycle, boat, kayak, stargaze and sheep trek (p109).

Swansea, the Gower & Carmarthenshire

Beaches and dunes to run wild across, hands-on fun at Swansea's National Waterfront Museum (p130), rambles in botanical gardens and off-grid glamping.

St Davids & Pembrokeshire

Quite the childhood dreams: hidden coves and broad sandy bays, ice-cream and sandcastles in Tenby, and activities from coasteering to sea kayaking and boat trips to puffin-filled islands.

Good to Know

Look out for the 🖼 icon for family-friendly suggestions throughout this guide.

Unique sleeps Kids will have a blast at farmstays, tepees, tree houses and the like.

Stuff for babies Pick up baby formula, nappies (diapers), ready-made baby food and sterilising solution at supermarkets and chemists.

Prams & pushchairs Prams and pushchairs (strollers) are suitable for towns and villages. Elsewhere, a front or back carrier is preferable.

Eating out Kids are generally welcomed, but double-check the high chair situation in advance. Some places offer children's meals.

Car travel Children must use a child car seat until they're 12 years old or 135cm. They must be rear-facing until 15 months.

Sight discounts/family tickets Kids under five generally get free entry and family tickets are readily available.

Useful Resources

Lonely Planet Kids (www.lonelyplanetkids.com) Loads of activities and great family travel blog content.

National Trust Days Out Wales (www.national trust.org.uk/days-out/wales) Woods and wildlife, beaches, castles and nature reserves.

Visit Wales (www.visitwales.com) Plenty of inspiration for family-friendly breaks and activities.

Kids' Corner

Say What?

Good morning.	Bore da. *Bo-re da*
Goodbye.	Hwyl fawr. *hueyl vowr*
Hello/ How are things?	Sut mae. *shu-mae*
My name is ...	Fy enw i yw ... *vuh e-noo ee yu...*

Did You Know?

• There are 600 castles in Wales.

• Wales has more sheep than people: some 10 million.

Have You Tried?

FANFO/SHUTTERSTOCK ©

Welsh Rarebit
A fancy version of cheese on toast..

Regions at a Glance

Cardiff

···

**Architecture
Sport
Nightlife**

···

Urban Showcases

From the neoclassical glory of the Civic Centre, to dainty Victorian shopping arcades and Cardiff Bay's edgily regenerated waterfront, the architecturally striking Welsh capital strides effortlessly between past and present with one icon after the next.

Rugby Fever

The scrum is in Cardiff's blood, with the city leaping to life during a rugby international, when the singing from the stands resonates through the streets. And Cardiff is the home of Welsh sport, with Principality Stadium dwarfing the city centre and three other major stadiums nearby.

Bar Scene

Cardiff ramps up the after-dark action with an exciting live music scene, raucous pubs, craft-beer bars and an ever-growing crop of ubercool cocktail bars and speakeasies.

p50

Brecon Beacons & Southeast Wales

···

**Walking
History
Mines & Forges**

···

Hiking Trails

Bring walking boots, waterproofs and stamina for hikes up into the moors, glacial valleys and mountains of Brecon Beacons National Park. You'll find terrific trails along the riverside Wye Valley and south coast, too.

Hilltop Castles

Wales is the world's most castellated country, and never is this clearer than here, where ruins and forts seem to crest almost every hillside. Top billing goes to remote Carreg Cennen.

Industrial Heritage

Victorian Britain was built on Welsh coal and iron; its legacy is captured at the Blaenavon World Heritage Site and in the beating industrial heart of the valleys.

p82

Swansea, Gower & Carmarthenshire

···

**Beaches
Gardens
Rural Life**

···

The Gower

Just a pebble's throw from Swansea, you'll find some of Wales' most fabulous dune-backed beaches. Most magical of all is Rhossili Bay, at the Gower's western tip.

Botanical Wonders

How do Welsh gardens grow? Find out at Aberglasney's Elizabethan walled gardens. Or devote a day to the National Botanic Garden of Wales, crowned by Norman Foster's Great Glasshouse.

Market Towns

The small rural towns of Carmarthenshire such as Llandeilo and Llandovery are full of genteel charm, Georgian architecture and friendly pubs. Carmarthen's market is a centre for fine Welsh products.

p126

St Davids & Pembrokeshire

Coastal Scenery
Beaches
Wildlife

Pembrokeshire Coast

Though it receives just a trickle of Cornwall's crowds, Pembrokeshire's coastline is every bit as enthralling. Its 186-mile coast path ribbons together cliff-rimmed bays, headlands and hill forts.

Hidden Bays

Backed by cliffs, caves, woods and waterfalls, Pembrokeshire's off-the-radar coves and bays look freshly minted for a Famous Five novel. The water may be freezing, but who cares?

Island Escapes

Take a bumpy boat trip to one of the offshore islands for gasp-eliciting encounters with seals, porpoises, dolphins and whales. The cliffs are home to millions of seabirds; on Skomer you'll see puffins galore.

p152

Mid-Wales

Nature
Market Towns
Food

Wildlife Spotting

The once-rare red kite is now the very symbol of Powys. Coastal Ceredigion shelters important wetland habitats, while Cardigan Bay attracts bottlenose dolphins, harbour porpoises, Atlantic grey seals and leatherback turtles.

Rural Heartland

You'll often see more sheep than people in the agricultural heart of Powys, scattered with quaint market towns, many of which still serve as farming hubs.

Local Produce

Mid-Wales has come on in culinary leaps and bounds in recent years, with suppliers of everything from goats cheese to craft beer, venison to wine (yes, really...). Things taste best at the source.

p190

Snowdonia & the Llŷn

Mountains
Quarries
Beaches

Snowdonia

Snowdonia is Wales at its dramatic best, rippling with the highest peaks in the country. Hike from mountain brook to moor, forest to summit, and embrace activities from white-water rafting to zip-lining.

Slate Quarries

Welsh slate once roofed much of the world and Snowdonia's quarries bear witness to the sweat and blood of generations of workers. Some have been converted into museums, while freight railways now shunt travellers through spectacular terrain.

Surf & Sand

Snowdonia is where the mountains collide with the coast. From the sands of Barmouth to the surf and bays of the Llŷn Peninsula, northwest Wales has a range of dreamy beaches.

p226

Anglesey & the North Coast

Castles
Coastal Scenery
Stately Homes

Edward I's Legacy

While there are castles all over Wales, the whopping great medieval fortresses masterminded by Edward I in North Wales are the only ones to be recognised as World Heritage Sites. Perched on crags and lonely coastlines, they truly are exemplars of the castle-makers' craft.

Isle of Anglesey

At times wild and rugged, at times gentle and restrained, the Druids' Isle is an instant heart-stealer and rates among the nation's most beautiful stretches of coast.

Menai Mansions

Barons, marquesses and slate magnates all chose to build grand testimonies to their good fortune along the Menai Strait – some of which are now open for all to enjoy.

p270

On the
Road

Anglesey & the
North Coast
(p270)

Snowdonia &
the Llŷn
(p226)

Aberystwyth &
Mid-Wales
(p190)

St Davids &
Pembrokeshire
(p152)

Swansea,
Gower &
Carmarthenshire
(p126)

Brecon Beacons &
Southeast Wales
(p82)

Cardiff ⭐
(p50)

AT A GLANCE

POPULATION
335,000

OLDEST STANDING BUILDING
Cardiff Castle keep
(late 11th century)

BEST UP-AND-COMING NEIGHBOURHOOD
Cathays (p63)

BEST CRAFT-BEER BAR
Tiny Rebel (p73)

BEST CITY VIEW
From Cardiff Bay
Barrage (p61)

WHEN TO GO

➡ **Jan–Mar** The coldest months; Wales' home matches in the Six Nations Rugby Championship warm local spirits.

➡ **Jul** Warmth and sunshine are enlivened by foodie calendar highlight Cardiff International Food & Drink Festival.

➡ **Oct** Autumn colours brighten tree-studded Bute Park; Cardiff's best music festival animates venues citywide.

Cardiff Bay (p61)
BILLY STOCK/SHUTTERSTOCK ©

Cardiff

V acillating between gritty and glitzy, the Victorian and the voguish, Cardiff is a master of reinvention. Wales' capital since just 1955, it has embraced the role with vigour.

The two top sights between which this chameleon-like city spreads embody its verve for innovation. An ancient fort forms Cardiff Castle's foundation but the flamboyant 19th-century rethinking of the fortress captivates most. Cardiff's creativity and confidence is embodied in the radical transformation of Cardiff Bay from unsightly mudflats to Europe's biggest, boldest waterfront development. Come weekends the area buzzes as shoppers hit the Hayes, rugby supporters' roars resound through the centre and revellers relish the thriving nightlife.

Cardiff makes an excellent base for day trips to surrounding valleys and coast, bombastic castles and intriguing industrial sites.

Cardiff Highlights

① Cardiff Castle
(p57) Marvelling at the Victorian extravagances grafted onto the city's ancient citadel.

② National Museum Cardiff
(p55) Taking an engrossing journey through Welsh culture via the Big Bang and seminal fine art.

③ Live Music
(p75) Checking out the bright young indie acts detonating central-city bars and clubs such as Clwb Ifor Bach.

④ Bute Park (p59) Promenading or relaxing on the lush lawns surrounded by trees, flower beds, the Taff and Cardiff's iconic castle.

⑤ Rugby (p59) Getting swept up in the mania of a Six Nations rugby game at Principality Stadium.

⑥ Pontcanna
(p71) Brunching or lunching in this lovely leafy suburb, then taking a turn in its parks.

⑦ Cardiff Bay
(p61) Admiring the architectural showpieces that transformed this waterfront precinct.

⑧ St Fagans National History Museum (p63) Exploring the transplanted historic buildings, Elizabethan manor house and gorgeous gardens of this world-class museum.

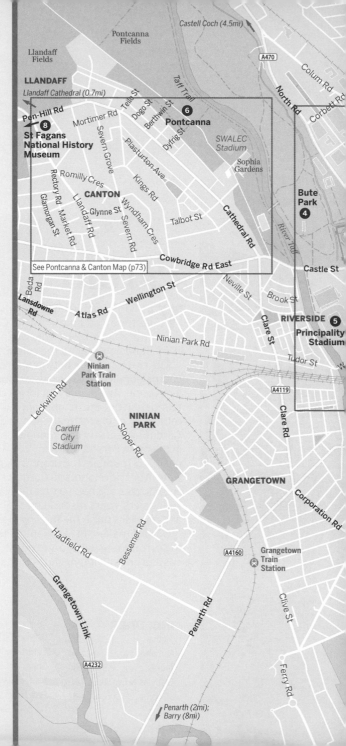

History

The name Cardiff probably derives from Caer Tâf (Fort on the River Taff). In CE 75 the Romans built a fort where Cardiff Castle now stands. After the Romans abandoned the site around 375, it remained unoccupied until the Norman Conquest. In 1093 a Norman knight named Robert Fitzhamon (conqueror of Glamorgan and later earl of Gloucester) built himself a castle within the Roman walls and a small town grew up around accordingly. Both were damaged in a Welsh revolt in 1183 and the town was sacked in 1404 by Owain Glyndŵr during his ill-fated rebellion against English domination.

The first of the Tudor Acts of Union in 1536 put the English stamp on Cardiff and brought stability. But despite its importance as a port, market town and bishopric, fewer than 10,000 people were living here in 1801.

The city owes its present stature to iron and coal mining in the valleys to the north. Coal was first exported from Cardiff on a small scale as early as 1600. In 1794 the Bute family – which owned much of the land from which Welsh coal was mined – built the Glamorganshire Canal for the shipment of iron from Merthyr Tydfil down to Cardiff. In 1840 this was supplanted by the new Taff Vale Railway.

A year earlier the second marquess of Bute had completed the first docks at Butetown, just south of Cardiff, getting the jump on other South Wales ports. By the time it dawned on everyone what immense reserves of coal the valleys contained, precipitating a kind of black gold rush, the Butes were well positioned to insist it be shipped from Butetown. Cardiff was off and running.

The docklands expanded rapidly, the Butes grew staggeringly rich and the city boomed, its population mushrooming to make it the biggest town in Wales by the 1880s and reaching almost 250,000 by 1931. A large, multiracial workers community known as Tiger Bay grew up in harbourside district Butetown. In 1905 Cardiff was officially designated a city and in 1913 the world's top coal port, exporting over 10 million tonnes of the stuff.

The post-WWI slump in the coal trade and the Great Depression of the 1930s slowed this expansion. Calamities accumulated as the city was badly damaged by WWII bombing. Shortly afterwards the coal industry was nationalised, which led to the Butes leaving town in 1947, donating the castle and a large chunk of land to the city.

Wales had no official capital and the need for one was seen as an important focus for Welsh nationhood: Cardiff had the advantage of being Wales' biggest city and boasted significant architectural riches. It was proclaimed Wales' first-ever capital in 1955, chosen via a ballot of the members of the Welsh authorities. Cardiff received 36 votes to Caernarfon's 11 and Aberystwyth's four.

Reinvention has been the city's mantra ever since, epitomised in the development of Europe's largest waterfront regeneration project, Cardiff Bay, during the 1990s and 2000s.

CARDIFF IN...

Two Days

Start with a stroll around the historic city centre, stopping to explore **Cardiff Castle** (p57) and **National Museum Cardiff** along the way. Lunch could be picnicking in **Bute Park** (p59) with treats acquired at **Cardiff Market** (p76) or, if the weather's not cooperating, a meal at any of the wondrous, dynamic, central-city eateries. On day two, either head back to the future at **Cardiff Bay** (p61), reconnoitring a remarkable mix of 19th-century and contemporary architecture backed by brilliant bayside vistas, or saunter through Wales' variegated past at the nation's foremost museum, **St Fagans National History Museum** (p63).

Four Days

Spend day three heading over to the Vale of Glamorgan, scouting out venerable seaside resorts **Penarth** (p79) and **Barry Island** (p80). On your last day, venture north to **Llandaff Cathedral** (p64), then continue on to **Castell Coch** (p58) and **Caerphilly Castle** (p125). For your last night, have a blast in one of the city's endlessly inventive bars (p72) or live-music venues (p74).

THE BEAUT BUTES

In Cardiff, the Bute name is inescapable. No family has had bigger impact on the city. An aristocratic Scottish brood related to the Stuart monarchy, the Butes arrived in Cardiff in 1766 in the shape of John, Lord Mount Stuart. He married a local heiress, Charlotte Hickman-Windsor, acquiring vast estates and mineral rights in South Wales in the process. Like his father of the same name (a prime minister under George III), he entered politics and became a Tory MP, privy councillor and ambassador to Spain. Eventually he was awarded the title marquess of Bute.

Their grandson, the second marquess of Bute, grew fabulously wealthy from coal mining and then in 1839 gambled his fortune to create a large complex of docks in Cardiff. The gamble paid off. The coal-export business boomed, and his son, John Patrick Crichton-Stuart, the third marquess of Bute, became one of the planet's richest people. He was an intense, scholarly man with a passion for history, architecture, ritual and (Catholic) religion, supporting the antivivisection movement and campaigning for a woman's right to a university education. In 1887 he gifted Roath Park to the town. His architectural legacy ranges from the colourful kitsch of Cardiff Castle and Castell Coch to the neoclassical elegance of the Civic Centre.

The Butes had interests all over Britain and never spent more than about six weeks at a time in Cardiff. By the end of WWII they had sold or given away all their Cardiff assets, with the fifth marquess gifting Cardiff Castle and Bute Park to the city in 1947. The present marquess, the seventh, lives in the family seat at Mount Stuart House on the Isle of Bute in Scotland's Firth of Clyde. Another maverick, he's better known as Johnny Dumfries, the former Formula One racing driver.

◉ Sights

◉ City Centre

In retail-mad Cardiff even some shopping areas are must-see sights. The covered Victorian Cardiff Market (p76) and the seven arcades dating from between 1858 and 1921, Castle Arcade (p77), High St and Duke St Arcades (p77) in the Castle Quarter, along with **Morgan Arcade** and **Royal Arcade** in the Morgan Quarter (p77), **Wyndham Arcade** (Map p56; btwn St Mary St & Mill Lane, CF10 1FJ; ⊗8am-7pm) and **Dominions Arcade**, are aesthetically pleasing enclosed alleys filled with the city's most iconic independent businesses. They're worth an eyeball even if you're determined to keep purse in pocket.

★**National Museum Cardiff** MUSEUM
(Map p56; ☑0300 111 2333; www.museum. wales/cardiff; Gorsedd Gardens, CF10 3NP; ⊗10am-5pm Tue, Thu, Sat & Sun; P⊕) FREE
Devoted mainly to art and natural history, this grand neoclassical building is the centrepiece of several institutions countrywide that together form the Welsh National Museum. It's among Britain's best museums; devote at least three hours to doing it justice. Boasting one of the world's most significant impressionist and post-impressionist collections, the **main gallery** rooms exhibit treasures such as Monet's *Water Lilies*, alongside his scenes of London, Rouen and Venice; a cast of Rodin's *The Kiss*; and van Gogh's anguished *Rain, Auvers*.

Then there are the Welsh scenes by Sisley (the artist was married in Cardiff!) and Renoir's shimmering *La Parisienne*. Many pieces were bequeathed to the museum in the 1950s and 1960s by the Davies sisters, Gwendoline and Margaret, granddaughters of 19th-century coal and shipping magnate David Davies. These include their seven paintings by British master JMW Turner, dismissed as fakes in the 1950s but subsequently reappraised as genuine.

Welsh artists, such as Gwen and Augustus John, Richard Wilson, Margaret Lindsay Williams and Ceri Richards, are well represented, along with famous names from across the border, such as William Hogarth, Thomas Gainsborough, John Constable, Francis Bacon and Lucian Freud. Add to that the likes of Van Dyck, Poussin, Rembrandt, Cézanne, Degas and Picasso, and you've got some seriously impressive works.

The equally absorbing **Evolution of Wales** exhibit scoots onlookers through 4600 million years of geological history, its

Central Cardiff

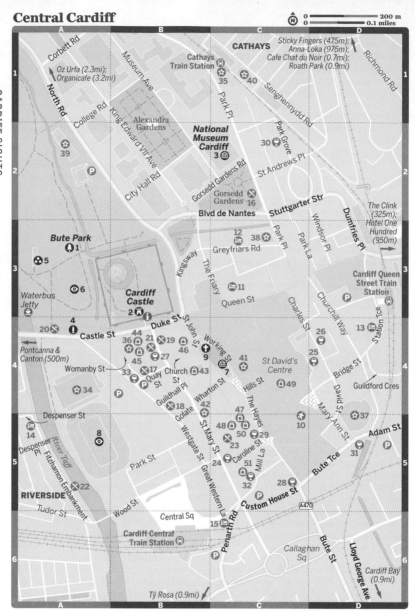

rollicking multimedia display placing Wales into a global context. Films of volcanic eruptions and aerial footage of the Welsh landscape explain how its scenery was formed, while model dinosaurs and woolly mammoths help keep the kids interested. Even more whizz-bang is **Mission: Planet Earth**,

a 15-minute virtual-reality experience (£10) at the beginning of the Evolution section that children will especially love.

The natural-history displays range from brightly coloured insects to the 9m-long skeleton of a humpback whale that washed up near Aberthaw in 1982. The world's

Central Cardiff

largest leatherback turtle (914kg), found on Harlech beach, is also here, suspended on wires from the ceiling.

One of the large upstairs galleries is devoted to Welsh ceramics, while others are set aside for temporary exhibitions. A new one-way system leads visitors throughout. Book online before visiting.

On-site parking, behind the museum, costs £6.50; you'll need to purchase an exit token from the gift shop.

★**Cardiff Castle**   CASTLE
(Map p56; ☎029-2087 8100; www.cardiff castle.com; Castle St; adult/child £14.50/10, incl guided tour £19.50/14; ☺9am-6pm Mar-Oct, to 5pm Nov-Feb) There's a medieval keep at its heart, but it's the later additions to Cardiff Castle that really capture the imagination. In Victorian times, extravagant mock-Gothic features were grafted onto this relic, including a clock tower and lavish banqueting hall. Some of this flamboyant fantasy world can be accessed for free from the castle courtyard; the rest on highly recommended guided tours. Explore, and you may finish up concurring with the fortress's claim to be the most fascinating castle in Wales.

From 1766 to 1947, when it was donated to the city, the castle was the private palace of the Butes, the family who transformed Cardiff from small town into the world's biggest coal port. It's far from a traditional Welsh castle; more a collection of disparate 'castles' scattered around a central green, but encompasses practically the whole history of Cardiff. The most conventionally castle-like bits are the well-preserved motte-and-bailey **Norman shell keep** at its centre (built in wood around 1081, rebuilt in stone in 1135) and the 13th-century **Black Tower** that forms the entrance gate. William the Conqueror's eldest son, Robert, Duke of Normandy, was imprisoned in the wooden fort by his brother, England's Henry I, until his death at the age of 83.

A grand house was built into the western wall in the 1420s by the Earl of Warwick

WORTH A TRIP

CASTELL COCH

Castell Coch (Cadw; ☎029-2081 0101; www.cadw.gov.wales; Castle Rd, Tongwynlais; adult/child £6.50/3.90; ⏲10am-1pm & 2-5pm Mar-Oct, 10am-4pm Wed-Sun Nov, Dec & Feb, closed Jan; ℗; 🚌26,132) Cardiff Castle's fanciful little brother sits perched up a thickly wooded crag on the northern fringes of Cardiff. It was the summer retreat of the third marquess of Bute and, like Cardiff Castle, was designed by oddball architect William Burges in gaudy Gothic-revival style. Raised on the ruins of Gilbert de Clare's 13th-century Castell Coch (Red Castle), the Butes' Disneyesque holiday home is a monument to high camp. An excellent audio guide is included in the admission price.

Lady Bute's bedroom, huge and circular, is pure fantasy – her bed, with crystal globes on the bedposts, sits beneath an extravagantly decorated and mirrored cupola, with 28 painted panels around the walls depicting monkeys (fashionable at the time, apparently). The corbels are carved with images of birds nesting or feeding their young, and the washbasin is framed between two castle towers.

Lord Bute's bedroom is small and plain in comparison, but the octagonal drawing room is another hallucinogenic tour de force, the walls painted with scenes from *Aesop's Fables*, the domed ceiling a flurry of birds and stars, and the fireplace topped with figures depicting the three ages of men and women.

While Castell Coch was closed at the time of research due to Covid-19 restrictions, it is still a worthwhile run out here just to see it, and for the beautiful **walking trails**, including part of the Taff Trail (p66), in the surrounding forest.

Stagecoach buses 26 and 132 (£2.50, 30 minutes, half-hourly) head from Greyfriars Rd in Cardiff to Tongwynlais, a 10-minute walk from the castle. Bus 26 continues to Caerphilly Castle (p125); the two castles can be combined in a day trip.

and extended in the 17th century by the Herbert family (the earls of Pembroke), but by the time the Butes acquired it, it had fallen into disrepair. The first marquess of Bute hired architect Henry Holland and Holland's father-in-law, famous landscape architect Lancelot 'Capability' Brown, to get the house and grounds shipshape.

It was only in the 19th century that it was discovered that the Normans had built their fortifications on top of Cardiff's original 1st-century Roman fort. The high walls that surround the castle now are largely a Victorian reproduction of the 3rd-century, 3m-thick Roman walls. A line of red bricks, clearly visible from the city frontage, marks the point where the original Roman section ends and the reconstruction commences.

Also from the 19th century are the towers and turrets on the western side, dominated by the colourful 40m clock tower, that constitute perhaps the most eye-catching part of the site today. This faux-Gothic extravaganza, known as the **Castle Apartments**, was dreamed up by the mind-bendingly rich third marquess of Bute and his architect William Burges, a passionate eccentric who used to dress in medieval costume and was often seen with a parrot on his shoulder. Both were

obsessed with Gothic architecture, religious symbolism and astrology, and influences are intricately incorporated into the designs both here and at the Butes' second Welsh pad at Castell Coch. Yet along with the focus on the past, the plans included all Victorian era mod cons, such as electric lighting (it was the second house in Wales to feature this newfangled wizardry) and running water in the en suite attached to the upper-floor bedroom.

Entry to the wide grassy courtyard, from where the Norman, 17th-century and Victorian exteriors can be enjoyed, is free. Here is Cardiff's main tourist information office (p77), a **shop** and a **cafe**. This, too, is where you sign up for castle tours. Standard entry gains you admittance to the Norman Keep, the Firing Line and Wartime Shelters, the Roman remains and selected rooms in the lavish Castle Apartments, with an audio guide to aid you. Start your visit in the **WWII air-raid shelter**, preserved in a long, cold corridor within the castle walls, then proceed to the **Firing Line**, a small but interesting museum devoted to the Welsh soldier.

An hour-long **guided tour** (it's £1 extra if you want to ascend the clock tower) takes you through the interiors and their fascinating associated stories in much more depth. Discover rooms such as the **library**, with its intricate bird and insect motifs on the shelves and walls, and Burges' humorous dig at Darwin's *Origin of the Species* (published just prior to the room's decorative construction), with monkeys stealing an apple from the Tree of Knowledge and squabbling over a book carved into the doorway.

Heading upstairs, the **banqueting hall** boasts Bute family heraldic shields and a fantastically over-the-top fireplace (look for the image of the imprisoned duke of Normandy) and is overlooked by that medieval must-have, a minstrels' gallery. Marble, sandalwood, parrots and acres of gold leaf create an elaborate Moorish look in the **Arab room**. The neighbouring **nursery** is decorated with fairy-tale and nursery-rhyme characters, while the small **dining room** has an ingenious table, designed so that a living vine could be slotted through it, allowing diners to pluck fresh grapes as they ate. The decor of the **winter smoking room** in the clock tower expounds on the theme of time (zodiac symbols grouped into seasons, Norse gods representing days of the week, and a fright for anyone who dares listen at the door – look up as you pass through the doorway), while the mahogany-and-mirrors narcissism of **Lord Bute's bedroom** features a gilded statue of St John the Evangelist (the marquess' name saint) and 189 bevelled mirrors on the ceiling, which reflect the name 'John' in Greek. The Roman-style **roof garden** seemingly underlines what a fantasy all this really was – designed with southern Italy in mind, rather than Wales.

★ **Bute Park**   PARK
(Map p56; www.bute-park.com; ⊙ 7.30am-30min before sunset; ⊕) Flanked by the castle and the River Taff, Bute Park was donated to the city along with the castle in 1947. With Blackweir Fields, along with Sophia Gardens, Pontcanna Fields and Llandaff Fields on the Pontcanna (west) side of the river, it forms a ravishing green corridor stretching northwest 1.5 miles to Llandaff – all this was once part of the Butes' vast holdings – and on again to Castell Coch in Cardiff's far north, then out into open countryside.

In the main, the park forms the city's gills – a tranquil place to walk, run or cycle – but minor sights are also scattered throughout.

In the part of the park just west of the castle are some **Gorsedd Stones** (Map p56), a stone circle erected in 1978 when Cardiff hosted the National Eisteddfod. Gorsedd stones are found all over Wales where eisteddfodau have been held. Marked out in brick on the lawn nearby are the dimensions of 13th-century **Blackfriars Friary** (Map p56), destroyed in 1404 when Owain Glyndŵr attacked Cardiff. There are also a couple of places to eat, including highly recommended Pettigrew Tea Rooms (p70) at the Castle St entrance and, close by, the water-bus jetty, from where you can take a boat to Cardiff Bay (a far lovelier journey than the bus or train).

Principality Stadium   STADIUM
(Millennium Stadium; Map p56; ✆ tickets & tours 029-2082 2432; www.principalitystadium. wales; Westgate St; tours adult/child £13.75/9.90; ⊙ tours 10am-5pm, 10.15am-4pm Sun) Also known as Millennium Stadium ('Principality' is the current naming-rights sponsor), this spectacular venue is Welsh rugby's heart and soul, squatting like a stranded spaceship on the River Taff's east bank. Seating 74,500 and built at a cost of £168 million, the three-tiered, retractable-roofed arena was completed in time to host 1999's Rugby World Cup. If you can't get match tickets, it's well worth taking a tour – book online for the best prices.

Rugby is Wales' national game and when the Principality crowd begins to sing, all Cardiff resonates. To watch a match here is to catch a glimpse of the Welsh psyche, especially when the Six Nations tournament (p66) is on. Tickets for international fixtures are difficult to obtain. Other matches at adjacent Cardiff Arms Park (p76), Principality's famous predecessor and home to the Cardiff Blues rugby team, are easier to pick up.

The stadium is additionally used for mammoth events and concerts. Like other similarly sized venues, it was adapted into a hospital during the Covid-19 pandemic to treat patients, and both matches and tours were temporarily suspended.

Museum of Cardiff   MUSEUM
(Map p56; ✆ 029-2034 6214; www.cardiff museum.com; Yr Hen Lyfrgell, The Hayes; ⊙ 10am-4pm) FREE This excellent little museum within Cardiff's beautiful Yr Hen Lyfrgell (The Old Library) building uses interactive displays, free audio guides, video footage

Cardiff Bay

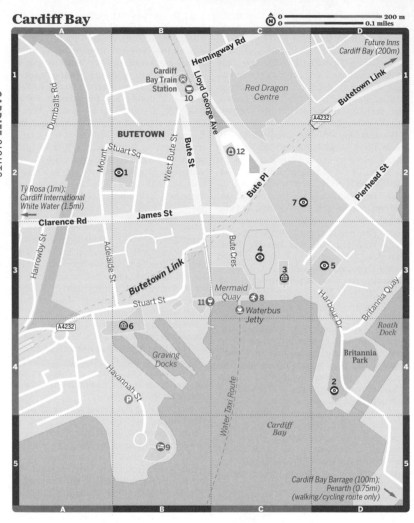

N
0   200 m
0   0.1 miles

and everyday objects to tell the story of the city's transformation from small market town into the world's biggest coal port and then into the Welsh capital city. Be sure to check out the 'tiled corridor', the library's original entrance, lined with gorgeous Victorian tiles.

There is a small gift shop and, downstairs, the City Lab, with kids' activities and exhibits on the history of protest in Cardiff, as well as Welsh-language lessons. There's also a left-luggage desk (each piece £5 to £10 per day).

Animal Wall   SCULPTURE

(Map p56; Castle St) This section of wall on Bute Park's southern edge is topped with stone figures of lions, seals, bears and other creatures (a seahorse was proposed but sadly never made the cut). Designed by architect William Burges and sculpted by Thomas Nicholls, the figures were originally erected when the castle was redeveloped in the late 19th century.

In the 1930s they were moved to their present site and became the subject of a newspaper cartoon strip. As a result, many Cardiff kids grew up thinking the animals came alive at night!

Cardiff Bay

◎ Cardiff Bay

Lined with important national institutions, Cardiff Bay is where the modern Welsh nation is displayed in an architect's playground of interesting buildings, open spaces and public art. The bay's main commercial centre, Mermaid Quay, is less forward-thinking, packed with predominantly chain restaurants, bars and shops.

It wasn't always thus. By 1913 more than 13 million tonnes of coal were being shipped from Cardiff's docks. Following the post-WWII slump the docklands deteriorated into wasteland. The bay outside the docks, which has one of the highest tidal ranges in the world (more than 12m between high and low water), was ringed for up to 14 hours a day by sewage-contaminated mudflats; nearby Butetown became a neglected slum.

Beginning in 1987, the area has been radically redeveloped. The real turning point came with the completion of state-of-the-art Cardiff Bay Barrage in 1999, with landmark buildings popping up in the early 2000s, and is ever-evolving even today.

While there is astounding architecture here, most can be adequately appreciated from outside, or from further afield such as on the Cardiff Bay Barrage.

Cardiff Bay Barrage   DAM
(www.cardiffharbour.com/barrage-story; ♿) Completed in 1999 at a cost of £220 million, this large dam plugged the gap between Penarth and Porth Teigr, containing the waters flowing out from the mouths of the Rivers Taff and Ely, and transforming stinky Cardiff Bay into a freshwater lake. It includes sluice gates to control the water flow, three lock gates to allow passage for boats, and a fish pass that lets migrating salmon and sea trout pass between the rivers and the Bristol Channel.

When it was built, the barrage was a controversial project, as its construction flooded 200 hectares of intertidal mudflats, which, despite their unpleasant aspects, were an important habitat for waterfowl. Like it or loathe it, it was what paved the way for Cardiff Bay's revival, as gleaming waterfront was a sight more attractive to developers than smelly mudflats.

A walking and cycling track heads over the barrage, providing easy access to Penarth (allow 40 minutes from the Norwegian Church if walking). This is part of the **Bay Trail**, a 6-mile loop that follows the shoreline back around to Butetown. Along the way there's a skate park, a playground and display boards by the sails at the midway point telling the story of Captain Robert Scott's expedition to the Antarctic, which departed from Cardiff in 1910. Two years later Scott and his men were dead, having been pipped to the pole by a Norwegian team led by Roald Amundsen.

Coal Exchange   NOTABLE BUILDING
(Map p60; https://coalexchangecardiff.co.uk; Mount Stuart Sq, Butetown) This imposing Renaissance Revival building was once the Welsh coal trade's nerve centre, and for a time the place where international coal prices were set. It was here in March 1908 that a coal merchant wrote the world's first-ever £1 million cheque. The building narrowly missed becoming the home of the Welsh government in 1979, fell into disrepair, got spectacularly refurbished between 2016 and 2020 and has, as of October 2020, opened as a luxury hotel-cum-restaurant.

It might be worth the price of a drink to get an interior peep: the best features are the exquisite dark wood panelling, carved balconies and Corinthian columns.

Wales Millennium Centre ARTS CENTRE
(Map p60; ☑029-2063 6464; www.wmc.org.uk;
Bute Pl, CF10 5AL; ☺10am-6pm, later on show
nights) FREE The centrepiece of Cardiff
Bay's regeneration is this £106-million
edifice, an architectural masterpiece of
stacked Welsh slate in shades of purple,
green and grey topped with an overarching
bronzed steel shell. Designed by Welsh architect Jonathan Adams, it opened in 2004
as Wales' premier arts complex, housing
major cultural organisations such as the
Welsh National Opera and National Dance
Company Wales.

The roof above the main entrance is
pierced by 2m-high letter-shaped windows,
spectacularly backlit at night, which spell
out phrases from the work of Welsh poet
Gwyneth Lewis. Beneath it are housed a
1900-seat theatre, a recital hall, a studio
theatre, a cabaret venue and other performance and recording spaces.

At the time of research it was closed until at least early 2021. When it's open you
can wander around the impressive inside,
where you'll find a decent **cafe** and **shop**.

Outside, **Roald Dahl Plass** (Map p60), a
square honouring the famous Cardiff-born
writer and with an unusual shape due to
its past life as the basin of the West Bute
Dock, stretches south to the Pierhead
Building and Senedd. The square starred
in the *Doctor Who* spin-off series as the secret entrance to *Torchwood's* underground
headquarters.

Pierhead Building MUSEUM
(Map p60; ☑0300 200 6565; www.senedd.wales/
en/visiting; Pierhead St, CF10 4PZ; ☺9.30am-
4.30pm Mon-Fri, from 10.30am Sat) FREE One
of the waterfront's few Victorian remnants,
Pierhead is a red-brick French Gothic con-
fection, built in 1897 with Bute family money to impress the maritime traffic. Its ornate
clock tower earned it the nickname 'Wales'
Big Ben'. Once headquarters of Cardiff
Railway, it now shows a short film of what
Cardiff Bay looked like pre-refurb, from the
1800s onwards, complemented by interactive displays and artefacts.

It's an offshoot of the Senedd, Wales' National Assembly, next door.

Senedd NOTABLE BUILDING
(Map p60; ☑0300 200 6565; www.assembly.
wales; CF99 1SN; ☺9.30am-4.30pm Mon-Fri,
from 10.30am Sat & Sun) FREE Designed by
Lord Richard Rogers (the architect behind

London's Millennium Dome and Paris'
Pompidou Centre), the home of the National Assembly for Wales' Siambr (debating
chamber) is a striking structure of concrete,
slate, glass and steel, with an undulating
canopy roof. It has won awards for its environmentally friendly design, which includes
a gutter system that collects rainwater for
flushing the toilets.

The lobby is dominated by the 'meeting
place', a curved bench made of 3-tonne slate
blocks from Blaenau Ffestiniog, thoughtfully provided as a place for protesters to rest
their legs.

When they're not in recess, the National
Assembly meets in a plenary session from
1.30pm on Tuesday and Wednesday. In
non-Covid-19 times, seats are usually available in the public gallery.

Techniquest MUSEUM
(Map p60; ☑029-2047 5475; www.techniquest.
org; Stuart St; adult/child/under 4 £9.59/7.73/
free; ☺10am-1pm & 2-5pm Wed-Sun; ℙ 🖖) With
the goal of introducing kids to science,
Techniquest is jam-packed with engrossing,
hands-on exhibits that are equally enjoyable for under-fives and inquisitive adults.
The digital planetarium stages star tours
and science shows. A flash new discovery
centre, the Science Capital, aimed at making science-based fun accessible to a more
diverse audience, opened in late 2020.
Prebooking tickets via the website is currently essential.

**Norwegian Church
Arts Centre** ARTS CENTRE
(Map p60; ☑029-2087 7959; www.norwe
gianchurchcardiff.com; Harbour Dr; ☺10.30am-
4pm) FREE Looking like it's popped from
the pages of a storybook, this white-slatted
wooden building with a black witch's-hat
spire was modelled on a traditional Norwegian village church. It was built in 1868
to minister to Norwegian sailors and remained a place of worship until 1974. It's
now an arts centre hosting exhibitions, concerts, markets and the like, and has a sweet
cafe. Cardiff-born writer Roald Dahl, whose
parents were from Norway, was christened
here.

Dahl served as president of the preservation trust that restored and renovated the
church. It was closed at the time of research
due to Covid-19 restrictions.

ST FAGANS

St Fagans National History Museum (☑ 0300 111 2333; https://museum.wales/st
fagans; St Fagans; parking £6.50; ☺ 10am-5pm Tue, Thu, Sat & Sun; 🅿 🚹; 🚍 32, 32A, 320)
Historic buildings from all over the country have been dismantled and re-erected in
the semirural surrounds of St Fagans village, 5 miles west of central Cardiff. Almost 50
buildings are on show, including thatched farmhouses, barns, a watermill, a school, an
18th-century Unitarian chapel and shops selling period-appropriate goods. Buses 32,
32A and 320 (£2, 25 minutes) head here from Cardiff. By car it's reached from the continuation of Cathedral Rd (which becomes Pencisely Rd then St Fagans Rd).

You'll need at least half a day to do the whole complex justice and you could easily
spend longer, picnicking in the grounds.

It's a super place for kids, with special events in the summer, tractor-and-trailer rides
and an old-time fun fair. Craftspeople are often on hand, demonstrating how blankets,
clogs, barrels, tools and cider were once made. In winter, fires are stoked by staff in period costume, and there's a high-ropes course through the beeches, CoedLan, between
May and October (£12 per person).

Highlights include a **16th-century farmhouse** imbued with the smell of old timber,
beeswax and wood smoke. A row of six **miners' cottages** from Merthyr Tydfil has been
restored and furnished to represent different periods in the town's history, from the austere minimalism of 1805 to all the mod cons of 1985. It took 20 years to move **St Teilo's
Church** (built 1100 to 1520) here, stone by stone. It's been restored to its original look,
before Protestant whitewash covered the vividly painted interior. Then there's the museum's six-year multimillion-pound redevelopment, completed in 2019, which has added
two **Iron Age roundhouses** and a re-creation of the **Ilys** (court) of medieval prince
Llywelyn Fawr (Llywelyn the Great), one of the last kings of Wales, as well as three new
indoor **galleries** charting Wales' social history through experiential exhibits (from prehistoric times right up to a beautifully tiled coal-fired, deep-fat fryer) and a **restaurant**.

St Fagans Castle is no johnny-come-lately to this site, either. It was originally built
by the Normans in 1091 as a motte-and-bailey castle before being rebuilt in stone. The
manor house (1580) at its heart is recognised as one of Wales' finest Elizabethan houses.

The property was donated by the earl of Plymouth in 1946, along with its lovingly
maintained formal gardens and the grounds that encompass the site. Despite inside
areas being closed to the public due to Covid-19 at the time of research, the grounds
remained open. A walk around them still shows most of the enthralling edifices.

⊙ Northern Suburbs

Some of Cardiff's most intriguing areas lie
in the suburbs immediately north of the
city centre. Directly north of the centre, and
east of Bute Park, proximity to the university makes up-and-coming **Cathays** and
Maindy with their tightly packed Victorian
terrace houses popular with students. It's
fabulously multicultural and still gritty in
parts. For a broader (and very tourist free)
taste of Cardiff life, stroll along the thor-
oughfare that starts as City Rd, morphing
into Crwys Rd and then Whitchurch Rd. In
the north, these areas become more well-
heeled as they merge with more affluent
Roath, arranged around one of Cardiff's
loveliest parks. Meanwhile, northwest of
the centre, and backed by fetching fecund
parkland, is **Pontcanna**. Come here to

see upmarket Cardiff, ensconced among
leafy streets, where some of the city's best
places to brunch, lunch and dine await. To
the north, Pontcanna bounds **Llandaff**, a
handsome former village enfolding Cardiff's most eye-catching ecclesiastical sight,
Llandaff Cathedral (p64).

Roath Park   PARK
(www.outdoorcardiff.com/parks; Lake Rd, Roath;
☺ 7.30am-sunset) Long, narrow Roath Park
rivals Bute Park (p59) as Cardiff's favourite
green space. The third marquess of Bute
gifted the land to the city in 1887, when the
marsh at its northern end was dammed to
create the 12-hectare Roath Park Lake, the
park's central feature. The rest was laid
out in Victorian style, with rose gardens,
tree-lined paths, lawns and wild nooks. A
lighthouse was added to the lake in 1915 as

a memorial to ill-fated Antarctic explorer Robert Scott.

The park is a lovely spot for a stroll and a picnic. If you fancy something a little more diverting, there are cafes, playgrounds, bowling greens, tennis courts and basketball courts, along with boating and fishing opportunities on the lake.

Llandaff Cathedral
CATHEDRAL

(☑029-2056 4554; www.llandaffcathedral.org.uk; Cathedral Close, CF5 2LA, Llandaff; ⊙2-4pm Mon-Fri, to 5pm Sat & Sun) This venerable cathedral is set in a hollow near the River Taff, on the site of a 6th-century monastery founded by St Teilo, a leading figure in early Welsh Christianity. The present building was begun in 1120, but it crumbled throughout the Middle Ages, and during the Reformation and Civil War was used as an alehouse and then an animal shelter. It was largely rebuilt in the 19th century, and then repaired again following a German bombing raid in 1941.

The towers at the western end epitomise the cathedral's fragmented history – one was built in the 15th century, the other in the 19th. Inside, a giant arch supports Sir Jacob Epstein's huge aluminium sculpture **Majestas**, its modern style a bold contrast in this gracious, vaulted space. Pre-Raphaelite fans will appreciate the Burne-Jones reredos (screen) in **St Dyfrig's chapel** and the stained glass by Rossetti and William Morris' company.

Medieval effigies recline beneath tattered and tasselled Union flags, **St Teilo's tomb** is located on the south side of the sanctuary, and other signs of early Christianity – a **Celtic cross** near the chapter-house door and **St Teilo's Well** on the Cathedral Close approach to the holy building – are visible.

Cathedral clocked, you might fancy a mooch and a bite to eat around the pleasant village of Llandaff. Buses 25, 61 and 63 head here every 15 minutes from Westgate St in the city centre.

🏃 Activities

Cardiff International White Water
ADVENTURE SPORTS

(☑029-2082 9970; www.ciww.com; Watkiss Way, CF11 0SY, Cardiff Bay; 2hr rafting £40-55, 2hr kayaking from £10; ⊙9.30am-4.30pm; 🔊) This Olympic-standard artificial white-water complex offers adrenaline-fuelled rafting, canoeing, kayaking, river boarding, stand-up paddleboarding and hot-dogging (inflatable

---

🏃 City Walk
Historic Cardiff

START CARDIFF CROWN COURT
END THE HAYES
LENGTH 1.5 MILES; 1½ HOURS

Among Britain's most elegant administrative quarters, Cardiff's Civic Centre encompasses formal parks and a grand array of early 20th-century buildings, finished in gleaming white Portland stone. Start outside neoclassical ❶ **Cardiff Crown Court**, continue past the baroque-style ❷ **City Hall** and bear right into ❸ **Gorsedd Gardens**. Here you'll find a *gorsedd* stone circle, raised for 1899's National Eisteddfod.

Head towards the neoclassical facade of the ❹ **National Museum Cardiff** (p55) and then turn into Park Pl. Next is the imposing main building of ❺ **Cardiff University**. Head through its black gates and enter through the central door into the short corridor leading to the foyer (after hours you'll need to circle around the building). In the centre is a white marble statue of John Viriamu Jones, the institution's first principal.

Head through the door on the other side, curve to the left, cross the road and enter ❻ **Alexandra Gardens**. Amid the formal lawns and colourful flower beds is an interesting set of war memorials, respectively to Britons killed in the Falklands War, Welsh volunteers who fought against fascism in the Spanish Civil War and the Welsh National War Memorial, erected in 1928 in memory of WWI dead.

Exit the gardens onto King Edward VII Ave. Straight ahead is the old ❼ **Glamorgan County Council Building** (now part of Cardiff University), fronted with Corinthian columns and elaborate statuary (Minerva, to the left, represents mining; Neptune, on the right, navigation). The ❽ **Bute Building**, to the right, also belongs to the university and features Doric columns and a red dragon on its roof.

Turn right, then left onto College Rd. You'll see, straight ahead of you, the impressive new home of the ❾ **Royal Welsh College of Music and Drama** (p75). Cross towards it, turn right and then left past the curved, timber-clad

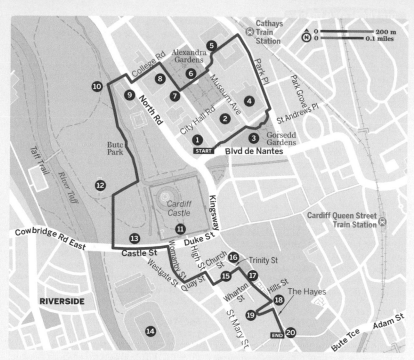

end of the building and enter **10 Bute Park** (p59). Cross the little bridge, turn left and follow the canal towards the rear of **11 Cardiff Castle** (p57). At the next bridge take the path to the right; you'll shortly come to the foundations of **12 Blackfriars Friary** (p59; on your right).

Veer left and exit through the West Lodge gate. Turn left on Castle St and look at the magisterial menagerie perched atop the **13 Animal Wall** (p60). Originally positioned by the castle's main gate in late Victorian times, the animals were moved here after WWI. Cross the road and continue to Womanby St. Lined with warehouses, with many reincarnated as bars, this is among Cardiff's oldest, most storied streets. Historically linking Cardiff Castle with the docks, it was privy to many colourful incidents in its legend-steeped pubs, not least a full-scale brawl in 1759 between two rival ships' crews armed with muskets and cutlasses. Today's revellers are a marginally more placid crowd. As you head down the street, **14 Principality Stadium** (p59) is on your right.

Take a left on Quay St – Cardiff's original quay stood here before the River Taff was realigned to make way for the railway in 1860. Turn right on St Mary St, then left to enter

15 Cardiff Market (p76). This cast-iron market hall has been trading since 1891. Before that, the site was the city gaol. The market's St Mary's entrance was where Dic Penderyn, instrumental in the Merthyr Rising that battled against mining injustices, was hanged in 1831.

Exit on the far side on Trinity St and admire 15th-century **16 St John the Baptist Church** (p75), one of the few remnants of medieval Cardiff. Turn right and head towards the beautiful sandstone building of Yr Hen Lyfrgell, the old city library, now housing the intriguing **17 Museum of Cardiff** (p59).

Continue down the street and into the heart of the Hayes. The name derives from a Norman-French word relating to the small garden enclosures that would once have stood here. It's now Cardiff's pedestrianised main shopping strip. Glitzy **18 St David's** (p77) mall occupies the entire left-hand flank, but more interesting is the Victorian-era **19 Morgan Quarter** (p77) on your right. It's the prettiest and best-preserved of Cardiff's Victorian/Edwardian shopping arcades and contains many iconic independent shops and eateries. Finish back on the Hayes under the hoop and arrow of sculpture **20 Alliance**.

OFF THE BEATEN TRACK

TAFF TRAIL

Following canal towpaths, country lanes and disused railway routes, the 55-mile **Taff Trail** (www.mytafftrail.co.uk) walking and cycling route connects Cardiff Bay with Brecon, passing Castell Coch (p58), Merthyr Tydfil (p121) and much of the Brecon Beacons National Park on the way. Starting from Brecon will ensure more downhill runs. The Taff Trail also forms the southern end of National Cycle Network Route 8 (Lôn Las Cymru), which runs all the way north to Holyhead.

kayaking) experiences without having to leave the city. It also runs kayaking trips into Cardiff Bay – the very best way to see it. Then there's indoor surfing, a high-ropes course and climbing wall, plus gorge-walking expeditions in the Neath Valley.

Cardiff Jet   CRUISE
(Map p60; ☑ 07496 620379; https://cardiffjet. co.uk; Mermaid Quay) Offers superfast speedboat trips within Cardiff Bay (the 'Bay Blast' at 15 minutes for £12), plus speedy sojourns further afield.

Treetop Adventure Golf   MINIGOLF
(Map p56; ☑ 029-2022 6590; www.adventure golf.com; level P3, St David's; adult/child under 5 £9/4; ☺ 11am-9pm Mon-Wed, to 10pm Thu & Fri, 10am-10pm Sat, 10am-9pm Sun) The mega St David's shopping mall (p77) really does have everything – as this jungle-themed minigolf course aptly demonstrates.

⌖ Tours

Dark Wales   HISTORY
(☑ 07707 711088; www.darkwalestours.co.uk; £16; ♿) Matthew and Luke bring several years' worth of ghost-tour experience in the Cardiff area to these haunting jaunts to discover the city's spookiest places. They run St Fagans National History Museum and Cardiff Castle ghost tours (unfortunately not running at the time of research due to Covid-19) and feature regular ghostly podcasts on their Facebook page. Over 12s only.

Loving Welsh Food   FOOD & DRINK
(☑ 07810 335137; https://lovingwelshfood.uk; ☺ 9.15am-5.15pm Mon-Fri) Brilliant range of tours introducing you to the capital's diverse eating scene, with plenty of tastings

along the way. Great-value, four-hour tasting tours, leaving every Saturday from the castle at 10.30am are £45.

Wandering Bard Tours of South Wales BUS
(☑ 07854 194982, 07725 849121; https://toursof wales.co.uk/wandering-bard; per day £60) You are just not going to get more personalised, insightful tours of Wales than these run by Gareth Bates. He is a fluent Welsh speaker with a huge passion for Wales. Only one of his three set South Wales tours, the Welsh Valleys Tour, leaves from Cardiff, but he's very adaptable if you have different plans. Pickup/drop-off at your Cardiff digs.

Gareth's other set tours focus on Swansea Bay and Pembrokeshire.

Cardiff on Foot   WALKING
(www.cardiffwalkingtours.com; adult/child £45/10) Leads guided strolls around the city centre and Cardiff Bay. The quoted price is for two-person minimum tours of the city centre and bay; prices come down a lot (to as little as £5) when group size gets to six.

See Wales   BUS
(www.seewales.com; adult/child £45/30) Themed day tours include Mines & Mountains (visiting Big Pit in Blaenavon before heading through Brecon Beacons National Park to the town of Brecon), Romans & Ruins (Caerleon, Tintern Abbey and Raglan Castle) and Golden Gower (Swansea and the Gower Peninsula). Tours, cancelled during the Covid-19 pandemic, were starting again in 2021 at the time of research.

✷ Festivals & Events

Six Nations   SPORTS
(www.sixnationsrugby.com; ☺ Feb & Mar) The premier European rugby championship, with Wales taking on England, Scotland, Ireland, Italy and France. Cardiff normally hosts two or three home games at Principality Stadium (p59) – the atmosphere is supercharged, and accommodation should be booked well in advance.

Cardiff Children's Lit Fest   LITERATURE
(www.cardiffkidslitfest.com; ☺ Apr) Nine days of storytelling, reading and activities: great if you're in the city that reared Roald Dahl with the little'uns.

**Everyman Open Air
Theatre Festival**   THEATRE
(www.everymanfestival.co.uk; ☺ Jun & Jul) Five weeks of theatre, held in Sophia Gardens.

Cardiff International Food & Drink Festival FOOD & DRINK
(⌚early Jul) Held over a long weekend (Friday to Sunday), this festival sees Roald Dahl Plass filled with producers' stalls, a farmers market, street food and craft stalls. One of Wales' better gastronomy-focused festivals.

Welsh Proms MUSIC
(www.welshproms.com; ⌚mid-Jul) A week of classical concerts at St David's Hall.

Pride Cymru PARADE
(www.pridecymru.co.uk; ⌚late Aug) Also known as the Cardiff-Wales LGBT Mardi Gras, this annual lesbian, gay, bisexual and transgender pride festival includes a street parade and a ticketed day-long celebration in Bute Park.

Sŵn Festival MUSIC
(www.swnfest.com; ⌚Oct) New music from Wales and further afield is the thing here, backed by a little film and art, held in venues across Cardiff each October. Sŵn means 'noise' in English, by the way.

Festival of Voice MUSIC
(www.festivalofvoice.wales; ⌚Oct-Nov) The Welsh have always excelled at vocalising, from medieval bards to rock bands. Held in even-numbered years at venues across Cardiff, this four-day festival celebrates that heritage, and in a wider sense the human voice generally over many genres. Past line-ups have included gospel choirs, the Welsh National Opera and solo luminaries such as Van Morrison and John Cale.

Note there will be a festival in 2021 (to compensate for the lack of one in 2020).

Cardiff Christmas Market CHRISTMAS MARKET
(www.cardiffchristmasmarket.com; The Hayes; ⌚10am-6pm Mon-Sat, to 5pm Sun mid-Nov–Dec 23rd) Cardiffians embrace Christmas early, but with 200-plus stalls festively festooning the Hayes – the majority independents selling mainly traditional products you just can't source on the high street – you can see why.

Sleeping

Cardiff has Wales' broadest range of accommodation, spanning luxury hotels to personable guesthouses. It has several decent hostels too, but due to Covid-19 many were closed at the time of research, and not recommended due to the difficulty of social distancing.

Most places have higher rates on Friday and Saturday nights. It can be almost impossible to find a bed anywhere near the city on big sporting weekends, especially rugby internationals – book well ahead if your visit coincides with one.

City Centre

The central city has an OK selection of budget and upmarket accommodation, though it's predominantly in big chain hotels. Light sleepers, take note: it can be noisy.

Hotel One Hundred HOTEL £
(☎029-2010 5590; www.hotelonehundred.com; 100 Newport Rd, Adamsdown, CF24 1DG; r from £45; P 📶) Patterned metallic wallpaper and chandeliers add a touch of glam to the rooms of this small B&B-like hotel. It's on a busy arterial road, so expect some street noise in the front rooms. A continental breakfast is included in the rates. A minimum two-night stay applies, but one-night bookings are accepted for any unsold rooms three days prior to arrival.

It's self check-in with a code provided before arrival. Book in advance.

Sleeperz HOTEL £
(Map p56; ☎029-2047 8747; www.sleeperz.com/cardiff; Station Approach, Saunders Rd; r from £38.70; 📶) Some of the best budget private rooms in the city, small but clean, are provided in trademark style by the Sleeperz chain, which has four hotels across the UK. Cardiff's is right by (as in, alongside) Cardiff Central station in a large, five-floor contemporary building. Breakfast is £7.95 extra. Book online for cheapest rates.

Premier Inn Cardiff City Centre HOTEL £
(Map p56; ☎0333 777 3981; www.premierinn.com; Helmont House, 10 Churchill Way; r without breakfast from £35; 📶) The Cardiff branch of Britain's biggest chain has some 200 beds in a squat, mirror-clad city-centre former office tower. It's not flash, but it's comfortable, clean and rooms are decently sized – though you'll need to book in advance online for the cheapest rates. Higher-floored rooms can be quieter. Breakfast is £8.99.

There's no on-site parking, but parking is available nearby at a guest rate of £12.50 per day.

★**Hotel Indigo** BOUTIQUE HOTEL ££
(Map p56; ☎0871 942 9104; www.ihg.com; Dominions Arcade, Queen St; r/ste from £62/103; 📶)

The Indigo Hotel Group (IHG) has over a dozen hotels UK-wide, but only this one in Wales. Like other IHG offerings, it tailors itself uniquely to Cardiff and Welsh culture. Spacious rooms cleverly include aspects such as traditional Welsh fabrics above bed headboards, pictures of old industrial scenes and crockery decorated with sheep. Insanely good value.

Expect in-room coffee machines, welcome sweets, Myddfai toiletries and voluminous, retro-tiled showers. Staff are eager to please and the top-floor breakfast room metamorphoses in afternoons/evenings into a Marco Pierre White Steakhouse. The entrance is inside a Queen St shopping mall.

Park Plaza HOTEL **££**
(Map p56; ☑029-2011 1111; www.parkplaza cardiff.com; Greyfriars Rd; r £79-134, ste £149-169; ✳🛜🛋) Luxurious without being stuffy, the Plaza has all the five-star facilities you'd expect from an upmarket business-oriented hotel, including a gym for guests, a spa, a restaurant/bar (open to all) and Egyptian cotton on the beds. The slick reception has a gas fire blazing along one wall, and rear rooms have leafy views over the Civic Centre.

Rates can be a smidgeon cheaper if you book online, in advance, and midweek. No parking, though – despite the name.

🛏 Pontcanna & Canton

Long, leafy Cathedral Rd is lined with B&Bs and small hotels, nearly all in restored Victorian town houses. It's only a 15- to 20-minute walk from the city centre, or a £10 taxi ride from the train and bus stations. Street parking is mostly unrestricted, but check signage carefully.

Cathedral 73 BOUTIQUE HOTEL **££**
(Map p73; ☑029-2023 5005; http://cathe dral73.com; 73 Cathedral Rd, Pontcanna, CF11 9HE; d/ste from £99/179; 🅿🛜) Bedecked in mirrored fittings and silver tones, this stylish little hotel has nine rooms, suites and apartments in a beautifully restored Victorian town house. Downstairs there's a restaurant (two-course meal £25), chi-chi tearoom and piano bar specialising in gin, while out back there's a pretty garden terrace. There are also gin-making classes. Spot the gin theme? There's a mini-distillery next door.

Parking is £10 per night.

Lincoln House HOTEL **££**
(Map p73; ☑029-2039 5558; www.lincolnhotel. co.uk; 118-120 Cathedral Rd, Pontcanna, CF11 9LQ; r £100-135, 2-4-person penthouse £190-290; 🅿🛜) Walking a middle line between a large B&B and a small hotel, Lincoln House is a generously proportioned Victorian property with heraldic emblems in the stained-glass windows of its book-lined sitting room, and a separate bar. There are 21 rooms and a loft penthouse sleeping up to four. For added romance, book a four-poster room.

Saco Cardiff APARTMENT **££**
(Map p73; ☑0845 122 0405; www.sacoapart ments.co.uk; 76 Cathedral Rd, Pontcanna, CF11

9LN; 1-/2-bedroom apt from £105/129; [P][🛜])
This large town house has been given a
contemporary makeover by Saco, which
operates in several UK cities, and converted
into one- and two-bedroom serviced apartments with comfortable lounges and fitted
kitchens. The place is set up for longer visits: one-night stays are possible midweek,
but rates can increase at weekends. The
two-bedroom apartments are good value
for families with kids.

Courtfield Hotel
B&B ££

(Map p73; ☑029-2022 7701; www.courtfield
hotel.com; 101 Cathedral Rd, Pontcanna, CF11 9PH;
s/d from £40/80; 🛜) It's the friendliness of
hosts, Keith and Norman, and the hearty
breakfasts that distinguish this Victorian
town house B&B from the Cathedral Rd
pack. The decor is suitably old-fashioned,
with moulded cornices, chandeliers and
heavy red carpets.

🛏 Riverside & Grangetown

Tŷ Rosa
B&B ££

(☑029-2022 1964; www.tyrosa.com; 118 Clive St,
Grangetown, CF11 7JE; s/d from £64/79; 🛜) A
good 30 minutes' walk from either the Bay
or central Cardiff, and just south of Grangetown railway station (four minutes from
Cardiff Central by regular direct train),
this gay-friendly B&B is noted for sumptuous breakfasts and affable hosts. The neat,
thoughtfully equipped rooms, named after South Wales sights, divide between the
main house and an annexe across the road.
Some rooms share bathrooms.

Riverhouse
B&B ££

(Map p56; ☑029-2010 5590; www.icardiff.
co.uk/riverhouse; 59 Fitzhamon Embankment,
Riverside, CF11 6AN; d £64-68, tr/q £85/131; 🛜)
Professionally run by a helpful young broth-
er-and-sister team, the Riverhouse is a mix
of small, clean doubles, triples and quadru-
ples in a genteel terraced Victorian property
right across the Taff from Principality Stadium. A good free breakfast is provided if you
book through the website. Parking outside
is £9 per day.

🛏 Cardiff Bay

Choices are surprisingly thin here, and predominantly chains, though the impressively
refurbished Coal Exchange (p61) opened
in late 2020, adding some much-needed
variety. If you want seaside lodgings close to
Cardiff, also consider Penarth.

Future Inns Cardiff Bay
HOTEL £

(☑029-2048 7111; www.futureinns.co.uk; Hem-
ingway Rd, CF10 4AU; r without breakfast from
£58; [P][🛜]) Of the Bay's lower midrange
chain hotels, this is most interesting,
though its location feels more rounda-
bout-side than bayside. It's one of three
of Canada-originating Future's UK hotels.
Digs are large and finished to three-star
standard, there's a restaurant-bar and –
perhaps deal-clinchingly – free parking.
Don't like your room? There are 196 others.
  Breakfast is £12 if you want it.

Voco St David's Hotel & Spa
SPA HOTEL ££

(Map p60; ☑029-2045 4045; www.thestdavids
hotel.com; Havannah St, CF10 5SD; d from £100;
[P][@][🛜][🏊]) One of the few five-star hotels
in Cardiff, this high-end modern hotel
favoured by corporate types and couples
occupies the water's edge in Cardiff Bay.
Its location offers panoramic views across
Cardiff Bay, Penarth and over the Bristol
Channel towards England. Rooms are
plush and spacious and the design, with its
dramatic, futuristic central atrium, is a bit
different.
  The spa is one of Wales' best. Parking
spaces go for a premium £20.

🛏 Northern Suburbs

The New House
HISTORIC HOTEL £££

(☑029-2052 0280; https://townandcountry
collective.co.uk; Thornhill, CF14 9UA; s/d from
£110/138; [P][🛜]) A delightful discovery if you
prefer being based out of Cardiff in a characterful manor, but with spectacular city
views nevertheless (doesn't sound terrible,
right?). The New House is actually pretty
old (1730s) and from its ivy-trailed facade
through its sumptuous rooms and elegant
Sequoias restaurant, it's a class above.
  Even topographically it presides over
Cardiff's other accommodation, perched
on the slopes of Caerphilly Mountain on
the capital's northern limits. Stagecoach
bus 86X from Greyfriars Rd in central Cardiff stops nearby on the Cardiff–Caerphilly
Thornhilll Rd.

🍴 Eating

As Cardiff has become more glossy, cosmopolitan and multicultural, so have its eateries. There are myriad cafes and restaurants

firing confidence and creativity on all cylinders across all cuisines, with Wales and its wondrous produce championed, too.

✗ City Centre

The centre is strong on cafes and chains, but it can be harder to find a memorable meal. Options exist if you know where to look.

Brodies Coffee Co
CAFE £

(Map p56; ☑07414 963591; www.facebook.com/ brodiescoffee; Gorsedd Gardens, CF10 3NP; toasties £3.50; ☺10am-4pm) A charming New Zealand–trained barista serves amazing coffee from this cute little Gorsedd Gardens kiosk. Food is limited to toasted sandwiches, cookies, muffins and slices – tasty accompaniments to those silky flat whites. No issues with social distancing at tables dotted across a pretty park terrace, though if it rains you'll get wet. For this coffee, we'd chance it!

Pettigrew Tea Rooms
CAFE £

(Map p56; ☑029-2023 5486; www.pettigrew -tearooms.com; West Lodge, Castle St; mains £6-12, afternoon tea for one £17.50; ☺10am-6pm, closes 30min before dusk in winter) Cuppas and cakes are served on delicate china at this atmospheric little tearoom within the crenellated confines of Bute Park's 1863 gatehouse. Cucumber sandwiches, fabled afternoon teas, scuffed vintage furniture and crackly '20s tunes accompany the extensive range of beverages on offer – or try the ploughman's platter if you're after something more hearty.

Book afternoon teas in advance; there is a pleasant park-abutting terrace.

Uncommon Ground
Coffee Roastery
CAFE £

(Map p56; www.uncommon-ground.co.uk; 10-12 Royal Arcade; sandwiches & snacks £3-7; ☺7.30am-6.30pm Mon-Sat, 10am-5pm Sun; 🛜) Highly accomplished coffee roasters with a dark, debonair, bare-brick interior in one of Cardiff's classiest retail settings. The speciality teas and coffees are a welcome pick-me-up, the brownies are veritable slabs and a panini/salad selection completes the billing.

Madame Fromage
DELI £

(Map p56; ☑029-2064 4888; www.madame fromage.co.uk; 21-25 Castle Arcade; mains £6-15; ☺11am-4pm Mon-Sat) One of Cardiff's best delicatessens, with a wide range of charcuterie and French and Welsh cheese, the Madame also has a cafe with tables spilling into the arcade. Here you can read French newspapers and eat a mixture of Breton and Welsh dishes, including rarebit, lamb *cawl* (a stew-like soup) and *bara brith* (fruit cake).

★Curado
SPANISH ££

(Map p56; ☑029-2034 4336; www.curadobar. com; Guildhall Pl; pintxos £3.50, other dishes £7-15; ☺5-10pm Tue-Thu, noon-10pm Fri & Sat, to 6pm Sun) This ranks among central Cardiff's best places to eat right now. Elegant Spanish food personally sourced by the owners is Wales' finest, served in the divine forms of pintxos, northern Spain's answer to tapas. Big glass windows and metro-tiled walls enclose two floors and a downstairs deli. We recommend *morcilla*, Spanish black pudding with goats cheese and peppers.

Staff are also incredibly knowledgable, and the Spanish wine selection is eclectic. You need perhaps four small dishes for a filling meal, making this a brilliant mid-range dining option.

Pasture
STEAK ££

(Map p56; ☑07511 217422; www.pastureres taurant.com; 8-10 High St; mains £14-36; ☺noon-10pm Mon-Sat, 11.45am-7pm Sun) The classy steakhouse that began in Bristol now has its second home in Cardiff – it was the Welsh capital's see-and-be-seen place as we went to press. Its glitzy presence on High St has dated most of its neighbours. Steak, steak, steak is the raison d'être, whether that's chateaubriand, tomahawk or porterhouse. Meats are dry-aged for 35 days minimum.

Your mouth will water as serving staff showcase the 'prize cuts' priced per 100g and served in portions big enough for two. Book in advance.

The Clink
EUROPEAN ££

(☑029-2092 3130; https://theclinkcharity.org; Knox Rd, HMP Cardiff; breakfast £6-9, mains £14-17, 3-course dinner £39.95; ☺breakfast 9-11am Mon-Sat, lunch noon-3pm daily, dinner 6.30-9.30pm Thu-Sat) 🌿 This joint gives a whole new meaning to 'lockdown' as, despite smart dining environs (leather seats, glass tables, exposed brick and lofty pitched ceilings) and suave British-European cuisine (perhaps crispy pork belly with apricot, pancetta and thyme sauce), you're here for the fact that the ex-cell-ent food is prepared and served by prisoners in the last stages of their sentences.

Your money contributes towards improving their futures.

Potted Pig
MODERN BRITISH ££

(Map p56; ☑ 029-2022 4817; www.thepotted pig.com; 27 High St; starters £8, mains £19-28; ☺ 5-8.30pm Tue, noon-2.30pm & 5-8.30pm Wed-Fri, noon-8.30pm Sat, to 3.30pm Sun) Intimately located in the vaulted basement of a former bank, the Potted Pig is a thoroughly British bistro, serving the likes of ham hock, quail, Welsh lamb and steak. It's also known for its vast range of gins and speciality tonics. Dine here and feel all sorts of elite and exclusive.

Casanova
ITALIAN ££

(Map p56; ☑ 029-2034 4044; www.casanova cardiff.co.uk; 13 Quay St; 2-/3-course lunch £16/20, mains £16-21; ☺ noon-2.30pm & 5.30-10pm Mon-Sat) Rather than offering generic Italian dishes or the specialities of just one region, this little charmer offers a selection of authentic regional dishes from all over Italy. The result is a varied menu with half-a-dozen options for each course, served in a compact, romantic setting.

✘ Pontcanna & Canton

Here, Pontcanna is the verdant, well-to-do part; Canton the energised multiethnic part. Makings of a memorable food scene? We believe so.

Milkwood Bistro
BISTRO £

(Map p73; ☑ 029-2023 2226; www.milkwood cardiff.com; 83 Pontcanna St, Pontcanna, CF11 9HS; plates £4-11; ☺ 5-10pm Wed, noon-10pm Thu-Sat) Brunch, lunch or dine here and feel the Pontcanna love. It advertises itself as modern Welsh, but while many ingredients fit the bill, the small plates, pizzas, burgers and sandwiches are pan-European, or even pan-world, encompassing buffalo wings, celeriac and schnitzel burgers, cod fritters and ox-cheek fries.

Purple Poppadom
INDIAN ££

(Map p73; ☑ 029-2022 0026; www.purplepop padom.com; 185a Cowbridge Rd E, Canton CF1 9AJ; mains £11-20; ☺ 5-10pm Tue-Sat, 1-9pm Sun; ☑) Trailblazing a path for 'nouvelle Indian' cuisine, chef and author Anand George adds his own twist to dishes from all over the subcontinent – from Kashmir to Kerala. The emphasis is on perfecting tried-and-tested regional delights rather than anything unnecessarily wacky. Plump for a *nadan kozhi* chicken thigh and coconut curry. Flavours are thought-provokingly rich.

La Cuina
CATALAN ££

(Map p73; ☑ 029-2019 0265; www.lacuina.co.uk; 11 Kings Rd, Pontcanna, CF11 9BZ; mains £13-23; ☺ 5.30-9.30pm Wed & Thu, to 10pm Fri & Sat) This cute Catalonian restaurant is *so* Pontcanna: a desirable, unpretentious place that passersby look longingly upon from the leafy streets, and which bursts with culinary love. Start with octopus, pea puree and paprika, then proceed with Aragón mountain lamb, washed back by vino from Catalan micro-producers. Chef-owner Montserrat has made this one of the neighbourhood's longest-running success stories. *Bravissimo.*

Dusty Knuckle
PIZZA ££

(☑ 07506 659306; www.dustyknuckle.co.uk; The Boneyard, Paper Mill Rd, Canton, CF11 8DH; pizza £8-15; ☺ 5-9pm Wed & Thu, noon-9pm Fri-Sun) Cardiff's coolest pizza outfit spreads its doughy fingers far across the city: it's also at Sticky Fingers (p72) in Roath. But we like this colourful, low-fi al fresco location on an industrial estate on the edge of Canton best (as do the hipsters) to wolf down wood-fired Neapolitan-style pizza. Bookings advised.

It's its offerings from the 'filthy' and 'fancy' lists, such as the gorgonzola, pear and walnut pizza, that distinguish the place.

✘ Riverside & Grangetown

Riverside Market
MARKET

(Map p56; www.riversidemarket.org.uk; Fitzhamon Embankment, Riverside, CF11 6AN; ☺ 10am-1.30pm Sun) Every Sunday, this street market takes over the embankment across the Taff from Principality Stadium. Independent producers flaunt their wares, from speciality cheeses, homemade sourdough bread and cured meats to fresh vegetables, jars of jam and hefty cronuts. Seating lets you watch the river go by while sipping great coffee and scoffing your goodies.

✘ Cardiff Bay

A breeding ground for exceptional restaurants that have developed to counter the bland bay-fronting chains of the Mermaid Quay complex, the scene here is nevertheless ever-changing to the verge of erraticism, not helped by Covid-19, which kept tourists away from an area reliant on them and destroyed many businesses.

✗ Northern Suburbs

Ranging between the gritty and the glam, the area stretching north of the city centre has seemingly endless supplies of exciting eats.

Sticky Fingers
STREET FOOD £

(☑ 029-2047 0803; www.stickyfingersstreetfood. com; 199-201 Richmond Rd, Roath, CF24 3BT; ⊙5-10pm Mon-Fri, noon-10pm Sat & Sun) Based in Roath, this permanent one-stop address for Cardiff street food has ever-changing stalls such as Cardiff classics Dusty Knuckle (p71) and Tukka Tuk with its Indian fare from Anand George of Purple Poppadom (p71). At the bar, Cardiff breweries Pipes and Crafty Devil preside on the taps and there are good cocktails, too. Food Thursday to Sunday only.

Organicafè
CAFE £

(104 Caerphilly Rd, Birchgrove, CF14 4AG; breakfast £3-4, panini £6-7; ⊙8am-5.30pm Tue-Sat) This proper Italian-style deli-cafe, with its sunny tables out the back entertaining expats and language students, serves panini, *cornetti* (Italian-style croissants), salads, salumi platters and Italian-style home baking. It also stocks Italian cheeses and cold cuts, organic coffee, jams and cereals.

Cafe Chat du Noir
FRENCH ££

(☑ 029-2048 8993; 6 Wellfield Court Arcade, Wellfield Rd, Roath, CF24 3PB; mains £7-15; ⊙4-9pm Wed & Thu, noon-9pm Fri & Sat, noon-4pm Sun) Eating out on trendy Wellfield Rd should start with this elegant French-Mediterranean-focused bistro that is forever making 'best in Cardiff' lists. You might opt for a croque – not just the standard monsieur, but also the likes of the Breton (with salmon) or *du Chat noir* special (chicken and goats cheese), or plump for paella.

The setting in a quiet set-back courtyard dispenses with the only downside of dining hereabouts: traffic noise.

Anna-Loka
VEGAN ££

(☑ 029-2049 7703; www.anna-loka.com; 114 Albany Rd, Roath, CF24 3RU; mains £11-13; ⊙noon-3pm & 5-10pm Wed-Fri, 11am-10pm Sat, 11am-5pm Sun; ☑) Wales' first 100% vegan restaurant, Anna-Loka offers breakfast baps and wraps, wholefood bowls, battered tofu, wraps, seitan burgers, irresistible triple-cooked chips

and desserts: hearty, healthy food in a vibrantly ethnic interior you wouldn't guess could be so convivial from the ordinary exterior.

Oz Urfa
MIDDLE EASTERN ££

(☑ 029-2062 0912; https://ozurfa.co.uk; 148 North Rd, Maindy, CF14 3BH; mains £10-14; ⊙2-10pm Tue-Sun) This family-run restaurant specialises in 'traditional Mediterranean and Mesopotamian food', which translates as delicious mezze, *güveç* (casseroles), whole roast lamb, fish dishes and shish kebabs cooked over a charcoal grill. Excellent-value lunch specials at £9 for two courses.

🍷 Drinking & Nightlife

Cardiff is a prodigiously boozy city, but there are two sides to the fun. Friday and Saturday nights see the centre invaded by hordes of generally good-humoured, beered-up lads and ladettes tottering from bar to club to kebab shop, whatever the weather. The lively alternative scene, including some of the most stylish and unusual bars in Britain and some great old-fashioned pubs, is harder to tap into, but brilliant once you do.

🍷 City Centre

Porter's
BAR

(Map p56; www.porterscardiff.com; Harlech Ct, Bute Tce; ⊙5-10pm Sun-Wed, 4-10pm Thu & Fri, noon-10pm Sat) Owned by a confessed 'failed actor', this friendly, attitude-free bar has something on most nights, whether it's a quiz, live music, comedy, theatre or movie screening (there's a little cinema attached). Local drama is showcased in the 'Other Room', the adjoining 44-seat theatre, while there's a wonderful beer garden out back.

Dead Canary
COCKTAIL BAR

(Map p56; ☑ 029-2023 1263; www.thedead canary.co.uk; Barrack Lane; ⊙5-10pm Tue-Sun) Inspired by Prohibition-era bars, this swanky speakeasy is hidden behind a narrow city-centre lane. Find the bell with a feather painted nearby (it's near a fire-exit sign). You'll then enter the dimly lit bar, with low seats, a jazz-club vibe and the best cocktails in town. Book ahead.

Lab 22
COCKTAIL BAR

(Map p56; ☑ 029-2039 9997; www.lab22cardiff. com; 22 Caroline St; ⊙2-10pm) The decor's all over the place (Prohibition speakeasy meets Buddha bar meets mad-scientist's lair) but

Pontcanna & Canton

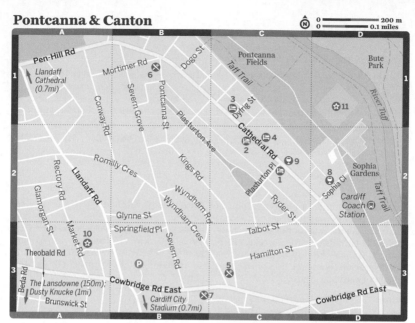

the bar staff are slick and the cocktails are famous far beyond the city limits.

Tiny Rebel   CRAFT BEER

(Map p56; ☑029-2039 9557; www.tinyrebel. co.uk; 25 Westgate St; ◷5-10pm Mon-Thu, noon-10pm Fri-Sun; 🖥) Slathered in graffiti art, this sprawling grunge-chic corner bar is the Cardiff outpost of an award-winning craft brewery from neighbouring Newport. Expect 15 craft beers on keg, 10 on cask and others by the bottle (we love an Easy Livin' pale ourselves). Good whiskies and regular gigs (from punk to cabaret) in non-Covid-19 times.

Gin & Juice   JUICE BAR

(Map p56; ☑029-2022 1556; www.ginand juice.com; 2-6 Castle Arcade; ◷8.30am-10pm) In seriously beautiful, tile-festooned, old-photograph-studded premises where historic Castle Arcade meets High St, and with tables spilling out onto the latter, Gin & Juice is an exuberant all-day affair. By day it's a juice, coffee, smoothie and bagel bar, and by night a gin den lovingly nursing some 400 varieties of gin.

Cambrian Tap   PUB

(Map p56; ☑029-2064 4952; www.sabrain.com; St Mary St; ◷noon-10pm Mon-Fri, 11am-10pm

Pontcanna & Canton

Sat & Sun; 🖥🖥) Cardiff's main brewery's unlikely contribution to the craft-beer revolution, this old-style corner pub serves up to 18 draught taps and a rotating selection of guest ales and local boutique beers. It's a lovely interior, attracting the usual city-pub assortment of odd characters.

Pen & Wig   PUB

(Map p56; ☑029-2037 1217; www.penand wigcardiff.co.uk; 1 Park Grove, CF10 3BJ;

LGBTIQ+ CARDIFF

Cardiff's small LGBTIQ+ scene is focused on a cluster of venues on Churchill Way and Charles St. The big event is the annual Pride Cymru (p67) in late August.

Eagle (Map p56; ☑029-2114 0000; www.eaglecardiff.com; 39 Charles St; ⊗5-10pm Thu-Sat) This friendly little basement bar is a bastion for blokiness, and considered by many to be Cardiff's best gay hang-out. Special events cover the spectrum from kink to karaoke. It also operates the Eagle 50 sauna across the road. Check the website for updates on opening hours.

Golden Cross (Map p56; ☑029-2115 1517; 283 Hayes Bridge Rd; ⊗noon-10pm; 🖥) One of the city's oldest pubs and a long-standing gay venue, this Grade II-listed Victorian bar retains its handsome stained glass, polished wood and ceramic tiles. It hosts drag, cabaret, games and karaoke nights, and there's a little dance floor.

⊗noon-10pm) Latin legal phrases (a nod to the many patrons from the legal profession) are printed on the walls of this solidly traditional pub. Large beer garden, weekly entertainment (in non-Covid-19 times) featuring a cask-ale club, quiz and live music, and straightforward pub grub.

Retro CLUB
(Map p56; ☑029-2034 4688; www.retrocardiff.co.uk; 7 Mill Lane; ⊗9pm-4am Wed, 6pm-2am Thu, 6pm-4am Fri & Sat, noon-4am Sun) The 'home of the party vibe' is exactly what you'd expect it to be. If you were around in the Britpop heyday, prepare to bop around your handbag all night long.

Pontcanna & Canton

The Lansdowne PUB
(☑029-2022 1312; www.facebook.com/thelansdownecardiff; 71 Beda Rd, cnr Lansdowne Rd, Canton, CF5 1LX; ⊗noon-10pm) With charmingly scruffy rooms sprawling around a central bar painted racing green and festooned with hops, the Lansdowne is esteemed for its CAMRA-acknowledged dedication to craft beer and cider and open-mic nights. It even runs its own mini beer festival every June.

The Cricketers PUB
(Map p73; ☑029-2034 5102; www.cricketerscardiff.co.uk; Cathedral Rd, Pontcanna, CF11 9LL; ⊗noon-10pm) The Cricketers marks a start (or end) to the Cathedral Rd pub crawl (a civilised affair compared to the more beered-up stagger on the city-centre equivalent). It feels like drinking in some urbane city dweller's private Victorian town house. There's a flagstoned beer garden, Evan Evans beers on tap and decent pub grub (mains £11 to £19).

Brewhouse & Kitchen PUB
(Map p73; ☑029-2037 1599; www.brewhouseandkitchen.com/venue/cardiff; Sophia Close, Pontcanna, CF11 9HW; ⊗11am-10pm Sun-Fri, from 10am Sat; 🖥) Right by SWALEC Stadium in an intriguing timber-framed edifice, this outpost of UK-wide Brewhouse & Kitchen is in pole position for thirsty cricket lovers, with an on-site microbrewery, conservatory, beer-garden seating and food (pub classics with a bit of barbecue thrown in). We'd say it's best for a sunny-afternoon pint stop while exploring Pontcanna.

Cardiff Bay

Academy @ Platform CAFE
(Map p60; www.academycoffee.co.uk/academy-platform; Bute St, Cardiff Bay railway station, CF10 5LE; ⊗9am-5pm Mon-Thu, to 10pm Fri & Sat, 10am-5pm Sun) Alighting from the train at Cardiff Bay, you won't find a better place for java than this swish platform new-build. Beans get sustainably sourced in Minas Gerais, Brazil, and consequent cuppas are pretty darned special (remember this as you invariably shun our advice and stray to the waterside vainly searching for nicer drinking spots). Come for craft beer and cocktails, too.

The Dock BAR
(Map p60; ☑029-2045 0947; www.sabrain.com; Mermaid Quay, CF10 5BZ; ⊗noon-10pm) If you must visit the chain-heavy wasteland of Mermaid Quay, you might as well drink overlooking the water at a place with slightly more personality. This gleaming, glassy, vaguely ship-shaped two-floor bar is captained by big Cardiff brewery SA Brain & Co, but stocks gins and cocktails, too.

☆ Entertainment

It's really important, especially when much entertainment has been disrupted by Covid-19, to get an up-to-the-minute take on what's happening. Pick up a copy of *Buzz* (www.buzzmag.co.uk), a free monthly magazine with up-to-date entertainment listings, available from tourist offices, bars, theatres and the like. Staff at the tourist office (p77) at Cardiff Castle can also help out with recommendations.

Live Music

Massive rock and pop concerts are staged at Principality Stadium (p59) and **Motorpoint Arena** (Map p56; ☑ 029-2022 4488; https://motorpointarenacardiff.co.uk; Mary Ann St), plonking the city on the map of Britain's best live-music destinations. If you're after a more intimate experience, try one of the many bars hosting live bands.

Pandemic-less times see Llandaff Cathedral (p64) and **St John the Baptist Church** (Map p56; ☑ 029-2039 5231; www.st johnscardiff.wales; 3 St John St, CF10 1GL; ☺ 10am-3pm Mon-Sat, to 6pm Sun) hosting regular classical-music concerts.

★ Clwb Ifor Bach   LIVE MUSIC
(Map p56; ☑ 029-2023 2199; www.clwb.net; 11 Womanby St; cover from £5; ☺ 7-10.30pm Sun-Wed, to 4am Thu-Sat) Named for 12th-century Welsh rebel Ifor Bach, the legendary Clwb ('Club') has broken many a Welsh band since it first opened its doors in 1983, building a reputation as Cardiff's most important indie-music venue. It now hosts bands performing in many tongues – from young upstarts to more established acts – along with regular club nights (Saturday is the big one).

Cardiff University
Students' Union   LIVE MUSIC
(Map p56; ☑ 029-2078 1400; www.cardiff students.com; Park Pl) The students' union hosts regular live gigs by big-name bands, usually of an alternative bent. The 'What's On' section of its website details the where and when.

St David's Hall   CLASSICAL MUSIC
(Map p56; ☑ 029-2087 8444; www.stdavids hallcardiff.co.uk; The Hayes) As the National Concert Hall of Wales, this address hosts the Welsh Proms in July and has a year-round roster of classical-music performances and other music from '80s to folk to jazz, comedy... the list is lengthy.

Royal Welsh College of
Music & Drama   LIVE PERFORMANCE
(Map p56; ☑ 029-2034 2854; www.rwcmd.ac.uk; Bute Park, CF10 3ER) All manner of performances are staged in this impressive, spacious building's state-of-the-art venues, including theatre from the college's in-house Richard Burton Company and music from jazz to classical.

The Deep   LIVE MUSIC
(Map p56; ☑ 07958 211744; www.thedeepvenuc. co.uk; 21 St Mary St; ☺ 3-10pm) Formerly the city's long-standing jazz venue, this is under brand-new management and has widened its repertoire to include all sorts of live music – both local acts and names from further afield – plus resident DJs at weekends.

Theatre, Comedy & Cinema

The Wales Millennium Centre (p62) is the home of the Welsh National Opera, BBC National Orchestra, National Dance Company Wales and other bastions of the arts.

Chapter   ARTS CENTRE
(Map p73; ☑ 029-2031 1050; www.chapter.org; Market Rd, Canton, CF5 1QE; ☺ 9am-9pm; ☎) Established in 1972 and still Cardiff's edgiest arts venue, Chapter masterminds a varied rota of art exhibitions (often free), art house cinema (tickets £6), contemporary drama, workshops and dance performances. There's also a very popular cafe-bar, with a big range of international beers and real ale on tap.

Also stop by just to find a recommendation of somewhere to eat or drink locally: it's a proper community hub.

New Theatre   THEATRE
(Map p56; ☑ 07367 629234; www.newtheatre cardiff.co.uk; cnr Park Pl & Greyfriars Rd) This pretty, restored Edwardian playhouse sporting two cupolas atop its roof hosts various touring productions, including theatre, musicals and pantomime.

Sherman Theatre   THEATRE
(Map p56; ☑ 029-2064 6900; www.sherman theatre.co.uk; Senghennydd Rd, Cathays, CF24 4YE) Reopening for spring 2021, South Wales' leading theatre company, Sherman, stages a wide range of material from classics and children's theatre to works by new playwrights.

Sport

Cardiff Arms Park
SPECTATOR SPORT

(Map p56; ☑ 029-2030 2000; www.cardiffrfc.com; Westgate St; tickets £12-24) In one handy space are some of the country's most important rugby venues. Cardiff Arms Park is home to both the Cardiff Rugby Football Club (www.cardiffrfc.com), aka the Blue and Blacks, founded in 1876, and the Cardiff Blues (www.cardiffblues.com), the professional regional side.

While the big rugby union test matches held next door at Principality Stadium (p59) provide a more thrilling spectacle, you're far more likely to be able to score tickets to a game here.

Cardiff City Stadium
SPECTATOR SPORT

(☑ 0333 311 1927; www.cardiffcityfc.co.uk; Leckwith Rd, Canton, CH11 8AZ) This 33,300-seater is home to Cardiff City Football Club, a big team that currently seesaws between the Championship and English Premier Leagues. Matches are usually on Saturday afternoons – catch the full schedule online.

Glamorgan County Cricket Club
SPECTATOR SPORT

(Map p73; ☑ 029-2040 9380; www.glamorgancricket.com; Sophia Gardens) Wales' leading cricket club: get match tickets and related info through the website.

 Shopping

Cardiff's market and Victorian and Edwardian shopping arcades give the city centre's retail action a touch of class: they're buildings to be admired in their own right. There are seven historic arcades in total: check out City of Arcades (https://thecityofarcades.com) for full details.

Cardiff Market
MARKET

(Map p56; www.cardiffcouncilproperty.com/cardiff-market; St Mary St, CF10 1AU; ⊙ 8am-4.30pm Mon-Sat) There's been a market here since the 18th century, but the current iron-framed covered market dates to 1891. Stalls sell everything from fresh fish to knitting supplies, and there's inspirational fare for a Bute Park picnic. Top stalls? Ashton's (fishmongers; supposedly trading on this spot 150-plus years), Noglu (delicious gluten-free treats), Hatts Emporium (vintage clothes

---

LOVE SPOONS

All over Wales, craft shops turn out wooden spoons with contorted handles in a variety of different designs at a speed that would have left their original makers – village lads with their eyes on a lass – gawking in astonishment. The carving of these spoons seems to date back to the 17th century, when they were made by men to give to women to mark the start of a courtship. If you want to see carving in progress, the St Fagans National History Museum (p63) can usually oblige. Any number of shops will be happy to sell you the finished product.

Various symbols are carved into the handles; the meanings of a few of them are as follows:

Anchor I'm home to stay; you can count on me.

Balls in a cage, links in a chain Captured love, together forever; the number of balls or links may correspond to the number of children desired, or the number of years already spent together.

Bell Marriage.

Celtic cross Faith; marriage.

Double spoon Side by side forever.

Flowers Love and affection; courtship.

Horseshoe Good luck; happiness.

Key, lock, little house My house is yours.

One heart My heart is yours.

Two hearts We feel the same way about one another.

Vines, trees, leaves Our love is growing.

and accessories) and upstairs, Kelly's Records (vinyl).

St David's
MALL
(Map p56; ☑029-2036 7600; https://stdavids cardiff.com; The Hayes; ⊘9.30am-8pm Mon-Fri, to 7pm Sat, 11am-5pm Sun; ☎) St David's is central Cardiff's biggest, slickest shopping centre, with all the famous chains you could name and even a golf course (p66) up top.

Bodlon
GIFTS & SOUVENIRS
(www.bodlon.com; 12 Park Rd, Whitchurch, CF14 7BQ; ⊘9am-4pm) Chasing a properly Welsh souvenir that isn't too cheesy? This shop, named for the Welsh for 'satisfied', is a good start. It stocks locally made art and craft, Welsh-language greeting cards and books, and has that all-important cafe, too.

Craft in the Bay
ARTS & CRAFTS
(Map p60; ☑029-2048 4611; www.makers guildinwales.org.uk; The Flourish, Lloyd George Ave, Cardiff Bay, CF10 4QH; ⊘11am-3pm Thu-Sun) This contemporary retail showcase for the Welsh Makers Guild cooperative is across from the Wales Millennium Centre, selling a wide range of authentic ceramics, textiles, jewellery, glassware and ironwork created by its members.

Morgan Quarter
SHOPPING CENTRE
(Map p56; www.morganquarter.co.uk; btwn St Mary St & The Hayes) Cardiff's oldest arcade, the Royal (1858), connects with Morgan Arcade via a series of covered lanes, forming a ritzy shopping precinct called the Morgan Quarter, which is the most beautiful of the city's arcade experiences. Along with name-brand fashion, shops sell skateboards, vintage books and antiques. Look for Spillers Records and excellent **Wally's Delicatessen** (Map p56; ☑029-2022 9265; www.wallys deli.co.uk; 38-46 Royal Arcade; ⊘9am-5.30pm Mon-Sat, 11am-4pm Sun) for scoffable takeaway goodies or foodie souvenirs.

Spillers Records
MUSIC
(Map p56; ☑029-2022 4905; www.spillers records.co.uk; 27 Morgan Arcade; ⊘10.30am-5pm Mon-Sat) The world's oldest record shop, founded in 1894 (when it sold wax phonograph cylinders), deserves special mention: *lots* of non-mainstream records and CDs for browsing and buying.

Castle Quarter
SHOPPING CENTRE
(Map p56; www.castlequarterarcades.co.uk; btwn High, Womanby, St John, Duke & Church Sts; ⊘8.30am-6pm Mon-Wed & Sat, to 9pm Thu & Fri, 10am-5pm Sun) Three more historic arcades comprise the Castle Quarter. The most decorative is the lovely **Castle Arcade** (btwn High & Womanby Sts), built in 1882 and housing Troutmark Books (Cardiff's best secondhand bookshop) among other stores. There are also the almost-as-venerable **High St and Duke St Arcades** (btwn High, Duke & St John Sts), dating from 1885 and 1902 respectively, on the other side of High St, completing the trio of arty shopping spaces.

ⓘ Information

Tourist Office (Map p56; ☑029-2087 2167; www.visitcardiff.com; Cardiff Castle; ⊘9am-5pm Mar-Oct, to 4pm Nov-Feb) In the Cardiff Castle courtyard, this is Cardiff's key tourist information centre. Souvenir shop and eateries adjacent.

University Hospital of Wales (☑029-2074 7747, 029-2074 4095; https://cavuhb.nhs. wales; The Gateway, Heath Park) Cardiff's main accident and emergency department, located 2 miles north of the city centre.

ⓘ Getting There & Away

AIR

Cardiff Airport (☑01446-711111; www. cardiff-airport.com; Rhoose, CF62 3BD) is 12 miles southwest of Cardiff, past Barry. The airlines with regular scheduled flights into Cardiff include the following:

Eastern Airways (www.easternairways.com) Belfast, Anglesey, Teeside

KLM (www.klm.com) Amsterdam

Loganair (www.loganair.co.uk) Edinburgh, Glasgow

Ryanair (www.ryanair.com) Málaga, Faro

TUI Airways (www.tui.co.uk; Mar-Oct only) Alicante, Gran Canaria, Lanzarote, Málaga, Tenerife, Rhodes, Antalya, Paphos, Dubrovnik, Corfu

Vueling (www.vueling.com) Alicante, Málaga, Palma de Mallorca

BUS

Cardiff's big new bus station is due to open in Wood St in 2023. In the meantime, buses call at stops scattered around the city; see www. traveline.cymru for details. Welsh destinations served include Caerphilly (£5.60, 45 minutes, half-hourly), Newport (£2.30, one hour, frequent) and Brecon (£7.20, two hours, five daily). Swansea (£5, 1¼ hours, every one to two hours) is best for points further west.

National Express (www.nationalexpress.com) coaches depart from **Cardiff Coach Station**

(Map p73; Sophia Gardens). Destinations include Swansea (from £5.50, 1¼ hours, two daily), Bristol (£7.60, 1¼ hours, seven daily) and London (£15 to £25, 4½ hours, three daily).

If you're connecting between Cardiff and London Heathrow Airport, you don't need to go via central London but can take the direct bus (from £14, 3½ hours, three daily).

Megabus (www.megabus.com) coaches stop on Kingsway. Destinations include Swansea (from £5, one hour, one daily) and Newport (from £3, 30 minutes, five daily). Services to Bristol (from £5, 1¼ hours, every two hours) usually continue to Heathrow Airport (from £17.50, 3¾ hours, six daily) and London (from £15, 4½ hours, six daily).

TRAIN

Trains from major British cities arrive at Cardiff Central station, on the southern edge of the city centre. Direct services to/from Cardiff include London Paddington (from £27.60, two hours, hourly), Abergavenny (£14.70, 40 minutes, at least hourly), Swansea (£12, one hour, at least

hourly), where you can change for points further west such as Tenby and Fishguard Harbour, and Shrewsbury (£48.60, two hours, hourly), where you can change for points in North Wales. For the latest timetables and bookings, see www.thetrainline.com.

ⓘ Getting Around

TO/FROM THE AIRPORT

The T9 Cardiff Airport Express bus (£5, 44 minutes, every 20 minutes) heads between the airport and Cardiff Bay via the city centre, though this was suspended at the time of writing due to Covid-19. The 304 Cardiff-Llantwit Major service (£2.65, one hour, hourly) stops at the airport, too.

The 905 shuttle bus (£1, nine minutes) links the airport terminal to nearby Rhoose Cardiff Airport railway station. Trains from Rhoose to Cardiff Central station (£4.80, 35 minutes) run hourly Monday to Saturday and every two hours on Sunday.

Around Cardiff

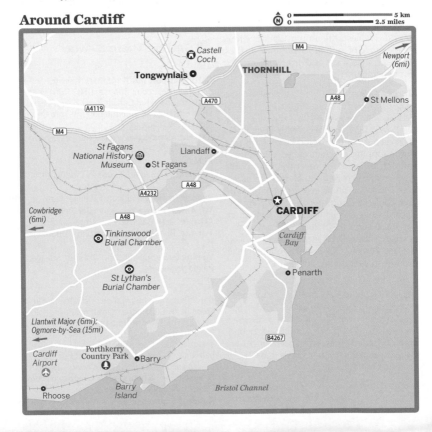

FlightLink Wales (☎ 01446-728 500; www.flightlinkwales.com) has the airport taxi concession, providing minibus shuttles to the city for £33.

BICYCLE

Cardiff Council's transport website (www.keepingcardiffmoving.co.uk) has lots of cycling information, including lists of bike shops and route maps. The city also has a bike-share scheme called **nextbike** (☎ 029-2248 1736; www.nextbike.co.uk); download its app and use it to unlock bikes parked in stations positioned around the city (£1 per 30 minutes, or £10 per 24 hours).

CAR & MOTORCYCLE

Cardiff doesn't pose many difficulties for drivers, though most central-city streets between Westgate St, Castle St and St David's are closed to traffic, meaning a cross-centre car journey often takes longer than the walk because of the circuitous, around-the-houses vehicular detour. City-centre parking is about £12 per day. It can be better (cheaper, and certainly less hassle) to jettison your car in the suburbs where there is some free parking available, such as in Pontcanna's Cathedral Rd, then walk or take public transport to the centre.

PUBLIC TRANSPORT
Boat

Aquabus (☎ 029-2034 5163; https://aquabus.co.uk; adult/child £4/2) and **Cardiff Boat** (☎ 07445 440874; www.cardiffboat.com; adult/child £5/2) run alternating water-bus services along the River Taff between Bute Park and Cardiff Bay's Mermaid Quay, departing every half-hour from 10am to 5pm. The journey takes about 25 minutes and is accompanied by a commentary on the sights.

Bus

Most local buses are operated by **Cardiff Bus** (☎ 029-2066 6444; www.cardiffbus.com; single trip/day pass £2/4); buy your ticket from the driver (cash or contactless; no change given). Useful routes from the city centre:

➡ **6** ('The Baycar') and **8/8S/9** to Cardiff Bay (from Customhouse St)

➡ **28** to Cathays and Roath Park (from the Fitzalan Pl stop on the A4161 just north of Queen St train station)

➡ **61** and **63** via Cathedral Rd to Llandaff (from Westgate St)

➡ **32A** (operated by Easyway) and **320** (operated by New Adventure Travel) to St Fagans (from Westgate St)

Train

Trains can (sometimes) be as convenient as buses for some cross-Cardiff trips. Useful routes:

➡ Cardiff Queen St–Cardiff Bay (£2.30)

➡ Cardiff Queen St–Llandaff (£3.20)

➡ Cardiff Central–Penarth (£3.20)

Journey time is about seven minutes for any of these.

TAXI

Cabs can be hailed in the street, ordered by phone, or picked up at taxi ranks, including outside Cardiff Central train station, in Duke St opposite the castle, and at the corner of Greyfriars Rd and Park Pl. Reliable companies include **Capital Cabs** (☎ 029-2077 7777; www.capitalcabs.co.uk) and **Dragon Taxis** (☎ 029-2033 3333; www.dragontaxis.com). Uber also operates in Cardiff.

VALE OF GLAMORGAN

Merging into the western flank of Cardiff, the largely rural Vale of Glamorgan is a county in its own right. Penarth is a stone's throw across the Ely River from Cardiff, while Barry Island is more or less Cardiff-by-the-beach.

You'll find a diverting selection of day-trip destinations from Cardiff in the Vale, from the British seaside's peculiar time-warped traditions through to ancient monuments lurking in lonely fields.

Penarth

POP 22,100

Well-heeled Penarth has transformed from an old-fashioned seaside resort to a virtual suburb of Cardiff, despite being in the

---

DON'T MISS

UNVEILING THE VALE

Curiosity aroused by the Vale of Glamorgan, with all its rural and small-town charm? Here are our top picks for further explorations.

Llantwit Major The Vale's third-largest town, abounding in history from Roman to Victorian, with a beautiful parish church.

Cowbridge Handsome town known for its Georgian architecture, independent shops and great eateries.

Ogmore-by-Sea Delightful seaside village alongside one of the Vale's loveliest beaches.

neighbouring county. It's connected to Cardiff Bay by Cardiff Bay Barrage (p61), with the Penarth side sporting a busy marina.

◉ Sights

Penarth Pier & Pavilion PIER

(☑029-2071 2100; The Esplanade, CF64 3AU; ☺10am-5pm) FREE Penarth's rock-and-sand shoreline may not drop jaws but it is Cardiff's closest beach. In 1894 it was graced with that obligatory Victorian seaside icon: a pier. This has been elegantly restored to art deco glory and makes a focus for beachside wanderings. The Pier Pavilion at the landward end was closed at the time of research due to Covid-19.

🛏 Sleeping & Eating

Penarth's has an ample scattering of hotels and B&Bs. There's a history of good eating options, too – the town held Cardiff area's only Michelin Star until recently – though these change like the tides.

Holm House SPA HOTEL **£££**

(☑029-2070 6029; www.holmhousehotel.com; 11 Marine Pde; d/ste £140/180; P🛜🐕) This spick-and-span hotel hogs an enviable location, with its gardens stretching high above the seafront. Built by a fishing magnate in the 1920s, it nevertheless feels contemporary. It has a good spa (Friday to Sunday, prebookings only) and restaurant (noon to 10pm Friday and Saturday, to 5pm Sunday, prebookings only).

ℹ Getting There & Away

Buses 92/93/94 head to/from Cardiff half-hourly (£2, 25 minutes). There are trains to/from Cardiff Central (£3.20, 11 minutes) roughly every 15 minutes.

You can walk/cycle along the barrage from Cardiff Bay to Penarth Marina (allow 40 minutes on foot). Then it's a steep 10-minute walk up into Penarth town centre, or a 20-minute walk around to Penarth Pier and beach.

Barry (Y Barri)

POP 51,500

Nowhere have the triumphs of the BBC Wales television department been more keenly felt than in Barry, a seaside town 8 miles southwest of Cardiff. If you watch *Doctor Who* or *Being Human*, you'll no doubt be aware that the town is infested with aliens, zombies, werewolves and vampires. Yet it's the massive popularity of the altogether-more-down-to-earth comedy *Gavin & Stacey* that has given the town a new cachet. The staff at Island Leisure (on the Promenade) are used to fans of the

---

OFF THE BEATEN TRACK

MYSTERIOUS MONOLITHS

Neolithic standing stones, stone circles and burial chambers are ubiquitous in Wales – so much so that many don't even make it onto tourist brochures and maps. That's the case with the mysterious millennia-spanning duo of Tinkinswood and St Lythans burial chambers, each standing in fields 7 miles west of Cardiff, orientated towards the rising sun.

The 6000-year-old **Tinkinswood chamber** (Duffryn Lane) FREE consists of a wall of stones supporting a mammoth 7.4m-long, 36-tonne limestone capstone, thought to be the largest of its kind in Britain. Meanwhile, dating from around 4000 BCE, the **St Lythans chamber** (St Lythans Rd) FREE is a cromlech consisting of three supporting stones capped with a large, flat stone, forming a chamber nearly 2m high. As with many such pre-Christian/pre-Celtic sites, St Lythans is connected with numerous local legends. It was once thought to be a Druid's altar, and on midsummer's eve the capstone supposedly spins around three times...

While located on private farmland, both sites are freely accessible to the public and each has an information post with a wind-up device that plays a recorded commentary.

You'll need your own wheels to get here and preferably GPS or a detailed road map. Head west of Cardiff to Culverhouse Cross and continue west on the A48 to St Nicholas, where the sites are signposted. Turn left at the lights and look for a parking area to the right of the road where you can walk across the field to the Tinkinswood site. Continue down this road another mile and turn left at the end for St Lythans.

show converging on the booth where Nessa worked, and other pilgrimage sites include nearby Marco's Cafe, where Stacey worked, and Trinity St, where Stacey's mum and Uncle Bryn lived.

The other big attraction here is the beach at **Barry Island** (CF62 5AJ), signposted at the south end of town. To spy it from afar, look over the urban sprawl to the big wheel marking the amusement park and the lovely sandy beach beyond.

◉ Sights

Porthkerry Country Park   PARK
(Park Rd, CF62 3BY; ℗ 👪) Spanning 90 hectares, this large expanse follows a lush wooded valley terminating at a pebbly beach, overshot by an impressive Victorian railway viaduct. There are trails, a cafe, a children's playground and a ruined 13th-century mill. The park is well signposted from the road to Barry Island.

🍴 Sleeping & Eating

Barry has moderately priced chain hotels, but we recommend staying in Cardiff and visiting on a day trip.

Once (OK, and still) the domain of typical seaside tack tucker, a new side to Barry's dining scene is emerging a few streets back from the beach around the cool Pumphouse

and Goodsheds developments. This has been heralded (slightly prematurely) as the 'next Cardiff Bay': see what you think of the exciting new options that might sway you away from Cardiff for a meal.

★ **Hangfire**
Southern Kitchen   BARBECUE **££**
(www.hangfiresouthernkitchen.com; Pumphouse, CF62 5BE; mains £15-25; ⊘ 5-10pm Wed & Thu, noon-10pm Fri & Sat, noon-5.30pm Sun; ℗) Visit the trendy Pumphouse development to discover Barry's culinary crowning glory. This former industrial complex, topped by a massive chimney and once the linchpin in Barry's coal-exporting prowess, now fires another sort of business: fine dining. Hangfire's Sam and Shawna learned the art of great barbecue travelling the southern USA and now they've brought their moreish meaty cooking knowledge home.

For £25, you get a choice of three meats from the likes of smoked brisket, spare ribs, pulled pork and smoked sausage. Barbecue in Britain doesn't get better. Booking a table through the website is currently essential.

❶ Getting There & Away

The best approach is by the half-hourly trains heading to Barry and Barry Island stations from Cardiff Central (£3.80, 29 minutes).

CARDIFF BARRY (Y BARRI)

AT A GLANCE

POPULATION
Newport: 145,700

HIGHEST MOUNTAIN
Pen-y-Fan
(886m/2907ft)

BEST HIKE
Tintern Abbey to the
Devil's Pulpit (p114)

BEST COUNTRY PUB
Newbridge on Usk
(p120)

BEST WILD SWIM
Ystradfellte (p107)

WHEN TO GO

➡ **Apr, May & Sep**
Reasonable weather
and fewer visitors
in Brecon Beacons
National Park.

➡ **May–Sep** Narrow
country roads
become congested
during peak holiday
season; most major
festivals take place
during this period.

➡ **Nov–Mar** Snow
regularly clads high
hills, remote roads
may close and many
tourist attractions
shut.

Crickhowell Bridge (p97)

Brecon Beacons & Southeast Wales

Wales' southeast corner, where the moorland expanses of the magnificent Brecon Beacons National Park, brushed by vertiginous mountain roads that dip to remote hamlets and forest-fringed country houses, is foot-itchingly fantastic hiking terrain. Meanwhile, to the southeast, the misty River Wye meanders along the border with England through the picturesque birthplace of British tourism. For over 200 years travellers have visited this winsome waterway and its steeply sloping surrounding woods, where romantically ruined Tintern Abbey has inspired poets and artists like Wordsworth and Turner. And wander west of here, too. You will then discover, in the dramatically serried South Wales valleys divulging the story of the Industrial Revolution, that southeast Wales is a juxtaposition of both jaw-dropping nature and human attempts to work it to their advantage – with some astounding results.

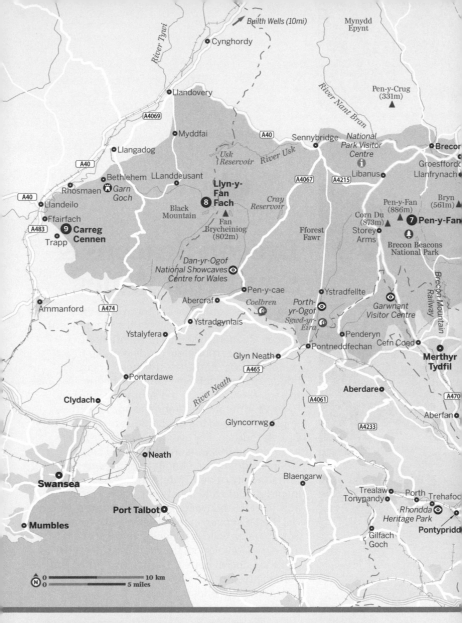

Brecon Beacons & Southeast Wales Highlights

1 **Tintern Abbey** (p113) Strolling among riverside ruins in the glorious Wye Valley.

2 **Blaenavon** (p123) Feasting on World Heritage Sites and world-class cheese.

3 **Caerphilly Castle** (p125) Crossing the moat and wandering into a fairy tale.

4 **Crickhowell** (p97) Winding down to a village pace in the

proudly independent heart of Brecon Beacons National Park.

5 **Black Mountains** (p90) Taking a spectacular, hair-raising drive through the chapel-dotted Vale of Ewyas.

BRECON BEACONS NATIONAL PARK

Snowdonia might have the height edge, but go off-the-beaten track, or *igam-ogam* as the Welsh say, and the Brecon Beacons can feel every bit as wild. Rippling from the English border all the way west to Llandeilo, this 520-sq-mile national park bombards you with lonely, moody beauty: remote single-track lanes twist and turn up to heather-flecked moors where rowan trees tremble in the breeze and sheep brazenly block roads. Hiking trails lead up through glacier-carved valleys to crest fin-shaped mountains. In between, the ramparts of Iron Age hill forts and the skeletal remains of medieval castles await. While in tiny villages, glorious old coaching inns welcome passers-by – their blazing fires and local ales taking the edge off a bracing, often wet and windy, walk.

There are four distinct regions within the park: the wild, lonely **Black Mountain** (Mynydd Du) in the west, with its high moors and glacial lakes; **Fforest Fawr** (Great Forest), whose rushing streams and spectacular waterfalls form the headwaters of the Rivers Tawe and Neath; the **Brecon Beacons** (Bannau Brycheiniog) proper, a group of very distinctive, flat-topped hills that includes Pen-y-Fan (886m), the park's highest peak; and the rolling heathland ridges of the **Black Mountains** (Y Mynyddoedd Duon) – not to be confused with the above-mentioned Black Mountain to the west.

Abergavenny (Y Fenni)

POP 12,500

Abergavenny is a classically idiosyncratic Welsh market town, replete with independent shops and businesses and sporting a higgledy-piggledy look that works its workaday charm on you the longer you linger. It has played many roles on history's stage: Roman fort, Norman stronghold, tanning and weaving centre, and prison for Hitler's deputy – and interesting remnants of its past remain. But, nestled between three shapely peaks – the Blorenge, Ysgyryd Fawr (Skirrid) and Sugar Loaf – it's mainly an excellent base for walkers, with uplifting greenery everywhere around. Hosting some acclaimed Michelin-starred restaurants on its fringes, as well as Wales' leading annual food festival, it also lures devotees of Welsh produce and cooking.

Its ancient name, Y Fenni (Welsh for 'place of the smiths'), was given to a stream that empties into the River Usk here, and later anglicised to Gavenny (Abergavenny means 'mouth of the Gavenny'). The Romans established Gobannium Fort here, exactly a day's march from their garrison at Caerleon, which they maintained from CE 57 to 400. Not long after the Norman Conquest, a marcher lord, Hamelin de Ballon, built the castle and inflated the town's importance.

⊙ Sights

★**St Mary's Priory Church** CHURCH
(⏷ 01873-858787; www.stmarys-priory.org; Monk St; ⊙ 9am-4pm Mon-Sat) FREE Although you wouldn't guess it from the outside, this large stone church has been described as the 'Westminster Abbey of South Wales' because of the remarkable treasury of aristocratic tombs that lies within. It was founded at the same time as the Norman castle (1087) as part of a Benedictine priory, but the present building dates mainly from the 14th century, with 15th- and 19th-century additions and alterations.

St Mary's survived Henry VIII's dissolution of the monasteries by being converted into a parish church, making it an interesting counterpoint to the ruins of nearby Tintern and Llanthony abbeys. In the northern transept is one of the most important medieval carvings in Europe – a monumental 15th-century wooden representation of the biblical figure of Jesse (commonly called a Jesse Tree). It was the base of what must have been a mighty altarpiece showing the lineage of Jesus all the way back to Jesse, father of King David. It's the only such figure in England, and may well be unique globally. Nearby, a graceful, worn, carved-oak effigy (1325) commemorates Sir John de Hastings, who was responsible for the church's 14th-century transformation.

The church's oldest memorial (1256) is the stone figure near the sanctuary of Eva de Braose, Lady Abergavenny, portrayed holding a shield. Her husband, William, was hanged after being found in the bedchamber of Prince Llywelyn the Great's wife, daughter of England's King John. The family tradition of royal adultery and execution continued with their direct descendant, Anne Boleyn.

Abergavenny

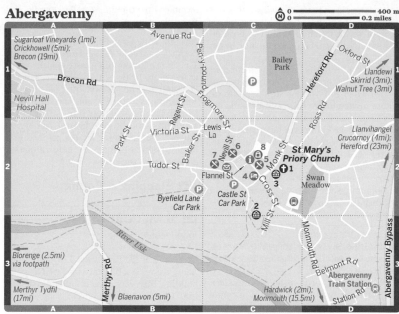

The Herbert Chapel is packed with recumbent effigies. Most depict members of the Herbert family, starting with Sir William ap Thomas, founder of Raglan Castle, and his wife, Gwladys, who was re-interred in accordance with pre-Reformation ritual following restoration in 2001. The oak choir stalls were carved in the 15th century (note the lively misericords and the little dragons at the ends).

Tithe Barn   HISTORIC BUILDING
(☑ 01873-858787; www.stmarys-priory.org; Monk St; ◷ 9am-4pm Mon-Sat) **FREE** The large blocky building next to the church is the former abbey's 12th-century tithe barn, the place where people brought their obligatory contributions to the church, usually 10% of whatever they produced. It has now been fully restored and converted into a **heritage centre** and Welsh-produce-focussed **food hall**. Pride of place goes to the painstakingly detailed and complex **Abergavenny Tapestry**, produced by more than 60 local volunteers over six years to mark the new millennium and reflect the town's heritage. The tapestry is located upstairs and a member of staff will often be around to explain its intricacies. Look for faint messages from the stitchers in the borders. Elsewhere on this floor a combination of artefacts and

Abergavenny

touch-screen monitors tells the story of the town and the abbey in an excellent interactive display.

Abergavenny Museum & Castle   MUSEUM
(☑ 01873-854282;   www.abergavennymuseum. co.uk; Castle St; ◷ 11am-2pm Thu, 1-4pm Sun) **FREE** Abergavenny castle's keep now houses a small museum. It tells the history of the castle and the town, and includes recreations of a 19th-century Welsh farmhouse kitchen, a saddlery workshop and the fascinating Basil Jones' grocery shop, with many

items dating back to the 1930s and '40s. Not much remains of the actual castle except for an impressive stretch of curtain wall on either side of the gatehouse on the northwest side.

The scant ruins belie a drama-charged past. This was the site of a notorious event in 1175 when the Norman lord William de Braose invited his Welsh rivals for a Christmas dinner and had them massacred. Frequently besieged but never taken, the castle was wrecked by royalist forces in 1645 during the Civil War in order to keep it out of parliamentary hands.

For the museum, prebooking via the Visit Monmouthshire website (www.visitmonmouthshire.com) was obligatory at the time of research.

Sugarloaf Vineyards   WINERY
(☑ 01873-853066; www.sugarloafvineyard.co.uk; off Pentre Lane, NP7 7LA; tastings from £3; ☺ 11am-5pm Tue-Sat, to 4pm Sun; 🅿) FREE Established in 1992, this vineyard on the northwestern edge of town produces a variety of white and red wines, including an award-winning sparkling. You can take a free self-guided tour before sampling the goods at the cafe and store. Prebooking a visit was essential at the time of research.

🏃 Activities

Much of Abergavenny's appeal admittedly lies in its eye-popping setting in-between three skyline-defining summits: the Sugar Loaf (p90), the Skirrid (p90) and the Blorenge (p99), all within the Brecon Beacons National Park. If hiking up these sounds too strenuous, you can plump for a promenade along easy paths beside the banks of the River Usk, or explore the towpath of the Monmouthshire and Brecon Canal, which passes 1 mile southwest of the town.

✨ Festivals & Events

South Wales Three Peaks Trial   SPORTS
(www.threepeakstrial.co.uk; ☺ Mar) An annual walking challenge held in March to test your endurance and map-reading skills.

Abergavenny Festival of Cycling   SPORTS
(www.abergavennyfestivalofcycling.co.uk; ☺ mid-Jul) This festival incorporates youth and professional races and the Monmouthshire and Iron Mountain Sportifs, plus participatory

events with 20-mile, 40-mile, 70-mile and 100-mile courses.

Abergavenny Food Festival   FOOD & DRINK
(www.abergavennyfoodfestival.co.uk; ☺ mid-Sep) The most important gastronomic event in Wales is held on the third weekend in September, with demonstrations, debates, competitions, courses, stalls and the odd celebrity. But the real drawcard is that this is an enthusiastically local festival, run by volunteers, and not some big-budget food producer's showcase. At night there's a market and events at the castle.

🛏 Sleeping & Eating

🛏 Town Centre

Angel Hotel   HOTEL £££
(☑ 01873-857121; www.angelabergavenny.com; 15 Cross St; r £135-195, cottages £255-295; 🅿🔁) Abergavenny's top hotel is a fine Georgian building that was once a famous coaching inn. Choose between sleek, sophisticated rooms in the hotel itself, in an adjoining mews, in a Victorian lodge near the castle or in the 17th-century Castle Cottage (sleeping four). There's also a good restaurant and bar, serving modern British food and elaborate afternoon and high teas.

Room prices do increase slightly on weekend nights.

Cwtch Cafe   CAFE £
(☑ 01873-855466; 58 Cross St; snacks & mains £5-6; ☺ 9am-5pm Mon-Sat; 🔁) Stylish and wonderfully friendly, Cwtch (Welsh for 'hug') entices a scrum of regulars through the doors with its homemade cakes, coffee, and lunchtime dishes such as rarebit, Canadian pancakes (with crispy bacon and maple syrup), quiche and gourmet pasties. There are plenty of gluten-free options, too.

Gurkha Corner   NEPALI £
(☑ 01871-855800; www.gurkhacorners.co.uk; 10 Nevill St; mains £7-10; ☺ noon-2.45pm & 5.30-11pm) Like its sister restaurant in Brecon, Gurkha Corner makes Abergavenny visitors' jaws drops slightly when they see high-quality ethnic food flourishing in the provinces, but in fact the Nepalese Gurkhas of eastern Wales have been an established community since the 1970s. And the food here spices up Abergavenny's options no end with feisty vegetable, prawn and fish curries.

King's Arms Hotel PUB FOOD **££**
(📞 01873-855074; www.kingsarmsabergavenny.
co.uk; 29 Nevill St; mains £8.95-19.95; ☺noon-
3pm & 5-8pm Mon-Thu. noon-8pm Fri & Sat,
noon-4pm Sun; 🛜🐾) Abergavenny's most
appealing pub dates from the 16th century
and has a cosy bar area with low ceilings
and a fabulously incongruous oil painting
of Martin Scorsese. The neighbouring dining room takes pub food to the next level
of sophistication, while still keeping a rustic
edge. Upstairs there are 11 comfortable en-
suite rooms (doubles £95 to £110).

🛏 Around Abergavenny

Hardwick MODERN BRITISH **£££**
(📞 01873-854220; www.thehardwick.co.uk; Old
Raglan Rd; mains £17-27, 2-/3-course Sun lunch
£26/30; ☺noon-2.30pm & 5.30-8pm Wed-Fri,
noon-2.30pm & 6-9pm Sat, noon-3.30pm Sun;
P) This traditional inn – with its old stone
fireplace, low ceiling beams and burnished
copper bar – has become head chef Stephen
Terry's showcase for the best of unpretentious country cooking. Dishes such as
braised rabbit with fried polenta are deeply
satisfying, but you need to save room for the
homemade ice cream. Attached are eight elegant rooms (from £135).

The Hardwick is 2 miles south of Abergavenny on the B4598.

★ Walnut Tree MODERN BRITISH **£££**
(📞 01873-852797; www.thewalnuttreeinn.com; Old
Ross Rd, Llanddewi Skirrid; mains £28-32,
2-/3-course lunch £30/35; ☺noon-2.30pm &
6-10pm Wed-Sat; P) Established in 1963, the
Michelin-starred Walnut Tree serves the
cuisine-hopping meat and seafood creations
of chef Shaun Hill, with a focus on fresh, local produce. If you're too full to move far after feasting on dishes such as middle white
pork loin with glazed cheek and cauliflower,
elegant cottage accommodation is available
(from £175).

The Walnut Tree is 3 miles northeast of
Abergavenny on the B4521.

🔒 Shopping

Abergavenny Market MARKET
(📞 01873-735811; Cross St; ☺9am-4pm market days) The 19th-century Market Hall is
a lively place, hosting a general market
(food, drink, clothes, household goods) on
Tuesday, Friday and Saturday, a flea market (bric-a-brac, collectables, secondhand
goods) on Wednesday, regular weekend

craft and antiques fairs, and a farmers market on the fourth Thursday of each month.
Stalls spill out onto the square behind.

ℹ Information

Nevill Hall Hospital (📞 01873-732732; www.
wales.nhs.uk; Brecon Rd; ☺24hr) Full emergency service.

Tourist Office (📞 0785-499 7541; abergaven
nytic@yahoo.com; Cross St, by Abergavenny
Market; ☺10am-4pm Mon-Sat) The tourist
office was in the process of relocating to new
premises next to Abergavenny Market and
the Town Hall at the time of research, and
also becoming a National Park Centre for the
surrounding Brecon Beacons National Park.

ℹ Getting There & Away

BICYCLE

National Cycle Route 42 passes through Abergavenny, heading south to Chepstow and north
to Glasbury-on-Wye near Hay-on-Wye, where it
connects with National Cycle Route 8 (Lôn Las
Cymru).

BUS

Direct services at Abergavenny's **bus station**
(by Swan Meadow) include the X3 to/from Hereford (£5.90, 55 minutes, six daily); the hourly
X4 service to/from Cardiff (£8.10, 2¾ hours),
via Merthyr Tydfil (£7, 1¾ hours); four daily 83
services to/from Monmouth (£3.90, 45 minutes); and 10 daily X43 services to/from Brecon
(£3.90, 40 minutes to one hour).

BEACONS WAY

The 99-mile, eight-day **Beacons Way**
trail wends its way across the national
park from Skirrid (Ysgyryd Fawr) near
Abergavenny to the village of Bethlehem
on the edge of the Black Mountain,
knocking off all the highest summits,
and immersing you properly in the wilds
of the region's sweeping peaks, starkly
beautiful moors and glacier-carved
valleys.

Needless to say, this is a stretching
walk and requires proper walking gear
as well as a good Ordnance Survey (OS)
map – the moorland sections can be
hard to navigate. The route is manage-
able in eight taxing days, but you may
want to take a little longer to make it
more enjoyable and less of an endurance test.

DON'T MISS

STAR LIGHT, STAR BRIGHT

The Brecon Beacons is just one of a handful of places in the world to be awarded 'Dark Sky Reserve' status. With almost zero light pollution, this is one of the UK's finest places for stargazing. Meteor showers, nebulae, strings of constellations and the Milky Way twinkle brightly in the night sky when the weather is clear. Among the 10 best spots are Carreg Cennen (p106), Sugar Loaf and Llanthony Priory.

Visitor centres throughout the park can give you information about stargazing events, or check out www.brecon beacons.org/stargazing.

TRAIN

There are direct trains from Abergavenny's train station to/from Cardiff (£14.70, 45 minutes, hourly), Swansea (£27.20, 1¾ hours, up to 16 daily), Manchester (£65, 2¾ hours, hourly), Tenby (£46, 3¾ hours, up to five daily changing at Carmarthen) and Holyhead (£78.60, 4¾ hours, up to 15 daily changing at Shrewsbury).

Black Mountains (Y Mynyddoedd Duon)

Puckering up between Abergavenny and Hay-on-Wye, the Black Mountains are untamed and largely uninhabited (if you ignore sheep and red kites, that is). They top out at 811m at the windswept summit of Waun Fach and its graceful sweep of gold-green moorland. Getting lost on single-track lanes is part of the fun: this is remote road-trip country, with drives making their way through forgotten valleys to lookouts with soul-stirring views, walking trails where you'll be accompanied by the skylark's serenade, and medieval ruins that fired the imaginations of the great romantics.

◎ Sights

Skirrid   MOUNTAIN
(Ysgyryd Fawr) Of the glacially sculpted hills rising above Abergavenny, the Skirrid (486m) is most dramatic. You can trek here from Llanvihangel Crucorney (5.5 miles) or take the B4521 from Abergavenny to the lay-by at the base of the hill (4 miles). It's a steep climb from here through broadleaf woods

thick with ferns. The final climb brings you to the wind-beaten summit, where you'll be rewarded with far-reaching views west to the Brecon Beacons and south to the Severn Estuary.

A cleft in the rock near the top was once believed to have split open at the exact time of Christ's death and a chapel was built here on what was considered a particularly holy place (a couple of upright stones remain). During the Reformation as many as 100 people would attend illegal Catholic Masses at this remote spot. Look out for the ruins of a medieval chapel and an Iron Age hill fort.

Sugar Loaf   MOUNTAIN
(Mynydd Pen-y-Fâl) There are many higher mountains in Wales, but few are more distinctive than the conical Sugar Loaf (596m). Hiking to the top is a 4.5-mile round trip from the Mynydd Llanwenarth viewpoint car park. Take the middle track that follows a stone wall, skirts a wood and rambles steeply uphill, turning right to bisect a grassy ridge before a final steep summit scramble. The descent route flanks the head of the valley.

To reach the car park, head west from Abergavenny on the A40. At the edge of town turn right for Sugarloaf Vineyards, then go left at the next two junctions.

★ Llanthony Priory   RUINS
(Cadw; www.cadw.gov.wales; ⊙10am-4pm; P 🚻 🐾) FREE Halfway along the impossibly beautiful Vale of Ewyas lie the wildly romantic ruins of this Augustinian priory, set among pasture and wooded hills by the River Honddu. Perhaps the second most important abbey in Wales when completed in 1230, it was abandoned after Henry VIII dissolved Britain's monasteries in 1538. Running a close second to Tintern for grandeur, Llanthony's setting is even more arresting, and you won't have crowds to fight. JMW Turner was impressed, too: he painted the scene in 1794.

St Issui's Church   CHURCH
(Patrishow) Tucked away on a thickly forested hillside in the Vale of Ewyas, this tiny, weathered, 11th-century church is a time capsule of Welsh faith and culture. Inside its wonders reveal themselves: a finely carved wooden rood screen, medieval frescoes of biblical texts, coats of arms and a red-ochre skeleton. The church is usually open

and empty. Immediately downhill from the church is the **Holy Well of St Issui**, which is believed to have healing powers and has long been a pilgrimage site.

🏃 Activities

The Black Mountains' wind-scoured summits and verdant valleys are ideally explored on foot, hoof or two wheels. One highlight is the drive through the bleakly beautiful, sheer-sided **Vale of Ewyas**, whose remote uplands and dark peaks inspired Bruce Chatwin to put pen to paper when writing *On the Black Hill* (1982).

★ Gospel Pass   SCENIC DRIVE
Pray for clement weather, well-behaved sheep and excellent reversing skills on this sensational drive through the upper reaches of the wild Vale of Ewyas. A single-track lane unspools through harsh but beautiful moorland to climb the 549m Gospel Pass, Wales' highest road. As you crest the pass, views crack open of 677m Hay Bluff to the east and 690m Twmpa (better known as, ahem, Lord Hereford's Knob).

Black Mountains
Cycle Centre   MOUNTAIN BIKING
(📞07946 123234; www.blackmountainscycle centre.com; Great Llwygy Farm; day pass push-up/ uplift £15/13; ⏱10am-dusk) Located in farmland near Llanvihangel Crucorney, this centre ramps up the action on downhill tracks complete with berms, bridges and jumps. Five are rated blue (intermediate), four red (advanced) and six black (expert). On weekends you can pay extra for 'uplift' transport to the top of the trailheads (includes 10 to 12 transfers).

🛏 Sleeping & Eating

★ Llanthony Priory Hotel   HOTEL ££
(📞01873-890487; www.llanthonyprioryhotel.co. uk; Llanthony; s/d from £75/95; 🅿) Seemingly growing out of the priory ruins and incorporating some of the original medieval buildings, this insanely atmospheric hotel has four-poster beds, stone spiral staircases and rooms squeezed into turrets. Bathrooms are shared and there's no TV or wi-fi. The logburner-warmed bar in the vaulted undercroft serves simple meals (mains £4.50 to £12) and a solid selection of real ales.

Celyn Farm   B&B ££
(📞01873-890894; www.celynfarm.co.uk; Forest Coal Pit; d £85-95) If you like to get away from all neighbours, you'll love Celyn ('Holy') Farm. Set in 120 hectares of farmland reached by narrow lanes from either Llanvihangel Crucorney or Crickhowell (make sure you print the directions), this remote country house offers four handsome rooms, excellent breakfasts and idyllic views over Sugar Loaf and the Gwryne Fawr River below.

Skirrid Mountain Inn   PUB FOOD £
(📞01873-890258; www.skirridmountaininn.co.uk; Hereford Rd, Llanvihangel Crucorney; mains £8-12; ⏱5.30-11pm Mon, 11am-2.30pm & 5.30-11pm Tue-Fri, 11.30am-11pm Sat, noon-10pm Sun; 🅿🍴) Possibly Wales' oldest and most haunted boozer, the Skirrid Inn's woodsmoke-blackened beams prop up 900 years of history. Lore has it that Shakespeare himself enjoyed a pint here, and the hangman's noose above the stairwell recalls the pub's former life as a courthouse. Downstairs it serves hearty grub (steak pie, leek-and-pork sausages with mash and the like) in front of roaring fires.

Snag a table by the inglenook fireplace on a cold winter day or on the garden terrace in summer.

ℹ Getting There & Away

Bus X3 runs frequently between Abergavenny and Llanvihangel Crucorney (£3.20, 12 minutes) and Hereford (£5.90, 55 minutes).

Hay-on-Wye (Y Gelli Gandryll)
POP 1598

Straddling the banks of the River Wye, just inside the Welsh border, Hay-on-Wye steals your heart with its location, then sends your soul winging straight to book heaven. This handsome Georgian market town exploded onto the literary scene in the 1970s when Richard Booth, self-proclaimed King of Hay, put it on the map as the centre of the secondhand book trade.

This newfound literary fame was the impetus for the festival of literature and culture founded in 1988, which has grown in stature each year to embrace all aspects of the creative arts. Today the 11-day Hay Festival is a massive draw every May and June, endorsed by former US president Bill Clinton, a high-profile guest in 2001, as 'the Woodstock of the mind'.

The town's old-school centre has narrow sloping lanes peppered by bookshops, antique shops, galleries, craft shops, delis and artsy cafes. Even outside festival time its alternative ambience lingers. Hay is a place to browse, dream, philosophise and crack the spine on a musty novel, with all the joy of reading it yet to come.

🏃 Activities

It's easy for a bibliophile to drift into insolvency here, but Hay is also an excellent base for active pursuits, whether you wish to mount Lord Hereford's Knob (a 690m swelling less humorously known as Twmpa) or strike out on the Offa's Dyke Path as it follows the Black Mountains towards Kington.

Celtic Canoes CANOEING

(☑ 07515 905419; www.celticcanoes.co.uk; The Bont, Glasbury; half-/full day £25/35) Half-day excursions take to the Wye waters at Glasbury for a 5-mile paddle to Hay-on-Wye, taking in rapids and river wildlife (kingfishers are often spotted). Full-day trips end over the border in Whitney-on-Wye in England, where you are collected. It can also help organise overnight paddling trips (from £35 per day).

✪✦ Festivals & Events

★ Hay Festival LITERATURE

(☑ box office 01497-822629; www.hayfestival. com; ticket prices vary; ⊘late May-early Jun) The 11-day Hay Festival is Britain's leading festival of literature and the arts – a kind of bookworms' Glastonbury. Like an iconic music festival, it has the gravity to attract the brightest stars in its corner of the artistic galaxy. Entry to the festival site is free; individual events are ticketed.

As well as readings, workshops, book signings, concerts and club nights, there's also a parallel children's program called **Haydays**, where youngsters can meet famous children's authors and enjoy workshops, games and other distractions. There are shuttle buses from Hay-on-Wye and surrounding towns to the site, in fields on Hay's southwestern fringe.

It's proved such a popular formula that there are now Hay Festivals in Mexico, Spain, Peru and Colombia.

HowTheLightGetsIn CULTURAL

(www.howthelightgetsin.org; ticket prices vary; ⊘May) Billed as the word's largest festival of philosophy and music, HowTheLightGetsIn hits Hay each May with a high-profile line-up of music events, debates, readings and talks with world-leading thinkers. Held to coincide with the Hay Festival, it attracts thousands to a site on the banks of the Wye.

🛏 Sleeping

Old Black Lion PUB ££

(☑ 01497-820841; www.oldblacklion.co.uk; Lion St; s/d £70/120; 🅿 🛜) Quite the medieval dream, parts of this traditional coaching inn date from the 13th century. Expect ceilings so low you crack your head on them, blackened beams and creaky, uneven floors. The accumulated weight of centuries of hospitality is cheerfully carried by the current staff. The food (p95) is excellent as well.

Maesyronnen B&B ££

(☑ 01497-842763; www.maesyronnenbandb.co.uk; Glasbury; s/d £70/95; 🅿 🛜) Secluded and relaxed, this 19th-century stone house sits in pretty, rambling gardens with views of the Wye Valley and Black Mountains. Only one of the four rooms is en suite, but all feature antique furnishings and a sense of past generations of peaceful country life. Breakfast features local and homemade produce. Maesyronnen is close to Glasbury, 5 miles from Hay.

★ By the Wye B&B £££

(☑ 01497-828166; www.bythewye.uk; The Start; safari tents £130-195) 🍃 Reclining in ancient native woodland on the banks of the River Wye, this ecominded escape takes glamping to a whole new luxury level. Perched on stilts high in the tree canopy, the safari tents are sublime, with fantasy-like beds handmade from gnarly driftwood and lots of above-and-beyond details, including welcome baskets with local goodies, firepits, decks overlooking the river and binoculars for bird-spotting.

The family that runs the place aims to please while protecting the environment – trees and plants on the footpath that follows the river have been carefully labelled, the tents run on solar power, and luggage is transported using – like it! – wheelbarrows.

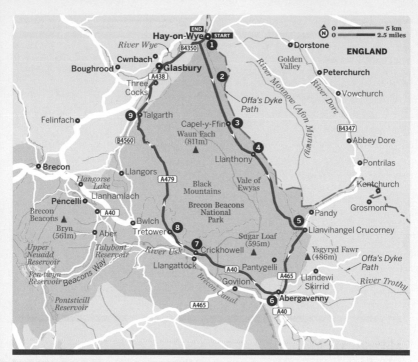

🏃 Driving Tour
Black Mountains Circuit

START HAY-ON-WYE
END HAY-ON-WYE
LENGTH 49 MILES; ONE DAY

Thanks to tractors and narrow single tracks, you can slow right down for this deliciously remote drive through the Black Mountains. Patrolled by unruly sheep in parts, the road climbs to dizzying heights and drops into a lonely valley. It returns via a much easier route, stopping in the charming village of Crickhowell and at an intriguing stately home.

The route kicks off in handsome border town Hay-on-Wye, of literary-festival and secondhand-bookshop fame. However, you could begin at Abergavenny or Crickhowell.

From **1 Hay-on-Wye** head south on Church St. Turn sharply left onto Forest Rd at the edge of town. The road narrows to a single lane (watch for oncoming cars) and quickly leads up to desolate moors as it crosses the 549m **2 Gospel Pass**. To the east is Hay Bluff and England; everywhere are

epic views of the Black Mountains. You might encounter wild ponies.

The country gets greener as you head down the other side into the Vale of Ewyas, via a couple of remote little churches in **3 Capel-y-Ffin** and onto the austere ruins of **4 Llanthony Priory**, which will drive Romantic poets into flurries of metaphor.

Pause at the ancient and creepy Skirrid Mountain Inn at **5 Llanvihangel Crucorney**. Beyond the village, turn right onto the A465, the main road into **6 Abergavenny** to see a priory church with graceful effigies, a ruined castle and a busy market hall. Take the A40 west out of town and stop at attractive **7 Crickhowell**. Continue along the A40 and turn right onto the A479. Soon you'll come to **8 Tretower Court & Castle**, a combination of Norman castle, Tudor manor and drowsy sheep farm.

Head back onto the A479, then stop at stone town **9 Talgarth**, with its restored mill and bakery-cafe. From Talgarth, follow the signs back to Hay-on-Wye via the A4078, A438 and B4350.

Hay-on-Wye

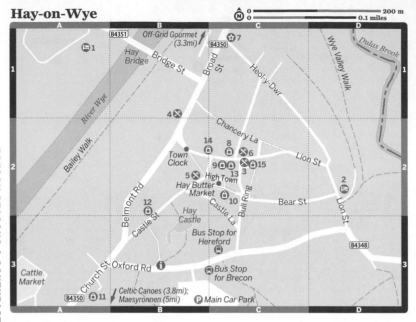

Hay-on-Wye

Eating

Old Electric Shop   VEGETARIAN £

(☏01497-821194; www.oldelectric.co.uk; 10 Broad
St; light bites £4-8; ☺10am-4pm Thu-Mon; ☎🖊)
Hay's hippest hang-out is this fabulously
quirky old curiosity shop of a cafe, crammed
with studios selling new and vintage clothing, furniture, crafts and books. There's a
nicely chilled boho vibe and a blackboard
menu putting creative riffs on vegetarian
soups, salads and curries – all made with
locally sourced ingredients. The delicious
homemade cakes go well with locally roasted coffee and loose-leaf teas.

Shepherds Parlour   ICE CREAM £

(☏01497-821898; www.shepherdsparlour.com; 9
High Town; ice cream £3; ☺10am-5pm; 🖈) This
quaintly old-fashioned parlour tearoom
serves freshly roasted coffee, lunches and
awesome homemade sheep's-milk ice cream
in original flavours like gooseberry and elderflower, Lebanese coffee, and damson and
sloe gin. The menu makes best use of local
deli ingredients in dishes like toasted focaccia with Hay charcuterie, Hereford ham, fig
relish and tomato.

Tomatitos Tapas Bar   SPANISH ££

(☏01497-820772; www.haytomatitos.co.uk; 38
Lion St; tapas £3-5.50; ☺noon-9pm Wed-Sat, to

3.30pm Sun; 🛜) There's always a good buzz at Tomatitos, which brings together a cosily beamed interior with an España-centric menu. Staples such as tortilla and chorizo in cider aside, daily specials feature guest stars such as roasted *piquillo* peppers stuffed with beef, and even lamb tagine. The food is great, and tastes even better washed down with Spanish wine by the glass.

Old Black Lion   PUB FOOD **££**
(📞 01497-820841; www.oldblacklion.co.uk; 26 Lion St; mains £15-22; ⊘noon-2.30pm & 6.30-9pm Wed-Sat, noon-3.30pm Sun) Walkers, book browsers and the literati all flock to this creaky 17th-century inn, with heavy black beams, and low ceilings keeping things cosy. The food swings global, from Goan-style prawn curry to pan-seared calf's liver in red-wine gravy. There are always a couple of vegetarian options.

★Off-Grid Gourmet   GASTRONOMY **£££**
(📞 07538 037770; www.walkers-cottage.co.uk; Walkers Cottage, Locksters Lane; menus £40-50) 🌱 If ever there was proof that all you need to knock up a gourmet meal is canvas, sustainable energy, a wood fire and a degree of talent, Hugh Sawyer is it. Setting up camp in a field 3 miles north of Hay-on-Wye, he wows with expertly crafted menus that are a true off-grid feast of sensational Welsh produce (including lobster in season).

Book well ahead as space is limited to a lucky few.

Chapters   WELSH **£££**
(📞 07855 783799; www.chaptershayonwye.co.uk; Lion St; menus £35; ⊘5-9pm Thu-Sat) 🌱 Atmospherically lodged in the beautifully converted meeting rooms of St John's Chapel, this intimate yet understated bistro-style restaurant is a real gourmet find. The seasonally changing menu spotlights sustainable regional produce in gorgeously presented, ingredient-led dishes such as heritage beetroot with radish and soy, and pork loin with spicy nduja sausage and cider.

☆ Entertainment

Globe at Hay   LIVE PERFORMANCE
(📞 01497-821762; www.globeathay.org; Newport St; ⊘cafe 11am-11pm Fri & Sat, 10am-4pm Sun, see website for event times; 🛜) Run by the Institute of Art and Ideas, the people behind Hay's HowTheLightGetsIn (p92) festival, this con-verted Methodist chapel wears many hats: cafe (mains £12 to £16), bar, live-music venue, theatre, club and all-round community hub. It's a wonderfully intimate place to catch a gig or listen to a tub-thumping political debate.

🛍 Shopping

There are dozens of secondhand and antiquarian bookshops in Hay, with hundreds of thousands of tomes stacked floor-to-ceiling across town. There are also excellent stores selling antiques, local produce, art and historic maps.

★Richard Booth's Bookshop   BOOKS
(📞 01497-820322; www.boothbooks.co.uk; 44 Lion St; ⊘9.30am-5pm Mon-Sat, 11am-5pm Sun) The most famous and still the best, Booth's is a thing of beauty – from the exquisite tiling outside to the immaculately catalogued shelves within (a far cry from the teetering piles of its early years). There's a sizeable Anglo-Welsh literature section, a Wales travel section, a great little cafe (mains £8 to £9) and an art-house cinema.

Eighteen Rabbit   ARTS & CRAFTS
(www.eighteenrabbit.co.uk; 2 Lion St; ⊘10am-5.30pm Mon-Sat, 11am-3pm Sun) 🌱 One of the coolest fair-trade shops you're ever likely to happen upon, Eighteen Rabbit has a terrific array of gifts and crafts from across the globe, from jewellery to ceramics, wooden toys for children to vegan-friendly wallets and bags. You'll also find a good selection of secondhand vinyl and CDs.

Welsh Girl   TEXTILES
(www.thewelshgirl.com; St John's Chapel, Lion St; ⊘11am-4pm Fri & Sat) 🌱 Julie is a whizz when it comes to heritage Welsh weaves. After a long career in fashion in London, she returned to her home in the Black Mountains to pursue textiles and design. Now she puts her own spin on traditional fabrics at this studio, where you can buy beautifully made, one-of-a-kind ponchos, scarves, totes and cushions.

Mostly Maps   MAPS
(📞 01497-820539; www.mostlymaps.com; 2 Castle St; ⊘10.30am-5.30pm Tue-Sat) Behind this boldly painted blue-and-red timber shopfront you'll find exquisite antiquarian maps and illustrative plates, many hand-coloured.

BRECON BEACONS & SOUTHEAST WALES HAY-ON-WYE (Y GELI GANDRYLL)

Murder & Mayhem BOOKS
([☎]01497-821613; 5 Lion St; ⊘10am-5.30pm Mon-Sat, to 5pm Sun) Over the road from its parent store, this specialist branch of Addyman Books has a body outline on the floor, monsters on the ceiling and stacks of detective fiction, true crime and horror.

Hay Antiques Market ANTIQUES
([☎]01497-820175; www.hayantiquemarket.co.uk; 6 Market St; ⊘10am-5pm Mon-Sat, 11am-5pm Sun) Seventeen little shops in one, this is a great place to look for a memento with an extra bit of mileage on it.

Hay Cinema Bookshop BOOKS
([☎]01497-820071; www.haycinemabookshop.co.uk; Castle St; ⊘9am-6pm Mon-Sat, 11.30am-5pm Sun) Hay's oldest and one of its biggest bookshops, this converted cinema is jam-packed with books on all manner of obscure subjects. There's also an antiquarian department and plenty of foreign-language titles.

Addyman Books BOOKS
([☎]01497-821136; www.hay-on-wyebooks.com; 39 Lion St; ⊘10am-5.30pm) A rabbit warren of a shop spread over several levels, with rooms devoted to sci-fi, myths, horror, music and art, among other subjects. Its speciality is rare, out-of-print books.

❶ Information

Police Station ([☎]101; www.dyfed-powys.police.uk; 5 Lion St)

Tourist Office ([☎]01497-820144; www.hay-on-wye.co.uk; Chapel Cottage, Oxford Rd; ⊘10am-1pm Mon-Sat) Stocks a map showing all of Hay's bookshops, as well as copious literature and advice on the town and surrounding area.

❶ Getting There & Away

Bus 39 runs six times a day (except on Sunday) to/from Talgarth (£5.70, 17 minutes), Felinfach (£6.30, 30 minutes), Brecon (£6.80, 37 minutes) and Hereford (£8.10, 57 minutes).

National Cycle Route 42 passes through Hay-on-Wye, heading south to Abergavenny. At nearby Glasbury it also connects with National Cycle Route 8 (Lôn Las Cymru), which heads southwest to Brecon and through Brecon Beacons National Park.

Talgarth

POP 1724

A handsome little market town of greystone buildings gathered around a gurgling stream at the head of the Black Mountains

(the name means 'end of the ridge'), Talgarth has a sprinkling of historic buildings to explore, along with woods and waterfalls in its hinterland. In the 5th century it was the royal capital of the kingdom of Brycheiniog.

◉ Sights

Talgarth Mill HISTORIC BUILDING
([☎]01874-711352; www.talgarthmill.com; High St; adult/child incl tour £5/1; ⊘10am-4pm Tue-Sun) Talgarth's 17th-century watermill is one of the few in the country to still grind wheat into flour, which is used by the neighbouring bakery and sold in the little craft shop at the front. Thirty-minute guided tours depart on the hour. Otherwise, grab a pamphlet and show yourself around. If you're extremely lucky, you might spot an otter in the pretty mill garden.

Bronllys Castle CASTLE
(Cadw; www.cadw.gov.wales; Bronllys Rd; ⊘10am-4pm) [FREE] Looking like it's slid straight off a chessboard, Bronllys' circular tower was built in 1230 on the site of an earlier Norman motte-and-bailey castle. You can climb up inside, wander around its three floors and gaze out over the verdant countryside through its little Gothic windows. It's just outside town, on the A479 heading northwest.

⚡ Activities

Black Mountain Adventure OUTDOORS
([☎]01497-847897; www.blackmountain.co.uk; The Activity Centre, Three Cocks; ⊘9am-5.30pm) Black Mountain ramps up the adventure with a flurry of activities in the mountains, rivers and rocky terrain in the Brecon Beacons. The outfit offers everything from canoe, kayak and mountain-bike hire (from £26) to white-water rafting (£65), caving (£46) and gorge adventures (£46).

🛏 Sleeping & Eating

Draen B&B ££
([☎]01874-713102; www.thedraen.co.uk; Llanfilo; d/ste/tr from £80/95/100; [P][🛜]) Set down a narrow lane 3 miles west of Talgarth, this old stone farmhouse is the very picture of Welsh country comfort. Of the three guest bedrooms, the most substantial has its own sitting room. All are decorated in soft pastels and with painted wooden furniture. Homemade marmalade is a nice touch at breakfast.

Bakers' Table CAFE £

(📞01874-711125; www.talgarthmill.com; Talgarth Mill, High St; lunch mains £5-7.50; ⊙10am-2pm Tue-Fri, 9.30am-2pm Sat; 📶🚹) Housed within Talgarth Mill, this cafe uses its own stone-ground flour to bake beautiful scones, *bara brith* (Welsh tea bread) and crusty bread. All the food and drink sold is sourced locally, including a delicious array of sandwich fillings from the likes of Crickhowell's Black Mountains Smokery.

★ **Felin Fach Griffin** GASTROPUB ££

(📞01874-620111; www.felinfachgriffin.co.uk; Felinfach; mains £16.50-20; P🚹🐾) True country pubs with outstanding food are as rare as gold dust, but the Felin Fach Griffin nails it. Go for a pint of real ale in the beamed, fire-warmed bar before lunch or dinner. The kitchen garden is regularly raided for ingredients used in season-driven stunners like smoked duck with feta and pickled garden berries, and halibut with broad beans, hazelnut fricassee and truffle.

Should you wish to stay the night, it has a handful of stylish doubles (£145 to £185), with vintage Roberts radios, homemade biscuits, local art and photography, and Welsh blankets. As you might expect, breakfast is superb, with local produce and homemade bread.

ℹ Information

Tourist Office (📞01874-712226; www.visittalgarth.co.uk; 10 High St; ⊙10am-4pm Apr-Oct, 10.30am-3.30pm Mon-Sat Nov-Mar; 📶) Pop in for local information, maps and books.

ℹ Getting There & Away

There are several T14 buses per day to/from Brecon (£2.50, 19 minutes) and Hay-on-Wye (£5.70, 17 minutes), and a daily bus to/from Builth Wells (£2.70, 29 minutes) and Llandrindod Wells (£4.40, 50 minutes). No Sunday services.

Crickhowell (Crughywel)

POP 2060

Sitting astride the River Usk, Crickhowell is as pretty as can be, with its neat rows of Georgian houses in chalk-box colours, sloping lanes and wide mountain views all around. Its high street has scooped awards for its old-fashioned flair, with independent shops including a butcher, baker and book-

shop. There are fabulous walks in the surrounds, such as the climb up to Crug Hywel Iron Age hill fort.

◉ Sights & Activities

Crug Hywel MOUNTAIN

(Table Mountain) Though not in the same league as its Cape Town cousin, Crickhowell has its very own Table Mountain, 451m Crug Hywel. Rising to the north, the distinctive hump of old red sandstone gave the town its name. The short-but-steep hike to the top is a rite of passage for local ramblers, heading through a wooded dingle and over stile and field to the remains of an Iron Age hill fort. The summit commands tremendous views of the Brecons and Black Mountains.

The tourist office has a leaflet detailing the 4.5-mile, three-hour round-trip route.

Crickhowell Castle & Bridge CASTLE

Once a mighty stronghold, now a pretty ruin, this Norman motte-and-bailey castle affords views of the Usk Valley. All that remains of the castle are a few tumbledown towers. Wander down to the nearby river, where a ford was superseded in the 17th century by the elegant stone bridge leading to the neighbouring village of Llangattock. The bridge is famous for having 12 arches on one side and 13 on the other.

Old Market Hall HISTORIC BUILDING

(High St) Built in the 1830s by the Duke of Beaufort, Crickhowell's small but grandiose open-fronted market hall hosts an arts-and-craft market most Saturdays. Upstairs there's a cafe in a space that originally served as the town hall.

Tretower Court & Castle HISTORIC BUILDING

(Cadw; www.cadw.gov.wales; Tretower; adult/child £6.50/3.90; ⊙10am-1pm & 2-5pm Mon-Wed, Sat & Sun) Originally the home of the Vaughan family, Tretower gives you two historic buildings for the price of one: the sturdy circular Norman keep, now roofless and commanding only a sheep-nibbled bailey, and a 15th-century manor house with a fine garden and orchard (now furnished with picnic tables). Together they illustrate the transition from military stronghold to country house that took place in the late medieval period. It's 3 miles northwest of Crickhowell on the A479. Prebook tickets online.

Beacon Park Day Boats BOATING, CANOEING
(☑ 01873-858277; www.beaconparkdayboats.co.uk; Hillside Rd, Llangattock; per day boat £90-120, canoe £50-60; ☺ Easter-Oct) 🌿 Rents six- to eight-seater electric-powered boats and three-seater Canadian canoes. In a day you can cruise southeast to Llangattock and back. It also has a fleet of luxury narrowboats (including an ecofriendly hybrid-electric one) for longer live-in voyages.

Golden Castle Riding Stables HORSE RIDING
(☑ 01873-812649; www.golden-castle.co.uk; 1hr lesson adult/child £25/20, pub ride £75; 🖐) Offers pony trekking, hacking and trail riding in the countryside surrounding Llangattock.

🎊 Festivals & Events

Crickhowell Walking Festival SPORTS
(www.crickhowellfestival.com; ☺ Mar) Held on the second week in March, this eight-day festival features guided treks, workshops on outdoorsy themes and music. The thigh-burning highlight is arguably the Table Mountain Challenge, where you walk or run up and down Table Mountain five times in 10 hours. Phew! Book on the website.

Green Man Festival MUSIC
(www.greenman.net; Glanusk Park; ☺ mid-Aug; 🖐) 🌿 This four-day, sustainably minded music festival has a sterling reputation for its mellow, family-friendly vibe and green ethos. It attracts A-list indie acts like Lamb and the Wedding Present, interesting electronic artists and the occasional dead-set rock legend. Tickets include camping on the riverside site 2 miles west of Crickhowell.

🛏 Sleeping

Bear PUB ££
(☑ 01873-810408; www.bearhotel.co.uk; Beaufort St; s £99-192, d £123-248; 🅿🛜) If only every village in Wales had a pub like this... Looking back on 600 years of history, the Bear was once an overnight stop on the horse-drawn coach journey from London to West Wales. Now a delightfully old-school gastropub and hotel, it's full of creaky character, with blackened-oak beams, log fires and cosy nooks.

The rooms are appealingly old-fashioned, with stone walls, antiques and blousy florals, while those in the converted courtyard stables are more contemporary. For romance, splurge on the best room in the house, with a four-poster and freestanding tub.

Downstairs, the restaurant (mains £14 to £25) places the accent on local sourcing in dishes like game terrine with real ale chutney, and braised Welsh lamb shank with spring-onion mash.

Old Rectory HERITAGE HOTEL ££
(☑ 01873-810373; www.rectoryhotel.co.uk; Llangattock; s £75, d £99-124, ste £139) Reclining peacefully in 17 acres of grounds and orchards, this 16th-century country abode was once home to the Welsh metaphysical poet Henry Vaughan. You'll find dashes of period charm in the warm-toned, plushly furnished rooms. Overlooking the Black Mountains, the conservatory restaurant (mains £16 to £20) serves the sophisticated likes of maple-glazed pork belly with fondant potato and cider sauce.

Ty Croeso B&B ££
(☑ 01873-740173; www.ty-croeso.co.uk; Dardy; d £95, ste £115-165; 🅿🛜) Once the infirmary at a Victorian workhouse, this handsome grey-stone house is now an elegant retreat, with a relaxed atmosphere, country-chic interiors and gorgeous mountain views. The welcome is warm and breakfast is delicious.

★**Gliffaes** HOTEL £££
(☑ 01874-730371; www.gliffaeshotel.com; r £135-290; 🅿🛜🐾) Winging you back to a more graceful era, Gliffaes is a class act. Set in grounds bristling with rare and exotic trees on the banks of the River Usk, this Italianate Victorian manor has elegant rooms full of period character – the pick of which overlook the gardens and wooded hills beyond. It's about 4 miles northwest of Crickhowell, off the A40.

Staying here is a proper dose of the country good life, with such leisurely pleasures as afternoon tea on the terrace, croquet and fly fishing. The restaurant (mains £19 to £28) has season-driven produce in its traceable menu, and dishes like supreme of guinea fowl with spring-vegetable broth are served with panache.

🍴 Eating & Drinking

Book-ish CAFE £
(☑ 01873-811256; www.book-ish.co.uk/cafe; 18 High St; mains £5-7; ☺ 10am-4pm Sun-Fri, to 5pm Sat; 🛜🖐) Attached to the independent bookshop of your wildest dreams, this cafe has a strong local following. Browse your latest paperback purchase over brunch (with tempting options like smashed avocado on

toast and buttermilk pancakes with fruit compote); a ploughman's platter with local Perl Las cheese, ham, pork pie and pickles; or homemade cake with local Black Mountain Roast coffee.

Vine Tree   WELSH ££
(☏ 01873-812277;   www.thevinetreellangattock.com; Llangattock; mains £17-22; ⏱ noon-10pm Wed-Sat, to 4pm Sun; ☕ ♿) Going strong since 1857, the Vine Tree blends the period flair of a historic building with post-industrial cool. Leather banquettes, bare-wood bistro tables and brass-cage pendant lights glam up the exposed-brick interior. Swinging with the seasons, the menu has local produce and snappy flavours in dishes like gin-cured salmon with lemon gel and pan-cooked duck with fondant potato and baby beets.

Nantyffin Cider Mill   PUB
(☏ 01873-810775; www.cidermill.co.uk; Brecon Rd; mains £13-18; ⏱ noon-11pm Wed-Sat, to 9pm Sun; ♿) Dishing up good old-fashioned pub grub in rustic surrounds, this 16th-century drovers' inn features an original cider press. Classics like minted lamb burger, and local Welsh ham, egg and homemade chips, go brilliantly with real ales and ciders. There's a kids' menu and playground, too. It's 2 miles northwest of Crickhowell on the A40.

🛍 Shopping

Black Mountains Smokery   FOOD
(☏ 01873-811566; www.smoked-foods.co.uk; Elvicta Estate; ⏱ 9am-5pm Mon-Fri) 🌿 On the edge of Crickhowell and in the foothills of the Black Mountains, this sustainably focused smokery is the brainchild of Jo and Jonathan Carthew. Besides 10,000 sides of salmon a year, they gently smoke chicken, duck, quail, trout and haddock over Welsh oak, and make pâtés and terrines. Stop by the shop for delicious picnic fixings.

Visit the website for details on smokery tours and tastings.

BEST ALTERNATIVE HIKES IN THE BRECON BEACONS

Pen-y-Fan gets all the fuss, but the Brecon Beacons offer plenty of alternative mountain hikes that are every bit as spectacular if less well known. For fewer crowds, take the backroad to one of these favourite trails.

Llyn-y-Fan Fach Out on its lonesome in the Black Mountain range, Llyn-y-Fan Fach is well hidden and worth seeking. Starkly beautiful peaks sweep abruptly down to this steel-blue glacial cirque lake, which is steeped in the legend of the Lady of the Lake. Traipse the 4-mile trail along the sheep-grazed valley, following the river upstream to the lake, ridge and high moors beyond. The views are sensational.

Twmpa More humorously nicknamed Lord Hereford's Knob, this distinctive 690m, cairn-topped peak rearing up just south of Hay-on-Wye forms the northwest scarp of the Black Mountains. The 6-mile, 4½-hour hike along high ridges makes for an excellent half day's ramble, with broad views across the Brecon Beacons.

Blorenge On the southeastern cusp of the Brecon Beacons National Park, the 561m Blorenge has tremendous views of the Usk Valley, Black Mountains and Severn Estuary on cloudless days. The rounded summit is brushed with heathery moorland and the trail path can get boggy when wet. At the top, look out for the remains of a Bronze Age burial chamber. A 4-mile, two-hour circular hike of the peak begins at the Keeper's Pond on the B426, 5 miles south of Abergavenny.

Fan Brycheiniog Capping off the Black Mountain in spectacular fashion, the dramatic escarpment of Fan Brycheiniog (802m) is reached via a fairly strenuous 11.5-mile loop from Glyntawe on the A4067. An initial precipitous ascent of the Fan Hir eases into an impressive ridge walk, with views of the Llyn-y-Fan Fawr glacial lake to the east.

Waun Fach Bare, brooding and thrillingly remote, 811m Waun Fach is the highest peak in the Black Mountains and can be reached on a full day hike. The 9-mile loop trail begins at Castell Dinas, where Norman castle ruins sit high atop an Iron Age hill fort. The trail climbs the imposing Dragon's Back ridge before cresting minor summits and ridges to reach the top. On the way down, Pen Trumau has phenomenal views of the Bristol Channel, Brecon Beacons and Shropshire Hills on clear days.

ℹ Information

Tourist Office (☑ 01873-811970; www.visit-crickhowell.co.uk; Beaufort St; ⊘10am-3pm Thu & Sat; 🕾) Shares a building with an art gallery and stocks leaflets for local walks.

ℹ Getting There & Away

Direct services include 12 daily 43/X43 buses to/from Abergavenny (£2.20, 15 minutes), Llanfrynach (£2.50, 33 minutes) and Brecon (£2.70, 45 minutes). No Sunday services.

Llangorse Lake

Reed-fringed Llangorse Lake may be Wales' second-largest natural lake (after Llyn Tegid), but it's barely more than a mile long and half a mile wide. Despite its diminutive size, it's Brecon Beacons National Park's main watersports location, used for sailing, windsurfing, canoeing and waterskiing.

Close to the northern shore is a **crannog**, a lake dwelling built on an artificial island. Such refuges were used from the late Bronze Age until early medieval times. Tree-ring dating shows that this one (of which only the base remains) was built around CE 900, probably by the royal house of Brycheiniog.

🏃 Activities

Llangorse
Multi Activity Centre   ADVENTURE SPORTS
(☑ 01874-658 272; www.activityuk.com; The Gilfach, Llangors; half/full day £36/64; ⊘9am-10pm Mon-Fri, to 9pm Sat, to 5pm Sun) Set on a hillside overlooking the lake, this centre ramps up the action with indoor and outdoor adventure activities, plus horse riding for beginners and pros. The outdoor 'challenge' course involves clambering up cargo nets, balancing along logs, swinging on tyres and using Indian rope bridges. There's also a set of 14 linked zip wires that stretch for over 3km.

The indoor facility has rock-climbing walls, a log climb, an abseil area, a rope bridge and even an artificial caving area.

🛏 Sleeping

New Inn & Beacons
Backpackers   HOSTEL £
(☑ 01874-730215; www.beaconsbackpackers.co.uk; Bwlch; dm £20-22; 🅿🕾) The one thing better than a good hostel is a good hostel inside a 14th-century pub. This compact, friendly place comes with comfy bunks, reliable hot showers, a crackling wood fire and a warm welcome from knowledgeable owners. With

---

ℹ BRECON BEACONS ACTIVITIES

Hiking & Biking

The national park is traversed by hundreds of walking routes: from gentle strolls to strenuous climbs. Walking cards, maps and guides are stocked in tourist offices as well as at the National Park Tourist Centre near Libanus.

Likewise, there are many excellent off-road mountain-biking routes, including 14 graded and waymarked trails detailed in guides available from tourist and national-park offices.

The **National Park Tourist Office** (☑ 01874-624437; www.breconbeacons.org; Libanus; ⊘10am-4pm) has details of walks, hiking and biking trails, outdoor activities, wildlife and geology. There's also a cafe. It's located off the A470, 4 miles southwest of Brecon and 15 miles north of Merthyr Tydfil. Any of the buses on the Merthyr Tydfil–Brecon route stop at Libanus village, a 1.25-mile walk away.

Wilderness Survival

The Brecon Beacons dish up a proper slice of wilderness once you get off the beaten track, making them perfect for going off grid, brushing up survival skills and camping in the wild.

A number of reputable academies put you through the paces in tucked-away locations in the Brecons (often only revealed when you book). Among them is the **Bear Grylls Survival Academy** (www.beargryllssurvivalacademy.com), which offers 24-hour crash courses that cover the whole survival shebang – from building emergency shelters to fire lighting, navigation, waterfall jumps and river runs. Meals are included and it costs £349 per person.

Other contenders include **Blue Ocean Activities & Adventure** (www.blue ocean-adventure.co.uk), offering half- and full-day bushcraft courses (£40 and £65 respectively) and wild camping (£35) including meals, drinks and firewood.

a couple of good hikes at its doorstep, it's a great place to mingle with fellow ramblers and local drinkers.

🛈 Getting There & Away

The lake is accessed from the village of Llangors. To get here, turn off the A40 at Bwlch. There's no public transport to Llangors.

Talybont-on-Usk

POP 720

Dwarfed by the highest peaks of the Brecon Beacons, tiny Talybont-on-Usk has a venerable transport heritage for its size: an aqueduct takes the canal over the Caerfanell River here, and a disused railway bridge cuts dramatically across the village. Just to the south, the steel-blue, forest-rimmed Talybont Reservoir beckons hikers and cyclists (p104). A handful of decent pubs makes the village an appealing base for an outdoorsy break.

◎ Sights

Talybont Reservoir   LAKE
(🖫) With its backdrop of forest and rolling hills, this glittering reservoir is made for outdoor escapades. These swing from gentle family walks to mountain biking (though swimming is firmly off limits). It's also a popular spot for birdwatching and stargazing, with incredibly dark night skies. A beautiful 5-mile circular walk leads from Talybont-on-Usk to the reservoir and back.

🏃 Activities

Bikes + Hikes   OUTDOORS
(🖉 07909 968135; www.bikesandhikes.co.uk; Talybont Stores; bikes per half/full day £25/30; ◷ 9am-5pm Wed-Sun) This knowledgeable outfit rents out mountain bikes, kids' bikes and tag-alongs and is spot on with local trail advice. It's also good for service, sales and repair, and it contributed to the creation of the Bike Hub in Talybont's nearby village hall, where muddy riders can get a shower for themselves and their mounts.

🛏 Sleeping & Eating

Hawthorns   B&B £
(🖉 01874-676337; www.hawthornstalybont.co.uk; s £58, d £65-75; 🖭) This sweet, simple and spotless B&B occupies a cottage next to the canal in the heart of Talybont. The

sash-windowed rooms are quiet, bright and comfortable. There's a shared guest lounge and bike storage, too.

Star Inn   PUB FOOD £
(🖉 01874-676635; www.thestarinntalybont.com; mains £8.50-12; ◷ 5-9pm Tue-Thu, noon-9pm Fri-Sun) This prettily whitewashed pub is a joy after a bracing hike in the hills. There's a log burner keeping things cosy in the old-school interior in colder months, and a large garden for summer-day drinks. Real ales pair nicely with excellent homemade grub from pies and fish and chips to Sunday roasts with all trimmings.

🛈 Getting There & Away

Three buses a day (except on Sunday) head to Talybont-on-Usk from Abergavenny (£3.10, 45 minutes), Crickhowell (£2.40, 30 minutes), Llangattock (£2.30, 22 minutes), Llanfrynach (£1.70, nine minutes) and Brecon (£2.20, 20 minutes).

Llanfrynach

POP 571

Tucked away in the countryside only 3 miles southeast of Brecon, sleepy little Llanfrynach feels much remoter than it really is, due in part to its only road access being narrow country lanes. It makes a good target for a short walk or bike ride from Brecon, or a quiet place to decamp to for a few days.

🏃 Activities

★**Brecon Beacons Foraging**   WALKING
(www.breconbeaconsforaging.com; The Bookhouse, Tregaer Rd; half-day foraging experience from £35; 🖫) 🖉 Get acquainted with wild food on a half-day, child-friendly foraging walk with Adele Nozedar. Bring along a basket or canvas bag and prepare to find a feast of wild ingredients in the surrounding moors, mountains, hedgerows and woodlands. Depending on the season, you can hope to pick everything from wild garlic to young nettles, bilberries and mushrooms.

Three-hour foraging with kids walks are also available (one adult plus two children costs £40), introducing children to edible plants. At the other end of the spectrum, for adults only, Adele offers botanical gin workshops, which start with a forage and end with cocktails.

**Cantref Adventure
Farm & Riding Centre**   HORSE RIDING
([📞]01874-665223; www.cantref.com; Upper Cantref Farm; £6-12; [🕐]10.30am-5.30pm Easter-Oct, weekends & school holidays only Nov-Easter; [👶]) This child-focused fun farm entertains the little 'uns with pig races, lamb and goat feeding, and play areas with zip wires, trampolines, slides and crazy golf. The adjoining riding centre offers equestrian lessons, pony rides and treks into the Brecon Beacons. Basic camping (per site £23) is also available. It's located in farmland west of Llanfrynach; follow the horseshoe signs.

[🛏] Sleeping

**Pencelli Castle
Caravan & Camping Park**   CAMPGROUND £
([📞]01874-665451; www.pencelli-castle.com; Pencelli; site per adult/child £12.50/5.25, caravans £25) On the site of a former castle and hugging the banks of the Monmouthshire Canal, this family-run site 1½ miles east of Llanfrynach is a tranquil delight. Come to canoe or cycle along the canal or hike into the surrounding heather-cloaked mountains. Besides knock-out views, there are pretty gardens, picnic areas, a well-stocked farm shop, nature trail and playground.

**Camp Cynrig
Glamping Village**   CAMPGROUND ££
([📞]01874-665751; www.breconglampingvillage. co.uk; Cantref; per weekend/week tepee £180/360, cabin £250/500, bell tent £200/420; [🕐]Easter-Oct; [P]) [🚣] Gazing up to the slopes of Pen-y-Fan, this off-grid, eco-aware glamping site is a lovely back-to-nature escape, with easy access to hikes, horse riding, kayaking and scores of other activities. Sioux-style tepees huddle beside the River Cynrig, each with futon beds, firepit and gas-cooking stove. Alternatively, stay in a boutique bell tent, shepherd's hut or riverside log cabin.

The Lodge   B&B ££
([📞]01874-665714; www.thelodgebreconbandb. co.uk; d £75-85; [P][📶]) Blissfully located on the village's rural fringes, this B&B has four spacious, warm-hued, country-style guest rooms. Relax in the gazebo in the lovingly tended garden with views out across the meadows and up to the high, high hills. Breakfast is a treat with locally sourced bacon and eggs. The drying room for wet, muddy gear is a bonus for hikers.

[ℹ] Getting There & Away

Buses stop in Llanfrynach seven times a day (except Sundays), heading to Brecon (£1.70, 11 minutes), Talybont-on-Usk (£1.70, nine minutes), Llangattock (£2.60, 34 minutes), Crickhowell (£2.70, 40 minutes) and Abergavenny (£3.70, 56 minutes).

Brecon (Aberhonddu)

POP 8250

The call of the mountains is irresistible in Brecon. Sitting astride the convergence of the rushing Rivers Usk and Honddu, this appealing little market town is laced with canals and capped off by an impressive cathedral. The real thrills here, however, are in the national park, hence the reason why hiking boots and backpacks are warmly welcome. If you're looking to combine outdoor adventure with a dash of culture, this is the place.

History

An Iron Age hill fort on Pen-y-Crug (331m), northwest of town, and the remains of a Roman camp at Y Gaer, to the west, nod to Brecon's rich history. After the Romans, the area was ruled by the Irish-born king and the town's namesake, Brychan, who married into a Welsh royal house in the 5th century. His kingdom, Brycheiniog, gave its name to the old county of Brecknockshire.

[◉] Sights

Brecon Cathedral   CHURCH
([📞]01874-623857; www.breconcathedral.org.uk; Cathedral Close; [🕐]11am-4pm Mon-Sat, to 3pm Sun) Perched above the River Honddu, Brecon Cathedral was founded in 1093 as part of a Benedictine monastery, though little remains of the original Norman church, except the elaborately carved font. Most of the Gothic structure standing today is early 13th century. Modern additions include its impressive vaulted timber roof. Look out for the stone cresset by the entrance. This rare ancient lighting device contains 30 cups that were once filled with oil and lit to illuminate dark corners or steps.

Monmouthshire & Brecon Canal   CANAL
Brecon is the northern terminus of this canal, built between 1799 and 1812 to transport coal, iron ore, limestone and agricultural goods. The 33 miles from Brecon to Pontypool is back in business, shifting a generally less grimy cargo of holidaymakers and river-dwellers. A peaceful 8.5-mile walk along

Brecon

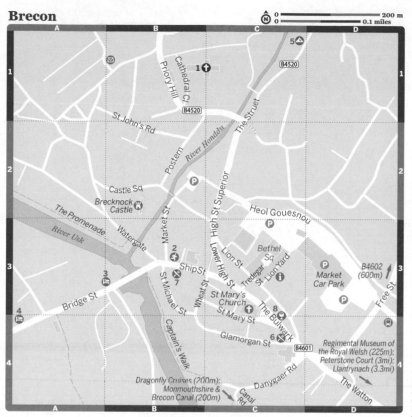

N 0 _____ 200 m
   0 _____ 0.1 miles

the towpath leads to the picturesque village of Talybont-on-Usk (p101).

Regimental Museum of the Royal Welsh
MUSEUM

(☑ 01874-613310; www.royalwelsh.org.uk; The Barracks, The Watton; adult/child £5/2; ☉10am-5pm Mon-Fri) More fascinating than it sounds, this museum at Brecon's early-19th-century military barracks zooms in on the history of the Royal Welsh. The highlight is the Zulu War Room – the Borderers (then the 24th Regiment) fought in the 1879 Anglo-Zulu war in South Africa, inspiration for the 1964 film *Zulu* starring Michael Caine.

Brecon is still an active military base. Many of the soldiers are Gurkhas (Nepalese soldiers fighting in the British Army), often seen in their civvies around the town.

🏃 Activities

Visit Brecon (p106), the town's unofficial but passionate tourist office, is the place to pick

Brecon

◎ **Sights**
1 Brecon Cathedral C1

✪ **Activities, Courses & Tours**
2 Biped Cycles B3

🛏 **Sleeping**
3 Bridge Cafe B3
4 Coach House A4
5 Priory Mill Farm C1

✖ **Eating**
6 Gurkha Corner C4
7 Hours B3

🍷 **Drinking & Nightlife**
8 Brecon Tap C3

up national-park walking cards and other information on nearby activities.

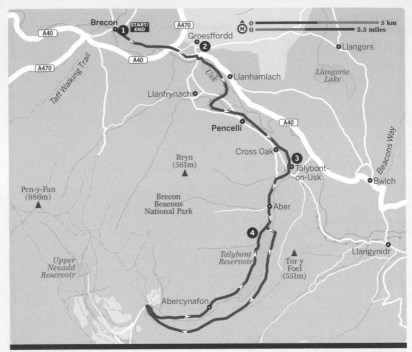

Cycling Tour
Talybont Reservoir

START BRECON
END BRECON
LENGTH 26 MILES; ONE DAY

This moderately challenging ride demands reasonable fitness and is a cycling route of two halves. The first leg – the easy part – whizzes along the canal to pretty Talybont-on-Usk, where you can stop at a pub. Beyond Talybont, a much more challenging pedal loops around the vast Talybont Reservoir. Overall there is 460m of ascent. The trail can get narrow and muddy so choose your wheels wisely.

Bike hire is available in ❶ **Brecon**. The cycle route proper starts near Theatr Brycheiniog with its cluster of canal boats. As you leave town, the houses dwindle and the scene rapidly becomes more rural.

At the first lock at ❷ **Groesffordd**, ignore cycle-route signs and continue on the canal towpath – the signed Taff Trail follows a similar route, but it's nicer to stick to the canal. For the next few miles follow the left-hand bank of the tranquil, tree-lined waterway, catching glimpses of the sinuous and rushing River Usk. You pass the small settlements of Llanfrynach, Pencelli and Cross Oak, but they're barely perceptible from the path.

Eventually you come to ❸ **Talybont-on-Usk**. Opposite the village shop, leave the path and join the lane over the drawbridge. Talybont has dining options, from the handy Talybont Stores with cafe to a few pubs (the best is the Star Inn).

Follow the country road through Aber, beyond which is the ❹ **Talybont Reservoir**. Follow the signs left off the road towards Danywenallt YHA; once you've crossed the water, take the lane to the right, which loops right round the reservoir. At the furthest point you're on the fringes of the Taf Fechan Forest – a steep 275m climb takes you back to the west bank of the reservoir.

The return route – back along the canal the way you came – is easy. Nearing home, at the bridge numbered 162, remember to cross the canal, following the signs to Brecon.

Dragonfly Cruises
BOATING

(☑ 07831 685222; www.dragonfly-cruises.co.uk; Canal Basin, Canal Rd; adult/child £9/5; ⊘ Mar-Oct; ♿) Runs 2½-hour narrowboat cruises on the Monmouthshire and Brecon Canal. There are trips twice daily in July and August, fewer in the cooler months – ring or see the website to enquire.

Biped Cycles
CYCLING

(☑ 01874-622296; www.bipedcycles.co.uk; 10 Ship St; bike hire per day £35; ⊘ 9am-4pm Mon, Tue & Thu-Sat, to 1pm Wed) Rents mountain and road bikes, performs repairs and can arrange guided rides. You'll need to leave two forms of ID in the shop.

✯ Festivals & Events

Brecon Fringe Festival
MUSIC

(www.breconfringe.co.uk; ⊘ Aug) Brecon swings to everything from acoustic blues to folk, gypsy and Latin jazz at this high-spirited festival, which brings a wide range of musical styles to pubs and other venues in and around town over four days in August.

Brecon Jazz
MUSIC

(www.breconjazz.org; ⊘ Aug) Brecon leaps to life for this jazz festival, held on the second weekend in August, with a smorgasbord of live bands, parades, open-mic events and DJs on several stages across town.

Beast of the Brecons
SPORTS

(www.limitlesstrails.co.uk; ⊘ Jul) If you're made of tough stuff, pit yourself against some of the region's fittest trail runners in this 20-mile trail-running race through the heart of the national park. The cut-off time for taming the 'beast' is eight hours. The starting point is Gilestone Farm in Talybont-on-Usk.

🛏 Sleeping

Priory Mill Farm
CAMPGROUND £

(www.priorymillfarm.co.uk; Hay Rd; sites per adult £10; ⊘ Easter-Sep; ℗) ✹ With a cobbled courtyard, an ancient mill, free-range chickens and a lush camping meadow by the Honddu, this is camping heaven, all just a 10-minute riverside walk from Brecon. Local wood and charcoal are supplied for campfires, plus there's a semi-enclosed shelter for cooking and chatting, and a covered bike locker for riders. Children aged 13 and over only.

Coach House
B&B ££

(☑ 01874-620043; www.coachhousebrecon.com; 12 Orchard St; d £89-150; ☎) This appealing 19th-century coaching inn is well attuned to the needs of walkers, with a drying room for hiking gear, generous breakfasts (including good vegetarian options) and packed lunches should you so wish. The six stylish, modern rooms, decorated in soothing taupes and creams, have ultra-comfy beds and great showers.

Bridge Cafe
B&B ££

(☑ 01874-622024, 07531 110358; www.bridgecafe.co.uk; 7 Bridge St; d £80; ☎) Owned by keen mountain bikers and hillwalkers who can advise on local activities, the Bridge has three simple but attractive and comfortable bedrooms by the river, with down-filled duvets and crisp cotton sheets. Only one has an en suite; the other two share a bathroom.

Peterstone Court
HOTEL £££

(☑ 01874-665387; www.peterstone-court.com; Llanhamlach; d £155-235, ste £275; ℗ ☎ ☙) This elegant Georgian manor house on the banks of the Usk offers large rooms brimming with period charm and affording superb views across the valley to the Beacons. The spa is another big draw, with organic beauty treatments, a Moroccan-style relaxation room and a heated outdoor pool. There's also a separate three-bedroom cottage and an excellent restaurant.

Llanhamlach is 3 miles southeast of Brecon, off the A40.

🍴 Eating

★ Hours
CAFE £

(☑ 01874-622800; www.thehoursbrecon.co.uk; 15 Ship St; mains £5.75-8.25; ⊘ 11am-4pm Tue-Sat; ☎) You might happily linger for hours in this little dream of an indie bookshop and cafe, lodged in an endearingly wonky olive-green cottage. The cafe takes pride in local sourcing. Besides fair-trade coffee, it does a fine line in lunches and light bites, from homemade soups, quiche and sandwiches to halloumi with roasted veg. The cakes are delicious, too.

Gurkha Corner
NEPALI £

(☑ 01874-610871; 12 Glamorgan St; mains £8-12; ⊘ noon-2.30pm & 5.30-11pm Tue-Sun; ✍) Rustic scenes of the Himalayas brighten the windowless dining room of this friendly Nepalese restaurant. The delicious food dishes –

WORTH A TRIP

PEAK BAGGING PEN-Y-FAN

No trip to the Brecons is complete without puffing up to **Pen-y-Fan** (886m), the highest peak. On cloud-free days, views stretch all the way to the Cambrians, Black Mountains and the Bristol Channel. It's popular, so avoid weekends and holidays when the biggest crowds descend. The quickest stomp to the top begins at the Pont ar Daf car park on the A470, 10 miles southwest of Brecon. It's a steep but straightforward ascent to the summit of Corn Du (873m), followed by a short dip and final ascent to Pen-y-Fan (4.5 miles return; allow three hours).

A slightly longer (5.5 miles return) but just as crowded path starts at the **Storey Arms** outdoor centre, 1 mile to the north. The T4 bus stops here. (Note: the Storey Arms is not a pub!)

Avoid the crowds by choosing one of the longer routes on the north side of the mountain. The best starting point is the **Cwm Gwdi** car park, at the end of a minor road 3.5 miles southwest of Brecon. From here, you follow a path along the crest of the Cefn Cwm Llwch ridge, with great views of the neighbouring peaks, and then there's a final steep scramble to the summit. The round trip from the car park is 7 miles; allow three to four hours.

Ticking off a quartet of summits – Corn Du, Pen-y-Fan, Cribyn and Fan y Big – the 10-mile **horseshoe walk** is a longer, more dramatic alternative. Pick a clear day for the solid five-hour trek, which begins at the Lower Neuadd Reservoir. The trail climbs steeply along a ridge, with phenomenal views of the bald, sheer mountains and moraine-strewn valleys.

curries, fried rice, lentils and rich veg side dishes – are influenced by, but not identical to, Indian food. The *sisnu* (stinging nettle) curry is a good example.

🍷 Drinking & Nightlife

Brecon Tap　　　　　　　　　　　BAR
(☎ 01874-622353; www.facebook.com/brecontap; The Bulwark; ⊘noon-8pm Mon-Thu, to 9.30pm Fri & Sat, to 2pm Sun; 🛜) Originally crowd-funded into being by the lads at Brecon Brewing, the Tap is a treasure trove of craft beer, traditional cider, estate wines and locally baked meat pies. Occasionally, live music intrudes on the happy hum of locals polishing their favourite bar stools.

ℹ️ Information

Visit Brecon Tourist Office (☎ 01874-620860; www.visitbrecon.org; 11 Lion Yard; ⊘10am-4pm) Visit Brecon is run by volunteers who are passionate about the towns and its surrounds. The centre is well stocked with information.

ℹ️ Getting There & Away

Direct bus services run to/from Brecon's **bus interchange** (Heol Gouesnou). Services include up to 12 43/X43 buses per day to/from Crickhowell (£3, 30 to 45 minutes) and Abergavenny (£3.90, 45 minutes), up to six T14 buses per day to/from Hay-on-Wye (£7, 37 minutes), and up to eight T4 services per day to/from Llandrindod Wells (£5.30, 55 minutes) and Cardiff (£7.20, 1¾ hours). Smaller routes run no Sunday services.

The Market car park offers short-stay pay-and-display parking. There are long-stay lots on Heol Gouesnou and near the canal basin.

Western Brecon Beacons & Black Mountain

Narrow single-track lanes, forested hills and moor after sweeping, sheep-nibbled moor lend a thrillingly remote feel to the sparsely inhabited western half of the Brecon Beacons. Rolling across the western fringes of the national park, the Black Mountain (Y Mynydd Du) is a lonely expanse of barren peaks that throws down an irresistible gauntlet to intrepid hikers. Scoured by glaciers and shaped by human action from prehistory through the Romans to today, it's a bleak, wild and utterly captivating place.

👁 Sights

⭐**Carreg Cennen**　　　　　　　CASTLE
(Cadw; ☎ 01558-822291; www.cadw.gov.wales; Trapp; adult/child £5.50/3.50; ⊘9.30am-5pm) Dramatically perched atop a steep limestone crag high above the River Cennen are the brooding ruins of Wales' ultimate romantic castle, visible for miles in every direction.

Originally a Welsh castle, the current structure dates to Edward I's conquest of Wales in the late 13th century. It was partially dismantled in 1462 during the War of the Roses. On a working farm of the same name, Carreg Cennen is well signposted from the A483 heading south from Llandeilo.

The castle's most unusual feature is a stone-vaulted passage running along the top of the sheer southern cliff, which leads down to a long, narrow natural cave; bring a torch or hire one (£1.50) from the ticket office. Next to the ticket office there's also a 12th-century longhouse (a kind of elongated barn in which people lived with their livestock), filled with darting swallows and the ephemera of rural times past.

Ystradfellte Waterfalls   WATERFALL

(☀) A series of dramatic falls lies between the villages of Pontneddfechan and Ystradfellte, where the Rivers Mellte, Hepste and Pyrddin pass through steep forested gorges. The finest is **Sgwd-yr-Eira** (Waterfall of the Snow), where you can actually walk behind the torrent. At one point the River Mellte disappears into **Porth-yr-Ogof** (Door to the Cave), the biggest cave entrance in Britain (3m high and 20m wide), only to reappear 100m further south.

The gentle **Elidir Trail** (2½ miles each way) starts from Pontneddfechan and connects with various other trails. Take special care – the footpaths can be slippery, and there are several steep, stony sections. The **Four Falls** walk, which takes in everything, is a hard 5.5 miles and demands proper footwear.

Defynnog Yew   NATURAL FEATURE

(St Cynog Church, Church Row, Defynnog; ☀ daylight; ☀) FREE Spreading its 5000-year-old majesty across a quiet churchyard in the unassuming little hamlet of Defynnog, this ancient yew is one of Britain's oldest trees. Yew trees were held sacred by the Druids, symbolising immortality and reincarnation, with roots that reached deep into the underworld. This one inspires wonder with its immense canopy and gnarled roots.

Dan-yr-Ogof National Showcaves
Centre for Wales   CAVE

(✆ 01639-730284; www.showcaves.co.uk; A4067, Abercraf; adult/child £15.50/12.50; ☀ 11am Tue-Thu, 11am & noon Sat & Sun; ☀) The limestone plateau of the southern Fforest Fawr is riddled with some of the largest and most complex cave systems in Britain. Most can only be visited by experienced cavers, but this set of three caves is well lit, spacious and easily accessible, even to children. The complex is just off the A4067, north of Abercraf. Tickets must be prebooked online in advance.

The highlight of the 1.5-mile self-guided tour is the **Cathedral Cave**, a high-domed chamber with a lake fed by two waterfalls that pour from openings in the rock. Nearby is the **Bone Cave**, where 42 Bronze Age skeletons were discovered. **Dan-yr-Ogof Cave**, part of a 10-mile complex, has glistening limestone formations.

Fforest Fawr   NATURE RESERVE

(www.fforestfawrgeopark.org.uk; ☀) 🍃 A dramatic mix of stark moorland, lushly wooded ravines, fern-flecked forest and fin-shaped

---

THE PHYSICIANS OF MYDDFAI

Tucked away in glorious seclusion at the foot of the Black Mountain, Llyn-y-Fan Fach (p99) is steeped in the legend of the Lady of the Lake, which appears in the Welsh folk epic, *The Mabinogion*. As the story goes, in the mid-13th century, a young farmer grazing cattle by here saw the fairest maiden he had ever seen, coaxed her to the shore and begged her to marry him. Her fairy father agreed, on the condition that if the man were to ever strike her three times she would return to the fairy world. The couple lived happily near Myddfai (p108) for many years and raised three healthy sons. But the spell was broken when the farmer broke his promise and struck her thrice. She and her cattle returned forever to the lake, leaving the farmer heartbroken.

The three sons often visited the lake and one day their mother appeared. She handed them a leather bag containing secrets of the lake's medicinal plants and informed them that they should heal the sick. At this point history merges with fact as in the 13th century Myddfai did indeed become a celebrated centre of herbalists and healing.

The Pant-y-Meddygon (Physicians' Valley) on Mynydd Myddfai is still rich in bog plants, herbs and lichens and is worth visiting for a scenic walk.

peaks, Fforest Fawr (Great Forest) was once a Norman hunting ground and is now a Unesco Global Geopark. Underpinned by Old Red Sandstone, seriously ancient rocks have been eroded by the elements over 470 million years to create what you see today. A series of paths thread through the park (visit the 'geotrails' section on the website for details).

Penderyn Distillery
DISTILLERY

([📞] 01685-810650; www.penderyn.wales; Penderyn; tours adult/child £9.50/4.50; ⊗ shop 9am-5pm; [P]) Wales has carved out its own niche for Brecon Botanicals gin and award-winning single malts thanks to the Penderyn Distillery. What began as a pub chat about whisky back in the 1990s swiftly evolved when Alun Evans bought a copper-pot still. He chose the foothills of the Brecon Beacons for its spring water and produced the first bottle of Welsh whisky in a century in 2004. Stop by the shop or visit the website for details on tours, tastings and more in-depth masterclasses.

Myddfai
VILLAGE

Little Myddfai on the northwestern edge of the national park might seem quaintly sleepy today, but back in medieval times it was a hotbed of herbalist activity, famed for the prowess of the Physicians of Myddfai and their powerful natural remedies. Pant-y-Meddygon (Physicians' Valley) on Mynydd Myddfai is still rich in bog plants, herbs and lichens, and is well worth visiting for the scenery alone. Beginning in the village centre, an 8-mile circular walk takes you up to the trig point and back.

Garn Goch
RUINS

[FREE] You're likely to have the impressive remains of Garn Goch to yourself. One of the largest Iron Age sites in Wales, it comprises a smaller hill fort covering 1.5 hectares, and a much larger one of 11.2 hectares. While what you now see are immense piles of rubble, it's sobering to know that these were once 10m-high ramparts, faced with stone and 5m thick. From the top, jaw-dropping views of Black Mountain country roll to every point of the compass.

To get here, follow the signs from Llangadog through Bethlehem village and into the hills beyond.

Red Kite Feeding Centre
BIRD SANCTUARY

([📞] 01550-740617; www.redkiteswales.co.uk; Llanddeusant; adult/child £5/3; ⊗ 3pm Apr-Oct, 2pm Nov-Mar) A multitude of majestic birds of prey swoop in daily for their afternoon meal of manky meat scraps at this remote feeding centre. You're likely to see upwards of 50 red kites, alongside buzzards and ravens, all from a hide mere metres from the meat-munching action.

🍴 Sleeping & Eating

There are some good hostels and campgrounds scattered about this section of the national park. Alternatively, you could base yourself in Llandovery or Llandeilo.

Coed Owen Bunkhouse
HOSTEL £

([📞] 01685-722628, 07508 544044; www.brecon beaconsbunkhouse.co.uk; Cwmtaff; dm/r £30/60; [P]) On a working sheep farm just south of the Cantref Reservoir, this excellent custom conversion of an old stone barn offers smart six- and 10-bed bunk rooms and two small private rooms. There's an excellent kitchen, a common area, outdoor tables, a boot room and a laundry. At weekends it's usually booked up by groups, but solo travellers shouldn't have trouble midweek.

Brecon Beacons YHA
HOSTEL £

([📞] 0345-371 9029; www.yha.org.uk; Libanus; sites per adult £10, r £29-59, camping pods £29-79; [P]) Set in six hectares of woodland, 6 miles southwest of Brecon on the A470, this 18th-century farmhouse hostel has had its facilities smartened up but still has plenty of historic character courtesy of flagstone floors and rough stone walls. The location is ideal for hikers – particularly for ascents of Pen-y-Fan. Private rooms, camping pods (sleeping four) and camping are available.

Dan-yr-Ogof
CAMPGROUND £

([📞] 01639-730284; www.showcaves.co.uk; A4067, Abercraf; sites per adult/child £10/5; ⊗ Apr-Oct) Part of the Dan-yr-Ogof (p107) cave attraction, this is a verdant family-friendly site with a play barn for kids. It's also a great spot for walkers, and includes riverside woodland pitches as well as space for motorhomes.

Mandinam
CABIN ££

([📞] 01550-777368; www.mandinam.com; Llangadog; huts £100 per night; ⊗ Easter-Oct; [P]) 🌿 This wonderfully remote estate on the park's northwestern fringe offers a bohemian back-to-nature experience in gypsy vans, shepherd's huts and coolly converted wagons, complete with kitchens and wood-fired hot tubs for romantic stargazing. You

DON'T MISS

SHEEP TREKKING

With sheep outnumbering people by around three to one, Wales is one seriously wet and woolly land. But one organic farm in particular has raised the baaa (pardon the pun) when it comes to sheep farming. At **Jacob Sheep Trekking** (☑01874-636797; www. sheeptrekking.co.uk; Aberhyddnant Organic Farm, Crai; £30; ☉Feb-Sep; 🏍), you can take a sheep for a walk. Besides the novelty value, it's a terrific way to motivate little ones to slap on the wellies and get out for a ramble in the Brecon Beacons National Park.

Ah, but these are no ordinary sheep – the flock of piebald Jacob, Ouessant (the world's smallest) and Valais Blacknose (the world's shaggiest and quite probably cutest) sheep are very easygoing and – dare we say it – friendly. Bring solid footwear and water-proofs just in case.

And if you're not up for trekking, it offers other sheep-related experiences – from lambing sessions to 'shear a sheep' workshops.

needn't worry about privacy, as the huts are well spaced within the vast, bucolic proper-ty. The kind family that owns the farm has made something very special here. Three-night minimum stay.

The estate is a joy to explore on foot, with its own sessile oak wood and plenty of wild-life (keep an eye out for otters, red squirrels, peregrines and red kites as you wander).

⭐**International Welsh
Rarebit Centre**   CAFE **£**
(☑01874-636843; High St, Defynnog; rare-bits £5.50-7.50; ☉10am-5pm Wed-Sat; 🏍) 🍽
Dutch owner Roos pulled a rabbit out of a hat when she transformed a dilapidated schoolhouse into this unique cafe, art gal-lery and cultural hub combination. Served with garden-grown salads and chalked up on a blackboard, the menu is school-dinner fantasy stuff. The delicious rarebits often deviate from the traditional, with the likes of Guinness-laced 'Stout Rarebit', feisty jal-apeño and coriander 'Mexican Rarebit' and Caerphilly, leek and chive 'Spring Rarebit'.

Save room for the outstanding homemade cakes whipped up with seasonal fruits.

Carreg Cennen Tearoom   WELSH **£**
(☑01558-822291; www.carregcennencastle.com; Trap; mains £6-7; ☉11am-4pm; 🅿) Possibly the best castle tearoom anywhere. The farm-er-owner's longhorn beef is on the menu as cottage pie and beef salad, plus it serves warming *cawl* (traditional Welsh stew) and excellent homemade cakes. The location is in an impressive converted barn that sits just below the castle (p106).

❶ Getting There & Away

The only useful bus routes through this region are the 63 between Brecon and Ystradgynlais, which stops at the Dan-yr-Ogof National Show-caves Centre when it's open; and bus T4 be-tween Cardiff and Newtown (via Merthyr Tydfil, Brecon and Llandrindod Wells).

MONMOUTHSHIRE (SIR FYNWY) & SOUTHEAST WALES

You need only ponder the preponderance of castles to realise that this pleasantly rural county was once a wild frontier. The Nor-man marcher lords kept stonemasons ex-tremely busy, erecting mighty fortifications to keep the Welsh at bay. Despite this stone line marking out a very clear border along the Rivers Monnow and Wye, the 1543 sec-ond Act of Union left Monmouthshire in a kind of jurisdictional limbo between Eng-land and Wales. This legal ambiguity wasn't put to rest until 1974, when Monmouthshire was definitively confirmed as part of Wales.

The River Wye, Britain's fifth longest, flows from the mountains of Mid-Wales, tootles its way into England and then re-turns to the middle ground – forming the border of the two countries – before emp-tying into the River Severn below Chep-stow. Much of it is designated an Area of Outstanding Natural Beauty (AONB; www. wyevalleyaonb.org.uk), famous for its lime-stone gorges, dense broadleaved woodland and epic medieval ruins.

Chepstow (Cas-gwent)

POP 12,400

Stick to the several remaining unspoilt historic thoroughfares snaking about its bulky castle battlements and you will see how Chepstow is clinging on to some of its centuries-old good looks. Its main attraction is its magnificent 11th-century fortress: the town was first developed as a base for Norman conquest of southeast Wales (and was only narrowly 'Welsh', with the Wye cutting its eastern edge made the Wales–England boundary by kingdom-forming King Athelstan, in 982). Chepstow later prospered as a timber and wine port, but as river-borne commerce gave way to the railways, its importance diminished to reflect its name, which means 'market place' in Old English. Its status as a major hiking centre, however, means it's well worth staying the night.

◉ Sights

★ Chepstow Castle   CASTLE

(Cadw; ☑ 01291-624065; www.cadw.gov.wales; Bridge St; adult/child £6.50/3.90; ⊙ 10am-1pm & 2-5pm Wed-Sun Mar-Oct, to 4pm Nov-Feb; ⊕) Imposing Chepstow Castle perches atop limestone cliffs overhanging the river, guarding the main river crossing from England into South Wales. It is among Britain's oldest castles – building started in 1067, under a year after William the Conqueror invaded England – and the nation's oldest post-Roman stone-built structure. The impressive Great Tower dates from the 1060s and includes bricks plundered from Caerwent, a nearby Roman town. It was extended over the centuries, resulting in a long, narrow complex snaking along the hill.

There are plenty of towers, battlements and wall walks to explore, and lots of green space in between. Keep an eye out for the primitive latrines extending over the river and for Europe's oldest surviving castle door, a massive wooden barrier dated to before 1190 and used in the main gateway until 1962.

A cave in the cliff below the castle (sadly, no longer accessible to the public) is one of many places where legend says King Arthur and his knights are napping until the day they're needed to save Britain.

Once the entire town was wrapped in fortified walls, bolting it to the castle. Vestiges of the 13th-century **Port Wall** (High St) edge the western side of the town centre, while Chepstow's main street, High St, passes through the Gate House, the original city gate, which was restored in the 16th century.

Tickets must be purchased in advance via the Cadw website.

Chepstow Museum   MUSEUM

(☑ 01291-625981; www.visitmonmouthshire.com; cnr Bridge St & Gwy Ct; ⊙ 11am-2pm Tue, to 4pm Sat) **FREE** Housed in an 18th-century town house just across the road from the castle, this small, child-friendly museum covers Chepstow's industrial and social history. A collection of 18th- and 19th-century prints and drawings reflects the area's importance to early tourists and students of the picturesque. Prebook your visit via website or phone.

St Mary's Priory Church   CHURCH

(Upper Church St; ⊙ hours vary) Elements of this venerable church, including the wonderful zigzag-patterned arches of its Romanesque doorway, date from the 11th century. It was once part of a Benedictine Abbey established by the Normans at the same time as the castle.

Black Rock Picnic Site   VIEWPOINT

(www.visitmonmouthshire.com; Black Rock Rd, NP26 5TW; ℗ ⊕) **FREE** The Severn Bridge, which you will likely have crossed to make it into Wales, is an impressive and graceful feat of modern engineering, spanning some delightful estuary landscapes invariably bathed in the rare and special light the area is blessed with. But if you are thundering over at 60mph+, you are not best positioned to appreciate all this. Come down to the Black Rock Picnic Site and do just that. Pick up the Wales Coast Path here too.

It's 5 miles southwest of Chepstow, near Portskewett, off the B4245 before you hit Caldicott.

🏃 Activities

Chepstow teems with walking possibilities, with the winding Wye offering scenic strolls close to town along its verdant banks.

The **Wales Coast Path** (www.walescoast path.gov.uk), the world's first hiking trail to traverse all of a country's coastline, begins (or ends) beneath the grassy slopes of Chepstow Castle.

The Wye Valley Walk (p112) has one of its trailheads near the castle in Chepstow, while the 177-mile Offa's Dyke Path (p217) starts just over the river at Sedbury Cliffs. For a

Chepstow

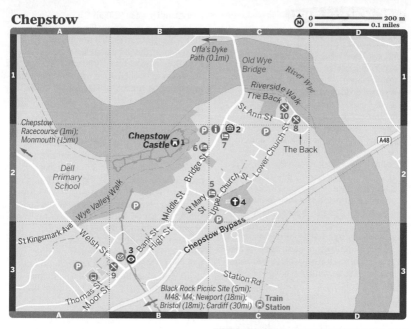

taste of both, you can walk upriver to Tintern Abbey on the former, cross the bridge just past the abbey and take the path to Devil's Pulpit, where you can join the latter for the return leg. The total distance is around 13 miles; allow a full day, with lunch at Tintern. Ordnance Survey (OS) Explorer map OL14 is recommended. You can cut the walk short at Tintern and return to Chepstow (or continue to Monmouth) by bus.

✹ Festivals & Events

Chepstow Farmers' Market   FOOD & DRINK
(High St; ⊙9am-1pm market days) Held on the morning of the second and fourth Saturdays of the month.

Chepstow Festival   PERFORMING ARTS
(www.chepstowfestival.co.uk; ⊙ Jun & Jul) A four-week-long festival held in even-numbered years, with medieval pageantry, drama and music, outdoor art exhibits, comedy, street entertainment and Shakespeare in the castle.

Chepstow Show   FAIR
(www.chepstowshow.co.uk; ⊙Aug) An agricultural one-dayer, with the usual array of livestock, craft and kennel-club competitions, held at the nationally famous Chepstow Racecourse.

Chepstow

◎ Top Sights
1 Chepstow Castle B2

◎ Sights
2 Chepstow Museum C2
3 Gate House & Port Wall D3
4 St Mary's Priory Church C2

⊜ Sleeping
5 First Hurdle Guest House C2
6 Three Tuns B2
7 Woodfield Arms C2

⊗ Eating
8 Boat Inn C1
9 Mythos! B3
10 Riverside Wine Bar C1
Stonerock Pizza .... (see 5)

🛏 Sleeping & Eating

First Hurdle Guest House   GUESTHOUSE £
(☎01291-622189; www.thefirsthurdle.co.uk; 9-10 Upper Church St; r from £55; ☎) One of the best-value bed-and-breakfasts in town is on a pretty street leading along to the castle. There are 12 spick-and-span rooms here, including a cute family room tucked up in the eaves. These guys run an award-winning pizzeria situated next door, too: what's not to love?

OFF THE BEATEN TRACK

WYE VALLEY WALK

Wye Valley Walk (www.wyevalleywalk.org) This 136-mile riverside trail runs from Britain's fifth-longest river, the Wye, which forms much of the boundary between Wales and England in its lower course. It begins high on the lonely slopes of Pen Pumlumon Fawr at the Wye's source and follows the river downstream via Llangurig, Rhayader, Builth Wells, Hereford and Ross-on-Wye in England, Monmouth, Tintern and Chepstow.

The section downstream from Monmouth, past Tintern, is particularly beautiful, through winsome woodsy valley landscapes. At Tintern, the Old Station Tintern visitor centre has further information on the walk. More information can also be obtained online.

Three Tuns
PUB £

(☏ 01291-645797; 32 Bridge St; s/d from £45/65; 🕾) This mid-17th-century pub by the castle is Chepstow's best watering hole to grab a pint or take your pick from the pie-heavy pub menu (mains £10.50). With Tintern-based Kingstone Brewery beers, and an artful makeover, with rugs and antique furniture complementing the more rugged features of the ancient building, it's equally conducive to stay in one of the three en-suite guest rooms.

The flowery, castle-backed beer garden is a boon, and there's an animated atmosphere at weekends.

Woodfield Arms
PUB ££

(☏ 01291-620349; www.thewoodfieldarms.com; 16 Bridge St; s/d from £55/£75; 🕾) The 300-year-old Woodfield Arms has intriguing historic details, including 18th-century wall paintings in two bedrooms and hand-painted glass in the back door. One bedroom sports a carved four-poster bed, although overall accommodations are small and creaky. But there's bags of atmosphere, at its utmost in the bar (open Friday to Sunday), which is full of beams, exposed stonework, nooks, crannies and venerability.

The Sunday lunch is excellent here.

★ Stonerock Pizza
PIZZA ££

(☏ 01291-621616; www.stonerockpizza.co.uk; 9-10 Upper Church St; pizzas £13-15; ⊗ 5-9pm Mon-Thu, to 9.30pm Fri, noon-9.30pm Sat, noon-9pm Sun) Those with a penchant for pizza will know that while you can grab a doughy, cheesy circle down at the supermarket for a pittance, it makes a world of difference having an artisan one cooked for you by people that have studied the art of Neapolitan pizza for 18 months. This little place's 'best pizzeria in the UK' awards' stand testament.

Riverside Wine Bar
TAPAS ££

(☏ 01291-628300; www.theriversidewinebar.co.uk; 18a The Back; tapas £4.95-5.95, mains £10-15; ⊗ 10.30am-11pm Tue, Wed & Fri-Sun, food served noon-3.30pm & 5.30-9pm; 🕾) Quaff a glass of wine while grazing your way through antipasto and cheese platters, skewers, tortillas, pizza and tapas at this refined and newly refurbished Wye-side locale. If the weather is anything approaching decent, the riverbank terrace under draping willows lets you gaze across to England as you drink and dine. Best to book in advance for inside meals.

Boat Inn
PUB FOOD ££

(☏ 01291-626548; www.theboatinnchepstow.co.uk; The Back; mains £10-16; ⊗ 11.30am-11pm Thu-Mon) Strewn with nautical knick-knacks, this riverside pub dishes up better-than-average pub grub and a good menu of daily specials. The best tables are upstairs, overlooking the river. Entertainment includes open-mic and quiz nights.

Mythos!
GREEK ££

(☏ 01291-627222; www.themythos.co.uk; Welsh St; mains £10-14; ⊗ noon-midnight Tue-Thu, to 2am Fri & Sat, 5pm-midnight Sun; 🖉) Exposed beams, stone walls and dramatic lighting make this lively and lovingly decorated Greek bar and restaurant memorable, but it's the authentic, delicious food that justifies that exclamation mark in the name: tzatziki, grilled halloumi, spanakopita, lamb and chicken souvlaki, moussaka and *stifatho* – served as meze or main-sized portions.

☆ Entertainment

Chepstow Racecourse
HORSE RACING

(☏ 01291-622260; www.chepstow-racecourse.co.uk; A466) Set in riverside parkland north of the town centre, Chepstow Racecourse is one of Britain's most famous horse-racing venues. It's home to Wales' most prestigious race meeting, the Welsh Grand National – a roughly 3-mile steeplechase held between Christmas and New Year since 1949. Racing was behind closed doors at time of research due to Covid-19.

ⓘ Information

Tourist Information Centre (☑ 01291-623772; Bridge St; ⊙10am-1.30pm & 2-4pm) One of the most helpful centres in South Wales, with a shop showcasing Welsh produce. Across from the castle.

ⓘ Getting There & Away

BICYCLE

National Cycle Route 42 starts at Chepstow and heads northwest through Abergavenny to Glasbury-on-Wye (near Hay-on-Wye). Route 4 (London, Bristol, Swansea, St Davids, Fishguard) also passes through.

BUS

From Chepstow's **bus station** (Thomas St), frequent X74 and 73 services head to/from Newport (£3.80, 45 minutes to an hour); up to 10 daily 69 services head to/from Tintern (£2.95, 16 minutes) and Monmouth (£4.20, 45 minutes); and up to 12 X7 services head to/from Bristol's Clifton Down station (£6.50, 40 minutes). Sunday services are limited.

National Express (www.nationalexpress.com) has at least a couple of coaches a day to/from London (from £15, three hours), Cardiff (from £5.90, one hour) and Swansea (from £16, two hours).

TRAIN

There are frequent direct trains to/from Newport (£8, 23 minutes), Gloucester (£10.90, 30 minutes) and Cardiff (£10.60, 40 minutes), but only one direct service per day to Swansea (£29.70, 1¾ hours). Change in Cardiff or Swansea for direct services to Carmarthen, Tenby and Fishguard Harbour.

Lower Wye Valley

The A466 road follows the meandering, steep and tree-cloaked valley of the River Wye from Chepstow to Monmouth, passing through the village of Tintern, strung out around its famous abbey as it was in the late-18th-century heyday of tourism here. This is a beautiful and little-visited pocket of Wales, rendered particularly mysterious when a twilight mist rises from the river and shrouds the illuminated ruins.

Much of this fecund area is now part of the Wye Valley AONB, and the countryside here is likely to be the highlight of your trip to southeast Wales. Tiny lanes and pathways thread through dense woods to reach serendipitous ancient sites, gastronomic gems and picturesque panoramas.

It's now almost impossible to see the vestiges of the surprisingly robust industries that flourished here in the 18th and 19th centuries: wire, paper and boat-making. It's still a great place for boats, though – kayaking on the Wye provides just the pace and perspective to tune into the blissful rhythms of this special place.

⊙ Sights

★**Tintern Abbey**   ABBEY
(Cadw; ☑ 0300-025 2239; www.cadw.gov.wales; Tintern; adult/child £5/2.30; ⊙10am-1pm &

THE WYE TOUR

The Wye Valley has a valid claim to being the birthplace of British tourism. Boat trips along the River Wye began commercially in 1760, but a bestselling book – in fact, one of the first-ever travel guidebooks – William Gilpin's *Observations on the River Wye and Several Parts of South Wales* (1771), inspired hundreds of people to take the boat trip down the river from Ross-on-Wye (in England) to Chepstow, visiting the various beauty spots and historical sites en route. Early tourists included many famous figures, such as poets William Wordsworth and Samuel Taylor Coleridge, painter JMW Turner and Admiral Lord Nelson, who made the tour in 1802. Doing the Wye Tour soon became *de rigueur* among English high society.

Local people made good money providing crewed rowing boats for hire, which were equipped with canopies and comfortable chairs and tables where their clients could paint or write, while inns and taverns cashed in on the trade by providing food, drink and accommodation. It was normally a two-day trip, with an overnight stay in Monmouth and stops at Tintern Abbey and Chepstow Castle, among others. In the second half of the 19th century, with the arrival of the railways, the hundreds of tourists increased to thousands, and the tour became so commercialised that it was no longer fashionable.

You can still do the Wye Tour, but these days it's a less glamorous, more DIY affair.

2-5pm Wed-Sun Mar-Oct, to 4pm Nov-Feb; P) The haunting riverside ruins of this sprawling monastic complex have inspired poets and artists through the centuries, notably William Wordsworth, who penned 'Lines Composed a Few Miles Above Tintern Abbey' during a 1798 visit, and JMW Turner, who made many paintings and drawings of the site. It was founded in 1131 by the Cistercian order and fell into picturesque ruin after the monks were booted out by Henry VIII in 1536. Tickets must be booked in advance via the website.

The huge abbey church, closed for repairs at the time of research, was built between 1269 and 1301, its soaring Gothic arches testament to the pre-Reformation monastic wealth and the power the king so coveted. The finest feature is the ornate tracery that once contained the magnificent west windows. Spreading to the north are the remains of the cloisters, the infirmary, the chapter house, the refectory, the latrines, and a complex system of drains and sewers.

The site is clearly visible from the road, but if you want to explore it properly, you'll need a good hour to do it justice. It's best visited either early or towards the end of the day, after the coach-tour crowds have dispersed.

Prices reflect the fact that the abbey church is currently off-limits.

Old Station Tintern NOTABLE BUILDING
(📞 01291-689566; www.visitmonmouthshire.com; parking per 3hr/day £2/4; ⏰ 10am-5.30pm Apr-Oct; P 🚼) FREE About 1 mile upstream from Tintern Abbey, this fetchingly restored Victorian train station has old railway coaches housing a tourist information desk, temporary exhibitions and a cafe. There is a large grassy play area for kids, as well as picnic spots and easy riverside walks.

You can walk between here and the abbey along the river.

Kingstone Brewery BREWERY
(📞 01291-680111; www.kingstonebrewery.co.uk; NP16 7NX; ⏰ noon-4pm Mon-Wed, Fri & Sat; P)
FREE Kingstone Brewery has something of the maverick about it, making takes on traditional ales and often according to archaic recipes. That would be enough to warrant visiting, but the pretty complex of wood-ensconced buildings, engaging explanations of the brewing process and on-site canoe hire (£45 for a 2½-hour paddle) and bike rental (£24 per day) seal the deal.

Tours and tastings weren't possible at the time of research but the brewery shop remained open. The brewery's driveway entrance is opposite that of the Old Station Tintern, a mile upstream of the village.

Parva Vineyard WINERY
(📞 01291-689636; www.parvafarm.com; Parva Farm; self-guided tour £2; ⏰ 1-5pm Thu-Mon Apr-Oct, 11.30am-4pm Thu-Mon Nov-Mar) Grain comes before grape in Wales where the climate doesn't exactly lend itself to vineyards, but nevertheless there are good wineries here, and it is worth the jaunt from the abbey to the northern edge of Tintern to this one. Views through the vines to Tintern are a delight and best between April and September. Tours include a tasting afterwards.

🏃 Activities

There is no shortage of options for valley **walks** around Tintern: a well-maintained trail waymark seemingly springs up every few metres. One of the best begins at the old railway bridge just upstream from the abbey and leads up to the **Devil's Pulpit** (⏰ 24hr), a limestone crag on the eastern side of the river with a soul-stirring view over the abbey (3 miles out and back). This combines elements of the Wye Valley Walk (p112) and Offa's Dyke Path (p217), the long-distance trails which can both be picked up here.

Canoeing on the Wye is fantastic. Get paddling with the folks at Kingstone Brewery, who can arrange 2½-hour self-guided canoe trips for £45.

🛏 Sleeping & Eating

★**Hop Garden** CABIN ££
(📞 01291-680111; www.thehopgarden.co.uk/glamping; Kingstone Brewery, NP16 7NX; d £115; P) The serene meadows and copses encompassing Kingstone Brewery secrete five creaky glamping retreats, collectively called the Hop Garden: two shepherd's huts and three cabins, all isolated from each other, each sleeping two and abounding with their own fabulous quirks. Escaping the day-to-day is the point, so there's no wi-fi, but each has a wood-burning stove or outside firepit, which is much more fun!

Tintern Old Rectory B&B ££
(📞 01291-689920; www.tintern-oldrectory.co.uk; Monmouth Rd, Tintern Parva; r £88-93; P 🐾 🐶)
Dressed in pale pink, blue and cherry-

TRELLECH: THE LOST CITY

The Wye Valley AONB extends into the forested hills way out of sight of the river, although far fewer visitors venture up here. For the curious, though, the fascinating village of Trellech (often anglicised to Trelleck) is a tranquil spot to begin explorations, more than justifying the trip here along woodsy back lanes. In a field on the outskirts, archaeology graduate Stuart Wilson begun discovering fragments of medieval pottery dug up by moles and, convinced that this was indicative of far more extensive ruins below, sunk his life savings into buying the land in 2004. His hunch proved correct and, in subsequent years, artefact after artefact has been uncovered here, including remains of a manor house and a stone tower. Trellech, it appears, was among Wales' most thriving towns in the 13th century, and bigger than Cardiff in size. The only way of experiencing Stuart's considerable findings is to sign up to one of his **archaeological experience days** (☑ 01291 -625831; www.lostcityoftrellech.org; Trellech; per person £50; ☉ Apr-Oct). Trellech likely derives its name from the trio of gutturally leaning megalithic standing stones, **Harold's Stones** `FREE`, in a field close by. The village also boasts a lovely country pub, an ancient healing well and the nearby viewpoint and walking trails just east at **Beacon Hill**.

blossom wallpaper, the four sweet rooms in this Tudor-inspired 18th-century house either look over the river or have access to the rear garden. The breakfast menu offers impressive options, including Welsh classic cockles and laverbread, served on potato pancakes, and the Scottish smoked fish delicacy, Arbroath smokies.

Parva Farmhouse   GUESTHOUSE ££
(☑ 01291-689411; www.parvafarmhouse.co.uk; Monmouth Rd; s/d from £75/90; ☎) This cosy 17th-century farmhouse has low oak-beamed ceilings, Chesterfield sofas, a bar and a wood-burning stove in the lounge, and a garden with beautiful valley views. The eight bedrooms are chintzy and appealingly old-fashioned; one has a four-poster. Better yet: if you book in advance they rustle up exquisite evening meals (7pm to 8.30pm, available to nonguests too).

It's at the northern end of Tintern, opposite the Wye Valley Hotel.

★ **Whitebrook**   MODERN BRITISH £££
(☑ 01600-860254; www.thewhitebrook.co.uk; Whitebrook, NP25 4TX; 3-course menu/lunch/dinner £35/55/85, d incl dinner from £330; ☉ noon-2pm & 7-9pm Wed-Sun; P ☎) Hidden down green-canopied country lanes in a remote part of the Wye Valley, this wonderful Michelin-starred restaurant-with-rooms is well worth the effort to find. Every plate proceeding from the kitchen is a little work of art, made largely with what can be sourced from within 12 miles and adorned

with foraged herbs such as monkwort, nettles, wild garlic and elderflower.

If a sober driver is an unlikely prospect, book one of the eight elegant rooms upstairs.

❶ Getting There & Away

Eleven Bus 69 services a day (fewer on Saturday, none on Sunday) stop here on their journey between Chepstow (£2.95, 16 minutes) and Monmouth (£3.95, 30 minutes). You may want your own wheels.

Monmouth (Trefynwy)

POP 10,500

Against a background of pastel-painted Georgian prosperity, the agreeable market town of Monmouth bustles and thrives. It sits at the confluence of the Rivers Wye and Monnow, and has hopped in and out of Wales over the centuries as the border shifted back and forth. Today it feels more English than Welsh and makes an attractive base for forays into the nearby Wye Valley AONB and blissfully rural landscapes beyond.

History

There was a Roman fort, Blestium, at Monmouth, although the settlement really became a major player on the Wales stage in medieval times, famous as the birthplace of King Henry V, victor at the Battle of Agincourt in 1415 and immortalised by Shakespeare. Other locals who have passed into history include the 12th-century historian

Monmouth

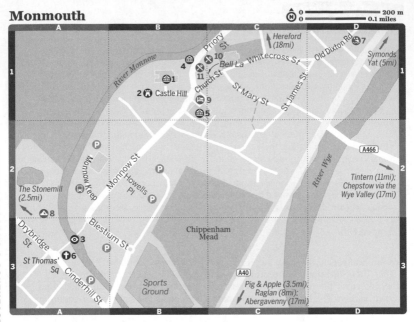

Monmouth

👁 Sights

1 Castle & Regimental Museum B1
2 Monmouth Castle B1
3 Monnow Bridge A3
4 Nelson Museum & Local History
    Centre B1
5 Shire Hall B1
6 St Thomas the Martyr's Church A3

🚴 Activities, Courses & Tours

7 Monmouth Canoe & Activity
    Centre D1

🛏 Sleeping

8 Monnow Bridge Caravan &
    Camping Site A2
9 Punch House B1

🍴 Eating

10 Misbah Tandoori C1
11 Whole Earth Thai Bistro B1

Geoffrey of Monmouth and Charles Stewart Rolls, co-founder of Rolls-Royce.

When Catholicism was banned in Britain, Monmouthshire was a notable pocket of resistance. In 1679 a Catholic priest, Fr (later St) David Lewis, was discovered, tried in Monmouth and hung, drawn and quartered in nearby Usk.

One of Monmouth's more recent claims to fame is Rockfield Studios, a few miles to the northwest. Established in the 1960s, the studio has since produced a string of hit albums, including Queen's *A Night at the Opera*, Oasis' *(What's the Story) Morning Glory?* and Super Furry Animals' *Rings Around the World*, and has been used by artists from Iggy Pop to Coldplay.

👁 Sights & Activities

There are sufficient diversions within town, if you happen to be here, although the real allure is the tranquil Wye-threaded countryside just outside.

Monnow Bridge   BRIDGE
Monmouth's main drag, such that it is, starts at car-free Monnow Bridge, a useful point of orientation and indeed the UK's only complete example of a medieval fortified bridge. It was built in 1272 to protect the English town from the Welsh, but it was later used to extract tolls from people entering the town. Much of what you see now dates from a 1705 restoration.

St Thomas the Martyr's Church   CHURCH
(www.monmouthparishes.org.uk; St Thomas' Sq; ⏱hours vary) Positioned by the Monnow Bridge, sweet little St Thomas dates from

around 1180. Inside highlights include a distinctive Norman Romanesque arch, and pews and a gallery fashioned out of dark wood.

Castle & Regimental Museum
MUSEUM
(☑ 01600-772175; www.monmouthcastlemuseum. org.uk; Castle Hill; ⊙ 2-5pm Apr-Oct) **FREE** Inside Great Castle House, this volunteer-run regimental museum traces the history of the Royal Monmouthshire Royal Engineers (doubly royal!) from its 16th-century militia origins to its current role as the senior regiment of the reserve army, all within a cupboard-sized space. There is little beyond a shell to **Monmouth Castle** (www. monmouthcastlemuseum.org.uk; Castle Hill) **FREE** next door, despite it being the birthplace of King Henry V.

Closed until April 2021 due to Covid-19.

Shire Hall
HISTORIC BUILDING
(Agincourt Sq) **FREE** Fronting Agincourt Sq at the north end of Monnow St, this handsome Georgian building (1724) originally housed sittings of the assizes court. Outside is a statue of former Monmouth resident Charles Stewart Rolls (1877–1910), co-founder of Rolls-Royce. He was the first Brit to die in an air accident, and thus depicted clutching a model of the Wright biplane in which he died.

The historic courtroom upstairs, holding cells below, ground-floor archaeological display and tourist information desk, were closed at the time of research.

Nelson Museum & Local History Centre
MUSEUM
(☑ 01600-710630; www.visitmonmouthshire.com; Priory St; ⊙ 11am-2pm Tue, to 4pm Sat) **FREE** Admiral Horatio Nelson visited Monmouth twice in 1802, officially en route to inspect Pembrokeshire forests for ship timber, though it may have had more to do with his affair with local heiress Lady Emma Hamilton. Despite this tenuous connection, Lady Llangattock, mother of Charles Stewart Rolls (of Rolls-Royce fame), became an obsessive collector of 'Nelsoniana'. The results of her obsession can be seen in this endearing museum. Monmouth history also features, including a display on Rolls and interesting old photographs.

It's fascinating to see how fanatical Nelson-worship was in 19th-century Britain, with forged items, such as locks of his hair,

displayed alongside banal relics of the great man himself. Prebook via phone or website.

Symonds Yat
VIEWPOINT
(www.wyedeantourism.co.uk; Symonds Yat, GL16 7PW; ℗ 🚻) From Monmouth it's a jump over the Wye to the English side of the AONB to one of its most majestic viewpoints at the forest-ensconced hamlet of Symonds Yat, divided into an 'east' settlement and a 'west' either side of the river. Symonds Yat Rock (east side) is the beauty spot where the impressive river gorge vistas reveal themselves. There are great hiking trails here, including one connecting the rock with Symonds Yat East village.

From outside the Saracens Head pub in Symonds Yat East a historic hand-pulled **ferry** (£1/50p adult/child) connects east side with west side.

The red-and-white house nestling in the trees above the Saracens Head pub has recently starred as Otis and Jean's house in popular Netflix TV series *Sex Education*.

Symonds Yat is 5 miles northwest of Monmouth on the A40.

Monmouth Canoe & Activity Centre
CANOEING
(☑ 01600-716083; www.monmouthcanoe.co.uk; Castle Yard, Old Dixton Rd; guided paddles from £35) Perhaps the best thing to do in Monmouth is to come here, rent a two-person Canadian canoe (half-/full day £50/60), single kayak (£35/45) or double kayak (£50/60), with prices including return transport, to float gently downstream on the Wye. You can reach Whitebrook in half a day, or Chepstow in a day.

However, you'll need a guide to navigate the tidal section of the river downstream from Bigsweir Bridge, near Tintern.

🛏 Sleeping & Eating

Sleeping and eating options are both limited in town. Monmouthshire is bejewelled by Michelin-starred restaurants such as the Whitebrook (p115) within an easy drive, and yet central Monmouth doesn't conjure up much that's memorable. The best options are outside town.

Monnow Bridge Caravan & Camping Site
CAMPGROUND £
(☑ 01600-714004; Drybridge St; tent sites from £7; ℗) Just across Monnow Bridge from central Monmouth, this tiny campground has a

quiet riverside location, despite being only a short stroll from the town centre.

Punch House
PUB **££**

(☑ 01600-713855; www.sabrain.com/punchhouse; Agincourt Sq; s/d £50/70) Monmouth is the town of plenty until you're looking for a place to stay – and then options get oddly sparse. One exception is this venerable boozy building, a pub run by the SA Brain brewery, where the rooms are neat if small save for the more sizeable, pricier four-poster room (£85).

★ Pig & Apple
CAFE **£**

(☑ 0786-813-8286; www.thepigandapplemonmouth. co.uk; Upper Meend Farm, NP25 4RP; light bites & mains £5.95-12.95; ⊗ noon-9pm Thu-Sat, noon-3pm Sun; ℗ ♿) Situated on TV presenter Kate Humble's 117-acre smallholding Humble By Nature, the Pig & Apple utilises farm-grown produce in its salads, baps and multifarious burgers (served noon to 3pm and 5pm to 8pm) and keeps you sustained in-between with coffee and homemade cakes. Sunday lunches are a treat too and the hilltop farm setting makes everything more special. Four miles south of Monmouth.

Call ahead to book a table as opening hours can be erratic. The farm has several accommodation options available too.

Whole Earth Thai Bistro
THAI **£**

(☑ 01600-715555; www.facebook.com/pg/the wholeearththai; 10 White Swan Ct; mains £7.95-11.95; ⊗ 9am-4pm Mon-Thu, to 10.30pm Fri & Sat; ♿) Refreshing Thai food in a lovely courtyard arcade, dishing up six sorts of *pad* (stir-fry) and three sorts of *gaeng gati* (Thai curry) among its scrumptious repertoire.

Misbah Tandoori
BANGLADESHI **££**

(☑ 01600-714940; www.themisbah.com; 9 Priory St; mains £10.95-19.95; ⊗ noon-2.30pm & 5.30-11pm; 🍴♿) Longstanding Misbah is an authentic Bangladeshi family curry house with a large, loyal and sometimes famous following. Paul Weller, REM, Oasis and Arthur Scargill have all dined here. Vegetarians are well looked after.

Stonemill
MODERN EUROPEAN **£££**

(☑ 01600-716273; www.thestonemill.co.uk; B4233, Rockfield, NP25 5SW; lunch mains £13-27, 2-course dinner £27-31; ⊗ noon-2pm & 6-9pm Wed-Sat, noon-2pm Sun) Housed in a 16th-century barn, 2.5 miles northwest of Monmouth, this upmarket restaurant showcases Welsh produce in Italian- and French-influenced dishes. It prides itself on making all of its own bread, pasta, pastries, jam, chutneys, ice cream and sorbets. The complex also has six stone and oak-beamed cottages for hire.

❶ Getting There & Away

From the central **bus station** (Monnow Keep), buses head to/from Chepstow (£4.20, 45 minutes, about hourly) via Tintern (£3.95, 30 minutes); as well as Caerleon (£5.50, 45 minutes, three daily); Newport (£5.50, one hour, three daily); Abergavenny (£3.90, 45 minutes, four daily), where the nearest mainline railway station is; and Hereford (£5.50, one hour, five daily). Sunday services are limited.

There's free parking on Cinderhill St, near St Thomas the Martyr's Church.

WORTH A TRIP

RAGLAN

The last great medieval castle to be built in Wales, **Raglan Castle** (Cadw; ☑ 01291-690228; www.cadw.gov.wales; Castle Rd; adult/child £6.50/3.90; ⊗ 10am-1pm & 2-5pm Wed-Sun Mar-Oct, 11am-4pm Wed-Sun Nov-Feb; ℗) was designed more as a swaggering declaration of wealth and power than a defensive fortress. A magnificent, sprawling complex built of dusky pink and grey sandstone, it was constructed in the 15th and 16th centuries by Sir William ap Thomas and his son William Herbert, the first earl of Pembroke.

Its centrepiece, the lavish Great Tower, a hexagonal keep ringed by a moat, bears a savage wound from the civil wars of the 1640s, when it was besieged by Cromwell's soldiers. After the castle's surrender, the tower was undermined, until eventually two of the six walls collapsed. The impressive courtyards beyond the Great Tower display the transition from fortress to grandiose palace, with ornate windows and fireplaces, gargoyle-studded crenellations and heraldic carvings.

Raglan Castle is on the busy A40, 8 miles southwest of Monmouth and 9 miles southeast of Abergavenny. Buses heading between the two stop at Raglan village, which is a five-minute walk from the castle. Book tickets in advance via the website.

Caerleon (Caerllion)

POP 8070

Plonked between Monmouthshire and the south coast conurbation of Newport, the small, genteel town of Caerleon fans around one of the largest, most important Roman settlements in Britain. After the Romans invaded in CE 43, they controlled their new territory through a network of forts and military garrisons. The top tier of military organisation was the legionary fort, of which there were only three in Britain – Isca (Caerleon), Eboracum (York) and Deva (Chester).

Caerleon ('Fort of the Legion') was the headquarters of the elite 2nd Augustan Legion for more than 200 years, from CE 75 until the end of the 3rd century. It wasn't just a military camp but a purpose-built township some 9 miles in circumference, complete with a large amphitheatre and a state-of-the-art Roman baths complex.

Caerleon's place in history did not wane with the Romans' departure: several sources point towards this being the legendary location of King Arthur's court of Camelot.

◉ Sights & Activities

★ National Roman Legion Museum
MUSEUM

(☑ 0300-111-2-333; www.museum.wales/roman; cnr High & Museum Sts; ⊘10am-5pm Wed, Fri & Sat) FREE Put your Caerleon explorations into context at this excellent museum, which paints a vivid picture of what life was like for soldiers in one of the empire's remotest corners. It displays intriguing Roman artefacts uncovered locally, including jewellery, armour, a section of mosaic floor found in the neighbouring churchyard and one of the largest known caches of Roman gems, found under the nearby baths. Book tickets in advance via the website.

There's also a recreation of a Roman garden, featuring trees and herbs first introduced to Britain by the invaders. Kids will relish the costumed character (a soldier usually) who answers the questions of the curious, and the opportunity to try on armour.

Closed at time of research.

Caerleon Roman Fortress & Baths
RUINS

(Cadw; ☑01633-422518; www.cadw.gov.wales; High St; adult/child £3.80/2.20; ⊘10am-4pm; 🅿♿) Like any good Roman town, Caerleon had a grand public bath complex. Parts of

THREE CASTLES WALK

West of the Wye Valley AONB and east of the Brecon Beacons National Park lies a wide band of winsome borderland displaying many of the finest features of both regions: gentle river valleys, green hills and castles. Lots of castles. Three of its finest fortresses are now connected by one hiking trail, the **Three Castles Walk** (www.visitmonmouthshire. com/things-to-do/three-castles-walk). This 19-mile circular meander is a hard day hike or a leisurely weekender, with the rugged trio of ruins **Grosmont Castle** (Cadw; https://cadw.gov.wales; ⊘10am-4pm) FREE, **Skenfrith Castle** (Cadw; www.nationaltrust.org.uk; ⊘dawn-dusk) FREE and **White Castle** (Llantilio Crossenny; ⊘10am-4pm) FREE as the highlights. Drop-dead gorgeous country inns queue up to waylay walkers, including the especially well-regarded **Bell at Skenfrith** (☑01600-750235; www.skenfrith.co.uk; r £175-230; 🅿🛜🐾), right besides the River Monnow in chocolate-box-pretty Skenfrith, and with an upmarket restaurant.

the outdoor swimming pool, *apodyterium* (changing room) and *frigidarium* (cold room) remain under a protective roof, and give some idea of the scale of the place. Projections of bathers splashing through shimmering water help bring it to life, and there are touch-screen quizzes and dress-ups for the kids.

Closed at time of research.

Roman Amphitheatre
RUINS

(Cadw; www.cadw.gov.wales; Broadway; ⊘10am-4pm) FREE These turf-covered terraces edged in brick and stone represent the only fully excavated Roman amphitheatre in Britain. It was positioned just outside of the Roman fortress walls and had a capacity of 6000 people. Follow the signs on the other side of the Broadway to see the foundations of the Roman military barracks: the only one open to the public in Europe. Twelfth-century scholar Geoffrey of Monmouth fancifully cites this as the location of King Arthur's Round Table.

The site, though, is no longer quite as spectacular as its grand history might imply.

BRECON BEACONS & SOUTHEAST WALES CAERLEON (CAERLLION)

TREDEGAR HOUSE

The seat of the Morgan family for more than 500 years, **Tredegar House** (NT; ☑ 01633-815880; www.nationaltrust.org.uk; park free, formal gardens £5, house £7.50, parking £2; ☉ park dawn-dusk year-round, formal gardens 9.30am-4pm, house by hourly guided tour 11am-4pm Wed-Sun Easter-Sep; P) is a stone and red-brick 17th-century building set amid extensive gardens, 2 miles west of Newport city centre. It is among the finest examples of a Restoration mansion in Britain and the oldest parts date to the 1670s. The National Trust took over management of the property in late 2011 and has done a great job bringing the fascinating stories of its owners to life.

The Morgans, once one of Wales' richest families, were an interesting lot. Sir Henry was a 17th-century pirate (Captain Morgan's Rum is named after him); Godfrey, the second Lord Tredegar, survived the Charge of the Light Brigade; and Viscount Evan was an occultist, a Catholic convert and a twice-married homosexual who kept a boxing kangaroo.

Ground-floor highlights include the sumptuous grand dining room and adjoining 'gilt room', blanketed in gold-leaf and with paintings of bare-breasted mythological figures.

The decor of the upstairs bedrooms fast-forwards in time to the 1930s, when Evan Morgan was hosting his fabulous parties at Tredegar. For the full *Downton Abbey* experience, head 'below stairs' to explore the preserve of the Morgans' numerous servants.

The house was temporarily closed at the time of research; grounds remain open.

Usk Valley Walk   WALKING
(www.visitmonmouthshire.com) The Usk Valley does not receive nearly the attention that the close-by Wye Valley does, but this long-distance path begs you to think differently, running from Caerleon to Abergavenny and onto Brecon through gently rural emerald-green terrain alongside the River Usk, and thankfully festooned with some magical pubs (especially on the river's lower reaches) to refresh the footsore.

🛏 Sleeping & Eating

Priory Hotel & Restaurant   HISTORIC HOTEL ££
(☑ 01633-421241; www.thepriorycaerleon.co.uk; High St; d from £95; P ☎) This 12th-century Cistercian monastery is now one of the fanciest addresses to stay at in Caerleon, with 27 rooms done gracefully in classic contemporary style and muted blues, pale pinks and beiges. Features include antiques, beams and – in our favourite – a stand-alone bath in a floor-to-ceiling window recess. The decent restaurant serves Spanish-British food (mains £15 to £26).

Hanbury Arms   PUB FOOD £
(☑ 01633-420361; www.sabrain.com/hanbury; Hanbury cl; mains £8-15; ☉ noon-10pm) This 16th-century coaching inn is owned by one of Wales' biggest breweries, SA Brain, which homogenises its individuality a

little, but in a Caerleon dining scene which changes like the wind, offers consistency, cracking riverside panoramas and the historic environs in which poet Alfred Lord Tennyson lodged while penning *Idylls of the King*. Food here is hearty and traditionally pubby.

An occasional Welsh theme is evident in dishes like the steak-and-ale pie, made with the brewery's Rev James, or in Wales' own version of the meatball: faggots.

Newbridge on Usk   PUB FOOD ££
(www.celtic-manor.com; Newbridge-on-Usk; mains £15-26; ☉ noon-9.30pm) The River Usk secretes many riverside pubs, but the greatest is 5 miles northeast of Caerleon, commanding a dreamy location by a centuries-old stone river bridge. Run by the Celtic Manor Resort, it presents exquisitely cooked food many steps up from standard pub grub: the likes of tender duck breast or lamb rump with truly creative sides.

The things they can do with simple veg such as cauliflower have to be tasted to be believed. You could walk here from Caerleon along the Usk Valley Walk.

ℹ Getting There & Around

Caerleon is 3 miles northeast of central Newport. Buses head to Caerleon from Newport's bus station adjacent to Friar's Walk Shopping

Centre (£1.80, 20 minutes, frequent). Local bus 60 runs from Caerleon to Monmouth (£5.50, one hour, three daily), operated by Newport Bus (www.newportbus.co.uk).

Newport is the key transport hub for southeast Wales. From the bus station here there are also long-distance connections to London (from £22, three hours, every two hours) as well as Swansea (£10, 1½ hours, four daily), Cardiff (£3, 30 minutes, four daily), Bristol (£9, 40 minutes, four daily) and Birmingham (£21, 2¼ hours, four daily).

The bus station is a seven-minute walk from Newport train station. Here, direct trains run to London Paddington (from £43, two hours, at least hourly), Chepstow, Cardiff, Swansea, Tenby and Holyhead on Anglesey.

SOUTH WALES VALLEYS

The valleys fanning north from Cardiff and Newport were once the heart of industrial Wales, playing a part in national (and world) history that can't be overstated. Although the coal, iron and steel industries have withered, the valley names – Rhondda, Cynon, Rhymney, Ebbw – still evoke a world of tight-knit working-class communities, male-voice choirs and rows of neat terraced houses set amid a scarred, coal-blackened landscape. Today the region is fighting back against a very noticeable and tragic decline by creating a tourism industry celebrating and preserving its industrial heritage – places such as the Big Pit and Blaenavon Ironworks are among Wales' most impressive and historically poignant tourist attractions.

History

The valleys' industrial economy emerged in the 18th century, based on the exploitation of the region's rich deposits of coal, limestone and iron ore. At first the iron trade dictated the need for coal, but by the 1830s coal was finding its own worldwide markets and people poured in from the countryside looking for work. The harsh and dangerous working conditions provided fertile ground for political radicalism – Merthyr Tydfil elected Britain's first-ever Labour Party MP, Keir Hardie, in 1900, and many locals went to fight in the Spanish Civil War in the 1930s.

Merthyr Tydfil (Merthyr Tudful)

POP 43,800

Merthyr Tydfil (*mur*-thir *tid*-vil; Merthyr for short) occupies a spectacular if eerie site, sprawled across a bowl at the head of the Taff Valley, ringed and pocked with quarries and spoil heaps. It was even more spectacular 200 years ago when the town was at the heart of the Industrial Revolution, and this bowl was a crucible filled with the fire and smoke of the world's biggest ironworks.

Perhaps unusually for such an industrial town, Merthyr Tydfil has produced two internationally famous fashion designers – the late Laura Ashley (famed for her flowery, feminine designs in the 1970s) and Julien Macdonald (he of the shimmery, figure-hugging dresses favoured by Kylie and Britney).

History

Merthyr's history is as singular as its appearance. Merthyr Tydfil means 'the place of Tydfil's martyrdom' – the town was named in honour of a Welsh princess who, according to legend, was murdered for her Christian beliefs in the 5th century. St Tydfil's Church is said to mark the spot where she died.

In the late 18th century Merthyr's proximity to iron ore, limestone, water and wood led to it becoming a centre of iron production. The subsequent discovery of rich coal reserves upped the ante, and by 1801 a string of settlements, each growing around its own ironworks – Cyfarthfa, Penydarren, Dowlais, Pentrebach and others – had merged together to become the biggest town in Wales (population 10,000, eight times the size of Cardiff at that time). Immigrants flooded in from all over Europe, and the town's population peaked at 81,000 in the mid-19th century.

By 1803 Cyfarthfa was the world's biggest ironworks. Ever more efficient ways to make iron were pioneered, on the backs of overworked labourers (including, until 1842, women and children as young as six) who lived in appalling, disease-ridden conditions.

By the 19th century Merthyr was a centre of political radicalism. The Merthyr Rising of 1831 was the most violent uprising in Britain's history – 10,000 ironworkers, angry over pay cuts and lack of representation, faced off against a handful of armed soldiers, and rioting continued for a month.

During the protest a red flag was raised; it went on to become an international symbol of the workers' movement.

As demand for iron and steel dwindled in the early 20th century, the ironworks closed down. Unemployment soared, reaching as high as 60% in 1935. In 1939 a Royal Commission even suggested that the whole town should be abandoned, but community ties were strong and people stayed on.

Today unemployment still runs at 8%, nearly twice the UK average, and it became one of Britain's worst-hit towns during the 2020 Covid-19 pandemic.

◉ Sights & Activities

Merthyr is certainly jaw-dropping: mostly, you're not drinking in the beauty so much as gazing around with a sort of appalled awe at how humankind can radically alter a landscape.

If you like industrial heritage with your hike or bike ride, a section of the 55-mile Taff Trail (p66) between Cardiff Bay and Brecon follows the river that runs along the western edge of town. It's crossed by the handsome railway viaducts of Cefn-Coed (the third biggest in Wales) and Pontsarn, both completed in 1866. One of Wales' best mountain-biking trail systems, **BikePark Wales** (☑07730 382501; www.bikeparkwales.com; Gethin Woods, Abercanaid; day pass £14, incl uplift £41-48, bike hire per half-/full day from £40/60; ⊗10am-4pm Thu-Mon), is in Gethin Woods 2 miles south of central Merthyr: check the website for the latest opening hours, which were to be reviewed every couple of weeks post-lockdown.

Cyfarthfa Castle   CASTLE
(☑01685-727371; www.cyfarthfa.com; Brecon Rd; adult/child £2.30/free; ⊗11am-4pm; P) For a measure of the wealth that accumulated at the top of the industrial pile, check out this castle built in 1825 by William Crawshay II, overlooking his ironworks. The house is now jam-packed with interesting stuff, from ancient Egyptian and Roman artefacts, to Laura Ashley and Julien Macdonald frocks. The basement houses an excellent exhibition on Merthyr's gritty history, taking in the struggles of the Chartists, trade unions and suffragettes. The house is surrounded by a beautiful public park.

Set into the hillside across the river from the castle are all that remains of the Cyfarthfa blast furnaces.

Brecon Mountain Railway   HERITAGE RAILWAY
(☑01685-722988; www.bmr.wales; CF48 2DD; adult/child £15.75/6.75) Between 1859 and 1964 this narrow-gauge railway hauled coal and passengers between Merthyr and Brecon. It's a nice urban-to-rural transition. A 5.5-mile section of track, between Pant Station and Torpantau at the head of Pontsticill Reservoir, has been restored and steam locomotives operate on the line. The trip takes 65 minutes with a 20-minute stop at Pontsticill (you can stay longer if you like and return on a later train). Check timetables online. Closed until April 2021.

Pant Station is 3.5 miles north of Merthyr bus station; take bus 35 (20 minutes, departs every 20 minutes, hourly on Sunday) to the Pant Cemetery stop.

🛏 Sleeping & Eating

Grange Guesthouse   GUESTHOUSE ££
(☑01685-359750; www.thegrangecefncoed.wales; Pont y Capel Rd, Cefn-Coed-Y-Cymmer; r £95) Cyclists will love this guesthouse with views opening onto the impressive Cefn-Coed viaduct, and the five rooms decorated red, black, yellow, green and blue to reflect the five colours on the cycling world champion's 'Rainbow Jersey'. The homemade slabs of cake are welcome hunger-busters upon arrival.

★Mango House   INDIAN ££
(☑01685-388085; www.mangohouse.co.uk; 91 High St, Cefn-Coed-Y-Cymmer; mains £9.95-16.95; ⊗6-10.30pm; ☑) Bringing the subcontinent to the suburbs, this snazzy Indian eatery serves up a huge menu of delicious and complex curries, including an extensive vegetarian selection. Don't confuse the address with High St in the town centre; this High St is the continuation of Brecon Rd west of Cyfarthfa Castle.

Woodfired   BURGERS, PIZZA ££
(☑01685-359435; www.woodfiredmt.com; 62 High St; breakfasts £3-7, lunches £4.50-10, dinner mains £7.95-19.95; ⊗10am-10pm Mon-Sat, noon-5pm Sun; ☑) Bringing a dose of industrial-chic to Merthyr's tired shopping strip, this cool-looking restaurant-bar serves good breakfasts and lunches; a fancy burger, wood-fired pizza and grill menu come evening; plus craft ale and some original cocktails. One of our favourite Merthyr hang-outs.

ℹ️ Getting There & Away

Merthyr Bus Station is in Victoria St, in the town centre. Direct buses head to/from Cardiff on the dependable X4 service (£5.80, 60 minutes, at least hourly) as well as to Abergavenny (£7, 1¾ hours) in the other direction. Other destinations you can bus to direct include Brecon (£3.30, 35 minutes) and Llandrindod Wells (£8, 1¾ hours) on the T4 service, running every two hours.

Trains head to/from Cardiff (£5, 50 minutes) every hour. The train station is right in the centre of town, by the giant Tesco supermarket on Tramroadside North.

Blaenavon (Blaenafon)

POP 6050

Of all the valley settlements that were decimated by the demise of heavy industry, the one-time coal and iron town of Blaenavon shows the greenest shoots of regrowth, helped in large part by the awarding of Unesco World Heritage status in 2000 to its unique conglomeration of industrial sites. Its proximity to Brecon Beacons National Park and Abergavenny doesn't do it any harm either. Anyone with an interest in industrial history (or social history, for that matter) will find plenty to see and consider here.

◉ Sights & Activities

Blaenavon World Heritage Centre MUSEUM
(📞 01495-742333; www.visitblaenavon.co.uk; Church Rd; ⊙10am-5pm Tue-Sun) FREE Housed in an artfully converted old school, this centre contains a cafe, a tourist office, a gallery, a gift shop and, more importantly, excellent interactive audiovisual displays that explore the industrial heritage of the region. If you're going to explore any of the World Heritage venues, this is the place to start to contextualise it all.

Blaenavon Ironworks HISTORIC SITE
(Cadw; 📞 01495-792615; www.cadw.gov.wales; North St; adult/child £5.20/3.10; ⊙10am-5pm Easter-Oct, 11am-4pm Fri-Sun Nov-Easter) When it was completed in 1789, this ironworks was among the most advanced in the world. Today the site is among the best preserved of all its Industrial Revolution contemporaries, with a motion-activated audiovisual display within the hulking remains of one of the blast furnaces. Also on display, but temporarily closed at time of research, are the ironworkers' tiny terraced cottages, furnished as

they would have been at different points in history.

Blaenavon Ironworks' three huge coal-fired blast furnaces were provided with air by a steam engine, making them much more powerful than older, smaller furnaces fired with charcoal and blasted with air from waterwheel-powered bellows. Within a few years of construction, it was the world's second-biggest ironworks, after Cyfarthfa at Merthyr Tydfil. Innovation and development continued here until 1904, when the last furnace was finally shut down.

You can follow the whole process of production, from the charging of the furnaces to the casting of molten iron in the casting sheds. The surrounding hillsides are pitted with old tramlines, mines, tunnels and 'scouring' sites, where water was released from holding ponds to wash away topsoil and expose ore seams.

Pontypool &
Blaenavon Railway HERITAGE RAILWAY
(📞 01495-792263; www.bhrailway.co.uk; Furnace Sidings, Garn-Yr-Erw; per 8-person compartment £32) Constructed to haul coal and passengers, this railway has been restored by local volunteers, allowing you to catch a train 3.5 miles from the town centre (Blaenavon High Level Station) to Furnace Sidings (near Big Pit) and then on to Whistle Halt, which at 396m is one of Britain's highest stations. Check online for running days and times; most journeys involve restored steam locomotives.

At the time of research, Covid-19 restrictions meant that each separate group needs to book an entire train compartment, seating up to eight people (regardless of their group size).

★ Big Pit National Coal Museum MINE
(📞 0300-111 2333; www.museum.wales/bigpit; car park £3; ⊙10am-5pm Tue, Wed, Fri & Sat, guided tours 10am-3.30pm; 🅿🚻) FREE Fascinating Big Pit provides an opportunity to explore a real coal mine and taste what life was like for the miners working here between 1880 to 1980. At the time of research, the biggest attraction, the Real Underground Experience, where tours descend 90m into the mine and explore the tunnels and coalfaces guided by an ex-miner, was closed. Nevertheless, there's plenty going on above ground. You can visit numerous colliery buildings, including the 1939 pithead baths.

DON'T MISS

AFAN FOREST PARK
....

A welcome contrast with the grim industry of Port Talbot to the south, the **Afan Forest Park** (www.afanforestpark. co.uk; SA13 3HG) shores up beyond the built-up M4 corridor of South Wales in word-defying shades of green forest and hills. The A4107 traverses the south of the park, which feels vast and stretches north to the edge of the Brecon Beacons National Park, and off this road is the main **visitor centre**, opening onto an array of mountain-bike trails and hikes.

At the visitor centre there is bike hire (£30 to £65 per day), a cafe and ample parking (£2.50 for four hours). The outdoor activities here attract visitors from far and wide. Bus 83 stops here from Port Talbot bus station (20 minutes); if driving, take the A4107 north from Port Talbot via Pontrhydyfen.

The baths are filled with displays on the industry and the evocative reminiscences of ex-miners. Lots of discarded industrial mining equipment adds to the interest.

It's sobering to experience something of the dark, dank working conditions below ground, particularly considering that children once worked here by candlelight. When the underground tour reopens, if you choose to do it you'll be decked out in a hard hat, power pack and other safety gear weighing some 5kg, and you won't be allowed to bring matches or anything electrical (including photo equipment and watches) down with you. It's cold down here, so take extra layers and wear sturdy shoes. Children must be at least 1m tall. Visitors with disabilities can arrange tours in advance.

For some extra fun, you can take the heritage Pontypool & Blaenavon Railway (p123) here from Blaenavon.

👉 Tours

Mountain Tours   CYCLING, HIKING
(☑ 01495-793123; www.chunkofwales.co.uk; 80 Broad St; bike hire per half-/full day £14/20) Operated in conjunction with the folks at Blaenavon Cheddar Company, this crew hires bikes and can arrange guided walks (from £10 per adult) to suit all abilities (strongly advised to book well in advance through the website).

🛏 Sleeping & Eating

Oakfield   B&B ££
(☑ 01495-792829; www.oakfieldbnb.com; 1 Oakfield Tce, Varteg Rd; d £75; P 🛜) Paula and Heidi, clued-up owners of this spick-and-span B&B, are a fount of local knowledge. Three well-appointed rooms have a fresh, modern feel. Two have en-suite bathrooms, with the third an interconnected family suite having a bathroom on the landing. At the time of research they were only offering one room (or permitting one household group) at any one time.

The family suite is £112.50 for a family of four.

Butterflies   PUB FOOD ££
(☑ 01495-791044; www.butterfliesblaenavon. co.uk; 31 Old Queen St; mains £13-18, 3-course Sun lunch £16.95; ⊙ kitchen 6-9pm Tue-Sat, noon-3pm & 6-9pm Sun; 🍴) Serving surprisingly decent food for a small-town pub in a former mining town, cosy Butterflies specialises in meat, especially burgers, lamb and steak. If that all sounds a bit too much, there are fish and vegetarian options to fall back on. Inside it's all very sophisticated and there is an outside terrace too.

🛍 Shopping

Blaenavon Cheddar Company   CHEESE
(☑ 01495-793123; www.chunkofcheese.co.uk; 80 Broad St; ⊙ 10am-3pm Mon-Fri) Showcasing the company's range of award-winning handmade cheese, some of which is matured down in the Big Pit mine shaft, this little store also stocks a range of Welsh speciality ale, chutney, mustard and other local produce.

ℹ Getting There & Away

Frequent (one or two hourly) X24 bus services head to/from Newport (£7.70, one hour).

Caerphilly (Caerffili)
POP 41,400

The town of Caerphilly, centred on a massive masterpiece of a castle that would be too flamboyant for most fairy tales, guards the entrance to the Rhymney Valley to the north of Cardiff. Its name is synonymous with a popular variety of mild, slightly crumbly, hard white cheese that was once made in farmhouses all over South Wales.

Its other claim to fame is as the birthplace of Tommy Cooper, a much-loved

British comedian. A statue of Cooper in his trademark fez and with a rabbit at his feet overlooks the castle from near the tourist office. Unfortunately, nothing else in town remotely approaches the castle (or the cheese, for that matter) for interest and significance – it's a definite day-trip candidate.

◎ Sights

★ Caerphilly Castle   CASTLE
(Cadw; www.cadw.gov.wales; Castle St; adult/child £8/4.80; ⊘ 10am-1pm & 2-5pm Wed-Sun; ⊞) You could be forgiven for thinking that Caerphilly Castle – with its profusion of towers and crenellations reflected in a duck-filled lake – was a film set rather than an ancient monument. While it is often used as a film set, it is also one of Britain's finest examples of a 13th-century fortress with phenomenal water defences, and the largest castle in Wales. Most construction was completed between 1268 and 1271 by powerful English baron Gilbert de Clare (1243–95), marcher lord of Glamorgan.

The fortress was built in response to the threat of attack by Prince Llywelyn ap Gruffydd, prince of Gwynedd (and the last Welsh Prince of Wales), who had already united most of the country under his control at the time. Edward I's subsequent campaign against the Welsh princes put an end to Llywelyn's ambitions and concluded Caerphilly's short-lived spell on the front line (the leaning tower at the southeastern corner is a result of subsidence rather than battle).

In the 13th century Caerphilly was state-of-the-art, being one of the earliest castles to use lakes, bridges and a series of concentric fortifications for defence. To reach the inner court you had to overcome no fewer than three drawbridges, six portcullises and five sets of double gates. In the early 14th century it was remodelled as a grand residence and the magnificent great hall was adapted for entertaining, but from the mid-14th century the castle began to fall into ruin.

Much of what you see today is the result of restoration by the fortress-loving Bute family (p55). The third marquess of Bute purchased and demolished houses built up against the walls, and in 1870 the great hall was given a magnificent wooden ceiling. The fourth marquess instituted a major restoration from 1928 to 1939, giving jobs to many Great Depression–affected locals in the process. Work continued after 1950, when the fifth marquess gifted the castle to the state. In 1958 the dams were reflooded, creating the castle's current fairy-tale appearance.

You can enter through the outside gate and into the first tower before reaching the ticket office. Upstairs are detailed displays about the castle's history. A cartoonish film projected onto the walls of one of the inner towers tells a truncated version of the same story.

On the south dam platform you can see reconstructions of medieval siege weapons; they are working models that lob stone projectiles into the lake during battle re-enactments. Fans of toilet humour should seek out the communal latrine in a small tower nearby.

The castle was temporarily closed due to a local Covid-19 lockdown at the time of research. check the website for details of what parts are opening when. Even when closed, it's still very much worth clapping eyes on.

✯ Festivals & Events

Big Cheese   FAIR
(www.caerphilly.gov.uk; ⊘ Jul) Any festival that includes a Cheese Olympics and a Tommy Cooper Tent has got to be worth a look. On the last weekend of July Caerphilly welcomes more than 80,000 people to the grassy grounds around the castle for three days of family-oriented fun and games that offer everything from fireworks to falconry and comedy acts to cheese-tasting.

ℹ Getting There & Away

The easiest way to reach Caerphilly from Cardiff – and particularly because the buses are almost as expensive and not always direct – is by train (£4.60, 24 minutes, up to three per hour) from Cardiff Central station.

AT A GLANCE

POPULATION
Swansea: 238,000

**NUMBER OF
GOWER PENINSULA
BEACHES**
30

LONGEST BEACH
Cefn Sidan (p144),
Pembrey Country
Park (8 miles)

**COOLEST COUN-
TRY RESTAURANT**
Wright's Food
Emporium (p147)

BIGGEST CASTLE
Kidwelly Castle
(p144)

WHEN TO GO

➜ **Apr** Perfect
surf on the Gower
Peninsula; a famous
music-poetry
celebration in
Laugharne.

➜ **May–Jun &
Sep–Oct** Often
this region's best,
least rainy weather;
perfect for hiking
among spring/
autumn colours.

➜ **Jul & Aug** The
year's greatest
concentration of
sunny days make
for prime beach-
going weather.

Dylan Thomas Boathouse (p145), Laugharne

Swansea, Gower & Carmarthenshire

Enfolded within broad beaches and framed by fecund hills, this region has an utterly cut-off feel, with many visitors rushing through between the Brecon Beacons and Pembrokeshire National Parks lying either side.

Spectacularly set Swansea acts as a magnet for devotees of bad-boy bard Dylan Thomas, with many sights linked to Wales' most famous writer, and the city is your multicultural starting point. Beyond sweeps the Gower Peninsula's craggy coastline and epic sandy bays, whilst inland, rural Carmarthenshire boasts nationally significant parks and gardens, castle ruins and untrammelled uplands to get explorers' feet itching.

Some of Wales' most fabled produce also awaits to whet the palate: Gower salt-marsh lamb, Penclawdd cockles and Carmarthen ham. Tuck in.

Swansea, Gower & Carmarthenshire Highlights

1 Swansea (p130) Acquainting yourself with writerly sights in the Uplands synonymous with literature luminary, Dylan Thomas.

2 The Mumbles (p135) Wine-swilling, beer-supping, caffeine-quaffing, ice-cream-licking and beachgoing in Swansea Bay's apotheosis.

3 Rhossili (p140) Wandering along the sand and watching waves crash over mighty Worms Head.

4 Laugharne (p145) Finding inspiration in the time-lost estuary town that stimulated Dylan Thomas.

5 National Botanic Garden of Wales (p147) Marvelling at Norman Foster's intriguing sunken greenhouse dome and the rare and endangered plants that it harbours.

6 Aberglasney Gardens (p148) Channelling your inner Jane Austen within walled gardens and yew tunnels.

7 Dinefwr (p148) Roaming the expansive grounds, encompassing a ruined castle, manor house, deer park and ancient woods.

8 Upper Tywi Valley (p149) Veering off-piste on a glorious green journey up to South Wales' largest, loveliest lake on the cusp of Mid-Wales.

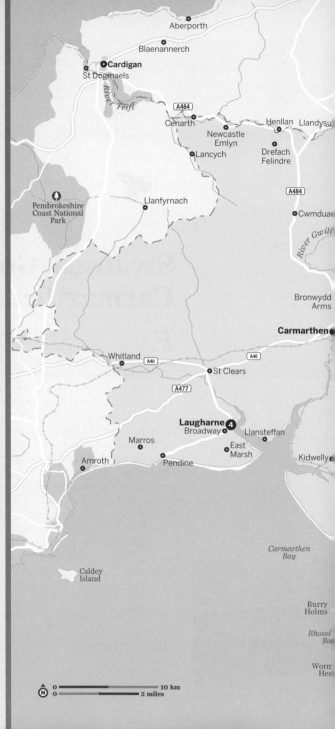

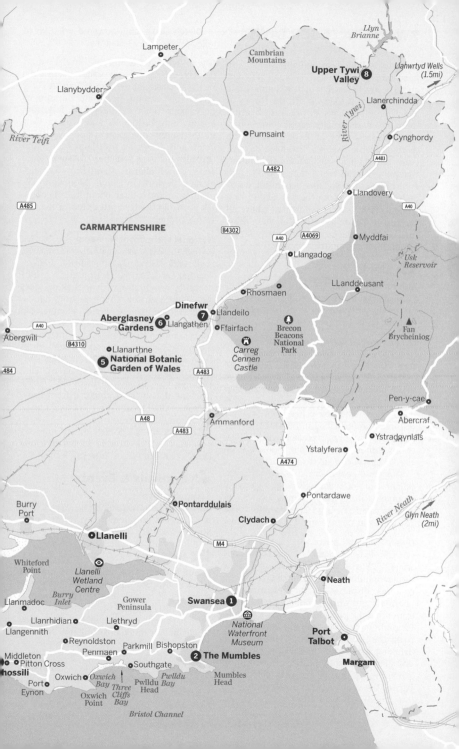

SWANSEA (ABERTAWE)

POP 238,000

Swansea is Wales' second-largest city; its most famous son Dylan Thomas called it an 'ugly, lovely town', which remains a fair description of it today. It's in the throes of a regeneration that's slowly transforming the drab, postwar city centre into something more worthy of its setting on the glorious 5-mile sweep of Swansea Bay. Already present is a hefty student population that buoys a lively restaurant, nightlife and entertainment scene, and expanding pockets of hipness in suburbs like Sketty and Uplands (which is, conveniently, where all the best B&Bs are located). The main draw for visitors in the city are the many Dylan Thomas–related sights.

◉ Sights

Almost any other UK city would covet Swansea's sandy **beach**, but if you're bound for the Gower Peninsula, there is little point tarrying on it.

Dylan Thomas Birthplace   HOUSE
(✆01792-472555; www.dylanthomasbirthplace.com; 5 Cwmdonkin Dr, Uplands, SA2 0RA; adult/child £8/6; ☺10.30am-4.30pm) The bad boy of Welsh poetry was born in this unassuming Uplands house and wrote two-thirds of his poetry here. The house has been lovingly restored and furnished in period style; Dylan's bedroom, preserved as it was in 1934, is tiny. Guides are on hand (bookings advised) but you can also explore solo.

The same people are still operating excellent tours of Dylan's Swansea stomping grounds (£18 for the Uplands locales) including lovely nearby **Cwmdonkin Park**. You can even stay the night if you're keen.

Dylan Thomas Centre   MUSEUM
(✆01792-463980; www.dylanthomas.com; Somerset Pl; ☺10am-4.30pm) FREE Housed in the former guildhall, this absorbing museum contains displays on the Swansea-born poet's life and work. It pulls no punches in examining the propensity of Dylan Thomas for puffing up his own myth; he was eventually trapped in the legend of his excessive drinking. Aside from the collection of memorabilia, what really brings his writing to life are recordings of his work performed, part of the centre's permanent, interactive 'Love the Words' exhibition.

There's also a high-powered calendar of talks, drama and workshops.

Glynn Vivian Art Gallery   GALLERY
(✆01792-516900; www.swansea.gov.uk/glynnvivian; Alexandra Rd; ☺11am-3.30pm Wed-Sun) FREE This elegant Italianate building is once again open to the public following lengthy refurbishment, and with a Covid-19-friendly one-way system whisking you round. There is a prestigious collection of Welsh art here – Richard Wilson, Gwen John, Ceri Richards, Shani Rhys James – along with works by Claude Monet and Lucien Freud and a large ceramics collection. It's probably the best attraction in the city centre proper.

National Waterfront Museum   MUSEUM
(✆0300-111 2333; www.museum.wales/swansea; South Dock Marina, Oystermouth Rd; ☺11am-4pm Thu, Sat & Sun) FREE Housed in a 1901 dockside warehouse with a striking glass and slate extension, this museum's hands-on galleries explore Wales' commercial maritime history and the impacts of industrialisation on its people, using interactive computer screens and audiovisual presentations. There's some fascinating stuff here. A highlight is the Penydarren Steam Locomotive, Richard Trevithick's steam machine that in 1804 chugged from Penydarren to the Merthyr-Cardiff Canal on the world's first railway journey.

Displays on the Welsh music industry (artefacts include Bonnie Tyler's gold and Duffy's platinum discs) also catch the eye.

✯ Festivals & Events

Escape Festival   MUSIC
(www.escapefestival.co.uk; ☺Sep) Wales' biggest dance event, held every September in Singleton Park.

🛏 Sleeping

Grand Hotel   HOTEL £
(✆01792-645898; www.thegrandhotelswansea.co.uk; Ivey Pl, High St; d £55-70) This hotel is conveniently right by the train station, and close to the city centre, which in most cities would be advantageous (but not in Swansea, where the chief appeal lies on its periphery). It's more make-up-smudged old crone than grande dame but clean and with personality. Loud air-con is more noise nuisance than outside traffic.

DYLAN THOMAS

Dylan Thomas is a towering figure in Welsh literature, one of those poets who seemed to embody what a poet should be: chaotic, dramatic, drunk, tragic and comic. His work, although written in English, is of the bardic tradition – written to be read aloud, thunderous, often humorous, with a lyrical sense that echoes the sound of the Welsh voice.

Born in Swansea in 1914, he lived an itinerant life, shifting from town to town in search of cheap accommodation and to escape debt. He married Caitlin Macnamara (a former dancer, and lover of Augustus John) in 1936 but had numerous infamous affairs. Margaret Thomas, who was married to the historian AJP Taylor, was one of his admirers and paid the rent on his house in Laugharne (mysteriously enough, AJP detested him). Thomas' dramatic inclinations sometimes spilt over into real life: during a stay in New Quay he was shot at by a jealous local captain.

Thomas was also a promiscuous pub-goer, honing in an astonishing number of taverns the habit that eventually killed him. By 1946 he had become an immense commercial success, making regular book tours to America, but his marriage was suffering. In December 1952 his father died – his failing health had inspired one of Thomas' most resonant poems, 'Do Not Go Gentle into That Good Night'. Less than a year later, a period of depression while in New York ended in a heavy drinking spell, and he died shortly after his 39th birthday.

Whether you're a fan or just interested to know what all the fuss is about, you'll find plenty of sites in Swansea to stalk the shade of the maverick poet and writer. When you've exhausted them, you can always head on to his haunts in Laugharne (p145).

In Uplands you can visit the Dylan Thomas Birthplace, an unassuming terraced house where he wrote two-thirds of his poetry, then take a tour of the surrounding Dylan locales there. Also stop by the Dylan Thomas Centre and check out his statue gazing across the marina outside the Dylan Thomas Theatre (p134).

Perhaps the places where you're most likely to feel his presence are his beloved drinking hang-outs, which include No Sign Bar (p133), Uplands Tavern (p134) and **Queen's Hotel** (☑01792-521531; Gloucester Pl; ⊗11am-10pm).

SWANSEA, GOWER & CARMARTHENSHIRE SWANSEA (ABERTAWE)

There are good breakfasts, though, and all told it's an OK one-night base.

Mirador Town House   B&B **££**
(☑01792-466976; www.themirador.co.uk; 14 Mirador Cres, Uplands, SA2 0QX; s/d from £60/80; ☎) Kooky and kitsch in the extreme, all seven B&B rooms here are fancifully and elaborately themed – Roman, Mediterranean, African, Venetian, Egyptian, Asian and French – with murals on the walls and sometimes the ceilings. The exuberant hosts are enthusiastic cheerleaders for the bars, restaurants and general buzz of the area. Reopening spring 2021.

Dylan Thomas Birthplace   GUESTHOUSE **£££**
(☑01792-472555; www.dylanthomasbirthplace.com; 5 Cwmdonkin Dr, Uplands, SA2 0RA; r from £179) Dylan Thomas fans now have the unique opportunity to stay in the house where the poet was born and spent his first 23 years. The house has been diligently maintained in period style, and you'll have the choice of staying in the bedrooms once occupied by Nancy (his sister), DJ and Florrie (his parents), and of course Dylan himself.

Booking a room entails exclusive use of the house, so solo travellers will get it all to themselves! At the time of research there is a two-night minimum stay, although the price given is for one/two people for one night.

Morgans   HOTEL **£££**
(☑01792-484848; www.morganshotel.co.uk; Somerset Pl; r £150-300; ℗☎) The city's first boutique hotel, set in the gorgeous red-brick and Portland-stone former Ports Authority building, Morgans combines historic elegance with contemporary design and a high pamper factor. An annexe across the road has lower ceilings but similar standards.

✖ Eating

★**Square Peg**   CAFE **£**
(☑01792-206593; www.squarepeg.org.uk; 29b Gower Rd, Sketty, SA2 9BX; mains £6-10; ⊗8am-3pm Mon-Sat; ☎☑) With mismatched stools

Swansea

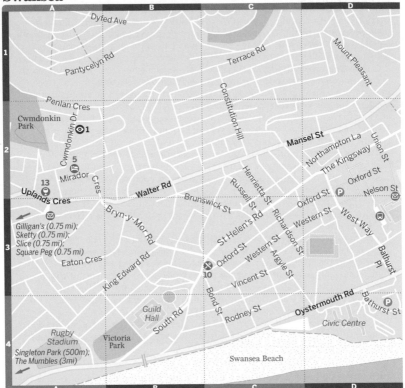

re-upholstered in recycled denim and kooky local photography blanketing the walls, this is exactly the hip kind of place you'd expect to deliver seriously good coffee. It doesn't disappoint. But the menu surprises: tasty light breakfasts, salads, soups... and deliciously inventive naans combining the likes of masala yoghurt, Gower bacon and beetroot puree.

There's now a sister cafe in the Mumbles that's equally excellent.

Joe's Ice Cream Parlour   ICE CREAM £
(☏ 01792-653880; www.joes-icecream.com; 85 St Helen's Rd; 2 scoops from £3.15; ⊘ noon-7pm) For an ice-cream sundae or a cone, locals flock to Joe's, a Swansea institution founded in 1922 by Joe Cascarini, son of immigrants from Italy's Abruzzi mountains. So beloved is this gelato that outlets have sprung up elsewhere across South Wales, including in the Mumbles (p137).

★ **Gigi Gao's Favourite**   CHINESE ££
(☏ 01792-653300; www.favouritechinese.co.uk; 18-23 Anchor Ct; mains £6-20; ⊘ noon-10pm; 🛜🍴) In a new centre-stage waterfront location, this passionately loved Chinese kitchen eschews the batters, all-purpose sauces and replica menus of many Westernised Chinese restaurants to produce food that does justice to China's deep culinary treasures. Homemade organic noodles are served with unapologetically funky Beijing-style sauce, the pork is sweet-braised Hunan style, and the higher-end fish dishes are good too.

Hanson at the Chelsea   SEAFOOD ££
(☏ 01792-464068; www.hansonatthechelsea.co. uk; 17 St Mary's St; mains £15-26, 2-/3-course lunch £16.95/21.95; ⊘ noon-2pm & 7-9.30pm Mon-Sat) Perfect for a romantic liaison, this elegant little dining room of mustard-yellow walls and stiff napery is tucked away behind the

Swansea

◎ Sights

🛏 Sleeping

✕ Eating

🍷 Drinking & Nightlife

✪ Entertainment

🛍 Shopping

3-/6-course dinner £46/60; ⊙ 6.15-9.15pm Thu & Sun, 12.30-1.45pm & 6.15-9.15pm Fri & Sat) The simple decor – wooden floors and furniture, and pale walls – stands in contrast to the elaborate dishes emanating from Slice's kitchen. Its elegantly presented food spans locally sourced meat, fish, cheese and beer, plus homemade bread and home-grown herbs, the foundation of successful adventures such as suckling pig, loin, shoulder and faggot, savoy cabbage, celeriac terrine and caramelised apple puree.

🍷 Drinking & Nightlife

Swansea's main boozing strip is Wind St, and on weekends it can be a zoo, full of generally good-natured alcopop-fuelled teens. *Buzz* magazine (available for free from cafes and bars around town) has its finger on the local scene's pulse.

★ No Sign Bar

WINE BAR

(☑ 01792-465300; www.nosignwinebar.com; 56 Wind St; ⊙ noon-10pm Mon-Sat, to 8pm Sun; 🤏) Once frequented by Dylan Thomas (it appears as the Wine Vaults in his story 'The Followers'), the No Sign stands out as the only vaguely traditional bar left on Wind St. Formerly a wine merchant's, it's a haven of dark-wood panelling, old boys in deep

---

frenzy of Wind St. Seafood dishes star, such as the grilled swordfish with Welsh cheese carbonara, but the menu also contains plenty of less challenging meaty dishes, and blackboard specials are chalked up daily. Unfortunately, vegetarians have few options.

Gilligan's   EUROPEAN **££**

(☑ 01792-203767; www.gilligansrestaurant.com; 100 Eversley Rd, Sketty, SA2 9DF; 2-/3-course lunch £16.95/19.95, dinner £23.95/27.95; ⊙ 5.30-10pm Wed-Fri, noon-4.30pm & 5.30-10pm Sat, noon-4.30pm Sun) You'd be pretty darned happy to have Gilligan's as your local neighbourhood bistro. Expect simple French- and Mediterranean-influenced dishes served in pleasant surrounds, with friendly and attentive service.

Slice   MODERN BRITISH **£££**

(☑ 01792-290929; www.sliceswansea.co.uk; 73-75 Eversley Rd, Sketty; 2-/3-course lunch £32/36,

conversation, friendly staff and a long, lovely wine list (a dozen by the glass).

There's also good pub grub, great beers on cask and tap and, at weekends in non-Covid-19 times, live music downstairs in the 1690s wine vaults.

Uplands Tavern PUB
(☑ 01792-458242; www.facebook.com/theuplandstavern; 42 Uplands Cres, Uplands, SA2 0PG; ⊘ noon-10pm) As the pub sign intimates, this is a former Thomas hang-out, and Uplands still serves a quiet daytime pint in the 'Dylan Thomas' snug. Sober enough by day, come nightfall it turns into the hub of the city's live-music scene, attracting a crowd of students and local regulars. Check the Facebook page for upcoming events.

☆ Entertainment

Dylan Thomas Theatre THEATRE
(☑ 01792-473238; www.dylanthomastheatre.org.uk; Gloucester Pl; tickets around £12) Home to Swansea Little Theatre, an amateur dramatic group of which Dylan Thomas was once a member, this company stages a wide repertoire of plays, including regular performances of your man's *Under Milk Wood*. Endlessly inventive, they were even doing virtual shows whilst kept closed by Covid-19.

🛍 Shopping

★ **Swansea Market** MARKET
(www.swanseaindoormarket.co.uk; Oxford St; ⊘ 8.30am-4.30pm Mon-Sat) There has been a covered market in Swansea since 1652, and at this site since 1830. Rebuilt in 1961 after being bombed in WWII, the current version is a buzzing place to sample local specialities, like Penclawdd cockles, laver bread and Welsh cakes hot from the griddle. However, it's hard to resist stall 58d, Thai Taste (mains £4 to £5).

ⓘ Orientation

The city centre clusters around Castle Sq and pedestrianised Oxford St on the River Tawe's west bank. Just south is the Maritime Quarter, with most central places of interest.

Uplands neighbourhood is 1 mile west of the city centre, along Mansel St/Walter Rd, with Sketty west beyond that. From the southern edge of the city centre, Oystermouth Rd runs 5 miles west then south along Swansea Bay to the Mumbles.

ⓘ Information

Swansea has several points city-wide with desks where tourist information can be obtained: try those at Swansea train station (p134), National Waterfront Museum (p130) and Dylan Thomas Centre (p130).

Morriston Hospital (☑ 01792-702222; www.sbuhb.nhs.wales; Heol Maes Eglwys, Morriston, SA6 6NL) Has an accident and emergency department; 5 miles north of the centre. Bus 4 from the bus station (35 minutes) heads here regularly.

ⓘ Getting There & Away

BUS

Swansea's **bus station** (Plymouth St) is by the city centre's Quadrant shopping centre.

National Express (p333) coaches serve bigger, further-away destinations. Services head to/from Tenby (£9.10, 1½ hours, one daily), Cardiff (from £5.50, 1¼ hours, two daily), Bristol (£14, 2¾ to 3½ hours, one daily, sometimes changing in Cardiff) and London (£16 to £23, five hours, two direct daily).

Other direct services include the X10 to/from Cardiff (£5, 1¼ hours, every one to two hours), frequent 110/X11 services to/from Llanelli (£5.90, one to 1½ hours), half-hourly X11 services to/from Carmarthen (£5.90, 1¾ hours) and the X13 to/from Llandeilo (£5.90, 1½ hours, five daily).

TRAIN

Swansea's **train station** (High St) is 600m north of Castle Sq along Castle St and High St.

Direct services to/from Swansea include (heading east) Cardiff (£12, one hour, two per hour), Abergavenny (£27, 1¾ hours, up to 11 per day) and London Paddington (£37 to £53, three hours, hourly).

Heading west, you can reach Tenby (£16.80, 1½ hours, three daily) and Fishguard Harbour (£17.30, two to three daily, 1¾ hours) and, heading north via Llanelli on the Heart of Wales Line, Llandeilo (£8, one hour, two daily) and Llandovery (£9.60, 1½ hours, two daily).

ⓘ Getting Around

You can negotiate the city centre and the Maritime Quarter on foot, but buses come in handy for the Uplands and even Sketty, as they do for the Mumbles.

BICYCLE

Part of the Celtic Trail (National Cycle Network Route 4) hugs the bay for the lovely stretch from downtown Swansea to the Mumbles.

BUS

First Cymru (www.firstgroup.com) runs most local services:

10/20 Uplands and Sketty (from Christina St)

2/2B/2C The Mumbles (from the bus station)

Drivers accept cash for single fares (it's £4.30 from the city centre to the Mumbles). Alternatively, pay slightly less via a mobile-phone app (see the website).

THE MUMBLES (Y MWMBWLS)

POP 16,600

Strung out along the shoreline at the southern end of Swansea Bay, the Mumbles has been Swansea's seaside retreat since 1807, when the Oystermouth Railway, built three years previously for transporting coal, was adapted for human cargo. Closed in 1960, it claims to have been the world's first passenger railway service.

It is today a very fashionable district, with bars and restaurants vying for trade along the promenade, and celebrities such as Hollywood actor and local gal Catherine Zeta Jones and singer Bonnie Tyler buying homes here.

The origin of the Mumbles' unusual name is uncertain, although one theory is that it's a legacy of French seamen who nicknamed the twin rounded rocks at the tip of the headland *Les Mamelles* – 'the breasts'.

◉ Sights

Going west from Mumbles Head, there are two small bays, **Langland Bay** and **Caswell Bay**, which expose hectares of golden sand at low water. Both are popular with families and surfers. About 500m west of Caswell Bay is beautiful **Brandy Cove**, a tiny secluded beach away from the crowds.

★ Clyne Gardens   GARDENS

(www.swansea.gov.uk/clyne; Blackpill) **FREE** Spanning 20 hectares, these magnificent gardens are particularly impressive in spring, when the azaleas and rhododendrons are at their most spectacular. Plus there are delicate pieris and enkianthus, bluebell woods, wildflower meadows, a bog garden and even a dogs' graveyard. The entrance is by the Woodman Pub near the junction of Mumbles Rd and Mayals Rd, about halfway between central Swansea and the Mumbles.

Oystermouth Castle   CASTLE

(☑ 01792-635478; www.swansea.gov.uk/oyster mouthcastle; Castle Ave) It wouldn't be Wales without a castle, and sure enough the trendy shops and bars of Newton Rd are guarded broodingly by a majestic ruin – appreciable from outside at the time of research but closed within due to maintenance work. When it's open, there's a fine view over Swansea Bay from the battlements.

Mumbles Pier   PIER

(☑ 01792-365200; www.mumbles-pier.co.uk; Mumbles Rd; ⊗ noon-10pm Mon-Fri, 10am-10pm Sat & Sun) The Mumbles' mile-long strip of pastel-painted houses, pubs and restaurants reaches its picturesque denouement with a rocky headland, a pretty sandy beach and two tiny islands, the furthermost one topped with a lighthouse. Built in 1898, Mumbles Pier juts out jauntily from the headland, housing the usual amusement arcade, a fish-and-chip shop and a once-grand cafe festooned with chandeliers.

🛏 Sleeping & Eating

Tides Reach Guest House   B&B ££

(☑ 01792-404877; www.tidesreachguesthouse. com; 388 Mumbles Rd; s/d from £65/80; [P] 🛜) Tides Reach has maintained the same friendly service and delicious breakfasts across the years. Some rooms have sea views; we dig sea-facing Room 6. Two-night minimum stays can apply in peak periods.

Patricks with Rooms   HOTEL £££

(☑ 01792-360199; www.patrickswithrooms.com; 638 Mumbles Rd; r £125-185; 🛜) Patricks has 16 individually styled bedrooms in bold contemporary colours, with art on the walls, fluffy robes and, in some rooms, roll-top baths and sea views. Some rooms are set back in an annexe. Downstairs are the (excellent) restaurant, in which Patrick cooks (mains £17 to £20), and a bar that practically insists you linger, perhaps with afternoon tea (£17.50).

There's also a small gym that guests can use.

Front Room   BISTRO £

(☑ 01792-362140; www.thefrontroomcafe.co.uk; 618 Mumbles Rd; brunch £5.50-8.50, lunch £8.50-11, dinner £10-14; ⊗ 9.30am-4pm Tue-Sun, plus 6.30-9.30pm Fri & Sat; 🛜) With seashell chandeliers and local art on the baby-blue walls, this convivial bistro is a pleasant place to

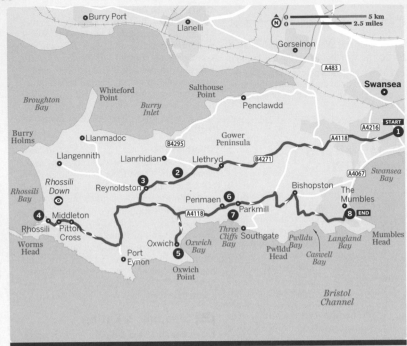

Driving Tour
Gower Circuit

START SWANSEA
END THE MUMBLES
LENGTH 40 MILES; ONE DAY

This drive takes you onto the Gower's narrow back roads, which are crowded in summer but otherwise have an enjoyably remote feel. The itinerary explores the area's ancient past and also acquaints you with two sweeping sandy beaches and a Tudor castle, winding up in picture-perfect Mumbles.

Take the A4118 (the continuation of Uplands Cres and Sketty Rd) west from **1 Swansea** and turn right onto the B4271, the secondary road traversing the centre of the Gower Peninsula. After 4.5 miles turn left onto the back road signposted to Reynoldston. Before you descend to the village itself, look for a rough parking area to the right of the road and stop here to take a walk across the heath to the neolithic tomb known as **2 Arthur's Stone** (p143). The **3 King Arthur Hotel** (p143) down the hill in Reynoldston makes for a great traditional pub-lunch stop and serves real ales too.

Head south on the A4118 and B4247 to **4 Rhossili**, where wide, sandy Rhossili Bay, with its dramatic waves, provides a haven for surfers. Walkers are well looked after too. The best leg-stretch is to the undulating headland of Worms Head; if the tide is right you can walk onto the head itself. Backtrack to the start of the Rhossili turn-off road, continuing on smaller lanes along the peninsula's south to **5 Oxwich**, for fine seafood right on the lovely beach. Detour at Parkmill to another mesmerising prehistoric monument: the Long Cairn at **6 Parc-le-Breos** (p138). Nearby, the Cathole Rock Cave once sheltered mesolithic hunters. Then walk down to **7 Three Cliffs Bay** (p138), one of Britain's most beautiful beaches. It's only accessible on foot and is presided over by a picture-perfect ruined castle.

Take the A4118 and B4436 east to the **8 Mumbles**, Swansea's charming seaside suburb, sporting a castle, pier and long promenade. Finish off in one of its many enticing cafes or pubs, or explore Mumbles Head, snapping photos of the late-18th-century lighthouse offshore.

feast on a cooked breakfast, Welsh rarebit, ploughman's lunch, sandwich (toasted or doorstop) or traditional high tea (£16.50 per person). On the more adventurous evening menu you might find anything from boat-fresh squid to a lovely squash-and-goats-cheese tart.

Joe's Ice Cream Parlour ICE CREAM £
(☑ 01792-368212; www.joes-icecream.com; 526 Mumbles Rd; ☉ 10.30am-5.30pm Mon, from 10am Tue-Fri, to 6.30pm Sat & Sun) The most popular branch of the Swansea institution (p132).

★ **Môr** SEAFOOD ££
(☑ 07932 385217; www.mor-mumbles.co.uk; 620 Mumbles Rd; mains £12-20; ☉ 5.30-9pm Tue, 12.30-3.30pm & 5.30-9pm Wed-Sat, 12.30-8pm Sun) Some of the area's scrummiest seafood is proffered at this slick restaurant, such as succulent sea bass with bacon and *dashi* (Japanese stock), although there is also turf beside the surf on the menu. Book in advance. 'Môr' in Welsh simply means sea.

🍺 Drinking & Nightlife

Pilot PUB
(☑ 07897 895511; www.thepilotofmumbles.co.uk; 726 Mumbles Rd; ☉ noon-10pm; 🍴🍷) Stained glass, polished wood and a roaring fire set an immediately comforting tone, but it's the beer that the punters are here for. Sample from the Pilot's own microbrewed range or choose from its select set of guest ales.

Cakes and Ale WINE BAR
(☑ 01792-363828; www.cakesandale.wales; 29 Newton Rd; ☉ 10am-10pm Wed-Sat, to 5pm Sun) We confess to gravitating to Cakes and Ale because the sign promised to offer our favourite things: why not, indeed, bridge the gap between cake-stacked cafe and cool evening bar? But it's actually the wine that impresses more than the beer: a discerning old world–new world selection to enjoy with tapas or burgers in friendly, fun-loving environs.

🛍 Shopping

Lovespoon Gallery GIFTS & SOUVENIRS
(www.welshlovespoon.com; 492 Mumbles Rd; ☉ 10.30am-4pm Mon-Sat year-round, also Sun Easter-Sep) If your curiosity has been fed by that classic Welsh souvenir, the Welsh love spoon, then this is your place. It's one of Wales' only shops dedicated to this actually very traditional, authentic and skillfully carved item. There are no tacky, mass-produced spoons here.

ⓘ Getting There & Away

Regular 2/2B/2C buses run between Swansea and the Mumbles (£4.30, 30 to 45 minutes). Regular 2C buses run between Oystermouth Sq on Mumbles Rd and Caswell Bay (£2.60, 12 minutes).

GOWER PENINSULA (Y GŴYR)

With its broad butterscotch beaches, pounding surf, precipitous clifftop walks and rugged, untamed uplands, the Gower Peninsula feels a million miles from Swansea's urban bustle – yet it's on the doorstep. This 15-mile-long thumb of land stretching west from the Mumbles was designated the UK's first official Area of Outstanding Natural Beauty (AONB) in 1956. You can hike all of the Gower's enchanting seaboard on the Wales Coast Path, and the peninsula has Wales' best surfing outside Pembrokeshire.

The main family beaches, patrolled by lifeguards during summer, are (just west of the Mumbles and easily visited from there) **Langland Bay** and **Caswell Bay**, along with Port Eynon (p139). The most impressive, and most popular with surfers, is the magnificent 3-mile sweep of Rhossili Bay (p140) at the peninsula's far end. Much of the Gower's northern coast is salt marsh, which provides an important habitat for wading birds and wildfowl, not to mention sheep: salt-marsh-grazed lamb is a Gower culinary delicacy.

A **Gower Explorer** (day pass adult/child £7.50/5) is worth purchasing if you're taking two or more bus connections. Buy online (www.firstgroup.com) or on the bus. Buses don't run Sundays.

Parkmill & Around

Some of the Gower's best, most secluded beaches are here on the stretch between the Mumbles and Oxwich Bay, particularly in the area around the small tourist village of Parkmill.

⊙ Sights

Three Cliffs Bay
BEACH

Three Cliffs Bay is named for the pyramid-like, triple-pointed crag pierced by a natural arch that juts into the water at its eastern point. It's regularly voted one of the most beautiful beaches in Britain, and it's particularly impressive when viewed from the picturesquely broken ruins of 13th-century **Pennard Castle**. The craggy headland is a popular rock-climbing site, although bay swimmers should be wary of some dangerous currents.

The only way to reach the beach is on foot. Look for the path across the road and down a bit from Shepherd's Coffee Shop in Parkmill. Cross the bridge, turn right and then take the next left-hand fork heading up the hill. You'll skirt some houses and Pennard Golf Course before reaching the castle. For a flatter, quicker path, take the right-hand fork instead and follow the stream. Another approach is via the mile-long track along Pennard Cliffs from the National Trust car park in Southgate.

Gower Heritage Centre
HISTORIC BUILDING

(☑01792-371206; www.gowerheritagecentre. co.uk; Parkmill; adult/child £6.75/5.75; ☉10am-5.30pm; 🖼) Housed in a restored 12th-century mill with a working waterwheel, this complex has plenty to keep kids entertained when the weather drives you off the beaches. There's a puppet theatre, craft workshop, petting zoo, fish pond, bouncy castle, medieval armour display, gold panning and 'Wales' smallest cinema', housed in a converted railway carriage. Adults might be more interested in the mill itself, which served as both a corn- and a sawmill, and the non-operational heritage-listed toilet.

Tickets must be purchased online and include parking charges for nearby Three Cliffs Bay.

Parc-le-Breos
PARK

(Parkmill) Nestled in a tiny valley between wooded hills, this verdant park contains the **Long Cair**, a 5500-year-old burial chamber consisting of a stone entryway, a passageway and four chambers. It once contained the skeletons of 40 people, but these were removed, along with its protective earth mound, after it was dug out in 1869.

Further into the park, a natural limestone fissure houses **Cathole Rock Cave**, home to hunter-gatherers up to 20,000 years ago. Flint tools were found in the cave, alongside the bones of bears, hyenas and mammoths.

The turn-off for Parc-le-Breos is right beside the Gower Heritage Centre in Parkmill; the park is less than half a mile further on.

🛏 Sleeping

Nicholaston Farm
CAMPGROUND £

(☑01792-371209; www.nicholastonfarm.co.uk; Penmaen; tent sites £18-26, caravan sites £35-45; ☉Easter-Sep; 🅿🛜) This working farm overlooking Oxwich Bay has offered pea-green field camping with a view since the 1920s, and knows the ropes well. There's an excellent ablutions block (with under-floor heating!) and an attractive little farm shop-cafe too. Nicholaston is signposted on the southern side of the A4118, just west of Penmaen and 1.7 miles west of Gower Heritage Centre.

★Llethryd Barns
B&B ££

(☑01792-391327; www.llethrydbarns.co.uk; Llethryd; s/d from £80/105; 🅿) Arranged in a horseshoe around a central courtyard, this handsome set of late-Georgian farm buildings has been converted into seven guest suites, each with living area and mezzanine bedroom and all with their own entrance, making them feel utterly private. Breakfasts are indulgent. It's 2 miles north of Parkmill on the B4271.

Parc-le-Breos House
HOTEL ££

(☑01792-371636; www.parc-le-breos.co.uk; Parkmill; r £105-150, ste £232; 🅿🛜) Within its own private estate north of the main A4118, Parc-le-Breos offers 16 en-suite rooms in a Gothic Victorian hunting lodge. The majestic lounge, conservatory and dining room have grand fireplaces that crackle into action in winter, and there are great walks nearby, including to Cathole Rock Cave. Book ahead for the two-course dinner (£20), served Wednesday to Monday from 6pm to 8pm.

It's a mile (north then west) further down the turning for the Gower Heritage Centre.

✕ Eating

For food, the **Joiners Arms** (☑01792-232658; www.thejoiners.info; 50 Bishopston Rd, Bishopston; ☉3-10pm Mon & Tue, noon-10pm Wed-Sun) in Bishopston does good pub food and also boasts a microbrewery, Parc-le-

Breos House produces fancier fare, Nicholaston Farm has a cafe and **Little Valley Bakery** (☑01792-371346; www.littlevalleybakery.com; Gower Heritage Centre, Parkmill; ⊙9am-4pm Wed-Sun; ℗) at the Gower Heritage Centre has great baked treats.

⊙ Getting There & Away

Nine direct buses head to/from Swansea (£4.60, 36 minutes) and west to Perriswood (for Oxwich, £2.90, 11 minutes) and Rhossili (£4.60, 31 minutes).

Jump off at Scurlage for Port Eynon. It may be quicker to walk from here than wait for the connecting bus.

Oxwich Bay

Oxwich Bay is a windy, 2.5-mile-long curve of sand backed by dunes. Road access and a large car park (£6 per day) make it popular with families and watersports enthusiasts (although there's no lifeguard). Behind the beach lies **Oxwich Nature Reserve**, an area of salt and freshwater marshes, oak and ash woodlands and dunes; it is home to a variety of birdlife.

⊙ Sights & Activities

Oxwich Castle   CASTLE
(www.cadw.gov.wales; Oxwich; adult/child £3.80/2.20; ⊙10am-5pm Wed Sun Mar-Nov) On a hillside above the beach, ruined Oxwich Castle is less castle and more sumptuous 16th-century, mock-military Tudor mansion.

Oxwich Watersports   WATER SPORTS
(☑07740 284079; www.oxwichwatersports.co.uk; ⊙Mar-Oct) Rents surfboards, kayaks and stand-up paddleboards for £15/50 per hour/day from a beachside shack.

Gower Coast Adventures   CRUISE
(☑01792-348229; www.gowercoastadventures.co.uk) Speedboat trips blast along from Oxwich Bay to Worms Head at the Gower Peninsula's westernmost point (adult/child £45/25, two hours return).

⊨ Sleeping & Eating

Oxwich Bay Hotel   HOTEL **££**
(☑01792-390329; www.oxwichbayhotel.co.uk; Oxwich; d from £79; ℗☎) Some rooms at this bay-hugging hotel look onto sandy beach on two sides, they're that close to the coast. The bright, modern-looking premises is ac-

tually on its own 3.2-hectare grounds and has a bistro-restaurant (mains £7.75 to £15) and pretty beachside garden where you can also eat. Six garden pods are additionally available on a room-only basis (from £52).

Beach House   WELSH **£££**
(☑01792-390965; www.beachhouseoxwich.co.uk; Oxwich Bay, SA3 1LS; mains £29-34; ⊙noon-2.15pm & 6-8.45pm Wed-Sat, noon-4pm Sun) Wales is famous for having Michelin-starred restaurants in unexpected locations, and of the lot of them, this is perhaps the most serendipitous. The Beach House offers wondrous, maritime-rich dishes such as pink grapefruit, sea fennel, charred lettuce and laver bread, or octopus with oregano, Kalamata olives and cauliflower, from a photogenic stone building right on the beach.

⊙ Getting There & Away

You'll need to come under your own steam to Oxwich – or get to Port Eynon or Perriswood Turning on the Parkmill–Knelston section of the A4118 (both with bus connections), then walk.

Port Eynon

The three-quarter-mile stretch of rock-strewn Blue Flag beach at Port Eynon is the Gower's busiest summer swimming destination. The town swells dramatically with the rising mercury, as holiday parks, self-catering cottages, pubs and hostels brace themselves for the seasonal strain. Whatever the time of year, and however fierce the competition for a lunchtime table at the pub or towel space on the beach, it's a thoroughly pleasant little seaside village.

⊨ Sleeping

Port Eynon accommodation comes at a beachside premium, with two-night minimum stays. Choice of self-catering lets and holiday parks there is, but for regular B&Bs and hotels, precious little.

Culver House   APARTMENT **££**
(☑01792-720300; www.culverhousehotel.co.uk; apt £99-179; ☎) A stone skim from the beach, this renovated 19th-century house offers eight self-contained apartments with all the mod cons, finished in fairly minimalist Scandi style. The upper apartments have balconies, while most of those on the ground floor open onto cute little gardens.

Two-night minimum stays are usually required.

✕ Eating & Drinking

Ship Inn   PUB FOOD **££**
(☑ 01792-390204;   www.shipinngower.co.uk;
mains £12-22; ⊘ noon-10pm; ☎🐕) A large
rusty anchor sets an appropriately nautical tone for this appealing local pub, which
serves the Gower Brewery's range of real
ales as well as pizzas, grills and other regular pub classics.

① Getting There & Away

Buses serving Port Eynon are sporadic. For
Rhossili (£2.10, 15 minutes) there is one direct
bus daily, otherwise travellers can take the 119
to Reynoldston (£3.90, 20 minutes, four daily),
which continues to Swansea (£4.90, one hour),
and change to backtrack with the westbound
118 to Rhossili. You will pay the £3.90 fare
twice this way though. You could also change
at Scurlage, the nearest point on the A4118,
but there's less to do whilst you wait for the
next bus.

Change in Reynoldston for buses through
Parkmill to Swansea, which run in the mornings
and evenings only. For Llangennith, take that
Reynoldston/Swansea 119 service and jump off
at Llanrhidian for one of the two daily services
back west to Llangennith.

It's easier to come with a car or bike!

Rhossili

Saving the best for last, the Gower Peninsula ends spectacularly with the three miles
of golden sand that edges Rhossili Bay. Facing nearly due west towards the very bottom of Ireland, this is one of Britain's best
and most popular surfing beaches. But be
warned: when the surf's up, swimming can
be dangerous. At low tide the stark, ghostly
ribs of the *Helvetica,* a Norwegian barque
wrecked in a storm in 1887, protrude from
the middle of the beach.

Rhossili village spreads out along the
road approaching the beach for some way
and is a pleasant place to eat, drink or
spend the night.

◉ Sights

★ Worms Head   NATURAL FEATURE
The western extremity of the Gower is
guarded by this mile-long tentacular promontory, which turns into an island at high
tide. Worms Head takes its name from

the Old English *wurm,* meaning 'dragon'.
Seals bask around its rocks, and the cliffs
are thick with razorbills, guillemots, kittiwakes, fulmars and puffins during nesting
season (April to July).

There is a five-hour window of opportunity (2½ hours either side of low tide)
when you can walk out across a causeway
and along the narrow crest of the Outer
Head to the furthest point of land. Check
the tide tables posted at the Rhossili Visitor
Centre (p142) carefully. Among those who
have spent a cold, nervous night trapped
here was the young Dylan Thomas, as he
relates in 'Who Do You Wish Was With
Us?', from *Portrait of the Artist as a Young
Dog.* If you do get stuck, do not try to wade
or swim back: currents are fierce and the
rocks treacherous.

Rhossili Bay   BEACH
Just think: three miles of wide, curving
golden sands with abundant surf to the
north and the dramatic headland, Worms
Head, showing off to the south. No wonder
this beach is the Gower's best and most
popular. Rhossili village at the southern
end of the beach makes the best base for
most, with the Rhossili Visitor Centre
(p142), plus good places to eat and drink.
Surfers tend to base themselves at Llangennith at the beach's northern end.

Rhossili Down   HILL
Rhossili beach is backed by the steep slopes
of this humpbacked, heather-covered ridge
(193m), whose updraughts create perfect
soaring conditions for hang-gliders and
paragliders. On the summit are numerous
Iron Age earthworks, a burial chamber
called **Sweyne's Howe** and the remains of
a WWII radar station. The path to the top is
easily accessed from the village.

🛏 Sleeping & Eating

Among other options, the Worms Head Hotel, at the road's end above the beach, has
digs and dining with views.

Rhossili Bunkhouse   HOSTEL **£**
(☑ 01792-391509;   www.rhossilibunkhouse.com;
Rhossili Village Hall, Middleton; per person in bunk
room from £20; P🐕) Located in Middleton,
within easy walking distance of Rhossili, this community-run bunkhouse is well
equipped, clean and comfortable. There are
seven rooms: four two-bed, two three-bed
and a four-bed. At the time of research it

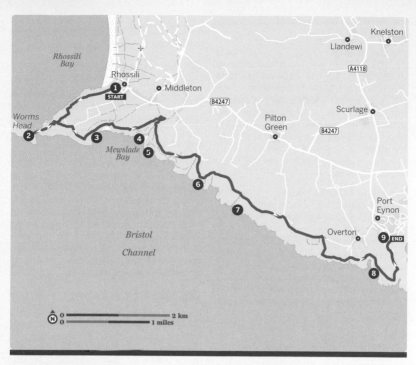

Coastal Walk
A Wild Stretch

START RHOSSILI
END PORT EYNON
LENGTH 7 MILES; THREE HOURS

This walk takes in a precipitous stretch of Gower coastline, topped with ancient hill forts and punctuated by beautiful sandy coves. There are no refreshments except at the beginning and end: take food and water with you.

The walk starts at the Worms Head Hotel, **1** **Rhossili**, at a high vantage point overlooking both beautifully sandy Rhossili Bay, voted one of the best beaches in the world, and Rhossili Down, with its Iron Age earthworks and incredible views, to the north. **2** **Worms Head** is visible too to the southeast. It's possible to walk out to the Worms Head headland, but only at low tide or it will be partly submerged. On the high point facing the head is a Victorian coastguard station, still very much in use.

The route then pivots east/southeast and follows the coast above the golden beaches of **3** **Fall** and **4** **Mewslade** bays, with **5** **Thurba Head** beyond. More ancient

history is evident at the 10,000-year-old **6** **Knave Promontory Fort**, the largest of several Iron Age structures you'll see on the walk. Shortly afterwards you'll pass above the **7** **Goats Hole**, a cave in the cliff (only accessible from the water) that was the site of a hugely significant prehistoric burial: the Red Lady of Paviland.

Beyond this point the cliffs descend and the going is easier for a long stretch until you begin to climb to Port Eynon Point. There's an interesting detour near the summit – a steep descent to **8** **Culver Hole**, a ruined medieval dovecote crammed into a fissure in the cliff. Bear in mind, though, that it's unsigned and the path down is steep.

On the fringes of **9** **Port Eynon** you'll pass the Salt House, a salt-extraction unit built in the 16th century. In the village you can stop for a celebratory drink or meal in the Ship Inn. Note: only one direct bus a day heads between Port Eynon and Rhossili (6.07pm at the time of research), so you may need to change in Reynoldston/Little Reynoldston if you've left your car at the starting point.

was catering to one group from one household at a time.

The Coach House APARTMENT **££**
(☑ 01792-390172; www.broadparkrhossili.com; ste £90; P ☎) This self-contained two-floor converted coach house in Rhossili village is self-check-in, and you'll be stocked up with coffee, tea and biscuits until you can make it down to the cafe/pub. It's one of the few places in Rhossili that you can stay in by the night.

It has a decent kitchen too, so bring self-catering food.

Bay Bistro & Coffee House BISTRO **£**
(☑ 01792-390519; www.thebaybistro.co.uk; mains £7-15; ☺ 10am-4pm Mon-Fri, 9am-5pm Sat & Sun; ☑) This buzzy beach cafe has a sunny terrace, good surfy vibrations and the kind of drop-your-panini views that would make anything taste good – although the roster of burgers, sandwiches, salads, cakes and coffee stands up well regardless. On summer evenings it opens for al fresco meals.

ⓘ Information

Rhossili Visitor Centre (☑ 01792-390707; www.nationaltrust.org.uk/rhosili-and-south-gower-coast; Coastguard Cottages; ☺ 11am-5pm daily Mar-Sep, Fri-Sun Oct) The National Trust's centre has information on local walks and wildlife, and an audiovisual display upstairs. Grab souvenirs, fill your water bottles and check the tides here. Parking is a minimum of £3 (per half-day).

ⓘ Getting There & Away

The 118/119 to/from Swansea (£4.90, one to 1¼ hours, up to 11 daily) usually runs via Parkmill (£4.50, 30 to 45 minutes).

Reynoldston (£3.90, 20 minutes, up to five daily) is where you will need to change for services to Port Eynon (20 minutes) if you don't want to wait for the one direct connection daily.

Walking the three miles along the coast for Llangennith is simpler than bussing there.

Llangennith

Surfers flock to this pretty village at the northern end of Rhossili Bay, where there's a good local pub and a large campsite right by the beach. There are some unforgettable beach-dominated vistas around here. Centred on the weathered, 12th-century church of St Cenydd, Llangennith has a

local produce market from 10am to 1pm on the last Saturday of the month from April to September.

🏃 Activities

Progress Surf SURFING
(☑ 01792-410825, 07876 712106; www.swansea surfing.com; lessons 2hr/day £35/65) This mobile outfit offers introductory surf lessons, mostly at Llangennith unless conditions aren't favourable.

PJ's Surf Shop SURFING
(☑ 01792-386669; www.facebook.com/pjs.s.shop; per day wetsuits £12, surfboards £12-15; ☺ 9am-5.30pm Mar-Oct, 10am-5.30pm Mon-Fri Nov-Feb) Run by former surfing champion Peter Jones, this is a very friendly centre of activity for local surfers. Check the Facebook page for current local surfing conditions. In winter it also offers extra protective cold-weather gear (£9 per day).

🛏 Sleeping & Eating

Hillend Caravan & Camping CAMPGROUND **£**
(☑ 01792-386204; www.hillendcamping.com; site tents with 2 adults £21-26; ☺ Easter-Oct; P) As close to the beach as you can get, this large campground can accommodate 300 tents and motorhomes. On-site surfy-style Eddy's Restaurant has brilliant views and rustles up meals for under a tenner.

King's Head HOTEL **££**
(☑ 01792-386212; www.kingsheadgower.co.uk; r £125-155; P ☎☎) Up the hill behind (and run by) the pub of the same name, these two stone farm buildings have been simply but stylishly fitted out with modern bathrooms and underfloor heating. As well as the 20 rooms here, there are more in a nearby house. Look online for weekly, five-night and weekend deals that run year-round.

Come down to the picturesque pub for breakfast (included) or to have wholesome meals with a spicy bent towards curries.

ⓘ Getting There & Away

The 116 service runs once in the morning and once in the evening direct to Swansea (£4.90, 1¼ to 1½ hours). It heads there via Llanrhidian (change for connections to the southern Gower, though it's a convoluted process and you're better off with your own wheels) and Penclawdd.

For Rhossili, just walk the three miles along the beach.

Reynoldston

At the heart of the Gower Peninsula is Cefn Bryn, a ruggedly beautiful expanse of moorland. Tucked below it is this lost-in-time collection of stone houses, benefiting from a popular pub and from being a nexus for a fair few of the Gower's fairly limited bus connections.

◎ Sights

Arthur's Stone   TOMB
(Coeten Arthur) On a desolate ridge near Reynoldston stands this mysterious neolithic burial chamber capped by a 25-tonne quartz boulder. The view from here is fantastic. In legend, the capstone is a pebble that King Arthur removed from his boot; the deep cut in the rock was either made by Excalibur or by St David, and the muddy spring beneath the stone grants wishes.

To find it, turn right (east) on the road leaving the King Arthur Hotel in Reynoldston and look out for a rough parking area on your left after about 0.6 miles. Looking north, you can see the stone on the horizon.

⌷ Sleeping & Eating

King Arthur Hotel   PUB **££**
(☑ 01792-390775; www.kingarthurhotel.co.uk; Higher Green; d £90-125, cottages £135, P ⋒) As traditional as swords in stone and ladies of the lake, the King Arthur serves real ales in a cosy, wood-panelled bar and offers many tasty, rustic dishes in its restaurant (mains £7.25 to £18.95). Accommodation is split between the pub's 1st floor and a neighbouring annexe, and it also rents a handful of romantic, stone-walled cottages in the village.

❶ Getting There & Away

Buses head to/from Swansea (£4.90, 50 minutes, nine daily), Parkmill (£3.40, 16 minutes, six daily), Port Eynon (£3.90, 15 minutes, four daily, some via Rhossili) and Rhossili (£3.90, 16 minutes, three to five daily).

Llanmadoc

Pretty little Llanmadoc sits beside Whiteford Burrows, a nature reserve composed of sand dunes and pines. Check the tide tables before walking to the **lighthouse** on the point, the only cast-iron lighthouse in the UK. It's about a 6-mile circular **walk** from the Britannia pub. There is a handy all-in-one store, post office and cafe in Llanmadoc too.

⌷ Sleeping & Eating

Phillistone Farm   CAMPGROUND **£**
(☑ 07967 820990; www.phillistonegower.co.uk; sites £22.50; ⊘ Apr-Oct; P) This place offers micro-camping, with caravans or tents and a lovely low-key grassy field with electrical hook-ups, but no showers or toilets. There are amazing sea views though.

Cwm Ivy Cafe & Crafts   CAFE **£**
(snacks £2-4; ⊘ noon-5pm Wed-Fri, 10am-5pm Sat & Sun Apr-Oct) It doesn't serve much food, but in this sweet spot you will be very content ogling the views and lingering over tea, coffee, sandwiches and cakes in the beautiful garden.

Britannia   PUB FOOD **£**
(☑ 01792-386624; www.britanniainngower.co.uk; mains £10-12, 2-/3-course meals £19/25; ⊘ noon-3pm & 5-10pm Mon-Thu, noon-10pm Fri & Sat, noon-8pm Sun; P) The food at this 18th-century inn is a cut well above average pub grub: there's roasted veg Thai curry, salt-marsh lamb shank and other appetite-inspirers. There are gorgeous green-rimmed sea views from the back garden terrace.

❶ Getting There & Away

A couple of buses daily serve Llanrhidian, from where you can pick up onward connections to Swansea (the total fare is £8 and it takes anything from one to three hours including waiting time). Your own wheels are best for getting here.

CARMARTHENSHIRE (SIR GAERFYRDDIN)

The castle-dotted county of Carmarthenshire enfolds gentle valleys washed by abundant rivers, dense woods and bald yellow hilltops, but most of the action is on and around the wide crescent of Carmarthen Bay (Bae Caerfyrddin), carved up like a crazy jigsaw into wide, winding, sand-flanked estuaries. Caught between attractive neighbours – the Brecon Beacons lie on Carmarthenshire's eastern border whilst Pembrokeshire kicks off to the west

DON'T MISS

LLANELLI WETLAND CENTRE

Llanelli Wetland Centre (☎01554-741087; www.wwt.org.uk/llanelli; Llwynhendy; adult/child £9/7.68; ⊗9.30am-5pm; P 🚻) Llanelli might be an unsightly urban sprawl, but do not let this dissuade you from visiting this 97-hectare reserve sharing nothing in common save the name. On the north shore of the River Loughor across from the Gower Peninsula, this is one of Wales' most important habitats for waders and waterfowl. Up to 60,000 birds converge on the salt marsh and mudflats here in winter. There are many hides and observation points, and you can hire binoculars (£5). Book ahead.

The big attraction for birdwatchers is the resident population of little egret, as well as oystercatchers, greylag geese, gadwalls, wigeons, teals, black-tailed godwits – and flashiest of all – a flock of pink Caribbean flamingos. There are summertime kids activities on offer. as well.

Approaching from the southeast, take the A484 and turn left onto the B4304. The centre's a 2.5-mile walk from Llanelli train station.

– it is often wrongly overlooked. This much calmer and less-explored pocket of Wales is predominantly tinted in dazzling green. It sates those in need of drama-charged castles, glorious landscaped gardens, quietly confident market towns and, importantly for the back of beyond, seriously great cuisine where 'farm to fork' is often a distance no greater than a hedgerow hop.

Kidwelly

Kidwelly is probably South Carmarthenshire's most likeable locale, and steps up with more smiles than far-larger nearby Llanelli as county ambassador. Bounded by the rivers of Gwendraeth Fach and Gwendraeth Fawr, its prize attraction is heavyweight fortress Kidwelly Castle.

👁 Sights

Kidwelly Castle   CASTLE
(Cadw; ☎01554-890104; www.cadw.gov.wales; Castle Rd; adult/child £5.10/3.10; ⊗10am-1pm & 2-5pm Wed-Sun) Rising above a narrow waterway dotted with gliding swans, this forbiddingly fortified grey eminence was founded by the Normans in 1106, but most of the system of towers and curtain walls was built in the 13th century in reaction to Welsh uprisings. If it looks familiar, that may be because it featured in the opening scene of *Monty Python and the Holy Grail*. The castle is a 14-minute walk northeast from Kidwelly railway station.

Pembrey Country Park &
Cefn Sidan Beach   PARK
(☎01554-742435; www.pembreycountrypark. wales; parking 2hr/all day £3/5.50; ⊗6am-10pm;

🚻) **FREE** This woodsy 200-hectare park four miles southeast of Kidwelly is a great place to come with the kids, who can let off steam on the footpaths, cycling trails, playgrounds and – best of all – the adjacent 8-mile golden band of sandy beach called **Cefn Sidan**, one of Wales' longest. There is a visitor centre and a ski slope too.

The park/beach begin a 2.5-mile walk west from Pembrey & Burry Port railway station, served by Kidwelly–Llanelli trains.

ℹ Getting There & Away

Kidwelly has a railway station on the tracks between Llanelli (£4.90, 15 minutes, 14 trains daily) and Carmarthen (£5.40, 20 minutes, 12 daily). Llanelli-bound services continue east to at least Swansea where you can pick up other connections nationwide.

Carmarthen (Caerfyrddin)

POP 14,200

Carmarthenshire's county town is a place of legend and ancient provenance, but that was then and this is now – a time when it's handy for a journey-breaker or as a transport/shopping hub, but little else.

Most intriguingly, Carmarthen is reputed to be the birthplace of the most famous wizard of them all (no, not Harry Potter) – Myrddin of the Arthurian legends, better known in English as Merlin. An oak tree planted in 1659 for Charles II's coronation came to be called 'Merlin's Tree' and was linked to a prophecy that its death would mean curtains for the town. The tree died in the 1970s. The town still stands...

◉ Sights

Carmarthenshire
County Museum   MUSEUM
(☑ 01267-228696; www.discovercarmarthenshire.
com; Abergwili; ⊙ 10am-4.30pm Tue-Sat; [P])
FREE In a 13th-century country house and
bishop's palace, this museum is an emporium of archaeology, Egyptology, pottery
and paintings, with recreations of a Victorian schoolroom and a collection of carved
Roman stones. A major refurbishment, including opening a cafe and walks around
the fecund grounds, was happening at the
time of research, with the museum due to
reopen in June 2021. It's two miles east of
Carmarthen on the A40 at the Abergwili
roundabout.

✖ Eating

Carmarthen's key contribution to Welsh
gastronomy is a salt-cured, air-dried ham.
Local legend holds that the Romans liked
the recipe so much they took it back to Italy, where it is now known as Parma ham.
Find it at the **market** (www.carmarthenshire.
gov.wales; Market Way; ⊙ 9.30am-4.30pm Wed &
Sat) **FREE**.

The Warren   CAFE ££
(☑ 01267-236079; www.warrenmanselst.co.uk;
11 Mansel St; lunch £7-9, dinner £14-20; ⊙ 10am-
3pm Wed, Thu & Sun, to 9pm Fri & Sat; 🖥) In a
culinary desert, the Warren's lively atmosphere and menu are shining stars. There's
nothing complicated, but even the simpler
dishes have exceptional ingredients and
thought in them: Thai beetroot curry with
turmeric rice, coconut raita and courgette
bhaji, for example.

❶ Information

Tourist Office (☑ 01267-231557; www.dis
covercarmarthenshire.com; Old Castle House;
⊙ 9.30am-4.30pm Mon-Sat) In Carmarthen
Castle. Closed at the time of research.

❶ Getting There & Away

Carmarthen is Carmarthenshire's main regional hub. The bus station is on Blue St. Direct
services go to/from Swansea (£5.90, one hour
and 10 minutes, half-hourly) via Llanelli, Llandeilo (£3.90, 40 minutes, seven daily), Llandovery (£4.60, one hour 5 minutes), Laugharne
(£3.30, 30 minutes, five daily), Haverfordwest
(60 minutes, three daily) via Narberth, and
Aberystwyth (£6.25, 2¼ hours, hourly).

National Express (p333) coaches head to/
from London (from £20, six hours) and Tenby
(from £7, 45 minutes) once daily.

The train station is 300m south of town
across the river. There is one direct service
to/from London Paddington (from £70, four
hours); change in Swansea for more frequent
services. The very regular trains to Swansea
(£10.20, 50 minutes, at least hourly) serve
Kidwelly (£5.20, 15 minutes), Pembrey & Burry
Port (£8.50, 21 minutes) and Llanelli (£9.60, 28
minutes). There are also trains to Abergavenny
(£40, 2½ hours, hourly), Cardiff (£21, 1¾ hours,
hourly) and Tenby (£10.40, 45 minutes, seven
daily).

Laugharne (Talacharn)

POP 1220

Handsome little Laugharne (pronounced
'larn') sits above the wide, sand-banded
tidal shores of the Taf Estuary, overlooked
by a Norman castle. Dylan Thomas, one of
Wales' greatest writers, spent the last four
years of his life here, during which time he
produced some of his most inspired work,
including *Under Milk Wood*. The town is
one of the inspirations for the play's fictional village of Llareggub (spell it backwards
– you'll get the gist).

On Thomas' first visit to Laugharne he
described it as the 'strangest town in Wales',
and in many ways it still is: a cut-off back-
water nevertheless pulsating with culture
that hinges around its connection to 'Dylan', as locals touchingly refer to him.

◉ Sights

The main focus are the places connected
with Dylan Thomas. In addition to the bigger sights, devotees Dylan devotees should
stop by **Brown's Hotel** (King St), his one-
time local, and the **grave** in St Martin's
Church where he and his wife Caitlin are
buried.

★ Dylan Thomas Boathouse   MUSEUM
(☑ 01994-427420; www.dylanthomasboathouse.
com; Dylan's Walk; adult/child £4.75/3.75; ⊙ 2-
5pm Fri-Mon) Dylan Thomas, his wife, Caitlin, and their three children lived in this
cliff-clinging house from 1949 to 1953. It's a
beautiful setting, looking out over the estuary that Thomas, in his 'Poem in October',
described as the 'heron-priested shore'. The
parlour has been restored to its 1950s appearance, with a desk that once belonged to
Thomas' schoolmaster father. Upstairs are

photographs, letters, a video about his life, and his death mask, which once belonged to Richard Burton.

Along the lane from the Boathouse is the old shed where Thomas did most of his writing. It looks as if he has just popped out, with screwed-up pieces of paper littered around the sea-facing table where he wrote *Under Milk Wood* and poems such as 'Over Sir John's Hill' (which describes the view).

The on-site cafe, where you can gaze at the residence from the patio, was open at the time of research, but it wasn't possible to look around inside the house.

Laugharne Castle CASTLE
(Cadw; 01994-427906; www.cadw.gov.wales; cnr King & Wogan Sts; adult/child £3.80/2.20; 10am-1pm & 2-5pm Thu-Mon) Built in the 13th century, picturesque Laugharne Castle was converted into a mansion in the 16th century for John Perrot, thought to be the illegitimate son of Henry VIII. Gazing out over the estuary, it was landscaped with its current lovely lawns in Victorian times.

The adjoining **Castle House** was leased in 1934 by Richard Hughes, author of *A High Wind in Jamaica*. It was Hughes who first invited Dylan Thomas to Laugharne. Thomas stayed with Hughes at Castle House and wrote some of his short-story collection, *Portrait of the Artist as a Young Dog*, in the little gazebo looking over the estuary.

Activities

The estuary-indented coast of Carmarthen Bay, with wide sands and glimmering shallow waters creating a marbled expanse of blue, with yellow, green and grey, is perhaps best appreciated from a coastal stroll around Laugharne. The Taf, Tywi and Loughor river mouths can be descried from here.

Dylan Thomas Birthday Walk WALKING
(www.laugharnetownship-wcc.gov.uk) This scenic 1.7-mile loop starts at the foreshore car park below the castle, skirting the bottom of the castle before heading up to Dylan Thomas' writing shed and Boathouse. It then cuts inland to St Martin's Church and returns via the main street. It's clearly signposted. A brochure can be downloaded from the town's website.

Extend the walk into a 5-mile circuit traipsing more of the pretty surrounding estuary countryside.

Festivals & Events

Laugharne Weekend MUSIC
(www.thelaugharneweekend.com; weekend tickets £100; Apr) This vibrant, small-scale festival held over the first weekend in April concentrates on music and writing by artists with Welsh connections.

Sleeping & Eating

Boat House B&B ££
(01994-427263; www.theboathouselaugharne. co.uk; 1 Gosport St; r £90-120;) Friendly, homely and tastefully decorated, Laugharne's smartest B&B offers four well-appointed colour-themed guest rooms – the Purple, a suite, plus the Scarlet, Olive and Blue. The building was formerly the Corporation Arms pub, where Dylan Thomas told stories in exchange for free drinks. The current owner's exceptional home-cooked breakfasts would surely assuage even Thomas' legendary hangovers.

Carpenter's Arms PUB FOOD £
(01994-427435; www.facebook.com/carpentersbroadway; Broadway; mains £8-17, 2-course Sun lunch £10.50; 4.30-10pm Mon-Sat, noon-5pm Sun;) This community pub has a cast of local characters to share a yarn with as you tuck into simple grills, burgers, lasagne, battered fish etc. Rooms are available too (from £58).

Castle View FISH & CHIPS £
(01994-427445; Grist Sq; fish & chips £7.50-9, snacks/meals £3-6; noon-2pm & 5-7.30pm Mon-Sat, noon-6pm Sun) For a serve of cod, chips and mushy peas bigger than your head, this upmarket chippie is the 'plaice'. All fish is sustainably caught and the menu also stretches to faggots, curry and a rather lovely cod chowder. Try takeaway on one of the estuary-facing picnic tables below the castle if it's clement.

Arthur's ITALIAN ££
(01994-427422; www.facebook.com/arthurs laugharne; 6 Grist Sq; mains £12-18; 11.30am-4pm Mon & Wed, 6-9pm Thu, 11.30am-3pm & 6-9pm Fri & Sat, 11.30am-4pm Sun) Arthur's is among Carmarthenshire's best Italian restaurants, and certainly the best located. Prettily flanking Grist Sq overlooking the estuary, it is only loosely Italian, and might

serve up a baked fig and goats-cheese salad or freshly caught mackerel as easily as a pizza.

ⓘ Getting There & Away

Bus 222 runs between Carmarthen and Laugharne (30 minutes, five daily).

Llanarthne

POP 760

Tiny Llanarthne (often anglicised as Llanarthney) is as pleasantly rural and slow-paced as dozens of other Carmarthenshire villages, and would perhaps have remained indistinguishable from the pack if it hadn't been for the National Botanic Garden of Wales opening nearby, along with the presence of probably the county's two top places to eat.

◉ Sights

★National Botanic Garden of Wales
GARDENS

(☏01558-667149; www.botanicgarden.wales; adult/child £12.65/6.05; ⊙10am-6pm Apr-Oct, to 4pm Nov-Mar; ℗♿) Concealed in the rolling Tywi valley countryside, this lavish complex opened in 2000 and is still maturing. Formerly an aristocratic estate, the garden has a broad range of plant habitats, from lakes and bogs to woodland and heath, with lots of decorative areas and educational exhibits. The centrepiece is the Norman Foster–designed **Great Glasshouse**, a spectacular glass dome sunken into the earth. The garden is 2 miles southwest of Llanarthne village, signposted from the main roads.

Themed spaces include a historic double-walled garden, a **Japanese garden** and an **apothecaries' garden**, and there are fascinating displays on plant medicine in a recreated chemist shop. The 110m-wide Great Glasshouse shelters endangered plants from Mediterranean climes sourced from all over the world. Children will love the **Birds of Prey Centre**, home to more than 20 British raptor species. There are additional fees for the falconry and owl demonstrations, and for learning how to fly the birds yourself.

This estate once belonged to Sir William Paxton, the man responsible for transforming Tenby into a tourist resort. His grand manor house, built in the 1790s, burnt down in 1931, but you can still see the outline of the foundations, and the old

---

WORTH A TRIP

COALTOWN COFFEE

Ammanford, where the understatedly slick **Coaltown Coffee Roastery** (Foundry Rd, Ammanford; coffee/cakes/pizzas from £3/3/8; ⊙10am-4pm; ℗⎙) is based, was once a flourishing coal-mining town, then once that stopped it was deprived for a long time. With the mantra 'new black gold' (the name given locally to coal back in the day, and here meaning coffee beans), Scott and crew concoct standout java in chic premises that wouldn't look amiss in Brooklyn.

Some wonderful coffee-making contraptions are on site, where the roasting magic is conducted in a massive old-school Italian roaster. And the pizza is almost as sensational as the coffee. Barista courses too. One of South Wales' best cafes.

---

servants' quarters: pretty impressive in themselves. The original Regency-era landscaping, comprising a chain of decorative lakes, was restored during 2020.

On the hill in the distance is **Paxton's Tower**, a folly built by Paxton with superb panoramic views across Carmarthenshire.

🛏 Sleeping & Eating

Llwyn Helyg Country House
B&B £££

(☏01558-668778; r £125-145; ℗⎙) This modern, Georgian-look stone house on the village fringes has three guest bedrooms luxuriously decked out with dark wooden furniture, white Italian marble en suites and spa baths. Audiophiles can make advance requests to use the state-of-the-art 'Listening Room', which has a system that must be heard to be believed.

★Wright's Food Emporium
CAFE ££

(☏01558-668929; www.wrightsfood.co.uk; Golden Grove Arms, B4300; 2-course meal £22; ⊙noon-3pm Thu-Sun, also 6-8pm Sat; ℗⎙♿🐾) Sprawling through the rooms of an old village pub, this hugely popular deli-cafe serves elaborate sandwiches, salads and massive antipasto platters packed full of top-notch local and imported ingredients (with a French bent). Follow up with a craft beer or something from its range of small-estate organic wine, then browse crates of vinyl records and shelves of the area's best produce.

Set two-course menus only were available at the time of research, with prebooking advised.

Y Polyn WELSH, EUROPEAN **££**
(www.ypolyn.co.uk; Capel Dewi; mains £18-27; ☉noon-2.30pm & 6.30-9pm Tue-Sat, noon-2.30pm Sun; **P** **🎵**) Most things are understated at Y Polyn. Tables are mismatched bare wood, the staff dress casually, you pour your own wine, and it's emphasised that this place is just about cooking well and unpretentiously with magic local ingredients. But the results are brilliantly flavoursome and highly rated by many top gastronomes.

Bite into chargrilled Welsh sirloin with chimichurri sauce, candied walnuts and local cheesemaker Caws Cenarth's Perl Las in the dressing. Veggie? How about roast cauliflower steak with toasted almond salad?

It's three miles west of Llanarthne in Capel Dewi.

❶ Getting There & Away

Up to two 278/279 buses a day stop here en route between Carmarthen (£2.85, 35 minutes) and Llandeilo (£2.30, 20 to 30 minutes). The 279 stops at the botanic garden.

Llandeilo

POP 1800

On a hill encircled by bedazzling green fields and the charmingly meandering River Tywi, Llandeilo is a cute collection of narrow streets lined with grand, vibrant Victorian and Georgian buildings. The surrounding region was once dominated by large country estates, and though they have long gone, the deer, parkland, trees and winsomely agricultural character of the landscape are their legacy.

Used by many travellers as a springboard for the wilder terrain of Brecon Beacons National Park, it's within a short drive of numerous outstanding sights – Elizabethan gardens, rolling country estates, castles and more.

⊙ Sights

★**Dinefwr** PARK, HISTORIC BUILDING
(NT, Cadw; ☑01558-824512; www.nationaltrust.org.uk; adult/child £8/4; ☉grounds 10am-4pm, house 11am-4pm Sat & Sun; **P** **♿** **🐕**) This idyllic, 324-hectare, beautifully landscaped estate on the edge of Llandeilo incorporates a deer park, an Iron Age fort, pasture, woods, a 12th-century castle and a 17th-century manor with a Victorian Gothic facade. The highlight is the serene parkland, though. There are several marked walks: keep your eyes peeled for fallow deer and one of only a few remaining herds of the very rare White Park cattle, an ancient breed once common in Britain.

Most visitors will want to clamber to the substantial ruins of Dinefwr Castle, on a hilltop in the southern corner of the estate. Fantastic views fall away from its battlements across the Tywi to Brecon Beacons National Park. Once the seat of the lords of Deheubarth, whose power and influence spread across South Wales, in the 17th century it suffered the indignity of being converted into a picturesque garden feature.

WORTH A TRIP

ABERGLASNEY GARDENS

Aberglasney Gardens (☑01558-668998; www.aberglasney.org; Llangathen; adult/child £8.55/free; ☉10am-6pm late Mar-Oct, 10.30am-4pm Nov-Feb, to 5pm early-late Mar; **P**) Entering these formal walled gardens feels a bit like wandering into a Jane Austen novel. The gardens date originally from Elizabethan times, evolving continually since then, and contain a unique cloister built solely as a garden decoration. There's also a lake, a 250-year-old yew tunnel, a 'wild' garden in the bluebell woods to the west and various other horticultural havens. In the summer exhibitions and musical events bring further life and gaiety.

At its heart stands a semi-restored **manor house** (Georgian, over an Elizabethan core) with temporary art exhibitions and installations. The derelict kitchens have been converted into a glass-roofed **atrium garden** full of subtropical plants. Out on the flower-bedecked terrace, a whitewashed and flagstoned **tearoom** sells cakes and snacks.

Aberglasney is in Llangathen, just off the A40, 4 miles west of Llandeilo. Llandeilo–Carmarthen buses stop at Broad Oak, seven minutes' walk away.

17th-century Newton House is presented as it was in Edwardian times. Other rooms recall Newton's WWII incarnation as a hospital, and the former Billiard Room is now a tearoom.

Book in advance via the website to visit the house.

🛏 Sleeping & Eating

Cawdor   HOTEL **££**
(☑ 01558-823500; www.thecawdor.com; Rhosmaen St; r £125-175, apt £225; P 🛜) Walking through the broad entrance into the bright-red, quite posh Cawdor, you get some sense of the Georgian house of assembly it once was. The very well-appointed rooms, some with beautiful wooden beams, have Egyptian cotton bed linens and marble in the bathrooms.

Downstairs a snug lounge bar, with a roaring fire in winter, and a more contemporary courtyard cafe flank a more formal dining room (mains £8.50 to £12.50). Book in advance for food and rooms.

★ Ginhaus Deli   DELI **£**
(☑ 01558-823030; www.ginhaus.co.uk; 1 Market St; ⊙ 8am-5pm Mon-Thu, to 10pm Fri & Sat; 🛜) Specialising in two of the very finest things in life (gin and cheese), this hip deli-cafe also serves cooked breakfasts, filled baguettes, quiches, tarts, fresh juices and delicious British food such as smoked haddock with poached egg. Charcuterie and cheese platters are offered too. On Friday and Saturday nights there's pizza from 5pm to 8pm.

The charming traffic-free side street it spills out onto enhances the appeal.

The Hangout   CAFE **£**
(www.thehangoutllandeilo.co.uk; Beechwood Industrial Estate; light lunches £4-8; ⊙ 10am-4pm; P 🛜 ✏) This industrial chic joint is justly popular for its varied brunches (veggie included), shelves of gooey cakes and – of course – wonderful coffee. It's worth the 10-minute walk from the town centre.

ℹ Getting There & Away

The main buses are the eight daily 280/281 to/from Llandovery (£3.25, 45 minutes) and Carmarthen (£3.60, 45 minutes). Seven daily X13 buses head via Ammanford to Swansea (£5.90, 1½ hours).

Llandeilo is also on the Heart of Wales railway line (Swansea–Shrewsbury). Heading south, direct trains run to/from Swansea (£8, one hour, two daily). Northbound, you can reach Llandovery (£3.90, 20 minutes), Llandrindod Wells (£8.60, 1¼ hours) and Shrewsbury (£15.40, three hours).

Llandovery (Llanymddyfri)
POP 2070

The lovely, unhurried market town of Llandovery puts on no shows for tourists but furnishes all comers with a taste of real, workaday rural Wales. It makes an excellent base for exploring the western fringes of Brecon Beacons National Park (just south of town) or the Cambrian Mountains (just north). The name means 'the church among the waters', and the town is indeed surrounded by rivers: the Tywi, Bran and Bawddwr.

It was once a key assembly point for drovers taking their cattle towards the English markets.

◉ Sights & Activities

The highlight is the fine hill country around town, with the Brecon Beacons just south (Myddfai is only 3.5 miles) and the Cambrian Mountains immediately north. Llandovery is also a good place to join the **Cambrian Way**, a tough 298-mile trail across Wales' mountainous midriff from Cardiff to Conwy.

Llandovery Castle   CASTLE
(Castle St) Very ruined Llandovery Castle, originally dating from 1100, looms ineffectually over the town car park. The disembodied stainless-steel knight statue commemorates Llywelyn ap Gruffydd Fychan, gruesomely executed by Henry IV for refusing to lead him to Welsh independence leader Owain Glyndŵr's base.

Upper Tywi Valley   SCENIC DRIVE
Twisting immediately north from Llandovery, a web of charmingly rural lanes traces the upper course of the River Tywi up to the valley's highlight, the lofty reservoir **Llyn Brianne**, near the river's source. South Wales' biggest body of water, the reservoir also boasts the UK's highest dam and, with spinach-coloured forest fringing the stark hills above, feels more like Canada than Carmarthenshire.

At the lake, you're on the border between Carmarthenshire and Mid-Wales counties Ceredigion and Powys.

✻ Festivals & Events

Sheep Festival FAIR
(www.llandoverysheepfestival.co.uk) This centuries-old drovers' town celebrates all things sheep each September, from how to shear one of the woolly beasts to sheepdog trials and sheep-themed food. Brilliant.

🛏 Sleeping & Eating

Castle Hotel PUB £
(☑01550-720343; www.castle-hotel-llandovery. co.uk; Kings Rd; s/d from £50/65; 🛜) This large, handsome old pub has many strings to its bow. Foremost for travellers, perhaps, are the 15 contemporary guest bedrooms: a surprise given the rambling sequence of venerable, beamed, low-ceilinged rooms with log fires downstairs where you encounter two bars, the restaurant, function rooms and even the Red Giraffe antique shop.

The restaurant food is decent (mains £10 to £21), and is especially hot on burgers and steaks from the town's butchers (which must be good; those guys have the Royal Warrant).

Drovers B&B ££
(☑01550-721115; www.droversllandovery.co.uk; 9 Market Sq; s/d from £65/88; P🛜) This attractive Georgian house on the town's main square has a comfortably old-fashioned feel with its ancient stone hearth, antique furniture and simply, tastefully furnished bedrooms.

ⓘ Getting There & Away

Buses head to/from Carmarthen (£4.50, 1½ hours, eight daily) via Llandeilo (£3.15, six daily) and Broad Oak (£3.50, 50 minutes, eight daily), for Aberglasney Gardens.

Llandovery is on the Heart of Wales line, with two direct trains to/from Swansea (£9.60, 1½ hours), Llandeilo (£3.90, 20 minutes), Llandrindod Wells (£6.70, one hour) and Shrewsbury (£15.60, 2¾ hours).

Pumsaint

A cluster of dwellings on the surprisingly busy A482 between Llanwrda and Lampeter, Pumsaint is distinguished largely by one important historical site in the pretty woodland nearby.

◉ Sights

Dolaucothi Gold Mines MUSEUM
(NT; ☑01558-650177; www.nationaltrust.org.uk; adult/child £9.25/4.95; ⊙11am-5pm Easter-Oct; P♿) Enfolded in a wooded estate, this is the only known Roman gold mine in the UK. The main attraction is the chance to go underground on a guided tour of the old mine workings, although the exhibition and the mining machinery above ground, where you can try panning for gold, are interesting. The mines were closed at the time of research.

The Romans left around 120 CE, but locals carried on for another two centuries. Mining recommenced with the Victorians, stopping for good in 1938. There's also a tearoom and short walking trails here.

ⓘ Getting There & Away

Your own wheels only, folks. Pumsaint is 12 miles northwest of Llandovery via Llanwrda on the A482.

Newcastle Emlyn & Around

POP 1190

Most travellers head west from Carmarthen towards the temptations of beach-blessed Pembrokeshire, leaving the lush hills and valleys of northern Carmarthenshire relatively unexplored. The River Teifi forms much of the border with Ceredigion, and a particularly pretty stretch of the river passes through Newcastle Emlyn, the big settlement hereabouts, with its main street of brightly hued houses. Scattered around the surrounding countryside are a few prepossessing sights.

◉ Sights

Cenarth VILLAGE
Three miles downstream from Newcastle Emlyn, Cenarth hogs a picturesque spot by an old stone bridge, straddling some rapids on the River Teifi, **Cenarth Falls**. Cenarth is known for its legacy of coracles: rounded, ungainly looking traditional boats still used on West Wales rivers for fishing via a method little-changed since Roman times: hand-holding nets extended between two vessels and floating slowly downstream by nightfall. In fact, coracle-caught sewin (the sea trout coracle fishermen catch) has EU Protected Food Name status.

The **National Coracle Centre** (☑01239-710980; www.coraclemuseum.co.uk; adult/child £3.50/1.50; ☺10.30am-5.30pm Sun-Fri Easter-Sep), on Cenarth's south bank, tells the fascinating story.

Caws Cenarth FACTORY
(☑01239-710432; www.cawscenarth.co.uk; Fferm Glyneithinog, Pontseli, Lancych; ☺10am-5pm Mon-Sat; [P]) **FREE** One of Wales' most acclaimed organic cheesemakers, Caws Cenarth produces its own take on Caerphilly as well as many others, such as award-winning washed-rind Golden Cenarth. It is possible to watch cheese being made, peruse informative cheesemaking displays and buy the cheese in the shop. You can also order via the website. It's located in the countryside, 4 miles southwest of Newcastle Emlyn.

National Wool Museum MUSEUM
(☑0300-111-2333; www.museum.wales/wool; Drefach Felindre; ☺11am-1pm & 2-4pm Thu-Sat) **FREE** The Cambrian Mills factory, world famous for its high-quality woollen products, closed in 1984 and this interesting museum has taken its place. Former mill workers are often around to get the remaining machines clickety-clacking, but there's also a working commercial mill next door where you can watch operations, and a shop selling snug woollen blankets. Prebooking

tickets online was essential at the time of research. It's off the A484 four miles east of Newcastle Emlyn.

🛏 Sleeping & Eating

★Larkhill Tipis YURT **££**
(☑01559-371581; www.larkhilltipisandyurts.co.uk; Cwmduad; tepees & yurts £70-90; [P]) 🍃 Chickens and ducks escort guests around the fairy-lit grounds of this off-the-grid glamping site, set in farmland and a 1.6-hectare wood. Five styles of tepee and yurt are available, from Iranian to Native American, all comfortably furnished with their own beds, gas cookers and wood fires. Remotely located 7 miles southeast of Newcastle Emlyn, it's ideal for families.

Gwesty'r Emlyn Hotel HOTEL **££**
(☑01239-710317; www.emlynhotel.co; Bridge St; s from £72, d £85-125; [P]🛜) This 300-year-old coaching inn has been transformed into a slick mini-hotel with well-presented rooms, a restaurant and a 'fitness suite', with gym equipment, a spa pool and a sauna.

ℹ Getting There & Away

Direct hourly buses connect Newcastle Emlyn with Cenarth (5 minutes, £1.80), Carmarthen (one hour, £4.15) and Cardigan in Ceredigion (25 minutes, £3.15).

AT A GLANCE

★

POPULATION
122,439

CAPITAL
Haverfordwest

BEST BEACH
Barafundle Bay
(p179)

**BEST SEAFOOD
SHACK**
Café Môr (p181)

**BEST COASTAL
THRILL**
Preseli Venture
(p164) coasteering

📅

WHEN TO GO
➡ **Mar–May**
Peaceful hiking on
the Coast Path,
wildflowers, puffins
returning to their
summer shores.

➡ **Jul & Aug**
Festivals aplenty.
Rush hour on the
coast. Crowds swell,
beaches are at their
busiest and room
rates peak.

➡ **Sep–Feb** Autumn
foliage, big swells
for surfers, quiet
time for exploring;
some sights and
accommodation
closed.

St David's Cathedral, St Davids (p156)
HARTMUT ALBERT/SHUTTERSTOCK

St Davids & Pembrokeshire

T he Pembrokeshire coast is what you imagine the world would look like if God were a geology teacher with artistic yearnings. There are knobbly hills of volcanic rock, long, thin, glacier-scoured inlets, and stratified limestone eroded into arches, blowholes and sea stacks. All along the shoreline towering red and grey cliffs are interleaved with perfect sandy beaches. This phenomenally wild landscape is the county's greatest asset and in summer it beckons with spectacular walking, surfing, coasteering and sea kayaking.

Natural assets aside, Pembrokeshire offers a wealth of Celtic and pre-Celtic sites, forbidding castles, fascinating islands and little St Davids – the magical mini-city with its chilled vibe, medieval cathedral and abiding association with Wales' patron saint.

St Davids & Pembrokeshire Highlights

❶ St Davids (p156)
Clicking into the laid-back groove of Britain's smallest city with the spectacular cathedral and gnarly surf beach.

❷ Pembrokeshire Coast Path (p173)
Heading over cliff and kissing gate on the upliftingly beautiful trail wrapping around the county's entire coast.

❸ Tenby (p175)
Joining the summer fun in a colourful seaside resort flanked by velvety sand beaches.

❹ Newport (p167)
Tapping into the food and arts scene in this pretty coastal town, with cracking coastal and hill walks nearby.

❺ Water sports (p181) Hitting the surf at Freshwater West, sea kayaking at Fishguard and coasteering at Abereiddi.

❻ Skomer Island (p187) Spotting puffins galore on a cruise around one of the richest wildlife habitats in Britain.

❼ Castell Henllys (p170) Slipping back to the Iron Age at this reconstructed Celtic fort.

❽ Pentre Ifan (p170) Feeling the mystery at Wales' loftiest dolmen, a prehistoric chamber tomb formed from the same rock as Stonehenge.

NORTH PEMBROKESHIRE

Where Cardigan Bay slings its hook into the wind-whipped, spindrift-flecked Irish Sea, the country's northern reaches reveal Pembrokeshire's wild side. Bookended by the tiny cathedral-topped city of St Davids in the south, birthplace of Wales' patron saint, the coast is shaped by starkly eroded rock formations: stratified cliffs cloaked in heather and gorse, caves and arches, stacks and skerries. These rocks are a geologist's dream, since many have been around since dinosaurs walked the earth. There is history of the human kind here, too, with many a hill and promontory graced by Iron Age hill forts, dolmens, standing stones and holy wells, all pointing to a rich and mysterious past. Inland, the rolling moors of the remote Preseli Hills unfurl, home to the same sacred bluestones used to form Stonehenge.

Much of the coastline from St Davids onwards is inaccessible by car. If you're only going to walk part of the Pembrokeshire Coast Path (p173), this is an excellent section to tackle.

St Davids (Tyddewi)

POP 1841

Capped off by the country's most impressive Norman cathedral, St Davids is officially Britain's smallest city, though it's no bigger than a village. On a fiercely beautiful stretch of the Pembrokeshire coast, this is the birthplace of Wales' patron saint (and his final resting place). And as such it has attracted pilgrims for 1500 years. Back in the Middle Ages, this was a pilgrimage destination to rival Santiago in Spain.

In summer, St Davids becomes a full-on coastal honeypot, attracting hordes of non-religious pilgrims, drawn by the town's laid-back vibe, buoyant food and drink scene, and the excellent hiking, water sports and wildlife-watching right on the doorstep.

History

Dewi Sant (St David) founded a monastic community here in the 6th century, only a short walk from where he was born at St Non's Bay. In 1124 Pope Callistus II declared that two pilgrimages to St Davids were the equivalent of one to Rome, and three were equal to one pilgrimage to Jerusalem. The cathedral has seen a constant stream of visitors ever since.

◉ Sights

★ **St David's Cathedral**   CATHEDRAL
(www.stdavidscathedral.org.uk; The Pebbles; ⊙10am-3pm Mon-Sat, 1-4pm Sun) `FREE` Hidden in a hollow and behind high walls, St David's Cathedral is built on the site of a 6th-century chapel. The valley location was chosen in the vain hope the cathedral would be overlooked by Saxon raiders, but it was ransacked at least seven times. When you pass through the gatehouse and its stone walls come into view, the 12th-century Norman cathedral is astonishingly impressive, its distinctive west front embellished with four pointed towers of purple stone.

The **nave** is the oldest surviving part of the cathedral, with massive, purplish-grey pillars linked by semicircular Norman Romanesque arches. Above is a richly carved 16th-century oak ceiling, adorned with pendants. At the far end of the nave is a delicately carved 14th-century Gothic **pulpitum** (screen), which bears a statue of St David dressed as a medieval bishop. Beyond the pulpitum is the magnificent **choir**. Check out the mischievous carved figures on the 16th-century misericords (under the seats), one of which depicts pilgrims being seasick over the side of a boat.

Between the choir and the high altar is the object of all those pilgrimages: a **shrine** containing the bones of St David and St Justinian. Destroyed during the Reformation, it was restored and rededicated in 2012, adorned with five new Byzantine-style icons by artist Sara Crisp.

Towards the rear of the cathedral is the low-lit **Holy Trinity Chapel**, distinguished by a superb fan-vaulted ceiling dating from the early 16th century, and the light-filled **Lady Chapel**.

Lord Rhys ap Gruffydd, the greatest of the princes of South Wales, and his son Rhys Gryg are known to be buried in the cathedral, although their effigies in the south choir aisle date only from the 14th century. Gerald of Wales, an early rector of the cathedral, has a gravestone here, but scholars suggest he is actually buried at Lincoln Cathedral.

St Davids Head   AREA
The National Trust tends this heather-wreathed promontory, formed from the oldest rock in Wales and once fortified by

St Davids

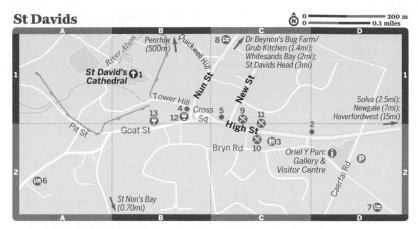

St Davids

the Celts. A magnificent circular 3.5-mile, two-hour hike leads up and over clifftops with staggering views of Whitesands Bay, Ramsey and Skomer Islands and, on clear days, the Wicklow Mountains in Ireland across the water. For prehistory fans, the highlights are **Coetan Arthur**, a burial chamber dating to 3500 BC, and the neolithic chambered tombs below the rocky fin-shaped peak of **Carn Llidi** (181m).

The tip of the headland is a series of rock and turf ledges, a great place for a picnic or wildlife spotting – in summer you can see gannets diving and choughs soaring, while dolphins and porpoises can often be spotted out at sea.

St Non's Bay   RUINS
Immediately south of St Davids, this ruggedly beautiful spot is named after St David's mother and traditionally accepted as his birthplace. A path leads to the 13th-century **ruins of St Non's Chapel**. Only the base of the walls remains, along with a

stone marked with a cross within a circle that's believed to date from the 7th century. Standing stones in the surrounding field suggest that the chapel may have been built within an ancient pagan stone circle.

On the approach to the ruins is a pretty little **holy well**. The sacred spring is said to have emerged at the moment of the saint's birth and the water is believed to have curative powers.

Whitesands Bay   BEACH
(Porth Mawr) Swimming, surfing and coastal hiking are the big draws at this mile-long sandy beach. At extremely low tide you can see the wreck of a paddle tugboat that ran aground here in 1882, and the fossil remains of a prehistoric forest. If Whitesands is really busy – and it often is – escape the worst of the crowds by walking north along the coastal path for 15 minutes to the gorgeously secluded cliff-rimmed bay at **Porthmelgan**.

Whitesands, 2 miles northwest of St Davids, has lifeguards, toilets and a cafe between May and early September. If you drive, expect to pay for parking (£5 per day). Otherwise, catch the Celtic Coaster bus from the Oriel y Parc centre (summer only) or walk.

Ramsey Island   BIRD SANCTUARY
🍃 Reclining off the coast of St Davids like a sleeping dragon, Ramsey Island (Ynys Dewi) is ringed by dramatic sea cliffs and an offshore armada of rocky islets and reefs. The Royal Society for the Protection of Birds (RSPB) reserve is seabird nirvana, famous for its large breeding population of choughs, as well as peregrine falcons, ravens, guillemots, razorbills, fulmars and kittiwakes. The island is also home to one of Britain's largest populations of Atlantic grey seals (and in autumn their adorable pups).

Operators whisking you across to the island include Thousand Islands Expeditions (p159) and Voyages of Discovery (p159).

🏃 Activities

★ **Wild About Pembrokeshire**   OUTDOORS
(📞01437-721035; www.wildaboutpembrokeshire.co.uk; foraging per person from £12; ☉Apr-Oct; 🚶) 🍃 Passionate foragers Julia and John know the shores and hedgerows around St Davids like the backs of their hands. For the inside scoop on edible seaweeds, wild plants and herbs, hook onto one of their informative, sustainably minded foraging walks. These range from beginner's walks to a seashore forage and wild picnic, and family-focused seashore and rock-pool discovery walks.

Walks vary in length from 1½ to two hours. See the website for exact times, dates and locations. Advance booking is essential. The Really Wild Emporium (p160) is their centre-of-town HQ.

Dr Beynon's Bug Farm   WILDLIFE
(📞07966 956357; www.thebugfarm.co.uk; Lower Harglodd Farm; adult/child £7/4.50; ☉10.30am-4.30pm Thu-Sun; 🚶) 🍃 It sure is a bug's life on this working farm just outside of

SEVEN HEAVENLY BEACHES IN PEMBROKESHIRE

Pembrokeshire's most wild and wonderful beaches are accessible only on foot or by boat. If you're up for an off-the-radar adventure, here's our pick of the most memorable bays.

Druidston Haven If you like your beaches wild and wave lashed, this gold-sand bay is the ultimate haven. The geology is spectacular, with caves, rock arches and Ordovician shale cliffs buckled into spectacular faults and folds.

Westdale Just south of Marloes Sands (p189), this seductively wild beach reveals a generous scoop of sand and jagged cliffs at low tide. It's a fabulous spot to watch the sun set.

Abermawr & Aberbach Just north of Abercastle, this twinset of crescent-shaped pebble bays sit below a lush wooded valley, misted with bluebells in spring. Low tide reveals golden sand, and very low tide the stumps of an ice-age forest.

Pwll Deri This deliciously under-the-radar pebble-and-sand bay is tucked into the cliffs below the Iron Age hill fort of Garn Fawr. Reach it on foot through coastal woods or by kayak.

Ceibwr Mawr Rugged cliffs rear up above this wild horseshoe-shaped bay, notched into the coastline just south of St Dogmaels. You might share the beach with seals and seabirds. It's a 40-minute walk from here to Pwll y Wrach (the Witches' Cauldron), a striking collapsed cave.

Skrinkle Haven & Church Doors This duo of ravishingly beautiful cliff-backed coves sit midway between Manorbier and Lydstep on the Pembrokeshire Coast Path. Access Skrinkle Haven through a gap in the rocks at low tide. Steps lead down to Church Doors, where stratified limestone and sandstone cliffs tower to form a natural rock arch.

Watwick Bay Powdery blonde sands and rust-red rocks await at this lovely secluded beach – your reward for hiking the coast path around St Ann's Head. It's rarely busy, even in summer.

THE COASTAL WAY

Taking the length of Cardigan Bay in its stride, the 180-mile **Coastal Way** is designed to show off the Welsh coast from its most flattering angles. Part of the Wales Way (three national driving routes), this is a road trip to remember, stitching together some of Britain's most phenomenal coastal scenery, bounded by the Irish Sea to the west and high mountains to the east.

Moving south to north, the route begins in St Davids before diving straight into the Pembrokeshire Coast National Park, ticking off one incredible beach, headland and prehistoric site after the next. From here, it swings north to Ceredigion and Snowdonia before ending in prettily whitewashed Aberdaron on the surf-lashed, wildlife-rich coastline of the Llŷn Peninsula. See www.visitwales.com for more details and inspiration.

St Davids. The brainchild of academic entomologist, ecologist and farmer Dr Sarah Beynon, the Bug Farm raises awareness about the importance of insects and their planet-saving role in its tropical bug zoo, museum, gallery and play barn, plus trails zooming in on wildflowers, wetlands and arable plants. Book tickets in advance online.

Part of the same concept, the Grub Kitchen (p160) is a terrific choice for a gourmet bug-inspired lunch.

Thousand Islands Expeditions   BOATING
(☑ 01437-721721; www.thousandislands.co.uk; Cross Sq; ☺ Apr–Oct) Look out for guillemots, razorbills, peregrines and choughs on the cliffs and (in September and October) Atlantic grey seal pups on the beaches of Ramsey Island on a 90-minute cruise around it. This highly regarded operator also offers one-hour jet-boat trips (adult/child £26/13), 2½-hour whale- and dolphin-spotting cruises (£60/30), and two-hour trips to see the puffins of Skomer (£50/22). Book in advance.

Voyages of Discovery   BOATING
(☑ 01437-721911; www.ramseyisland.co.uk; 1 High St; ☺ Easter–mid-Nov; ⛵) Offers trips to the waters around Ramsey Island (adult/child £27/15), as well as 2½-hour whale- and dolphin-watching trips (adult £62) and shearwater and puffin voyages (adult £33).

Aquaphobia   BOATING
(☑ 01437-720471; www.aquaphobia-ramseyisland. co.uk; Grove Hotel, High St; ☺ Easter–Oct) Wildlife-spotting powerboat trips to the coast of Ramsey (adult/child £27/11) and bouncy 2½-hour rides over to Ramsey and Grassholm (£60/30) islands in search of whales, dolphins, seals, seabirds and porpoises.

Ma Sime's Surf Hut   SURFING
(☑ 01437-720433; www.masimes.co.uk; 28 High St; 2hr group lesson £40; ☺ 11am-5.30pm Mon, from 10am Tue-Sun Easter-Oct) Established in 1978 (the first surf shop in St Davids), Ma Sime's rents wetsuits (£10), surfboards (from £15), body boards (£10), stand-up paddleboards (£25) and kayaks (£25 to £40) from both its shop in St Davids and, in the summer holidays, from the beach at Whitesands (p157). Also runs a surf school at Whitesands from May to October.

TYF Adventure   ADVENTURE
(☑ 01437-721611; www.tyf.com; 1 High St; half-/full-day activities £70/120; ☺ 10.30am-3.30pm Easter-Oct; ⛵) ✎ Ramp up the adventure along the coast by popping into this one-stop shop, offering everything from coasteering to surfing to sea-kayaking, rock climbing, cycle tours and family-friendly rock-pool safaris from its St Davids base.

✯ Festivals & Events

St Davids Cathedral Festival   MUSIC
(www.stdavidscathedralfestival.co.uk; St David's Cathedral; ☺ May-Jun) Ten days of classical and contemporary music performances, starting on the Spring Bank Holiday weekend at the end of May. The Irish-oak ceiling gives the cathedral fine acoustics, so if you're not here for the festival, check out one of the many other concerts performed here throughout the year.

🛏 Sleeping

Ramsey House   B&B ££
(☑ 01437-720321; www.ramseyhouse.co.uk; Lower Moor; d £90-135; 🅿🛜) Owners Shaun and Suzanne have poured love and creativity into this boutique-style B&B in their duck-egg-blue house on the outskirts of town. The six rooms are all different but feature

bold Designer's Guild and Zoffany wallpapers, leather tub chairs, solid oak furniture, goose-down duvets and stylish bathrooms clad in Italian tiles. First-floor rooms afford lovely views of the sea or St Davids Cathedral.

Waterings
B&B ££

(☑ 01437-720876; www.waterings.co.uk; Anchor Dr; s £50-80, d £90-100; P 🗢) This incredibly welcoming B&B has two loft-conversion rooms in the main house and five others gathered around a garden courtyard. All have a nautical theme, decorated in blues and whites, with coastscapes and maritime knick-knacks. The garden rooms are large and suite-like, with a semi-separated sitting area. Breakfasts are excellent, with local produce and eggs from their own chickens.

Y Glennydd
HOTEL ££

(☑ 01437-720576; www.glennyddhotel.co.uk; 51 Nun St; s/d from £55/75; 🗢) Decorated with maritime memorabilia, this 1880s terraced house was built to accommodate coast guard officers and has a traditional, bordering on old-fashioned, feel. Some of the 11 smallish, unfussy bedrooms have views over Whitesands, and there's a cosy lounge-bar downstairs.

★Penrhiw
BOUTIQUE HOTEL £££

(☑ 01437-725588; www.penrhiwhotel.com; Pen Rhiw; d £190-240, ste £260; P 🗢) Serenely tucked away in grounds with landscaped gardens, wildflower meadows and woodlands, this late-Victorian priory turned boutique hotel is one of St Davids' most fabulous escapes, with its air of understated sophistication, minimalist-chic interiors bearing the imprint of Welsh-born architect Keith Griffiths, and original features from stone arches and stained glass to exquisitely tiled arts and crafts fireplaces.

Twr y Felin
HOTEL £££

(☑ 01437-725555; www.twryfelinhotel.com; Caerfai Rd; d £250-290, ste £320-420; P 🗢) Pembrokeshire-born architect Keith Griffiths put his stamp on Twr y Felin, using a 19th-century windmill as the impetus for this slickly modern hotel in private landscaped grounds. A collection of specially commissioned, large-scale contemporary art (including works by Welsh street artist Pure Evil) enlivens the monochrome, distinctly minimalist interiors. All rooms are luxurious, but top billing goes to the

spectacular three-level circular suite in the tower itself.

Enjoy an aperitif in the subtly lit, gallery-style lounge bar before dinner at Blas, hands down one of the top tables in town.

✖ Eating & Drinking

Really Wild Emporium
CAFE £

(☑ 01437-721755; www.thereallywildemporium. co.uk; 24 High St; cakes £2.50-3, mains £8.50; ☺ 10am-4pm) 🍃 Wild About Pembrokeshire (p158) foragers Julia and John have had fun converting a high-ceilinged art-deco building into this fabulous emporium in central St Davids. Exposed brick, reclaimed wood and corrugated iron set an industro-cool scene for dishes peppered with foraged ingredients – from pad thai with wild garlic seeds to insanely delicious seaweed brownies.

Upstairs is given over to nature-inspired workshops and a store brimming with homemade soaps and skincare products infused with wild plants, herbs and algaes.

St Davids Food & Wine
DELI £

(☑ 01437-721948; www.stdavidsfoodandwine. co.uk; High St; light bites £3-4.50; ☺ 9am-3.15pm Mon-Thu, to 5pm Fri & Sat) Stock up on picnic supplies (including lavish hampers) at this delicatessen, which specialises in local organic produce. Or you can grab a pastry or a made-to-order gourmet sandwich – slow-cooked Pembrokeshire pork in Welsh cider or Solva crab, for instance – and dig in at the benches out front.

Gianni's
ICE CREAM £

(11 High St; ice cream £3; ☺ noon-5.30pm; 👪) What do you get when you combine the finest organic Pembrokeshire cream and milk with an Italian gelato maker? Answer: Gianni's. For the smoothest ice cream in flavours swinging from rhubarb and custard to limoncello and cherry Bakewell, stop at this hole-in-the-wall for a cone. It does bacon-flavoured gelato for dogs, too (yes, it's a thing...).

★Grub Kitchen
INTERNATIONAL ££

(☑ 07986 698169; www.grubkitchen.co.uk; Lower Harglodd Farm; mains £14.50-17.50; ☺ 10.30am-4.30pm Thu-Sun) 🍃 The grub is excellent at the sustainably minded restaurant at the Bug Farm (p158). With a little help from his entomologist (insect scientist) wife Dr Sarah Beynon, Andy Holcroft rustles up highly original dishes featuring edible insects. Spicy crickets, say, might be the prelude for smoked chipotle cricket and black bean chilli, signature bug burgers with polenta chips, and cricket-cardamom carrot cake.

If the food puts a spring in your step, so too does the location – the restaurant is housed in a renovated 18th-century cowshed (the kitchen used to be a pigsty in a former life), with bug-themed art hanging on exposed walls.

The one-of-a-kind concept is part of a grander plan to raise awareness of entomophagy (insect eating) and tackle issues of sustainability in the food chain.

Blas GASTRONOMY £££
(☑ 01437-725555; www.blasrestaurant.com; Caerfai Rd; mains £22-34, 7-course tasting menu £69)
🖋 The dark-walled, softly lit, art-slung restaurant at Twr y Felin (p160) is deliciously intimate. The chef takes pride in local, seasonal, sustainable sourcing. Homemade sourdough bread piques the appetite for starters like Solva lobster with cucumber, dill and sea vegetables, and mains like lamb rump with hen-of-the-woods mushrooms and black garlic – all big on integral flavours and exquisitely served on slate, wood and bespoke crockery.

Bishops PUB
(☑ 01437-720422; www.thebish.co.uk; 22-23 Cross Sq; ⊙ 11am-midnight; 🖥) A friendly, rambling pub full of locals, walkers and blow-ins, this place has a roaring fire in winter, a decent pint and pub grub offer, plus great cathedral views from the beer garden.

Farmer's Arms PUB
(☑ 01437-721666; www.farmersstdavids.co.uk; 14-16 Goat St; ⊙ 11am-10pm; 🖥🏴) This gregarious boozer has real ale and Guinness on tap, regular live music at weekends, and is *the* place to be when the rugby's playing. A basic pub menu (mains £10 to £14) is served noon to 2.30pm and 6pm to 9.30pm daily.

❶ Information

Oriel Y Parc Gallery & Visitor Centre
(☑ 01437-720392; www.orielyparc.co.uk; High St; ⊙ 10am-4pm) Oriel y Parc encompasses the National Park tourist office and St Davids' landscape art gallery, showing some terrific exhibitions throughout the year, often with a strong focus on Graham Sutherland and landscape-inspired pieces from the National

Museum of Wales. It also has a gift shop and a cafe that stages live music and cultural events throughout the year.

❶ Getting There & Away

Public transport is limited, especially on Sunday and in winter.

The main Pembrokeshire coastal bus services (p183) stopping here are the Strumble and Puffin Shuttles. From late July to late September there's also the Celtic Coaster, which circles between St Davids, St Non's Bay, St Justinian and Whitesands.

Up to nine 411 buses per day go to/from Solva (£1.65, 11 minutes), Newgale (£2.50, 21 minutes) and Haverfordwest (£3.40, 43 minutes, 10 daily), while 413 buses run to/from Fishguard (£3.80, 40 minutes, six daily).

❶ Getting Around

The Celtic Trail West (National Cycle Network Route 4) passes through St Davids. There's pleasant cycling on minor roads around the peninsula but no off-road action.

St Davids and the surrounding area suffer from parking problems and congestion in summer.

Tony's Taxis (☑ 07816 991548, 01437-720931) provides a luggage-transfer service for Pembrokeshire Coast Path walkers, covering the area from Little Haven to Fishguard.

Solva (Solfach)

POP 865

Enclasped in a deep inlet, Solva is quite the coastal dream with its sprinkling of cottages in chalk-box colours, galleries and inviting pubs. Lower Solva sits at the head of an L-shaped harbour, where the water drains away completely at low tide, leaving its flotilla of yachts tilted on the sand.

Clifftop walks along the coast towards Newgale (east) and St Davids (west) reveal hidden coves, some impressive rock formations and big sea views.

❂ Sights & Activities

Caer Bwdi BEACH
Sandwiched between Solva and St Davids on the Pembrokeshire Coast Path, this wild, rugged cove is at its best at low tide when its seaweed-ensnared rock pools shimmer with life. Climbers can sometimes be spotted hauling themselves up its stacks and columns. The Pembrokeshire purple stone, used to build St David's Cathedral, was once quarried here.

Solva Woollen Mill HISTORIC BUILDING

(☎01437-721112; www.solvawoollenmill.co.uk; Middle Mill; ⊙10am-5.30pm Mon, to 4pm Tue-Fri) **FREE** It's a pleasant walk of just over a mile upriver from Solva to Middle Mill, where you'll find the oldest working woollen mill in Pembrokeshire. Fine fabrics have been woven on its historic looms for more than a century. You can see the weavers at work and browse in the shop.

🛏 Sleeping & Eating

Haroldston House B&B ££

(☎01437-721404; www.haroldstonhouse.co.uk; 29 High St; 3-night stay from £264; P🐾) 🐾 Occupying a Georgian merchant's house, this eco-aware B&B has a dash of contemporary boutique style. The tasteful self-catering apartments feature art by owner Ian Mc-Donald as well as other Wales-based artists. Quarters are big on charm, whether you opt for the deep-blue Blue Room, with original floorboards, shutters and log burner, or the Stable Studio in a stylishly converted 18th-century stable pigsty.

★ Mrs Will the Fish SEAFOOD £

(☎01437-721571; https://mrs-will-the-fish.business.site; dressed crab/lobster/seafood platter for 2 from £5/18/30; ⊙9am-6pm Mon-Sat) Mrs Will the Fish is something of a local legend, preparing fresh-from-the-boat dressed crab and generous seafood platters for takeaway. Cheerful Mrs Will operates from her home in Upper Solva: simply call ahead, place your order and rock up at the arranged time for your fishy feast. Enjoy with cold drinks down by the harbour or on the beach.

MamGu Welshcakes CAFE £

(☎01437-454369; www.mamguwelshcakes.com; 20 Main St; lunch mains £5.50-7, box 6 welshcakes £4; ⊙9.30am-5pm Mon-Sat, 10am-4pm Sun) You'll see the humble welshcake in a whole new light after a visit to MamGu. Friends Becky and Thea travelled the world before landing in the fishing village of Solva and working their magic with a griddle. At this rustic-cool coastal cafe, welshcakes traverse the entire taste spectrum, with flavours from leek and cheese to ginger and chilli-chocolate. All are delicious.

Cambrian Inn PUB FOOD ££

(☎01437-721210; www.thecambrianinn.co.uk; 6 Main St; mains £14-25; ⊙noon-3pm & 6-9pm; 🐾) The Cambrian Inn is a delicious mix of old and new, with exposed stonework, original beams, modern, muted colours and bistro tables. Pub classics include pies and steaks, plus winningly fresh seafood (including St Brides Bay Lobster) and delicious gourmet burgers (try the Fat Cow). There are also five bright, slickly contemporary guest rooms (doubles from £100).

❶ Getting There & Away

Both the Puffin Shuttle (p183) and bus 411 between Haverfordwest and St Davids stop here. Alternatively, you can walk along the coast path from St Davids and then bus it back. Join the coast path at Caerfai Bay (signposted from Oriel y Parc), then pick up the eastbound path. It's about 5 miles in total.

Porthgain

For centuries, the tiny harbour of Porthgain consisted of little more than a few sturdy cottages wedged into a rocky cove. From 1851 it began to prosper as the port for shipping out slate quarried just down the coast at Abereiddi, and by 1889 its own deposits of granite and fine clay had put it on the map as a source of building stone and brick until the post-WWI slump burst the bubble.

Today Porthgain is a surprisingly picturesque little port, home to a couple of art galleries, pubs and restaurants, making it an appealing stopover for walks along the Pembrokeshire Coast Path.

◉ Sights

Blue Lagoon BAY

(Abereiddi) In a flooded former slate quarry, the shockingly turquoise Blue Lagoon is a magnet for brave wild swimmers who don't mind the water being deep and bitterly cold. Slate was quarried at this site on the water's edge in Abereiddi up until 1910 and then transported by tramway to the harbour at Porthgain. After the mining stopped, a channel was blasted through to the sea, creating this brilliant blue-green pool surrounded by a bowl of sheer stone walls.

From Porthgain, the Blue Lagoon is best reached via a spectacular 30-minute walk west along the coast path, past the ruins of workers' cottages and quarry buildings.

Carreg Samson TOMB

FREE Sitting in a farmer's field, with terrific views of Strumble Head, this 5000-year-old dolmen is quite remarkable. The

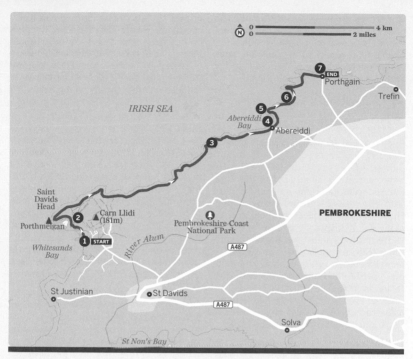

🏃 Coastal Walk
Whitesands to Porthgain

START WHITESANDS
END PORTHGAIN
LENGTH 10 MILES; FOUR TO SIX HOURS

Covering a beautiful but remote stretch of coast, this rewarding walk takes you over rugged headlands and past dramatic cliffs, pretty coves and flooded quarries. It's a taxing route with several steep descents and ascents, but it's well worth the effort. Bring provisions, as it's a long way between villages.

Start out at busy ❶ **Whitesands Bay** (p157) and head west onto wild and rocky St Davids Head. The start of the route is fairly easy, with a good path, wide open views and craggy volcanic outcrops to admire. The only signs of human habitation here are ancient, with the simple ❷ **neolithic burial chamber** on the headland predating the surrounding remnants of Celtic forts.

The path soon becomes more rugged, with a rock scramble down to and up from the lovely little cove at ❸ **Aberpwll**. Continue on past crumbling cliffs to ❹ **Abereiddi**, looking out for seals in the coves, gannets,

and possibly porpoises diving for fish out at sea. The beach at Abereiddi is famous for its black sand full of tiny fossils. Ruined quarry buildings and slate workers' cottages flank the path beyond the beach that leads to the ❺ **Blue Lagoon** (p162), a deep, turquoise flooded slate quarry. It's now popular with coasteerers and, in early September, cliff divers from all over the world, who compete here, diving 27m into the icy water below.

The 45-minute walk from Abereiddi to Porthgain is one of the best stretches along the entire coast path, following a clifftop plateau past the often deserted ❻ **Traeth Llyfn**, an astonishingly lovely beach of fine dark sand, wave-smoothed rocks and looming cliffs. A flight of steep stairs leads down to the golden sand, but beware of strong undercurrents and the tide, which can cut off parts of the beach from the steps.

Continue on for the last descent into the tiny harbour of ❼ **Porthgain**, where you can reward yourself with some superb seafood at the Shed (p164) or a cold beverage at the welcoming Sloop Inn (p164).

massive capstone seems to be only just touching the stones that it is balanced on. It's off the minor road between Trefin and Abercastle, 3 miles east of Porthgain. Look out for the small walker's signpost pointing to the farm.

🏃 Activities

★ Preseli Venture   ADVENTURE
(☑ 01348-837709; www.preseliventure.co.uk; Parc-y-nole Fach, Mathry; coasteering & kayaking from £52; ☺ office 9am-5pm; 🚹) 🅿 Beautifully positioned above the coast, this eco-aware retreat is a fantastic place to escape into the wilds and ramp up the adventure with water-based activities. Owner Sophie Hurst was among the original coasteering pioneers and knows the area inside out, so you're in good hands to go kayaking, surfing and coasteering at secluded bays, caves and cliffs nearby. It's roughly a 10-minute drive north of Porthgain via the A487, just inland from Abercastle.

Should you wish to stay the night, there's a low-carbon backpackers lodge, geodesic dome and camping in a woodland glade.

Celtic Quest   ADVENTURE SPORTS
(☑ 01348-837337; www.celticquestcoasteering.com; coasteering £55; 🚹) Coasteering specialists Celtic Quest provide heavy-duty wetsuits, helmets and buoyancy aids to let you hit the cliffs and waters around Abereiddi at all times of the year. Families are welcome (suitable for children of aged eight and above). The starting point is Abereiddy beach.

🛏 Sleeping

Old School Hostel   HOSTEL £
(☑ 07845 625005; https://oldschoolhostel.com; Ffordd-yr-Afon, Trefin; s/d £30/44; 🅿 🖥) 🅿 Set in a rambling old school building in Trefin, 2 miles east of Porthgain, this is one of the new breed of independent, brightly painted, personally run backpackers. The six rooms have en-suite showers but communal toilets. A great collection of games and a good-quality self-service breakfast are included in the price.

Crug Glâs   HOTEL £££
(☑ 01348-831302; www.crug-glas.co.uk; Abereiddy Rd; r £150-210; 🅿 🖥) Set on a big beef and cereal farm that has existed here since at least the 1100s – there's a reference to it in the 12th-century Black Book of St David's – this opulent country house offers rooms

decked out with rich fabrics, ornate beds, enormous bathrooms and elegant period grandeur. Five rooms are in the main house, two in converted farm buildings.

There's also a highly regarded restaurant (three-course menu £35). Crug Glâs is 3 miles south of Porthgain, off the A487.

✕ Eating

Shed   SEAFOOD ££
(☑ 01348-831518; www.theshedporthgain.co.uk; fish & chips £11-14, mains £16-24; ☺ noon-8pm; 🖥🚹) Housed in a quirkily converted machine shop right by the harbour, this funky little shack is renowned as one of Pembrokeshire's best seafood restaurants. Fish and chips get their own separate menu, while the main menu relies where it can on the day's fresh catch, alongside favourites such as Porthgain lobster and crab. It gets insanely busy on sunny holiday days.

Sloop Inn   PUB FOOD ££
(☑ 01348-831449; www.sloop.co.uk; mains £12-23; ☺ 11am-11pm Mon-Fri, 9.30am-midnight Sat, 9.30am-11pm Sun; 🖥🚹) With wooden tables worn smooth by many a bended elbow, timber beams and old photos of Porthgain in its industrial heyday, this nautical-flavoured tavern opened its doors to thirsty seamen back in 1743. The hearty, home-cooked grub will satisfy even the hungriest Coast Path walker, with specials like Pembrokeshire crab salad and beer-battered cod. On summer weekends there's often live music.

ℹ Getting There & Away

The only bus heading here is the Strumble Shuttle, one of the Pembrokeshire coastal bus services (p183).

Fishguard (Abergwaun)
POP 3419

Perched on a headland between its modern ferry port and former fishing harbour, Fishguard is often overlooked by travellers on the mad dash to and from Ireland. It doesn't have any standout sights, but it's nevertheless an appealing, culturally vibrant town (which, incidentally, holds the distinction of being the setting for the last foreign invasion of Britain).

Fishguard is split into three distinct areas. Right in the heart is the main town, centred on the Town Hall in Market Sq. To the east is the charming harbour of the

Lower Town, used as a setting for the 1971 film version of *Under Milk Wood* (starring Richard Burton, Peter O'Toole and Elizabeth Taylor). The train station and ferry terminal lie a mile northwest of the town centre, down on the bay in Goodwick.

History

In 1078, the marshy plain of Goodwick was the site of a battle between the northern and southern Welsh lords (as if they didn't have enough to worry about from the encroaching Normans), culminating in a bloody massacre of the southerners.

⊙ Sights

Strumble Head   VIEWPOINT
On wild, lonely, rocky Strumble Head, a lighthouse beams out its signal as high-speed ferries thunder past on their way to Ireland. Jutting into the wave-hammered sea, the headland makes a good vantage point for spotting dolphins, seals, sharks and sunfish; below the parking area is an old coast-guard lookout that now serves as a shelter for observing wildlife. It's located 4 miles northwest of Goodwick and the route is well marked.

The Strumble Shuttle (bus 404 between St Davids and Newport) stops here.

St Gwyndaf's Church   CHURCH
(Llanwnda) At the heart of the tiny village of Llanwnda, 2 miles northwest of Goodwick, 8th-century St Gwyndaf's showcases its antiquity in the carved stones, inscribed with crosses and Celtic designs, set into the outside walls. Inside, look up at the timber roof beams; at the far end of the third beam from the west (door) end, facing the altar, is a 15th-century carving of a tonsured monk's head.

A mile-long track leads from Llanwnda to Carreg Wastad Point, the site of the 1797 invasion.

🏃 Activities

Marine Walk   WALKING
This path follows the coast from the car park on the Parrog in Goodwick and traces the cliffs flanking Fishguard, offering great views of the harbour, the Lower Town and along the coast to Dinas Head. There's an option to take a detour into the Lower Town before heading up and circling back to Goodwick.

Kayak-King   KAYAKING
(☑07967 010203; www.kayak-king.com; tours £45; ◷9.30am-noon & 2-4pm) Twice-daily sea-kayaking tours, tailored to either family groups or adults. Kayak-King is a mobile outfit; its conspicuously painted van can be found in Lower Fishguard Harbour when it's running tours, but it's easier to ring or use the online form to make a booking.

Mayberry Kayaking   KAYAKING
(☑01348-670364, www.mayberrykayaking. co.uk; ⊞) These Fishguard-based pros get you out on the water and along the rugged, cave-indented coastline with guided kayaking tours suitable for either adults (half-/full day £70/117) or families (half-day £127). Keep your eyes peeled for seals and dolphins.

🎭 Festivals & Events

Fishguard Folk Festival   MUSIC
(☑07934 418186; www.fishguard-folk-music. co.uk; ◷late May) Forging the Welsh–Irish connection, this four-day shindig in late May immerses you in Celtic music traditions. A number of performances are free, and they include pub sessions, dance displays, open-mic events, workshops and a rip-roaring festival *twmpath* (traditional community dance). Tickets for the few charged events can be bought from the Royal Oak hotel on Market Sq.

Fishguard International Music Festival   MUSIC
(www.fishguardmusicfestival.co.uk; ◷Jul-Aug) A two-week festival of mainly classical-music performances starting in late July, including opera, choirs, solo pianists, string quartets and other ensemble groups.

Aberjazz   MUSIC
(www.aberjazz.com; ◷Aug) This five-day jazz and blues festival takes local theatres, pubs and cafes by storm.

🛏 Sleeping

Fishguard has a flurry of cracking B&Bs, and staying central will give you easy access to the pick of the bars and restaurants. Goodwick is full of budget hotels and B&Bs catering to passengers catching the Irish ferries or overnight visitors walking the Coastal Path. There are also some enticing camping options in the surrounding countryside.

ST DAVIDS & PEMBROKESHIRE FISHGUARD (ABERGWAUN)

Fishguard Bay Resort
CAMPGROUND £

(☑01348-811415; www.fishguardbay.com; site for 2 incl car £29.50, pods £77; 🛜📶) Dramatically positioned on a clifftop overlooking Fishguard Bay, this large complex offers tent sites, static caravans, sea-facing cottages, luxury lodges and barrel-shaped 'glamping pods'. There's also a shop, a small playground, a games room, a laundry and a 'pamper pod' used for massage. It's located 2.5 miles east of Fishguard, signposted from the A487.

Hill Fort Tipis
CAMPGROUND £

(☑01348 891497; www.hillfortcampingandyurts. co.uk; Penparc, Pencaer, Goodwick; sites adult/ child £15/6, tepees per night/week from £75/490; ⊙May-Sep; 📶) 🌿 A staggering panorama of Strumble Head and the Irish Sea greets you from this ecofriendly hilltop campground, 4 miles west of Goodwick. Positioned by an Iron Age hill fort, there are 11 camping pitches, each with fire pit, alongside well-furnished tepees and bell tents, sleeping four or six. They can provide fresh eggs, milk and organic veggies on request.

★ Manor Town House
B&B ££

(☑01348-873260; www.manortownhouse.com; 11 Main St; d £80-160, extra bed £25; 🛜) Sea views enthral at this graceful Georgian house, with a garden terrace for gazing across the harbour and Cardigan Bay. With a mix of antiques, upcycled finds and eye-catching fabrics, the spacious rooms have boutiquey flair, tastefully done out in crisp whites, blues and dove greys, with nice touches like Welsh honesty hampers, Noble Isle vegan toiletries and waffle robes.

The charming owners have created a genuine home-from-home and bend over backwards to please – whether you want to borrow books, organise activities or have a cream tea on the terrace – just say the word.

Fern Villa
B&B ££

(☑01348-874148; www.fernvillafishguard.co.uk; Church Rd, Goodwick; s/d from £50/70; 🛜) Situated on the slopes in Goodwick (head towards the church), this large cream Victorian offers clean en-suite rooms, some with exposed stone walls and sea views. It's a great option if you want to be close to the train station and ferry port, and especially to the coastal path.

🍴 Eating & Drinking

Gourmet Pig
DELI, CAFE £

(☑01348-874404; www.gourmetpig.co.uk; 32 West St; mains £5-7; ⊙9.30am-5.30pm Mon-Fri, to 4.30pm Sat; 🛜📶) Delicious sandwiches, samosas, Iberian-accented deli platters (laden with chorizo, jamón, sobrassada and manchego), pies and pastries are the main attractions at this relaxed deli-cafe, along with barista-made locally roasted coffee. Grab a window seat and watch Fishguard go about its business.

Hooked @ 31
FISH & CHIPS £

(☑01348-874657; www.hookedat31.co.uk; 31 West St; fish suppers £5-8; ⊙noon-8.30pm Tue-Sun; 📶) For a proper taste of the briny blue, stop by this excellent little chippie and take your fish-and-chip supper down to the harbour or one of the nearby beaches. They also make their own ice cream with Pembrokeshire milk (dairy-free alternatives are available). There's a kids' menu, too.

Mannings
DELI £

(☑01348-874100; 18 West St; lunch mains £6-10; ⊙8.30am-5.30pm Mon-Sat; 📷📶) 🌿 Lodged in a funkily converted former bank, this high-ceilinged grocers and deli-cafe is one of Fishguard's most happening hubs. Pop in for a sourdough loaf, lunch specials (frittatas, paninis), homemade cake with locally roasted coffee, or a takeaway picnic box with treats for two (£22). The emphasis is on sustainable local sourcing and organic produce, with plenty of options for vegans.

Peppers
BRITISH ££

(☑01348-874540; www.peppers-hub.co.uk; 16 West St; mains lunch £6.50-10, dinner £16-19; ⊙6-10pm Mon-Wed, 10am-3pm & 6-10pm Thu-Sat; 📷) This hip hub includes an interesting gallery (the streetside West Wales Art Centre), a restaurant, a peaceful terrace area and an inviting tile-floored bar. The restaurant whips up sharing platters, quesadillas and ciabatta sandwiches at lunch, while dinner has a pinch more sophistication, with the likes of beef baked in pork, Guinness and pickled walnuts, and millet burgers with spicy sauce.

Ship Inn
PUB

(☑01348-874033; 3 Old Newport Rd, Lower Town; ⊙5-11pm Wed-Fri, noon-midnight Sat, noon-10pm Sun) This tremendously snug and convivial little 250-year-old pub has an open fire in winter and walls covered in memorabilia, including photos of Richard Burton filming

Under Milk Wood outside (the street and nearby quay haven't changed a bit).

Shopping

Melin Tregwynt   ARTS & CRAFTS
(☑01348-891288; www.melintregwynt.co.uk; ⊙10am-4pm Mon-Sat) Since 1912 the same family has run this traditional woollen mill, which churns out some of Wales' best blankets, cushions and upholstery fabrics. New designs have brought the traditional weaves bang up to date and the full range includes clothing and bags, all of which are on display in the mill shop.

You can watch the looms and giant waterwheel in action on weekdays and there's also a small cafe on site.

ℹ Getting There & Away

BOAT

Stena Line (☑08447 707 070; www.stena-line.co.uk; Fishguard Harbour; pedestrian/car & driver from £32.50/95; ☎) has two ferries a day year-round between Rosslare in the southeast of Ireland and Fishguard Harbour.

BUS

Direct services to/from Fishguard include the frequent T5 to Haverfordwest (£3.50, 33 minutes), Newport (£2.50, 15 minutes), Cardigan (£3.85, 37 minutes) and Aberystwyth (£6.10, 2½ hours); the 413 to St Davids (£3.80, 50 minutes, up to six daily); and the useful Pembrokeshire coastal bus services (p183).

TRAIN

There are frequent direct trains between both Fishguard and Goodwick Station and Fishguard Harbour Station (both of which are actually in Goodwick) and destinations including Swansea (£17, 1¾ hours, three daily), Cardiff (£28, 2½ to three hours, two daily), Newport (£33, 3¼ hours, daily) and Manchester (£94, 6¼ hours, daily).

Cwm Gwaun

Hidden away in glorious seclusion, this narrow valley of the River Gwaun, thickly wooded with ash, beech, hazel and oak, curves southeast from Fishguard to its source in the Preseli Hills. Despite its proximity to Fishguard, Cwm Gwaun feels strangely remote and mysterious. Ancient sites litter the valley and, famously, its inhabitants retain an idiosyncratic soft spot for the Julian calendar, abandoned by the rest of Britain in 1752. During their New Year's celebrations (on 13 January, according to the usual calendar), local children walk from house to house singing traditional Welsh songs and are rewarded with sweets and money.

The valley's narrow lanes are best explored by bicycle or on foot. The valley has no public transport links.

St Brynach's Church   CHURCH
(www.fishguardanglicanchurch.org.uk; Pontfaen) Humble yet beautiful, this tiny church in Pontfaen was founded in AD 540 by St Brynach. Ruined and then rescued in the late 19th century, it has two 9th-century stone crosses in the graveyard.

Dyffryn Arms   PUB
(☑01348-881305; Pontfaen; ⊙11am-10pm) If the step-back-in-time feel of Cwm Gwaun isn't visceral enough, drop into the Dyffryn Arms. Better known as Bessie's after its legendary 90-year-old landlady, this rare survivor of yesteryear occupies what's basically the front room of her house. Beer is served from jugs filled straight from the barrel; no hand pumps here!

Newport (Trefdraeth)
POP 1161

As different from the industrial city of Newport near the English border as chalk is to cheese, the Pembrokeshire Newport moves to a deliciously relaxed coastal beat, with a pretty cluster of flower-bedecked cottages huddled beneath a small Norman castle. It sits at the foot of Mynydd Carningli, a large bump on the seaward side of the Preseli Hills, and in recent years it has seriously upped its hospitality game, with restaurants playing up regional sourcing and foraged ingredients, and a peppering of boutiquey guesthouses.

Newport makes a pleasant base for walks along the coastal path or south into the Preseli Hills.

◎ Sights

Newport Sands   BEACH
(Traeth Mawr; ♿) This half-mile sweep of golden, dune-backed beach sits just across the River Nevern from the town. You can wade across the river at low tide. It's a wonderful spot for rockpooling, gathering shells, or launching a canoe, kayak or sailing boat. On clear days you can see the faint outline of Ireland across the water, and the

WORTH A TRIP

EXPLORING DINAS ISLAND

For some of the most ravishing coastscapes in Pembrokeshire, make your way to the rugged headland of **Dinas Island**, midway between Fishguard and Newport. Though technically more a headland than an island, it is framed on either side by pretty coves – the sandy strand of Pwllgwaelod to the west, and the rocky inlet of Cwm-yr-Eglwys to the east, where you can see the ruin of 12th-century **St Brynach's Church**, destroyed by the great storm of 1859.

The 3-mile circuit of the headland is an outstanding walk, heading up and over vertiginous cliffs cloaked in gorse, blackthorn and bramble, and indented with largely inaccessible coves. The rumble of the sea is your constant companion on the trail, where there is the chance of spotting seals and dolphins from **Dinas Head**, the northernmost point, and, in late spring and summer, puffins at **Needle Rock**. A path across the neck between Pwllgwaelod and Cwm-yr-Eglwys allows you to return to your starting point.

Either bring picnic provisions or stop for lunch and a pint at the waterfront **Old Sailors** (☑ 01348-811491; www.theoldsailors.co.uk; Dinas Cross; mains £12-20; ⊙ 11am-8.30pm Wed-Sun; 🐾). There's a lovely beach-facing beer garden for warm days.

Buses between Newport and Fishguard stop at Dinas Cross, which is just over a mile from Pwllgwaelod.

peachy sunsets reflected in the estuary waters are quite something.

Carreg Coetan Arthur   TOMB
(Cadw; www.cadw.gov.wales; 1 Carreg Coetan; ⊙ 10am-4pm) **FREE** Now surrounded by fields and houses, this little dolmen has been here for 5000 years. At first glance it looks like the capstone is securely supported by the four standing stones; closer inspection suggests that some old magic has held it together all these thousands of years, as it's balanced on only two of them. Archaeological investigations have uncovered the remains of cremated bones and urns. It's well signposted down a side road on the town's eastern edge.

St Brynach's Church   CHURCH
(Nevern) Two miles east of Newport, St Brynach's beautifully melancholic **churchyard** dates from around the 6th century, predating the 13th-century church itself. Within the graveyard is a tall **Celtic cross**, one of Wales' finest, decorated with interlace patterns. According to tradition, the first cuckoo that sings each year in Pembrokeshire does so from atop this cross on St Brynach's Day (7 April). The churchyard's gloomy alley of yew trees is estimated to be upwards of six centuries old.

Inside the church, the **Maglocunus Stone** in the south transept dates from around the 5th century, and is one of the few carved stones that bears an inscription in both Latin and Ogham. Stones like these were important tools for deciphering the meaning of the ancient Celtic script.

Up on the wooded hill behind the church you'll find a pilgrims' cross and the scant remains of **Nevern Castle**, originally a Welsh stronghold, then rebuilt by the Normans and eventually destroyed by the Welsh in 1195.

🏃 Activities

If you keep walking past Carreg Coetan Arthur (p168), you'll come to Feidr Pen-Y-Bont – an iron bridge over the **Nevern Estuary**, a haven for birds, especially in winter. Cross the bridge and turn left for an easy walk along the shoreline to the beach at **Newport Sands**.

Mynydd Carningli   WALKING
In the 6th century, St Brynach of Nevern supposedly used to head up 346m Mynydd Carningli ('Mountain of Angels') to commune with angels. You can clamber up to the craggy outcrop from town (a 3.5-mile, roughly two-hour return trip). Work your way up grassy paths to the summit of this extinct volcano, the site of an Iron Age hill fort, with great views of Newport Bay and Dinas Head. On a fine day you might spot Ireland.

Carningli Bike Hire   CYCLING
(☑ 01239-820724; www.carninglibikehire.com; Carningli Centre, East St; per half-day/day/week £15/22/60; ⊙ 10am-5.30pm Mon-Sat) Offers bike rental with free delivery within the

local area, provides route maps and leads guided rides.

🛌 Sleeping

★ Llys Meddyg
HOTEL ££

(☑ 01239-820008; www.llysmeddyg.com; East St; s £105, d £120-160; P 🗢 🐾) This classily converted Georgian coach house takes contemporary big-city cool and plonks it firmly by the seaside. The rooms ooze boutique flair, with original art gracing the walls, painted wainscotting, locally woven blankets, reclaimed wood furnishings and bright pops of colour. Many bathrooms have freestanding tubs and monsoon showers. Downstairs there's an excellent restaurant (p169) and snug bar for pre-dinner cocktails.

Owner Ed takes guests on half-day foraging expeditions with a simple lunch (£70 per person, minimum of two people) on request.

Cnapan
B&B ££

(☑ 01239-820575; www.cnapan.co.uk; East St; s/d £75/98; ☉ Mar-Jan; P 🗢) This diligently maintained, listed Georgian town house has a flower-filled garden and five light-filled rooms. Renovations have freshened up the decor and left brand-new bathrooms in their wake; ask for room 4 – it's a little bigger than the others. Downstairs was once a restaurant, and restaurant standards carry over into the excellent breakfasts.

Golden Lion
PUB ££

(☑ 01239-820321; www.goldenlionpembrokeshire.co.uk; East St; s/d/tr/f £100/110/130/150; P 🗢) This old-school country inn has bright, clutter-free rooms, decked out in contemporary style, restful colours and fabrics from local woollen mill Melin Tregwynt. Downstairs there's a cosy traditional bar with a log fire and low ceilings, serving real ales and tasty pub grub like beer-battered cod and chips, Thai green curry and gourmet burgers. Kids are well catered for.

✖ Eating

Canteen
PIZZA £

(☑ 01239-820131; www.thecanteennewport.com; cnr Market & East Sts; mains £8-12; ☉ 4-9pm Tue-Sat; 🖋 🖐 🐾) With names like Strumble Head, Mae Hen Wlad Fy Nhadau (Land of My Fathers) and Costa del Newport, the Canteen's lip-smacking range of thin, crispy, stone-baked pizzas has been suitably Welshified with the addition of locally sourced quality toppings. It also serves burgers, salads, better-than-average coffee and a range of Welsh craft beer.

Tides Kitchen & Wine Bar
BISTRO £

(☑ 01239-820777; www.facebook.com/marketstreetnewport; mains lunch £8-12.50, dinner £12-20; ☉ 9am-3pm Tue-Sat; 🖐) Bare-wood floors, cheek-by-jowl tables, banquette seating and local art dangling on walls create a modern boho-chic feel at Tides. Dig into imaginative takes on local fish and shellfish from Cardigan Bay, plus other well-prepared dishes from Welsh fillet of steak to Black Mountain smoked duck with beetroot crisps. The simpler lunch mains, homemade cakes and sourdough bread are delicious, too.

Blas at Fronlas
CAFE £

(☑ 01239-820065; www.blasatfronlas.com; Market St; lunch mains £6.50-11; ☉ 9am-4.30pm Sun-Thu, 9am-4.30pm & 6.30-9pm Fri & Sat; 🖐) With its shelves stacked high with tempting local produce, this nicely chilled deli-cafe rolls out yummy breakfasts, light lunches and tasting platters of freshly baked bread and Welsh cheeses, hams, pâté and smoked salmon. There's live music at 'tapas and tunes' on Friday evenings, and it does a cracking Sunday roast (slow-roast lamb rubbed with garlic and rosemary if you're lucky).

Llys Meddyg
MODERN BRITISH ££

(☑ 01239-820008; www.llysmeddyg.com; East St; mains £15-23; ☉ 5-9pm; P 🗢 🖐) Low ceilings, reclaimed wood and soft, flattering lighting create an urban-cool-meets-mountain-chalet vibe at this restaurant at Llys Meddyg. Kitchen garden and locally sourced and foraged ingredients are cooked with imagination and delivered with panache in dishes that reveal clean, bright flavours, such as home-smoked salmon with cucumber, apple and wasabi, and Welsh shoulder of lamb with goat's cheese, butternut squash and sea vegetables.

🏠 Shopping

Carningli Centre
ANTIQUES

(☑ 01239-820724; www.carninglicentre.com; East St; ☉ 10am-4pm Mon-Sat) This rabbit warren of a shop is packed with interesting oddments, including art, antique homewares, books and loads of railway paraphernalia. It also hires bikes.

Newport Collective
ARTS & CRAFTS

(☑01239-821056; www.newportcollective.co.uk; East St; ⊙10am-5pm Mon-Sat) The showcase for nearly two dozen North Pembrokeshire artists, this interesting little store sells jewellery, pottery, clothing, paintings, photography and hand-turned wooden objects.

Wholefoods of Newport
FOOD & DRINKS

(☑01239-820773; www.wholefoodsofnewport. co.uk; East St; ⊙9am-4pm Mon-Sat) 🌱 The place to go to stock up on organic picnic supplies, planet-friendly provisions and vegan ice cream. There's a selection of ethical gifts at the rear, including Pembrokeshire wool, pottery and hippyish knick-knacks.

🛈 Getting There & Away

Direct services to/from Newport include the frequent T5 to Dinas Cross (£1.65, six minutes), Fishguard (£2.50, 16 minutes), Haverfordwest (£4.15, 52 minutes), Cardigan (£3.45, 23 minutes) and Aberystwyth (£6, 2¼ hours, nine daily). The Pembrokeshire coastal bus services (p183) are also useful, especially in summer.

Preseli Hills

The only upland area in Pembrokeshire Coast National Park, this wild ripple of craggy hills, bogs and heather-flecked moorland tops out at 536m at Foel Cwmcerwyn. The Preseli Hills encompass a fascinating prehistoric landscape that is positively littered with hill forts, standing stones and burial chambers. Most famously, they are said to be the source of the mysterious bluestones of Stonehenge. The ancient Golden Road track runs along the crest of the hills, taking cairns and stone circles in its stride.

🅞 Sights & Activities

★Pentre Ifan
TOMB

(Cadw; www.cadw.gov.wales; ⊙10am-4pm) The largest neolithic dolmen in Wales, Pentre Ifan is a 5500-year-old neolithic burial chamber set on a remote hillside with superb views across the Preseli Hills and out to sea. The huge, 5m-long capstone, weighing more than 16 tonnes, is delicately poised on three tall, pointed upright stones, made of the same bluestone that was used for the menhirs at Stonehenge. The site is about 3 miles southeast of Newport, signposted off a minor road south of the A487.

Castell Henllys
HISTORIC SITE

(☑01239-891319; www.castellhenllys.com; Meline; adult/child £5.50/3.50; ⊙10am-5pm Apr-Oct, reduced hours Nov-Mar; ♿) If you've ever wondered what a Celtic village looked, felt and smelt like, rewind time at this Iron Age settlement, 4 miles east of Newport. From 600 BC and right through the Roman occupation there was a thriving settlement here – now reconstructed on its original foundations. The buildings include three thatched roundhouses, animal pens, a smithy and a grain store, all of which you can enter. There are even Iron Age breeds of pigs and sheep and reconstructions of Celtic gardens.

Buses between Newport and Cardigan stop nearby on request. At the time of writing, time slots needed to be reserved by calling ahead.

★Golden Road
HIKING

Wending its way through the wild open moors of the Preseli Hills, the 7-mile Golden Road is a fascinating ramble through prehistory. Once part of a 5000-year-old trade route between Wessex and Ireland, it runs along the crest of the hills, beginning at Bwlch Gwynt near the summit of Foel Eryr.

The route passes the Carn Bica standing stones (supposed resting place of King Arthur), the tors of Carn Menyn (thought to be the source of the bluestone for Stonehenge), and an Iron Age hill fort at Foeldrygarn. Take a map as the path isn't fully waymarked.

🛌 Sleeping & Eating

★Llama Lodge
CABIN ££

(☑07539 892519; www.llamas.wales/llamalodge; Glanrhydwilym Rhydwilym Llandysilio, Llandissilio; lodge £70-130) 🌱 Wake up to views of grazing llamas at this eco-aware escape in a peaceful spot just south of the Preseli Hills. All rustic timber, the lodge sits surrounded by native woodland and is as cosy as can be, with a log burner for chilly nights. It's a surefire hit with kids, too: the family that runs the farm offers guided llama walks and has a menagerie of friendly animals to pet.

Tafarn Sinc
PUB FOOD ££

(☑01437-532214; www.tafarnsinc.cymru; Rosebush; mains £10-17; ⊙noon-10pm Tue-Thu & Sun, noon-11pm Fri & Sat) Deep in the heart of the Preseli Hills, Tafarn Sinc is a fabulously

BLUESTONE MYSTERY

There are 31 bluestone monoliths (plus 12 'stumps') at the centre of Stonehenge, each weighing around 4 tonnes. Geochemical analysis shows that the Stonehenge bluestones originated from outcrops around Carnmenyn and Carn Goedog at the eastern end of the Preseli Hills. Stonehenge scholars have long been of the opinion that Preseli and the bluestones held some religious significance for the builders of Stonehenge, and that they laboriously dragged these monoliths down to the River Cleddau, then carried them by barge from Milford Haven, along the Bristol Channel and up the River Avon, then overland again to Salisbury Plain – a distance of 240 miles.

An alternative theory is that the bluestones were actually transported by ice-age glaciers, and dumped around 40 miles to the west of the Stonehenge site some 12,000 years ago – although there is no evidence of any similar glacial transportation in southern Britain.

eccentric blast from the past. Outside it's all red corrugated tin and weird statues recalling the old train line. Inside it is even more bonkers, with sawdust on the floor, flitches of ham hanging from the ceiling and an attic's worth of old furniture, farming and mining curios.

After a blustery walk up on the surrounding moors, stop by for a pint of its own locally brewed bitter and hearty traditional faves like cawl and faggots in rich onion gravy.

St Dogmaels (Llandudoch)

POP 1353

Unfurling along the banks of the Teifi Estuary and but a joyous pebble-throw away from dune-backed Poppit Sands, St Dogmaels is a low-key coastal charmer. Walkers and muddy boots are welcome everywhere as the village marks the end of the Pembrokeshire Coast Path. From as early as the 5th or 6th century there was a Celtic monastic community here, which the Normans replaced with French Tironian monks. The remains of their beautiful abbey still stand today.

⊙ Sights

St Dogmaels Abbey　　　RUINS
(☑ 01239-615389;　www.stdogmaelsabbey.org.uk; ⊙ 9am-3pm Mon & Wed-Sat) FREE Built by a reforming Benedictine community from France in 1120 on the site of an already-ancient Celtic monastery, St Dogmaels' active life lasted until 1538, when it fell to Henry VIII's dissolution of the monasteries. Cut off from community and purpose, it declined into the photogenic ruin you see today. The small museum in the coach house tells the abbey's story and includes a cafe and gallery. A vibrant Local Producers Market (p172) is held here every Tuesday from 9am to 1pm.

Welsh Wildlife Centre　　WILDLIFE RESERVE
(☑ 01239-621600; www.welshwildlife.org; Cilgerran; parking £3; ⊙ 10am-4pm Wed-Sun; P ⊕) FREE Bordering the River Teifi just south of Cardigan, the **Teifi Marshes Nature Reserve** is a haven for kingfishers, owls, otters, badgers and butterflies. You can find out more about the critters that live in the surrounding river, marsh and woodland habitats at this striking glass-walled information centre, which also houses a shop and cafe. There are several short waymarked trails nearby, most of them wheelchair accessible.

Poppit Sands　　　BEACH
(⊕) Right at the end of the road that follows the river north from St Dogmaels, this terrific sweep of blonde sand backed by dunes commands terrific views over the estuary to Cardigan Island and out to sea. It's an extremely popular spot for swimmers, surfers, sun seekers and dog walkers. Lifeguards patrol here at the height of summer and facilities include a cafe and toilets. It's about 2 miles north of St Dogmaels; the Poppit Rocket (p183) bus stops here.

Y Felin　　　HISTORIC BUILDING
(www.yfelin.co.uk;　tours adult/child £2.50/1; ⊙ 9am-1pm & 2-4pm Mon-Fri, 9am-1pm Sat) Sidling up to the 12th-century abbey of St Dogmaels, this is one of the last working watermills in Wales, dating to the 1640s. Y Felin is still used to make stoneground flour today, which you can purchase at the mill door.

ST DAVIDS & PEMBROKESHIRE ST DOGMAELS (LLANDUDOCH)

🍴 Sleeping & Eating

Bethsaida
B&B £

(☑ 01239-615479; www.bethsaida.wales; High St; s/d/tr £69/99/129; ☎) Praise be for this beautifully converted blue-and-white Baptist chapel, now a heavenly little B&B brimming with original features that evoke its former life, from its wooden pulpit to its pew headboards. With names like Gobaith (Hope) and Ffydd (Faith), its five guest rooms are dressed in contemporary style, with calming colours, local art and books on Welsh history. Walkers, cyclists and families are warmly welcome.

Fforest Farm
CAMPGROUND ££

(☑ 01239 -623633; www.coldatnight.co.uk; Cilgerran; 3-night stay from £280; ☎) 🚲 On the edge of Teifi Marshes Nature Reserve, Fforest challenges the notion that camping means roughing it. Stay in large tents, tepees or geodesic domes and enjoy the country air. Simple, wholesome breakfasts are served at the lodge, and the owners run a second site further up the coast at Manorafon. There's a seven-night minimum stay during summer holidays.

Local Producers Market
MARKET £

(www.stdogmaelsabbey.org.uk; St Dogmaels Abbey; ⊙ 9am-1pm Tue) Every coastal village ought to have a food market like this. Held by the abbey ruins (p171), the market keeps things local and sustainable, championing produce from Pembrokeshire's sea, pastures, forests and rivers. Fill your picnic basket with the likes of crab hummus and potted lobster, organic preserves and pickles, freshly baked bread, homemade cakes, honey, Welsh sheep's cheese and charcuterie.

Ferry Inn
PUB FOOD ££

(☑ 01239-615172; www.ferry-inn.com; Poppit Rd; mains £13-24; ⊙ 5-10pm Mon, from noon Tue-Sun; P 🚲 ♿ ☎) Peering dreamily out across the Teifi Estuary, this glorious pub has heaps of coastal character. The interior is a melange of historic flair and contemporary chic, with beams, exposed stone, bistro tables and prettily painted wainscotting. Snag a conservatory or terrace table for creative takes on classics: from Ferry tempura fish and chips to Cardigan Bay mackerel with spicy Mexican salsa.

In summer, this is one of the very few places you might be lucky enough to try coracle-caught sewin (the increasingly rare but utterly delicious local sea trout).

ℹ️ Getting There & Away

The Poppit Rocket (p183) stops here, as does the 408 bus (Poppit Sands–Cardigan; hourly, no Sunday service).

SOUTH PEMBROKESHIRE

South Pembrokeshire is necklaced with some of Wales' most gorgeous sandy beaches and limestone formations, making it an impressive starting point for the Pembrokeshire Coast Path (p173).

Once known as Little England Beyond Wales, it was divided from the north by the Landsker Line – a physical and then a linguistic barrier roughly following the old Norman frontier. The divide is less pronounced now, but there's a noticeable English feel to places like Tenby, especially in summer, when the masses descend with their buckets and spades, building miniature replicas of the castles their ancestors once used to keep the Welsh at bay. Those sturdy fortifications are still visible in Tenby, Manorbier, Carew and Haverfordwest, reaching their apotheosis at Pembroke Castle.

Saundersfoot

POP 3361

Bright and breezy Saundersfoot has a long, broad curve of beach with a sweet little harbour at one end, built in 1829 for the shipment of coal. Nowadays the only mining activity hereabouts is carried out by the toddlers digging in the golden sand. Well-kept old houses cling to the hilly streets radiating up from the town centre, where there are some interesting shops to peruse.

It makes for a quieter base than neighbouring Tenby, which is only an hour's walk away along the coast path.

◉ Sights

Saundersfoot Beach
BEACH

(♿) Bookended by a harbour, this wide, long ribbon of butterscotch sand is at its best at low tide. The gently sloping beach is ideal for families, with water shallow enough for swimming and plenty of space

PEMBROKESHIRE COAST PATH

Straddling the line where Pembrokeshire drops suddenly into the sea, the Pembrokeshire Coast Path is one of Britain's most spectacular long-distance walking trails. Established in 1970, it meanders along 186 miles of Britain's most dramatic coastal scenery, running from Amroth to St Dogmaels, taking in vertiginous clifftops and endless beautiful beaches.

Hugging Wales' wild Atlantic coast, this two-week ramble dips and rises over cliff, bluff and headland to coves, prehistoric standing stones and dune-backed bays of astonishing beauty. The route takes you from seaside honeypots to hidden bays where Celtic hill forts are the only human trace. Marine life is plentiful, and rare birds find a safe haven in the remote cliffs: peregrine falcons, red kites, buzzards, choughs, puffins and gannets can be spotted.

Despite the lack of heart-pumping climbs, the constant up-and-down rhythm is not to be underestimated – the total ascent and descent amount to 35,000ft, the equivalent of climbing Mt Everest. If you don't have the time or the stamina for the full path, split it into smaller chunks. You can walk it in either direction, but south–north allows for an easy start, building up to longer, more isolated stretches.

Some sections look deceptively short, but expect endless steep ascents and descents where the trail crosses harbours and beaches. Referring to a tide table is essential.

The weather can be incredibly fickle and mobile-phone coverage is unreliable; come prepared, and bring wet-weather gear and something warm, even in summer. The path has a dedicated website (www.pembrokeshirecoast.wales/coast-path) that's ideal for planning your trek. If you want to skip a stage, there are coastal buses (p183) covering the entire route.

Maps

Ordnance Survey (OS) Explorer 1:25,000 maps No 35 (North Pembrokeshire) and No 36 (South Pembrokeshire) cover the route in detail. *Pembrokeshire: Wales Coast Path Official Guide* (2015), by Vivienne Crow, and *Pembrokeshire Coast Path* (2017), by Brian John, have detailed route descriptions.

When to Walk

Spring and early summer are good times to walk, when wildflowers dot the hills, birdlife is abundant and the school holidays are yet to begin in earnest. Late summer tends to be drier and you might spot migrating whales out to sea, but it can be busy and hard to find a bed for a single night. In autumn crowds and temperatures dwindle and seals come ashore to give birth to their pups. Many hostels and campgrounds close from October to Easter and buses are far less frequent at this time. Although walking in winter can be exhilarating, it may not be the most enjoyable or safest experience. High winds can easily turn a backpack into a sail, which can be extremely dangerous on the cliff-top sections.

Best Sections

Dale to Broad Haven (six hours, 15.4 miles) A wonderful walk along dramatic clifftops ending at an impressive beach. Many access points and regular public transport make it good for short circular walks, too.

Whitesands to Porthgain (four to six hours, 10 miles) A beautiful but taxing section worth tackling if your time is limited. It's within easy reach of St Davids and offers the reward of some excellent nosh at the end of your day.

Porthgain to Pwll Deri (four to six hours, 12 miles) An exhilarating section with sheer cliffs, rock buttresses, pinnacles, islets, bays and beaches but some steep ascents and descents in between. Magnificent views of St Davids and Strumble Head.

Newport to St Dogmaels (six to eight hours, 15.5 miles) A tough, roller-coaster section with frequent steep hills but spectacular views of the wild and rugged coast and its numerous rock formations, sheer cliffs and caves.

for free play. For more seclusion, follow the coast path around to pretty Coppet Hall Beach, where you can paddle among rockpools and go for a cracking lunch at Coast.

Colby Woodland Garden GARDENS
(www.nationaltrust.org.uk/colby-woodland-gar den; Amroth; ⊙10am-5pm; ⊞) ⚑**FREE**
Tucked away in a hidden forested valley 4 miles northeast of Saundersfoot, these National Trust gardens are a riot of fragrance and colour in spring and summer, when the bluebells, rhododendrons, camellias, azaleas and hydrangeas bloom. Once a working coalfield, the estate now has acres of gardens to roam, including a wildflower meadow, walled garden and woodland trails fringed by mighty oaks and Japanese redwoods. The summer house commands uplifting views along Carmarthen Bay.

🛌 Sleeping

Trevayne Farm CAMPGROUND £
(☑01834-813402; www.trevaynefarm.co.uk; Monkstone; sites per tent/campervan £18/28; ⊙Easter-Oct; ⊞) Based on a working 40-hectare permaculture farm, this large clifftop site has beautiful sea views and two separate fields so back-to-basics campers can avoid the looming motorhomes. Perfect, secluded Monkstone Beach feels like the farm's private water frontage, and it's just a mile south of central Saundersfoot via the coast path, or 2 miles by road.

Cliff House B&B ££
(☑01834-813931; www.cliffhousebbsaundersfoot. co.uk; Wogan Tce; s £80-90, d £100-120; ☎) It's well worth lugging your bags up the short but steep road from the town centre to this wonderful little Victorian-era B&B. There are five light, bright rooms, and the two on the top have glorious sea views. A guest lounge keeps the vibe relaxed, and there's a handy communal fridge, DVD library and book exchange. Pembrokeshire produce stars at breakfast.

★St Brides Spa Hotel HOTEL £££
(☑01834-812304; www.stbridesspahotel.com; St Brides Hill; r from £190; ⓟ☎☒) Perched on headland with uplifting sea views, this stylishly contemporary spa hotel is one of Wales' finest. Seascapes hang on walls in the light-flooded rooms decked out in breezy blues and whites; the best have terraces overlooking the harbour. The spa is a huge draw, with its hydrotherapy infinity

pool, thermal suite and coast-themed treatments reaching from seaweed wraps to lava shell massages.

By night, you can see Saundersfoot twinkle when you dine on high at Cliff restaurant.

🍴 Eating

Cŵlbox STREET FOOD £
(www.cwlbox.com; Saundersfoot Beach; mains £9-12; ⊙10am-4pm Fri-Sun) The hippest joint on Saundersfoot beach bar none is this converted rice horse trailer, which dishes up terrific street food with a strong seafood slant when the weather permits. Stop by for the likes of crispy halloumi with skin-on fries, bang-bang prawns, popcorn cockle and shredded Tenby lobster with its own riff on mayo.

Cliff MODERN BRITISH ££
(☑01834-812304; www.stbridesspahotel.com; St Brides Hill; mains £16-30; ⊙6-9pm; ☎) Candles flicker and the views stretch for miles across Saundersfoot harbour and Carmarthen Bay from the dining room of this chic appendage to St Brides Spa Hotel (p174). Outstanding local produce, especially seafood, is finessed into modern British dishes such as scallops sliding decadently into confit lamb belly, celeriac and hazelnut, and tandoori spiced monkfish with crispy capers and charred baby leeks.

★Coast MODERN BRITISH £££
(☑01834-810800; www.coastsaundersfoot.co.uk; Coppet Hall Beach; mains £24-30, tasting menus £35-70; ⊙noon-2.15pm & 6-9pm Wed-Sun; ☒) The sea views are unbeatable at this curving, glass-fronted, sunlit restaurant, dreamily plonked on Coppet Hall Beach. The streamlined design is Scandi-style minimalist, and there's a great terrace for when the weather behaves. Head chef Fred Clapperton plays up locally foraged ingredients and sustainably sourced seafood in ingredient-led menus, delivered with skill and panache.

Dishes like salmon, oyster and cucumber, and brill, Indian spice, carrot and mussels are fresh and punchy, and the Welsh cheese selection is second to none.

ℹ Getting There & Away

Saundersfoot's request train stop is a mile from the centre of town. Direct services head to/from Swansea (£16.30, 1½ hours, seven

Tenby

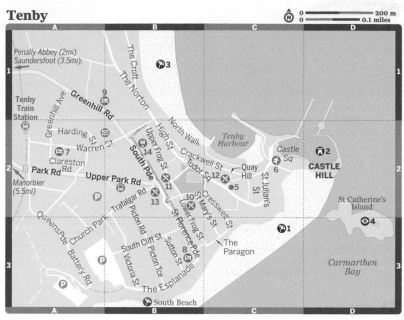

daily), Tenby (£3.80, eight minutes, nine daily) and Pembroke (£8.30, 32 minutes, nine daily).

Regular 381 buses head to/from Tenby (£2.50, 18 minutes), Narberth (£3.55, 34 minutes) and Haverfordwest (£5.10, one hour).

Tenby (Dinbych Y Pysgod)

POP 4696

Held high on a headland with magnificent sandy beaches either side, Tenby is the Pembrokeshire of a million postcards, with Georgian houses lavishly painted in pastels gathered around a harbour where fishing boats bob. Tenby's heart is still rimmed by Norman-built walls, funnelling holidaymakers through medieval streets lined with pubs, ice-cream parlours and gift shops.

Without the tackiness of the promenade-and-pier beach towns, it tastefully returns to being a sleepy little place in the low season. In summer it has a more boisterous, boozy, holiday-resort feel.

History

Tenby boomed in the 15th century as a centre for the textile trade, exporting cloth in exchange for salt and wine. Cloth making declined in the 18th century, but the town soon reinvented itself as a fashionable

Tenby

watering place. The arrival of the railway in the 19th century sealed its future as a resort, and William Paxton (owner of the Middleton estate in Carmarthenshire, now home to the National Botanic Garden of Wales) developed a saltwater spa here.

PEMBROKESHIRE COAST NATIONAL PARK

Britain's only true coastal national park, the astoundingly beautiful Pembrokeshire Coast National Park, founded in 1952, takes in the full sweep of the coast and its offshore islands, as well as the moorland Preseli Hills in the north. Pembrokeshire's sea cliffs and islands support huge breeding populations of sea birds, while seals, dolphins, porpoises and whales frequently splash around offshore.

Available at visitor centres, *Coast to Coast* (online at www.pembrokeshirecoast. wales), the free annual publication and app, gives the inside scoop on park attractions, a calendar of events and details of park-organised activities, including guided walks, themed tours, cycling trips, pony treks, island cruises, canoe trips and minibus tours. It's worth getting *Coast to Coast* for the tide tables alone – they're a necessity for many legs of the coast path.

Anxiety over a possible French invasion of the Milford Haven waterway led to the construction in 1869 of a fort on St Catherine's Island.

Among those who have taken inspiration or rest here are Horatio Nelson, Jane Austen, George Eliot, JMW Turner, Beatrix Potter and Roald Dahl.

◉ Sights

Castle Beach   BEACH
(🏊) The most central of Tenby's beaches, cliff-backed Castle Beach is a pretty curve of golden sand for a stroll, ice cream or sand-castle building session, with fine views over to St Catherine's Island. It's in the northern crook of the vast South Beach, a mile-and-a-half long swathe of dune-backed sand.

Castle Hill   CASTLE
Separating North Beach from Castle Beach, this modest headland is capped by the scant remains of Tenby's 11th-century Norman castle. On the very top is a large memorial to Prince Albert (captioned 'Albert Dda', meaning Albert the Good). The breezy views along the coast and out to sea make it a prime spot for a picnic.

St Catherine's Island   ISLAND
(www.saintcatherinesisland.co.uk; adult/child £5/2.50; ⊙ late Mar-Dec) At low tide you can walk across the sand to little St Catherine's Island, but it's a long, cold wait if you get trapped by the tide – check tide tables online. The Victorian fort on the island is open to the public, but the exhibition is a half-hearted attempt to explain its history (save your money and enjoy the view from the outside).

North Beach   BEACH
(🏊) A broad arc of sand that is particularly appealing at low tide, Tenby's North Beach is bookended at one end by cliffs and at the other by the harbour. It's defining feature is the Goskar rock.

☞ Tours

Tenby Boat Trips   CRUISE
(☏ 07980-864509; www.tenbyboattrips.co.uk; Tenby Harbour; ⊙ Apr-Oct; 🏊) This boat trip operator runs seal safari cruises (adult/child £18/10) around monastic Caldey Island in search of Atlantic grey seals. The Caldey and St Margaret's cruise (adult/child £15/8) takes in impressive cliffs and caverns that are home to thousands of seabirds, including puffins, razorbills, cormorants and gannets. See the website for times and bookings.

Tenby Watersports   WATER SPORTS
(☏ 07826-306566; www.tenbywatersports.co. uk/kayak-hire.html; Tenby Harbour; 🏊) This water-sports provider offers kayak and paddleboard hire (£12 to £15 per hour) as well as action-based activities such as 30-minute RIB rides (£15).

Guided Tours Wales   WALKING
(☏ 01834-845841; www.guidedtourswales.co.uk; adult/child £6.50/4, private tour £65; ⊙ Easter-Oct) Marion Davies brings Tenby's history to life with a variety of guided town tours. Adults with an interest in history will get a great insight into the town's past from the Story of Tenby walk, while families will enjoy the tales of smugglers and shipwrecks on the Pirates tour, and those of fairies, apparitions and witches on the Ghost Walk. See the website for times and dates.

✨ Festivals & Events

Tenby Arts Festival　　PERFORMING ARTS
(📞01834-845277;　www.tenbyartsfest.co.uk;
🕐late Sep) A week-long celebration in a variety of venues around town, the annual arts fest features everything from poetry readings by Caldey Island monks to sandcastle competitions. Expect classical concerts, talks on seaweed, piano recitals and Tenby's fine male voice choir in between.

🛏 Sleeping

Coach　　B&B ££
(📞01834-842210; www.coachhousetenby.co.uk; 11 Deer Park; d/f from £70/85; 🛜) Standing head and shoulders above most B&Bs in Tenby, the Coach extends the warmest of welcomes in a lovingly restored Victorian building. The cosy rooms have plaid throws, plenty of homey touches and pops of bright colour, and a generous breakfast is included.

Panorama　　HOTEL ££
(📞01834-844976; www.panoramahotel.co.uk; The Esplanade; d £135; 🛜) Overlooking Tenby's south beach, the Panorama is the pink slice in a pastel row of Victorian town houses. The convivial, family-run hotel has eight guest rooms with a dash of old-school style, some with chintzy flock wallpaper and flouncy curtains. Bathrooms could do with an update. Try to snag a front room with sea view.

Langdon Villa Guest House　　B&B ££
(📞01834-849467; www.langdonguesthousetenby. co.uk; 3 Warren St; r £68-78; 🛜) Right in the heart of town and just a couple of minutes' walk from the beach, this traditional and very comfortable B&B has tasteful decor, great breakfasts (vegetarian on request), and incredibly friendly and accommodating owners.

⭐ Penally Abbey　　HOTEL £££
(📞01834-843033; www.penally-abbey.com; Penally; r from £165; 🅿🛜🐾) One of Pembrokeshire's most alluring escapes, this ivy-wreathed fantasy of a Strawberry Gothic country house sits on a hillside amid acres of gardens and woodland, with soul-stirring views across Carmarthen Bay. Rooms blend calm colours and contemporary style with period charm, arched windows, embroidered white bedspreads and espresso machines. Built on the site of an ancient abbey in the village of Penally, it is 2 miles southwest of Tenby along the A4139.

For romance, top billing surely goes to the superior double with four-poster bed and dreamy views across the bay to Caldey Island. The country house's restaurant, Rhosyn (p178), is well suited for special occasions, too.

🍴 Eating & Drinking

Tenby's Fish & Chips　　FISH & CHIPS £
(Trafalgar Rd; mains £6-8; 🕐4-8.30pm Mon-Sat; 🍴) For a fresh-as-it-comes fish-and-chip supper down by the seafront, pop into Tenby's. Besides all the usual classics, it has a menu for children.

Billycan　　BISTRO ££
(📞01834-842172;　www.billycan-tenby.co.uk; Lower Frog St; mains £10-16; 🕐9am-midnight; 🍴) This family-friendly, bistro-style place is one of the better picks in the heart of town, with a pleasingly relaxed vibe. Opt for a window seat and dig into the likes of piri-piri roast chicken, burgers, pies, seafood platters and fish and chips. Produce is sourced locally. It also does an impressive Sunday roast.

Should you fancy staying the night, upstairs has been given over to a nouveau-rustic guesthouse with boutique flair (doubles £110 to £130).

Blue Ball Restaurant　　INTERNATIONAL ££
(📞01834-843038; www.theblueballrestaurant. co.uk; Upper Frog St; mains £11-21; 🕐1-8pm Tue-Sat, noon-2pm Sun) Polished wood, old timber beams and exposed brickwork create a rustic atmosphere in this cosy restaurant. The menu makes good use of local produce in everything from Asian-influenced dishes such as spicy Thai-style chicken to Pembrokeshire lobster with garlic aioli and new potatoes, and moules-frites.

Plantagenet House　　MODERN BRITISH £££
(📞01834-842350; www.plantagenettenby.co. uk; Quay Hill; mains lunch £10-12, dinner £25-28; 🕐noon-2.30pm & 6-9pm, reduced hours in winter; ✏🍴) Atmosphere-wise, this place sure has the wow factor, ramping up the romance with cheek-by-jowl tables and candlelight. Tucked down an alley in Tenby's oldest house, parts of which date to the 10th century, it's dominated by an immense 12th-century Flemish chimney hearth. Tenby-caught fish, seafood and lo-

cal organic beef are seasoned with freshly picked herbs, and the wine list is second to none.

Rhosyn

GASTRONOMY £££

(☑ 01834-843033; www.penally-abbey.com; Penally; mains £25-31; ⊙ 2-4.30pm & 6.30-9pm Wed-Sat) At Strawberry Gothic country house Penally Abbey (p177), Rhosyn is perfect afternoon tea, date night or romantic dinner material. The lavishly muralled, chandelier-lit dining room is a riotously romantic backdrop for food prepared with the seasons and local sourcing in mind. Expect artistically presented taste sensations such as pan-fried scallops with Carmarthen ham and crispy bacon and salt-aged steak with roast mushroom and onion jam.

★ SandBar

BAR

(☑ 01834-844068; www.tenbybrewingco.com; The Mews, Upper Frog St; ⊙ 11am-11pm Tue-Sun) The coolest kid on Tenby's block by a long shot, this retro-hip bar always has a great buzz and mellow sound track. It's the baby of Tenby Brewing Co, so you'll find a cracking assortment of craft beers, including tropical ones like Son of a Beach and Yeah Mango, which pair brilliantly with delicious street food from the Cŵlbox (p174) pop up.

There's a cute courtyard terrace for summer imbibing.

ℹ Getting There & Away

BUS

The **bus station** (Upper Park Rd) is next to the tourist office on Upper Park Rd.

Tenby's direct bus connections include two services per day to/from Narberth (£5, 45 minutes), regular 381 buses to/from Saundersfoot (£2.50, 17 minutes), the hourly 349 to/from Manorbier (£3.60, 19 minutes) and Pembroke (£4.30, 48 minutes), and the hourly 381 to/from Haverfordwest (£5.25, 1¼ hours).

National Express (p333) coaches head to/from Swansea (£9.20, 1½ hours, two daily), Cardiff (£19, 3½ hours, one direct daily), Birmingham (£42, six hours, one direct daily) and London (£32, seven hours, one direct daily).

CAR

If you come in high season, expect to pay for parking. There are several multistorey car parks dotted around the centre charging £4 per day.

TRAIN

There are direct trains to/from Pembroke (£6, 22 minutes, nine daily), Narberth (£5.40, 21 minutes, nine daily), Swansea (£16.80, two hours, seven daily) and Cardiff (£28.20, three hours, seven daily).

Manorbier (Maenorbŷr)

POP 1327

Capped off by a high-and-mighty medieval castle, Manorbier (man-er-*beer*) is a little village of leafy, twisting lanes that curl down to a 12th-century Norman church. Its beach is a gorgeous buttery scoop of sand, backed by dunes and cliffs and pounded by waves that attract surfers. If it's busy, walk a couple of pretty miles west along the coast path to deliciously remote and tranquil Swanlake Bay, where low tide reveals a fine sweep of sand.

A COTTAGE OF YOUR OWN

Pembrokeshire has a raft of self-catering cottages that make a terrific base for a longer stay in the area.

Quality Cottages (www.qualitycottages.co.uk) Has an excellent range of cottages throughout Pembrokeshire.

Coast & Country Holidays (☑ 01239-801580; www.welsh-cottages.co.uk) Holiday digs in well-kept cottages throughout the area.

Coastal Cottages (☑ 01437-765765; www.coastalcottages.uk) An extensive portfolio of Pembrokeshire cottages.

National Trust Cottages (www.nationaltrust.org.uk/holidays) Characterful cottages big on historic charm – from former dairies to converted granaries.

Welsh Country Cottages (☑ 03452-688734; www.welsh-country-cottages.co.uk) A collection of mostly rural cottages across Pembrokeshire.

◉ Sights

Manorbier Castle
CASTLE

(☑ 01834-871394; www.manorbiercastle.co.uk; adult/child £5.50/3; ☺ 10am-4pm Apr-Sep; ☞)
Every inch the medieval castle dream with its sturdy battlements and turrets, this Norman fortification was the birthplace of Giraldus Cambrensis (Gerald of Wales; 1146–1223), one of the country's greatest scholars and patriots. The 12th- to 19th-century castle buildings are grouped around a pretty landscaped garden. Looks familiar? That's perhaps because the castle starred in the 2003 film *I Capture the Castle*.

Medieval music plays in the Great Hall and there's a murky dungeon, a smuggler's secret passage and a tableaux of wax figures in period costume. More impressive, however, are the coastal views from the turrets.

King's Quoit
TOMB

This simple neolithic dolmen, fashioned from slabs of rock, has sat here overlooking shell-shaped Manorbier Bay since around 3000 BC. The enormous capstone is supported by an earth bank and two small sidestones. To find it, head to the beach at Manorbier and turn left onto the coast path. You will see the dolmen before you round the headland.

⊨ Sleeping & Eating

Manorbier YHA
HOSTEL £

(☑ 0345-371 9031; www.yha.org.uk; campsite per person from £16, camping pod/r from £75/49; P 🛜) Looking like a cross between a space station and a motorway diner, this futuristic ex-Ministry of Defence building is 1.5 miles east of Manorbier, close to Skrinkle Haven's fabulously wild beach. It's a gloriously remote spot, with private rooms, family-sized camping pods and bell tents. Camping and dorms were not available at the time of writing.

Beach Break
CAFE £

(☑ 01834-871709; Manorbier House; snacks & light bites £4-7; ☺ 9am-4pm; ☞) This breezy blue-fronted coastal cafe is a delight. Inside it is big on rustic charm, with exposed stone, beams and cheek-by-jowl tables. When the sun's out there's a lovely garden. Stop by for breakfast, a light lunch or – best of all – tea with homemade cake. There are gluten-free and children's options available.

ⓘ Getting There & Away

Manorbier is 5.5 miles southwest of Tenby. It's served by bus 349, which heads to Tenby (£3.50, 19 minutes), Pembroke (£3.60, 30 minutes), Pembroke Dock (£4.20, 43 minutes) and Haverfordwest (£5.80, 1½ hours) hourly, except on Sunday.

There's also a train station, a mile north of the village, with direct services to Swansea (£16.80, 2¼ hours, five daily), Carmarthen (£10.40, one hour, seven daily), Narberth (£8.30, 35 minutes, eight daily), Tenby (£3.60, 10 minutes, nine daily) and Pembroke (£4, 11 minutes, nine daily).

Stackpole (Stagbwll)

The villages of Stackpole and Bosherston bookend the National Trust–run **Stackpole Estate** (NT; ☑ 01646-661359; www.nationaltrust. org.uk; ☺ dawn-dusk; FREE), a vast, formerly aristocratic property encompassing beaches, woodland and lakes. The coastline heading west from the estate is some of the most ruggedly beautiful in the entire country, with sheer cliffs dropping 50m into churning, thrashing surf. Unfortunately, much of it lies within the army's Castlemartin firing range and it's regularly closed to the public.

◉ Sights

Stackpole Quay
HARBOUR

The dinky harbour of Stackpole Quay marks the point where pink and purple sandstone gives way to the massive grey limestone that dominates the South Pembrokeshire coast from here to Freshwater West. There's a large car park and a good tearoom, and in the warmer months you can go kayaking or coasteering here. The quay itself isn't well signposted; instead look for signs pointing to the Boathouse.

★ Barafundle Bay
BEACH

(☞) Regularly topping polls as one of Britain's most sublime beaches, pinch-yourself-pretty Barafundle Bay is a highly scenic 10-minute walk south along the coast path from Stackpole Quay (turn right) or half an hour from the Stackpole Estate car park. Enveloped by dramatic, ragged cliffs and flanked by dunes, the beach is a perfect arc of golden sand sliding into clear turquoise sea. Avoid summer weekends when crowds descend. Barafundle is at its peaceful best in the low season.

If you're up for more walking, follow the coast path south of the beach out onto **Stackpole Head** with its impressive cliffs and rock arches. It's a 1.6-mile (30- to 40-minute) return hike.

Bosherston Lily Ponds   LAKE

(📷) `FREE` Criss-crossed by a network of footpaths and wooden bridges, these ponds are a serene spot for a dappled-shade stroll. The lilies bloom in June and July but the surrounding woodlands brim with wildlife year-round. The ponds are home to otters, herons and more than 20 species of dragonfly, while the ruins of the manor house are inhabited by the greater horseshoe bat.

The main car park for the ponds is in Bosherston village, but walking trails connect them to Broad Haven South (1 mile, 30 minutes) and Barafundle Bay (4 miles, 1¾ hours).

Broad Haven South   BEACH

(📷) A mile southeast of Bosherston village, this magnificent golden crescent of beach is backed by sand dunes and framed by grey limestone cliffs and pointed sea stacks. Most spectacular of all is Church Rock, so named because it resembles a submerged church at high tide. The beach was formed in the 1860s by the erection of the dam that created the Bosherston Lily Ponds.

St Govan's Chapel   CHURCH

(📞01646-662367) One of the most dramatic sights on this extraordinary stretch of coast is this 13th-century hermit's chapel, wedged into a slot in the cliffs, just out of reach of the sea. Steps hacked into the rock lead down through the empty shell of the structure and onto the rocks below, where there's a particularly picturesque rock arch, perpetually pounded by the waves.

The chapel is named for a 6th-century Irish preacher who, according to legend, was being pursued by pirates when the cliff conveniently opened and enfolded him, protecting him from his attackers. In gratitude, he built the original chapel and lived here until his death in 586.

St Govan's is well signposted from Bosherston and there's a car park at the top of the cliffs. The road to St Govan's passes through MOD land and is closed at certain times (call ahead to check it is open).

Huntsman's Leap   LANDMARK

A spectacular gash in the cliffs with near-vertical walls, Huntsman's Leap is famed as one of Britain's best sea-cliff climbing locations. The sheer sides are often dotted with rock climbers and it makes a good short walk if you're in the area. Park at the St Govan's Head car park and walk west along the coast path for about 10 minutes to get here.

Elegug Stacks   LANDMARK

Dramatic in the extreme, these two isolated pillars of rock rise abruptly from the sea. The rocks are an important nesting site for guillemots and kittiwakes, which can be seen throughout spring and early summer. Nearby is the **Green Bridge of Wales**, the biggest natural arch in the country. The access road to the Stack Rocks car park is off the B4319 between Stackpole and Castlemartin.

🛏 Sleeping & Eating

Stackpole Under the Stars   CAMPGROUND £

(📞01646-683167; www.stackpoleunderthestars. wales; North Lodge, Cheriton; 2-person sites from £25, glamping £110-130, minimum 3-night stay) Surrounded by pretty wildflower meadows, this glamping site is a terrific family find. Pitch a tent here or opt for more space and luxury in handmade yurts, glamping pods and safari tents complete with picnic areas and fire pits for gazing up at the bright night skies. There's a tiny shop on site, well stocked with Pembrokeshire produce and essentials.

Stackpole Inn   PUB FOOD ££

(📞01646-672324; www.stackpoleinn.co.uk; Jasons Cnr, Stackpole; mains £10-24; ⏱noon-8pm Mon-Sat, noon-3pm & 5-8pm Sun; 🅿🛜📷) This wonderful country pub is a real treat on a wet day, with a wood-burning stove and beamed ceilings, while the garden is perfect for a summer's pint. The food bigs up seasonal Welsh in dishes like perfectly pink pan-roasted rump of lamb with pearl barley, charred onions, baby carrots and locally foraged wild garlic. See the specials board for the catch of the day.

If you fancy staying overnight in the area and exploring the coast, there are four appealingly bright, wood-floored, seaside-themed rooms (singles/doubles from £75/120).

PEMBROKESHIRE ADVENTURES

With all that wild, rugged coastline, Pembrokeshire will have you itching to leap into the water (albeit in a wetsuit!). All across the region you'll find sailing, surfing, windsurfing, kite-surfing, diving and kayaking operators, as well as Pembrokeshire's very own home-grown invention, **coasteering**. A combination of rock climbing, gully scrambling, cave exploration, wave riding and cliff jumping, this demanding activity is the mainstay of the local adventure-sports scene.

The notorious **Bitches** in Ramsey Sound are known as one of Britain's best white-water play spots. This tidal race offers massive whirlpools, eddies, big wave trains and stoppers, and standing waves on higher tides. It's a dangerous place to play, however, so consider hiring a guide for your first attempt.

ⓘ Getting There & Away

The Coastal Cruiser (p183) stops at Stackpole Quay, Stackpole village, Bosherston and Broad Haven South, with additional stops at St Govan's Head and Elegug Stack Rocks on the weekends.

When the army's Castlemartin firing range is in use, the roads heading south to the coast at St Govan's Head, Stack Rocks, and the section of coast path that links them, are usually closed. Check the firing times online at www.gov.uk (search for Castlemartin). Red flags indicate that firing is taking place.

Angle

Out on its lonesome and all the more enticing for it, the village of Angle overlooks Wales' largest estuary and one of the world's deepest natural harbours. The big draw for beachgoers and surfers is wave-pummelled Freshwater West, but there's also the pretty horseshoe-shaped cove of West Angle Bay, peering across the mouth of Milford Haven to St Anne's Head. The peninsula offers terrific coastal walks with lots of rock pools to explore.

If you're walking the coast path, consider catching the Coastal Cruiser bus from Angle to Dale to skip two grim days passing the giant oil refineries lining Milford Haven.

Freshwater West   BEACH

Wild and windblown, this 2-mile strand of golden sand and silver shingle backed by acres of dunes is Wales' best surf beach, sitting wide open to the Atlantic rollers. But beware – although it's great for surfing, big waves, powerful rips and quicksand make it dangerous for swimming. Lifeguards patrol the beach from mid-June to August; swim only between the flags.

If it looks familiar, it may be because it was the setting for Dobby's sad demise in *Harry Potter and the Deathly Hallows.* Key scenes from Ridley Scott's *Robin Hood* were also filmed here.

★ Café Môr   STREET FOOD £

(☑ 07919 192771; www.beachfood.co.uk; Freshwater West; light bites £4.50-12; ◷ 9am-4pm Mon-Fri, 8.30am-5pm Sat & Sun) In the beach car park at Freshwater West, Café Môr is the world's first solar-powered, mobile-converted fishing boat and seaweed kitchen, headed up by passionate forager Jonathan Williams. The food truck weaves locally foraged ingredients into its menu, with takeaway treats like brekkie rolls with egg, cheese and laverbread, lobster rolls with Welsh Sea black butter, and fish butties with homemade pickles and seaweed-chilli sauce.

ⓘ Getting There & Away

The seasonal Coastal Cruiser (p183) bus stops at Freshwater West, Angle and West Angle Bay.

Pembroke (Penfro)

POP 7552

Pembroke is not much more than a single street of neat Georgian and Victorian houses guarded by a whopping great castle. This mighty fortress fell only once – in 1648, following a 48-day siege by Oliver Cromwell during the English Civil War. After this, the town was stripped of its encircling walls.

Nowadays more people live in Pembroke Dock, a sprawling expanse of grim housing abutting a commercial port, just down the hill from the historic town. Aside from a 19th-century Martello tower in the harbour, there's nothing to see down here.

Pembroke

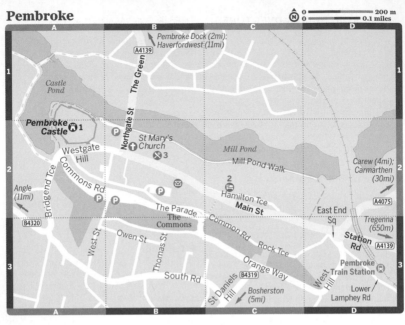

Pembroke

◉ Top Sights
1 Pembroke Castle A2

🛏 Sleeping
2 Woodbine C2

✖ Eating
3 Food at Williams B2

◉ Sights

★ Pembroke Castle
CASTLE
(☏ 01646-681510; www.pembroke-castle.co.uk; Main St; adult/child £7/6; ⊙ 10am-5pm; ♿) This spectacular and forbidding castle was the home of the earls of Pembroke for over 300 years and the birthplace of Henry VII, the first Tudor king. A fort was established here in 1093 by Arnulph de Montgomery, but most of the present buildings date from the 13th century. It's a great place for both kids and adults to explore – wall walks and passages run from tower to tower, and there are vivid exhibitions detailing the castle's history.

Free guided tours are offered daily; check the website for times. Falconry displays and costumed re-enactments are held in summer.

🛏 Sleeping & Eating

Woodbine
B&B ££
(☏ 01646-686338; www.pembrokebedandbreakfast.co.uk; 84 Main St; s/d £65/85; ☎) This well-kept, forest-green Georgian town house presents a smart face to Pembroke's main drag. The three pretty guest rooms are tastefully furnished, with original fireplaces, sash windows and bold colour schemes. A 17th-century Welsh slate floor and inglenook fireplace grace the breakfast room.

Tregenna
B&B ££
(☏ 01646-621525; www.tregennapembroke.co.uk; 7 Upper Lamphey Rd; s/d £50-80, d £65-90; 🅿️☎) If your image of B&Bs is tainted by creaky-floored, chintz-filled cottages run by cranky empty-nesters, prepare to have it challenged by this large, friendly, modern pick on Pembroke's eastern edge. There's a large, sun-filled breakfast room at the rear.

Food at Williams
CAFE £
(☏ 01646-689990; 18 Main St; light bites £3.50-8, mains £8.50-16; ⊙ 9am-3pm Mon-Sat, from 10am Sun; ☎) This cheerful cafe lodges in a funkily converted Georgian town house, now sporting claret-red walls, wood floors, exposed stone and a vintage wood-burning stove. Pop in for a breakfast special, like

eggy bread with maple syrup and streaky bacon, baguettes with hummus, halloumi and beetroot, and mains like gourmet burgers with brie and aioli.

ℹ Getting There & Away

BOAT

Irish Ferries (☑ 08717 300 400; www.irish-ferries.com; pedestrian/car & driver £32/122) has two sailings a day on the four-hour route between Pembroke Dock and Rosslare in the southeast of Ireland.

BUS

There are five direct 349 buses to/from Tenby (£4.30, 48 minutes, hourly), Manorbier (£3.60, 28 minutes, hourly), Pembroke Dock (£2.30, 16 minutes, hourly) and Haverfordwest (£4.90, 57 minutes, hourly). The seasonal Coastal Cruiser (p183) loops in both directions between Pembroke, Angle, Freshwater West, Bosherston and Stackpole, terminating at Pembroke Dock. National Express (p333) coaches head to/from London (from £22.50, 6½ hours, daily).

TRAIN

Trains stop in both Pembroke and Pembroke Dock. There are direct services to/from Cardiff (£28.20, 3¼ hours, daily), Swansea (£16.80, 2½ hours, seven daily), Narberth (£9.20, 43 minutes, eight daily) and Tenby (£6, 21 minutes, nine daily).

Narberth (Arberth)

POP 2489

An arty little hub of independent shops, cafes, restaurants and galleries, Narberth is a South Pembrokeshire market town full of history and charisma. Though light on standout sights (ruined Norman castle aside), it's nevertheless worth visiting for its burgeoning food scene and upbeat vibe, with butchers, delis, antique shops and boutiques lining its pretty pastel-painted streets.

◉ Sights

Narberth Museum   MUSEUM
(Amgueddfa Arberth; ☑ 01834-860500; www.narberthmuseum.co.uk; Bonded Stores, Church St; adult/child £4.50/1; ☺ 10am-5pm Thu-Sat; ☝) Housed in a wonderfully atmospheric restored bonded-stores building, this museum presents a fascinating romp through local history. You can learn about medieval siege warfare and Narberth Castle through models and interactive games,

PEMBROKESHIRE COASTAL BUS SERVICES

The hiker's best friend, Pembrokeshire's coastal buses operate on five main routes three times a day in each direction from May to September. For the remainder of the year the **Strumble Shuttle** (404, Fishguard–St Davids) and **Poppit Rocket** (405, Cardigan–Newport) operate two services a day on Thursday only, and the **Puffin Shuttle** (400, St Davids–Marloes) on Wednesday only. For timetables, see www.pembrokeshire.gov.uk or pick up a copy of the national park's *Coast to Coast* magazine.

walk historic streets, or listen to Welsh folk stories in the storytelling chair. There are lots of hands-on activities and dress-ups for children, plus a museum shop brimming with local crafts. It doubles as Narberth's tourist office.

⚔ Festivals & Events

Narberth Food Festival   FOOD & DRINK
(www.narberthfoodfestival.com; ☺ last weekend Sep) Narberth pulls out all the foodie stops for this small but friendly celebration of Welsh produce, good wine and the joy of cooking. The line-up offers everything from master classes and tutored tastings to free cookery demonstrations, workshops and talks, food stalls, live music, street theatre and children's activities.

🛏 Sleeping

Max & Caroline's   GUESTHOUSE £
(☑ 01834-861835; www.maxandcarolines.com; 2a St James St; s/d/f £55/75/95; 🛜) Why bother serving breakfast when you're situated directly above Plum Vanilla (p184), Narberth's best cafe? That's the philosophy at this excellent British- and German-run guesthouse, where the rooms are handsomely decorated with home-style flourishes – pastels, florals and coolly revamped vintage furniture.

Canaston Oaks   GUESTHOUSE ££
(☑ 01437-541254; www.canastonoaks.co.uk; Canaston Bridge; d £99-135, ste £120-190, f £189-260; 🅿🛜) 🏆 With rolling country views, this incredibly welcoming family-run bolthole on a farm is based on a refurbished rural longhouse, with cottage-style

CAREW

This sleepy little village situated on the tidal reaches of the River Carew between Tenby and Pembroke is completely dwarfed by its whooping great Norman castle. It's a pretty slice of rural Wales, with a sprinkling of big-hitter historic sights to explore.

Looming romantically over the River Carew and photogenically reflected in the glassy water, the formidable **Carew Castle** (☎ 01646-651782; www.carewcastle.com; adult/child £6/4; ⊙ 11am-4pm; ℗ ♿) often elicits gasps of wonder. The rambling limestone ruins range from functional 12th-century fortifications to Elizabethan country house, and there are plenty of towers, wall walks and dank basements to explore. A summer line-up of events includes archery, falconry, battle re-enactments and open-air theatre. Time slots and tickets need to be pre-booked online.

The mill at the castle is the only intact mill of this kind in Wales. The incoming tide would be trapped in a pond, which was then released through sluice gates to turn the waterwheels. For 400 years until 1937, the mill ground corn for the castle community, although the present building only dates from the early 19th century.

Near the castle entrance is the 11th-century **Carew Cross**. Covered in intricate Celtic carvings and standing 4m tall, it's one of the grandest of its kind.

Opposite Carew Castle, fabulously cosy **Carew Inn** (☎ 01646-651267; www.carewinn. co.uk; 1 Picton Terrace; mains £12-16; ⊙ 11am-11pm; ☑ ♿) has a timber-lined bar with a roaring fire to ward off the winter cold and an attractive beer garden with fortress views for summer days. The food is good old-fashioned pub grub (homemade pies and the like). It's also an appealing place to spend the night, with luxe self-catering cottages (from £90) full of period character.

rooms, suites and apartments built in local stone and timber gathered around a Celtic-cross-shaped garden. Lots of loving detail has gone into the bright, spacious, contemporary rooms. Top billing goes to those with spa baths and the rustic Barn Suites with conservatories for stargazing.

Breakfast is a wonderful spread, with Welsh jams, yoghurt and homemade fruit compote, fresh sourdough bread and proper coffee. Besides cooked options, you could opt for the most decadent porridge, made with brown sugar, cream and a dash of Penderyn whisky.

★ Grove of Narberth   HOTEL £££

(☎ 01834-860915; www.thegrove-narberth.co.uk; Molleston; r from £170; ℗ ☎) 🍽 Perhaps the escape of your wildest country dreams, the multiple award-winning Grove of Narberth has a pinch of timeless magic and luxury about it from the moment you glide up the drive. Its interiors are a clever warp-and-weft of Georgian elegance, Arts and Crafts flair, contemporary style and Welsh artwork, photography, furniture and pottery. The 28-acre grounds make for a delightful romp.

Spend a night or two here and you might not want to venture far. Go for walks in wildflower meadows and grounds plumed

with ancient oaks and beeches, take afternoon tea on the terrace, or grab a gourmet picnic and head for the hills. Evenings are given over to expertly crafted cocktails in the lounge, followed by dinner in the chicly relaxed Artisan Rooms or in the Fernery (p185), the pinnacle of fine dining in these parts.

🍴 Eating

Narberth's butchers, delis and cafes proudly tout their local sources.

Plum Vanilla   CAFE £

(☎ 01834-862762; 2a St James St; mains £8-10; ⊙ 9am-5pm Mon-Sat; ☑) Adorned with technicolor chandeliers and vividly painted walls, this friendly little bohemian cafe has a loyal local clientele who flock here for the cooked breakfasts, homemade soups, interesting wholefoods and salads, daily specials and luscious desserts (the salted-caramel vegan cheesecake is wonderful). You may have to wait for a table at lunchtime.

Fire & Ice   ICE CREAM £

(☎ 01834-861995; www.fireandicewales.co.uk; 65 St James St; ⊙ 10am-5pm Mon-Sat; ☑) 🍽 This cracking little bottle shop whips up the finest gelato in town, made with Welsh organic milk and Welsh organic double cream, with punchy flavours like blood orange and basil and spiced ginger apple. Vegan and dairy-free sorbets are also available. It's also a great place to stock up on Welsh craft beers, ciders, gins and spirits.

Ultracomida   SPANISH ££

(☎ 01834-861491; www.ultracomida.co.uk; 7 High St; tapas £5-9; ⊙ 10am-6pm Mon-Sat; ⊞) The aroma of cured meats, fine cheeses, olives and freshly baked bread hits you as you walk into the buzzy little deli and tapas bar. Stock up on supplies for a gourmet picnic or go for the delicious tapas. Welsh-influenced taste sensations include the likes of Swansea smoked salmon with Galician cream cheese and pickled cucumber.

Fernery   GASTRONOMY £££

(☎ 01834-860 915; www.thegrove-narberth.co.uk; 5-/10-course tasting menu £69/105; ⊙ 6.30-9pm Tue-Sat) One for special occasions or date-night decadence, this gourmet restaurant at the Grove of Narberth (p184) is a tucked-away delight. Ferns luxuriantly carpet the walls in the elegant, candlelit dining room. Tasting menus put creative riffs on local and kitchen-garden-grown produce, resulting in dishes as simply sophisticated as scallop with truffle and chive, and venison with blueberry, beetroot and pumpkin.

❶ Getting There & Around

Bus destinations include frequent services to/from Haverfordwest (£4.05, 21 minutes), Carmarthen (£5.35, 37 minutes), Saundersfoot (£3.55, 34 minutes), Tenby (£5, 45 minutes), and twice daily 430 services to Cardigan (£4.15, one hour).

There are good train connections to/from Newport (£33.30, 2¾ hours, seven daily), Cardiff (£28.20, 2½ hours, seven daily), Swansea (from £16.80, 1½ hours, eight daily), Tenby (£5.40, 20 minutes, nine daily) and Pembroke (£9.20, 48 minutes, eight daily).

Haverfordwest (Hwlffordd)

POP 12,042

A workaday town rather than a tourist hot spot, Haverfordwest is Pembrokeshire's main transport and shopping hub. Though it retains some fine Georgian buildings, many are in dire need of repair and it lacks the prettiness and historic atmosphere of most of its neighbours.

Founded as a fortified Flemish settlement by the Norman lord Gilbert de Clare in about 1110, its castle became the nucleus for a thriving market and its port remained important until the railway arrived in the mid-19th century.

◉ Sights

Today the Riverside Quay is the main focus of activity and home to an excellent farmers market with organic and local produce stalls every Friday from 9am to 2pm.

Haverfordwest Castle   CASTLE

(Castle St) The meagre ruins of Haverfordwest Castle consist of little more than three of its 13th-century walls. The castle survived an onslaught by Owain Glyndŵr in 1405, but according to one dubious local story it was abandoned by its Royalist garrison during the English Civil War, when its soldiers mistook a herd of cows for Roundheads.

⊨ Sleeping & Eating

★ Slebech Park Estate   BOUTIQUE HOTEL ££

(☎ 01437-752000; www.slebech.co.uk; The Rhos; d from £85) Dreamily perched on the shores of an estuary and surrounded by 650 acres of wooded grounds, this stylishly converted Georgian manor is 5 miles east of Haverfordwest but a world away in spirit. The rooms are rustic chic, with high ceilings and arched windows (luxurious suites come with terraces and jetted tubs). Walled gardens and forest trails invite exploration outside.

Warmed by an open fire during the cold months, the highly atmospheric restaurant is one of the area's finest, with a menu that places the accent on organic home-grown and foraged ingredients.

Georges   CAFE £

(☎ 01437-766683; www.thegeorges.uk.com; 24 Market St; mains £5.50-15; ⊙ 10am-5.30pm Tue-Fri, to 11pm Sat; ⊞) Gargoyles on leashes guard the door of this trippy, hippy gift shop that leads a double life as an offbeat cafe. The Georges has cosy nooks of stained glass and candlelight, lanterns and fairy lights, along with a simple menu of home-cooked food swinging from steak and Guinness pie to Thai-style chicken curry.

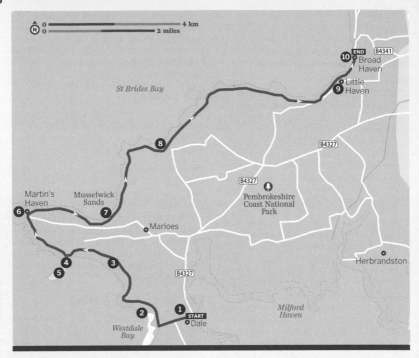

☆ Coastal Walk
Dale to Broad Haven

START DALE
END BROAD HAVEN
LENGTH 15.4 MILES; SIX HOURS

A wonderful but not too challenging walk along dramatic clifftops, this section of the Pembrokeshire Coast Path (PCP) is close to villages, bus routes and road access points, making it ideal for more leisurely walking but, particularly in midsummer, potentially busier than more remote sections of the path.

Start at ❶ **Dale** and cut across country to pick up the PCP in ❷ **Westdale Bay**. As you head up around the northern headland you'll skirt a disused WWII airfield before reaching the long curving stretch of beach at ❸ **Marloes Sands**. At the end of the beach you'll pass ❹ **Gateholm Island**, a major Iron Age Celtic settlement where the remains of 130 hut circles have been found. Although the island appears accessible at low tide, it is surrounded by slippery jagged rocks and steep cliffs. Walk on, though, and you'll soon pass the earthwork ramparts of a ❺ **promontory fort**. Atlantic storms batter this section of

coast and active erosion threatens the sheer red cliffs streaked with yellow algae.

Continue on, enjoying the views over Skomer and Skokholm islands, to ❻ **Martin's Haven**. This tiny harbour is the base for Skomer Island boat trips and the office of the Skomer Marine Nature Reserve, which has an interesting display on the underwater environment.

Around the headland the cliffs change from red to black, and after an hour you'll reach the deliciously wild ❼ **Musselwick Sands**. There are fine views over St Brides Bay and across to St Davids and Ramsey Island. ❽ **St Brides Haven** is a further 2 miles down the track, with the headland dominated by a Victorian faux-castle, once owned by the Barons of Kensington.

A reasonably easy 5-mile stretch leads to ❾ **Little Haven**, a pretty village with restaurants and B&Bs. It's separated by a rocky headland from ❿ **Broad Haven**; from the path you'll be able to assess the tide and decide whether to follow the busy road or cross via the beach.

ⓘ Information

Police Station (📞101; www.dyfed-powys.
police.uk; Merlin's Hill)
Withybush General Hospital (📞01437-
764545; www.wales.nhs.uk; Fishguard Rd)

ⓘ Getting There & Away

Direct buses head to Tenby (£5.80, 1¼ hours,
hourly), Pembroke (£4.90, 51 minutes,
half-hourly), St Davids (£3.30, 40 minutes, 10
daily), Carmarthen (one hour, three daily) and
Aberystwyth (£6.25, 3¼ hours, eight daily).
National Express (p333) coaches head to/from
London Victoria (£22.50, 7½ hours, daily).

There are direct trains to/from Newport
Gwent (from £33.30, three hours, 13 daily),
Cardiff (from £28.20, 2½ hours, nine daily),
Swansea (£17.30, 1½ hours, nine daily), Llanelli
(£17, one hour, nine daily) and Carmarthen
(£10.60, 38 minutes, nine daily).

Skomer, Skokholm & Grassholm Islands

Wales is at its wildest and most dramatic
best at these rocky islands, which lie in the
turbulent, tide-ripped waters at the south
end of St Brides Bay. In the nesting season,
these enchanting cliff-rimmed islands form
one of Britain's richest wildlife habitats, attracting more than half a million seabirds,
including guillemots, razorbills, puffins,
storm petrels and a significant colony of
Manx shearwaters.

While it was not possible to land on the islands at the time of research due to Covid-19
restrictions, boat trips to explore them from
the sea depart from Martins Haven.

⊙ Sights

★**Skomer**   ISLAND
(www.welshwildlife.org; ⊗Apr-Sep) Rimmed by
dramatic sea cliffs, Skomer is a real puffin
fest of an island, home to 24,000 individual puffins at the last count, as well as the
world's largest population of Manx shearwaters (350,000 pairs). Keep a close eye
out too for Atlantic grey seals down on the
rocks, which are especially plentiful during
pupping season (September), and porpoises and dolphins out at sea.

Skokholm   ISLAND
(📞01656-724100; www.welshwildlife.org; ⊗Apr-
Sep) 🏊 Hemmed in by cliffs of old red sandstone, this thrillingly wild, storm-battered
isle is capped off by a white lighthouse. The

marine nature reserve is seabird heaven,
with bays, gullies and cliffs that harbour
sizeable populations of Manx shearwaters,
storm petrels, puffins, razorbills and guillemots. Grey seals, porpoises and dolphins
can often be spotted too.

Grassholm   ISLAND
(🐦) 🏊 The furthest of the three outlying
islands off the coast of Marloes, Grassholm
is but a tiny speck of an island. On the approach by boat, the island looks white with
snow – in fact its white appearance comes
courtesy of its resident population of gannets (39,000 pairs at the last count), which
is one of Britain's largest. The island is
an RSPB reserve with a strict 'no landing'
policy.

☞ Tours

Dale Sailing   BOATING
(📞01646-603123; www.pembrokeshire-islands.
co.uk; ⊗Easter-Sep; 🐦) Dale Sailing is your
best bet for wildlife cruises and RIB safaris
to the islands. Its offers includes a one-hour
cruise around Skomer (adult/child £16/12)
in search of puffins, seals and more, a
sunset seabird spectacular (summer only)
around Skomer and Skokholm (adult/child
£20/16), and a two-hour Grassholm ganne-
try experience (£45/25). Advance bookings
are essential.

ⓘ Getting There & Away

The Puffin Shuttle (p183) heads to Marloe's
Haven, which is where the island cruises depart
from.

Little & Broad Haven

Shoehorned into the southern corner of St
Brides Bay, these two beaches are joined at
low tide but separated by a rocky headland
otherwise. Little Haven is the quainter of
the two, with a tiny shingle beach and a
low-key village vibe formed by a cluster of
pastel-painted holiday cottages and some
cracking pubs. The beach, however, is bigger and better at Broad Haven, backed by
tearooms, gift shops, and places selling
rubber rings, water wings and body boards.

🛏 Sleeping & Eating

Mill Haven Place   CAMPGROUND £
(📞01437-781633; www.millhavenplace.co.uk; Talbenny; yurts per weekend/week from £175/550,
cottages per week £450-1680) 🏊 A short stroll

from the serene cove of Mill Haven, this eco-aware camping and glamping site is decked out with bunting, brightly coloured tablecloths, solar-powered fairy lights and paper lanterns. There are two yurts (each with camp kitchen and fire pit) and a cool-but-compact mini gypsy wagon, plus a small cluster of whitewashed stone cottages. Talbenny is 1.4 miles west of Little Haven.

Anchor Guesthouse
GUESTHOUSE **££**
(☑01437-781476; www.anchorguesthouse.co.uk; Enfield Rd; d £90-100) Facing the beach in Broad Haven, this blue-fronted guesthouse commands mood-lifting views of the sea from many of its nine bright-and-breezy rooms, done out in greys, creams and blues. They are well geared up for families, and there's an Italian restaurant serving great homemade pizza (£9 to £13).

Lobster and Môr
CAFE **£**
(☑01437-781959; www.lobsterandmor.co.uk; Grove Pl; light bites £5.50-8.50; ⊙10am-4pm Tue-Sun) Live lobsters and crabs splash around at the back of this coolly nautical deli-cafe in Little Haven. You can buy them whole for a seafood feast or take away a delicious lobster brioche or crab sandwich. It also sells other picnic fixings, from local seaweed-infused ales and gins to Snowdonia cheeses, chilli jams and chocolate brownies. The nautical gift shop plays up local arts and crafts.

Saint Brides Inn
PUB FOOD **££**
(☑01437-781266; www.saintbridesinn.co.uk; St Brides Rd; mains £10-18; ⊙8am-11pm; 🖢) All blues, whites, beams and exposed stone, this cheery pub down by the front in Little Haven is as cosy as can be. A log fire burns in winter, while in summer the garden terrace hums with happy punters. Come for a pint and to dig into local seafood (lobster and crab in season), Welsh lamb and other pub-grub classics.

❶ Getting There & Away

The 311 bus connects Broad Haven with Haverfordwest (20 minutes, six daily except Sunday). The seasonal Puffin Shuttle (p183) stops in both Little and Broad Havens.

Newgale (Niwgwl)

Thrillingly wild, wind- and wave-battered Newgale is the biggest beach in St Brides Bay, a broad 2-mile-long ribbon of golden sand backed by pebbles and rimmed by cliffs honeycombed with caves. It's a cracking spot for beginner surfers, particularly on an incoming tide. As you pass over the bridge by the pub near the north end of Newgale, you're officially crossing the Landsker Line into North Pembrokeshire.

🏃 Activities

Newgale-Solva
WALKING
(🖢) Big sea views on repeat and briny breezes thrill on the 4-mile stretch of the Pembrokeshire Coast Path linking Newgale to Solva. Heading up and over the heather- and gorse-clad clifftops, the path reveals some incredible rock stacks, headlands, hidden coves and views of Ramsey Island.

Newsurf
WATER SPORTS
(☑01437-721398; www.newsurf.co.uk; ⊙10am-6pm; 🖢) Newgale is battered by some of Pembrokeshire's biggest waves. If you fancy hitting the surf, hire boards (£6/13 per hour/day), wetsuits (£5/12) or kayaks (£11/29 per two hours/day) here. It also offers 2½-hour group surfing lessons (£35).

Outer Reef Surf School
SURFING
(☑01646-680070; www.outerreefsurfschool.com; from £35) Learn to surf at Newgale Sands or Manorbier before hitting the big breaks at Freshwater West. Stand-up paddleboarding also offered.

🛏 Sleeping

Asheston Eco Barns
CABIN **££**
(☑01348-831781; www.eco-barns.co.uk; Penycwm; per week from £775; 🅿🛜) 🌿 With dreamy views across rolling Pembrokeshire countryside, these five beautifully converted barns (including an old cart house and cow shed) have tons of charm. They have impeccable eco credentials, too, running almost entirely on renewable energy. Welcome hampers with local produce are a nice touch. It's terrific for families, with a playground, a wildlife pond and acres of fields and woodland to explore.

★ Roch Castle
CASTLE **£££**
(☑01437-725566; www.rochcastle.com; Roch; r £240-270; 🅿🛜) It's not every night you get to stay in a 12th-century Norman castle. Perched on a crag providing far-reaching views across farmland and out to sea, this luxurious bolthole bears the slickly minimalist hallmark of Welsh-born architect Keith Griffiths. A spiral staircase twists up

from the lobby to zen-like rooms decorated in whites, dove greys and charcoals, with bespoke ceramics and rich fabrics.

All rooms have been designed with a razor-sharp eye for detail, and come with iPod docks, espresso makers, bathrobes and aromatherapy-infused toiletries. There are nods to the castle's history in the original details and design: from the arch stone windows in the guest lounge (where you can sip a drink from the honesty bar) to specially commissioned tapestries and the castle's foundations in the lobby.

❶ Getting There & Away

Both the Puffin Shuttle (p183) and bus 411 between St Davids, Solva and Haverfordwest (10 daily except Sunday) stop here.

Marloes Sands

In the southernmost crook of St Brides Bay, Marloes Sands is wonderfully wild, with its mile-long scoop of sand and pebbles, sandstone cliffs and jagged rock formations. The tang of salt in the air and the wind ripping across the ocean have all the senses on high alert. At low tide you can go rock-pooling and fossil hunting. If you strike out on the 5-mile walk that rims the peninsula, heading through pristine heathland and over the clifftops, bring binoculars and keep an eye out for marine- and birdlife. Peregrines, choughs, meadow pipits, stonechats and puffins can be spotted, as can dolphins, seals (and their pups, in autumn) and porpoises with any luck.

Heading south instead of north takes you on a phenomenally beautiful 12-mile, six-hour walk to the pretty coastal village of Dale, taking in lighthouse-topped St Ann's Head and the magnificently secluded beaches of Mill Bay and Watwick.

Clock House   B&B ££
(☑ 01646-635800;   www.clockhousemarloes. co.uk; Gay Lane; s/d £50/100) In the heart of the tiny village of Marloes, the Clock House offers spick-and-span rooms in breezy blues and whites, and a pretty cottage-style cafe for coffee, cake, light lunches and sharing platters.

Runwayskiln   CAFE ££
(☑ 01646-636545;   www.runwayskiln.co.uk; 2-/3-course lunch menu £20/25; ☉ noon-5pm Thu-Sun) 🍴 Sitting on a clifftop just above Marloes Sands and right on the coast path, the Runwayskiln lodges in a cluster of lovingly converted farm buildings (including an old piggery), with a courtyard for warm-day dining. The imaginative lunch menu keeps things winningly fresh, with farm-to-fork flavours shining through in dishes such as warm pulled lamb salad with puy lentils, cucumber, mint, tomato and za'atar.

Be sure to book well in advance, or just stop by for coffee and cake.

❶ Getting There & Away

Marloes Sands is accessed via the coastal path from the National Trust car park. Parking costs £3 for up to three hours and £6 for the day from March to October.

AT A GLANCE

POPULATION
Aberystwyth: 13,000

LONGEST RIVER
Teifi (76 miles)

**HIGHEST
MOUNTAIN**
Pen Pumlumon
Fawr (p206)
(752m/2467ft)

**HIGHEST WATER-
FALL**
Pistyll Rhaeadr
(p223) (73m/240ft)

BEST FESTIVAL
World Bog Snorkel-
ling Championships
(p214)

WHEN TO GO

➡ **Apr** The driest
month: great for
exploring outdoors.

➡ **Jul** Idiosyncratic
festivals reach their
zenith, including
wacky sporting
events in kooky
capital Llanwrtyd
Wells.

➡ **Sep** Summer
tourists have gone
but some of the
year's best weather
remains: opportune
for tackling hikes
such as Offa's Dyke
Path.

North Beach (p201), Aberystwyth
MILOSK50/SHUTTERSTOCK ©

Mid-Wales

Welcome to the gap: the giant, green empty middle of Wales between the national parks of Snowdonia, Pembrokeshire and Brecon Beacons, yet often with wilder, less-compromised nature than any of them. Such remoteness wins this rugged region the title 'Desert of Wales'.

Full of flurries of moor, picturesquely plunging coastline, wooded river valleys and lakes and bizarre back-of-beyond market towns, this is the Wales the Industrial Revolution bypassed.

Apart from exuberant, student-populated Aberystwyth, it's the places in between the bigger urban areas, and the people living there, that captivate most. Yes, unbelievably untraipsed country lanes, hiking and cycling routes unveil vistas too beautiful to countenance. But combined with a cast of characters, from struggling farmers to the wacky minds of Britain's smallest town, you have somewhere revealing more about the Welsh than you could ever have imagined.

20 km
10 miles

Penmaenpool
Barmouth
Dolgella
Cader Idris ▲ (893m)
Fairbourne
Corris
Abergynolwyn
Dolgoch
Centre for Alternative Technology
Tywyn
Machynlleth
A493
Forge
Aberdovey
Derwenla
Ynyslas Dunes
IRISH SEA
Borth
Nant-y-Moch Reservoir
Bwlch Na yr Arian
A44
River Rheidol
Aberystwyth ❸
Ysbyty Cynf
Cardigan Bay
Rheidol Falls
Devil Brid
Llanrhystud
A485
Llanon
Pontrhydfendigaid
Stra Flori Abbe
Aberaeron
◎ *Llanerchaeron*
New Quay
A482
Tregaron
CEREDIGION
A485
Cambria Mountai
Cardigan Bay ❶
Cwmtydu
Penbryn
Manorafon
Synod Inn
Temple Bar
River Teifi
Mwnt
Aberporth
Tresaith
A486
Lampeter
Poppit Sands
Glynarthen
A487
Blaenannerch
A475
Llanybydder
Cardigan
Croeslan
Llandysul
CARMARTHENSHIRE
Cenarth
Henllan
River Teifi
PEMBROKESHIRE
River Teifi

Aberystwyth & Mid-Wales Highlights

❶ **Cardigan Bay** (p198) Spotting dolphins and seals along this gloriously rugged stretch of coast by boat trip or kayak.

❷ **Strata Florida Abbey** (p199) Roaming the ruins of this peaceful but history-rich ruin, then hiking to the source of Wales' longest river.

❸ **Aberystwyth** (p200) Experiencing a collision of high culture, student high jinks and seaside fun in Aberystwyth, a colourful beach-abutting university town.

4 Cambrian Mountains (p211) Venturing into the unpeopled moorland massif dominating most of Mid-Wales for some really wild hiking.

5 Elan Valley (p212) Exploring mighty Victorian dams and magic trails in this lovely lake-dotted wilderness.

6 Powis Castle (p224) Discovering the magnificent gardens and ornate interiors of this castle near Welshpool.

CEREDIGION

Bordered by Cardigan Bay on one side and the Cambrian Mountains on the other, Ceredigion (pronounced with a 'dig', not a 'didge') is an ancient Welsh kingdom founded by the 5th-century chieftain Ceredig. The rural communities here escaped the population influxes of the south's coal-mining valleys and the north's slate-mining towns, and, consequently, the Welsh language is stronger here than in any other part of the country except Gwynedd and Anglesey.

The lack of heavy industry also left Ceredigion with some of Britain's cleanest beaches that, with no train access south of Aberystwyth, tend to be pleasantly uncrowded. Adding to the isolation is the massif known as the 'Desert of Wales' – the barren uplands of the Cambrian Mountains. All of this conspires to make Ceredigion's sandy coves, river valleys, quiet towns and wild plateaus as off-the-beaten-track as Wales gets.

Cardigan (Aberteifi)

POP 4180

Cardigan has the feel of a town waking from its slumber. An important trading port and herring fishery in Elizabethan times, it declined with the coming of the railway and the silting up of the River Teifi in the 19th century. By the late 20th century a shabbiness had encroached, exemplified by the ugly steel buttresses that held up its castle walls.

The new millennium saw the castle restored, buttresses removed and high street rejuvenated. Today's visitors will find a pretty riverside town with an attractive jumble of heritage architecture lining its streets and lanes. However, castle aside, the biggest attraction is still its proximity to the beautiful beaches and walking tracks of North Pembrokeshire and Cardigan Bay.

'Cardigan' is an anglicisation of Ceredigion, the place of Ceredig, but the Welsh name, Aberteifi, refers to its location at the mouth of the River Teifi.

⊙ Sights

Some of Cardigan's main sights are across the river in Pembrokeshire, including Cilgerran Castle, the ruins of St Dogmaels Abbey (p171) and Poppit Sands beach (p171).

Cardigan Castle　　　　　　　CASTLE
(Castell Aberteifi; ☏ 01239-615131; www.cardigancastle.com; cnr Bridge St & Quay St; adult/child £6/3; ⊙ 10am-4pm; ⦿) Cardigan Castle holds an important place in Welsh culture, having been the venue for the first competitive National Eisteddfod, held on Christmas Day 1176 under the aegis of Rhys ap Gruffydd, ruler of Deheubarth. Neglected for years, a multi-million-pound refurbishment has once again elevated it into a major centre of regional Welsh culture, with exhibitions on the castle, Cardigan and the Eisteddfod, live performances, festivals, language classes and more taking place within its lovely buildings and courtyard.

The Normans were the first to construct a castle on this site, building it out of wood. It was rebuilt in stone in 1171 after it fell to Rhys ap Gruffydd, making it the first stone castle erected by the Welsh.

The visit starts with the short film that plays in the room adjacent to the entrance. There is further interest in the displays in the Georgian Castle Green House on Eisteddfod history and, around the back, in the kitchen garden and circular medieval tower, parts of which survive from the 1171-built castle. The grounds also feature a playground, an oversized Eisteddfod chair and a WWII pillbox.

Lastly, there's an excellent restaurant (p196), and pleasant B&B accommodation in the castle's old stables, coach house and other outbuildings.

Mwnt　　　　　　　　　　BEACH
(NT; www.nationaltrust.org.uk; SA43 1QH; parking per day £4) Tucked within an arc of black cliffs, 5 miles north of town, this small stretch of golden sand is one of the region's most picturesque beaches, with a little stream cascading down at one end and frequent visits from dolphins, porpoises and seals. Sitting above it is lonely **Holy Cross Church**, striking for its simplicity and remoteness. Whitewashed, and dwarfed by its windswept setting, this 13th- or 14th-century church is thought to be Ceredigion's oldest.

Mwnt is reached by narrow country lanes, well signposted from Cardigan.

🏃 Activities

For a challenging but spectacular day's walk, head to St Dogmaels and tackle the last leg of the Pembrokeshire Coastal Path in reverse, catching the T5 bus back from

Newport (15.5 miles). In the other direction, the first day of the Ceredigion Coast Path ends up in Aberporth (17 miles), where you can also catch the T5 bus back.

Alternatively, **Cardigan Bay Coast & Country** (www.cardigan-bay.com) lists walks in the area, including a 10.5-mile circular walk to the gorgeous hidden cove at Mwnt.

If you don't fancy a full day's trek, you can walk or cycle from Cardigan through the **Teifi Marshes Nature Reserve** to the Welsh Wildlife Centre (p171). From the town centre, cross the river and take the pedestrian walkway leading left (east) along the riverbank, out of town, past the reed beds and along a wooded trail to the wildlife centre. The walk is about 1 mile long, but it's 4 miles by road.

A Bay to Remember WILDLIFE WATCHING
(☑01239-623558; www.baytoremember.co.uk; Prince Charles Quay; adult/child from £26/13; ⊘Apr–Oct; ▣) Running one- and two-hour trips into Cardigan Bay from St Dogmaels, Gwbert and Poppit Sands, this operation takes groups out in rigid-hulled inflatable boats to spot bottlenose dolphins, harbour porpoises, grey seals and seabirds; its dolphin-sighting rate is 60% on short trips and 90% on longer ones. There's a seasonal booking office at Prince Charles Quay in Cardigan.

Cardigan Bay Active ADVENTURE SPORTS
(☑01239-612133; www.cardiganbayactive.co.uk; Scout Hall Boat House, The Strand; per person/6-person group from £45/180; ⊘9am–5pm) CBA offers guided canoe trips through Cilgerran Gorge, plus climbing, coasteering, surfing, white-water rafting and sea and river kayaking. Stand-up paddleboarding and bushcraft sessions cost a little less (£30/120 per person/six-person group).

BikeBikeBike.Bike CYCLING
(☑01239-621275; www.bikebikebike.bike; 29-30 Pendre; per 3hr/day £17.50/23; ⊘10am–5pm Mon–Sat) Hire your ride here for cycling around Cardigan Bay and the Teifi Valley.

🛏 Sleeping

Cardigan is well supplied with traditional, good-value guesthouses, and can also accommodate campers. Bear in mind that across the river, Pembrokeshire's St Dogmaels also offers lovely places to stay, including the nearest hostel.

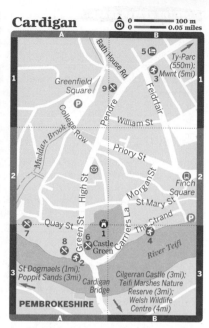

Cardigan

Cardigan

◉ Sights
1 Cardigan Castle...................................A2

⊕ Activities, Courses & Tours
2 A Bay to Remember.............................A3
3 BikeBikeBike.Bike...............................B1
4 Cardigan Bay Active...........................B3

⊟ Sleeping
5 Llety Teifi...B1

⊗ Eating
6 1176..A3
7 Abdul's Spice......................................A2
8 Fforest Pizzatipi..................................A3
9 Food for Thought................................B1

Gwbert Hotel HOTEL ££
(☑01239-612638; www.gwberthotel.com; Gwbert, SA43 1PP; s/d from £65/85; ▣🛜) With unspoilt views from the cliff-lined inlet through which the Teifi flows into Cardigan Bay, and 21 comfortable, understated en-suite rooms (many better and higher-priced than others), the Gwbert is among Cardigan's most appealing sleeps. There are hearty breakfasts and the Flat Rock bistro, which combines upmarket pub and bistro classics (mains £10 to £17). Located three miles north of Cardigan.

MID-WALES CARDIGAN (ABERTEIFI)

OFF THE BEATEN TRACK

CEREDIGION COAST PATH

....

Running for 60-odd miles up and down wave-washed headlands, along sweeping bays and through weathered fishing villages, this is one of Wales' classic walks. At a moderate pace, it takes around a week to complete, with plenty of accommodation available along the way.

A sensible six-day itinerary from Cardigan would see you stopping overnight in Aberporth (17 miles), New Quay (14 miles), Aberaeron (6.5 miles), Llanrhystud (seven miles), Aberystwyth (10 miles) and Borth (6 miles); each has its own sandy beach to relax on at the end of the day. This is part of the 870-mile Wales Coast Path (www.walescoastpath. gov.uk), so it's possible to tack Ceredigion's coast onto the end of the Pembrokeshire Coast Path or to continue up through Snowdonia National Park.

Borth and Aberystwyth are both connected to the train network, while the T5 bus stops in all of the main towns between Cardigan and Aberystwyth – making it easy to break up the route into day walks. If you'd rather not lug your own luggage, you can book a bag transfer service through a commercial operator such as Walkalongway (www. walkalongway.com).

Ty-Parc
B&B ££

(☑ 01239-615452; www.ty-parc.com; Park Ave; r £70-80; 🐾) This appealing Edwardian house just north of the town centre offers five bright, comfortable and scrupulously clean en-suite rooms decked out in pine furniture and shades of cream. Not suitable for pets or children.

Llety Teifi
B&B ££

(☑ 01239-615307; www.lletyteifi-guesthouse.co. uk; Pendre; s/d from £45/65; 🅿🐾) Don't be put off by the lurid pink exterior – this large Victorian guesthouse is well appointed and stylish, with plenty of period character. Expect bold patterned fabrics and wallpapers, giant windows and spacious bathrooms. Altogether it's a very good deal. Breakfast is served next door.

Eating

★ Fforest Pizzatipi
PIZZA £

(☑ 01239-612259; www.pizzatipi.co.uk; Cambrian Quay; pizza £7-9; ⊙ 4-9pm Thu & Fri, noon-9pm Sat & Sun) Run by four young brothers, this seasonal pop-up venue is the hottest ticket in town on summer nights. Pizzas pumping from two wood-fired ovens, craft beer, music, smartly chosen events and a buzzing atmosphere all set under a candlelit tepee in a hidden riverside courtyard: what more could you ask for? It's open roughly from April to October, weather-dependent.

Food for Thought
CAFE £

(☑ 01239-621863; 13 Pendre, SA43 1JL; mains £6-10; ⊙ 9am-5pm Mon-Sat; 🍴) A consistent local favourite, this cafe delivers a huge menu that ranges from light bites to *cawl* (Welsh stew), cockles with laver bread (a Welsh seaweed dish), gourmet burgers, homemade cakes and plenty of options for vegetarians and vegans. Arrive early at lunchtime or be prepared to wait for a table.

1176
GRILL ££

(☑ 01239-562002; www.cardigancastle.com/ dining; Cardigan Castle, SA43 1JA; breakfast £5-8, lunch £6-12.50, dinner £12-18; ⊙ 10am-4pm Sun-Wed, to 9pm Thu-Sat) This glass-and-slate cafe-steakhouse is an integral part of Cardigan Castle's rebirth. It opens at 8.30am for breakfast when there are guests staying in the castle B&B and has nice lunches, but really comes into its own with its evening incarnation: Holden's Steakhouse. Portions are huge, and served with grilled veggies and potatoes.

Abdul's Spice
BANGLADESHI ££

(☑ 01239-615371; www.facebook.com/AbdulsTandoori; 2 Royal Oak, Quay St; mains £7.95-14.95; ⊙ 5-10pm Tue-Sun; 🍴) Long-standing Abdul's enjoys a loyal local following, cheerfully serving a huge selection of tandoori dishes and curries, including an authentically spicy *achari gosht* (Punjabi-style pickled lamb curry). No alcohol is served.

ℹ Getting There & Away

Direct destinations from the **bus station** (Finch Sq) include hourly T5 services to New Quay (£4.15, 50 minutes), Aberaeron (£4.40, one hour) and Aberystwyth (£5.50, 1¾ hours), and services to Carmarthen (£5.10, 1½ hours, hourly) and Haverfordwest (£5.05, 1¼ hours, five daily).

Hire bikes from BikeBikeBike.Bike (p195) for cycling around this prettily countrified region.

Aberporth & Around

Dinky but bustling Aberporth is one of Ceredigion's most attractive seaside settlements. Once a major herring port, these days it just nets holidaymakers who are enticed by its two tandem sandy beaches, **Aberporth** and **Dolwen** (with Blue Flag status). With the village's facilities as a launch pad, this is also a place to make a voyage of discovery along a nearby coast boasting further sandy bays, waterfalls and more.

⊙ Sights

Traeth y Cribach   BEACH
(SA43 2DG) You need no guide to find Aberporth's two main beaches, but this sandy diamond requires a little delving: worth it for the dearth of other beachgoers. To find it, follow the coast path west beyond Traeth Dolwen for just under a mile.

Traeth Penbryn   BEACH
(SA44 6QL) The decent-sized sandy curve of Traeth Penbryn is an excellent focus for a walk from Aberporth: 2.5 miles one-way along the coast path heading east–northeast. The route is initially scarred with caravan parks until Tresaith, sporting a shoreline **pub** and one of Wales' most spectacular beachside **waterfalls**. The stretch onto Penbryn is beautiful though. Traeth Penbryn beach lies beneath a steep-sided wooded **valley**: walk about half a mile up to reach a lovely **cafe** beside the National Trust car park.

Traeth Penbryn is one of many beaches in Cardigan Bay where sightings of dolphins (p198) are common.

🛏 Sleeping

Highcliffe Hotel   HOTEL **££**
(🗷 01239-810534;   www.highcliffehotel.co.uk; Rhiw y Plas, SA43 2DA; s/d from £65/75; 🅿🛜) This whitewashed, 16th-century former ship owner's abode has clean, neat rooms finished in the buff-blue tones of Aberporth Beach on a summer's day. A restaurant, a bar and two beaches are within 200m.

❶ Getting There & Away

Eight buses daily run southwest to Cardigan (23 minutes) and northeast to Aberystwyth (1½ hours).

New Quay (Cei Newydd)

POP 1080

Distinguished by its candy-coloured Georgian houses and long sandy beaches, New Quay has successfully transformed from historic fishing village to 18th-century smuggler's lair, to 19th-century ship-building port, to present-day tourist destination. It's not as classy as nearby Aberaeron but the beaches are better.

New Quay's compact town centre is now lined with coffee shops, fish and chipperies, and pubs – ready to burst into life when the giant static caravan park blighting the backdrop of the main beach fills up in summer.

Dylan Thomas – who lived here for a year at the end of WWII and is thought to have gleaned inspiration for *Under Milk Wood* from the town's characters – described one pub here, the Black Lion, as 'waiting for Saturday night as an over-jolly girl waits for sailors'. Have a drink here and see what you think. The **Dylan Thomas Trail**, linking the poet's erstwhile abodes and hang-outs hereabouts, ends at New Quay.

⊙ Sights & Activities

**Cardigan Bay
Marine Wildlife Centre**   WILDLIFE RESERVE
(🗷 01545-560032; www.welshwildlife.org; Glanmor Tce, SA45 9PS; 2/4/8hr boat trip from £20/38/65; ⊙9am-5pm Easter-Oct) **FREE**
Learn about Cardigan Bay's marine life from volunteers in the visitor centre and, if you're feeling inspired to learn more, join a boat trip or a dolphin-survey boat trip, as researchers collect data on bottlenose dolphins and other local marine mammals. Trips vary in length and price; dates are posted on the website.

SeaMôr   CRUISE
(🗷 07795 242445; www.seamor.org; Sail House Gifts, South John St, SA45 9NP; adult/child £17/12; ⊙Apr-Oct; 🅰) SeaMôr runs 90-minute boat trips to the dolphin-feeding sites of Llanina Reef and New Quay Bay (at the time of research trips were £16 per person). Grey seals, bottlenose dolphins and harbour porpoises are commonly seen, and there are occasional sightings of sunfish, basking sharks, minke whales and even humpback whales. Departures are tide-dependent, and more frequent in summer.

ℹ Getting There & Away

From Monday to Saturday the hourly T5 bus stops here, heading along the Ceredigion coast's settlements to/from Aberystwyth (£4.10, one hour), Aberaeron (£2.30, 21 minutes) and Cardigan (£4.15, 50 minutes). Change in Cardigan for Fishguard (1½ hours) and Haverfordwest (two hours).

Aberaeron

POP 1420

Elegant Aberaeron, with its brightly painted Georgian houses, was once a busy port and ship-building centre, its genteel architecture the result of planned expansion in the early 19th century. The arrival of the railway then made it a popular holiday destination. With heavy industry long gone, today Aberaeron is quietly bucking the trend of economic decline; its stylish streets and much-admired harbour are lined with independent shops and cafes, some excellent restaurants and chic B&Bs and boutique hotels.

◎ Sights

Llanerchaeron   HISTORIC BUILDING
(NT; ☑ 01545-570200; www.nationaltrust.org.uk; SA48 8DG; Ciliau Aeron; grounds only £5/2.50; ☺ garden & grounds 10.30am-5pm, shorter hours winter, woodland walks daily year-round; ℗) This beautifully maintained Georgian country estate offers a fascinating insight into the life of the Welsh gentry and their staff 200 years ago. The villa, closed at the time of research, is among the most complete early works of architect John Nash, featuring curved walls, false windows and ornate cornices. The estate was originally self-sufficient and still is today: staff tend to the

rare-breed livestock and the fruit, veg and herbs in the walled garden.

There is an ornamental lake, pleasure gardens and woodland walks to stroll around. Llanerchaeron is 2.5 miles southeast of Aberaeron along the A482.

🛏 Sleeping & Eating

Carno House   B&B ££
(☑ 01545-571862; www.carnohouse.com; cnr North Parade & Bryn Rd; s/d from £72/82; ℗ 🛜) This friendly B&B offers four tidy en-suite rooms, two of which have sea views, with floral-feature walls and gauzy curtains. Thoughtful in-room extras include tea- and coffee-making facilities and Ferrero Rocher chocolates. Two-night minimum stays sometimes apply.

Harbourmaster Hotel   BOUTIQUE HOTEL £££
(☑ 01545-570755; www.harbour-master.com; Pen Cei, SA46 0BT; s/d from £140/150; 🛜) Standing proudly at Aberaeron's harbour entrance, this boutique hotel offers accommodation worthy of any chic city bolthole, besides its now famously fantastic food. The striking, indigo-painted Georgian buildings hold 13 singularly decorated rooms (seven in the main house) featuring Frette linens, Welsh blankets, bold colour schemes and high-tech bathrooms.

Rooms in the newly restored grain warehouse have the same contemporary styling, with excellent harbour views.

Downstairs, Harbourmaster's **restaurant** does delicious things with local seafood and Welsh beef, lamb and cheese (mains £12 to £28). Check the website for dinner-and-room packages and be aware that two-night minimums are sometimes in effect.

CARDIGAN BAY'S DOLPHINS

Cardigan Bay is home to an amazingly rich variety of marine animals and plants, but the star attraction is Europe's largest pod of bottlenose dolphins (more than 250). With reliable sightings from May to September, there are few places where these sociable creatures are more easily seen in the wild. Along with the dolphins, harbour porpoises, Atlantic grey seals and a variety of birdlife are regularly seen, as well as seasonal visitors such as sunfish, basking sharks and leatherback turtles.

Some of the best places to spot dolphins from the shore are the beaches around New Quay: **New Quay North**, **Little Quay**, **Cwmtydu** and **Llanina** are good bets, as are the beautiful sandy beaches at Mwnt (p194), Penbryn (p197) and Aberporth (p197) north of Cardigan.

You can learn more about Cardigan Bay's marine life at the Cardigan Bay Marine Wildlife Centre (p197) in New Quay.

The Cellar
BISTRO ££

(☑ 01545-574666; www.thecellar-aberaeron.co.uk; 8 Market St; mains £14-29; ☺ 9am-late) Up-market yet informal, this award-winning bistro serves a solid, crowd-pleasing menu including the likes of pork belly, chicken breast, mushroom risotto, steak, salmon and curry. As the name implies, it is located in a basement, but there are windows gazing over the harbour and, in summertime, tables on the terrace.

ⓘ Information

Aberaeron Tourist Information Centre
(☑ 01545-570602; www.discoverceredigion.co.uk; Pen Cei; ☺ 10am-5pm Mon-Sat) In the old General Storehouse building by the harbour; closed at the time of research.

ⓘ Getting There & Away

Hourly T5 buses head to/from Aberystwyth (£3.80, 40 minutes) and Cardigan (£4.40, one hour) calling at points in between. There are also direct buses to Carmarthen (£5.85, 1½ hours, hourly) via Lampeter. Change in Cardigan for services to Pembrokeshire.

Tregaron

POP 1210

Positioned on the River Brenig in the hilly Ceredigion hinterland, historic market town Tregaron is a picturesque jumble of coloured houses set around an imposing stone church that may have been built on a Bronze Age barrow. The settlement scenically shelters below the western edge of Britain's greatest unbroken moorland area south of the Scottish Highlands, and with your own wheels (or hardy pair of feet) exploring this is the big adventure Tregaron can offer. You can also pick up the Ystwyth Trail (p203) here, which runs 21 miles along riverbanks and disused railway lines to Aberystwyth.

◉ Sights & Activities

Cors Caron
NATURE RESERVE

(Tregaron, SY25 6LG) A mile north of Tregaron on the A485, Cors Caron's wetlands support one of Wales' biggest and best-preserved raised bog ecosystems. Boardwalk trails and information boards lead you around and offer insights into the wildlife. Autumn is great for spotting over-wintering wildfowl species.

Strata Florida Abbey
RUINS

(Abaty Ystrad Fflur; Cadw; ☑ 01974-831261; www.cadw.gov.wales; Abbey Rd, Pontrhydfendigaid, SY25 6ES; adult/child £4.20/2.50, Nov-late Mar free; ☺ 10am-5pm Apr-Oct, to 4pm Nov-Mar) The elegiac remains of this Cistercian abbey can't quite compete with Monmouthshire's famously picturesque Tintern Abbey, but you'll have Strata Florida ('Valley of the Flowers' in Latin) almost to yourself, which makes it as special. It holds a unique place in Welsh hearts too. Although founded in 1164 by a Norman lord, the Cistercians won the support of the Welsh princes, and their abbeys became a focus for Welsh literary activity and culture.

Lord Rhys ap Gruffyd – of Cardigan Castle (p194) and National Eisteddfod fame – was a powerful patron of Strata Florida, and various dignitaries from one-time South Wales superpower Deheubarth are interred here. The great 14th-century poet Dafydd ap Gwilym is said to be buried under the yew tree in the neighbouring churchyard.

The best-preserved remnant of the abbey is the arched entrance portal, decorated with lines in the shape of knotted rope. Otherwise it's mainly just low foundations tracing the outline of the church, cloister and other buildings. Also, two chapels at the rear still retain some of their 14th-century tiling, with interesting depictions including one with a man admiring himself in a mirror.

Get a further sense of the wild surrounding countryside with the wonderful clamber up a lonely valley to the Teifi Pools, source of Wales' longest river. The walk starts behind the abbey.

This isolated abbey lies a mile down a rural road from Pontrhydfendigaid, which itself is 5.5 miles northeast of Tregaron along the B4343.

Teifi Pools
HIKING

The hike up to the Teifi Pools, a scattering of lakes making up the source of Wales' longest river, the Teifi, is a fittingly dramatic accompaniment to Strata Florida Abbey where it begins.

Follow the dead-end lane bending around the north of St Mary's church and ascend to the hand-painted sign to the pools at a stile on the left near the lane's end. Then take the distinct path up a wild

RURAL RETREATS

Some of Ceredigion's best accommodation is hidden away in its rural hinterland, far from the main coastal towns, and presents an excellent opportunity for forays into rarely visited regions.

Penbontbren (☑01239-810248; www.penbontbren.com; Glynarthen, SA44 6PE; ste £190–290; P 🛜 🐾) Surrounded by green fields and hills 9 miles northeast of Cardigan, pretty Penbontbren offers five spacious, sumptuous modern suites, each with its own little kitchen, coffee machine and private terrace. The romantic garden room has a big brass bed and prints of butterflies and birds on the walls. Groups should enquire about renting the entire pale-pink, slate-roofed four-bedroom farmhouse.

Delicious breakfasts can be served on your own private terrace and they do evening meals for you to heat up in your own suite.

Falcondale (☑01570-422910; www.thefalcondale.co.uk; Falcondale Dr, Lampeter, SA48 7RX; s/d/4-poster ste from £110/135/210; P 🛜) Nestled between wooded hills on a still-working farm estate, this grade II–listed Victorian Italianate country house once belonged to the Harford family, Lampeter's lords of the manor in the 19th and early 20th centuries. The decor is a little dated but the rooms are spacious, and the setting could hardly be more peaceful and bucolic.

Enjoy croquet on the hotel lawns or nearby canoeing and horse-riding for daytime diversions.

valley beside the thunderously churning stream.

Cross the steam at a bridge to continue far above the right bank, which you remain on all the way up to the first pool, **Llyn Egnant**. Views looking back down the valley epitomise Mid-Wales moorland at its best.

🛏 Sleeping & Eating

Y Talbot PUB ££
(☑01974-298208; www.ytalbot.com; Y Sgwâr, SY25 6JL; s/d from £75/95; P 🛜 🐾) Filling one flank of Tregaron's main square, this heritage-listed hotel displays its venerable age in its elegant whitewash and barestone exterior and wonky corridors. The bedrooms, above, are modern and less characterful, but all have en-suite bathrooms, and superior rooms are spacious. Even if you're passing through, it's worth stopping for refreshments in this atmospheric low-beamed, slate-floored pub (mains £11 to £22).

🛍 Shopping

Craft Design Centre Wales ARTS & CRAFTS
(Canolfan Cymllun Crefft Cymru; ☑01974-298415; http://oriel.rhiannon.co.uk; Y Sgwâr, SY25 6JL; ⊙9.30am-5pm) If you're after a Welsh-language edition of Scrabble or a bottle of spiced rum flavoured with Pembrokeshire seaweed, you'll find them here. Welsh

artists are showcased in Oriel Rhiannon, the fine-art gallery on the mezzanine level.

Jane Beck Welsh Blankets HOMEWARES
(Ty Zinc; ☑01570-493241; www.welshblankets. co.uk; Llwyn-y-Groes, SY25 6QB; ⊙10am-5.30pm Mon-Sat) Hidden away in a kooky tin shed bedecked in vintage advertising signs, in a village 7 miles southwest of Tregaron, this quirky shop is equal parts store, museum and shrine to the humble but famously snuggly Welsh woollen blanket. New and vintage blankets are sold, sorted into eras, with some dating back to the 19th century.

❶ Getting There & Away

From Monday to Saturday there are eight to 10 buses per day between Tregaron and Aberystwyth (£3, one hour).

Aberystwyth

POP 13,000

Spread out along a shingle beach, Aberystwyth is the largest and by far the liveliest town in Mid-Wales – which, admittedly, isn't saying much. Credit for this is largely due to its sizeable student population, courtesy of Aberystwyth University. During term time the bars are buzzing and students play football on the promenade, while in summer the bucket-and-spade brigade enjoys the beach. Meanwhile, the vestiges of a stately seaside resort can be glimpsed in the terrace of grand houses that line the promenade.

History

Aberystwyth's now mainly ruined castle was erected from 1277; like many other castles in Wales, it was captured by Owain Glyndŵr at the start of the 15th century and slighted by Oliver Cromwell in the 17th. By the beginning of the 19th century, the town's walls and gates had completely disappeared and much of the stone was repurposed by locals.

The town developed a fishing industry, and silver and lead mining were also important here. With the arrival of the railway in 1864, the town reinvented itself as a fashionable seaside destination. In 1872 Aberystwyth was chosen as the site of the first college of the University of Wales (Aberystwyth University now has around 8000 students). In 1907 it became home to the National Library of Wales and in 1955 it was in the running for the honour of national capital.

◉ Sights

North Beach, with its lovely lengthy sweep of imposing pastel-hued houses and hotels, harks back to the town's Victorian heyday as a fashionable resort – although some buildings have clearly seen better days. When you reach the Constitution Hill end of the 1.5-mile prom, it's customary to kick the white bar, although the locals can't seem to explain the rationale behind this ritual.

The prom pivots around the Old College and Aberystwyth Castle before leading along **South Beach** – a quieter but still attractive seafront. Many locals prefer the stony but emptier **Tanybwlch Beach**, just south of the harbour, where the Rivers Rheidol and Ystwyth meet. **Pen Dinas**, the upland rising behind Tanybwlch, is the site of the important Iron Age hill fort **Dinas Maelor**. The peak is now dominated by a monument to the Duke of Wellington.

National Library of Wales
LIBRARY
(Llyfrgell Genedlaethol Cymru; ☑ 01970-632800; www.llgc.org.uk; Penglais Rd; ⊙ 9am-6pm Mon-Fri, to 5pm Sat) FREE On a hilltop east of town with a sensational view of Cardigan Bay, the National Library is a cultural powerhouse. Founded in 1916, it holds millions of books in many languages – as a copyright library it has copies of every book published in the UK. Among its 25,000 manuscripts are such gems as the 13th-century *Black Book of Carmarthen* (the oldest existing Welsh text), a text of Chaucer penned by his scribe Adam Pinkhurst, and a 1st edition of *Paradise Lost*.

Another highlight is the Nanteos Cup – one of many candidates across Europe for the Holy Grail. Other galleries display an ever-stimulating set of changing exhibitions (some of which charge fees) featuring the library's collection and Welsh heritage in general. Check the website for the latest opening times.

Aberystwyth Castle
CASTLE
(King St) FREE Erected between 1277 and 1289 by England's Edward I, Aberystwyth Castle was captured by Owain Glyndŵr in 1404, then retaken by the future Henry V in 1407. Slighted by Oliver Cromwell in 1649, the castle retains three partial towers and some outer wall, and offers expansive seaward views. A stone circle planted in the castle's centre remains from a 1915 eisteddfod, while the large war memorial in front of it features a surprisingly saucy nude.

Old College
HISTORIC BUILDING
(☑ 01970-628692; www.aber.ac.uk/en/oldcollege; 6 King St) Built around a late-18th-century John Nash–designed structure, this stunning Gothic-revival building flaunts castellated towers, conical spires and flamboyant gargoyles. It was intended as a grand hotel in the mid-19th century, but it was sold to Aberystwyth University's founders before receiving a single guest. It is due to open as a major new cultural centre, museum and cafe-bar with artists' spaces and other facilities for the building's sesquicentennial celebrations, in 2022–23. It already hosts sporadic exhibitions and events (see the website for details).

Royal Pier
PIER
(☑ 01970-636101; www.royalpier.co.uk; Marine Tce; ⊙ 10am-9pm; ⊛) A much-truncated version of the 242m pleasure pier opened in 1865, the Royal Pier, repeatedly shortened by storm damage, lumbers 91m out to sea under the weight of a restaurant, pub, nightclub, billiard parlour, amusement arcade and the town's best fish-and-chip stop. As Wales' oldest pleasure pier, it has Grade II heritage listing.

Aberystwyth

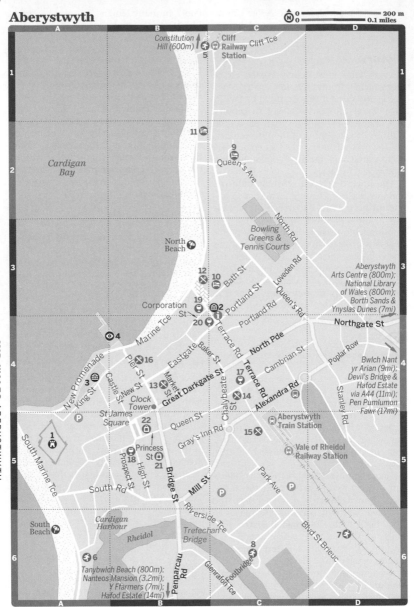

Cardigan Bay

Ceredigion Museum   MUSEUM
(📞 01970-633088; www.ceredigionmuseum. wales; Terrace Rd; ⏰ 10am-5pm Mon-Sat) FREE Ceredigion's county museum inhabits the Coliseum, which opened in 1905 as a theatre, then from 1932 served as a cinema promising 'amusement without vulgarity'.

The elegant interior retains its stage, with exhibits from the museum's collection of 60,000-plus artefacts positioned around its three tiers – everything from old chemist furnishings and a replica 1850s cottage to a Bronze Age burial urn and a Roman cooking pot. It was closed at the time

Aberystwyth

of research. Aberystwyth's tourist office (p205) is located here.

Constitution Hill HILL
Constitution Hill rises from the northern end of the seafront promenade; on a clear day you can see the Llŷn Peninsula from its blustery top. After you've walked or ridden the Cliff Railway up, there's a cafe (open 10am to 4pm) and the world's largest camera obscura (closed at the time of research), a 1980s recreation of the Victorian original.

🏃 Activities

Vale of Rheidol Railway RAIL
(☎01970-625819; www.rheidolrailway.co.uk; Park Ave; return adult/child £26/11; ☺mid-Feb–Nov; 🚉) Due to reopen in March 2021, this scenic narrow-gauge railway is one of Aberystwyth's most popular attractions. Steam locomotives built between 1923 and 1938 have been lovingly restored by volunteers and chug for almost 12 miles up the beautiful wooded valley of the River Rheidol to Devil's Bridge. There's car parking at the Aberystwyth terminus. Timetables vary throughout the year; check the website.

Cliff Railway CABLE CAR
(☎01970-617642; www.aberystwythcliffrailway.co.uk; Cliff Tce; adult/child one-way £4.50/3, return £5.50/4; ☺10am-5pm Apr-Oct, reduced hours Nov-Mar; 🚉) If your legs aren't up to the climb of Constitution Hill (it's 130m, and you can't drive), catch a lift on the trundling Cliff Railway, the UK's longest electric funicular (and possibly its slowest, too, at a breakneck 4mph). It must have

been glacial when first built, in 1896, when it was powered by a water-balance system.

Rheidol Cycle Trail CYCLING
(🚲) Sticking mainly to designated cycle paths and quiet country lanes, the 17-mile Rheidol Cycle Trail climbs from Aberystwyth Harbour to Devil's Bridge through the beautiful Rheidol Valley. Along the way it passes side-routes to sights such as picturesque lake-spotted woodland Bwlch Nant yr Arian (p206).

A trail map and directions can be downloaded from the Cardigan Bay website (www.cardigan-bay.com).

Ystwyth Trail CYCLING
(www.discoverceredigion.co.uk; 🚲) This 21-mile waymarked hiking and biking route mainly follows the former Great Western Railway from Aberystwyth southeast to Tregaron, shadowing the River Ystwyth for the first 12 miles and ending in the Teifi Valley. Pick up the trail from the footbridge on Riverside Tce in Aberystwyth, or start from Tregaron if you prefer heading downhill.

🛏 Sleeping

You will never be lost for lodgings in Aberystwyth, with its glut of hotels and B&Bs of widely varying standards, many refusing to give up their old-fashioned decor and attitudes. We've listed some of the few that stand out from the many.

Maes-y-Môr GUESTHOUSE £
(☎01970-639270; www.maesymor.co.uk; 25 Bath St; s without bathroom £45, d with bathroom from £55; 🅿🛜) Above a laundrette you'll find nine clean, bright rooms, basic self-catering

equipment and a warm welcome. Bathrooms and kitchen are shared – only the family room has an en-suite bathroom – and there's a locked shed for bicycles.

Bodalwyn
B&B **££**

(☑ 07969-298875; www.bodalwyn.co.uk; Queen's Ave; s/d from £49/69; ☎) Simultaneously upmarket and full of home comforts, this handsome Edwardian B&B offers tasteful rooms with sparkling bathrooms and a hearty cooked breakfast (with vegetarian options). Three of the rooms have sea views, but ask for room 3, with the bay window.

The Glengower
HOTEL **££**

(☑ 01970-626191; www.glengower.co.uk; 3 Victoria Tce; s/d from £57.50/87.50; ☎) This pastel-blue building at the quiet (north) end of the promenade is perhaps Aberystwyth town centre's best hotel. Downstairs, it's a very nice pub (food is served from noon to 8.30pm) with a narrow seafront terrace, whilst upstairs the usual Aber Victorian townhouse makeover ensures crisp, spacious bay-windowed rooms in neutral beiges and whites. Good breakfasts too.

★Nanteos Mansion
HERITAGE HOTEL **£££**

(☑ 01970-600522; www.nanteos.com; Rhydyfelin, SY23 4LU; d & ste from £129; P☎☰) The stately 18th-century residence of the locally prominent Powell family for 180 years, Nanteos is an excellently executed country-house hotel where equal attention is lavished on the rooms (most graced with astounding individual features such as hand-painted wallpaper, ornate chandeliers and silk-lined wardrobes), the restaurant (with some of the best steaks we've ever eaten) and the serene, seemingly endless woodland-dotted estate.

It's located three miles southeast of Aber. Take the A487 south, turn off on the B4340 – the access lane is 1km on the left. It's possibly Mid-Wales' finest lodging.

✖ Eating

Aber's dining scene has some high points that wouldn't be amiss in a much larger city.

Medina
MIDDLE EASTERN **£**

(☑ 01970-358300; www.medina-aberystwyth.co.uk; 10 Market St; meze £6-7, set meals £11, mains £8-12; ⊙9.30am-8.30pm Mon-Fri, to 9.30pm Sat) Hummus, feta and tabbouleh it up with Aberystwyth's de facto Middle East, a

large, lively space spread-eagling across the ground floor of the old Talbot Hotel serving the best-value food in town. It's fresh, flavour-packed and there's a shop showcasing more of the same, along with Welsh speciality products.

Treehouse
VEGETARIAN, VEGAN **£**

(☑ 01970-615791; www.tcth.co.uk; Unit 6, Yr Hen Ysgol; meals £8-10; ⊙8am-8pm Mon-Sat; ✍) This long-standing Aber organic grocer has moved to smart new premises alongside the train station. It cooks a range of wholesome, tempting dishes catering equally to vegetarians, vegans and meat-lovers for a takeaway picnic on the beach – imaginative fare such as harissa roast chicken and brown-lentil dal with spicy bean fritters – alongside a mean cup of coffee.

Roisin's Tea & Coffee Room
CAFE **£**

(☑ 07765 606974; www.facebook.com/Caffi Roisins; 13 Cambrian Pl; snacks & light meals £2-4; ⊙8.30am-2.30pm Mon-Sat) Aberystwyth doesn't have as many great cafes as it should, but while the tables and chairs are out at this perky little place, painted pillar-box red, who cares? Shakes, pancakes, fish-finger wraps, burgers and egg-and-bacon muffins are an absolute steal at £2 to £4, and there's oodles of atmosphere too.

★Ultracomida
TAPAS **££**

(☑ 01970-630686; www.ultracomida.co.uk; 31 Pier St; tapas £4-10; ⊙10am-4pm Mon-Sat; ✍) Aber is lucky to have Ultracomida – an importer, deli and restaurant motivated by a personal love of all things Iberian. Out front is an exceptional collection of Spanish charcuterie, cheese, dry goods and sweetmeats (with nods to France and Wales), while out back is a convivial little dining room serving great tapas and wine without pretension.

Tapas range from innovative (carpaccio of smoked salt cod with capers, oil and grated tomato) to classic (*tortilla española*). In non-Covid-19 times, it opens evenings at weekends too.

Baravin
ITALIAN **££**

(☑ 01970-611189; www.baravin.co.uk; Terrace Rd, Llys y Brenin; mains £8.50-14; ⊙10am-10pm Mon-Sat; ☎) If you've ever wondered how Italian food tastes when made with Welsh ingredients – such as pizzas and calzones with Welsh pork sausage or Perl Wen cheese – this stylish see-and-be-seen bistro occupying a prime spot on Aber's seafront terrace

MID-WALES ABERYSTWYTH

can help satisfy your curiosity. It's good! As are the craft beers and cocktails.

Drinking & Nightlife

Thanks to its large student population, during term time Aberystwyth has livelier nightlife than anywhere else in the northern half of the country.

Bottle & Barrel CRAFT BEER
(📵07788 585443; www.bottleandbarrel.cymru; 14 Cambrian Pl; ☺1-10pm) Mid-Wales' best craft-beer bar serves predominantly Welsh brews – a selection from across the country, from Cardiff's Crafty Devil to Gwynedd's Geipel Brewing – displayed in detail above their bar. There are 30-odd Welsh gins too and the cosy rambling rooms of a Victorian town house to partake in.

The Libertine COCKTAIL BAR
(📵01970-611331; www.facebook.com/TheLibertineAberystwyth; 54-56 Terrace Rd, SY23 2AJ; ☺noon-10pm) Going for a suitably louche look – with portraits of Lord Byron and Frida Khalo above the bar, and tatty rolled-arm leather chairs – this hip cocktail bar shakes up concoctions with names such as Under Milk Wood and 50 Shades of Earl Grey.

Ship & Castle PUB
(📵07773 778785; 1 High St; ☺4-10pm Mon, 2-10pm Tue-Sun; 🍴🐾) A sympathetic renovation has left this 1830 pub as cosy and welcoming as ever, while adding big screens for watching rugby. It's the place to come for real ales, with a large, constantly revolving selection on tap, plus a few ciders.

White Horse PUB
(📵01970-615234; www.whitehorseaberystwyth.co.uk; Upper Portland St; ☺10am-10pm; 🍴) Spacious, simple and welcoming to all comers, the Horse makes the most of its plum crossroads location with its open, modern feel and picture windows for idly watching passers-by outside. Relaxed and sport focused during the day, it gets rowdy on weekend nights.

☆ Entertainment

Aberystwyth Arts Centre PERFORMING ARTS
(Canolfan Y Celfyddydau; 📵01970-623232; www.aberystwythartscentre.co.uk; Penglais Rd, SY23 3DE; ☺box office 10am-8pm Mon-Sat, noon-5.30pm Sun) The largest arts centres in Wales, and part of Aberystwyth University, this cultured complex stages excellent opera, drama, dance and concerts, plus it has an art gallery, a quality bookshop and crafts shop, a bar and a cafe. The cinema shows a great range of cult and foreign-language movies, and there are always creative workshops to sign up for.

The centre is on the Penglais campus, half a mile east of town.

🛍 Shopping

Ystwyth Books BOOKS
(📵01970-639479; 7 Princes St; ☺11am-3.30pm Mon-Sat) One of the very best Welsh-interest and rare secondhand bookshops in Wales.

Coastal Antiques VINTAGE
(📵01970-358100; www.coastalantiques.co.uk; 23 Bridge St; ☺10am-5pm Mon-Sat) This place is an Aladdin's cave of curios, records and retro clothing.

ℹ Information

Bronglais Hospital (📵01970-623131; www.hduhb.nhs.wales; Caradoc Rd, SY23 1ER; 🛜) Has a 24-hour accident and emergency department.

Tourist Office (📵01970-612125; www.discoverceredigion.co.uk; Terrace Rd, SY23 2AQ; ☺10am-5pm Mon-Sat; 🛜) Within Ceredigion Museum, this office stocks pamphlets, maps and books on local history. It was closed at the time of research.

ℹ Getting There & Away

BUS

The bus station is next to the train station, on Alexandra Rd.

National Express coaches run a daily service to/from Newtown (£13, 80 minutes), Welshpool (£15, 1¾ hours), Shrewsbury (£15, 2¼ hours), Birmingham (£21, four hours) and London (£29, seven hours).

The T1 service connects Aber with Cardiff once daily Thursday to Sunday (£11, 3½ hours). On other days, change in Carmarthen for Swansea and Cardiff buses. Other Welsh destinations served include Carmarthen (£6.25, 1½ hours, every one to two hours), Dolgellau (£5.60, 1¼ hours, four daily) and Bangor (£6.70, 3¼ hours, three daily).

More locally, buses also run to Ceredigion destinations Tregaron (£3, one hour, up to 10 daily) and all main points down the coast to Cardigan (£5.50, 1¾ hours, hourly) including Aberaeron (£3.80, 40 minutes, hourly).

TRAIN

Aberystwyth is the terminus of the Arriva Trains Wales Cambrian Line, which crosses

WORTH A TRIP

LLANFIHANGEL Y CREUDDYN

Y Ffarmers (☑01974-261275; www.yffarmers.co.uk; Llanfihangel y Creuddyn, SY23 4LA; mains £12-18; ⊙6-10pm Tue-Fri, noon-10pm Sat, noon-3pm Sun), an outstanding whitewashed pub with a cosily contemporary interior, is the main reason to visit the pretty hamlet of Llanfihangel y Creuddyn, 7 miles southeast of Aber. Prepare for fantastic Welsh pub food: cockle cakes with laver-bread sauce, guinea fowl with tarragon and shallots, and other delicious creations.

Take the B4340 to New Cross, then follow signs.

Mid-Wales to Shrewsbury (£22, 1¾ hours) eight times a day, via Machynlleth (£7.20, 33 minutes), Newtown (£14.50, 1¼ hours), Welshpool (£16.30, 1½ hours). There are three trains to Birmingham (£34, three hours). Change in Shrewsbury or Birmingham for other destinations UK-wide.

Around Aberystwyth

The area around Aberystwyth is rural, with about half the population speaking Welsh. Many of the key sights will be instantly familiar to fans of the locally made bilingual detective series *Hinterland/Y Gwyll* (which screened from 2013 to 2016). If you've got your own vehicle, Bwlch Nant yr Arian, Devil's Bridge and Hafod Estate can easily be combined on one outing.

◉ Sights

St John the Baptist Church   CHURCH
(A4120, Ysbyty Cynfyn, SY23 3JR) The churchyard at Ysbyty Cynfyn (es-*bet*-ty *kun*-vin) offers a fascinating example of the grafting of the Christian onto the pagan, so widely evident in Wales. Here, the remains of a stone circle are clearly visible within the Georgian churchyard walls. Earlier, the site was a hospice *(ysbyty)*, run by the Knights Hospitaller for travellers making their way to the Strata Florida Abbey (p199).

Borth Sands & Ynyslas Dunes   BEACH
(B4353, Borth) The stretch of golden sand at Borth, 7 miles north of Aberystwyth, is Ceredigion's longest beach. Low tides expose the gnarled stumps of a prehistoric forest, swallowed by the waves 4500 years ago, linked in local lore to the 'drowned kingdom' of Cantre'r Gwaelod. Cross to the beach opposite Borth train station and trace it either south along the town beach or, better, three miles north to lovely Ynyslas Dunes, one of West Wales' most extensive sand dune systems.

Ynyslas Visitor Centre (Ynyslas Dunes, SY24 5JZ; ⊙9am-5pm Easter-Sep) is tucked amid the sandy mounds here, which are part of the 2000-hectare Dyfi National Nature Reserve.

Bwlch Nant yr Arian   FOREST
(☑0300 065 5470; www.naturalresources.wales; Ponterwyd, SY23 3AB; parking 1hr/3hr/day £1.50/3/5; ⊙visitor centre 10am-5pm; **P**) **FREE** This is a picturesque piece of woodland set around a lake, ringed with mountain-biking and walking tracks. There's also a mountain-biking skills park complete with berms and bowls, and a red-kite feeding station, with feeds taking place at 2pm daily year-round (3pm British summer time). It's located 9 miles east of Aberystwyth, along the A44.

These raptors were once almost extinct, decreasing UK-wide to some 20 pairs in the Mid-Wales valleys, but thanks to re-introduction efforts they're now a common sight in Mid-Wales.

Pen Pumlumon Fawr   MOUNTAIN
(Plynlimon) Mid-Wales' highest point at 752m (2467ft) is a bald, wind-blasted yellow-green summit that is a fair representation of what the wild Cambrian Mountains offer far more of: lovely, unpeopled moorland panoramas. There are views from the summit cairns up to Snowdonia and the Brecon Beacons on a clear day. Within a couple of miles of here are the sources of the Rivers Wye and Severn (the latter Britain's longest river and marked with more fanfare).

Access is from the remote hamlet of Eisteddfa Gurig, on the border with Powys, 17 miles east of Aber on the A44. Trail signage is non-existent but the track up, once you negotiate the farm buildings by the car park, is distinct. Bring an OS map. The out-and-back route is 5 miles. Bus service 525 (Aberystwyth–Llanidloes) stops at Eisteddfa Gurig five times daily.

Devil's Bridge   GORGE
(Pontarfynach; ☑01970-890233; www.devilsbridgefalls.co.uk; SY23 4QY; adult/child £4/2.50; ⊙24hr, staffed 9.30am-5pm Mar-Oct)

Mysterious Devil's Bridge spans the lush Rheidol Valley where the Rivers Mynach and Rheidol tumble together in a narrow gorge. Just above the confluence, the Mynach drops 90m in a series of waterfalls. Devil's Bridge is itself a famous crossing point, where three bridges are stacked above each other. The lowest was built supposedly by the Knights Templar before 1188, the middle one in 1708 and the uppermost road-bridge in 1901.

It's one of many bridges associated with a legend that involves the devil building a bridge on the condition that he gets to keep the first living thing that crosses the bridge. An old lady then outwits the devil by throwing some food over, which her dog chases and everybody's happy – except the devil and, presumably, the dog.

Access to the waterfalls and old bridges is from beside the top-most bridge. There are two possible walks: one, just to view the three bridges, takes only 10 minutes (bring a £1 coin for the turnstile). The other, a half-hour walk, descends 100 steps (Jacob's Ladder), crosses the Mynach and ascends the other side. When the entrance isn't staffed (in winter and outside business hours) you can still enter through the turnstile by inserting two £1 coins.

Hafod Estate PARK
(☏ 019/4-282568; www.hafod.org; SY25 6DX) FREE Nearly 200 hectares of picturesque grounds await at this lovely Georgian park, not far from Devil's Bridge. Five walks (totalling 15 miles) weave around the landscape, showing off its different aspects. Open year-round, and free to access, Hafod is off the B4574 between Pontrhydygroes and Cwmystwyth; park at the church and walk from there.

❶ Getting There & Away

The Vale of Rheidol Railway (p203) (reopening in March 2021) heads to Devil's Bridge from Aberystwyth, as does the Rheidol Cycle Trail. There are regular trains from Aberystwyth to Borth (£4, 15 minutes).

POWYS

Small villages, quiet-but-quirky market towns and an abundance of sheep litter the undulating hills and moorland of predominantly rural Powys, by far Wales' biggest county. Named after an ancient Welsh kingdom, this modern entity was formed in 1974 from the historic counties of Montgomeryshire, Radnorshire and Brecknockshire. Ideal for walking and cycling, Powys isn't just green in a literal sense – Machynlleth has become a focal point for the nation's environmentally friendly aspirations. The red kite – a once-threatened bird, for which the county went to outstanding lengths to save from extinction – is now the very symbol of Powys.

Machynlleth

POP 2200

Little Machynlleth (ma-*hun*-khleth) is saturated in historical significance: the town was the site where nationalist hero Owain Glyndŵr established the country's first parliament in 1404. Oddly, that legacy is not widely known or enthusiastically celebrated, and Machynlleth is perhaps better known as the country's green capital – thanks to the Centre for Alternative Technology, 3 miles north, and its proximity to cycle-path-laced forested hills.

Machynlleth is a surprisingly cosmopolitan local town, with some fantastic sleeping and eating options scattered about.

◉ Sights

★ **Centre for Alternative Technology** SCIENCE CENTRE
(CAT; Canolfan y Dechnoleg Amgen; ☏ 01654-705950; www.cat.org.uk; Pantperthog, SY20 9AZ; adult/child £6.50/5.50; ⊙10am-5pm; ⓟ♿) ✦ A small, dedicated band of enthusiasts have spent 40 years practising sustainability at the thought-provoking CAT, set in the Dyfi Unesco Biosphere Reserve, north of Machynlleth. Founded in 1974 (well ahead of its time), it's an education/visitor centre that demonstrates practical solutions for sustainability. Nearly 3 hectares of displays deal with topics such as composting, organic gardening, environmentally friendly construction, renewable energy sources and sewage treatment.

To explore the whole site takes about two hours – take rainwear, as it's primarily outdoors. Kids will love the interactive displays and adventure playground and there's a great organic wholefood restaurant.

The visit starts with a 60m ride up the side of an old quarry in an ingenious water-balanced cable car (closed in winter to save water). A drum beneath the

Machynlleth

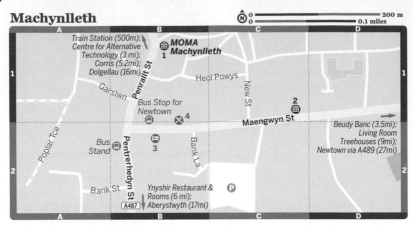

Machynlleth

top car fills with stored rainwater and is then drawn down while the bottom car is hauled up. At the top you disembark by a small lake with great views across the Dyfi Valley.

There are workshops and games for children during the main school holidays and an extensive programme of residential courses for adults throughout the year. Volunteer helpers are welcome, but you'll need to apply.

To get to the CAT from Machynlleth (seven minutes) you can take the 34 bus. Buses T2 stops close by too, on the A487.

⭐ **MOMA Machynlleth** GALLERY
(☑ 01654-703355; http://moma.machynlleth. org.uk; Penrallt St; ⊙ 10am-4pm Mon-Sat) **FREE** Housed partly in a former Wesleyan chapel, the Museum of Modern Art exhibits work by contemporary Welsh artists in a permanent collection supplemented by ever-changing temporary exhibitions. The chapel itself has superb acoustics – it's used for concerts, theatre and August's annual celebration of international music, the Machynlleth Festival.

Owain Glyndŵr Centre MUSEUM
(Canolfan Owain Glyndŵr; ☑ 01654-702932; www. canolfanglyndwr.org; Maengwyn St; ⊙ 11am-3pm Jul, Aug & school holidays) **FREE** Housed in a rare example of a late-medieval Welsh town house, this centre contains an exhibition telling the story of the Welsh hero's fight for independence and starring the Pennal letter, written by Glyndŵr in pursuit of an alliance with the French. It's best to email in advance to book a look round, or ask for the keys at Caffi Alys alongside.

Closed at the time of research.

🏃 **Activities**

The Machynlleth region has some of Wales' best mountain biking, with numerous tracks and bridleways and four excellent trails to follow. Beicio Mynydd Dyfi Mountain Biking has information and maps.

Sustrans National Cycle Network Route 8, leading off the A487 just north of the train station, leads you towards the Centre for Alternative Technology (p207).

Beicio Mynydd Dyfi
Mountain Biking MOUNTAIN BIKING
(www.dyfimountainbiking.org.uk) This local collective has waymarked four mountain-biking routes from Machynlleth: the Mach 1, 2, 3 and 4, each longer and more challenging than the last. In the Dyfi Forest, near Corris, is the custom-built, 9-mile, ClimachX loop trail. Routes are downloadable from the website.

🛏 Sleeping & Eating

⭐ Beudy Banc
CABIN **££**

(📞 01650-511495; www.beudybanc.co.uk; Abercegir, SY20 8NP; tree house/barn from £95/98) 🖉 Set on a working sheep farm in the Dyfi Valley, this wonderful solar- and wind-powered place offers two off-grid cabins, the stylishly converted 'barn' and 'tree house', with glorious views. There's a firepit and a walking trail across the farm that links up with Glyndŵr's Way (p224), plus two excellent mountain-biking descents and a network of other tracks and bridleways.

Beudy Banc is about 3.5 miles northeast of Machynlleth off the A489; look for the small turn-off signed simply 'Banc'.

Wynnstay
HOTEL **££**

(📞 01654-702941; www.wynnstay.wales; Maengwyn St; s/d from £65/95; 🅿🛜) This erstwhile Georgian coaching inn (1780) remains the best all-rounder in town, with 22 charming older-style rooms, one with a four-poster bed, and creaky, uneven floors. Downstairs there's a good restaurant (mains £11 to £22), a wine shop with Italian single-estate varietals and, in the courtyard on Friday and Saturday nights between Easter and October, a wood-fired pizzeria (pizzas £10).

⭐ Living Room Treehouses
CABIN **£££**

(📞 01172-047830; www.living-room.co; Bryn Meurig, SY20 9PZ; 3 days & 2 nights £379; 🅿) 🖉 Wonderfully designed, these six cosy, rustic-glam tree houses blend organically into an enchanted forest off the A470. You're as close to nature as can be (up a tree!), yet the beds are luxurious, the insulation and wood-burning stoves keep you warm all year, and the seclusion is glorious (all houses are set generously apart). Arrival days are Sunday, Wednesday and Friday.

These were the UK's first-ever rentable tree-house accommodations and they're still unique escapes today, sporting eco-friendly features such as composting toilets and fridges chilled by stream water. Magical for families, there are also woodlands and pasture to roam, with star-gazing platforms and outdoor hot tubs for fresh air.

Number Twenty One
WELSH **££**

(📞 01654-703382; www.numbertwentyone.co.uk; 21 Maengwyn St; mains £11.95-19.95; ⊘ noon-10pm Wed-Sun; 🖉) Run by a passionate, professional young foodie couple with ambitions exceeding the usual small-town bistro, Number Twenty One has been popular since day one, a status ensured by surprising dishes such as asparagus and sea spinach risotto with focaccia, goat's curd and liberal scatterings of fresh-grown garden herbs, or sourdough-encrusted catch of the day. Space is limited: book ahead.

⭐ Ynyshir Restaurant & Rooms
GASTRONOMY **£££**

(📞 01654-781209; www.ynyshir.co.uk; Eglwysfach, SY20 8TA; set dinner £200; ⊘ noon-2pm & 7-9pm Tue-Sat; 🅿🛜) Foraged wild foods, the best local meat and seafood and his own kitchen-garden produce (but mainly meat!) give Gareth Ward of Ynyshir Hall the foundations to concoct some of Wales' most wonderful food. A Michelin-starred restaurant within a luxurious country retreat, Ynyshir offers set, multicourse menus ever-changing in course number, content and composition, and herald total gastronomic joy.

The **rooms**, some in the original hall and some newly built in the grounds, are stylish and delightful (from £320 per person including dinner, bed and breakfast). An RSPB reserve immediately behind the property adds extra appeal. Ynyshir Hall is off the A487, 7 miles southwest of Machynlleth. Aberystwyth-bound buses stop on the main road 0.25 miles away.

ℹ Getting There & Away

On a bike? Sustrans National Cycling Network Route 8 passes through Machynlleth, heading north to Corris then southeast to Rhayader.

Bus routes include the X28 and T2 to Aberystwyth (£4.25, 40 minutes, at least hourly) and the two-hourly T2 to Dolgellau (£3.55, 30 minutes), Porthmadog (1¾ hours), Caernarfon (2¼ hours) and Bangor (2¾ hours); and up to nine 34 services per day to the Centre for Alternative Technology (£2.25, seven minutes) and Corris (£2.60, 15 minutes).

The bus stops for **Newtown** (Maengwyn St) and **other destinations** (Pentrerhedyn St) are either side of the market cross in the centre of town.

By train, Machynlleth directly serves Aberystwyth (£7.20, 35 minutes), Porthmadog (£15.90, two hours), Pwllheli (£18.40, 2½ hours) and Newtown (£10.70, 35 minutes). There are three trains daily to Birmingham (£25, 2½ hours).

Corris

POP 723

Tucked beneath looming slopes of pine on the edge of Snowdonia National Park, Corris is a peaceful former slate village. With subterranean tours of the village's old slate mine and caves, a one-time slate mining railway now open as a heritage run, a craft centre and great bike trails, it is well worth a stop.

🏃 Activities

Corris Mine Explorers   TOURS
(☑ 01650-511720; www.corrismineexplorers.co.uk; A487, Corris, SY20 9RF; 1hr mini mine explorer adult/child £13.50/8.50; ⊘ tours by appointment) The harsh working conditions and cramped depths of the slate mines are vividly brought to life on these tours. Braich Goch was abandoned over 40 years ago but everything is left just as it was when the miners last walked out. Reasonable fitness and the willingness to get wet and dirty are required. Advance bookings are essential: call the mine guide on the listed number.

Older children will love it! Enquire about longer mine tours that are also available.

Corris Railway   RAIL
(☑ 01654-761303; www.corris.co.uk; Station Yard, Corris, SY20 9SH; adult/child £6/3) Built in the 1850s to transport slate, the narrow-gauge Corris Railway now offers 50-minute trips, which include a guided tour of the sheds. Trains run every hour from 11am to 4pm on running days, which are generally weekends April to October (see the website for the days of operation). The attached museum is free to enter.

Bike Corris   MOUNTAIN BIKING
(☑ 07880 992552, 01654-761456; www.bikecorris.co.uk) This operation is your passport to the trails of the Dyfi Valley and Southern Snowdonia, host to some of the UK's most challenging downhill mountain-biking races. Packages are tailored individually to clients, and can include guided riding, accommodation and meals: enquire through the website. A guided ride for two riders costs about £160.

King Arthur's Labyrinth   TOURS
(☑ 01654-761584; www.kingarthurslabyrinth.com; A487, Corris, SY20 9RF; adult/child £12.65/8.40; ⊘ 10am-5pm Easter-Oct; 👣) Child-focused King Arthur's Labyrinth is an underground boat ride and walking tour through caves and tunnels where a sound-and-light show, mannequins and a hooded guide bring old Celtic tales and Arthurian legends to life.

🛏 Sleeping & Eating

Corris Hostel   HOSTEL £
(☑ 01654-761686; www.corrishostel.co.uk; Old School, Corris, SY20 9TQ; 8-person hostel sections from £150) Occupying an old slate schoolhouse uphill from the centre of town, this ecofriendly independent hostel is popular with walkers and mountain bikers. There's a self-catering kitchen.

In normal times there's a mix of dorms and private rooms; for the duration of Covid-19 the hostel was being divided into separate sections, each available for up to eight people from an extended household.

Do the maths: bigger groups can bag a beautifully located, very reasonable self-catering let.

Old Vicarage   B&B £££
(☑ 01654-761419; www.theoldvicaragewales.co.uk; A487, Corris, SY20 9RD; s/d from £105/130) The Old Vicarage is the village's nicest lodging, with four individually styled ensuite rooms. We liked Goddard, with its impressive bathroom boasting a big walk-in shower and a bath for soaking travel-weary bodies beneath a poster of the London Underground, which couldn't seem further away from this stone-built abode all alone below forested hills. It's half a mile south of Corris.

Slaters Arms   PUB FOOD £
(☑ 01654-761324; www.theslatersarms.com; Bridge St, Corris, SY20 9SP; mains £8-14) A convivial and old-fashioned Welsh village pub, Corris would not want to be without the Slaters. It has simple pub food (great-value pizzas and burgers for £8) and brilliant ales from an interesting line-up of breweries, from Snowdonia's Purple Moose to Liverpool's Big Bog Brewing Company. Stay locally and you'll likely end up here at some point.

🛍 Shopping

Corris Craft Centre   ARTS & CRAFTS
(☑ 01654-761584; www.corriscraftcentre.co.uk; A487, Corris, SY20 9RF; ⊘ 10am-5pm) A hive of interconnected workshops for potters, glassblowers, gin distillers, wood turners, candle-makers and chocolatiers, with a cafe to keep everyone productive, this is an excellent place to see craftspeople at work, join a workshop or pick up some souvenirs. It was hoped at the time of research that the centre would reopen in spring 2021.

CAMBRIAN MOUNTAINS

••

The Cambrian Mountains are an empty, starkly beautiful area of uplands running from Snowdonia down to the Brecon Beacons, and cover the majority of Mid-Wales, surrounding the few settlements in the valleys far below. Largely unpopulated and undeveloped, this plateau of yellow-green moorland is the source of both the Rivers Severn and Wye. Hidden in the folds of the hills are lakes, waterfalls and deserted *cwms* (valleys) plus hill farms that are home to thousands of sheep. The region sees few visitors except for around the Elan Valley; if you wish to get away from it all, there is no more majestic place in Wales in which to hike or bike in solitude. Many tracks criss-cross the area, including the 298-mile Cambrian Way, which thrusts across Wales from Cardiff to Conwy in the north; a good third of the route is in the Cambrian Mountains themselves. You can discover more about walking some or all of the lonely trail, not every stage of which has lodgings, at www.cambrianway.org.uk, and find more information about the region at www.cambrian-mountains.co.uk.

❶ Getting There & Away

Buses T2 and X27 northbound from Machynlleth (15 minutes) or southbound from Dolgellau (22 minutes) stop in Corris.

Rhayader (Rhaeadr Gwy)

POP 2100

Rhayader is a small, fairly uneventful livestock-market and former cattle-droving town. It's elevated to major status because of the lack of anywhere else nearby, and revolves around a central crossroads marked by a war-memorial clock and some rather venerable town houses. Wednesday – market day – sees the most action. What it lacks in urbanity, though, the town compensates for in stunning moorland countryside. The nearby Elan Valley, a series of immense nearby lakes hemmed in by imposing Victorian dams and full of thrilling hiking and biking trails, is the big lure, as is tackling the 136-mile Wye Valley Walk.

🏃 Activities

Gigrin Farm Red Kite Feeding Station
BIRDWATCHING

(☑ 01597-810243; www.gigrin.co.uk; South St, Rhayader, LD6 5BL; adult/child £7.50/4; ⊙ 1-5pm Sat-Wed, daily school holidays; 🅿) By the 1960s Britain's red kite population had been decimated to near-extinction (there were just 20-odd breeding pairs). Outstanding campaigns by centres like this across Powys, Ceredigion and Carmarthenshire have since brought the bird back to being a common sight in Mid-Wales: one of the greatest-ever UK conservation results. Hundreds of red kites arrive daily at 2pm (3pm British summer time) to gorge on meat scraps.

Watch the fray from strategically located viewing hides. Crows and ravens also try to partake, but the kites, with their 2m wingspan and raking claws, come out on top, mugging the passerines (and each other) to nab the meat.

There's also a coffee shop, a picnic area and nature trails and, for £20, you can access special photographers' hides. Gigrin is just off the A470, half a mile southeast of Rhayader (the turning is by the speed delimitation signs).

Clive Powell Mountain Bike Centre
MOUNTAIN BIKING

(☑ 01597-811343; www.facebook.com/ClivePowell Bikes; cnr West St & Church St; ⊙ 9am-1pm & 2-5.30pm) This centre is run by a former cycling champion and coach. Hire a mountain/road bike here (£32/24 per day, including helmet and puncture kit; most are new Giant models) or take it easier with an electric bike (£40 per day).

🛏 Sleeping & Eating

Rhayader has some decent guesthouses, a campsite by the Wye and more accommodation options a few miles up in the Elan Valley.

Camping & Caravanning Club
CAMPGROUND £

(Wyeside; ☑ 01597-810183; www.campingandcaravanningclub.co.uk; Llangurig Rd, Rhayader, LD6 5LB; tent & 2 adults unpowered site from £25; ⊙ Apr-Oct; 🅿🤝) A short walk from the centre of Rhayader, this relaxed, grassy campsite has river views, lots of trees, two shower blocks and a shop.

Horseshoe Guesthouse
B&B ££

(☑ 01597-810982; www.rhayader-horseshoe.co. uk; Church St; s/d £75/90; [P][⊚]) This 19th-century former inn now offers comfortable modern rooms (five of seven are en suite, one has disabled access) and plenty of communal space in the large dining room, garden, conservatory and walled courtyard. Heavy beams and other antique touches remain, there's a 20-seat restaurant (pre-booking advised), and packed lunches can be arranged (pre-ordering essential).

Lost ARC
CAFE £

(☑ 01597-811226; www.thelostarc.co.uk; Old Drill Hall; breakfasts £5-8, lunches £5-8, pizza £8-10; ⊗ 10am-4pm Sun, Mon & Thu, to 9pm Fri & Sat; [⊚]) A breath of fresh air in the Rhayader eating scene, this bright cafe in a stone building down by the river off Bridge St tantalises the town with smashed avocado on sourdough, breakfast wraps, Welsh rarebit and weekend wood-fired pizzas – it even has a 'region of the week' street-food special. The venue is an up-and-coming arts centre too.

Triangle Inn
PUB FOOD ££

(☑ 01597-810537; www.triangleinn.co.uk; Cwmdauddwr; mains £8-16; ⊗ 5-10pm Mon-Sat; [⊚]) This tiny 16th-century inn, just over the bridge to Cwmdauddwr (the village adjoining Rhayader), is the pick of the local dining choices. A very welcoming place, it serves real ales, including Rev. James, and excellent hearty pub classics. If there's no room in the snug interior, there's a pretty outside terrace.

Food is served from 5pm to 9pm every evening. Next door is a small stone-built self-catering cottage, refurbished in 2020 (£70 per night).

ⓘ Getting There & Away

Buses stopping here include the X47 to Llandrindod Wells (£2.40, 25 minutes, four to seven daily) and Aberystwyth (1¼ hours, four to seven daily), the X75 to Newtown (£4.35, one hour, two daily), Berriew, on the way to Welshpool (£6.70, two hours, one daily), and Shrewsbury (£9.60, 2¾ hours, one daily).

Elan Valley

The Elan Valley is filled with strikingly beautiful countryside, split by imposing Victorian and Edwardian dams and the lakes they've created. In the late 19th century, dams were built on the River Elan (pronounced 'ellen'), west of Rhayader, mainly to provide a reliable water supply for Birmingham. During WWII, the earliest of the dams was used to perfect the 'bouncing bomb' used in the storied Dambusters raids on targets in Germany's Ruhr Valley. In 1952 a fourth, large dam was inaugurated on the tributary River Claerwen. Together their reservoirs now provide over 70 million gallons of water daily for Birmingham and parts of South and Mid-Wales, and with their dams provide 3.9 megawatts of hydroelectric power.

The need to protect the 70-sq-mile watershed (called the Elan Valley Estate) has turned it and adjacent areas into an important wildlife-conservation area, and in 2015 it was awarded Dark Sky Park status.

🏃 Activities

The **Elan Valley Trail** is an 18-mile (return) traffic-free walking, horse-riding and cycling path that mostly follows the line of the long-gone Birmingham Corporation Railway alongside the River Elan and its reservoirs. It starts just west of Rhayader at Cwmdauddwr: see a route map at www.elanvalley.org.uk.

Up at the Elan Valley lakes, many more **hiking and cycling trails** can be picked up: ask at the visitor centre. Some continue right across the moors to the Teifi Pools (p199) and Strata Florida Abbey (p199).

🛌 Sleeping & Eating

Penbont House
B&B ££

(☑ 01597-811515; LD6 5HS; s £65, d £90-130; ⊗ tearoom 10am-6pm Apr-Sep, to 4.30pm winter; [P][⊚]) Delightfully situated on a verdant hillside below Pen y Garreg dam, this house has light, prettily refurbished rooms (four spacious doubles, one single) with pine furnishings, and makes for a memorable Elan Valley vacation, especially combined with the pine-beamed glass-roofed traditional tearooms. Enjoy *Bara brith* (rich fruit tealoaf), properly brewed tea and light lunches (£5 to £10) overlooking the gardens or in the charming interior.

The Clyn   ACCOMMODATION SERVICES **££**
([✆]01597-810120; www.clyncottages.co.uk; LD6 5HP; 1-/2-person cottages from £80; [P]) Two self-catering cottages, 'The Cottage' and 'The Granary', beautiful beamed refurbishments of buildings with 18th-century origins, sit in quiet hilly countryside two miles southwest of Elan Village. You'll get wood for the open fires, and use of the communal games room, which kids will love almost as much as seeing the animals on the farm.

See the website for the detailed arrival instructions.

ℹ Information

Elan Valley Visitor Centre ([✆]01597-810880; www.elanvalley.org.uk; B4518, Caban-coch Reservoir, LD6 5HP; ⊙9am-5pm Apr-Oct, 10am-4pm Nov-Mar) Operated by Dwr Cymru Welsh Water, this is a modern, vital visitor resource and recommended starting point for explorations. It houses displays, including an audiovisual show, on how the dams work and were built, plus information on native wildlife and local history. It also provides leaflets on the estate's 80 miles of hiking and cycling trails and rents bicycles (adult/child £26/14 per day).

It also offers activities like a September 'Walking Fest' and ranger tours inside Pen y Garreg dam.

Parking here costs £2.50. The centre is just downstream of the lowest dam, 3 miles from Rhayader on the B4518.

ℹ Getting There & Away

Unless you have your own transport, the only way into the Elan Valley is to walk, cycle (both very pleasant) or take a taxi from Rhayader.

Llanwrtyd Wells (Llanwrtyd)

POP 850

Llanwrtyd (khlan-*oor*-tid) Wells is an odd little town – placid except during one of its many unconventional festivals, when it's packed to the rafters with crazy contestants and their merrymaking supporters.

Apart from its status as the capital of wacky Wales, Llanwrtyd Wells is encircled by exquisite walking, cycling and horse-riding country, bounded by the Cambrian Mountains to the northwest and Mynydd Epynt to the southeast.

Theophilus Evans, the local vicar, first discovered the healing properties of the Ffynon Droellwyd (Stinking Well) in 1732

when he found it cured his scurvy. The popularity of the waters grew and Llanwrtyd became a spa town. Nowadays, however, its wells have been capped, and its madcap festivities are its main enticement.

To burst one bubble, though, it's not, as it sometimes claims, Britain's smallest town. Fordwich in Kent has fewer citizens.

◉ Sights & Activities

Sustrans National Cycle Route 43 passes through Llanwrtyd Wells, heading east to Builth Wells (from where Route 8, Lôn Las Cymru, continues north to Machynlleth or south to the Wye Valley). There's excellent mountain biking in the surrounding hills; enquire at the Drovers Rest (p214).

Llanwrtyd & District Heritage & Arts Centre   VISITOR CENTRE
([✆]01591-610067; www.history-arts-wales.org.uk; Ffoss Rd; ⊙10am-4pm Thu-Sun Apr-Oct) **FREE** This visitor centre and museum is in a refurbished chapel opposite the service station on the Builth Wells road, acting not just as an interesting insight into how Llanwrtyd developed as a fashionable tourist resort in bygone days but, with its helpful staff, doubling as an invaluable source of information on the surrounding area.

Abergwesyn   WALKING
The pretty hamlet of Abergwesyn, five miles north of Llanwrtyd, is a superb base for breathtaking hiking nearby in the Cambrians. Start off gently at **Abergwesyn Common**, a grassy riverside area below some sheer crags on the mountain road to Llyn Brianne a mile outside the village. Other walks lead north of Abergwesyn up to the upland's uppermost reaches, and the Elan Valley Lakes are accessible via longer cross-moor hikes.

★ Festivals & Events

While mulling over how to enourage tourism in Llanwrtyd, some citizens started an inspired roll call of unconventional celebrations. There's something strange on every month (see www.green-events.co.uk for more details).

Saturnalia World Mountain Bike Chariot Racing Championship   SPORTS
(www.green-events.co.uk; team entry £20; ⊙Jan) Specially designed chariots harnessed to two mountain bikes are raced by teams

of three during Llanwrtyd's revival of Saturnalia, the Roman festival of misrule. There's a 'best dressed Roman' competition, the devouring of stuffed bulls' testicles, rambling the course of old Roman roads and plenty of ale, of course.

Man vs Horse Marathon
SPORTS
(www.green-events.co.uk; ☺ mid-Jun) The event that instigated all the Llanwrtyd Wells craziness, the Man vs Horse Marathon has been held every year (except 2020) since 1980 and has resulted in some tense finishes. Two-legged runners have won only twice, most recently in 2007. The prize money currently jackpots £500 each year a biped doesn't win (the first winner trousered £25,000). In 2020 it stood at £3500.

World Bog Snorkelling Championships
SPORTS
(www.green-events.co.uk; adult/child £15/12; ☺ bank holiday Aug) The best-known of all Llanwrtyd's wacky events. Competitors are allowed wetsuits, snorkels and flippers to traverse a trench cut out of a peat bog, using no recognisable swimming stroke and surfacing only to navigate.

Welsh Open Stone Skimming
SPORTS
(www.green-events.co.uk; ☺ Aug) It's borderline whether stone skimming can be dubbed a 'sport'. Nevertheless the pursuit of bouncing pebbles across water that we've all tried at some point is made into competitive fun here with two categories: 'stoned' for the pros and 'stoneless' for the amateurs. Tossers can bring their own stones if so desired.

Real Ale Wobble & Ramble
SPORTS
(www.green-events.co.uk; 1-day ride £20, 1-/2-day ramble £11/18; ☺ Nov) In conjunction with the Mid-Wales Beer Festival (centre of action: Llanwrtyd's Neuadd Arms Hotel), every November cyclists and walkers follow waymarked routes (12 or 20 miles for ramblers; 15 or 28 miles for wobblers), supping real ales at the 'pint stops' en route.

Mari Llwyd
NEW YEAR
(New Year Walk In; www.green-events.co.uk; ☺ New Year's Eve) A revival of the ancient practice of parading a horse's skull on a pole house to house on New Year's Eve while reciting Welsh poetry. The procession leaves from the centre of Llanwrtyd Wells at 10.30pm.

🛌 Sleeping & Eating

Lasswade Country House
B&B ££
(☎ 01591-610515; www.lasswadehotel.co.uk; Station Rd; s/d from £70/85; P 🅟 🛜) 🅿 This excellent country restaurant (with rooms) makes great use of a handsome, three-storey Edwardian house looking over the Irfon Valley towards the Brecon Beacons. Committed to green tourism (it's won multiple awards, sources hydroelectric power and offers electric-vehicle recharging), it's also big on gastronomy: the chef-owner's three-course menu (£36) features Cambrian lamb, Tally goats cheese and other delights.

At the time of research the **restaurant** is open only to guests (7.30pm to 9.30pm Monday to Saturday); reservations are required.

Ardwyn House
B&B ££
(☎ 01591-610768; www.ardwynhouse.co.uk; Station Rd; s/d £60/80; P 🛜) The Arts and Crafts grandeur of this once-derelict house has been well and truly restored: there are rural views, parquet flooring and period wallpaper and furnishings throughout, and claw-foot baths in two of the three rooms. Then there is the oak-panelled guest lounge with a pool table and bar, and afternoon tea on arrival. Breakfasts are the stuff of legend.

★ Neuadd Arms Hotel
PUB FOOD ££
(☎ 01591-610236; www.neuaddarmshotel.co.uk; mains £8.50-14, 3-course meal £18.50; ☺ 9am-10pm) At this focal point for Llanwrtyd folks, there's above-average pub food, with delicious curries the stand-outs, and excellent beers brewed in the stables out back. Bed-and-breakfast rooms (singles/doubles £45/80) are nice enough too. Here, former landlord Gordon Green and his punters cooked up many of the kooky events that put Llanwrtyd Wells on the tourist trail. Full of bygone charm.

★ Drovers Rest
WELSH ££
(☎ 01591-610264; www.food-food-food.co.uk; The Square; 3 courses £35; ☺ noon-2pm & 7.30-9.30pm Wed-Sun; 🛜) One of Mid-Wales' best dining venues, this charming restaurant does fantastic things with local produce. Snugly perched by the Irfon, it has a relaxing riverside terrace and a few simple-but-cosy rooms (singles/doubles £45/85, some en suite). The owners also run regular one-day cooking courses (£165

to £195) featuring Welsh cuisine and game. Book ahead.

ℹ️ Getting There & Away

Bus 48 heads to Builth Wells (£3.80, 25 minutes, up to five per day).

Llanwrtyd is probably best approached on the Heart of Wales Line (www.heart-of-wales. co.uk), with up to four direct services daily to Swansea (£12.40, two hours) via Llandovery (£3.60, 25 minutes) and Llandeilo (£5.60, 45 minutes), and to Llandrindod Wells (£4.70, 50 minutes) and Shrewsbury (£15.60, 2¼ hours). Buses often replace trains, especially in winter months.

Builth Wells (Llanfair-Ym-Muallt)

POP 2600

Builth (pronounced 'bilth') Wells is perhaps the liveliest of the former spa towns of Mid-Wales, with a bustling, workaday feel – although the only attraction per se is July's mammoth agricultural show, Wales' most important. The town has a pretty location on the River Wye and prominence as a centre of local agriculture, whilst being a handy base for walkers or cyclists tackling the surrounding hill country.

◎ Sights & Activities

To sample the stunning surrounding hiking, why not do so with a theme? The greatest Llewelyn of them all, Llewlyn the Great (the last Welsh prince of Wales) was slain (unglamorously; in a chance encounter with an English soldier) two miles west of Builth at Cilmery, the site marked by an **obelisk**. To walk here, take the Wye Valley Walk northwest along the Wye until passing under the railway bridge, then follow the Heart of Wales Way through Dolyrerw Wood and along the railway line southwest to Cilmery.

🎊 Festivals & Events

Royal Welsh Show   FAIR
(www.rwas.co.uk; Llanelwedd; per day adult/child £26/5; ☺ Jul; 🐾) More than 200,000 people descend on Builth for four days every July for the Royal Welsh Show (founded in Aberystwyth in 1904) to see everything from gussied-up livestock to lumberjack competitions, falconry and a food hall bursting with farm produce.

The showgrounds – actually over the Wye in Llanelwedd – host numerous other events throughout the year, from antique fairs and garden shows to equestrian events.

🛏️ Sleeping & Eating

Bronwye   B&B ££
(☑ 01982-508002; www.bronwye.co.uk; Church St; s/d from £60/80; P 🛜) Not far from the River Wye, this imposing 19th-century house has five comfortable, modern rooms with good beds and bathrooms. It's cosily modern rather than rich with period character, but there's a warm welcome, a pleasant garden and excellent breakfasts, which, at these rates, make it good value.

Caer Beris Manor   HERITAGE HOTEL ££
(☑ 01982-552601; www.caerberis.com; A483, LD2 3NP; r £90-150) This 1896 mock-Tudor country manor lies at the end of a long driveway, winding through 7.3 hectares of parkland on the River Irfon. Classic styling, log fires and spacious rooms with swag curtains, heavy fabrics and tassled lamps await. The oak-panelled Restaurant 1896 dishes up a delightful seasonal menu featuring local produce (mains £13 to £19).

The hotel is on the west side of Builth, a mile from the centre, on the A483.

★ Drawing Room   MODERN WELSH £££
(☑ 01982-552493; www.the-drawing-room.co.uk; Cwmbach, LD2 3RT; 3 courses £40; ☺ from 7pm, last orders 8.30pm; P 🛜) Ensconced in a Georgian country house flanked by kitchen gardens, this two-rosette restaurant-with-rooms is one of Mid-Wales' finest. Prime Welsh black beef, Brecon lamb and Cardigan Bay crab feature on the locally sourced menu, while the three gracefully refurbished rooms are well worth considering (from £235, including dinner, bed and breakfast). It's 3 miles north of Builth, off the A470.

☆ Entertainment

Builth Male Voice Choir   PERFORMING ARTS
(www.builthmalechoir.org.uk; Garth Rd; ☺ from 8pm Mon) You can catch a rehearsal from 8pm on Monday nights in the Greyhound Hotel on Garth Rd, which is also one of the town's better pubs. Formed at the local rugby club in 1968, the choir now sings internationally.

Llandrindod Wells

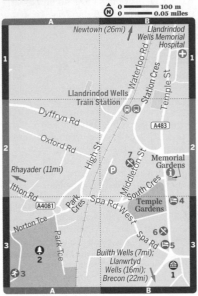

Llandrindod Wells

ℹ️ Getting There & Away

Buses stopping here include the three to four daily T4 services to Llandrindod Wells (£2.30, 20 minutes), Newtown (£6.30, 1¼ hours), Brecon (£3.90, 45 minutes) and Cardiff (£9, 2½ hours), and one X15 per day to Hay-on-Wye (£3.30, 30 minutes) and Hereford (£6.80, 1¼ hours).

Builth is on the Heart of Wales railway line, with two to four daily trains serving Swansea (south) and Shrewsbury (north), but Builth Road station is 2.5 miles outside town, which makes it less convenient.

Llandrindod Wells (Llandrindod)

POP 5309

The Victorian and Edwardian glory days of this pleasantly faded spa town live on in its delightful architecture – Queen Anne and Edwardian baroque hotels and terraces that are arrestingly grand to this day. However, once the allure of the iron-, sulphur- and saline-rich waters dwindled, Llandrindod relaxed into sleepy obscurity. Now you'd need to prod it with a sharp stick to rouse it on a Wednesday afternoon, when most of the shops close.

One absorbing museum and a couple of Victorian heyday attractions keep curious visitors coming – but it's a trickle, rather than the flood of past spa-seekers.

◉ Sights

National Cycle Museum MUSEUM
(📞 01597-825531; www.cyclemuseum.org.uk; cnr Temple St & Spa Rd East; adult/child £5/2; ⊙10am-4pm Tue & Wed, to 2pm Fri) Housed in the art nouveau Automobile Palace, the National Cycle Museum comprises more than 250 bikes. The exhibits show the progression from clunky boneshakers and towering penny-farthings to bamboo bikes from the 1890s and the vertiginous 'Eiffel Tower' of 1899 (used to display billboards), and on to slicker, modern-day versions. It's run with infectious enthusiasm.

Rock Park PARK
FREE Rock Park, the site of the earliest spa development, is an artfully wild, well-strewn oasis at the centre of town. The bathhouse is now a complementary **health centre** (www.therockpark.org; Winter Gardens Pavillion; ⊙9am-5pm Mon-Fri) and the pump room a conference centre. Fill your bottle at the rusty-looking, salty **Chalybeate Spring** beside the Arlais Brook – apparently the iron-rich water is good for treating gout, rheumatism, anaemia and more.

Llandrindod Lake LAKE
(LD1 5NU) Just southeast of the centre is a sedately pretty, tree-encircled lake, built at the end of the 19th century to allow Victorians to take their exercise without appearing to do so. The lake's centrepiece is a sculpture of a water-spouting Welsh dragon.

Sleeping & Eating

The Cottage B&B ££
(☎01597-825435; www.thecottagebandb.co.uk; Spa Rd; s/d £48/75) A really class B&B in a rambling, Arts and Crafts–style Edwardian house, the Cottage exhibits comfortable period-style rooms with heavy wooden furniture and myriad original features, set within a winsome garden. Reopening spring 2021.

Metropole Hotel HOTEL £££
(☎01597-823700; www.metropole.co.uk; Temple St; s/d from £98/129; P 🛜 ≋) This ostentatious, turreted – and turquoise, interestingly – late-Victorian hotel has spacious, corporate-style rooms and an excellent leisure complex with a swimming pool, sauna and gym. The Rock Spa offers a full treatment range (£100 for a 1½-hour hot-stone massage) and there are two restaurants.

Spencer's Bar & Brasserie has light bistro fare: burgers, grills, risotto and the like (mains £12 to £17). For something swankier, try Radnor & Miles Restaurant. Two-night minimum stays often apply.

Van's Good Food Shop DELI £
(☎01597 823074; www.organicfoodpowys.co.uk; Middleton St; ⊙9.15am-5pm Mon-Fri, 9.30am-3.30pm Sat; ✎) This top-notch vegetarian deli stocks the best of local produce, including organic fruit, cheese and wine, plus ecofriendly cleaning products and other ethically selected goods. It's been in business for around 40 years, so it must be doing something right. Load up for a picnic in Rock Park.

Fabian's Kitchen ITALIAN, INDIAN ££
(☎01597-824642; www.fabianskitchen.co.uk; Albion House, Temple St; mains £10-14; ⊙5.30-10pm Tue-Sat) Among Llandrindod's newest restaurants, Fabian's Kitchen, believe it or not, has a damned good crack at the two big Is: Italian and Indian. It's actually the Indian that is more interesting, with the fish and coconut curry especially fab, although the tagine is lovely too.

Information

Llandrindod Wells Memorial Hospital (☎01597-822951; www.powysthb.wales.nhs.uk; Temple St) Has a minor injuries unit and is open 7am to midnight.

Tourist Office (☎01597-822600; www.llandrindod.co.uk; Temple St; ⊙10am-4pm Mon-Sat) In the old town hall in the Memorial Gardens.

Getting There & Away

The **bus station** (Station Cres) is next to the train station. For places not served, call a **cab** (☎01597-822877).

Bus routes include the invaluable three to four daily T4 connections to Builth Wells (£2.30, 20 minutes), Newtown (£4.90, 45 minutes) and Brecon (£5.30, 1¼ hours), and the X47 (four to seven per day) to Rhayader (£2.40, 25 minutes) and Aberystwyth (£8.50, 1¾ hours).

By train, Llandrindod is on the Heart of Wales Line. Direct services reach Swansea (£14.20, 2½ hours), Llandeilo (£8.70, 1¼ hours), Llanwrtyd Wells (£4.70, 28 minutes), Knighton (£5.10, 36 minutes) and Shrewsbury (£13.20, 1½ hours).

Presteigne (Llanandras)

POP 2050

At the far east of the vanished county of Radnorshire, pressed right up against the English border, is Presteigne – its former county town. It's an appealing little place, lined with distinguished, sometimes strikingly decorated red-brick and timber-framed buildings, and dotted with tearooms, craft shops and farmers' pubs. The popular Offa's Dyke Path, running from South to North Wales through exquisite countryside, is a pleasant two-mile walk from town.

OFF THE BEATEN TRACK

OFFA'S DYKE PATH

The true purpose of Offa's Dyke, Britain's longest ancient monument, isn't known, although one theory is that the 2.4m-high earthwork was built in the 8th century by the Anglian king, Offa, to defend his kingdom (Mercia) from Welsh Powys. Knighton is the approximate halfway point of **Offa's Dyke Path** (www.nationaltrail.co.uk) and, helped by its excellent Offa's Dyke Centre (p218), is a great place to explore the path's southern or northern sections.

Running for 177 miles across river valleys and through handsome market towns from Sedbury Cliffs near Chepstow in the south to the coastal town of Prestatyn in the north, it's best tackled in 12 stages.

◉ Sights

Judge's Lodging   HISTORIC BUILDING
(📞01544-260650;   www.judgeslodging.org.uk;
Broad St; adult/child £8.95/4.95; ◎10.30am-
4.30pm Wed-Sun Mar-Oct) Presteigne's main
sight is pretty interesting. The Judge's
Lodging lends an intimate glimpse into
Victorian times through an audio-guided
wander through the town's 19th-century
courthouse and lock-up. The tour is enlivened by narrations from an array of Victorian characters and you'll explore the
apartments where circuit judges used to
stay and where the servants who tended
them lived.

🛏 Sleeping & Eating

You will find decent digs and dining in
town but the best place for both is in the
nearby countryside.

Harp Inn   PUB FOOD ££
(📞01544-350655; www.harpinnradnor.co.uk; Old
Radnor, LD8 2RH; mains £10-19; ◎6-10pm Wed &
Thu, 5-10pm Fri, noon-2.30pm & 5-10pm Sat, noon-
10pm Sun) One of the finest, most unspoilt
rural pubs hereabouts, the Harp Inn is a
treasure of a tavern in a stone-built Welsh
longhouse commanding beautiful bucolic
views over a melange of hiking trail-laced
hills. Savour a thoughtful menu that is
mainly pub food elevated several levels
above standard while quaffing a local ale
in snug, timber-framed, bare-stone-walled
surrounds.

And why not elongate the experience:
the five double rooms are £80 to £130 and
if you stay longer, you'll get the room price
discounted.

The inn is 6 miles southwest of Presteigne via the B4362 and 2 miles west of the
Offa's Dyke Path at Lower Harpton.

ℹ Getting There & Away

Bus 41, otherwise known as the 'Offa Hopper',
heads to Knighton (17 minutes) five or six
times every day except Sunday. At Knighton,
you can pick up more extensive bus and train
connections.

Knighton (Tref-Y-Clawdd)

POP 3000

Hilly Knighton (Tref-Y-Clawdd; the town
on the dyke) is so close to the border that
its train station is actually in England. It
is a dignified-looking but workaday place

of steep winding streets and half-timbered
houses, midway along the Offa's Dyke Path
National Trail (p217) and at one end of
the Glyndŵr's Way National Trail (p224).
Knighton was traditionally an agricultural
town, though tourism is as important today: it's a popular stopover for walkers.

The coming of the railway in 1861 and the
growth of livestock farming saw Knighton's
fortunes rise, but they fell again with failed
attempts to turn it into a spa town and the
population decline post-WWII.

One disturbing piece of local folklore
suggests that it was possible for a man to
obtain a divorce by 'selling' his wife at the
square where the 1872 clock tower now
stands. Husbands would bring their spouse
to the square at the end of a rope; the last
wife was sold in 1842.

◉ Sights

Offa's Dyke Centre   VISITOR CENTRE
(📞01547-528753;   www.offasdyke.demon.co.uk;
cnr West & Norton Sts; ◎10am-5pm Apr-Oct, to
3pm Mon-Sat Nov-Mar) **FREE** The wonderful
two-in-one Offa's Dyke Centre and tourist
office is full of information for walkers,
with interactive displays about the history
of the dyke, a section of which runs behind
the centre. There's also a basic cafe with
lovely cakes and free wi-fi. If you're going
a-walking, enquire about leaving your car
in the centre's car park (£5 per day, book in
advance). Donations towards centre maintenance are appreciated.

🛏 Sleeping & Eating

Offa Dyke House   B&B ££
(📞01547-428267; www.offadykehouse.com; 4
High St; s/d from £69/89; P🛜) Reached by
passageway from High St, this B&B offers
three sumptuous rooms, all attentively
decorated and with the comfort of hikers
in mind. Offa Dyke Room and Glyndŵr
Room feature views of the eponymous
trails, baths in two rooms soothe aching
bodies, and guests' needs are anticipated
with cheerful efficiency. Discounts for stays
of two nights or more.

The Banc   WELSH, BRITISH ££
(📞01547-520009;   www.facebook.com/thebanc
knighton; 5 Broad St; mains £10.95-15.95; ◎11am-
10pm) Whether it's a smattering of pan-fried
pheasant to start, a spicy duck breast or a
mushroom and quinoa burger for a main,
the Banc (occupying an imposing red-brick

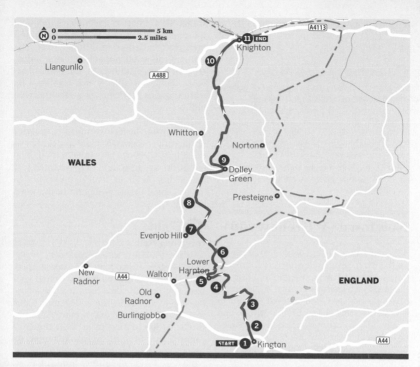

🏃 Walking Tour
Offa's Dyke Path

START KINGTON (ENGLAND)
END KNIGHTON
LENGTH 13.5 MILES; FIVE TO SEVEN HOURS

One of the most rewarding sections of Offa's Dyke Path, this route offers glorious views of the surrounding hills and passes some particularly well-preserved sections of the 8th-century defensive earthwork. This moderate walk begins across the border in Kington, Herefordshire and weaves between the two countries crossing remote hills to Knighton (Tref-Y-Clawdd; the town on the dyke).

From **1 Kington Museum** head towards the clock tower, turning left onto Church St then right onto Doctor's Lane. Continue along narrowing Crooked Well to traverse a footbridge over a stream, crossing the busy A44 to start your first ascent towards **2 Bradnor Green**. Skirting the edge of the golf course, keep climbing along the edge of Bradnor Hill and then **3 Rushock Hill**, enjoying wonderful views across the undulating landscape. Follow the path as it runs along a section of the dyke to reveal another impressive vista southwest to the Hergest Ridge and East Radnor Hills. Here the dyke itself runs near the summit of **4 Herrock Hill** but the path skirts the hill bending north then west to **5 Lower Harpton**, where you cross into Wales over an old packhorse bridge.

Follow the leafy lane uphill past the scant remains of **6 Burfa Camp**, an ancient hill fort. The path then negotiates **7 Evenjob Hill** where the dyke remains in remarkable condition, with wonderful westerly views. As you head up and over **8 Pen Offa** the easterly hills are revealed. It's downhill from here to the Lugg Valley past magnificent, towering sections of the dyke. Cross the field to the River Lugg, a small but beautiful river with deep pools and plenty of shade. From nearby **9 Dolley Green** it's a steep but scenic climb up **10 Furrow Hill** with more astonishing views west, although the dyke here is little more than a heaped earth mound. From here, it's a gentle stroll down into **11 Knighton**.

building that was formerly Knighton's HSBC bank) can oblige with its well-orchestrated Welsh-British dishes.

ℹ️ Getting There & Away

Knighton is a stop on the lovely Heart of Wales Line. Destinations include (northbound) Shrewsbury (£10.90, 54 minutes) and (southbound) Llandrindod Wells (£5.10, 40 minutes), Llanwrtyd Wells (£8.10, 1½ hours), Llandovery (£10.20, two hours), Llandeilo (£12.70, 2¼ hours) and Swansea (£18.50, 3¼ hours).

Bus 41 (the 'Offa Hopper') heads to Presteigne (17 minutes, five to six daily) every day except Sunday.

Newtown (Y Drenewydd)

POP 11,400

A former mill town and major textile centre on the River Severn, Newtown remains the largest town in Powys. It serves as a hub for the largely agricultural county, but is proud of its history, too, and showcases this in several diverting sights, from a culture hub in a handsome country mansion to a museum devoted to the town's most famous son, radical reformer Robert Owen.

History

Newtown was once the home of Welsh flannel – and partly as a result, a onetime hotbed of industrial protest. When competition began driving wages down,

THE ASHES OF ASHLEY

Textile town Newtown might have been forgiven for thinking its important 19th-century fabrics industry was gone for good when the renowned Cambrian Mills was destroyed by fire in 1912. But textiles would again bolster the local economy, when Merthyr Tydfil–born designer Laura Ashley set up her home and factory in Carno, 11 miles west of Newtown, in the 1960s, putting the town back at the forefront of international fashion. Until 2020, that was, when Laura Ashley PLC filed for administration, slashing hundreds of jobs in Newtown. Yet every cloud has a silver lining. Fabrics manufacturer and social enterprise Fashion-Enter Ltd is set to employ more than 70 former Laura Ashley staff at its premises in the town.

Wales' first Chartist meeting (a political movement calling for the vote for working men) was held here in October 1838. The acme of the woollen manufacturing industry was from 1856 to 1900, the boom period of Cambrian Mills, which produced its world-famous fabrics from a steam-driven mill on the banks of the Severn.

The town's biggest claim to fame is that Robert Owen, the factory reformer, founder of the cooperative movement and 'father of Socialism', was born here in 1771, though he left at the age of 10 and only returned just before his death in 1858. Monuments to his esteemed memory abound in the town centre.

👁 Sights

Gregynog Hall   GARDENS

(📞01686-650224; www.gregynog.org; Tregynon, SY16 3PL; formal garden £5, parking £2.50; ☉dawn-dusk) **FREE** While Gregynog Hall has been here in some form for 800 years, its current mock-Tudor manifestation dates to 1840. It's now the 300-hectare Grade 1–listed garden, dating to at least the 16th century, that's the major attraction. Walking tracks trace avenues of sculpted yews, banks of rhododendrons and azaleas, 300-year-old oaks and bird-filled beech woodlands. Aside from the formal garden, admission to the enchanting grounds is unrestricted.

From 1924 Gregynog was home to the Davies sisters, Gwendoline and Margaret, who bequeathed an extraordinary collection of paintings to the National Museum. The sisters intended to make the house an arts centre, and it's now owned by the University of Wales, who use the venue for the Gŵyl Gregynog, an annual classical-music festival held in mid-June. The house also has a renowned Welsh-interest library, which visitors can browse, and a cafe and shop (open 10am to 4.30pm from April to September).

The hall is 5 miles north of Newtown, signposted from the B4389.

Oriel Davies Gallery   GALLERY

(📞01686-625041; www.orieldavies.org; The Park, SY16 2NZ; ☉10am-5pm Tue-Sat) **FREE** One of Wales' leading contemporary spaces and the largest visual-arts venue in Mid-Wales, Oriel Davies hosts often edgy national and international exhibitions, and offers a range of talks, courses and workshops. It has a popular sunny, glassed-in, vegetarian-friendly cafe (Relish; open 10am to 4pm). The gallery sits within a leafy riverside park, which contains a mound that's all that remains of Newtown's 13th-century castle.

Robert Owen Museum — MUSEUM
(☑ 01686-625544; www.robert-owen-museum. org.uk; The Cross, Broad St; ☺ 11am-3pm Mon-Fri) **FREE** Housed in Newtown's Edwardian library and council chambers, this museum is the best place to bone up on the legacy of Robert Owen: the son of a saddler who became a successful cotton-mill owner and radical reformer. Owen's achievements included ensuring a 10- to 12-hour workday, a minimum working age of 10 and schools for his employees' children. Exhibits are rich in detail. The museum also serves as Newtown's tourist information point.

At the corner of Gas and Short Bridge Sts, a statue and garden herald Owen as a 'pioneer, social reformer and philanthropist'. His **grave** (St Mary's Old Parish Church) lies in St Mary's Old Parish Church on the south bank of the river.

✪ Festivals & Events

Gŵyl Gregynog Festival — MUSIC
(☑ 01686-207100; www.gwylgregynogfestival. org; ☺ Jun) Long-standing classical-music festival happening at various locales across rural northern Powys. The epicentre of it all is Gregynog Hall, near Newtown.

🛏 Sleeping & Eating

Old Vicarage Dolfor — B&B ££
(☑ 01686-629051; www.theoldvicaragedolfor. co.uk; Dolfor; r 1/2/4 people from £70/95/150; 🅿 🛜) A handsome rural red-brick Victorian house, the Old Vicarage offers four pretty rooms with muted colour schemes, subtle floral wallpapers, claw-foot bathtubs and an incredibly warm welcome. If you book, you can also dine here: there is an accomplished two-course dinner menu (£25). The Old Vicarage is 4 miles south of Newtown by the busy A483.

Elephant & Castle Hotel — HOTEL ££
(☑ 01686-626271; www.elephantandcastlehotel. co.uk; Broad St; s/d/ste from £60/90/120; 🅿 🛜) Occupying a sweet, central spot by the Severn, this refurbished stone pub offers five en-suite rooms with king-size beds in the hotel proper (will it be the 'Robert Owen' or the 'Laura Ashley'?), and another 10 (smaller, still very nice) in the bothy (outbuilding) out back.

There's also the in-house Riverside Restaurant, proffering a perked-up pub-food menu (mains £11 to £18). Oh, and a lounge bar.

Granary Wine Bar — TAPAS ££
(☑ 01686-621120; www.thegranarywinebar.com; 17 Parkers Lane; tapas £4-5; ☺ 5-9pm Fri & Sat) This refined address specialises in hand-picked wines, especially Spanish ones, but fleshes out the appeal for customers with a lovely tapas menu too (three to four dishes are needed to make it a meal). Book ahead.

🛍 Shopping

Market Hall — MARKET
(☑ 01686-622388; www.glanhafren.org; 26 Market St; ☺ 9am-5pm Tue-Sat) Dating to 1870, Newtown's handsome brick market hall has been extensively restored and now houses stalls selling antiques, Welsh woollen blankets and more.

ⓘ Getting There & Away

Bus routes include four daily services to Cardiff (£9, 3¾ hours), Brecon (£9, 1¾ hours) and Llandrindod Wells (£4.90, 50 minutes).

The daily National Express (p333) coach from Aberystwyth (from £10, 1¼ hours) to London (from £7, 5¾ hours), via Welshpool (£6, 25 minutes), Shrewsbury (£8.20, one hour) and Birmingham (£14, 2½ hours), stops here.

Newtown is on Arriva Trains Wales' Cambrian Line, crossing from Aberystwyth (£14.50, 1¼ hours) to Birmingham (£22, two hours) five times a day via Machynlleth (£11, 39 minutes), Welshpool (£5.70, 14 minutes) and Shrewsbury (£8.30, 40 minutes).

Montgomery

POP 990

Set around a market square lined with handsome stone-and-brick houses, and overlooked by the ruins of a Norman **castle** (☺ 10am-6pm Apr-Sep, to 4pm Oct-Mar) **FREE**, genteel Montgomery is one of Wales' prettiest small towns. An idiosyncratic mixture of Georgian, Victorian and timber-framed houses (many marked by helpful historical plaques) lines the streets and there are a number of excellent places to eat.

A mile east of town is one of the best-preserved sections of Offa's Dyke, with 6m-high ditches flanking the B4386

by opposing field gates, ensuring Montgomery is also a hit with hikers.

◉ Sights

Monty's Brewery
Visitor Centre
VISITOR CENTRE

(www.montysbrewery.co.uk; Forden Rd) If you have acquired a taste for Welsh craft beer, or want to, make the hop north of the centre to one of the country's most visitor-friendly breweries. The experience encompasses a visitor centre, a shop, a tasting room and a window onto their developmental brewery (their main brewery cannot be visited, but you can learn about the brewing process here). Walkers will cherish their 'Best Offa' as a beery souvenir: a golden bitter and official beer of the Offa's Dyke Path.

St Nicholas' Church
CHURCH

(Church Bank; ⊙9am-dusk) Evocative Norman St Nicholas' Church dates from 1226. Look out for the vaulted ceiling decorated with intricate coloured bosses, a beautifully carved pre-Reformation rood screen, striking mid-19th-century stained-glass windows and the canopied tomb of local landowner Sir Richard Herbert and his wife Magdalen, parents of Elizabethan poet George Herbert.

Cloverlands Model Car Museum
MUSEUM

(☑01686-668004; www.cloverlandsmuseum. wales; Montgomery Institute, Arthur St; adult/child £3/free; ⊙10am-noon & 1-3pm Fri, 10am-1pm & 2-5pm Sat; ⓓ) With some 4000 exhibits, Cloverlands is one of the most extensive collections of its kind in the UK, and a must for model-car lovers. Other viewing times are possible to arrange by prior appointment.

🛏 Sleeping & Eating

Dragon Hotel
INN ££

(☑01686-668359; www.dragonhotel.com; Market Sq; r from £63; ⓟ🛜🏊) Popular with walkers, this extremely noticeable 17th-century half-timbered coaching inn has some 20 en-suite rooms, a common snug (the Den), a pool (yes, really) and a restaurant (mains £13 to £17.50, kitchen open noon to 3pm and 6pm to 8.45pm). The bar is as good a place as any to try ales brewed at Monty's, just down the road.

⭐Checkers
FRENCH £

(☑01686-669822; www.checkerswales.co.uk; Broad St; lunch £5-10; ⊙10am-4pm Tue-Thu, from 9am Fri & Sat; 🛜) One of Montgomery's main drawcards is this truly excellent restaurant-with-rooms. With an inquisitive modern-French approach to fresh, locally sourced ingredients, and as a former Michelin-star-holder, it's earned a loyal fan base. It now concocts the likes of Gressingham duck salad with blackberries and smoky beef and chorizo chilli with feta, plus brunches and a few inspired puddings.

Upstairs, this 17th-century coaching inn still welcomes guests. Five quietly stylish rooms (£105 to £125) with extra-comfy beds, two of which are super-king, also sport blissful bathrooms.

Castle Kitchen
CAFE £

(☑01686-668795; www.castlekitchen.org; 8 Broad St; lunch £7-10; ⊙9am-4.30pm Mon-Sat, from 11am Sun) This lovely little deli-cafe overlooking Monty's picturesque heart is perfect for stocking up on bottles, butter, charcuterie and other supplies for a picnic on Offa's Dyke or in the surrounding hills. Or you can just relax in-house, enjoying the unforced friendliness of the service and a wonderful selection of soups, breads, sandwiches, luscious cakes and daily specials.

🛍 Shopping

Bunners
HOMEWARES

(☑01686-668308; www.bunners.co.uk; Arthur St; ⊙9am-5.30pm Mon-Fri, to 5pm Sat) This Aladdin's cave of an old-fashioned ironmongers attracts curious visitors from afar. Founded in a Georgian shop in 1892, it will still sell a single screw from among the unimaginable profusion of goods heaped on every surface.

ℹ Information

Tourist Information Point
(cnr Arthur & Princes Sts; ⊙24hr) A tourist-information point in a blue-painted phone box.

ℹ Getting There & Away

Up to seven X71/81 buses per day run to Welshpool (18 minutes) and Newtown (23 minutes) – at either of which you can connect to national rail services.

Berriew

POP 1330

Shortly before the River Rhiw empties into the Severn, it gurgles through this pretty village of black-and-white houses, grouped around an ancient oval churchyard. Tiny

PISTYLL RHAEADR

'I never saw water falling so gracefully, so much like thin beautiful threads, as here,' George Borrow, the Victorian writer who penned one of the best-known Welsh travelogues, *Wild Wales* (1862), says of **Pistyll Rhaeadr** (www.pistyllrhaeadr.co.uk; Llanrhaeadr-ym-Mochnant, SY10 0BZ; **P**) **FREE**, one of the country's highest waterfalls. In terms of an overall experience, this wonderfully tumbling cascade is certainly among the loveliest.

Reached from the lonely village of Llanrhaeadr-ym-Mochnant, and four miles up the valley from there, Pistyll Rhaeadr is in fact three separate falls dropping 73m (240ft) over a thickly, lushly vegetated cliff. The scene feels like some South American wilderness grafted onto the rarely visited and barren Berwyn Mountains, which rise up here. There are two waterfall viewing points: one easily accessed from the car park at the base, and one, a steep 20-minute walk, at the top. Also from here, further forays up into the bleak but beautiful Berwyns beyond are possible. The remote range features the highest point in Wales outside a national park, **Cadair Berwyn** (827m/2713ft).

Below the falls perches welcoming **Tan-y-Pistyll** (01691-780392; www.pistyllrhaeadr.co.uk; Llanrhaeadr-ym-Mochnant, SY10 0BZ; tent/2-person apt from £7/130; **P**), where travellers can tarry longer through camping, apartments (with a two-night minimum) and a pretty tearoom (open 9.30am to 6pm from April to September, to 4pm October to March).

Berriew is the unlikely location for the Andrew Logan Museum of Sculpture; when it's closed there's not much to do here except stroll around, sip a drink in the cafe-deli and take in the scenery.

Sights

Andrew Logan Museum of Sculpture   GALLERY
(ALMoS; 01686-640689; www.andrewloganmuseum.org; adult/child £5/3; 10am-5pm Sat & Sun May-Sep) The supremely flouncy and fascinating Andrew Logan Museum of Sculpture is a surprise find in this tiny village. Occupying a former squash court, it's the world's only sculpture museum devoted to a still-living artist. That, of course, is Andrew, and this temple to his work is a glorious celebration of the beautiful, frivolous and humorous, including his huge, glittering Cosmic Egg and a larger-than-life likeness of fashion designer Zandra Rhodes.

You can look around at other times if you reserve in advance.

Eating

Lychgate Cottage   CAFE £
(01686-640750; www.facebook.com/LychgateCottageTearoomDeli; mains £3-7.50; 9am-4pm Mon-Sat Oct-Mar, to 4.30pm Apr-Sep) This little tearoom by the village church serves delicious deli items, such as Welsh cheese, pâté platters and Ludlow olives, alongside sandwiches, cakes and other light bites and meals.

Getting There & Away

Berriew is 6 miles south of Welshpool, just off the A483. Buses T12/89/X75 from Welshpool (15 minutes) or T12/X75 from Newtown (25 minutes) stop at Berriew's Lion Hotel.

Welshpool (Y Trallwng)
POP 5950

The English originally called this place Pool, after the 'pills' – boggy, marshy ground (long since drained) along the nearby River Severn. It was changed in 1835 to Welshpool, so nobody would get confused with Poole in Dorset. Set below a steeply wooded hill, it's a smart, busy, unspectacular market town with a mixture of Tudor, Georgian and Victorian buildings along its main streets. It promotes itself as 'Gateway to Wales'. As with most entranceways, however, you won't dawdle here long.

Livestock lovers might be drawn by the Monday livestock market, one of the largest in Western Europe, but more compelling, to be sure, are Welshpool's peripheral sights, such as glorious Powis Castle (p224).

Sights & Activities

Welshpool sits on the longest navigable section of the Montgomery Canal, which originally ran for 33 miles, starting at Frankton

Junction in Shropshire, where it joined the Llangollen Canal, snaking past Welshpool to Newtown. A towpath still runs the whole length, and makes for a great hike or (between Welshpool and Newtown only) bike ride, and there are also occasional **canal boat trips** (www.heulwentrust.co.uk; boat trips per adult/child from £8/4).

★ Powis Castle

CASTLE

(NT; ☎ 01938-551944; www.nationaltrust.org.uk; castle & gardens adult/child £14.20/7.10; ⊙ gardens 10am-6pm Apr-Sep, to 4pm Oct-Mar, castle & Clive Museum noon-4pm; ℗ 🖭) Surrounded by magnificent gardens, the red-brick Powis Castle was originally constructed in the 13th century by Gruffydd ap Gwenwynwyn, prince of Powys, and subsequently enriched by generations of the Herbert and Clive families. The castle's highlight, the **Clive Museum**, houses exquisite treasures brought back from India and the Far East by Clive of India (British conqueror of Bengal at the Battle of Plassey in 1757) and his son Edward, who married the daughter of the first earl of Powys.

The extravagant mural-covered, wood-panelled interior, the mahogany beds, tiger skins and one of Wales' finest collections of paintings proclaim the family's opulence, while the Clive Museum, with its cache of armour, bejewelled weapons, precious stones, textiles, diaries and letters, is testament to a life richly lived in colonial India. You may spot a gold tiger's head encrusted with rubies and diamonds – one of only two to survive from the throne of Tipu Sultan – as well as a Chinese sword with snakeskin scabbard and finely carved ivory chess pieces.

Ridiculous wealth this may be, but it's worth remembering (the museum indeed points this out) that, as with many grand British residences popping up during the colonial era, the Clives looted many of the artefacts for their country pile – in this case during their power seizure and brutal resultant rule in India and Myanmar.

The baroque Italianate gardens are extraordinary, dotted with original lead statues, flowerbeds and ancient yews, with an orangery, formal and wild sections, terraces and orchards.

The castle is just over a mile south of Welshpool, off Berriew Rd, a pretty walk from the centre.

Welshpool & Llanfair Light Railway TOURS (☎ 01938-810441; www.wllr.org.uk; Raven Sq; adult/child £12/5; ⊙ Mar-Oct; 🖭) This sturdy narrow-gauge railway, completed in 1903 to bring livestock to market, chugs through the pretty Banwy Valley. It's an 8-mile, 50-minute journey up steep inclines from Raven Square Station to Llanfair Caereinion. Check online for departure times. Closed in 1956, the line was reopened seven years later by enthusiastic volunteers and now even offers courses in steam-engine driving (£395; drinks included).

🎊 Festivals

Welshpool Country Music Festival MUSIC (www.countrywestern.org.uk; evening/weekend ticket from £15/40; ⊙ mid-Jul) In mid-July, the Powis Castle Showfield becomes the unlikely venue for a weekend country-music hoedown. Proceeds benefit people with disabilities, through the Heulwen Trust, which runs two narrowboats to take its beneficiaries on canal trips.

🛏 Sleeping & Eating

Royal Oak HISTORIC HOTEL £ (☎ 01938-552217; www.royaloakwelshpool.co.uk; The Cross; d £62-81; ℗ 🛜) Occupying a former Georgian coaching inn and known by the honorific 'Royal' ever since Queen Victoria visited, this is easily the grandest hotel-restaurant in Welshpool. Adorned in bright patterns, rooms are comfortably

---

OFF THE BEATEN TRACK

GLYNDŴR'S WAY

Named for the last native Prince of Wales, **Glyndŵr's Way** (www.nationaltrail.co.uk/glyndwrs-way) meanders 135 miles from Welshpool, near the English border, to Machynlleth on the southern cusp of Snowdonia National Park. It then returns cross-country to Knighton, just below the dreamy Shropshire Hills. Allow nine days to complete the whole route, which is in parts a strenuous hike for experienced hikers only.

On the hike, you'll catch sight of iconic peaks such as Cadair Idris, Pen Pumlumon Fawr, and other bucolic delights, and see Glyndŵr-related sights including battle sites, an abbey the prince ransacked and the place where he established Wales' first parliament.

modern, while the public bar and restaurant serve the town both for casual get-togethers and destination dining (mains £15 to £19).

Corn Store   INTERNATIONAL **££**
(☑01938-554614; 4 Church St; 2-/3-course meal £21/26; ☉noon-2.30pm & 6-9.30pm Wed-Sat, noon-3pm-Sun) Run by chef-proprietor Rebecca for 30-odd years, Welshpool's best and friendliest restaurant has avocado walls and cheery round, rainbow mirrors that overlook families of regulars tucking into British-Med-Asian dishes such as sea bass with chilli and crayfish tails or duck breast in blackberry and sloe-gin sauce.

❶ Information

Tourist Information Centre (☑01938-552043; www.visitwelshpool.org.uk; 1 Vicarage Gardens, Church St; ☉9.30am-4.30pm Mon-Sat, 10am-4pm Sun) Has a bed-booking service, can sell bus and canal-boat trip tickets and proffers plenty of visitor information on Welshpool.

Victoria Memorial Hospital (☑01938-558900; www.powysthb.wales.nhs.uk; Salop Rd; ☉24hr) Central, with a 24/7 Minor Injuries Department.

❶ Getting There & Away

Bus X75 runs to Newtown (£2.80, 37 minutes, six to seven per day) and Shrewsbury (£3.20, 48 minutes); the daily National Express runs to Newtown and Aberystwyth (£15, 1¾ hours) in one direction and Shrewsbury (£6, 35 minutes), Birmingham (£13, 2¼ hours) and finally London (from £18, 5½ hours) in the other.

Welshpool is on the Cambrian Line. Eight daily services forge east from Aberystwyth (£16.30, 1½ hours) via Machynlleth (£14.20, 50 minutes), Newtown (£5.70, 15 minutes) and Shrewsbury (£6.70, 22 minutes). Birmingham is also served by direct train (£19, 1½ hours, five daily).

AT A GLANCE

POPULATION
Llanberis: 2112

LARGEST TOWN
Llanberis

TALLEST MOUNTAIN
Snowdon (1085m)

BEST OFF-THE-BEATEN-TRACK HIKE
Carnedd Loop (p251)

BEST ADRENALIN RUSH
Go Below Underground Adventures (p249)

BEST PANORAMIC VIEW
Tre'r Ceiri Hillfort (p269)

WHEN TO GO
May & Jun Warm daytime temperatures and few crowds mean it's the best time to hit the mountain trails.

Jul Llangollen rocks out with the International Musical Eisteddfod, Fringe Festival and Underneath the Arches.

Sep Offbeat Portmeirion hosts Festival No 6, an exuberant arts, music and food fest.

Snowdonia National Park (p226)
ANDREI DORAN/SHUTTERSTOCK ©

Snowdonia & the Llŷn

T wo sharply contrasting parts of north Wales, Snowdonia and the Llŷn share a proud identity as staunch enclaves of the Cymraeg language and culture. Mountainous Snowdonia is densely packed with sky-scraping peaks, post-glacial valleys with icy lakes or ancient forests, and former slate-mining towns turned adventure-tourism hubs celebrating their industrial heritage.

Away from the castles, heritage railways, and seaside towns along the coast further south, slow-paced Llŷn exudes a quiet Celtic spirituality. A pilgrims' destination for many centuries, it rewards slow travel and attracts those in search of paths less trodden, beguiled by myths of Avalon, plus a few surfers.

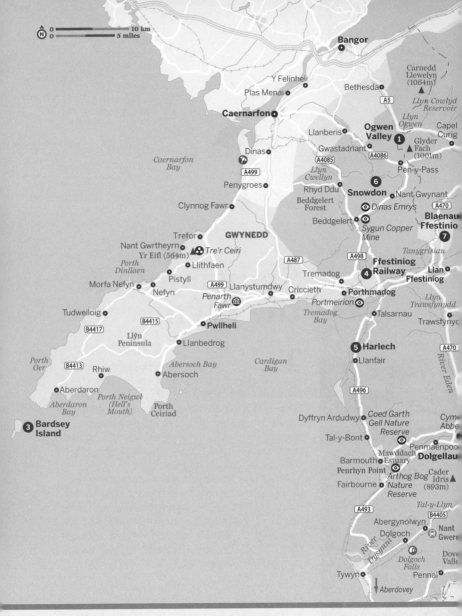

Snowdonia & the Llŷn Highlights

1 Glyder Traverse (p252)
Viewing some of Snowdonia's
most spectacular mountain
panoramas from the Castle of
the Winds and Devil's Kitchen.

2 Betws-y-Coed (p247)
Frolicking in fairy-populated

glens and partaking in
daredevil adventure.

3 Bardsey Island (p268)
Braving the crossing to
mythical Avalon from an end-
of-the-world headland.

4 Ffestiniog Railway
(p260) Riding the most scenic
of Welsh heritage railway
journeys from the sea to the
mountains.

5 Harlech Castle (p244)
Enjoying cliff-edge views of

Cardigan Bay and Snowdon, from the sturdy battlements.

6 Mount Snowdon (p255) Conquering the highest peak in Wales, via precipitous trails or a rack-and-pinion railway.

7 Blaenau Ffestiniog (p245) Exploring slate caverns and former mining tunnels, or zooming above them on zip lines.

8 Pontcysyllte Aqueduct (p232) Slow-boating or hiking across this lofty pinnacle of Georgian civil engineering.

NORTH WALES BORDERLANDS

Comprising a chunk of Welsh coast that leads east towards Chester, the Vale of Clwyd, fringed by the Clwydian range, and the broad Dee Valley, the Welsh borderland counties of Denbighshire and Flintshire are hard to pin down. It's well worth pausing here as you make your way towards Snowdonia to peruse the varied highlights: the stately market town of Ruthin with its handsome medieval buildings, a holy well that has drawn pilgrims for centuries, and a splendid aqueduct near Llangollen, a seat of Welsh culture.

Ruthin

POP 5723

Tucked away in the bucolic Clwyd valley, Ruthin (*rith*-in) is an attractive, lost-in-time hilltop settlement. In the Middle Ages it was an important market town and textile producer. There are still livestock markets held here three times a week, as well as a produce market on Friday morning and a general market on Thursday.

The heart of Ruthin is St Peter's Sq, lined with an impressive collection of heritage buildings, including a 1421 half-timbered Old Courthouse (now a bank), with the remains of a gibbet under the eaves, and St Peter's Collegiate Church, the oldest parts of which date from 1310.

WORTH A TRIP

THE SHOW MUST GO ON... IN MOLD

The unfortunately named town of Mold, 10 miles east of Ruthin, is the home of Wales' leading theatre company, Clwyd Theatr Cymru.

Founded in 1976, **Clwyd Theatr Cymru** (☑ box office 01352-701521; www.theatrclwyd.com; Raikes Ln, Mold) has five performance spaces, and stages a year-round program of old and new drama, mainly in English, including works for children and young people. It also offers opera, live music, dance, comedy, poetry and films. It's signposted off the A5119, a mile outside Mold, in Flintshire.

◉ Sights & Activities

Nantclwyd y Dre   HISTORIC BUILDING
(☑ 01824-706868; www.denbighshire.gov.uk; Castle St; adult/concession £7/6; ⊙ 11am-5pm Wed-Mon) Dating from 1435, half-timbered Nantclwyd y Dre is thought to be the oldest town house in Wales. It originally belonged to a family of weavers and the rooms have been restored and furnished to reflect the era of each addition, offering windows into the world of the various families that lived in them: a Victorian schoolroom, a Stuart study, Georgian and Jacobean bedchambers. The 13th-century Lord's Garden, behind the house, has also been restored.

A 'bat-cam' lets you peek into the world of the colony of lesser horseshoe bats that resides in the attic – they're the smallest (with bodies about the size of a plum) and rarest bat species in Britain.

Ruthin Craft Centre   ARTS CENTRE
(☑ 01824-704774; www.ruthincraftcentre.org.uk; Park Rd; ⊙ 10am-5.30pm; P) **FREE** This is an excellent gallery and arts hub. Aside from the three galleries – which do great work bringing the best of local photography, glasswork, painting and sculpture to light, and show many pieces for sale – the complex includes artists' studios, public workshops and talks, a very nice cafe and shop, and an unstaffed information centre.

Ruthin Gaol   HISTORIC BUILDING
(☑ 01824-708281; www.denbighshire.gov.uk; 46 Clwyd St; adult/concession £7/6; ⊙ 11am-5pm Wed-Mon Apr-Sep) This sombre building is the only Pentonville-style Victorian prison in Britain that's open to visitors. A free audio guide allows you to follow the sentence of an imaginary prisoner, 'Will the Poacher', while information panels in the cells fill you in on all the fascinating and grisly details of day-to-day prison life and the daring escapes of John Jones, the 'Welsh Houdini', banged up here in the 1870s. Pentonville-style prisons employed the 'separate system' of isolating and observing inmates.

Coed Llandegla Forest   OUTDOORS
(☑ 01978-751656; www.oneplanetadventure. com; Ruthin Rd, A525, Wrexham; car parking £5; ⊙ 9am-9pm Mon-Thu, to 6pm Fri-Sun Mar-Oct, shorter hours rest of year) Roughly equidistant from Ruthin, Wrexham, and Llangollen, Coed Llandegla Forest is home

to some of the best mountain biking you'll find in northeast Wales, ranging from a family-friendly loop to gritty, technically challenging black runs. There's plenty to keep two legs occupied as well, with almost 25km of walking trails, and two dedicated trail-runner trails. All are operated by One Planet Adventure.

🛏 Sleeping & Eating

Manorhaus BOUTIQUE HOTEL **££**
(☑ 01824-704830; www.manorhaus.com; 10 Well St; r from £80, ste £120; 🛜) This boutique restaurant with rooms offers eight individually styled bedrooms in a stately Georgian town house, each decorated by a different artist. Perks include a spa, library and private cinema, while the superb in-house restaurant (open 6pm to 9pm Tuesday to Saturday; two/three courses £25/30) dishes up the bold flavours of Modern Welsh cuisine for guests and nonguests alike.

Ruthin Castle Hotel HISTORIC HOTEL **£££**
(☑ 01824-702664; www.ruthincastle.co.uk; Castle St; r/ste from £170/240; P 🛜) The forlorn cries of peacocks strutting the gardens of this neo-Gothic mansion are the first hint of the offbeat luxury within. Making use of a Victorian 'castle' constructed amid the ruins of the real thing (built for Edward in 1277), its over-the-top grandeur includes a spa, a wood-panelled library and bar and a medieval banqueting hall that doubles as an atmospheric restaurant.

There's also a gym and spa (packages start at £69).

Leonardo's Deli DELI **£**
(☑ 01824-707161; www.leonardosdeli.co.uk; 4 Well St; sandwiches, wraps & salads £4; ⊙ 9am-4pm Mon-Sat) Run by a Welsh-German couple, this deli offers an abundance of local cheeses, free-range eggs, preserves, fresh sandwiches, and top-notch pies. Its chicken, leek and laverbread was champion of the 2011 British Pie Awards; pie day is Friday, so place your order on Thursday at the latest.

❶ Getting There & Away

Frequent bus X51 runs between Ruthin and Denbigh on weekdays (£2, 25 minutes), with nine services continuing to Wrexham (£2.70, one hour); the X1 runs to/from Chester (£2.90, 1¼ hours, two daily).

DON'T MISS

THE HOLY WELL OF HOLYWELL

The market town of Holywell, which bills itself 'the Lourdes of Wales', is named after its well, **St Winefride's Well** (☑ 01352-713054; www.saintwinefrideswell. com; Greenfield St; adult/child £1/30p; ⊙ 9am-5pm Apr-Sep, 10am-4pm Oct-Mar; P). The site where St Winefride was supposedly decapitated after spurning the amorous advances of Prince Caradoc (and revived by her uncle, St Bueno, using the miraculous waters) has been a place of pilgrimage since her death in the 7th century. Curative bathing dates to the Romans who allegedly cured gout and rheumatism here, and modern-day pilgrims still take the waters.

Llangollen

POP 3491

Curving around the banks of the tumbling River Dee (Afon Dyfrdwy) in a narrow valley, and with the mysterious hilltop ruins of Castell Dinas Brân as a backdrop, picturesque, compact Llangollen (khlan *goth*-len) is a seat of Welsh culture, and a jumping-off point for visiting a remarkable aqueduct.

Named after St Collen, a 7th-century monk who founded a religious community *(llan)* here, Llangollen has a growing summer walking and white-water-rafting scene, and the riverside walk, heading west from the 14th-century bridge, has been a popular promenading spot since Victorian times. Two major arts festivals boost tourism, as do railway and engineering enthusiasts interested in the area's industrial legacy. That legacy accounts for the town's present layout: housing was relocated to make way for locomotives.

⊙ Sights

⊙ Centre

⭐ **Plas Newydd** HISTORIC BUILDING
(☑ 01978-862834; www.denbighshire.gov.uk/heritage; Hill St; adult/child £6/5; ⊙ 10.30am-5pm Apr-Sep; P ♿) Plas Newydd is the 18th-century home of the Ladies of Llangollen (Irish aristocrat Lady Eleanor Butler and her companion, Sarah Ponsonby). The celebrated couple transformed the house from a simple cottage into an elaborate hybrid

Llangollen

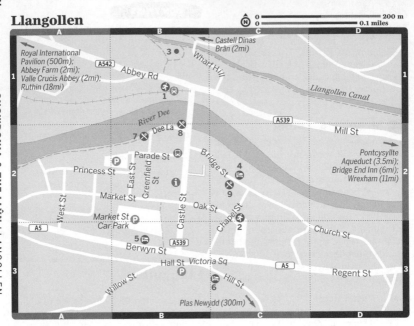

Llangollen

🏃 Activities, Courses & Tours

🛏 Sleeping

🍽 Eating

of Gothic and Tudor styles, complete with stained-glass windows, carved-oak panels and a knot garden out front. Informative self-guided audio tours of the house bring the half-dozen dark-wood-panelled rooms to life, including the pared-down attic room of the housekeeper. Access to the gardens is free.

⊙ Around Llangollen

★ Pontcysyllte Aqueduct & Canal World Heritage Site   CANAL
(🖳 visitor centre 01978-822912; www.pontcysyllte-aqueduct.co.uk; B5434; guided tours £3;

⊙ visitor centre 10am-4pm Easter-Oct, long weekends Nov, Dec & late Feb–Easter) **FREE** The preeminent Georgian engineer Thomas Telford (1757–1834) built the Pontcysyllte (pont-kus-*sulth*-teh) Aqueduct in 1805, 4 miles west of Llangollen, to carry the canal over the River Dee. At 307m long, 3.6m wide, 1.7m deep and 38m high, it is the most spectacular piece of engineering on the entire UK canal system and the highest canal aqueduct ever built. You can walk the Unesco-certified aqueduct and an 11-mile stretch of the canal, or sail it in a narrowboat.

In the 18th century the horse-drawn canal barge was the most efficient way of hauling goods over long distances, but, with the advent of the railway, most of them fell into disrepair. The Llangollen Canal fared better than most because it was used for many more years to carry drinking water from the River Dee to the Hurleston Reservoir in Cheshire. Today it's again in use, carrying visitors up and down the Vale of Llangollen. In addition, the old towpaths offer miles of peaceful, traffic-free walking.

Telford's goal was to connect up the haulage routes between the Rivers Dee, Severn and Mersey. To collect water for the canal from the Dee, he also designed an elegant

DON'T MISS

'YOU RANG, M'LORD?'

Situated on the Clywedog River, **Erddig** (NT; ☑ 01978-355314; www.nationaltrust.org.uk; A483, LL13 0YT; adult/child £13/6.30, grounds only £8/5; ⊙ house 12.30-3.30pm, grounds 10am-5pm, shorter hours winter; P ♿) was the Yorke family's ancestral home for over two centuries since 1680. It provides a unique insight into the life of the British upper class in the 18th and 19th centuries, and the 'upstairs-downstairs' social hierarchy of their bygone world. When the National Trust took over in 1973, it restored the 18th-century garden and the house to its 1922 appearance. Highlights include an intimate glimpse into the relationship that existed between masters and their servants, with the Servants' Hall featuring oil paintings of staff and poems by members of the Yorke family that honour some of their favourites.

The last Yorke to own Errdig left the country pile in a state of disrepair; the house, the earliest parts of which date from 1680, had no electricity, running water, or telephone line, and the garden was hopelessly overgrown. Today, the 486-hectare landscaped pleasure park and, in particular, the walled garden, are a delight to behold, with the walls covered with a mind-boggling 150 species of ivy, and trimmed yew hedges encircling a battalion of pleached trees.

Erddig is 12 miles northeast of Llangollen, signposted off the A483.

curving weir called Horseshoe Falls. The adjacent riverbank is a tranquil picnic spot.

Blue-badge guides run tours from near the aqueduct visitor centre, while canal boats offer trips along the 'stream in the sky' from the nearby quay and from Llangollen Wharf. Otherwise you can simply stroll across, free of charge. Whichever way you choose, you'll need a head for heights.

Horseshoe Falls is about 2 miles west of Llangollen (take the A5 west and after about 1.5 miles turn right across the river). Both the falls and aqueduct are easily reached by the canal towpath, if you're in no hurry.

Valle Crucis Abbey   RUINS
(Abaty Glyn y Groes; Cadw; www.cadw.gov.wales; A542; adult/concession £3.80/2.20; ⊙10am-5pm Apr-Oct, to 4pm Nov-Mar) The stark ruins of this Cistercian abbey are a 2-mile walk north of Llangollen. Founded in 1201 by Madog ap Gruffydd, ruler of northern Powys, its largely Gothic form predates its more famous sibling at Tintern (which, on the eve of Valle Crucis' 1537 dissolution, was its only rival as the richest Cistercian abbey in the land). The vaulted chapterhouse, the west wall, and the monks' gravestones are intact.

A small interpretive centre brings the monks' daily routines to life.

Castell Dinas Brân   RUINS
(off Wern Rd) FREE The ever-visible ragged arches and tumbledown walls of Dinas Brân (Crow Castle) mark the remnants of

a short-lived 13th-century castle of which it was said 'there was not a mightier in Wales nor a better in England'. Burnt by defenders in anticipation of capture by Edward I, there's little left of it today – fabulous 360-degree views over the Dee and surrounding countryside are the real reward for the steep 1½-hour return walk from town.

🏃 Activities

Welsh Canal Holiday Craft   BOATING
(☑ 01978-860702; www.horsedrawnboats.co.uk; Llangollen Wharf; ⊙mid-Mar–Oct) Peaceful horse-drawn narrowboats depart on 45-minute trips from Llangollen Wharf every half-hour during the school holidays, and hourly otherwise (adult/child £8/4). Two-hour journeys head to Horseshoe Falls and back, and motorised boats take you up to Pontcysyllte Aqueduct (adult/child £14.50/12, return journey by coach). Self-drive boats are £140/195 per day/weekend. Reservations strongly advised in busy periods.

Llangollen Railway   RAIL
(☑ 01978-860979; www.llangollen-railway.co.uk; Abbey Rd; adult/child return £16/8.50; ⊙daily mid-Feb–Oct, reduced services rest of year; ♿) This 10-mile jaunt through the Dee Valley via Berwyn (near Horseshoe Falls) and Corwen on the former Ruabon to Barmouth Line, hauled by a steam or diesel engine, is a superb day out for rail fans. There are theme days for children, and Driver

Experience Days (£260 to £445) for those wanting to drive a heritage railcar, steam locomotive or diesel locomotive.

Ty Nant Outdoors
ADVENTURE SPORTS

(☑07814 922437; www.tynantoutdoors.com; Sun Bank) This highly regarded local operator offers mostly water-based activities, such as canoeing, kayaking and SUP instruction, including half-day (£55) canoeing jaunts across the aqueduct. Fairly gentle whitewater rafting (£58) on the River Dee is also on offer (minimum age eight years), as well as climbing, abseiling and gorge walking.

Safe & Sound Outdoors
ADVENTURE SPORTS

(☑01978-860471; www.sasoutdoors.co.uk; Chapel St; ⊙9am-5pm Apr-Oct, to 4pm Mon-Sat Nov-Mar) This all-purpose adventure company rents out late-model Diamondback mountain and road bikes (£30 per day). It also does rafting (£58 per three hours), gorge walking (£50 per half-day), rock climbing, paintball and, should you be in the market, hen and stag dos.

★ Festivals & Events

International Musical Eisteddfod
PERFORMING ARTS

(☑01978-862000; www.international-eisteddfod.co.uk; ⊙Jul) The International Musical Eisteddfod was established after WWII to promote world harmony. Each July it attracts 4000 participants and 50,000 spectators from around 50 countries, transforming lovely Llangollen into an international village. In addition to folk music and dancing competitions, gala concerts at the

Royal International Pavilion feature global stars. IME was nominated for the Nobel Peace Prize in 2004.

During the festival, choral performances and dance are held in venues across town, and the small town receives up to 120,000 visitors. Tickets for all-day access can be bought on the day; book tickets well in advance for headliners.

Llangollen Fringe Festival
PERFORMING ARTS

(☑08001-455779; www.llangollenfringe.co.uk; ⊙Jul) Normally held in the town hall, this volunteer-run 'alternative' arts festival, held over 11 days from mid-July, manages to attract some big names: 2018's line-up included Lee 'Scratch' Perry and Linton Kwesi Johnson. There are also poetry readings, musical narrowboat cruises and steam-train trips, and a final concert in the atmospheric ruins of Valle Crucis Abbey (p233).

🛏 Sleeping

Book months in advance for the International Eisteddfod in July.

Llangollen Hostel
HOSTEL £

(☑01978-861773; www.llangollenhostel.co.uk; Is-allt, Berwyn St; dm/d/f £20/50/70; ℗ 🛜) This excellent independent hostel, based in a former family home, has friendly owners and a cared-for feel. It offers various rooms, from private en-suite doubles to a six-bed dorm, as well as an orderly kitchen and a cosy lounge. It actively welcomes cyclists, walkers and canoeists, offering laundry facilities and bike/boat storage. Prices

---

THE LADIES OF LLANGOLLEN
....

Lady Eleanor Butler and Miss Sarah Ponsonby, the 'Ladies of Llangollen', lived in Plas Newydd (p231) (New Home) from 1780 to 1829 with their maid, Mary Carryl. They had fallen in love in Ireland, but their aristocratic Anglo-Irish families discouraged the relationship. In a desperate bid to be allowed to live together, the women eloped to Wales, disguised as men, and set up home in Llangollen to devote themselves to 'friendship, celibacy and the knitting of stockings'.

At first scandalous, their 'model friendship' became well known and respected, as they were visited by many national figures of the day, including the Duke of Wellington, William Wordsworth and Sir Walter Scott. Wordsworth was even suitably moved to pen the following words: 'Sisters in love, a love allowed to climb, even on this earth above the reach of time'.

The ladies' relationship with their maid, Mary, was also close. Mary managed to buy the freehold of Plas Newydd and left it to the 'sisters' when she died. They erected a large monument to her in the graveyard at St Collen's Parish Church in Llangollen, where they are also buried. Lady Eleanor died in 1829; Sarah Ponsonby was reunited with her soulmate just two years later.

include a self-service cereal-and-toast breakfast.

Abbey Farm CAMPGROUND £
(☑ 01978-861297; www.theabbeyfarm.co.uk; camping/pods per night £18/50, cottages per week from £250; ℗) Two miles northwest of Llangollen, with three stone self-catering cottages (the largest sleeping 14), a campsite with grassy sites in the lee of Valle Crucis Abbey (p233), a farm shop and a tearoom-bistro, Abbey Farm covers many bases. If you're looking for a halfway house between camping and cottage, snug wooden pods are just the ticket (bring your own bedding).

★ **mh Townhaus** B&B ££
(☑ 01978-860775; www.manorhaus.com; Hill St; r from £90; 🐾) This ultra-stylish boutique guesthouse occcupies a multistorey Victorian town house, and comprises nine fairly minimalist rooms in slate greys and whites, a lounge and bar, a library and even a rooftop hot tub. Common spaces double as a gallery for art and installations by local artists and there's also a semidetached one-bedroom cottage for self-caterers.

Cornerstones COTTAGE £££
(☑ 01978-861569; www.cornerstones-guesthouse. co.uk; 19 Bridge St; whole house from £290 per night; ℗🐾) All stripped floorboards and heavy oak beams, this converted 16th-century house has charm and history in spades. It's now five-star self-catering accommodation, with a working fireplace – a boon in winter – fully-equipped kitchen, and three beautifully appointed rooms, one with a remarkable bathroom where the claw-footed tub sits on its own little 'stage'. Sleeps up to six.

✕ Eating & Drinking

★ **Gales Wine Bar** EUROPEAN ££
(☑ 01978-860089; www.gales.wine; 18 Bridge St; mains £6-22; ⊙ 9am-8.30pm Wed-Sat) Equal parts wine bar and bistro, Gales is something of a Llangollen institution. Perch in the smart bistro area, or the wine garden, and dig into 'simple food done well': haddock and clam stew, gourmet burgers, steak, charcuterie and cheese platters, accompanied by carefully chosen wines from around the globe. Or come for a breakfast brioche and single origin coffee.

The owners – who took a punt in the late 1970s by opening this, the first wine bar

in North Wales – also run the wine shop next door. They also own an excellent hotel, with eight of the rooms (from £50) located above the wine bar, all individually styled and retaining period features.

Corn Mill PUB FOOD ££
(☑ 01978-869555; www.brunningandprice.co.uk/ cornmill; Dee Lane; mains £14-19; ⊙ kitchen noon-9.30pm; 🐾) The water wheel still turns at the heart of this converted mill, now a cheerful, bustling pub and brasserie. The deck over the tumbling Dee is the best spot in town for an unfussy alfresco meal, perhaps braised lamb shoulder or smoked-haddock fishcakes. The bar stays open longer than the kitchen, serving cask ales and other quality local brews.

Dee Side Caffe Bistro CAFE ££
(☑ 07466-699269; www.deesidebistro.co.uk; Dee Lane; mains £9-14; ⊙ 9am-9pm) With a profound commitment to carbs and meat in the form of pies, pasta, steak and beer-battered fish, this cheerful little riverside cafe is traditional and unpretentious. Try to grab a table overlooking the kayaks as they shoot the rapids below.

Bridge End Inn PUB
(☑ 01978-810881; www.bridgeendruabon.co.uk; 5 Bridge St, Ruabon; ⊙ 4-9pm Wed & Thu, 3-10pm Fri, noon-10pm Sat, noon-7pm Sun) In 2012 this unassuming little place became the first Welsh pub to win the coveted Campaign for Real Ale (CAMRA) pub-of-the-year award. Run by the McGivern family, it's home to the McGivern microbrewery and also showcases craft beers from around the nation. Ruabon is 6 miles east of Llangollen, on the way to Wrexham.

ℹ Information

Tourist Office (☑ 01978-860828; www. llangollen.org.uk; The Chapel, Castle St; ⊙ 9.30am-5pm; 🐾) This helpful tourist office doubles as an art-and-craft gallery and is well stocked with maps, books and gifts. Download its *Llangollen History Trail* brochure, which details a 9.5km walking circuit taking in Valle Crucis (p233) and Dinas Brân (p233).

ℹ Getting There & Away

Bus T3 buses head to/from Wrexham (£2, 40 minutes, four to nine daily) and in the other direction to Barmouth (£2.90, two hours) via Bala (£2.20 one hour) and Dolgellau (£2.40, 1½ hours). Buses leave from **Parade**

SNOWDONIA & THE LLŶN LLANGOLLEN

DON'T MISS

TYDDYN LLAN

The glowing reputation of Michelin-starred **Tyddyn Llan Restaurant** (☏ 01490-440264; www.tyddynllan.co.uk; B4401, Llandrillo; 3-/8-course dinner £75/95; ⊘ lunch Fri-Sun, dinner daily), run by a husband-and-wife team, is well-deserved. The pairings of ingredients are classical rather than off-the-wall – spring asparagus, for example, with morels and duck egg – but some dishes border on extraordinary. It's set among gardens near the village of Llandrillo (located on the secondary B4401 route between Llangollen and Bala).

There's a handful of beautifully appointed rooms (£110 to £160) at this this former shooting lodge, if you'd prefer to stay overnight.

St (Parade St). The frequent 5E also serves Wrexham.

Car Parking is at a premium in Llangollen in summer. If your accommodation doesn't have its own parking, check whether it can provide a pass for the council car parks.

SNOWDONIA NATIONAL PARK (PARC CENEDLAETHOL ERYRI)

For the majority of visitors, Wales is synonymous with Snowdonia – 823 sq miles of mountain ranges, green hills, ancient forests, and coastline, bisected by several heritage railways. The country's first national park since 1951, dotted with walkers' hub villages, dark-stone market towns and former slate-mining centres, Snowdonia is a hiker's dream, and it's no accident that the Welsh for Snowdonia is Eryri (eh-ruh-ree) – 'highlands'.

While a disproportionate number of people zoom in on the venerable (and very well-trodden) Mt Snowdon, Wales' highest peak, those in search of greater challenges and relative solitude need look no further than the Glyder and Carnedd ranges. Some of the most popular attractions are human-made, and combine the slate-mining heritage of this region with adrenalin-packed subterranean assault courses and zip lines above defunct mining

pits. And if you wind your way to the coast, classic beachside towns and a formidable castle await you.

Bala (Y Bala)

POP 2094

Watersports enthusiasts and hikers will appreciate the quiet Welsh-speaking town of Bala. Here you'll find the River Tryweryn, hallowed in whitewater kayaking circles, as well as Wales' largest natural lake, Llyn Tegid (Bala Lake), allegedly home to Teggie, Wales' answer to the Loch Ness Monster.

Bala was a centre for the Welsh wool industry during the 18th century, but today it's better known as a gateway to Snowdonia National Park and the park's main watersports hub.

The Romans had a fort near the river here, and just behind the high street is a Norman motte (castle mound), Tomen-y-Bala, that would once have supported a wooden castle. Climb it for a panoramic view of the town.

⊙ Sights & Activities

Llyn Tegid   LAKE

(Bala Lake) Llyn Tegid was formed during the last ice age when glaciers blocked the valley of the River Dee with debris. The resulting rectangular lake is 4 miles long, three-quarters of a mile wide and, in places, more than 42m deep. It's also the only home of the gwyniad, an endemic fish isolated in the glacial depths. Coastal winds sweeping through the Talyllyn Valley make it ideal for windsurfing.

Take to the water on a variety of craft, from SUPs to kayaks, courtesy of the **Bala Adventure & Watersports Centre** (☏ 01678-521059; www.balawatersports.com; Pensarn Rd; ⊘ 9am-5pm, later in summer).

National White Water Centre   RAFTING

(Canolfan Dŵr Gwyn Genedlaethol; ☏ 01678-521083; www.ukrafting.co.uk; Frongoch, off A4212; rafting taster/full session £37/67; ⊘ 9am-4.30pm Mon-Fri) Due to the damming of the River Tryweryn in the 1960s, this and the River Dee are two Welsh rivers with fairly reliable white water year-round (rafting is possible around 200 days per year). Departing from 4 miles north of Bala, rafting, kayaking and canoeing trips traverse class III white water and class IV rapids along a 1.5-mile stretch of the Tryweryn.

Bala Lake Railway · RAIL

(✆ 01678-540666; www.bala-lake-railway.co.uk; adult/unaccompanied child return £12/6; ⊘ Feb-Oct) Operational between 1868 and 1964, the 4.5-mile stretch from Bala to Llanuwchllyn of this narrow-gauge railway was reopened by volunteers in 1972. Up to four vintage locomotives depart from the little station at Pen-y-Bont each day, skirting the southern shore of Llyn Tegid for a scenic 90-minute return journey. Pen-y-Bont is half a mile from Bala, off the B4391.

🛌 Sleeping

Bala Backpackers · HOSTEL £

(✆ 01678-521700; www.bala-backpackers.co.uk; 32 Tegid St; dm/tw from £21/49; ⊘ reception 8-10am & 5-10pm; 🛜) Spread over two restored 19th-century houses facing each other across Tegid St, conveniently located Bala Backpackers has brightly painted dorms (with a maximum of four single beds), private twins and renovated kitchen and bathrooms. If staying in a dorm, bring your own sheets and sleeping bag or pay £3 for hire. Owner won't win any congeniality prizes.

Plas-yn-Dre · HOTEL ££

(✆ 01678-521256; www.plasyndre.co.uk; 23 High St; s/d incl breakfast from £79/80; 🛜) About as central as can be, this is the nicest midrange hotel in town. Expect cosy, carpeted rooms with tartan upholstery and excellent showers. The owners pride themselves on their hearty pub fare (mains £11 to £15), with the menu celebrating local ingredients in the form of slow-cooked beef brisket, Welsh leg of lamb and other solid standards.

🍴 Eating

Y Cyfnod Cafe & Bistro · CAFE £

(✆ 01678-521260; www.cyfnod.com; 48 High St; mains £10-14; ⊘ 9am-9pm; 🖉) In its previous incarnations, Bala's oldest cafe has been a 19th-century pharmacy, a newspaper shop, and a bicycle repair place during WWII. Today, it's a popular gathering place for locals and visitors alike, drawn by the warmth of the owners, as well as homemade cakes, excellent burgers and a smattering of international dishes, such as risotto.

Eagles Inn · PUB FOOD ££

(Yr Eagles; ✆ 01678-540278; www.yr-eagles.co.uk; Church St, Llanuwchllyn; mains £11-18; ⊘ 11am-11pm Sun-Wed, to midnight Thu-Sat, closed lunch Mon; 🖉) In Llanuwchllyn, the village at the other end of the lake from Bala, this handsome stone pub is locally known for its Welsh-speaking regulars and hearty pub-grub classics, washed down with real ales. Most of the vegetables, the beef and the pork come from the family farm, and for dessert there's a delicious array of homemade pies and puddings.

ℹ️ Getting There & Away

Buses stop on the high street. Bus T3 (up to nine daily) heads to/from Barmouth (£2.20, one hour) via Dolgellau (£1.90, 35 minutes), and in the other direction to Wrexham (£2.40, 1½ hours) via Llangollen (£2.20, 52 minutes).

Dolgellau

POP 2672

Dolgellau (dol-*geth*-lye) is a charming little market town, boasting the highest concentration of heritage-listed buildings in Wales (more than 200). The county town of now-vanished Merionethshire, it was a regional centre for Wales' prosperous wool industry in the 18th and early 19th centuries and many of its finest buildings, made of dark, unadorned stone, were built at that time. Local mills failed to keep pace with mass mechanisation, however, and decline set in – preserving the town centre much as it was then.

The region bounced back when the Romantic Revival made Wales' wild landscapes popular with genteel travellers. There was also a minor gold rush in the 1860s. Today Dolgellau's main draw is its appeal as a base for fresh-air fiends, as its attractions lie largely outside town.

⊙ Sights

Mawddach Estuary · NATURE RESERVE

(www.mawddachestuary.co.uk) The wide, sandy Mawddach Estuary is a striking sight, flanked by woodlands, wetlands and the mountains of southern Snowdonia. There are two Royal Society for the Protection of Birds (RSPB) nature reserves in the valley, both reached on foot or by bike from Dolgellau or Barmouth via the Mawddach Trail (p238). Arthog Bog is 8 miles west of Dolgellau on the access road to Morfa Mawddach station, off the A493, while Coed Garth Gell is 2 miles west, on the A496.

Dolgellau

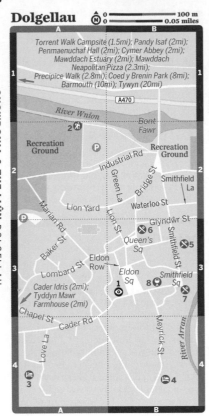

Torrent Walk Campsite (1.5mi); Pandy Isaf (2mi);
Penmaenuchaf Hall (2mi); Cymer Abbey (2mi);
Mawddach Estuary (2mi); Mawddach
Neapolitan Pizza (2.3mi);
Precipice Walk (2.8mi); Coed y Brenin Park (8mi);
Barmouth (10mi); Tywyn (20mi)

Dolgellau

Tŷ Siamas   CULTURAL CENTRE
(☎ 01341-421800; www.tysiamas.com; Eldon Sq,
Neuadd Idris; ⊙ 10am-4pm Tue-Fri, to 1pm Sat;
👪) Dolgellau has been a Welsh folk-music

hub since holding the first national folk
festival in 1952. The town's former market
hall now houses the volunteer-run National
Centre for Welsh Folk Music, named after
Dolgellau-born Elis Sîon Siamas, harpist
to Queen Anne and the first Welshman
to build a triple harp (now known as the
'Welsh harp'). There's a recording studio,
workshops and lessons on traditional instruments and a cafe and shop. Check the
website for upcoming performances.

Cymer Abbey   RUINS
(Cadw; www.cadw.gov.wales; off A470; ⊙ 10am-
5pm) **FREE** This Cistercian abbey, founded
in 1198, was once home to sheep-rearing
and gold-panning monks, and its ruined
walls and looming arches are still bleakly
picturesque, especially if you ignore the
surrounding caravan park. You can reach
the Precipice Walk from the abbey on foot.
The ruins are 2 miles northwest of Dolgellau, signposted from the A470.

🏃 Activities

Precipice Walk   HIKING
This 3-mile anticlockwise loop walk leads
you through woodland, and up a steeply
sloped hill, finally descending to the shores
of Llyn Cynwch lake. There are fantastic
views of the Mawddach estuary, Cader Idris
and Snowdon from the precipitous path,
and plenty of wild blueberries in July. The
walk starts from Saith Groesffordd car park,
Llanfachreth, 2.8 miles from Dolgellau.

Mawddach Trail   HIKING
(www.mawddachtrail.co.uk) The 9.5-mile Mawddach Trail is a flat walking and cycling
path that follows an old train line through
woods and past wetlands on the southern
side of the beautiful Mawddach Estuary,
before crossing over the train viaduct to
Barmouth (where you can catch the bus
back). The trail starts in the car park beside
the bridge in Dolgellau.

Mawddach Way   HIKING
(www.mawddachway.co.uk) Mawddach Way is
a moderately challenging 30-mile two- to
three-day loop track winding through the
hills on either side of the bird-filled and
extremely scenic Mawddach Estuary, starting in Barmouth and taking in Llanelltyd
and Dolgellau. Highlights include the Barmouth Bridge and views of the estuary
from ancient hill-fort remains.

🛏 Sleeping

🛏 Centre

⭐Tan y Gader   B&B ££
(☑ 01341-421102; www.tanygader.co.uk; Meyrick St; s/d from £80/90; 🅿 🛜) 🌀 There is much to love about this wonderful guesthouse. There are just three rooms, each playfully decorated to reflect a beloved children's classic (Alice, Secret Garden, Narnia); Narnia features a claw-footed tub. There are lots of thoughtful extras, and the owners go the extra mile when it comes to breakfast – a delicious gathering of locally sourced ingredients.

Ffynnon   B&B £££
(☑ 01341-421774; www.ffynnontownhouse.com; Love Lane; s/d from £100/160; 🅿 🛜) With an eye for contemporary design and a super-friendly welcome, this award-winning boutique B&B is homey and stylish. French antiques mix with modern chandeliers, claw-foot tubs and electronic gadgets, and each room has a comfy seating area for admiring the impressive vistas. There's a bar, a library, an outdoor hot tub, and Egyptian cotton and goose down in the bedrooms.

🛏 Around Dolgellan

Torrent Walk Campsite   CAMPGROUND £
(☑ 01341-422269; www.guesthousessnowdonia. com/en; off A470, Dolgun Uchaf; camping £10, glamping pod £90; 🅿 🛜) Run by the working Dolgun Uchaf farm and ideally situated for hiking and other outdoorsy pursuits, this grassy campsite offers tent pitches, caravan spots (May to October), and snug wooden glamping pods – perfect for hobbits or families of three.

It's 1.5 miles northeast of Dolgellau; turn left after the petrol station.

⭐Tyddyn Mawr Farmhouse   FARMSTAY ££
(☑ 07979 377306; www.wales-guesthouse.co. uk; off A496, Tal-y-Bont; r incl breakfast £105; ☺Feb-Nov; 🅿 🛜) Two miles southwest of Dolgellau, off the A496, this oak-beamed 18th-century farmhouse nestles on the southern slopes of Cader Idris, and is mere steps away from the Pony Path. The two large, atmospheric bedrooms overlook the mountain, the owners make you feel like a family friend and the cooked breakfasts are excellent.

Pandy Isaf   B&B ££
(☑ 01341-423949; www.pandyisaf-accommodation.co.uk; off A494; r/ste £100/130; 🅿 🛜) 🌀 This extended country house, set alongside the River Clewedog, started life as a 16th-century fulling mill. It's now a peaceful retreat straight out of the pages of *Country Living*, comprising two spotless doubles and a self-contained suite, amazing breakfasts made from local organic ingredients and a prime location for hiking. It's 2 miles northeast of Dolgellau.

Penmaenuchaf Hall   HOTEL £££
(☑ 01341-422129; www.penhall.co.uk; off A493, Penmaenpool; r from £276; 🅿 🛜 ❄) With grand furnishings, sculpted gardens and superb views, this upscale country hotel is the former pile of Bolton cotton magnate James Leigh. The 14 rooms have a lavish old-world air, with all the 21st-century conveniences and four-poster beds in some. Standards are similarly high in Llygad yr Haul, the hotel's garden **restaurant**. It's 2 miles west of Dolgellau, off the A493.

✕ Eating & Drinking

TH Roberts   CAFE £
(☑ 01341-423573; Parliament House, Bridge St; light mains £4-5; ☺9am-5.30pm Mon-Sat; 🛜) Occupying a Grade II–listed building fitted with its original counter, glass cabinets and a Gold Rush display, this charismatic cafe still looks a lot like the ironmonger's it once was. The coffee is the best in Dolgellau, there's a reading room with books and

---

THE DOLGELLAU QUAKERS

The Dolgellau area has historical links with the Society of Friends (the Quakers). After George Fox visited in 1657, preaching his philosophy of direct communication with God, free from creeds, rites and clergy, a Quaker community was founded here. Converts, from simple farmers to local gentry, were persecuted with vigour because their refusal to swear oaths – in particular to the king – was considered treasonous. Many eventually emigrated to William Penn's American Quaker community in 1689. *Y Stafell Ddirgel* (The Secret Room), local author Marion Eames' 1969 novel about the persecution, was curricular reading for many a Welsh schoolchild.

COED Y BRENIN FOREST PARK

Woodland **Coed y Brenin Forest Park** (☑01341-440747; www.naturalresources.wales/coedybrenin; A470; ☺9am-5pm Apr-Oct, shorter hours rest of year) offers some of Wales' best mountain biking. It comprises eight graded routes to suit everyone from beginners to guns. The more challenging trails, such as the Dragon's Back (20 miles; red) and the Beast of Brenin (25 miles; black), stage major mountain-biking events.

The T2 bus from Bangor to Aberystwyth stops here, 8 miles north of Dolgellau.

Covering 16 sq miles, the place is not just for bikers: there are also four waymarked running trails, ranging from the 2.7-mile Sarn Helen to the 13.7-mile half-marathon, plus three dedicated walking trails, the most strenuous of which, Pistyll Cain, leads to some beautiful waterfalls near the Gwynfynydd gold mine.

Housed under the tourist office (☑01341-440747; www.naturalresources.wales/coedy-brenin; car park per hour/day £1/5; ☺9am-5pm Easter-Oct, 9.30am-4.30pm Mon-Fri, 9am-5pm Sat & Sun rest of year), Beics Brenin (☑01341-440728; www.beicsbrenin.co.uk; per day from £25; ☺9am-5pm) rents out bikes, from simple hardtail Trek Xcaliber 7 mountain bikes (£20 per day) to serious motor-assisted Trek Rail eMTB bikes (£70 per day), as well as children's bikes.

papers, and the soup, sandwiches and rarebit (and Nan's scones) are all first rate.

Mawddach Neapolitan Pizza   PIZZA £

(Bwyty Mawddach; ☑01341-421752; www.mawddach.com; A496, Llanelltyd; pizza £7-12; ☺6-9pm Thu, 4-9pm Fri & Sat; ℗🚗🍴) 🍴 Occupying a smartly renovated former barn, fine-dining Mawddach has reinvented itself as a stellar 'pizza with a view' establishment, overlooking Cader Idris and the estuary 2 miles west of Dolgellau. The deftly executed wood-fired pizzas are authentic Neapolitan with a Welsh twist, and toppings include nduja sausage from a nearby farm and local Teifi cheese. Just wonderful.

★Tafarn y Gader   TAPAS ££

(☑01341-421227; www.facebook.com/dolgellau tapas; Smithfield St; tapas £5-11; ☺5-9pm Tue-Sat, 10am-2.30pm Sun; 🚗) Kicking Dolgellau's dining scene up a notch, this tapas bar is as ambitious as it is creative. Yes, there are some solid Spanish standards (*patatas bravas*, Serrano ham croquettes), but then dishes such as crispy rice with seared pigeon and marinated fennel and courgette carpaccio defy expectations, thrilling the tastebuds. A convivial atmosphere reigns amid the clinking of wine glasses.

Y Meirionnydd   EUROPEAN £££

(☑01341-422554; www.themeirionnydd.com; Smithfield Sq; 2/3 courses £24/29; ☺7-10pm Tue-Sat) This atmospheric medieval cellar of the former county jail is all exposed stone, white linen and quality local ingredients given the global treatment with

a light touch. So you might follow a first course of chilli-punched venison pâté with Welsh lamb rump with pomegranate relish and spiced potatoes. Dress nicely and book ahead.

Gwin Dylanwad Wine   WINE BAR

(☑01341-422870; www.dylanwad.co.uk; Porth Marchnad; snacks £1-5; ☺10am-6pm Mon-Thu, to 8pm Fri & Sat) The eponymous Dylan Rowlands knows his wines. This part-wine-merchant, part-bar showcases admirably select vintages from small producers across Europe and beyond, as well as Welsh wines. There are some nibbles available, but – as the title of Dylan's book, *Rarebit and Rioja*, suggests – they're there as supporting cast to a personally approved selection of wines by the glass.

❶ Getting There & Around

Bus Buses stop on Eldon Sq in the heart of town. The frequent T2 connects Dolgellau to Aberystwyth (£2.40, 1¼ hours, three to seven daily) via Machynlleth (£1.70, 30 minutes), and to Bangor (£2.90, two hours, three to nine daily) via Porthmadog (£1.90, 50 minutes) and Caernarfon (£2.40, 1½ hours). There's also the frequent T3 (five to nine daily) from Barmouth (£1.70, 30 minutes) to Llangollen (£2.90, 1½ hours) via Y Bala (£1.90, 35 minutes) and the 28 to Tywyn (£2, 55 minutes, six daily Monday to Saturday).

Bicycle Dolgellau Cycles (☑01341-423332; www.dolgellaucycles.co.uk; Smithfield St, The Old Furnace; half-/full-day rental £15/20; ☺9.30am-5pm Mon-Sat, 10am-4pm Sun) rents bikes, performs repairs and offers advice on local cycling trails.

Cader Idris (Cadair Idris)

Towering over southern Snowdonia, the distinctive peak of Cader Idris (893m) is visible both from Dolgellau and the seaside towns of Barmouth and Tywyn, and offers some of the most spectacular hiking in Wales.

Sights & Activities

★ **Cader Idris**   MOUNTAIN
(www.cadairidriswales.com) Cader Idris (893m) is a formidable mountain. It's named after the 7th century prince of Meirionnydd (c 630 CE), or perhaps Idris the giant, who allegedly created this landscape during boulder-throwing duels with rivals. It's also said to be the stomping ground of Gwyn ap Nudd, lord of the Celtic underworld, the howling of whose hounds is a portend of doom. Regardless of its repute, it's easily tackled in a day via one of three official trails.

The most scenic – and second-steepest – is the circular Minffordd Path (6 miles return, five hours), which begins from the Dol Idris car park, 6 miles south of Dolgellau at the junction of the A487 and the B4405. The trail takes you up steeply through some ancient oak forest, past waterfalls, and circles Llyn Cau, a beautiful mountain lake, before ascending climbing to Pen-y-Gader, the summit, where you'll find a basic stone shelter. The way down is steep and relentless.

Less challenging, 'Tŷ Nant' or **Pony Path** (6 miles return, five hours) begins from the Tŷ Nant car park, 3 miles southwest of Dolgellau. Formerly used by traders transporting their loads on pony-back, it's a well-marked, straightforward route (though you miss out on the scenic Llyn Cau).

The gentlest but longest route is the 'Tywyn' or **Llanfihangel y Pennant Path** (10 miles return, seven hours), a pony track that heads northeast from the hamlet of Llanfihangel y Pennant, joining the Tŷ Nant path at the latter's midpoint. Llanfihangel is 1.5 miles from the terminus of the Talyllyn Railway at Abergynolwyn. There are wonderful views of Castell y Bere and the Mawddach Estuary, and a final steep section near the top.

The OS (www.ordnancesurvey.co.uk/ OL23 (Cadair Idrid & Llyn Tegid) map is handy.

🛌 Sleeping

★ **Gwesty Minffordd Hotel**   HOTEL **££**
(☑ 01654-761665; www.minffordd.com; Tal-y-llyn, LL36 9AJ; s/d incl breakfast £65/130; 🐾) Looking for comfy digs to retreat to the minute you step off the Minffordd Path? Search no further. The individually styled, snug singles, doubles and twins (some with bathtub) all come with statement wallpaper, heavy wooden beams and comfy mattresses, while the restaurant menu is a pan-European melange of fish stew, Welsh lamb, moules marinière and pasta. Hearty breakfasts, too.

❶ Getting There & Away

Bus 30 connects Dolgellau with Tal-y-llyn (£3, 13 minutes) and Abergynolwyn (£3, 18 minutes) once daily from Monday to Saturday. The easiest way to reach the trailheads is with your own wheels.

Tywyn

POP 3093

At the mouth of the dramatically scenic Talyllyn Valley that leads inland towards the slopes of Cader Idris, the ho-hum resort town of Tywyn is renowned for two things: the narrow-gauge Talyllyn Railway, famous as the inspiration for Rev W Awdry's *Thomas the Tank Engine* stories, and the long, sandy Blue Flag beach.

Sights & Activities

Narrow Gauge Railway Museum   MUSEUM
(www.narrowgaugerailwaymuseum.org.uk; Station Rd, Tywyn Wharf; by donation; ☺10.30am-4.30pm Apr-Sep) At Tywyn Wharf Station, the terminus of the Talyllyn Railway, this museum, lovingly run by a dedicated charity, is one for steam-locomotive buffs. Its 1000-plus artefacts date as far as 200 years back, telling the stories of British narrow-gauge railways and the volunteers who fought to preserve Talyllyn. There are regular temporary exhibitions, and opening hours are coordinated with the train timetable.

Talyllyn Railway   RAIL
(Rheilffordd Talyllyn; ☑ 01654-710472; www. talyllyn.co.uk; Wharf Station; compartment per 1-3/4-6 people £44/66; ☺Easter-Oct, varies rest of year) A must for railway buffs, the narrow-gauge Talyllyn Railway opened in 1865 to carry slate and was saved in 1950 by the world's first railway-preservation society.

One of Wales' most enchanting railways, it puffs 7.3 miles up the Fathew Valley to Nant Gwernol. The round trip takes around 2½ hours. Tickets are valid all day.

✗ Eating

Proper Gander   MODERN BRITISH £
(☑ 01654-712169; www.propergandertywyn.com; 4 High St; mains £7-12; ⊙ noon-3pm & 6-9pm Tue-Sat) Crustacea from Cardigan Bay, including crab and lobster from Tywyn and Aberdyfi, are occasional highlights of the locally focused menu. Otherwise, the creative menu spans the globe, from glazed pork belly with Vietnamese-style vermicelli to linguine with duck and walnut ragu. Proper roast-beef lunches on Sundays, too.

Salt Marsh Kitchen   BISTRO ££
(☑ 01654-711949; www.facebook.com/thesalt marshkitchen; 9 College Green; mains £12-15; ⊙ 5-9pm Thu-Sun) Bare timber and blue paint give this ambitious little bistro an appropriately maritime feel, given the good things it does with fish. Inspiration is drawn from around the globe, with dishes such as bream with scallop butter and risotto, smoked-haddock chowder and a Thai-style curry with mussels and prawns. Locally smoked mackerel and potato salad make a great packed lunch.

❶ Getting There & Away

Bus Route 28 buses head to/from Dolgellau (£1.90, 55 minutes, six daily Monday to Saturday) via Fairbourne (£1.70, 30 minutes), route 30 serves Dolgellau (£2.20, 1¼ hours, once daily) via various stops in the Talyllyn Valley (four daily), while X29 runs to Machynlleth (£1.70, 35 minutes, three to nine daily).

Train Tywyn is on the Cambrian Coast Line, with direct, frequent trains to/from Machynlleth (£6.40, 27 minutes), Fairbourne (£4.40, 20 minutes), Barmouth (£6.40, 30 minutes), Porthmadog (£12.80, 1½ hours) and Pwllheli (£14.90, two hours). Note that due to repairs to Barmouth Bridge, services had been replaced by buses at the time of writing.

Barmouth (Abermaw)

POP 2221

With a Blue Flag beach and the beautiful Mawddach Estuary on its doorstep, the seaside resort of Barmouth has been a popular tourist destination since the coming of the railway and the bridge across the estuary in 1867. In summer it becomes a typical seaside resort – chip shops, dodgem cars, donkey rides and crabbing. Outside the brash neon of high season it's considerably mellower, allowing space to appreciate its Georgian and Victorian architecture, beautiful setting and superb walking trails up the Dinas Oleu hill and along the estuary.

◉ Sights & Activities

Barmouth Bridge   BRIDGE
You're unlikely to miss Barmouth's foremost landmark: in fact, you may arrive on it, by train, on foot or on two wheels. Sitting on wooden spans and curving scenically into town, it traverses the 699m of the Mawddach Estuary mouth, it was built in 1867 for the new railway and is one of the longest wooden viaducts in Britain. Originally incorporating a drawbridge, it now has a swing bridge to allow tall shipping into the estuary.

Tŷ Crwn Roundhouse   HISTORIC BUILDING
(www.barsailinst.org.uk/crwn.html; The Quay; ⊙ 10.30am-5pm) **FREE** This squat, early-19th-century stone prison has gender-segregated cells where drunk sailors and slatterns were once locked up for 'wanton mischief'.

Last Haul   MONUMENT
(The Quay) This pockmarked slab of marble salvaged from a nameless 700-ton Genoese galleon that sank in these waters in 1709, locally nicknamed the *Bronze Bell* – has been sculpted by local Franck Cocksey to depict three fishermen straining to haul in a catch.

Dinas Oleu   HILL
Rising behind Barmouth, rocky Dinas Oleu (258m) made history in 1895 by becoming the first property ever bequeathed to the National Trust, kick-starting a movement dedicated to preserving Britain's best landscapes and buildings. The most popular trail up the 'Fortress of Light' is the Panorama Walk (signposted from the A496 on the eastern edge of town along Gloddfa Rd), which has the best views of Mawddach Estuary.

✯ Festivals & Events

Three Peaks Yacht Race   SPORTS
(www.threepeaksyachtrace.co.uk; ⊙ late Jun) The arduous Three Peaks Yacht Race runs from Barmouth to Fort William, with two members of each five-strong crew running

up Snowdon, Scafell Pike and Ben Nevis – the highest peaks of Wales, England and Scotland – en route. In all, that's 389 nautical miles of sailing, 29 miles of cycling and 59 miles of fell running.

🛌 Sleeping

Hendre Mynach CAMPGROUND £
(📞 01341-280262; www.hendremynach.co.uk; Llan-aber Rd; sites/pods £28/55; 🅿️🐕) Right by the beach, this well-kept park has caravan sites marked out between manicured hedges and a couple of flat camping fields protected by windbreaks. It also has wonderfully cosy hobbit house pods for up to four people. It's just off the A496, immediately north of Barmouth.

Tilman HOTEL ££
(📞 01341-281888; www.facebook.com/thetilmanbarmouth; Church St; r incl breakfast from £110; 🅿️🛜) Part-watering hole, part-hotel, the Tilman succeeds in both categories. The contemporary, blond-wood-panelled bar downstairs is equally good for a coffee or a local brew on tap, and the rooms upstairs are spacious, understated, spotless, with quality furnishings and nice touches, such as Molton Brown toiletries. Cooked breakfast included.

🍴 Eating

★ Celtic Cabin Cafe CAFE £
(📞 07775 331241; www.facebook.com/celticcabinbarmouth; Marine Pde; wraps £5-8; ⏰ 10am-6pm; 🐕) A wonderful addition to Barmouth's dining scene, this beachside cafe and takeaway joint specialises in terrific filled wraps, freshly made and served on the picnic tables with a view of the dunes and the sea. Try wraps with slow-roasted pork shoulder, falafel and hummus or locally caught mackerel and couscous...don't forget to finish with the homemade banana bread!

Bistro Bermo BISTRO ££
(📞 01341-281284; www.bistrobermo.com; 6 Church St; mains £16-23; ⏰ 6-9pm Tue-Sat, noon-3pm Sun) Discreetly hidden behind an aqua-green shopfront, this intimate restaurant delivers a sophisticated menu chock-full of Welsh farm produce and fresh fish. Featuring dishes such as duck breast with walnut crust and daily seafood specials, the cooking is classical rather than experimental, and generally excellent. There are only half a dozen tables, so book ahead.

🍷 Drinking & Nightlife

Last Inn PUB
(📞 01341-280530; www.last-inn.co.uk; Church St; ⏰ noon-11pm; 🐕) In a 15th-century cobbler's home now lives Barmouth's most characterful pub, full of inglenooks, old ship timber and other eclectic nautical memorabilia. Unusually, the hillside forms the rear wall, with a spring emerging to create a gaudily decorated pond inside the building itself. Kids are welcome, there are real ales on tap, and there's occasional live music.

ℹ️ Getting There & Away

Bus Buses stop on Jubilee Rd, across Beach Rd from the **train station** (Station Rd). Services include the 38/39 to/from Harlech (£1.70, 30 minutes, two to six daily) and Porthmadog (£1.90, 50 minutes, one to four daily) and the T3 to Dolgellau (£1.70, 20 minutes, five to 12 daily), Bala (£2, one hour, five to eight daily) and Llangollen (£2.90, two hours, five to eight daily).

Bicycle Cycle path Lôn Las Cymru passes through Barmouth, heading north to Harlech and east to Dolgellau.

Train Barmouth is on the Cambrian Coast Line, with eight direct trains per day to Fairbourne (£3.20, seven minutes), Machynlleth (£10.30, one hour), Harlech (£5.40, 25 minutes), Porthmadog (£8, 50 minutes) and Pwllheli (£13, 80 minutes).

Harlech

POP 1618

Hilly Harlech is best known for the mighty grey-stone towers of its impressive castle that sits on a promontory overlooking Tremadog Bay, framed by the mountains of Snowdonia to the north. Some sort of fortified structure has probably surmounted the rock since Iron Age times, but Edward I removed all traces when he commissioned the castle that currently stands. Finished in 1289, Harlech Castle is the southernmost of four fortifications grouped as the 'Castles and Town Walls of King Edward in Gwynedd' Unesco World Heritage Site.

Castle aside, Harlech also has one of the finest beaches in the area, backed by the Morfa Harlech dunes. In summer, the place buzzes with day visitors. Accommodation is sparse, but the town makes an excellent base for walkers, too.

RAMBLES IN THE RHINOGS

Some 3 miles east of Harlech as the crow flies, lies the compact range of heather-covered granite hills, the Rhinogs, overlooked by the twin summits of **Rhinog Fach** (Cwm Nantcol) (682m) and **Rhinog Fawr** (Llyn Cwm Bychan) (720m). Both offer demanding ascents and fantastic views across glacial lakes and Cardigan Bay. And you're likely to have them to yourself. Arm yourself with the *OS 1:25,000 OL18 map (Harlech, Porthmadog & Bala)*.

The best hike up Rhinog Fawr (5 miles, three hours) is from the car park in Cwm Bychan, past the eponymous lake, through a grove of ancient oaks, across open moor and then steeply up almost 500 'Roman steps' (that are actually medieval in origin). Beyond the Bwlch Tyddiad saddle, scramble steeply over boulders to reach the summit. It's also possible to hike between the two peaks.

◉ Sights & Activities

★ Harlech Castle   CASTLE

(Cadw; www.cadw.wales.gov.uk; Castle St; adult/child £6.40/4.30; ⊙10am-1pm & 2-5pm Wed-Sun) Built on a promontory, Harlech Castle was once impregnable, made so by the sea and the moat. Edward I finished this mighty castle in 1289, the southernmost of his 'iron ring' of fortresses designed to keep the Welsh firmly beneath his boot. The grey-sandstone castle's massive twin-towered gatehouse and outer walls are still intact, giving the illusion of impregnability even now. The finest exterior view of the castle (with Snowdon as backdrop) is from a craggy outcrop on Ffordd Isaf.

Entry is through the interactive visitor centre, and a drawbridge leads through three sets of gates and portcullises to the compact inner ward, where four round towers guard the corners. Some of the ramparts are partly ruined and closed off, but you can climb other sections. The fortress' great natural defence is the seaward cliff face. When it was built, ships could sail supplies right to the base, but the sea has receded since.

Despite its might, this fortress has been called the 'Castle of Lost Causes' because it has been lucklessly defended so many times. Owain Glyndŵr captured it after a long siege in 1404. He is said to have been crowned prince of Wales in the presence of envoys from Scotland, France and Spain during one of his parliaments in the town. He was, in turn, besieged here by the future Henry V.

During the Wars of the Roses, the castle is said to have held out against a siege for seven years and was the last Lancastrian stronghold to fall. The siege inspired the popular Welsh hymn 'Men of Harlech', which is still played today in regimental marches and sung with patriotic gusto at rugby matches. The castle was also the last to fall in the English Civil War, finally giving in to Cromwell's forces in 1647, because sturdy architecture is no match for human treachery.

Snowdonia Adventure Activities OUTDOORS
(☑01341-241511; www.snowdoniaadventureactivities.co.uk; adult/child full day £80/50) George, a Snowdonia native and outdoor instructor, and his partner, Toni, offer customised adventures within the national park, including rock climbing, abseiling, canyoning, 'Xtreme' canyoning for adrenalin junkies, gorge scrambling, canoeing, kayaking, mountain biking and guided hiking. A full day's program combines two activities of your choice, and mountain-bike hire is an additional £25.

🛏 Sleeping

★ Maelgwyn House   B&B ££

(☑01766-780087; www.maelgwynharlech.co.uk; Ffordd Isaf; r £98-135; ⊙Feb-Oct; 🅿 🛜) A model B&B in an art-bedecked former boarding school, Maelgwyn has interesting hosts, delicious breakfasts and five elegant rooms (though attic Room 5 is rather snug) stocked with DVD players and tea-making facilities (ask for one of the three with sea views – they're definitely worth it). Bridget and Derek can also help arrange bird-watching trips and fungus forays.

Castle Cottage   COTTAGE ££
(☑01766-780479; Ffordd Pen Llech; s/d from £75/130; 🅿 🛜) Billing itself a 'restaurant with rooms', this 16th-century cottage has seven spacious bedrooms in a contemporary

style, with exposed beams, in-room DVD players and a bowl of fresh fruit for each guest. The award-winning fine-dining **restaurant** (two-/three-course dinner £39/42) is a great showcase for Welsh produce, featuring local rack of lamb and line-caught sea bass, and other delights.

✕ Eating

★ As.Is
BISTRO £

(☎ 01766-781208; www.asis-harlech.co.uk; The Square; mains £5-9.50; ⏱ 5-9pm Mon-Sat) Overlooking the castle, this welcoming bistro features a short and sweet menu of solid, belly- and palate-pleasing food that doesn't bang on about 'taking you on a journey'. Highlights include sourdough pizza and jerk chicken wings, their crisp skin an allspice and chilli kick. The pared-down decor – naked wires, oversized light bulbs and rough timber tables – is equally pleasing.

Castle Bistro
BISTRO ££

(☎ 01766-780416; www.castlebistroharlech.com; Stryd Fawr/High St; mains £12-17; ⏱ 5.30-10pm Wed-Sun) Beautifully executed comfort food is what you can expect at this justifiably popular bistro. There's the happy marriage of the Welsh lamb shank with the buttery mash and toothsome braised red cabbage, the cod loin risotto, smoky with haddock, and the pork belly with perfect, oven-crisped skin.

ℹ Getting There & Away

Bus The Harlech Hoppa bus runs half-hourly in summer to Barmouth and Porthmadog; tickets £1.50.

Bicycle National Cycle Network path 8 (Lôn Las Cymru North) passes through Harlech, heading north to Porthmadog and south to Barmouth.

Train Harlech is on the Cambrian Coast Line, with direct trains to Machynlleth (£13.90, 1½ hours, eight daily) via Barmouth (£5.40, 27 minutes) and Fairbourne (£6.60, 40 minutes); and Pwllheli (£9.20, 47 minutes, eight daily) via Porthmadog (£5.40, 27 minutes). The station is at the base of the rocks below the castle.

Blaenau Ffestiniog

POP 3813

Most of the slate used to roof 19th-century Britain came from Wales, and much of that came from the mines of Blaenau Ffestiniog. Even though Blaenau (blay-nye) is in the centre of Snowdonia National Park, the grey mountains of shattered slate that surround the town prevent it from being officially included in the park, much to the fury of this close-knit community. To them, these monolithic heaps of slate, dug out by hand, are part of their heritage and testimony to the herculean efforts of the miners.

Although the slate industry has been reduced to a single surface mine, it continues to dominate Blaenau. Adrenaline junkies pursue subterranean adventures in the abandoned tunnels and caverns, the surrounding landscape attracts mountain bikers, and train buffs retrace slate's past journeys to Porthmadog aboard the historic Ffestiniog Railway.

◉ Sights

★ Llechwedd Slate Caverns
MINE

(☎ 01766-830306; www.llechwedd.co.uk; A470; tours £20; ⏱ 9.30am-5.30pm; P ♿) Blaenau's main attraction takes you into the depths of a Victorian slate mine. Donning protective gear, you descend the UK's steepest mining cable railway into the 1846, 25-mile network of tunnels and caverns, while 'enhanced-reality technology' brings to life the harsh working conditions of the 19th-century miners – be prepared to duck and scramble around dark tunnels. Knowledgeable guides relate stories of their own connections with the mines, and the softly lit caverns themselves are starkly beautiful.

You can also opt to join an overground, off-road Quarry Explorer tour in a 4WD military truck (£20 per person) that trundles up to the highest points of the human-made slate mountains, or stay overnight in the on-site glamping tents (£120).

Cellb
ARTS CENTRE

(☎ 01766-832001; www.cellb.org; Park Sq; ⏱ cafe-bar noon-10pm Tue-Sat, kitchen noon-3pm & 6-9pm Wed-Sat) Inside the Edwardian-era police station (hence 'Cell B'), this multifunction centre hosts everything from yoga to live bands to screenings in a 40-seat cinema. It's also the town's most appealing dining and drinking space, with a cafe and cocktail bar making clever use of original fittings. The final feather in Cellb's cap is hostel accommodation in three small dorms (created from the old magistrate's office and interview room, £25 per night), with a kitchen and stylish lounge.

✦ Activities

★ Zip World

Slate Caverns ADVENTURE SPORTS

(☑01248-601444; www.zipworld.co.uk; off A470, Llechwedd Slate Caverns; ⊘booking office 8am-6.30pm; ⊕) If you've ever wanted to practise trampoline tricks in a slate mine (and who hasn't?), then 'Bounce Below' – a 'cathedral-sized' cavern with bouncy nets, walkways, tunnels and slides – is your chance (adult/child one hour £25/20). There are also the caverns themselves, explored via zip wires (including the UK's steepest) through the semi-dark and wobbly rope bridges (£65 for two hours).

The latest attraction is Titan (£30 to £50), Europe's longest zip-line course that has you flying downhill above a disused slate quarry along three tracks – 890m, 630m and 450m, while the world passes you by in a blur at speeds of 70mph. Up to four people can take flight simultaneously.

Antur Stiniog MOUNTAIN BIKING

(☑01766-238007; www.anturstiniog.com; A470, Llechwedd Slate Caverns; 1 uplift £5, day pass from £31; ⊘8am-5pm Thu-Mon Apr-Aug & Thu-Sun Sep-Mar) Opened in 2012, Wales' most ambitious mountain-biking centre has been going from strength to strength. If you don't know the meaning of fear, check out these 14 blue, red and black downhill and free-ride runs down the mountainside near the slate caverns. The double-black jumps and rock sections host international championships.

There's a minibus uplift service (10am to 4.30pm) on-site.

⛺ Sleeping & Eating

★ Bryn Elltyd

Eco Guesthouse GUESTHOUSE ££

(☑01766-831356; www.ecoguesthouse.co.uk; Tanygrisiau; s/d from £60/90; ᴾ☎☀) ∅ Overlooking the Tanygrisiau reservoir, a mile south of Blaenau Ffestiniog, this wonderful guesthouse is 100% carbon-neutral, powered exclusively by renewables, and serving meals on request made from its own produce. Choose between the snug lake-view rooms in the main house or the two turf-roofed, sheep's-wool-insulated doubles in the garden. The location is great for bikers, hikers and canoe enthusiasts.

Pisgah Guesthouse B&B ££

(☑01766-831285; www.facebook.com/pisgah guesthouse; Maenofferen St; s/d from £50/80, tr £90; ᴾ☎) Run by the hospitable Doug and Glenys, this former chapel has been converted into a wonderfully homey B&B, with half a dozen snug, individually styled en suites. Mountain bikers are welcome (with ample storage space for bikes), room price includes a generous cooked breakfast and home-cooked evening meals can be arranged on request.

Caffi Kiki GREEK £

(☑07450-325119; www.kikis-cafe.com; Lakeside Cafe, Tanygrisiau; mains £10; ⊘5.30-8.30pm Fri & Sat; ⯑) Currently operating as a pop-up restaurant from the Lakeside Cafe in Tanygrisiau (its regular home is Newmarket Sq in Blaenau), Kiki's more than delivers on its promise of traditional Greek dishes with a Welsh twist. The moussaka will get you through a siege and the feta-stuffed lamb burger with black-garlic mayo is a thing of beauty and inspiration.

ⓘ Getting There & Away

Bus Services include the hourly (Monday to Saturday) 3/3B to/from Porthmadog (£1.75, 35 minutes), and three or four daily X19 services to Betws-y-Coed (£1.70, 30 minutes) and Llandudno (£2.50, 1½ hours).

Train Both the four or five daily trains running along the Conwy Valley Line from Llandudno (£8.70, 1½ hours) via Betws-y-Coed (£5.10, 35 minutes), and the seasonal, steam-powered Ffestiniog Railway (p260) from Porthmadog terminate at the **train station** (Cromwell St).

Penmachno

POP 634

Tucked away in the valley of the River Machno, the picturesque village of Penmachno dates to at least Roman times. Its population may have dwindled since its quarrying heyday in the '60s, but its location on the edge of Gwydir Forest attracts walkers, mountain bikers and horse riders.

◎ Sights & Activities

Conwy Falls WATERFALL

(Rhaeadr Y Graig Lwyd; www.conwyfalls.com; A5, LL24 0PN; adult/child £1.50/1; ⊘24hr; ⊕) Some 2 miles north of Penmachno, the frothing Conwy Falls cascade 50ft down a rock face into a deep pool, framed by forest greenery. There are several gentle walking trails through the woods here, as well as a children's playground.

Gwydyr Stables
HORSE RIDING

(☑ 01690-760248; www.horse-riding-wales.co.uk; Glasgwm Rd, Ty Coch Farm & Trekking Centre LL25 0HJ; 1hr/half-day £20/46) Offering rides on the plentiful bridle trails of the surrounding Gwydyr Forest throughout the year, Gwydyr is also known for its pub rides, which afford plenty of scope for refreshment along the way. To find the stables, follow the signs northwest towards Tŷ Mawr from Eagles inn for around 2.5 miles.

🛏 Sleeping

Eagles
HOSTEL £

(☑ 01960-760177; www.eaglespenmachno.co.uk; B4406; d/tr/q £44/66/82; ⊘ pub 7pm-late Wed-Fri, 2pm-late Sat & Sun; 🛜) A hand-painted sign depicting three black eagles hangs above the village pub, popular for its cask-conditioned ales, banter and (on Saturdays, plus Fridays from February to November) evening meals. Upstairs there's simple bunkhouse accommodation in nine private twins, triples and quads, plus a self-catering kitchen. It's well suited to mountain bikers, with a drying room and secure bike storage.

Penmachno Hall
B&B ££

(☑ 01690-760140; www.penmachnohall.co.uk; Glasgwm Rd; d £99 2-night minimum, cottages £625 per week; P🛜) Just over the bridge on the way to Tŷ Mawr, this ivy draped 1860s stone house has three vibrant colour-coded guest rooms and a separate two-bedroom coach-house cottage for longer, self-catered stays. 'Yellow' has a sleigh bed and 'Orange' has the best views, but both have claw-foot tubs. Packed lunches (£7.50) available on request.

ℹ Getting There & Away

Penmachno is 5 miles south of Betws-y-Coed; take the A5 and then turn right on to the B4406. From Monday to Saturday, bus 19 heads to/from Llandudno five times daily (£2.50, 1½ hours) via Betws-y-Coed (£1.30, 15 minutes) and Conwy (£2.25, 1¼ hours).

Betws-y-Coed

POP 1160

Betws-y-Coed (*bet*-us-ee-*coyd*) sits at the junction of three river valleys (the Llugwy, the Conwy and the Lledr) and on the verge

WORTH A TRIP

MOUNTAIN SURFING

Lying in the lush Conwy Valley, signposted off the A470 from Llandudno Junction to Betws-y-Coed, **Surf Snowdonia** (☑ 01492-353123; www.adventureparcsnowdonia.com; Conway Rd, Dolgarrog LL32 8QE; ⊘ 8am-11pm; 🚻), an unexpected slice of Maui, is an adventure park centred on a vast artificial wave pool. Choose between surfing (adult/child from £40/35) waves of different intensity, based on your ability, lagoon 'crash and splash' sessions (£25 per hour), kayaking, SUP, walking and more.

of the Gwydyr Forest. With outdoor-gear shops outnumbering pubs, gentle walking trails leaving right from the centre (though for any serious hikes you have to travel further out) and guesthouses occupying a fair proportion of its slate Victorian buildings, it's the perfect base for exploring Snowdonia.

Betws has been Wales' most popular inland resort since Victorian times, when a group of countryside painters founded an artistic community to record the diversity of the landscape. The arrival of the railway in 1868 cemented its popularity, and today Betws-y-Coed is as busy with families and coach parties as it is with walkers.

◉ Sights

Conwy Valley Railway Museum
MUSEUM

(☑ 01690-710568; www.conwyrailwaymuseum.co.uk; The Old Goods Yard; adult/child £2/1.50; ⊘ 10am-5pm) If you delight in dioramas and model train sets, this tiny museum is for you. And the model shop you have to pass through in order to enter might pose an unfair temptation. The big attraction for kids is the miniature steam-train (or sometimes diesel-powered) ride; the 1-mile round trip through manicured gardens costs £2.50, and there's a cafe in a full-sized carriage.

◉ Around Betws-y-Coed

★ Fairy Glen
WATERFALL

(A470, LL24 0SH; 50p) Reachable via a walking trail signposted off the A470, 2 miles south of Betws-y-Coed, this is a beautiful gorge, hemmed in by mossy rocks and a small waterfall. It's named after the Welsh

Betws-y-Coed

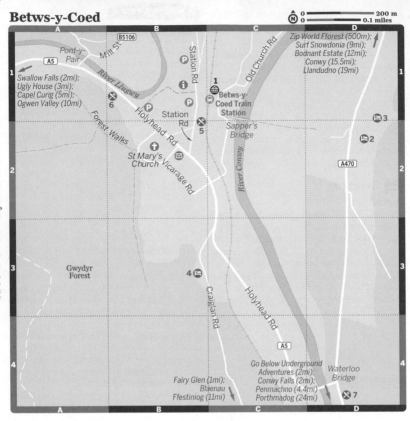

Betws-y-Coed

◎ Sights

1 Conwy Valley Railway Museum..........C1

◉ Sleeping

2 Maes-y-Garth.......................................D2
3 Tyn-y-Fron..D1
4 Vagabond..B3

◙ Eating

5 Hangin' Pizzeria..................................B2
6 Olif...B1
7 Tŷ Gwyn Hotel.....................................D4

sprites, the Tylwyth Teg, who allegedly live in these parts, and the pool at the confluence of Afon Lledr and River Cowny is a great swimming spot.

Gwydyr Forest FOREST

The 28-sq-mile Gwydyr Forest, planted since the 1920s with oak, beech and larch, encircles Betws-y-Coed and is scattered

with the remnants of lead and zinc mine workings. Named for a more ancient forest in the same location, it's ideal for a day's walking, though it gets very muddy in wet weather. *Walks Around Betws-y-Coed* (£5), available from the National Park Tourist Office (p250), details several circular forest walks.

Swallow Falls WATERFALL

(Rhaeadr Ewynnol; A5, LL24 0DW; adult/child £1.50/50p) Betws-y-Coed's main natural tourist draw is 2 miles west of town, alongside the A5 on the River Llugwy. It's a beautiful spot, with the 42m torrent, Wales' highest, weaving through the rocks into a green pool below. Outside seasonal opening hours, bring coins for the turnstile (no change is available).

Ugly House HISTORIC BUILDING

(Tŷ Hyll; www.theuglyhouse.co.uk; A5; ☺ 10.30am-4.30pm daily Easter-Oct, Mon-Fri Nov & Feb-

Mar) The Ugly House is a misnomer. This unusual cottage is constructed from huge boulders and is home to a characterful tea-room and, upstairs, the Honeybee Room, with displays devoted to the beleaguered insect, protected by the Snowdonia Society, an environmentalist group that sells locally produced honey in the garden. It's half a mile west of Swallow Falls on the A5.

🏃 Activities

★ Go Below Underground Adventures
ADVENTURE SPORTS

(☑ 01690-710108; www.go-below.co.uk; adventures £59-99; ☺ 9am-5pm) Head down an old slate mine and try your hand at scrambling along a subterranean via ferrata, zip-lining deep underground above abandoned mining pits, abseiling down shafts and plunging 70ft into darkness in underground freefall. There are three experiences of varying intensity and length; caving experience not required.

Meet at Conwy Falls, on the A5, at the turn-off to Penmachno.

Zip World Fforest
ADVENTURE SPORTS

(☑ 01248-601444; www.zipworld.co.uk; A470, LL24 0HX; 3 coaster rides £20, 2hr safari £40; ☺ 9am-5pm; ♿) Fun in the Fforest includes the 'Safari', a network of rope ladders and zip lines high in the treetops; the 'Coaster', a child-friendly toboggan ride on rails; and 'Skyride', an 80ft, five-person swing that reaches jaw-clenching velocity. The latest addition is 'Plummet', which is exactly what you do, for 100ft, dropping through a trapdoor on top of a tower.

🛏 Sleeping

Vagabond
HOSTEL £

(☑ 01690-710850; www.thevagabond.co.uk; Craiglan Rd; dm from £22; ᴘ 🛜 🐾) On the slopes below a forested crag, from which spills its own 'private' waterfall, the Vagabond is Betws' best hostel – and the only one within the town proper. It's a simple set-up, with freshly decorated six- to eight-bed dorms, two family rooms, shared bathrooms and an appealing bar (4.30pm to 11pm), kitchen and common room. Weekends mean pizza night.

Coed-y-Celyn Hall
APARTMENT £

(☑ 07821 099595; www.selfcatering-in-snowdonia.co.uk; A470, Coed-y-Celyn LL24 0SH; apt per week from £410; ᴘ 🛜) Built in the 1850s for a mining magnate, this grand pile has been converted into fully equipped apartments, five one-bedroom and one three-bedroom. Each of the six is different, but they're all huge – and terrifically good value. Apartment 4, with moulded ceilings, grand windows and views over the front lawns, is particularly appealing.

Maes-y-Garth
B&B ££

(☑ 01690-710441; www.maes-y-garth.co.uk; A470, Lon Muriau; s/d from £80/90; ᴘ 🛜) Off the A470, and accessible from Betws by a footpath (starting behind St Michael's Church) across the river, this top-notch B&B inhabits a 1970s Clough Williams-Ellis–designed 'alpine-style' house. A warm welcome and five quietly stylish guest rooms with gorgeous views await – perhaps the nicest is room 4, which has its own balcony and views of the valley. Two-night minimum.

Afon Gwyn Country House
B&B ££

(☑ 01690-710442; www.guest-house-betws-y-coed.com; A470, Coed-y-Celyn LL24 0SH; r from £105; ᴘ 🛜) Down in the valley, this old stone house has been skilfully converted into a grand boutique guesthouse. The decor is faultlessly tasteful, with hushed tones, white-painted wood panelling, glittering chandeliers, and bathrooms bedecked in Italian tiles and marble. While all the rooms are spacious, the Alice Suite, complete with free-standing bath and canopied bed, is particularly generously sized.

Bod Gwynedd
B&B ££

(☑ 01690-710717; www.bodgwynedd.com; Holyhead Rd; s/d from £80/95; ᴘ 🛜) Backed by towering pines and emerald fields on the western edge of town, this friendly B&B offers five tastefully furnished bedrooms in a mid-Victorian slate house, with creature comforts (king-sized beds) meeting modern tech (smart TVs). The welcoming owners keep everything spick and span and have plenty of local knowledge to impart. Adults only; two-night minimum.

Tyn-y-Fron
B&B £££

(☑ 01690-710449; www.snowdoniabedandbreakfast.co.uk; A470, Lon Muriau; s/d £170/190; ᴘ 🛜) This gracious old stone house has five spacious, individually styled rooms; the Valley View super-king room boasts expansive valley views. Friendly owners Barbara and Nigel serve an excellent breakfast, including award-winning sausages and bacon from the local butcher, and are full of advice on local walks. The B&B is off the A470 and accessible from Betws via a footpath.

✕ Eating & Drinking

★ Olif
TAPAS ££

(📞01690-733942; www.olifbetws.wales; Holyhead Rd; tapas £5-7; ⊘6-8.30pm Tue-Sun, noon-3pm Sat & Sun May-Oct, closed Mon-Wed Nov-Apr) Breakfast first up, burgers for lunch, and tapas and wine in the evening – Olif morphs to please throughout the day. The tapas has a distinctly Welsh flavour, without straying too far into fusion territory (the croquettes are made with Perl Wen cheese and the ham's from Camarthen) and fun finger foods, like popcorn cockles and cider-cooked mussels, abound.

Upstairs, there's a handful of light and bright boutique rooms, all en suite, with rain showers, and some with deep soaking tubs (rooms from £135).

Hangin' Pizzeria
PIZZA £

(📞01690-710393; www.hanginpizzeria.co.uk; Station Rd, The Old Railway Station; pizza £9-12; ⊘noon-8.30pm; 🅿) All industrial decor and cheerful, bustling staff, this pizzeria churns out crowd-pleasing, wood-fired pizza, with simple topping combos, some locally inspired (check out the Welsh rarebit pizza). Catering to a captive audience, since pretty much every visitor to Betws rocks up at the train station, but no worse for it.

Tŷ Gwyn Hotel
EUROPEAN ££

(📞01690-710383; www.tygwynhotel.co.uk; A5; mains £13-18; ⊘noon-2pm & 6-9pm; 🅿) This 400-year-old coaching inn with bare stone walls and exposed beams is hand-down the town's most characterful restaurant. The menu is creative without trying too hard, and the chef does wonderful things with local ingredients to conjure up the likes of slow-braised lamb shoulder and seafood gratin, and the quirky historic building only adds to the appeal.

ℹ Information

Snowdonia National Park Tourist Office
(📞01690-710426; www.eryri-npa.gov.uk; Royal Oak Stables; ⊘9.30am-12.30pm & 1.30-4.30pm) More than just a repository of books, maps and local craft, this office is an invaluable source of information about walking trails, mountain conditions and more.

ℹ Getting There & Around

Bus Snowdon Sherpa bus service S2 heads 12 times daily to Swallow Falls (seven minutes), Capel Curig (15 minutes), Pen-y-Pass (25 minutes) and Llanberis (35 minutes); all trips cost £2.

Other buses include 19 to Llandudno (£3.50, 55 minutes, seven daily Monday to Saturday) via Conwy (£3.30, 45 minutes) and to Pen-machno (15 minutes, five daily Monday to Saturday) and X19 services to Blaenau Ffestiniog (£2.70, 25 minutes, three daily) and Llandudno (£3.50, one hour, two to three daily).

Bicycle Beics Betws (📞01690-710766; www.bikewales.co.uk; Vicarage Rd; ⊘10am-5pm Mar-Nov, call ahead at other times) rent regular and electric mountain bikes.

Train Betws-y-Coed is on the Conwy Valley Line (www.conwyvalleyrailway.co.uk), with up to five trains every day to Llandudno (£6.30, 50 minutes) and Blaenau Ffestiniog (£5.10, 35 minutes).

Capel Curig

POP 222

Little more than a bustling intersection, complete with shops selling outdoor gear, tiny Capel Curig spreads out along the A5. Some 5 miles west of Betws-y-Coed, it's one of Snowdonia's oldest hill stations and has long been a magnet for walkers and climbers. The setting, in the midst of the Carneddau and Glyderau mountain ranges and overlooked by Snowdon, could hardly be more perfect.

🏃 Activities

Moel Siabod
HIKING

The one don't-miss walk from Capel Curig is the challenging ascent of Moel Siabod (5 miles, four hours, 872m). Start next to Plas y Brenin, cross the bridge and take the road south, following the signposts. The trail passes a disused slate quarry before climbing up the craggy ridge, with wonderful views of the Snowdon Horseshoe from the top.

Plas y Brenin National Mountain Sports Centre
OUTDOORS

(📞01690-720214; www.pyb.co.uk; A4086; 🅿) At the western edge of the village, this multi-activity centre has excellent facilities and a huge array of year-round courses on both land and water, ranging from rock climbing and summer and winter mountaineering, to kayaking, SUP, canoeing and abseiling.

🛏 Sleeping & Eating

★ Plas Curig Hostel   HOSTEL £

(📞 01690-720225; www.snowdoniahostel.co.uk; A5; dm/d/f from £25/60/110; 🅿🛜📶) Plas Curig is an exceptional hostel that has earned its five stars. Paying as much attention to comfort as decor, it has sturdy bunks with privacy curtains and storage space, a large, well-equipped kitchen, a drying room for soggy hiking gear, and hospitable owners who can sell you local craft beer at reception.

Bryn Tyrch Inn   HOTEL ££

(📞 01690-720223; www.bryntyrchinn.co.uk; A5; s/d/f from £75/90/155; 🅿🛜) Downstairs there's a restaurant and bar with a roaring fire and real ales – Capel Curig's liveliest spot after dark (mains £16 to £20). Upstairs the rooms are decked out in bright, cheery pastels, with feature wallpaper and exposed stonework, and some with sleigh beds. It also does packed lunches for walkers (£8 per person).

ℹ Getting There & Away

Snowdon Sherpa bus S2 runs roughly hourly to/from Betws-y-Coed (12 minutes), Pen-y-Pass (13 minutes) and Llanberis (35 minutes). Single trips cost £2.

Ogwen Valley

Hemmed in between the greenery-clad, rounded plateau of the Carnedd mountains to the north, and the rugged, spiky Glyderau range to the south, the Ogwen Valley is arguably Snowdonia's most beautiful. More importantly, several of Snowdonia's best and most challenging hikes are concentrated here, departing from the shores of the slate-hued Llyn Ogwen, and revolving around the triple-peaked **Tryfan** and the amphitheatre formed by the Carneddau range. Most of the valley's inhabitants are feral goats, descended from herds farmed here in the distant past. To experience the mountains without too much effort, take an hour-long return walk from Idwal Cottage to Cwm Idwal, an amphitheatre-shaped hanging valley sheltering the small and wonderfully scenic glacial lake, **Llyn Idwal** (A5), reflecting the Glyderau range.

The best map for Ogwen Valley hikes is the *OS 1:25,000 Explorer map OL17 (Snowdon/Conwy Valley)*.

◉ Sights & Activities

★ Tryfan   MOUNTAIN

(A5) If Snowdon gets more than its fair share of day trippers, then the menacing-looking, fractured rock spur of Tryfan (918m) draws only experienced mountaineers and hillwalkers, determined to conquer Snowdonia's most demanding peak. The summit is crowned by two massive boulders, Adam and Eve, and there are three tracks of varying difficulty leading to the top: South Ridge (aka Miners' Track), Heather Terrace and North Ridge. Climbing Tryfan is a serious undertaking, only to be attempted in fine weather.

The easiest way up is the **South Ridge track** (5 miles, five to six hours). It ascends from the Idwal Cottage car park towards Llyn Idwal, then climbs steadily past Llyn Bochlwyd towards Bwlch Tryfan, the saddle between Tryfan's peak and Glyder Fach. You then make your way past the Far Summit Peak and scramble up to the summit. If you're tempted to jump the 5ft gap between the Adam and Eve boulders (as some do!), consider the consequences of misjudging the distance.

The **Heather Terrace route** (4 miles, four to six hours) climbs up from the Gwern Gof Uchaf farm towards the 'Little Tryfan' rock slab, popular with rock climbers, cutting across Tryfan's east face, and culminating in a col between the Far South peak and the South peak, from where it's a short scramble up a broad, scree-covered slope to the summit.

Starting from a lay-by by Llyn Ogwen, the **North Ridge track** (3 to 4 miles, four to six hours) is the most challenging of the routes, starting as a scree-covered trail and becoming progressively steeper as you climb the ridge. There isn't a single formal path to follow, but thousands of feet have worn a rough trail among the boulders, and if you stick to the middle of the ridge, it's not difficult to follow. We recommend descending via one of the other two routes, though.

★ Carnedd Loop   HIKING

(A5, Tal-y-Llyn Ogwen Farm) Starting from the Tal-y-Llyn Ogwen farm, just east of Llyn Ogwen, this moderately strenuous 12-mile

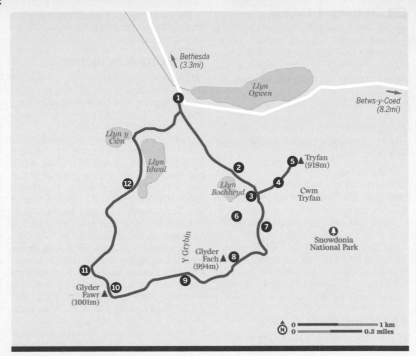

Mountain Walk
The Glyder Traverse

START IDWAL COTTAGE YHA
FINISH IDWAL COTTAGE YHA
LENGTH 6.5 MILES; SIX TO EIGHT HOURS

This rugged hike involves a little scrambling and takes in two of its greatest peaks – Glyder Fach and Glyder Fawr, with an optional scramble up Tryfan peak.

Cross the footbridge from the **1 Idwal Cottage** car park. At a **2 fork** in the path, go straight up the Miner's Track that crosses bracken-covered, boggy ground before climbing steeply up Cwm Bochlwyd to sheltered **3 Llyn Bochlwyd** lake. Ignore the track veering to the right and ascend towards the gap between Tryfan and Glyder Fach. Once you've reached the **4 ridge**, you have the option of detouring up the **5 South Ridge of Tryfan**. It's a 30-minute, straightforward scramble up some giant rocks to Tryfan's famous summit (918m) feature – the twin **6 Adam and Eve rocks**. If it's a windy day, don't climb up and try to jump the 5ft gap!

Once you've taken in the all-encompassing view of Llyn Ogwen below and the Carnedd mountains opposite, head back to the ridge. Use the ladder crossing and either scramble up the steep shortcut of **7 Bristly Ridge** or take the **8 footpath** that cuts across the eastern flank of Glyder Fach. Make a sharp right up towards the jumble of dark rock slabs that mark the **9 summit of Glyder Fach** (994m), with the famous Cantilever – a slab of rock balanced on two shorter rocks – nearby. It's a straightforward, cairn-marked walk across the bare, rock-strewn plateau to Glyder Fawr (1001m), passing the dramatic black rock spikes of **10 Castell y Gwynt** (Castle of the Winds). A steep, screen-strewn path zigzags down to **11 Devil's Kitchen** ridge. Head right along the path between the giant boulders to the shores of **12 Llyn Idwal**. Skirt the lake from the left for the best views of Cwm Idwal, cross the footbridge, turn left and follow the footpath back to the car park.

hike takes in four Carnedd peaks and two glacial lakes, with fantastic views of the Glyder range and Tryfan en route. It's a great mix of gentle ridge walks, plus a couple of challenging scrambles. Park by the trailhead along the A5.

The trail climbs steadily up the Afon Lloer valley before veering west by the Ffynnon Lloer lake, where you perform a short gully scramble up the rock spur. From **Pen-yr Ole Wen** (978m), it's an easy, cairn-marked ridge walk to **Carnedd Dafydd** (1044m), followed by a drop to Bwlch Cyfryd-drum and an ascent to **Carnedd Llewelyn** (1064m), Wales' third-highest peak. Another ridge walk and steep descent are followed by an exposed scramble up **Pen yr Helgi Du** (833m), then descending to the A5 via the gentle ridge of Y Braich.

🛏 Sleeping

Idwal Cottage YHA   HOSTEL £
(📞 0845 371 9744; www.yha.org.uk; A5, Nant Ffrancon LL57 3LZ; camping £12, dm/tw £25/59; ⊘ daily Mar-Oct, Fri & Sat Nov-Feb) Remote yet comfy Idwal Cottage, the oldest YHA hostel in Wales, makes a great base for walks in the Ogwen Valley or bagging Glyderau or Carneddau peaks. By the shores of Llyn Ogwen, it's smallish, with a mix of four-bed-dorms and two- and three-bed rooms, plus a drying room, bar and kitchen, and a wooded campsite. Booking conditions may apply.

ℹ Getting There & Away

From mid-April to late October, the Snowdon Sherpa bus S6 runs twice-daily on Saturday and Sunday from Bangor to Pen-y-Pass via Llyn Ogwen (25 minutes) and Capel Curig (35 minutes). Single trips cost £2. The rest of the time, you'll need your own wheels.

Llanberis

POP 1908

Right on the doorstep of Snowdonia National Park, Llanberis attracts a steady flow of walkers and climbers, particularly during the warmer months. It's a trekking base like no other, partly because of the Snowdon Mountain Railway, and partly because of its proximity to the most popular trails up Snowdon. Come evening, the main street's cafes and restaurants fill with Gore-Tex-wearing masses, returning from the slopes.

Llanberis originally housed workers from the Dinorwig slate quarry, and hillsides have been left deeply scarred by the mining. While tourism is the cornerstone of life these days, the town hasn't abandoned its industrial roots, and Dinorwig is now part of Europe's biggest pumped-storage power station. Some of the old quarry workshops have been reincarnated as a slate-industry museum, and the narrow-gauge railway that once hauled slate to the coast now transports day trippers along Llyn Padarn.

◉ Sights

★ National Slate Museum   MUSEUM
(📞 0300 111 2333; www.museum.wales/slate; off A4086; ⊘ 10am-4pm Sun, Mon, Wed & Thu; 🅿) FREE At Dinorwig Quarry, much of the slate was carved out of the open mountainside – leaving behind a jagged, sculptural cliff face that's fascinating if not exactly beautiful. This excellent museum, occupying the Victorian workshops beside the lake (Llyn Padarn), features video clips, a huge working water wheel, workers' cottages (progressively furnished in period decor from 1861 to 1969, when the quarries closed) and slate-cutting demonstrations.

The turn-off is along the A4086 between Electric Mountain and the Snowdon Mountain Railway station.

Llanberis Miners' Hospital   MUSEUM
(500m northwest of National Slate Museum; ⊘ 10am-5pm Easter-Oct, to 4pm Sun-Fri Nov-Easter) FREE Built in 1860 to care for workers injured in rockfalls and the other mishaps inseparable from slate mining, this museum provides a vivid insight into the sometimes gruesome medical care provided in Victorian times. Tuberculosis was a greater risk than blast-related dismemberment. Who knew?

The hospital is on the northeastern shore of Llyn Padarn, 500m northwest of National Slate Museum.

Dinorwig Power Station & Electric Mountain   MUSEUM
(📞 01286-870636; www.electricmountain.co.uk) More than just Dinorwig Power Station's public interface, Electric Mountain has interactive exhibits on hydropower that explain why the power station is worthwhile, even though it consumes more electricity than it produces. It's also the starting point for a fascinating guided tour through rock

tunnels into the power station's guts, 750m under Elidir mountain.

The centre is by the lakeside on the A4086.

Dolbadarn Castle CASTLE
(Castell Dolbadarn; Cadw; www.cadw.gov.wales; A4086; ⊙10am-4pm) [FREE] Built before 1230 by the Princes of Gwynedd, the keep of Dolbardarn rises like a perfect chessboard rook from a green hilltop between the two lakes, Llyn Padarn and Llyn Peris. If it seems spartan, spare a thought for Owain ap Gruffydd, imprisoned here for 20 years in the mid-13th century by his younger brother Llewellyn the Last. It's a brief stroll from town and you'll be rewarded with wonderful views of the lakes, quarries and Snowdon itself.

🏃 Activities

Paul Poole Mountaineering CLIMBING
(☑07786-360347; www.paulpoolemountaineering.co.uk; courses from £130) If you're looking to improve your mountain skills, from scrambling and rock climbing to winter ascents, reputable local mountain guide Paul can arrange a course to suit all abilities.

Boulder Adventures OUTDOORS
(☑01286-870556; www.boulderadventures.co.uk; Ty Du Rd; session/full day from £40/60) Small groups and families can work with Boulder to devise their own adventure from a list including rock climbing, abseiling, gorge walking, coasteering, orienteering and kayaking. It also offers hostel-style accommodation within the Bryn Du Mountain Centre, a spacious Victorian house on the slopes above Llanberis.

🛏 Sleeping

Snowdon Llanberis YHA HOSTEL £
(☑0845 371 9645; www.yha.org.uk; Llwyn Celyn, Ceunant St; dm/tw/tr/pods from £24/69/79/109; ⊙reception 8-10am & 5-10pm; P 🗢) Originally a quarry manager's house, this no-frills hostel with spartan six-bed dorms and various configurations of private rooms offers great views from its hillside locale, a self-catering kitchen, a drying room and four-person fixed camping pods. It's about a 10-minute walk above the town, signposted from High St.

★Beech Bank B&B ££
(☑01286-871085; www.beech-bank.co.uk; 2 High St; s/d from £70/80; P 🗢) First impressions of this double-gabled, wrought-iron-

trimmed stone house are great, but step inside and it just gets better. A stylish renovation has resulted in beautiful bathrooms and exuberant decor, which matches the gregarious nature of the host. Breakfasts can be packed for early-rising hikers and climbers. Thoughtful touches, such as lending flasks to hikers, are a boon.

Plas Coch Guest House GUESTHOUSE ££
(☑01286-872122; www.plascochsnowdonia.co.uk; High St; s/d from £70/90; P 🗢) More like a little hotel than a B&B, this large stone mid-Victorian guest house is operated by Jim and Eryl, a friendly couple with lots of local knowledge to impart. There's a slate-floored drawing room, and the eight bedrooms are smart, comfortable and in some cases large enough to qualify as suites. Breakfasts, including vegetarian and vegan options, are lavish.

Glyn Afon B&B ££
(☑01286-872528; www.llanberisguesthouse.co.uk; 72 High St; s/d from £55/65; P 🗢) On the main street, this boutique B&B comprises a handful of immaculate rooms decked out in neutral shades, along with nice extras. The hearty breakfast will set you up well for a day of hiking, and the owners are happy to help with information on walks (and will even lend you a compass or rucksack if you're missing gear).

Glyn Peris GUESTHOUSE ££
(☑01286-872711; www.glynperisguesthouse.com; A4086; s/d from £58/76; P 🗢) A 10-minute walk north of central Llanberis, this handsome guesthouse sits in a quiet spot off the main road, surrounded by woodland. Rooms are all en suite and a decent size. Owners Paul and Ceris are wonderfully hospitable and informative, there's a drying room for all-weather adventurers and packed lunches are arranged on request.

🍴 Eating & Drinking

★Pen-y-Ceunant Isaf CAFE £
(☑01286-872606; www.snowdoncafe.com; Llanberis Path; snacks £3-5; ⊙9am-10pm Apr-Oct, to 6pm rest of year) Imagine: you're descending from Snowdon through fog and drizzle, when this 18th-century cottage-cafe appears like a beacon of light, luring you in with an open fire, hot chocolate, herbal teas, doorstop wedges of *bara brith* fruitcake and steaming bowls of lobscouse soup.

In fine weather, have your craft beer and sandwiches on the picnic tables outside.

Pantri   CAFE £
(📞 01286-238070; www.facebook.com/pantrillanberis; High St; mains £5-7; ⊘ 9.15am-4.15pm Mon-Fri, 9am-4.30pm Sat & Sun; 🐾) Best coffee in Llanberis! After that, everything else this cruisy, pastel-hued, family-run cafe does is a bonus. But those extras – homemade cakes, sandwiches, soups and the like – are also top-notch, best enjoyed on the outdoor patio.

Pete's Eats   CAFE £
(📞 01286-870117; www.petes-eats.co.uk; 40 High St; mains £4-7; ⊘ 8am-8pm; 🛜) Pete's Eats is a local institution – a busy, primary-coloured cafe with a profound commitment to carbs, where hikers and climbers swap tips beneath photos of their mountaineering forebears over monster breakfasts, burgers and eggs and chips. There's a huge noticeboard full of travellers' information, a book exchange and a map and guidebook room.

There's also bunkhouse accommodation upstairs (dorm beds/doubles £22/49).

Gallt-y-Glyn   PUB FOOD £
(📞 01286-870370; www.galltyglyn.com; A4086; mains £11; ⊘ kitchen 6-9pm Wed-Sat; 🛏) Sure, it serves pasta, pies, burgers and salads, too, but almost everyone comes for the pizza and the free-pint-with-every-main deal. Simply tick the toppings you want on the paper menu and hand it over at the bar. It's a bit shabby, slightly eccentric, very family friendly and hugely satisfying. Find it on the A4086, half a mile towards Caernarfon.

There's also an eight-room bunkhouse upstairs (doubles £60).

Peak Restaurant   INTERNATIONAL ££
(Bwyty'r Copa; 📞 01286-872777; www.thepeakrestaurant.co.uk; 86 High St; mains £14-21; ⊘ 7-10pm Wed-Sat; 🖋) A chef-patron who once clattered the pans at the legendary Chez Panisse in California is behind this fine-dining restaurant's popularity and longevity. The open kitchen allows you to see her at work, turning good Welsh produce into internationally inspired dishes such as Anglesey sea bass with lemon butter or Welsh lamb rump with redcurrant jus. Book ahead.

ⓘ Getting There & Around

Bus Snowdon Sherpa buses stop by Joe Brown's on High St. S1 heads to Pen-y-Pass

(15 minutes, every 30 minutes), while S2 runs roughly hourly via Pen-y-Pass to Capel Curig (20 minutes) and Betws-y-Coed (35 minutes). Single tickets cost £2.

Other regular buses include the 88 to/from Caernarfon (£1.50, 25 minutes, four to eight daily) and the 85/86 to/from Bangor (£1.90, 50 minutes, four to nine daily).

Bicycle Llanberis Bike Hire (📞 07776 051559; www.llanberisbikehire.co.uk; 34 High St; £25/18 per day/3hr; ⊘ 9am-5pm) rents Genesis Core 30 and Core 20 hardtail mountain bikes, suitable for ascents/descents of Snowdon, and can deliver them to your lodgings (or up Snowdon for £50, including bike rental). Bear in mind that bikes are banned from Snowdon's trails between 10am and 5pm from May to September.

Train The Snowdon Mountain Railway (p256) whisks passengers up almost to the summit.

Snowdon (Yr Wyddfa)

No Snowdonia experience is complete without summiting Snowdon (1085m), one of Britain's most awe-inspiring mountains and the highest summit in Wales (it's actually the 61st highest in Britain; the top 60 are all in Scotland). 'Yr Wyddfa' in Welsh (pronounced uhr-*with*-vuh, meaning 'the Tomb'), it's the mythical resting place of the giant Rhita Gawr, who demanded King Arthur's beard for his cloak and was killed for his temerity.

On a clear day the views stretch to Ireland and the Isle of Man over Snowdon's fine jagged ridges, which drop away in great swoops to sheltered cwms (valleys) and deep lakes. Thanks to the Snowdon Mountain Railway the peak is extremely accessible when the winds aren't too high. On fine days, some of the trails leading to the summit get frustratingly crowded, so the big question is: which way up?

⊙ Sights & Activities

★ Mount Snowdon   MOUNTAIN
Summiting Wales' highest mountain (1085m) is neither a cakewalk nor an insurmountable obstacle, and is hugely worth it, in spite of occasional crowds. Seven trails of varying length and difficulty lead to Snowdon's summit, some more scenic than others. That the mountain has a train station and a cafe at its summit does not mean you should underestimate it. No route is completely safe, especially in winter, so sturdy

❶ BE PREPARED

Hikers have perished on Snowdon even in fine weather in summer and fog can descend on the summit within minutes. Regardless of the hiking route or the weather forecast, pack layers of clothing (including waterproofs), food and water, a torch and a decent map: *OS 1:25,000 Explorer map OL17 (Snowdon/Conwy Valley).*

footwear, extra layers, plenty of provisions and a torch are musts.

The longest and most straightforward (read: a bit boring) route to the summit is the **Llanberis Path** (5 miles one-way, three hours), a steady ascent that runs beside the train line, with a slightly steeper section once you pass Clogwyn station. This is also the route used by mountain bikes, and graded a black trail.

The two paths starting from Pen-y-Pass require the least amount of ascent but are nevertheless tougher walks. The **Miner's Track** (4 miles one-way, three hours) starts off wide and gentle, skirting part of Llyn Llydaw lake, then climbing to Cwm Glaslyn and proceeding steeply up via a series of switchbacks. The **Pyg Track** (3.5 miles one-way, 2½ hours) is shorter and steeper, climbing up to the Bwlch y Moch (Pass of Pigs), traversing a ridge above Llyn Lydaw and eventually joining the switchbacks of the Miner's Track.

The classic Snowdon Horseshoe (8 miles return), one of the most spectacular ways to see Snowdon and its glacial lakes, branches off from the Pyg Track to cross the precipitous ridge of **Crib Goch** (the knife-edge traverse, occasionally lethal in windy or wintry conditions, is only recommended for the experienced), with a descent over the peak of Y Lliwedd and a final section down the Miner's Track.

Two tracks start from the Caernarfon–Beddgelert road (A4085): the **Snowdon Ranger Path** (4 miles one-way, three hours) is a somewhat dull slog of the shores of Llyn Cwellyn, steep and boggy by turns, that skirts the Clogwyn Du'r Arddu cliffs and connects with the Llanberis Path. The **Rhyd Ddu Path** (4 miles one-way, three hours) has two starting points (Rhyl Ddu car park and Pitt's Head Rock) that shortly join up, and a particularly spectacular final

section that traverses the Cwm Clogwyn rim and Yr Wyddfa's south ridge.

The most rugged and scenic of the southern routes is the **Watkin Path** (4 miles one-way, three hours), involving an ascent of more than 1000m on its southerly approach from Nant Gwynant and finishing with a scramble to Bwlch Ciliau, the saddle between Y Lliwdd and the Snowdon summit.

★ **Snowdon Mountain Railway** RAIL
(☑ 01286-870223; www.snowdonrailway.co.uk; A4086; adult/child return diesel £29/20, steam £37/27; ☺ 9am-5pm mid-Mar–Oct) If you're not physically able to climb a mountain, short on time or just into conserving energy, those industrious Victorians have gifted you an alternative. Opened in 1896, the Snowdon Mountain Railway is the UK's highest – and only – rack-and-pinion railway. Vintage steam and modern diesel locomotives haul carriages from Llanberis up to Snowdon's summit (one hour one-way, 2½ hours return).

The train waits near the summit for half an hour before heading back down again. Single tickets can only be booked for the journey up (adult/child £27/20); if you want to walk up and ride down, you'll have to hope there's space. Tens of thousands of people take the train to the summit each season: make sure you book well in advance or you may miss out. Departures are determined by customer demand and are weather dependent. From March to May (or during high winds) the trains can only head as far as Clogwyn Station (adult/child £23/18) – an altitude of 779m.

🛏 Sleeping

Snowdon Pen-y-Pass YHA HOSTEL £
(☑ 0845 371 9534; www.yha.org.uk; A4086; dm/tw/tr/q £26/59/69/79; ℗) This superbly situated hostel has three of Snowdon's trails at its doorstep. It has a well-equipped kitchen, laundry and drying room; Mallory's Cafe& Bar (named for a past patron who perished on Everest); six-bed dorms and quiet, comfortable rooms, some en suite. Curfew 10.30pm. It's 5.5 miles up the A4086 from Llanberis; the Snowdon Sherpa buses stop here.

Snowdon Bryn Gwynant YHA HOSTEL £
(☑ 0845 371 9108; www.yha.org.uk; A498, Nant Gwynant; dm/r from £23/55; ☺ Mar-Oct; ℗) Bryn Gwynant has the most impressive

building and the most idyllic setting of all Snowdonia National Park's youth hostels, occupying a slate Victorian mansion overlooking Lake Gwynant to Snowdon. It's 4 miles east of Beddgelert, near the start of the Watkin Path. This 72-bedder has no wifi, but plenty of reading nooks.

Snowdon Ranger YHA   HOSTEL £
(☑ 0845 371 9659; www.yha.org.uk; A4085, Rhyd Ddu; ℗) On the A4085, 5 miles north of Beddgelert at the trailhead for the Snowdon Ranger Path, this former inn has its own adjoining beach on the shore of Llyn Cwellyn, and is close to the hiking and climbing centres of Llanberis and Beddgelert. The dorms and rooms at this 30-bed hostel are currently only available for exclusive (whole place) hire.

★ Pen-y-Gwryd   HISTORIC HOTEL ££
(☑ 01286-870211; www.pyg.co.uk; A4086, Nant Gwynant; r incl breakfast with/without bathroom from £115/95; ℗ 🛜 🐾) Eccentric and atmospheric, this creeper-clad Georgian coaching inn was used as a training base by the 1953 Everest team; spot Edmund Hillary's and James (now Jan) Morris' signatures on the restaurant ceiling. Traditional rooms are rather spartan, with washbasins; en suites are plusher, some with four-poster beds and claw-footed tubs. The hotel sits at the junction of the A498 and A4086.

Wi-fi in common areas only, and good luck getting a phone signal. But there's a comfy games room, a sauna and a lake for those hardy enough to swim. Solid meals and packed lunches are available. Two-night minimum on weekends.

ⓘ Information

Clad in granite and curved to blend into the mountain, **Hafod Eryri** (www.snowdonrailway.co.uk; ⊘10.30am-4.30pm May-Oct; 🛜) houses a cafe, toilets and ambient interpretive elements built into the structure itself. Closed in winter or if the weather's terrible, it's open whenever the train is running.

ⓘ Getting There & Away

Bus Snowdon Sherpa buses connect various destinations to Pen-y-Pass. S1 runs from Llanberis twice hourly (15 minutes); a dozen daily S2 buses run from Llanberis to Betws-y-Coed via Pen-y-Pass; S4 serves Caernarfon (one hour, five daily, Monday to Saturday) via Beddgelert, while S97 connects Porthmadog (one hour, seven daily Monday to Saturday) to

the trailhead via Tremadog. A Sherpa single/return/day ticket costs £2/3/5).

Bicycle Llanberis Bike Hire (p255) can deliver your rental bike up Snowdon for £50, including costs of hire. Bear in mind that bikes are banned from Snowdon's trails between 10am and 5pm from May to September.

Car It's worth considering public transport: car parks can fill up quickly and the Pen-y-Pass car park costs £10 per day.

Train The Welsh Highland Railway (p260) stops at the trailhead of the Rhyd Ddu Path, and there is a request stop (Snowdon Ranger Halt) for the Snowdon Ranger Path. Another option is to take the Snowdon Mountain Railway from Llanberis to the top and walk down. It's more difficult to do this the other way around; the train will only take on new passengers at the top if there is space.

Beddgelert

POP 468

Postcard-worthy Beddgelert consists of a tight clutch of stone cottages overlooking the River Colwyn and its ivy-covered bridge, upstream from where it meets the River Glaslyn. Flowers festoon the village in spring and the surrounding hills are covered in a purple blaze of heather in summer. The village is the starting point for several rewarding hikes, including a short stroll to the underwhelming **Gelert's Grave** (⊘24hr) FREE, allegedly the final resting place of the mythical hound of the 13th-century Prince of Gwynedd, Llywelyn the Great, after which Beddgelert supposedly takes its name. In warmer weather, the village teems with walkers and parking is tricky.

◎ Sights & Activities

Apart from hikes and gentle walks that originate in Beddgelert, you can also make use of the Welsh Highland Railway (p260) to ride one way to Waunfaur, returning along the Lon Gwyrfai walking/cycle track (9 miles, 2½ hours), or to Nantmor, walking back along the Fisherman's Path (one hour). The *OS 1:25,000 Explorer map OL17 (Snowdon/Conwy Valley)* is best for the area.

Sygun Copper Mine   MINE
(☑ 01766-890595; www.syguncoppermine.co.uk; A498; adult/child under 15yr £10/7.50; ⊘9.30am-5pm Apr-Sep, 10am-4pm rest of year; ℗ 🦽) This copper mine dates from Roman times,

although extraction was stepped up in the 19th century. Abandoned in 1903, it has since been converted into a family-friendly museum, with a half-hour self-guided underground tour containing dioramas that evoke the life of Victorian miners. You can also try your hand at metal detecting (£2.50) or panning for gold (£2). It's a mile northeast of Beddgelert.

Moel Hebog Ridge   HIKING

(off A4085) The ascent of Moel Hebog (783m) is relatively strenuous (8-mile loop, five hours) and includes a scenic ridge walk that encompasses lesser peaks. The trail begins at the Pont Alyn bridge, half a mile northwest of central Beddgelert. Follow the road to Cwm Cloch Isaf Farm, and then the signposted trail up along the northeast ridge of Moel Hebog.

Craflwyn & Dinas Emrys   WALKING

(NT; ☑ 01766-510120; www.nationaltrust.org.uk; A498) A mile northeast of Beddgelert, near Llyn Dinas, National Trust–owned Craflwyn Farm is the trailhead for the Dinas Emrys trail. It takes around 30 minutes to walk through fields, alongside a stream, past a waterfall and through woods to the summit. At the top are the remains of 12th-century and Roman-era fortifications and wonderful views over the valley of Nant Gwynant.

Aberglaslyn Gorge   WALKING

The gentle Aberglaslyn Gorge trail (3 miles return, two hours) runs from Beddgelert and follows the left bank of the Glaslyn downstream from the footbridge until it comes to the Welsh Highland Railway. Carry on until Pont Aberglaslyn, where the footpath meets the road, and then complete the walk along the right bank of the river.

🛏 Sleeping

Beddgelert Campsite   CAMPGROUND £

(☑ 01766-890288; www.beddgelertcampsite.co.uk; A4085; sites from £23; P @ 🐾) 🌿 Situated in the beautiful Beddgelert Forest, this site is well equipped, with a shop for contingencies, a children's play area and even a request stop on the Welsh Highland Railway. Find it 1 mile north of Beddgelert, off the A4085.

★ Plas Tan Y Craig   B&B ££

(☑ 01766-890310; www.plastanygraig.co.uk; Stryd Smith; r £124; 🐾) Super central and overlooking the Colwyn, this award-winning,

family-run B&B comprises five midsized rooms (twin and king) in cool slate-greys and creams. A generous cooked breakfast is served; other perks include an honesty bar and drying room for your wet gear. Packed meals prepared on request. Minimum of two nights.

Sygun Fawr
Country House   HISTORIC HOTEL ££

(☑ 01766-890258; www.sygunfawr.co.uk; A498; r incl breakfast £94; ☺ Mar-Nov; P 🐾) A warm welcome awaits at this sturdy 17th-century manor house, tucked away at the end of a narrow lane. Additions have been grafted onto the 1660s core over the centuries, so each of the dozen comfortable bedrooms is quite different; some have spectacular mountain views. No TV – blissful silence reigns. It's half a mile northeast of Beddgelert.

Coach House   GUESTHOUSE ££

(☑ 01766-890386; www.coachhousebeddgelert.co.uk; The Square; d/tr £105/120; 🐾) The former historic coach house is just steps from the bridge across the Colwyn. The handful of comfortable rooms have thick carpeting and classic decor, and hospitable owners Regan and Emma are happy to point you towards the walking and cycle trails. Continental breakfast included.

Plas Colwyn   LODGE £££

(☑ 01766-890276; www.plascolwyn.co.uk; Carenarfon Rd; r 4 nights £1700; 🐾) The nine rooms at this self-catering 18th-century stone house are large and very comfortable, with floral prints and punchy wallpaper, and there's a wooden-beamed lounge with a fireplace, fully equipped kitchen and comfy lounge. Perfect for large families and groups of friends; four-night minimum. Rooms at the front look out over the murmuring Colwyn and surrounding hills.

🍴 Eating

Glaslyn Ices & Cafe Glandwr   ICE CREAM £

(☑ 01766-890339; www.glaslynices.co.uk; 1 scoop £2.70; ☺ 9.30am-5.30pm Sun-Fri, to 8.30pm Sat; P ♿) In summer this excellent ice-cream parlour is the busiest place in the village. It serves some three dozen homemade flavours, some of which (mango sorbet, cinder toffee, banoffee) have won regional prizes.

Hebog   CAFE ££

(☑ 01766-890400; www.facebook.com/hebog beddgelert; Fford Caernarfon; mains £16-19;

noon-8pm Thu-Mon; 🛜) At the swankier end of Beddgelert's dining options, Hebog is an upmarket cafe serving the likes of braised lamb with samphire and homemade spinach-and-ricotta tortellini with red-pepper pesto. The scenic summer terrace by the babbling Glaslyn fills up quickly on warm days.

ℹ Information

Tourist Office (📞01766-890615; www.eryri
-npa.gov.uk; 3 Dolfair; ⏱9.30am-12.30pm &
1-4.30pm Easter-Oct) Great for information on hikes, cycling and accommodation in the area, and sells local produce.

ℹ Getting There & Around

Bus Snowdon Sherpa buses serve Beddgelert: the S4 (six daily) heads to/from Caernarfon (35 minutes) via Snowdon Ranger (10 minutes) and Rhyd Ddu (six minutes), while the S97 (seven daily) heads to Porthmadog (25 minutes) via Tremadog (18 minutes). Buses run Monday to Saturday; single tickets cost £2.

Bicycle Located near the train station, **Beddgelert Bikes** (Beics Beddgelert; 📞01766-890434; www.beddgelertbikes.co.uk; The Bike Barn, High St; per 4/8/24hr from £20/30/35) rents out mountain bikes, e-bikes, children's bikes, tandems and child seats, and can advise on the many trails in the area.

Train Beddgelert train station (off High St) is a stop on the historic Welsh Highland Railway (p260), which runs between Caernarfon and Porthmadog (£40 return) from Easter to October, with limited winter service, and stops at the Rhyd Ddu and Snowdon Ranger trailheads.

Porthmadog

POP 2905

Busy Porthmadog (port-*mad*-uk) enjoys an arresting estuarine setting overlooking the Glaslyn River, and even though the town itself has no discernible attractions, it's a convenient gateway for both the Llŷn Peninsula and Snowdonia National Park, and has the fantastical village of Portmeirion (p260) on its doorstep.

Porthmadog is also the starting place for heritage railways, one of them harking back to the the town's past as Wales' busiest slate port. There are 'little trains' all over Wales, a legacy of Victorian industry, but Porthmadog is triply blessed: it forms the southern terminus for two of Wales'

Porthmadog

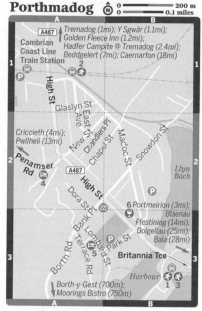

Porthmadog

⦿ **Activities, Courses & Tours**
1 Ffestiniog Railway B3
2 Welsh Highland Heritage Railway A1
3 Welsh Highland Railway B3

⦿ **Sleeping**
4 Tudor Lodge A2
5 Yr Hen Fecws A3

⦿ **Drinking & Nightlife**
6 Australia B3

⦿ **Shopping**
Purple Moose Brewery Shop ......(see 6)

finest narrow-gauge train journeys and has a third steam-train line connected to a rail-heritage centre.

The shallow Traeth Bach estuary abounds in mullet, which in turn attract ospreys. Keep an eye out for these large birds of prey as you walk around the cliffs of Borth-y-Gest and Portmeirion.

⦿ Sights

Borth-y-Gest VILLAGE
(Borth Rd) The best views over the estuary are from Porthmadog's Terrace Rd, which becomes Garth Rd above the harbour. At the south end of Porthmadog, a path heads

down to Borth-y-Gest, a pretty horseshoe of candy-coloured houses overlooking a sandy bay. At the other end of the crescent the path continues around the cliffs; you should be able to spot Harlech Castle in the distance.

🏃 Activities

★ Welsh Highland Railway   RAIL
(☑ 01766-516000; www.festrail.co.uk; £40 return; ☺ Easter-Oct, limited service winter) Originating in 1923, and departing from Porthmadog Harbour Station, the Welsh Highland Railway is the UK's longest, running for 25 miles to Caernarfon (2½ hours) via Beddgelert (£40 return) and Rhyd-Ddu, and skirting the southern slopes of Snowdon. Wonderfully scenic, the track runs through a river estuary and oak woods before steeply climbing some rugged mountainous terrain.

★ Ffestiniog Railway   RAIL
(Rheilffordd Ffestiniog; ☑ 01766-516024; www. festrail.co.uk; day ticket £25; ☺ daily Easter-Oct, reduced services rest of year; ♿) The world's oldest surviving narrow-gauge railway, the Ffestiniog wends its way from Porthmadog to the slate-mining town of Blaenau Ffestiniog. Long past its industrial heyday, the railway's 150-year-old steam locomotives and wooden carriages now ferry sightseers through oak woodlands, beneath towering

---

WORTH A TRIP

PORTMEIRION VILLAGE

Set on its own tranquil peninsula reaching into the estuary, **Portmeirion Village** (☑ 01766-770000; www.portmeirion.wales; Minffordd, off High St; adult/concession £13/11; ☺ 9.30am-5.30pm; Ⓟ) is a fantastical collection of colourful buildings with a heavy Italian influence that was masterminded by Welsh architect Sir Clough Williams-Ellis. Starting in 1925, Sir Clough collected bits and pieces from disintegrating stately mansions and set them alongside his own creations and, with a 'light-opera sort of approach', concocted this seaside utopia. At age 90, Sir Clough deemed Portmeirion to be complete – 50 years after he began.

It's really more like a stage set than an actual village and, indeed, it formed the ideally surreal set for cult TV series *The Prisoner,* which was filmed here from 1966 to 1967. It still draws fans of the show in droves, with rival *Prisoner* conventions held annually in March and April. The giant plaster-of-Paris Buddha, just off the piazza, featured in the 1958 film *The Inn of the Sixth Happiness,* starring Ingrid Bergman. Architecturally, it's a mishmash: there are Ionic columns topped with Thai figures, and a Jacobean town hall nestles alongside a Mediterranean piazza.

A documentary on Sir Clough and Portmeirion screens on the hour in a building just above the central piazza. Sir Clough's lifelong concern was with the whimsical and intriguing nature of architecture, his raison d'être to demonstrate how a naturally beautiful site could be developed without defiling it. His life's work now stands as a testament to beauty, something he described as 'that strange necessity'. He died in 1978, having campaigned for the environment throughout his life.

Most of the kooky cottages and scaled-down mansions scattered about the site are available for holiday lets (the Unicorn building, with its faux-Georgian facade, offers great views over the central village) and it's well worth experiencing Portmeirion after the day trippers have left. The other buildings contain cafes, restaurants and gift shops. Portmeirion pottery (the famously florid tableware designed by Susan, Sir Clough's daughter) is available, even though these days it's made in Stoke-on-Trent (England). A network of walking paths thread along the coast and through the forested private peninsula, which includes authentic castle ruins and a profusion of exotic plants, nourished by the warm microclimate of the peninsula.

Portmeirion is 2 miles east of Porthmadog. Public transport there isn't great, so if you don't fancy the walk, you're best to catch a taxi.

It's well worth staying on-site at **Hotel Portmeirion & Castell Deudraeth** (☑ 01766-770000; www.portmeirion.wales; Portmeirion; r from £184; Ⓟ🐾). Choose between over-the-top Hotel Portmeirion in a prime spot by the water, with individually styled rooms, a pool and a terrace bar, or fancifully Gothic Castell Deudraeth, just outside the village.

peaks and beside rivers. For an extra £7 each way, you can ride in giant-windowed observation carriages.

Children under 16 years travel for £1.

Welsh Highland Heritage Railway RAIL
(✆01766-513402; www.whr.co.uk; High St; adult/child £10.25/5; ✆Easter-Oct) Not to be confused with the Welsh Highland Railway, this volunteer-run 24in-gauge railway is a family-oriented attraction. Steam or diesel trains chug less than a mile up the track before heading back via the rail heritage centre and engine sheds. You can swap to a miniature railway here for a ride through the woods.

Passengers may also learn to drive a diesel train on select days.

✿ Festivals & Events

PortmeiriCon CULTURAL
(Prisoner Convention; www.portmeiricon.com; Portmeirion; ✆Apr) Here's one to either pencil in or avoid: fans of cult TV show *The Prisoner* converge on Portmeirion in April for a weekend of dress-ups and human chess. Indoor events are only open to members of the Six of One (the Prisoner Appreciation Society), but anyone can catch outdoor shows or glimpses of celebrities bussed in for the occasion.

🛏 Sleeping

Golden Fleece Inn PUB £
(✆01766-512421; www.goldenfleeceinn.com; Market Sq, Tremadog; s/d from £39/55, ste £114; P☎) Hop flowers hang from the ceiling of this former coaching inn, which offers real ales in a cave-like beer cellar, pub grub, an open fire on cold nights and live acoustic music. The rooms above the pub are snug and simply furnished; however, be prepared for noise. King rooms and king suites with whirlpool baths are in the nearby annex.

Hadfer Campsite @ Tremadog TENTED CAMP £
(✆07920 426660; www.hadfer.com; A498, Bwlch-y-Moch; camping £12, glamping tent £80; ☎) Some 3 miles northeast of Porthmadog, en route from Tremadog to Beddgelert, this welcoming campsite consists of a smattering of glamping tents with wood-burning stoves and separate bathrooms, and grassy camping pitched for those roughing it. Perfect location right in front of one of Wales'

best climbing sites, and the cafe serves generous portions of jacket potatoes and pies.

★ Yr Hen Fecws B&B ££
(✆01766-514625; www.henfecws.com; 16 Lombard St; s/d £80/90; P☎) Probably Porthmadog's nicest digs, 'The Old Bakery' is a stylishly restored stone cottage containing seven en-suite rooms, decorated in shades of grey, with crimson or exposed slate walls and fireplaces. Breakfast is served under the marigold walls and exposed beams of the downstairs bistro where the owner-chef whips up Welsh classics in the evenings (dinner mains £18 to £25).

Tudor Lodge B&B ££
(✆01766-515530; www.tudor-lodge.co.uk; Tan yr Onnen, Penamser Rd; s/d from £66/96; P☎) Friendly, spotless, family-run B&B in a handsome Tudor building, just off Porthmadog's High St. Snug rooms are all sweet pastels and greys, and the owners serve up a tremendous Scandinavian-style breakfast buffet alongside generous cooked Welsh breakfasts. A bonus for railway lovers is the 20% discount off Ffestiniog and Welsh Highland railway tickets.

🍴 Eating & Drinking

Moorings Bistro BISTRO ££
(✆01766-513500; www.facebook.com/mooringbistroborthygest; 4 Ivy Terrace, Borth-y-Gest; mains £9-14; ✆9am-9pm Mon-Sat, to 5pm Sun) This popular lunch stop for walkers draws in diners with its international menu of poached eggs on avocado and sourdough, cheese lamb burgers and the like for brunch and lunch, and more substantial dinners that include cod and chips and spiced-lamb tagine. Great views of the estuary from the terrace.

★ Y Sgwâr BISTRO £££
(✆01766-515451; www.ysgwar-restaurant.co.uk; 12-16 Market Sq, Tremadog; mains £18-28; ✆5-9pm Mon-Sat, noon-3pm Sun) On the main square in Tremadog, this cosmopolitan Welsh restaurant has the best food in either town. The service is attentive and friendly, and classics such as pork belly with dauphinois potatoes, and slow-roasted lamb shank with garlic mash are presented with flair and enthusiasm There's great value in the set menus offered between 6pm and 7pm (two/three courses £18.50/23).

Australia PUB

(📞 01766-515957; www.facebook.com/australia porthmadog; 31 High St; ⊙ noon-10pm Sun-Thu, to midnight Fri & Sat; 🛜) In a prime central location, the pub arm of the Purple Moose brewery proudly showcases its award-winning range of craft beers and real ales, all found on tap here. The brews are complemented by decent pub grub at mealtimes.

🛍 Shopping

★**Purple Moose Brewery Shop** DRINKS

(Bragdy Mŵs Piws; 📞 01766-512777; www.purple moose.co.uk; 27 High St; ⊙ 10am-5.30pm) This is the retail front for Purple Moose, an award-winning brewer supplying the better North Welsh pubs. Tipples include its five core brews: Snowdonia Ale, Madog's Ale, Glaslyn Ale, Dark Side of the Moose and Elderflower Ale, as well as craft beers such as Antlered IPA, seasonal Merry X-Moose and beer-emblazoned garb.

Ale aficionados can arrange a tour of the nearby brewery, which includes free tastings.

❶ Getting There & Away

Bus Buses stop on High St and most services pass through the satellite town of Tremadog. Routes include the T2 to/from Bangor (£2.25, 1¼ hours, three to nine daily) via Caernarfon (£1.90, 50 minutes), and in the opposite direction to Aberystwyth (£3.25, 2¼ hours, two to six daily) via Dolgellau (£1.90, 50 minutes, three to nine daily) and Machynlleth (£2.25, 1½ hours, three to seven daily); the frequent (Monday to Saturday only) 3/3B to/from Pwllheli (£1.70, 40 minutes) via Criccieth (£1.30, 15 minutes) and in the other direction to Blaenau Ffestiniog (£1.60, 35 minutes); and up to seven daily (Monday to Saturday) S97 (Snowdon Sherpa) services to/from Beddgelert (£2, 15 to 24 minutes).

Bicycle The Lôn Las Cymru (National Cycle Route 8) passes through Porthmadog, heading west to Criccieth and south to Harlech.

Train Porthmadog is on the Cambrian Coast Line; from the **train station** (High St) there are seven daily direct trains to/from Criccieth (£3.20, seven minutes), Pwllheli (£5.60, 25 minutes), and eight daily trains to Harlech (£4.40, 23 minutes) and Machynlleth (£15.30, two hours). The **Ffestiniog & Welsh Highland Railways** (www.festrail.co.uk) runs scenic services to Blaenau Ffestiniog, the Snowdon trailheads and Caernarfon.

LLŶN PENINSULA

Covered in a patchwork of pastureland and heather-covered hills, the green finger of the Llŷn (pronounced 'khleen') juts into the Irish Sea, its westernmost tip about as remote as you can get. Welsh is the Llŷn's lingua franca; the peninsula and adjacent island of Anglesey were the last to fall to both the Romans and Normans. Welsh culture and the slow pace of life are as much of a draw as the mysticism in which this unique part of Wales is shrouded: legends of King Arthur abound, and over the centuries the heaviest footfalls have been those of pilgrims heading to Bardsey Island.

The wildlife-rich coastline, remote beaches, Iron Age forts and end-of-the-world crags are best explored by bicycle, via a maze of narrow country lanes, or on foot, along the Llŷn Coastal Path.

Criccieth

POP 1792

Criccieth is an easygoing seaside town, made popular by the Victorians, its seaside lined with smart, pastel-coloured town houses. Overlooked by the ruins of a medieval castle on a promontory, it counts two sand-and-stone Blue Flag beaches among its attractions: one a tidy crescent, and the other a wild expanse stretching as far as the eye can see.

◉ Sights

Criccieth Castle CASTLE

(Cadw; www.cadw.gov.wales; Castle St; adult/child £5.10/3.10; ⊙ 10am-1pm & 2-5pm Wed-Sun) Ruined Criccieth Castle, perched on the seafront's most prominent headland, offers views stretching along the peninsula's southern coast and across Tremadog Bay to Harlech. Constructed by Welsh prince Llywelyn the Great in 1239, it was overrun in 1283 by Edward I's forces and recaptured for the Welsh in 1404 by Owain Glyndŵr, whose troops promptly reduced it to the still-standing gatehouse and some broken walls.

Lloyd George Museum MUSEUM

(📞 01766-522071; www.gwynedd.gov.uk/muse ums; Llanystumdwy; adult/child £6/4; ⊙ 10.30am-5pm Mar-Oct) Tiny Llanystumdwy, 1.5 miles west of Criccieth, was the boyhood home of David Lloyd George. The video, photos, posters and personal effects at this rustic house introduce the fiery orator and ladies' man who was largely responsible for introducing National Insurance in a two-pronged attack on unemployment and poverty. Later on in his career, his loyalty to Wales was challenged by his ambitions in Westminster and, though a friend of Churchill, by WWII Lloyd George became a shameless war apologist.

🛏 Sleeping

Caerwylan Hotel   HISTORIC HOTEL **££**

(☏ 01766-522547; www.caerwylan.co.uk; Beach Bank; s/d incl breakfast from £68/115; P 🛜) Overlooking Criccieth Beach, this lemon-yellow, rambling Victorian hotel is both well-located and wonderfully friendly. Carpeted, snug rooms of various sizes are reached via a maze-like assortment of staircases and corridors, or via the grand lounge. Tonnau, the on-site restaurant, is one of the best in town, serving extravagant breakfasts and superlative Welsh classics.

Glyn-y-Coed   B&B **££**

(☏ 01766-522870; www.gychotel.co.uk; Porthmadog Rd; s/d from £85/95; P 🛜) While the name alludes to a wooded glen, this 10-bedroom Victorian house sits right on the main road, gazing out to sea. The views through the bay windows in the elegant front rooms (worth the extra £10) encompass the castle, the bay and the mountains of Snowdonia, while inside you'll find individually styled rooms with quality beds.

🍴 Eating

Poachers Restaurant   INTERNATIONAL **£**

(☏ 01766 522512; www.poachersrestaurant.uk; 66 High St; mains £6-8; ◷ 5-8pm Tue-Sun) A likeable little family restaurant, Poachers sits in a converted grocer's on High St. Lo-cal produce, especially Welsh black beef, features in a menu that takes much from Europe (lasagne, Hungarian goulash), a little from Asia (Balti-style chicken curry) and a lot from Wales (braised Welsh beef, slow-roasted lamb shoulder). It was take-away only at the time of research.

Tir a Môr   CAFE **£**

(☏ 01766-523084; www.tiramor-criccieth.co.uk; 1 Mona Tce; mains £7-12; ◷ 8.30am-5pm Thu-Tue) Decked out in maritime cream and blue, the menu of the aptly named 'Land and Sea' runs the gamut from homemade quiche, croque-monsieurs, full Welsh breakfasts and gourmet burgers to smoked fish and seafood platters and beer-battered cod.

★ Dylan's   INTERNATIONAL **££**

(☏ 01766-522773; www.dylansrestaurant.co.uk; Maes y Mor; mains £13-25; ◷ noon-9.30pm; P 🛜♿) Making use of Morannedd – a light-filled, 1950s, deco-style beachside pavilion designed by Portmeirion architect Sir Clough Williams-Ellis and once used by Butlin's for afternoon tea dances – Dylan's also has a large alfresco sea-facing terrace. Like its siblings in Menai Bridge (p292) and Llandudno, it combines fantastic sea views with a crowd-pleasing, globe-trotting bistro menu spanning pizzas, burgers, curries and seafood.

ℹ Getting There & Away

Bus Buses passing along Criccieth's High St include the dozen daily 3 bus (five on Sunday) to/from Pwllheli (£1.50, 25 minutes), and also to Porthmadog (£1.30, 15 minutes), where you can switch to 3B services to Blaenau Ffestiniog. For services to other parts of the Llŷn, switch buses in Pwllheli.

Bicycle The Lôn Las Cymru (National Cycle Route 8) passes through Criccieth, heading north to Caernarfon and east to Porthmadog.

SNOWDONIA & THE LLŶN CRICCIETH

LLŶN COASTAL PATH

Starting from the Menai Bridge, the 110-mile **Llŷn Coastal Path** runs alongside the Menai Strait and Caernarfon Bay, via Caernarfon, before following the north coast of the Llŷn to the rugged westernmost tip of Mynydd Mawr, passing through seaside villages and sandy bays of the south coast and and finishing up in Porthmadog. The walk is typically done in nine days.

The less-peopled and most beautiful sections include Trefor to Nefyn, and Porth Colmon to Aberdaron via Mynydd Mawr, with epic views of Bardsey Island en route.

Official Guide: Llŷn Peninsula, part of the *Wales Coastal Path* series, is a good companion guide.

WORTH A TRIP

ART BY THE BEACH

A diverse collection of work by contemporary Welsh artists – all available for purchase – is only part of the attraction of Wales's oldest gallery, **Oriel Plas Glyn-y-Weddw** (☑01758-740763; www.oriel.org.uk; Glyn Weddw, Llanbedrog; ⊙10am-4pm). The flamboyant Victorian Gothic mansion it's housed in is striking, with exposed beams and stained glass. One room is devoted to the history of the house and a collection of porcelain. The two carved stones in the foyer date from the 5th or 6th century. Plas Glyn-y-Weddw is 3 miles east of Abersoch, in Llanbedrog.

Train Criccieth is on the Cambrian Coast Line, with direct services from the **train station** (High St) including eight direct trains each day to Pwllheli (£4,15 minutes), and to Machynlleth (£17.50, two hours) via Porthmadog (£3.20, nine minutes), Harlech (£6.60, 35 minutes) and Barmouth (£9.60, one hour).

Pwllheli

POP 4298

The Llŷn's main market town since the 12th century, public transport hub and unofficial capital, Pwllheli (poolth-*heh*-lee; meaning 'Salt-Water Pool') has a long sandy beach (blue-flagged Marian y De), a busy marina and a high concentration of Welsh speakers. The beach and the appealing Victorian high street aside, Pwllheli is really just a place to change buses, but there are some gorgeous, upscale lodgings a short drive away.

⊙ Sights & Activities

Penarth Fawr   HOUSE
(Cadw; ☑01766-810880; www.cadw.gov.wales; off A497, Chwilog; ⊙10am-5pm Apr-Oct) **FREE** Surrounded by stone farm buildings that time forgot, Penarth Fawr is a 15th-century manor that has somehow survived into the 21st century. Basically one large hall with an open hearth, stone flagging and a roof still supported by its original oak 'spere-truss', it gives a sense of how the Llŷn's better-heeled families lodged themselves in years gone by. Keep a third eye open for

the resident ghost. It's on a country lane, signposted from the A497 between Criccieth and Pwllheli.

🛌 Sleeping & Eating

Wern Fawr Manor Farm   COTTAGE **££**
(☑01758-740156; www.wernfawr.co.uk; off B4413, Lon Pin, Llanbedrog; s/d from £70/80, cottage per week from £415; 🅿🛜😻) ✈ Halfway between Pwllheli and Abersoch, a mile north of Llanbedrog and sitting amid 55 acres of woodland, these self-catering cottages and a B&B are an exceptional base for walkers and stargazers. The five cottages range from the snug two-person Forge to the 10-person Bragdy Wern. Alternatively, overnight in the wooden-beamed B&B doubles and enjoy a full Welsh breakfast in the Africa Room.

★**Plas Bodegroes**   HISTORIC HOTEL **£££**
(☑01758-612363; www.bodegroes.co.uk; Nefyn Rd; r 2 nights from £200, dinner £49, lunch Sun £24.50; ⊙restaurant 7-9pm Tue-Sat, noon-2pm Sun; 🅿🛜) Set in a stately 1780 manor house, this family-run restaurant with rooms has classically styled lodgings and Welsh art amid 2 hectares of immaculate gardens. The restaurant serves classic Welsh dishes with a contemporary touch, such as line-caught seabass with crab-crushed potato and roast Welsh lamb rump with artichoke gratin. It's a mile inland from Pwllheli, along the A497.

ⓘ Getting There & Away

BUS

Most of the Peninsula's services originate or terminate at Pwllheli's **bus station** (Station Sq). Route 3 (12 Monday to Saturday, five on Sunday) runs to Porthmadog (£1.60, 35 minutes) via Criccieth (£1.50, 25 minutes), 17/17B runs to Aberdaron (£1.70, 40 minutes, eight daily Monday to Saturday), route 8 to Morfa Nefyn (£1.40, 20 minutes, 10 daily Monday to Saturday), and route 12 to Caernarfon (£1.80, 45 minutes, 10 daily Monday to Saturday).

TRAIN

Pwllheli is the terminus of the Cambrian Coast Line, with eight direct trains daily from the **station** (Station Sq) to Criccieth (£4, 15 minutes), Porthmadog (£5.60, 23 minutes), Harlech (£9.20, 48 minutes) and Machynlleth (£18.40, 2½ hours).

Abersoch

POP 705

Abersoch is a former fishing port that's reinvented itself as a yacht and boat harbour, bona fide seaside resort and surfing hot spot that gets particularly busy in summer with wave-riders and sun-seeking families. The beaches are the main attraction here, though the smattering of good cafes and restaurants undoubtedly adds to the appeal.

◉ Sights

◉ Beaches

In town, the long, sandy Blue Flag **Abersoch Beach** (Lon Golff), is one of the most popular on the peninsula, and lined with photogenic beach huts. Surfers head further south for the springtime Atlantic swells at the wild **Porth Neigwl** (Hell's Mouth; Llanengan, LL53 7LG), 2 miles southwest of town, while **Porth Ceiriad** (Cilan, LL53 7BY), 2 miles directly south, attracts sunbathers in summer and surfers in springtime, when there are consistent barrel beach breaks, best around high tide.

🏃 Activities

Abersoch Sailing School BOATING
(☎07917-525540; www.abersochsailingschool.co.uk; LL53 7DP; ◐8.30am-7pm Mar-Oct) Operating from Abersoch's main beach, weather permitting, this outfit offers sailing and powerboating lessons (from £50) and joy rides (half hour £25). It also hires laser fun boats (one/two hours £60/80), catamarans (one/two hours £40/60), sea kayaks (single/double per hour £15/30), SUPs (one hour £20) and skippered yachts (2½ hours per person/boat £50/180).

Offaxis WAKEBOARDING, SURFING
(☎01758-713407; www.offaxis.co.uk; Lôn Engan; 2hr lessons incl equipment from £30; ◐10am-5pm Mon-Fri, 9am-6pm Sat, 10.30am-4pm Sun) This surf shop hires equipment (£10 per day for wakeboards and surfboards) and specialises in wakeboarding, SUP and surfing lessons. Most of the wakeboarding is run out of Offaxis Harbourside at the Pwllheli marina.

West Coast Surf Shop SURFING
(☎01758-713067; www.westcoastsurf.co.uk; Lôn Pen Cei; 2hr lessons incl equipment from £30;

◐10am-5pm Thu-Tue) Runs the not-at-all-intimidating-sounding Hell's Mouth Surf School and hires out boards (£10) and wetsuits (£8) year-round, as well as SUPs (£20 per two hours).

🛏 Sleeping

Angorfa B&B ££
(☎01758-712967; www.angorfa.com; Stryd Fawr, LL53 7EB; s/d from £70/80; ◐Mar-Sep; ⊛) Everything is ship-shape in this smart, beach-themed guesthouse, run by a welcoming couple who are happy to chat about the charms of the Llŷn Peninsula as they serve your breakfast. Popular with families, it's just up the High St (Stryd Fawr) from the town centre.

Egryn HOTEL ££
(☎01758-712332; www.egryn.com; Lôn Sarn Bach, LL53 7EE; s/d/ste from £95/119/220; P⊛) With tones as muted as its hosts are ebulliently welcoming, this Edwardian house has eight comfortable, modern rooms with marbled en suites and sea views, plus two spacious family suites. Spa breaks, complete with hydrotherapy and salt saunas, can be organised with a nearby spa on request.

★**Porth Tocyn** HISTORIC HOTEL £££
(☎01758-713303; www.porthtocynhotel.co.uk; Bwlchtocyn, LL53 7BU; s/d incl breakfast from £105/168, cottages £200; ◐mid Mar-Oct; P⊛) Near the south end of Abersoch beach and overlooking Cardigan Bay, this country hotel comprises 17 beautifully appointed rooms, all decked out with luxury fabrics and king-sized beds, and a fine restaurant. Families are welcome, with a dedicated children's play area, but if you're looking for luxurious seclusion and solitary walks, consider renting Bwthyn Bach, a beautifully renovated stone cottage.

At the on-site restaurant, open to nonguests, best bets include dependable classics such as pan-fried sea trout with samphire, moules marinière and lamb rump with colcannon mash (mains £17 to £28). Lighter bites are served at lunchtime.

🍴 Eating & Drinking

Fresh BISTRO ££
(☎01758-710033; www.fresh-abersoch.co.uk; Stryd Fawr, LL53 7DS; mains £13-26; ◐5pm-midnight, from 11.30am Jul & Aug; ⊛) A popular surfer's hang-out, whether for a beer on the front terrace or dinner, Fresh serves

ⓘ LLŶN COASTAL BUS

Between Easter and October, the **Llŷn Coastal Bus** (☑ 01758-721777; www. bwsarfordirllyn.co.uk) runs between Trefor and Llanbedrog, via Nefyn, Aberdaron and Abersoch, four times a day from Thursday to Monday. At only £2 per trip, it's a boon for walkers on some of the more remote stretches of the Llŷn Coastal Path. Booking 24 hours ahead is advised, and essential for prebook-only stops (see website).

hearty bistro food including lamb shanks, pan-seared haddock, burgers, sticky baby back ribs and steaks – exactly what you find yourself craving upon emerging from the sea.

★ **Dining Room** MODERN WELSH £££
(☑ 01758-740709; www.thediningroomabersoch. co.uk; Stryd Fawr, LL53 7DY; 3-course menu £30; ⊙ 7pm-midnight Wed-Sat, noon-5pm Sun) 🍴 At Abersoch's most creative dining space, the menu changes daily, depending on what's fresh and in season. Your plate may be graced by ox cheek in a red-wine and rosemary reduction, wood pigeon with black pudding, or hake, seared on the grill. The desserts are inspired, as are the samphire and blood-orange negroni aperitifs. Book ahead.

Zinc Bar & Grill BAR
(☑ 01758-713433; www.facebook.com/zincabersoch; Lon Pen Cei, LL53 7AW; ⊙ 9am-10pm) Zinc's riverside deck is one of the nicest places in town for a sundowner, when the weather's right. The short and sweet menu of Thai-tinged brasserie dishes includes red-curry pork belly and crab and glass-noodle salad, and there's a decent selection of local craft beers. Mind you, the place is equally good for breakfast and morning coffee.

ⓘ Getting There & Away

Bus 18 stops on Stryd Fawr (High St), heading to/from Llanbedrog (£1, seven minutes) and Pwllheli (£1.20, 15 to 20 minutes, seven daily Monday to Saturday). To reach Aberdaron, change to bus route 17 at Llanbedrog.

Aberdaron

POP 956

Aberdaron is an end-of-the-earth kind of place, with whitewashed houses weathering the squalls that blow in from the sweeping Aberdaron Bay. Overlooking a pebble beach, this fishing hamlet was traditionally the last resting spot before pilgrims made the treacherous crossing to Bardsey Island. The little Gwylan Islands, just offshore, are North Wales' most important puffin-breeding site, while choughs, peregrines, hares and grey seals all thrive in the surrounding wilderness. And hiking across wild country at the end of the peninsula, with its infinite variety of light, stone and seascape, is something that stays with you for a long time.

⊙ Sights

⊙ Centre

St Hywyn's Church CHURCH
(www.st-hywyn.org.uk; B4413; ⊙ 9am-6pm Easter-Oct, 10am-4pm rest of year) FREE Strategically positioned above a pebbly beach, St Hywyn's Church has a left half dating from 1100 and a right half that was added 400 years later to accommodate pilgrims. Inside there's information about local history; two remnants of the original, 6th-century Christian community here (the 'Veracius' and 'Senacus' memorial stones); and a medieval font and holy-water stoup. Welsh poet RS Thomas was the minister here from 1967 to 1978 – an appropriate setting for his bleak, impassioned work.

If the church is locked, ask to borrow the key from the adjacent Tŷ Newydd hotel.

Porth y Swnt CULTURAL CENTRE
(NT; ☑ 01758-703810; www.nationaltrust.org.uk; B4413; adult/child £2/1; ⊙ 10am-4pm Oct-Mar, to 5pm Apr-Jun & Sep, to 6pm Jul & Aug) Run by the National Trust, this rather impressionistic centre takes visitors deeper into the land and culture of the Llŷn through poetry, sound, light and artefacts. Its centrepiece is the magnificent optic of Bardsey Island lighthouse, which still bears bullet marks from being strafed during WWII.

⊙ Around Aberdaron

★ **Mynydd Mawr** HILL
(NT; www.nationaltrust.org.uk; Lon Uwchmynydd) Some 4km west of Aberdaron, the rugged, ethereally beautiful extremity of the Llŷn Peninsula is where medieval pilgrims set off to reach the holy island of Bardsey; one glimpse of their destination, rising out of the gunmetal-grey sea beyond the

surf-pounded rocks, hints at the drama of their final voyage. This hill, overlooking Bardsey Sound, is criss-crossed with walking trails, and while the car park at the top fills with day trippers, come dusk, you have the place to yourself.

From **Braich-y-Pwll**, the peninsula's westernmost tip, a path leads down past the remains of St Mary's Abbey to a neolithic standing stone known as Maen Melyn, suggesting that this was a holy place well before the Celts or their saints arrived.

A natural freshwater spring called St Mary's Well (Ffynnon Fair) issues from a cleft in the rock below the high-tide mark. It was held to be holy, and pilgrims would sip the water before setting out. There are sheer drops to the sea and high surf, so don't attempt to drink from the spring yourself.

Inland are strip fields that preserve many of the patterns of ancient land use. Keep an eye out for choughs, a cheeky red-legged relative of the crow, and the rare spotted rock rose – this is the only place on the British mainland where this yellow bloom is found.

Porthor BEACH
(Whistling Sands; NT; www.nationaltrust.org.uk; parking £4) This lovely, remote crescent of sand, some 5km north of Aberdaron, off the main coastal road, has oddly shaped sand that squeaks when you walk on it, giving it its English name, Whistling Sands. When the conditions are right, bodyboarders and surfers hit the waves. From here it's a 1.6-mile coastal walk southwest via the twin headlands of Dinas Bach and Dinas Fawr to the cove of Porth Orion.

Plas-yn-Rhiw HISTORIC BUILDING
(NT; 01758-780219; www.nationaltrust.org.uk; B4413; adult/child £6.80/3.40; noon-5pm Thu-Sun Apr, Oct & Nov, Wed-Mon May-Aug, Thu-Mon Sep) The three Keating sisters, Eileen, Lorna and Honora, friends of the poet RS Thomas, came to the rescue of this decaying Regency manor house in 1938, with the assistance of Portmeirion architect Clough Williams-Ellis. The lush gardens provide a sharp contrast to the surrounding moorland and views over Porth Neigwl to Cardigan Bay. The house retains many original furnishings, plus Honora Keating's landscape watercolours. It's near the hamlet of Rhiw, 5km east of Aberdaron; follow the signposts from the B4413.

Sleeping & Eating

Mynydd Mawr Caravan & Camping Site CAMPGROUND £
(01758-760223; www.aberdaroncaravanandcampingsite.co.uk; Mynydd Mawr; camping £15, static caravan £100) Some 3km west of Aberdaron, this is, hands down, the most scenic campsite on the Llŷn. Imagine waking up early in the morning and seeing the legendary Avalon across the silvery sea. Well, here it's a distinct possibility. On-site cafe serves simple meals and hot showers and electricity hook-up is available. The static caravan sleeps up to six.

PILGRIMAGE TO THE ISLAND OF 20,000 SAINTS

In the early Middle Ages, when journeys from Britain to Italy were long, perilous and beyond the means of most people, the Pope decreed that three pilgrimages to the holy island of Bardsey would have the same spiritual value as one to Rome. Tens of thousands of penitents took advantage of this, and many came here to die (hence the sobriquet 'Island of 20,000 saints'). The bones of pilgrims still periodically emerge from unmarked graves; it's said that in the 1850s they were used as fencing, there were so many of them.

Another appeal of a pilgrimage to Bardsey lay in the claim that if you died on the island, you would automatically not go to hell. The island's Welsh name means 'Isle of the Currents', a reference to the treacherous tidal surges in Bardsey Sound, which doubtless convinced medieval visitors that their lives were indeed in God's hands. In the 16th century Henry VIII's ban on pilgrimages stopped the practice – although pilgrims now defy him to walk the route today.

The traditional path stops at ancient churches and holy wells along the way. It's broken into nine legs on the **Edge of Wales Walk** (01758-760652; www.edgeofwaleswalk.co.uk) website, run by a cooperative of local residents. They can help to arrange a 47-mile, self-guided walking tour, including five nights' accommodation and baggage transfers (£376 per person).

HIGHLIGHTS OF NEFYN BAY

All rocky bluffs, tiny settlements and isolated sandy coves, the central part of Llŷn's north coast is very lightly trodden. If you're making your slow way through these remote parts, it's worth detouring to **Porthdinllaen** (parking summer/winter £5/1.50, free to NT members in summer), a hamlet on a tiny thumb of land jutting north into the Irish Sea from Morfa Nefyn. Its main attraction is the lovely, long, sheltered sandy beach, accessed via the car park in Morfa Nefyn.

Further east, swing by **St Beuno's Church** (☑ 07572 776225; www.facebook.com/bro madryn; B4417; ⊙ hours vary) FREE in tiny Pistyll – one of the main stops along the ancient Bardsey pilgrimage route. Founded by the eponymous 7th-century saint, this tiny stone church retains its original Celtic carved font and a window beside the 11th-century altar that allowed lepers standing outside to watch Mass (known as a 'leper squint'). St Beuno's really comes to life during the Christmas, Easter and harvest seasons when the floors are covered in reeds and fragrant herbs.

Both Morfa and Pistyll are served by bus 8 from Pwllheli (10 daily, except Sunday).

Tŷ Newydd   HOTEL ££
(☑ 01758-760207; www.gwesty-tynewydd.co.uk; r from £120; 🐾) The location is the clincher at this homey hotel. Right on the beach, it has comfortably kitted-out, spacious and light-drenched rooms, the pricier ones with wonderful sea views, plus contemporary touches like iPod docks. The tide comes in right under the terraced pub restaurant (mains £13 to £18), which seems designed with an afternoon G&T in mind.

Y Gegin Fawr   WELSH £
(The Big Kitchen; ☑ 01758-760359; mains £7-10; ⊙ 10am-5pm Fri-Wed) With their spiritual needs sorted, Bardsey-bound pilgrims could claim a meal at Y Gegin Fawr, a little thick-walled communal kitchen with tiny windows that sits prettily at the heart of Aberdaron. Dating from 1300, it now serves locally caught crab and lobster, homemade cakes and scones, filled jacket potatoes and the like.

ⓘ Getting There & Away

Buses calling at Aberdaron include eight 17/17B services per day (Monday to Saturday) to Llanbedrog (£1.50, 30 minutes) and Pwllheli (£1.70, 40 minutes). A weekday 8B service to Pwllheli passes through Aberdaron at 2.30pm and continues on to Portor/Whistling Sands (£1.30, 15 minutes); in the other direction, it runs to Morfa Nefyn at 12.32pm (£1.45, 23 minutes).

Bardsey Island (Ynys Enlli)

POP 11

This mysterious island, 2 miles off the tip of the Llŷn, is one of many candidates for the Isle of Avalon from the Arthurian legends – the final resting place of King Arthur.

Celtic druids believed the island to be holy, and the obscure St Cadfan founded a monastery here in 516 AD, giving shelter to Celts fleeing the Saxon invaders, and medieval pilgrims followed in their wake. Pirates claimed the island for over a century after the Augustine abbey was disbanded in 1536.

Modern pilgrims to Bardsey are nature lovers in search of solitude; during summer around 17,000 Manx shearwaters nest in burrows here. A colony of Atlantic grey seals lives here year-round; a pile of rocks by the harbour is a popular hang-out. Other attractions include 6th-century **carved stones**, the remains of a 13th-century **abbey tower** and a **lighthouse**.

🛏 Sleeping

Bardsey Lodge & Bird Observatory   HOSTEL £
(☑ 01626-773908; www.bbfo.org.uk; adult/child per week £210/130; ⊙ May-Oct) If your dream is to watch thousands of seabirds during the spring and autumn migrations, or the seals playing in the island's rocky coves, or perhaps photograph the rage of the stormy sea, then come stay at the Bird Observatory. Lodgings are hostel-style, with dorms, spartan singles and doubles, a kitchen, a dining room and a common area. Boat transfer costs £40.

ⓘ Information

Bardsey Island Trust (☑ 0845 811 2233; www.bardsey.org; 🐾) The Bardsey Island Trust can help arrange day trips to the island

and holiday lets in cottages for those who wish to linger beyond a day trip.

ℹ️ Getting There & Away

Two private boat services are the only way to reach Bardsey. In summer **Bardsey Boat Trips** (☑ 07971 769895; www.bardseyboattrips. com; adult/child £35/25) sails to Bardsey from Porth Meudwy, near Aberdaron.

Nant Gwrtheyrn

The village of Nant Gwrtheyrn (Vortigern's Valley) was built for quarry workers in the 19th century, when granite was dug out of the surrounding mountains and shipped to Liverpool, Manchester and elsewhere to be used in building roads. The quarries closed after WWII and the village was gradually abandoned, but was given a new lease of life when the Welsh Language & Heritage Centre opened in the restored buildings in 1982.

According to legend, Nant Gwrtheyrn is the burial place of the 6th-century Celtic King Vortigern, who features in many of the Arthurian legends, and who allegedly invited the Saxons to Britain following a prophecy by his mage, Myrddin (Merlin).

💿 Sights & Activities

★ **Tre'r Ceiri Hillfort**   ARCHAEOLOGICAL SITE
(⊘ 24hr) FREE Topping the second-highest mountain (489m) of the Yr Eifl trio, the Tre'r Ceiri ('Town of the Giants') hillfort is one of the best preserved Iron Age forts in Europe. A huge, intact stone rampart surrounds the remains of 150 stone huts. From the top there are tremendous views of both coasts of the Llŷn.

It's a 1.6-mile walk from the car park above Nant Gwrtheyrn, or a stiff 1 mile ascent from a layby on the B4417, between Llanaelhaearn and Llithfaen.

Welsh Language & Heritage Centre   LANGUAGE
(☑ 01758-750334; www.nantgwrtheyrn.org; Llithfaen; 5-day course incl full board £495; ⊘ call ahead for times) Aside from a small museum on the history of Nant Gwrtheyrn, this heritage centre offers Welsh language and literature courses to suit all levels of ability. For students, there is **self-catering cottage accommodation** (☑ 01758-750334; www.nantgwrtheyrn.org; Llithfaen; dm/d £25/50 per night, cottage from £435 per week; P @) on-site, plus shared rooms, all rented by the week.

ℹ️ Getting There & Away

The closest town to Nant Gwrtheyrn is Llithfaen on the B4417 (£1.50, 25 minutes from Pwllheli on bus 27), a 30-minute walk. Nant Gwrtheyrn is reached by a steep, narrow and hairpin bendy road down towards the sea. On-site parking is only for those taking multiday language courses. Otherwise it's a 15-minute walk from the car park at the top of the hill.

AT A GLANCE

POPULATION
Llandudno: 15,395

SPECIES OF MIGRATORY BIRDS
2000

BEST SCENIC LANDMARK
Great Orme (p286)

BEST LOCAVORE DINING
Moch a Môr (p294)

BEST WILDLIFE CRUISE
Seacoast Safaris (p295)

WHEN TO GO

➡ **May** Victorian Extravaganza in Llandudno, spring bird migration, and excellent walking weather for coastal paths.

➡ **Jun–Aug** Best beach months and the best time of year for water sports.

➡ **Oct** Gwledd Conwy Feast gives foodies an excuse to work on winter padding. Autumn bird migration.

Conwy Castle (p281)
ALEXANDER SPATARI/GETTY IMAGES ©

Anglesey & the North Coast

T his compact region can be boiled down to two essential ingredients: castles and coast. Yes, there are impressive castles all over Wales, but few can compete with the World Heritage trio of Caernarfon, Beaumaris and Conwy. On the north coast, bustling Llandudno exudes quintessential Victorian charm, its genteel appeal contrasting starkly with the wild beaches and the turbulent sea crashing against the cliffs of the Welsh stronghold of the Isle of Anglesey, its rolling pastures and woodlands dotted with ancient burial chambers.

Wilderness and the Welsh tongue aside, Anglesey also offers rich opportunity for surfing, windsurfing, kitesurfing and hiking, as well as some of the best dining in Wales.

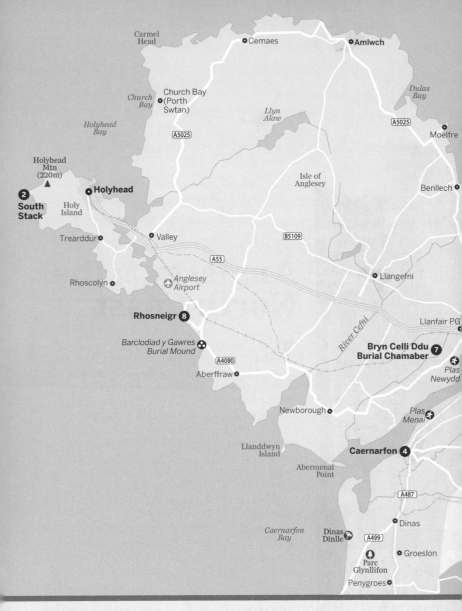

Anglesey & the North Coast Highlights

1 **Conwy** (p281) Admiring the mighty castle and enjoying the dining scene in the medieval walled town of Conwy.

2 **South Stack** (p298) Watching guillemots and razorbills wheel above a sea-battered clifftop lighthouse.

3 **Llandudno** (p285) Exploring Bronze Age mines and the windswept Great Orme plateau above this seaside resort's Victorian pier.

4 **Caernarfon Castle** (p274) Squeezing through wall passages of the mightiest castle built by Edward I.

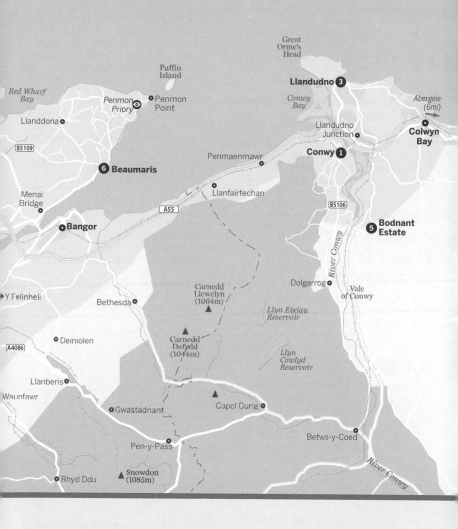

IRISH
SEA

Red Wharf
Bay

Puffin
Island

Penmon ● Penmon
Priory   Point

Llanddona ●

B5109

6 Beaumaris

Menai
Bridge

● Bangor

Y Felinheli

Bethesda ●

A4086

● Deiniolen

Llanberis ●

Waunfawr

● Gwastadnant

Pen-y-Pass ●

● Rhyd Ddu   ▲ Snowdon
                  (1085m)

Penmaenmawr

A55

● Llanfairfechan

Carnedd
Llewelyn
(1064m)
▲

▲
Carnedd
Dafydd
(1044m)

Llyn Eigiau
Reservoir

▲

Llyn
Cowlyd
Reservoir

Capel Curig ●

Great
Orme's
Head

Llandudno 3

Conwy
Bay

Llandudno
Junction ●

Conwy 1

Abergele
(6mi)
→

**Colwyn
Bay**

B5106

**5 Bodnant
Estate**

River Conwy

Dolgarrog ●

Vale
of Conwy

Betws-y-Coed ●

River Conwy

THE NORTH COAST

The North Wales coast has perennial natural charms, but seaside resorts of uneven appeal: some are outstanding examples of the genre, others more down at heel. The section west of Colwyn Bay includes glorious Unesco World Heritage–listed castles at Caernarfon and Conwy (p281) along with the Victorian resort of Llandudno, a favourite family-holiday hub. The sands stretch along a string of less-appealing resort towns east of the bay, but there are greater attractions to be discovered by turning south into the delightful Conwy Valley.

Caernarfon

POP 9859

Wedged between the gleaming Menai Strait and Snowdonia's bare hills, Caernarfon's main claim to fame is its magnificent castle, one of Edward I's finest fortress masterpieces. Given the town's antiquity and crucial historical importance (it's been a key strategic site since the Roman occupation), its proximity to Snowdonia and its reputation as a centre of Welsh culture, its lures are many and varied. The tight grid of narrow streets at the town's core, enclosed within medieval stone walls, is a joy to wander, as is the waterfront promenade. The Welsh Highland Railway draws steam buffs, and Caernarfon's strategic location makes it an excellent jumping-off point for some of Snowdonia's best hiking, as well as visits to the Llŷn Peninsula and the Isle of Anglesey.

History

Caernarfon Castle was built by Edward I as the last link in his 'iron ring' and it's now part of the 'Castles and Town Walls of King Edward in Gwynedd' Unesco World Heritage Site. In an attempt by the prime minister of the time, David Lloyd George (himself a Welshman), to bring the royals closer to their Welsh constituency, the castle was designated the venue for the 1911 investiture of the Prince of Wales. In retrospect, linking the modern royals to such a powerful symbol of Welsh subjugation may not have been the best idea. It incensed fervent nationalists and at the next crowning, that of Prince Charles in 1969, that sentiment climaxed with a thwarted bombing by the Mudiad Amddiffyn Cymru (Movement for the Defence of Wales).

◉ Sights

★ **Caernarfon Castle** CASTLE

(Cadw; www.cadw.gov.wales; adult/child £5.20/3.10; ⊙10am-1pm & 2-5pm Mon-Wed, Sat & Sun; ⊕) Majestic Caernarfon Castle was built by Edward I between 1283 and 1330 as a military stronghold, seat of government and royal palace. Designed by Master James of St George, from Savoy, its brief and scale were extraordinary. Today it remains one of the most complete and impressive castles in Britain – you can walk on and through the interconnected walls and towers gathered around the central green, admiring the defensive capabilities of the multiple gates and portcullises of the **King's Gate**.

Inspired by the dream of Macsen Wledig recounted in the *Mabinogion*, Caernarfon echoes the 5th-century walls of Constantinople (İstanbul), with colour-banded masonry and polygonal towers, instead of the traditional round towers and turrets.

Despite its fairy-tale aspect, it is thoroughly fortified with a series of murder holes and a sophisticated arrangement of multiple arrow slits. It repelled Owain Glyndŵr's army in 1404 with a garrison of only 28 men, and resisted three sieges during the English Civil War before surrendering to Cromwell's army in 1646.

A year after construction began, Edward's second son was born here, becoming heir to the throne four months later when his elder brother died. To consolidate Edward junior's power, he was made Prince of Wales in 1301, thus creating the tradition of English kings conferring that title on their heirs. As Edward II, he came to a very nasty end, possibly via a red-hot poker; his much-eroded statue is over the King's Gate. The first investiture that actually took place here (rather than in London), however, was that of his namesake, Edward VIII, in 1911 (coincidentally, his reign was also cut short, albeit less violently).

Start your inspection at the **Eagle Tower**, the one with the flagpoles to the right of the entrance. On the turrets you can spot the weathered eagle from which it gets its name, alongside stone-helmeted figures intended to swell the garrison's apparent numbers (they're easier to spot from the quay).

There's a film tracing the history of the site since Roman times in the **Northeast Tower**, while in the **Queen's Tower** (named after Edward I's wife Eleanor) is the rather dry **Regimental Museum of the Royal**

Caernarfon

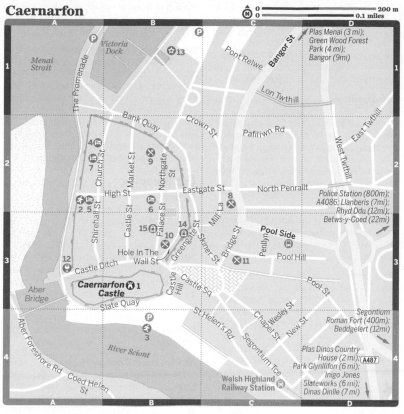

Caernarfon

Welch Fusiliers, filled with medals, uniforms, weapons and historical displays. The **Black Tower** exhibition is worth a peek for Edward I's riffs on Arthurian legend for propaganda purposes.

Segontium Roman Fort RUINS
(Cadw; www.cadw.gov.wales; Ffordd Cwstenin; ⊙10am-4pm) FREE Just east of the town centre, these low stone foundations represent the westernmost legionary fort of the Roman Empire. The fort dates back to AD

77, when General Gnaeus Julius Agricola completed the Roman conquest of Wales by capturing the Isle of Anglesey, though much of what you see is from the AD 364 rebuild. The on-site museum and visitor centre is open on weekdays. The site is half a mile along the A4085 (to Beddgelert).

Parc Glynllifon   GARDENS
(☑ 01766-771000; www.gwynedd.gov.uk/parcglyn llifon; Clynnog Rd; adult/child £4/2; ⊙ 10am-5pm daily Apr-Sep, Thu-Sun Oct-Mar) Strewn with rare plants, follies, sculptures and fountains, these historic gardens once formed part of the estate of the Lords Newborough. While the grand neoclassical manor house isn't open to the public, the woodland paths that criss-cross the park are. There's also a historic steam engine and the **Adra craft centre**, where resident artisans sell their wares. Parc Glynllifon is 6 miles south of Caernarfon, on the A499.

Dinas Dinlle   BEACH
Dolphins and porpoises can sometimes be spotted from this long, sandy, rock-fringed Blue Flag beach, 7 miles southwest of Caernarfon. The flatness of the surrounding land contrasts dramatically with the sculpted Llŷn Peninsula, visible across the water, and a solitary hill capped by the remains of an Iron Age fort.

🏃 Activities

Plas Menai   WATER SPORTS
(National Watersports Centre; ☑ 0300 300 3112, 01248-670964; www.plasmenai.co.uk; half/full day from £35/70; ⊙ office 8.30am-5pm) This excellent centre offers year-round courses in sailing, powerboating, sea kayaking and windsurfing for all ability levels (weekend packages from £190, advance reservations necessary). The on-site accommodation includes B&B rooms (singles/doubles £55/90) and a bunkhouse (£35), both with pool and gym access. It's located 3 miles along the A487 towards Bangor. Bus 5C (Caernarfon to Bangor) stops here.

GreenWood Forest Park   OUTDOORS
(☑ 01248-671493; www.greenwoodforestpark.co. uk; Bush Rd, Y Felinheli; adult/child/family £12.80/12/50; ⊙ 10am-5.30pm; ⛱) 🌿 Underpinned by a strong green ethos, GreenWood has a slew of rides and activities spread over 7 hectares of parkland. There's the Green Dragon, the world's first people-powered roller coaster, the solar-powered Sun Splash,

treetop walkways, archery and more. Green-Wood is signposted from the A487 near Y Felinheli, 4 miles northeast of Caernarfon.

Menai Strait Pleasure Cruises   CRUISE
(☑ 01286-672772; www.menaicruises.co.uk; Slate Quay; adult/child 40min cruise £10/5, 2hr £25/15; ⊙ every hour from 11.30am May-Oct) The 1937 ferry *Queen of the Sea* offers 40-minute cruises, with a full commentary, to the southwest entrance of the Menai Strait, and two-hour cruises in the other direction as far as the Menai Suspension Bridge. They leave from Slate Quay, beside the castle.

🛏 Sleeping

Totters   HOSTEL £
(☑ 01286-672963; www.totters.co.uk; 2 High St; dm/d £20/48; 🛜) Modern, clean and very welcoming, this excellent independent hostel is Caernarfon's best-value sleep. A 14th-century arch gives a sense of history to the communal kitchen in the basement, and continental breakfast is free. There are small dorms and doubles, an attic en-suite double overlooking the sea, a TV room and a library.

Over the road is a second property, sleeping up to six, which can be rented for £120 per night.

★ Plas Dinas Country House   B&B ££
(☑ 01286-830214; www.plasdinas.co.uk; A487, Bontnewydd; cottages/r/ste from £109/119/179; 🅿 🛜) Until the 1980s, this large 17th-century house belonged to Lord Snowdon's family. The ancestral portraits, the grand drawing room and antique furnishings give off the 'historic home' vibe, and the 10 individually decorated rooms range from snug attic luxury (Butlers) to somewhat austere (Major) to exuberantly grand (Princess Margaret suite with four-poster bed). It's 2 miles south of Caernarfon.

The Gun Room, the swanky in-house restaurant, serves upscale dishes such as Sirloin of Llanfair Hall beef with braised shin, tarragon, caramelised onion and bone-marrow jus. Self-catering cottages are also available.

★ Victoria House   B&B ££
(☑ 01286-678263; www.victoriahouse.wales; 13 Church St; s/d from £90/110; @ 🛜) This is pretty much the perfect guesthouse – a delightful, solid Victorian building in Caernarfon's old town, run by exceptionally hospitable and attentive hosts. The four spacious, Victorian-style rooms include thoroughly

contemporary touches, such as Chromecast. The Balcony Suite, with a private terrace looking across to Anglesey, is well worth the splurge, and breakfast is a joy.

Caer Menai
B&B ££

(☑ 01286-672612; www.caermenai.co.uk; 15 Church St; s/d/tr from £50/65/92; ☎) A former county school (1894), this elegant building is on a quiet street nestled against the western town wall. Owners Mark and Karen are happy to share their local knowledge and the seven renovated rooms are fresh, clean and snug; room number 7 has sunset sea views.

Ty Dre Town House
B&B ££

(☑ 01286-673604; www.black-boy-inn.com; 24-26 High St; r £75-108; P ☎) Just around the corner from the Black Boy Inn, where you'll find the reception and breakfast room, this handsome Edwardian town house comprises 14 well-appointed, carpeted rooms with bold splashes of crimson, extra-long beds and spacious bathrooms. We particularly like the memorable rooms under the eaves, with the heavy wooden beams. Complimentary cooked breakfast included.

✖ Eating

Y Gegin Fach
CAFE £

(☑ 01286-672165; www.facebook.com/karensgeginfach; 5-9 Pool Hill; mains £7-8; ⊘9am-4pm Tue-Sat) 'The Little Kitchen' is a proper old-fashioned Welsh-speaking caffi, right down to the net curtains and cheery red-polka-dot tablecloths. It's a great spot to tuck into traditional faves such as rarebit, faggots, lobscouse (lamb stew) and Welsh cakes, and wish you had a Welsh granny. Opens later in summer.

Ainsworth's Traditional Fish & Chips
FISH & CHIPS £

(☑ 01286-673151; https://ainsworthscaernarfon.co.uk; 41 Bridge St; mains £3-7; ⊘11.30am-9pm) This chippie, a stalwart on the Caernarfon dining scene for over 25 years, serves up crispy cod, scampi and fishcakes, along with burgers, Pukka pies and fried chicken. It's mainly a takeaway operation, ideal for consuming while sitting on the waterfront promenade on a sunny day.

★ Osteria
TUSCAN ££

(☑ 01286-238050; 26 Hole in the Wall St; mains £12-15; ⊘6-10pm Thu-Sat; ☑) Two Tuscan partners opened this excellent addition to Caernarfon's dining scene in a compact building hard up against the city walls. Specialising in classic carpaccios and interesting bruschette (try the gorgonzola with walnuts and honey), they import many of their ingredients and wines from Tuscany and prepare daily specials such as stuffed vegetables and pasta with cod and cherry-tomato ragu.

Black Boy Inn
PUB FOOD ££

(☑ 01286-673604; www.black-boy-inn.com; Northgate St; mains £10-18; ⊘noon-9pm; ☎🍴) Retaining many original 16th-century features, this charismatic pub consists of a warren of snug rooms, with low, warped roof beams, open fires and Welsh craft beer on tap. Dishes such as the lobscouse highlight local meats and seafood, while such satisfying pub-grub staples as the steak-and-ale pie will gently ease you into a food coma.

It's well worth staying overnight (singles/doubles from £54/76) in one of the pub's centuries-old rooms with their dark-wood furniture, heavy wooden beams, gilded mirrors and four-poster beds.

♟ Drinking & Entertainment

Anglesey Arms
PUB

(☑ 01286-672158; Harbour Front; ⊘11am-midnight; ☎) If you're not too fussy about what you're drinking (no craft beer here), the main appeal of this converted 18th-century waterfront customs house consists of its outdoor seating and views of the Menai Strait and Anglesey beyond. It's also a great spot for watching the sunset.

Galeri Caernarfon
THEATRE

(☑ 01286-685222; www.galericaernarfon.com; Victoria Dock; ⊘box office hours vary) This excellent multipurpose arts centre hosts exhibitions, theatre, films and events; check online for details.

🛍 Shopping

Iechyd Da!
ALCOHOL

(☑ 01286-675373; www.facebook.com/iechyddacaernarfon; 19 Hole in the Wall St; ⊘10am-4pm Thu & Fri, to 5pm Sat) Over 170 Welsh ales and ciders twinkle from the shelves of this Australian-owned hole-in-the-wall on Hole in the Wall St, alongside Welsh whisky, gin and vodka. Making ironic use of a former temperance hall, it even manages to find shelf space for that elusive beast: a Welsh wine. The name (pronounced ya-kee-da) is Welsh for 'good health!'.

Palas Print BOOKS
([✐] 01286-674631; www.palasprint.com; 10 Palace St; ⊙10am-5pm Tue-Sat) Everything you'd want from a local, indie bookshop, this little gem stocks English and Welsh books and CDs, with emphasis on local authors, Welsh folk and the history and landscape of the area. It's also a hub for readings, recitals and other events.

Inigo Jones Slateworks GIFTS & SOUVENIRS
([✐] 01286-830242; www.inigojones.co.uk; A487, Groeslon; tour per adult/child £6.50/6; ⊙9am-5pm Mon-Sat) Built in 1861 to provide slate for schools, this workshop now earns its coin making garden ornaments, cheeseboards, picture frames, cake stands, inscribed plaques and more from this most Welsh of materials. You can also take a self-guided tour of the works and have a go at chiselling your own slate. It's on the A487, 6 miles south of Caernarfon.

❶ Getting There & Away

Bus Local buses depart from the **bus station** (Pool Side). Routes include 1R/T2 to Porthmadog (50 minutes, five daily) via Criccieth (45 minutes) and Tremadog (45 minutes), hourly 5C to Llandudno (1½ hours) via Bangor (30 minutes) and Conwy (1¼ hours), 12 to Pwllheli (45 minutes, 10 daily) and 88 to Llanberis (30 minutes, four to eight daily). Snowdon Sherpa bus S4 heads to Beddgelert (30 minutes, seven daily Monday to Saturday) via the Snowdon Ranger (22 minutes) and Rhyd Ddu (24 minutes) trailheads.

Bicycle Beics Antur ([✐] 01286-802222; www.anturwaunfawr.org; Porth yr Aur, High St; half/full day £12/18; ⊙9.30am-5pm Tue-Sat) hires bikes and can advise on local cycle routes. Information on Gwynedd recreational cycle routes, including the 12.5-mile Lôn Eifion (starting near the Welsh Highland Railway station and running south to Bryncir) and the 4.5-mile Lôn Las Menai (following the Menai Strait to the village of Y Felinheli), can be found at www.gwynedd.llyw.cymru. Lôn Las Cymru passes through Caernarfon, heading northeast to Bangor and south to Criccieth.

Car Free street parking is at a premium, but it doesn't cost much to park just outside the walled town, just off Balaclava Rd.

Train Caernarfon is the **northern terminus** (Arthur St) of the Welsh Highland Railway, the scenic steam-train line that runs to Porthmadog (£40 return, 2½ hours) via Rhyd Ddu (£24 return, one hour) and Beddgelert (£31 return, 1½ hours) from Easter to October, with limited winter service.

Bangor

POP 18,709

Compared to the smaller towns and villages nestling in the valleys of neighbouring Snowdonia, Bangor feels like a metropolis. Though relatively compact in size, it has a lively arts and cultural scene, and is home to two of the region's best venues: Pontio and Storiel. Dominated by its university, it's the largest city in Gwynedd and a major transport hub for North Wales, but the cultural venues, cathedral, Victorian pier and nearby castle aside, there's little to detain visitors for long.

St Deiniol established a monastery here in the 6th century, which grew up into Bangor's sweet little cathedral. Bangor University, founded in 1884, sits on a ridge above town, its neo-Gothic contours aping those of the cathedral. During term time, over 10,000 students swell the city's population, bringing youthful vigour and the area's best nightlife.

◉ Sights & Activities

★**Penrhyn Castle** CASTLE
(NT; www.nationaltrust.org.uk/penrhyn-castle; A5, Llandygai; adult/child £10/5; ⊙castle noon-5pm Mar-early Nov, gardens 10am-4pm year-round; [P][♿]) Funded by the vast profits from the slate mine of Caribbean sugar-plantation owner and anti-abolitionist Baron Penrhyn, and embellished by his great-great-nephew, this immense 19th-century neo-Norman folly pushes the boundaries of good taste. Flanked by a magnificent Victorian walled garden, the creeper-clad stone walls of the Norman 'fortress' embower the neo-Gothic hall with its darkly extravagant rooms, carved ceilings, stained-glass windows, opulent furniture and early flushing toilets.

Penrhyn is 1.5 miles east of Bangor; Llandudno-bound buses stop at the gate.

Storiel MUSEUM
([✐] 01248-353368; www.storiel.cymru; Ffordd Gwynedd; ⊙11am-5pm Tue-Sat) FREE The title 'Storiel', a portmanteau of the Welsh words for 'story' and 'gallery', signals the combined historical and artistic focus of this well-curated institution. Essentially a folk museum for Gwynedd county, it makes great use of the former bishop's palace, with exhibitions of local artefacts (including the Roman 'Segontium sword'), photography, art and more. Guided tours and creative workshops are offered at times, and it's well

Bangor

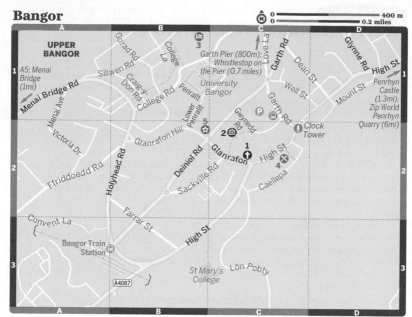

worth checking out the 'Object of the Month' – a stay busk most recently.

Garth Pier
PIER

(Garth Rd; adult/child 50/20p; ⊗8am-6pm Mon-Sat, 10am-5pm Sun) Given the large expanse of tidal mudflats here (a paradise for wading birds), it's surprising that the Victorians chose this site to build Britain's ninth-longest pleasure pier. Opened in 1896, Garth Pier strides on its original iron legs 458m into the Menai Strait – halfway to Anglesey. Ornate kiosks dot its length, including one of Bangor's best cafes.

You can park here for £1.50 per day.

Bangor Cathedral
CATHEDRAL

(https://bangorcathedral.churchinwales.org.uk; Glanrafon; ⊗10.30am-4.30pm Mon-Thu, to 1pm Fri & Sat) More formally known as the Cathedral Church of St Deiniol, this building occupies one of the oldest ecclesiastical sites in Britain, dating from AD 525, when the saint founded a monastic cell here. The beginning from which the city of Bangor grew, today's stone church dates to the 12th century, when Gruffudd ap Cynan rebuilt it following Viking raids. Later episodes of destruction followed, and much of today's cathedral is the work of Victorian architect Sir George Gilbert Scott.

Bangor

◉ Sights
1 Bangor Cathedral.................................C2
2 Storiel C2

⌂ Sleeping
3 Management Centre............................B1

✕ Eating
4 Blue Sky...C2

✸ Entertainment
5 Pontio...B2

Zip World Penrhyn Quarry ADVENTURE SPORTS
(☎01248-601444; www.zipworld.co.uk; Penrhyn Quarry, Bethesda; single ride £85; ⊗8am-6.30pm) The old Penrhyn slate quarry, nearly a mile long and 360m deep, is home to Europe's longest (and the world's fastest) zip line – Velocity 2. Bethesda is on the A5, 6 miles southeast of Capel Curig. Build up confidence on the 'Little Zipper' before shooting head first over the lake at the heart of the quarry at speeds of over 100mph.

🎇 Festivals & Events

Bangor Music Festival MUSIC
(Gŵyl Gerdd Bangor; ☎01248-382181; www.ban gormusicfestival.org.uk; ⊗Feb) Going strong for 20 years, this two-day festival sees

WORTH A TRIP

THE EARTHLY DELIGHTS OF BODNANT ESTATE

Whether you're a lover of gardens or fine food, Bodnant Estate (www.bodnant-estate.co.uk) should not be missed. While many large country estates fell on hard times in the 20th century, the McLaren family (holders of the title Baron Aberconway) managed to keep hold of theirs. Today it's a thriving seat of horticultural beauty, situated perfectly in the green and pleasant Conwy Valley. An excellent delicatessen on the premises, showcasing the best of regional produce, adds to the estate's appeal.

Bodnant Garden (NT; ✆01492-650460; www.nationaltrust.org.uk/bodnant-garden; Ffordd Bodnant, off A470; adult/child £8/4; ⏱9.30am-3.30pm; 🖐) Laid out in 1875 and painstakingly landscaped over 150 years, Bodnant is one of Britain's most beautiful gardens. Lord Aberconway of the McLaren family (which once lived in the gracious late-18th-century pile here) bequeathed the lush 32-hectare property to the National Trust in 1949. Italianate terraces overlook the River Conwy and Snowdonia's Carneddau Mountains, and rectangular ponds descend from the house into the picturesque wooded valley and wild garden.

Bodnant is 4 miles south of Conwy, just off the A470.

There's something to see in every season. Highlights include the 55m laburnum tunnel, a blaze of yellow when it blooms in May and June; fragrant rose gardens; great banks of azaleas and rhododendrons; and some of the tallest giant redwoods in Britain. Autumn is a riot of blues, pinks and reds, courtesy of the still-blooming hydrangeas and tree leaves changing colour.

Bodnant Welsh Food (✆01492-651931; www.bodnant-welshfood.co.uk; Furnace Farm, Tal-y-Cafn; ⏱farm shop 9.30am-5pm Mon-Sat, 10am-4pm Sun; 🅿) On the west side of the vast Bodnant Estate, a collection of lavishly restored 18th-century farm buildings now operates as Bodnant Welsh Food. One of the big attractions here is the **farm shop**, a wonderful showcase for Welsh produce comprising bakery, dairy, deli and the kind of butchery that knows the name of practically every animal that passes over the counter. Around half of what's sold here is produced on site or sourced in Wales.

If you want to do more than simply consume Welsh cheese, fresh produce, chocolate and ale, there's also a lively programme of food-and-wine events and a **cookery school** (✆01492-651108; www.bodnant-welshfood.co.uk; Bodnant Welsh Food, Furnace Farm, Tal-y-Cafn; courses £10-92) above the shop.

avant-garde recitals and contemporary compositions share the bill with chamber music, mixed-media performances, masterclasses, talks and other events. It's held in collaboration with Bangor University's Music School and makes use of the city's premier art space, Pontio.

🛏 Sleeping & Eating

Management Centre   HOTEL **££**
(✆01248-365900; www.themanagementcentre.co.uk; Bangor Business School, College Rd; s/d £83/92; 🅿🛜) Bangor isn't exactly blessed with accommodation options, but this university business centre has 57 modern ensuite rooms and makes for a comfortable stay. The on-site restaurant and bar, **1884** (mains £12 to £14), serves evening meals from 6pm to 9pm if you don't fancy the steep walk down into town and back.

⭐**Whistlestop on the Pier**   CAFE **£**
(✆07771 231463; Bangor Pier; mains £3.50-5) Don't let its appearance fool you: this humble kiosk halfway along the pier serves the best homemade scuffins (love child of muffin and scone) for miles around. Locals swear by them. If you're particularly hungry, Terry will feed you some moreish seafood chowder or steamed Menai mussels, with crusty homemade bread for mopping up every last drop.

Blue Sky   CAFE **£**
(✆01248-355444; www.blueskybangor.co.uk; Ambassador Hall, rear 236 High St; mains £7-11; ⏱9.30am-5.30pm Mon-Sat; 🛜✉) Blue Sky cafe hides down an alleyway in a former Jehovah's Witness Kingdom Hall, but the secret is out: it's hands down the best joint in town for breakfast, soups, sandwiches, burgers and salads, with all ingredients sourced

from local suppliers. The kitchen stops serving at 4pm, but the cafe stays open later when there's an evening gig.

☆ Entertainment

Pontio PERFORMING ARTS
(☑ 01248-383838, box office 01248-382828; www.pontio.co.uk; Deiniol Rd; ⊙ 8.30am-11pm Mon-Sat, noon-8pm Sun) Pontio cements Bangor's place as the cultural capital of North Wales. Within the fluid, Guggenheim-esque interior of this ambitious new multimillion-pound arts and innovation centre are a 450-seat main theatre, a 120-seat studio theatre and a cinema. Run by Bangor University, it stages drama in English and Welsh, classical-music and circus performances, and other arts events, film festivals and more.

❶ Getting There & Away

Bus The local **bus station** (Garth Rd) is located behind the Deiniol Shopping Centre. Bus routes include 5C to Caernarfon (30 minutes, every 30 minutes), X5 to Conwy (40 minutes, every 30 minutes) and Llandudno (one hour), 4H/42A to Menai Bridge (12 minutes, one to two hourly), X4 to Holyhead (1¾ hours) via Llangefni (40 minutes), 58 to Beaumaris (30 to 45 minutes, six daily), 85/86 to Llanberis (35 to 50 minutes, six daily), 5C/T2 to Caernarfon (25 to 35 minutes, every 30 minutes), T2 to Porthmadog (1¼ hours, three daily) and T2 to Dolgellau (two hours, eight daily), Machynlleth (2½ hours, seven daily) and Aberystwyth (3½ hours, seven daily).

Train Direct services from the **train station** (Holyhead Rd) head to/from Holyhead (£12, 30 to 45 minutes, 12 daily), Rhosneigr (£6.70, 25 minutes, nine daily), Conwy (£6.80, 18 minutes, 14 daily) and London Euston (£96, 3¼ hours).

Conwy

POP 4863

Sitting on the Conwy estuary, surrounded by medieval stone walls and dominated by a magnificent, World Heritage–listed castle, the compact town of Conwy punches above its weight. Its cluster of historic buildings, an attractive waterfront promenade and an abundance of good restaurants and lodgings make it a terrific base for exploring the surrounding coast.

The estuary was originally settled by mussel gatherers, joined in 1172 by Cistercian monks of Aberconwy, but the monastery was relocated upriver to make room for the castle when Edward I first planted it here in the late 13th century.

When approaching the town from the east, the scene is given another dramatic flourish by a tightly grouped trio of bridges crossing the Conwy, including Thomas Telford's 1826 suspension bridge (one of the first of its kind in the world) and Robert Stephenson's 1848 wrought-iron railway bridge (the first ever tubular bridge).

◉ Sights

★ Conwy Castle CASTLE
(Cadw; ☑ 01492-592358; www.cadw.wales.gov.uk; Castle Sq; adult/concession £8.80/5.40; ⊙ 9.30am-5pm Mar-Jun, to 6pm Jul & Aug, shorter hours rest of year; ℗) Caernarfon is more complete, Harlech more dramatically positioned and Beaumaris more technically perfect, yet out of the four castles that compose the Unesco World Heritage Site, Conwy is the most impressive to gaze upon. Exploring the castle's nooks and crannies makes for a superb living-history visit, but best of all, head to the battlements for panoramic views and an overview of Conwy's majestic complexity. Its historic role – to overawe and dominate the subjugated Welsh – couldn't be clearer.

At around £15,000 (over £45 million in today's money), Conwy was Edward I's most costly Welsh stronghold and part of his Iron Ring of fortresses. And if its crenellated turrets and towers call to mind romance and fairy tales rather than subjugation and oppression, that certainly wasn't the intention of its builders.

Constructed between 1283 and 1287, Conwy rises from a rocky outcrop with commanding views across the mountains of Snowdonia and the mouth of the River Conwy. With two barbicans (fortified gateways), eight fierce, slightly tapered towers of coarse, dark stone and a great bow-shaped hall within the elongated complex, it's very solid indeed.

After the Civil War in the 17th century, the castle fell into disrepair and the Council of State ordered it to be partly pulled down. But today it lives on and is a must-visit for anyone with an interest in Welsh history.

Town Wall HISTORIC BUILDING
(www.cadw.gov.wales; Rose Hill St) FREE The survival of most of its 1300m-long town wall, built concurrently with the castle, makes Conwy one of the UK's prime medieval sites. The 9m-tall wall, punctuated by 21 horseshoe towers, was erected to protect the English

ANGLESEY & THE NORTH COAST CONWY

Conwy

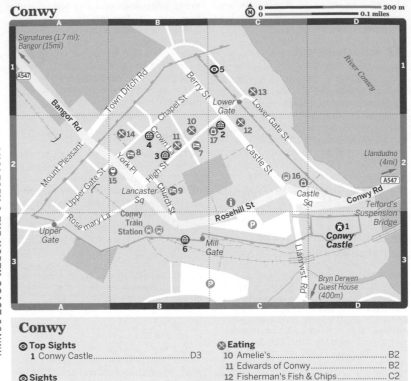

Conwy

◉ Top Sights
1 Conwy Castle.................................D3

◉ Sights
2 Aberconwy House................................C2
3 Plas Mawr...B2
4 Royal Cambrian Academy B2
5 Smallest House in Great Britain............C1
6 Town Wall...B3

🛏 Sleeping
7 Castle Hotel B2
8 Gwynfryn B2
9 Y Capel...B2

✕ Eating
10 Amelie's...B2
11 Edwards of Conwy................................B2
12 Fisherman's Fish & Chips....................C2
13 Parisella's of Conwy Ice Cream C1
14 Watson's Bistro...................................B2

◉ Drinking & Nightlife
15 Albion B2

🛍 Shopping
16 Knight Shop C2
17 Potter's Gallery C2

colonists from the Welsh, who were forbidden to live in the town and even the surrounding countryside. You can enter the town wall at Rose Hill St and walk along the battlements; the Porth yr Arden to Porth Uchaf section is particularly picturesque.

Plas Mawr   HISTORIC BUILDING
(Cadw; www.cadw.gov.wales; High St; adult/child £6.50/3.90; ⊘9.30am-5pm Easter-Sep, to 4pm Oct) Purchased in 1576 by one of the first Welshmen to live in Conwy – Robert Wynn, merchant and diplomat in the royal courts of Europe – Plas Mawr is arguably Britain's finest surviving Elizabethan town house. The discreet whitewashed exterior hides the vivid interior, with its colourful friezes, heraldic devices bearing the initials of the owner, and superb plasterwork that emphasises the noble Wynn dynasty and the owner's descent from the Princess of Gwynedd. An exhibition on 16th-century hygiene will raise eyebrows.

Conwy Nature Reserve   BIRD SANCTUARY
(📞01492-584091; www.rspb.org.uk; A55; adult/child £3/1.50; ⊘9.30am-5pm, closed Christmas Day; ♿) This Royal Society for the Protection of Birds (RSPB) sanctuary on the lovely Conwy estuary is home to lapwings, sedge warblers, shelducks and the superbly named black-tailed godwit. Hides and

wheelchair-accessible trails make for good going, while guided bird-spotting and family activities such as wildlife bingo keep interest levels high. There's a cafe (open 10am to 4pm) and easy access along the A55 from Llandudno Junction, 2 miles from Conwy.

Smallest House in Great Britain
NOTABLE BUILDING

(☎07925 049786; www.thesmallesthousein greatbritain.co.uk; Lower Gate St; adult/child £1/50p; ⊙10am-4pm Apr-Oct, to 6pm summer) This tiny red house is a quayside curiosity where the no-room-to-swing-a-cat bedroom and living room comprise a compact space measuring just over 3m high, 1.8m across and 3m deep, which has earned it a mention in Guinness World Records. Believe it or not, back in 1900, its last resident was a 1.91m-tall fisherman, who had a rather cramped time of it.

Aberconwy House
HISTORIC BUILDING

(NT; www.nationaltrust.org.uk; Castle St; adult/child £5/2.50; ⊙10am-5pm Mar-Oct) Timber-and-plaster Aberconwy House is the town's oldest, built as one of 20 merchants' houses when the town was fortified around 1300. Over the years it has been a coffee house, a temperance hotel, a bakery and an antique shop. Its past incarnations are recreated across several rooms, and an audiovisual presentation in the attic shows daily life from different periods of history.

Royal Cambrian Academy
GALLERY

(☎01492-593413; www.rcaconwy.org; Crown Lane; ⊙11am-4pm Thu-Sat) FREE Founded in 1881, given the royal imprimatur by Queen Victoria in 1882, and still going strong, the Cambrian runs a full calendar of exhibitions by its members in its twin whitewalled galleries, plus visiting shows from the National Museum Wales and elsewhere. Its excellent **Annual Summer Exhibition**, featuring the cream of contemporary fine art in Wales under one roof each August and September, has been a fixture from the academy's early days.

🎊 Festivals & Events

Gwledd Conwy Feast
FOOD & DRINK

(www.conwyfeast.co.uk; ⊙Oct) Held over a weekend in late October, this food festival, spiced up with music performances and a lantern parade, is the highlight of the Conwy calendar. It incorporates live music and the Blinc digital art festival, with images pro-

jected onto the castle walls at night. Around 25,000 people attend, so book accommodation well in advance; nearby Llandudno can accommodate spillover.

🛏 Sleeping

Bryn Derwen Guest House
B&B £

(☎01492-596134; www.conwybrynderwen.co.uk; Llanrwst Rd, Woodlands; s/d from £50/60; P🛜) Run by congenial, knowledgeable owners, this Victorian town-house B&B is barely a five-minute walk south of the walled town. The six cosy rooms are all individually conceived, some with iron bedsteads, others with boldly patterned wallpaper; the rooms at the rear are best described as snug. There's a decent breakfast thrown in, and guests must be 12 and over.

Conwy YHA
HOSTEL £

(☎08453-719732; www.yha.org.uk; Sychnant Pass Rd, Larkhill; dm/d/q £19/59/69; P🛜) Perched on a hill above the town, this former hotel has been converted into a typically utilitarian, minimalist YHA hostel with a fully equipped guest kitchen. Dorms have two or four beds; most of the private rooms have an en-suite bathroom. Head up to the large dining room for awesome mountain and sea views. There's wi-fi in the common areas only.

Castle Hotel
HOTEL ££

(☎01492-582800; www.castlewales.co.uk; High St; s/d/ste from £116/126/183; P🛜) This characterful coaching inn, built on the site of Conwy's vanished Cistercian Abbey, has been given a contemporary facelift without sacrificing its history. The bedrooms feature contemporary decor and Bose sound systems, while some boast castle views and free-standing baths, and there's an excellent on-site restaurant. Past guests have included William Wordsworth, Charlotte Brontë and Robert Louis Stevenson.

Gwynfryn
B&B ££

(☎01492-576733; www.gwynfrynbandb.co.uk; 4 York Pl; s/d from £75/80, ste £130; 🛜) With its cosy, individually decorated rooms and

---

ℹ CADW JOINT TICKET

Cadw (the Welsh historic monuments agency) offers combined tickets (adult/child £12/7) for the two historic properties it manages in Conwy: Conwy Castle (p281) and Plas Mawr.

ANGLESEY & THE NORTH COAST CONWY

comfy beds with plaid bedcovers, this friendly nine-bedroom B&B, set in a refurbished Wesleyan chapel house and vestry, is one of Conwy's best. You'll appreciate thoughtful extras such as fridges, biscuits, chocolates and earplugs, and the larger rooms in the main house come with deep soaking tubs. Guests must be 15 years and over.

Y Capel
GUESTHOUSE **££**

(☑01492-593535; www.ycapel.co.uk; Church St; s/d/f £100/120/220; ☎) In its past incarnation, this welcoming guesthouse used to be the Bethesda Baptist Chapel (1846), which fell into disuse and disrepair in the 1970s. Lovingly restored, it is now an 11-room B&B. Rooms are compact and decorated in neutral colours, some with exposed wooden beams. Complimentary full Welsh breakfast is served at the Erskine Arms opposite.

✕ Eating & Drinking

Edwards of Conwy
DELI **£**

(☑01492-592443; www.edwardsofconwy.co.uk; 18 High St; pies £6; ◷7am-5.30pm Mon-Sat, 10.30am-4.30pm Sun; ☑) While first and foremost a butchery with a great line in locally sourced Welsh meats, Edwards also sells savoury pies, local cheeses and freshly filled baps and sandwiches. Awards are continually bestowed on the deli for everything from its sausages to its pork pies.

Fisherman's Fish & Chips
FISH & CHIPS **£**

(☑01492-593792; http://thefishermanschipshop conwy.co.uk; 3 Castle St; mains £6-15; ◷11.30am-7pm) Bite into the beer batter, deep fried to a pleasing crunch, and reach the tender white flesh of the haddock or cod beneath, and you will understand why this family-run chippie (a rarity nowadays) has won many awards during its almost 40 years of existence. Whether you're after takeaway or a brisk sit-down meal, this is the place to come.

Parisella's of Conwy Ice Cream
ICE CREAM **£**

(www.parisellasicecream.co.uk; Conwy Quay; cone £2.70; ◷10.30am-5.30pm, longer hours high season) This kiosk on the quay sells a selection of what may well be the best ice cream in Wales. Among Parisella's 60-plus flavours are such delights as *stracciatella*, seriously awesome mint choc chip, lemon curd, and amaretto and black cherry.

★ Watson's Bistro
WELSH **££**

(☑01492-596326; www.watsonsbistroconwy.co.uk; Bishop's Yard, Chapel St; 2-course lunch £15, mains £17-25; ◷5.30-8.30pm Wed, Thu & Sun, 5.30-9pm Fri, noon-2pm & 5.30-9pm Sat) In the lee of the town wall, Watson's holds the crown for the most imaginative cooking in Conwy proper, conjured out of locally sourced produce. Prepare to woo your sweetie over treacle-cured lamb with port and blackberry sauce, or perfectly seared steak with wild mushrooms. Everything is homemade, including the ice cream. An early-bird menu (three courses £25) is served before 6.30pm.

Amelie's
FRENCH **££**

(☑01492-583142; 10 High St; lunch mains £7-9.50, dinner mains £14-17; ◷11.30am-2.15pm & 6-9pm Tue-Sat; ☑) Named after the Audrey Tautou film, and as friendly and beguiling as the film's star, this lovely boho bistro serves food that tastes as if it's been prepared by someone who really cares for you. This includes hearty homemade soup and open-faced crayfish sandwiches for lunch, and more substantial dinner mains, such as chicken cassoulet and other international dishes.

Signatures
MODERN BRITISH **£££**

(☑01492-583513; https://darwinescapes.co.uk/ aberconwy-resort-spa/facilities/signatures-restaurant; Aberconwy Park, Aberconwy Resort & Spa; mains £18-25; ◷noon-2.30pm & 6-9pm Wed-Sat, noon-8pm Sun; P☎) In a holiday park near the sea, 2 miles northwest of Conwy, this elegant restaurant doesn't stray far from classic dishes, but it does beautifully prepared comfort food really, really well. Dishes such as trio of lamb and pulled pork Wellington are deeply satisfying, and at lunchtime you can grab lighter bites, such as steak burgers and lobster bisque.

★ Albion
PUB

(☑01492-582484; www.albionalehouse.weebly. com; 1-4 Upper Gate St; ◷noon-11pm Sun-Thu, to midnight Fri & Sat; ☎) Born out of a collaboration between four Welsh craft breweries (Purple Moose, Conwy, Nant and Great Orme), this heritage-listed 1920s boozer is a serious beer-drinker's nirvana. Of the 10 hand pulls, eight are loaded with real ale and two with cider. Winner of multiple Wales and North Wales pub-of the-year awards, the Albion looks after wine and whisky drinkers, too.

🛍 Shopping

Knight Shop
GIFTS & SOUVENIRS

(☑01492-541300; www.theknightshop.co.uk; Castle Sq; ◷10am-5pm) Always buying boring, samey souvenirs for your loved ones? Or perhaps just looking to role play? Then why not go for a Henry VIII–era replica helmet, a ramshead heavy siege crossbow, a bottle of Conwy mead, a chainmail coif, or perhaps a Viking drinking horn?

Potter's Gallery   ARTS & CRAFTS
(✏ 01492-593590; www.thepottersgallery.co.uk; 1 High St; ⊙10am-5pm) Run by a cooperative of North Wales–based potters and designers, this gallery showcases the latest works from its members and is a mine of information about the local arts scene.

ℹ Information

Tourist Office (✏ 01492-577566; www.visit conwy.org.uk; Rose Hill St, Muriau Buildings; ⊙10am-5pm Mon-Sat Apr-Nov, shorter hours rest of year; ☎) This extremely busy office is well stocked with pamphlets and souvenirs and staffed by very helpful local experts. There's an interesting interactive exhibition on the princes of Gwynedd in the adjoining room.

ℹ Getting There & Away

BUS

Bus routes include the half-hourly 5/5C to Caernarfon (1¼ hours), Bangor (40 minutes) and Llandudno (22 minutes), and the thrice-daily 19 to Llandudno (20 minutes) and Betws-y-Coed (45 minutes).

Buses to Llandudno (Llanwrst Rd) leave from the stop near Castle Sq, while those to **Bangor and Caernarfon** (Rose Hill St) leave from outside the train station.

To catch a long-distance National Express coach, you have to go to Llandudno.

CAR

There are pay-and-display car parks on Mt Pleasant and by the castle. If you're after a free park and don't mind a 10-minute walk, turn right off Bangor Rd on the second-to-last street before you reach the town walls, cross the narrow rail bridge and park on residential Cadnant Park.

TRAIN

From Conwy's **train station** (Rose Hill St) direct services head to/from Holyhead (£17.40, one hour, 11 daily), Rhosneigr (£17.17, 45 minutes), Bangor (£6.80, 20 minutes, 12 daily) and Shrewsbury (£29, two to 2½ hours, six daily).

Llandudno

POP 15,395

When you think of grand Victorian seaside getaways of yesteryear, what comes to mind invariably looks like Llandudno, a purpose-built 19th-century resort town. Imagine: a sweeping seaside promenade with holidaymakers strolling unhurriedly past the long pebbled beach on one side and genteel, pastel-coloured hotels and town houses facing the sea on the other. Crinolines, bathing gowns and top hats wouldn't seem out of place here.

Alongside lost-in-time charms of the British seaside (long pier with arcades, Punch and Judy shows), Llandudno's most arresting feature is the near-wilderness of the Great Orme – a striking, rough-hewn headland offering breathtaking views of Snowdonia and miles of trails – looming above the town.

A slim connection to *Alice in Wonderland* (Alice Liddell, the inspiration for Lewis Carroll's fictional Alice, used to holiday here with her family) accounts for statues of the book's characters around the town, linked by a trail marked with 55 bronze rabbit footprints.

◎ Sights

◎ Centre

Llandudno Pier   PIER
(www.llandudnopier.com; North Pde; ⊙9am-11pm summer, to 6pm rest of year; ♿) FREE A trip to Llandudno isn't complete until you've strolled along the Victorian pier, eating ice cream and shooing away seagulls. At 670m, it's Wales' longest pier. When it opened in 1878 its main use was as a disembarkation point for passengers from Isle of Man steamers. Today it's lined with slot machines and booths selling candyfloss, with a gorgeous pavilion at the far end where brass bands used to play, and the odd angler trying his or her luck.

Oriel Mostyn   GALLERY
(www.mostyn.org; 12 Vaughan St; ⊙11am-4pm Tue-Sun) FREE A sensitively restored, heritage-listed 1901 terracotta-and-brick exterior hides the sharply angled interior of North Wales' leading contemporary art gallery. Its galleries house changing and often challenging exhibitions by leading Welsh artists, as well as international guests. It was among the first to exhibit female artists in Britain. It's well worth exploring the excellent shop, too.

ANGLESEY & THE NORTH COAST LLANDUDNO

Llandudno

Llandudno Promenade

WATERFRONT

(The Promenade) Llandudno's iconic 2-mile promenade is one of its distinctive sights. It was here that Queen Victoria herself watched Professor Codman's Punch & Judy Show (p290), performed by the same family since 1860 – let's hope she was amused by it. Mr Punch's iconic red-and-white-striped tent sits by the entrance to the Victorian pier.

◉ Great Orme & Around

★ Great Orme

NATURAL FEATURE

(Y Gogarth) From the top of the vast, wind-swept limestone plateau known as the Great Orme (Y Gogarth), you get all-encompassing views across the restless Irish Sea, the mountains of the Carneddau range, and Anglesey's shores. Named after an Old Norse word for 'sea serpent', this giant looms over Llandudno. Designated a Site of Special Scientific Interest (SSSI), the headland is home to a cornucopia of flowers, endemic butterflies and seabirds, and is best explored on three waymarked walking trails leading to the summit.

Great Orme Bronze Age Mines

MINE

(☏ 01492-870447; www.greatormemines.info; Bishop's Quarry Rd; adult/child £8/5.50; ⊙ 9.30am-5.30pm mid-Mar–Oct; P ☗) Sitting a short stroll from the Great Orme Tramway's Halfway Station is the largest prehistoric mine ever discovered. Roman remains were originally believed to be the oldest findings in this Bronze Age mine until 4000-year-old animal bones and stone scrapers were discovered some 60m below the ground in 1987. After watching an explanatory film, visitors are able to explore portions of more than 5 miles of tunnels dug over centuries in search of copper.

The self-guided tour explains how the ancients turned rock into copper at the smelting site. You then head underground

Llandudno

for about 200m into 3500-year-old tunnels, and get to peer down an open 145m Victorian mine shaft. The site, whose discovery moved Britain's metallurgic history back a mind-boggling 2000 years, was worked again from the 17th to 19th centuries. Spoiler alert: early copper extraction using very basic tools was made possible by dolomitisation, a geological process resulting in the softening of the rock.

Marine Drive　　　　WATERFRONT
(www.greatorme.org.uk/marinedrive.html; Marine Dr; drivers & cyclists £2.50; ⊙ 9am-8pm May-Sep, to 4pm Oct-Apr; P) Starting by the pier, this one-way, 4-mile narrow road loops anticlockwise around the Great Orme, with immense sea vistas opening up on your right-hand side. There are few places to pull over along the loop, but there's a cafe perched on the cliff edge. You can also take the branch road that heads up to the Great Orme summit a quarter of the way along.

Great Orme Tramway　　　　CABLE CAR
(☑ 01492-577877; www.greatormetramway.co.uk; Victoria Station, Church Walks; adult/child return £8.10/5.60; ⊙ 10am-6pm Easter-Oct) Head to the top of the Great Orme without breaking a sweat in an original 1902 tramcar. It's one of only three cable-operated trams in the world (the other two are in equally glamorous Lisbon and San Francisco). Trips head up the steep incline every 20 minutes, weather permitting; change to a second tram at the Halfway Station.

Great Orme Aerial Cable Car　　　　CABLE CAR
(☑ 01492-877205; Happy Valley Rd; adult/child return £11/9; ⊙ 10am-6pm Apr-Oct; P) Britain's longest cable car runs a mile from the Happy Valley Gardens, near the start of Marine Dr, and, if it's not too windy, whisks passengers up to the summit of the Great Orme in just 18 minutes in breezy four-seater pods, with superb sea views en route.

West Shore Beach　　　　BEACH
(West Pde; P) In stark contrast to the perpetually busy main beach, this quiet Blue Flag slice of shingle and sand sits beneath the Great Orme, overlooking Conwy Bay. It is found on the west side of Llandudno, near the end of Marine Dr. When the wind and tide conditions are right, kitesurfers take to the water. The views over Anglesey and the mountains of Snowdonia can be particularly bewitching as the sun sets.

⚒ Festivals & Events

Victorian Extravaganza　　　　FAIR
(www.victorian-extravaganza.com; ⊙ early May; 🖽) Llandudno plays dress-up for this annual event, held over the early May bank holiday weekend. Taking over Mostyn and surrounding streets, it's the social event of the year, with a daily parade, strolling Victorian characters, bands, funfairs and exhibitions of steam-powered machinery.

⊟ Sleeping

Llandudno Hostel　　　　HOSTEL £
(☑ 01492-877430; www.llandudnohostel.co.uk; 14 Charlton St; dm £25, s/d/f from £39/56/120; P 🛜)

Staking out the middle ground between hostel and budget B&B, this powder-blue Victorian town house offers tidy rooms, bike storage and a free continental breakfast. It's family run and very family friendly – not the kind of place for booze hounds, but neither is Llandudno. Kitchen facilities are limited to a microwave and kettle.

★ Escape B&B
B&B **££**

(☑ 01492-877776; www.escapebandb.co.uk; 48 Church Walks; r from £110; **P** 🛜) 🐾 Escape is the original design B&B in Llandudno, with nine individually styled double bedrooms brimming with boutique-chic ambience and a host of ecofriendly and quirky features. Even if you're not an interior-design geek, you'll love the honesty-bar lounge, Bose iPod docks, DVD library, stand-alone roll-top baths, tasty breakfasts and atmosphere of indulgence. Suitable for kids over 10 years.

Beach Cove
B&B **££**

(☑ 01492-879638; 8 Church Walks; r £70-80; 🛜) A stone's throw from both the Great Orme (p286) and the Promenade, this homey eight-room B&B represents excellent value for money, particularly for single travellers. The decor is all light wood and creams, breakfast is ample and if you're travelling with your sweetie, splurge a little on the four-poster room (£80).

St George's Hotel
HISTORIC HOTEL **££**

(☑ 01492-877544; https://stgeorgeswales.co.uk; St George's Pl; city-facing/sea-view r from £95/135; **P** 🛜) As central as can be, this mid-19th-century grand dame has been given a contemporary update, reflected in the decor of its rooms. The town-facing classics are perfectly comfortable but unlikely to

make your social-media posts, whereas the sea-view doubles with balconies overlooking the Promenade are well worth the splurge.

Can-y-Bae
HOTEL **££**

(☑ 01492-874188; www.can-y-baehotel.com; 10 Mostyn Cres; s/d from £45/80; 🛜🎭) The 'Song of the Bay' is a welcoming, gay-friendly hotel that numbers many a visiting thespian among its mainly older clientele. Rooms are somewhat dated but comfortable and it's hard to beat the sea views. Signed memorabilia blankets the walls of the little theatre-themed residents' bar and there's a piano if anyone wants to start a knees-up. Children over 14 years only.

★ Bodysgallen Hall
HISTORIC HOTEL **£££**

(NT; ☑ 01492-584466; www.bodysgallen.com; A470; r/ste from £275/510; **P** 🛜🛝) Owned by the National Trust but privately managed, this magnificent pink-stone 1620 country house set in French-style formal gardens lets you lose yourself in the wood-panelled world of the Jacobean gentry. The rooms, split between the main hall and outlying cottages, feature floral patterns, four-poster beds and antique furnishings. Bodysgallen is 3 miles south of Llandudno, on the A470.

Highlights include a spa and one of the best restaurants for miles around inside the formal dining hall. Modern Welsh dishes may include wild rabbit with pickled vegetables, maple-glazed duck and butter-poached sea bass with razor clams (three courses £49). Book ahead and dress nicely.

Cliffbury
B&B **£££**

(☑ 01492-877224; www.thecliffbury.co.uk; 34 St David's Rd; r from £162; **P** 🛜) Set on a quiet backstreet, this attractive corner house has six individually styled B&B rooms – two are suites and the remaining four are almost suite-like in their proportions. The friendly owners tactfully describe the place as 'mainly catering for over 25s'. Two-night minimum stay; complimentary cooked breakfast.

🍴 Eating

Loaf Coffee & Sandwich Bar
BRITISH **£**

(☑ 01492-338995; www.facebook.com/theloafcsb; 12-14 Gloddaeth St; mains £7-10; ⊙ 9am-5pm; 🐾) 🐾 This family-run cafe beguiles locals and visitors alike with its friendly, cheerful service, its commitment to high-quality local ingredients and its solid, no-nonsense cooking. Linger over a full Welsh breakfast (including vegetarian options) or freshly

---

DON'T MISS

STAY AT LAND'S END

Three rooms at the end of the world. Or so it feels at **Lighthouse** (☑ 01492-876819; www.bookalighthouse.com; Great Orme's Head, Marine Dr; ste £185), a blufftop abode at the tip of the Great Orme. Of the three individually styled suites, the Lamp Room is our favourite, and while the rooms are rather pricey, given the facilities, the location is unique and suits wilderness-loving types who enjoy surveying the sea through a telescope.

DON'T MISS

LLANDUDNO JUNCTION: UNLIKELY FOODIE MAGNET

Llandudno Junction, located across the estuary from Conwy and en route to Llandudno, grew around a major **train stop** (Conway Rd) en route from Cardiff, London or Holyhead, where passengers need to disembark and change if they're Llandudno- or Conwy-bound. Though the town itself is no looker, it (along with nearby Deganwy) punches way above its weight when it comes to dining out and gourmet coffee.

Paysanne (☑01492-582079; www.paysannedeganwy.co.uk; 147 Station Rd, Deganwy; mains £15-21; ☉6.30-8.30pm Wed-Fri, 5.30-8.30pm Sat, noon-2pm Sun; ℗) Going strong for 30 years, family-run Paysanne is all about prime Welsh ingredients put through the prism of rustic French cooking. Order the likes of bouillabaisse brimming with Menai Strait seafood, escargots amid fountains of garlic chilli butter, and bacon-enveloped guinea fowl bathed in a rich red-wine reduction, and pair them with a fine French vintage. Book ahead.

On Wednesday and Thursday, take advantage of the three-course prix fixe menu (£24).

Enochs (☑01492-581145; www.enochs.co.uk; 146 Conwy Rd; mains £6-12; ☉noon-8pm; ⊞) Customers come from miles around to this model of its kind – a fish-and-chip joint dedicated to sustainable fishing. The highlights are the cod and haddock fillets enveloped in crispy batter, with a supporting cast of thick-cut golden-fried chips, and peas of a satisfyingly mushy quality. There are also locally sourced sausages, burgers and pies for the non-pescatorially inclined.

Locals love Enochs so much it's opened a second cafe in Valley on Anglesey.

Providero (☑01492-338220; www.facebook.com/providero; 148 Conwy Rd; ☉8am-2pm Mon-Fri) What started out as a north-coast-plying coffee van has found a more permanent home in this wonderful, thimble-sized cafe. You may well find yourself lingering over a cup of locally roasted specialist coffee, or one of the 30-plus types of tea, propping up the bar and watching the friendly barista work latte-art magic.

---

baked scones and tea, or get freshly made sandwiches and cakes to take away.

Fish Tram Chips   FISH & CHIPS £
(☑01492-872673; 22-24 Old Rd; mains £7-10; ☉noon-2.30pm & 5-7.30pm Tue-Sat, noon 3pm Sun) Consistently serving up tasty, fresh fish and homemade side dishes with unaffected friendliness, this is where the locals head for slap-up fish-and-chip meals, either to take away or eat in the small dining room. Opening hours extend in summer.

Ham Bone Food Hall & Brasserie   DELI £
(☑01492-860084; 3 Lloyd St; mains £6-10; ☉8am-5pm Mon-Sat, 10am-4pm Sun; ☎) The best deli-cafe in Llandudno serves a huge range of freshly made sandwiches, perfect for a picnic on the Promenade. Breakfast is served until 11.30am, or come at lunchtime for burgers, fishcakes, steak-and-ale pies, huge pizzas and an ever-changing selection of specials.

★**Cottage Loaf**   PUB FOOD ££
(☑01492-870762; www.the-cottageloaf.co.uk; Market St; mains £13-17; ☉11am-11pm, kitchen noon-9pm; ☎❄) Tucked down an alleyway off Mostyn St, this charismatic pub has print-strewn walls, carpeted wooden floors and an atmosphere of genuine bonhomie. On the menu, traditional dishes such as steak-and-Conwy-ale pie mesh with more exotic offerings (try the Goan curry with Conwy mussels), and there are plenty of cask ales and good beers on tap.

There are also two flower-bedecked beer gardens (both dog friendly), and children are welcome as late as 9pm.

Johnny Dough's Woodfired Pizza   PIZZA ££
(☑01492 -871813; www.johnnydoughs.com; 129 Mostyn St; pizzas £10-11; ☉noon-9pm; ☑⊞) There's a lot to love about Johhny's: the inspired combination of superlative wood-fired pizza and the best of regional craft beer, the hit-the-spot cocktails, the cooking classes for kids... Pizza-wise, choose between old-school classics (pepperoni, Hawaiian) and more off-the-wall new-school offerings (Great Orme goat's cheese, Peking duck, beetroot pesto) to fill your belly.

WORTH A TRIP

COUNTRY COMFORT

The **Kinmel Arms** (☑ 01745-832207; www.thekinmelarms.co.uk; Primrose Hill, St George; ste 2-night stay from £125; ☺ Tue-Sat; P 🤝) is a rural enclave of fine food, real ales and four beautifully finished boutique suites. It's the restaurant (mains £14 to £28), one of Wales' most justly acclaimed gastropubs, that's the main attraction. Cooked breakfasts aren't offered, but room fridges are stocked with breakfast fare. St George is 15 miles east of Llandudno, off the A55.

Home Cookin'
INTERNATIONAL ££

(☑ 01492-876585; www.homecookin-llandudno.co.uk; 139 Upper Mostyn St; mains £9-16; ☺ 10.30am-9.30pm; ☑) This family-run bistro has won many loyal local fans with, as the name suggests, home cookin' with a flourish. Expect generous platefuls of comfort food, such as smoked haddock and spinach pie, or bangers and mash, at unthreatening prices, prepared with attention to detail and served in stylish surroundings.

Osborne's Cafe Grill
BRASSERIE £££

(☑ 01492-860330; www.osbornehouse.co.uk; 17 North Pde; 3-course set menu £25; ☺ 4-8.30pm Tue-Sat; 🤝) If you really want to live the grand Victorian fantasy, starch your shirt and head to Osborne House, where military types peer out of gilt frames from the walls, amid gilded mirrors and candle-powered chandeliers. The short-and-sweet menu includes slow-roasted lamb, steak frites and sticky toffee pudding and it's worth a visit for the ambience alone.

Seahorse
SEAFOOD £££

(☑ 01492-875315; www.the-seahorse.co.uk; 7 Church Walks; 1/2/3 courses £21/29/34; ☺ 4.30-10pm) Don, the chef at Llandudno's only dedicated seafood restaurant, is a keen fisherman, and the menu reflects his passion for the local catch: Menai mussels in white wine, or hake stuffed with crab and spinach. The restaurant is a split-level affair: upstairs is decorated with large Mediterranean murals, while the cellar room is more intimate.

Drinking

TAPPS Micropub
CRAFT BEER

(☑ 01492-870956; www.facebook.com/TAPPS35; 35 Madoc St; ☺ noon-9pm Mon, to 10pm Tue, Wed & Sun, to 11pm Thu-Sat) Their motto is 'No crapp at Tapp' and these guys mean business when it comes to craft beer. Their aim is to support local producers (and select breweries in Cheshire) and you'll find five rotating brews on tap, including the likes of Purple Moose elderflower ale, Crafty Devil coffee milk stout and Brew York 'Rhubarbara Streisand'. Good outdoor seating, too.

Wild Horse Brewing
MICROBREWERY

(☑ 01492-868292; www.wildhorsebrewing.co.uk; unit 4, Cae Bach, Builder St; ☺ 2-5pm Thu, 11am-5pm Fri, 9am-3pm Sat) Going strong since 2015 and inspired by American microbreweries, Wild Horse specialises in Nokota (session IPA) and Buckskin (lager). There are also nine rotating stouts, pale ales and IPAs, plus occasional special small batches. Come and try them at the buzzy taproom, or get a minikeg and fill up a growler to take away.

King's Head
PUB

(☑ 01492-877993; www.kingsheadllandudno.co.uk; Old Rd; ☺ noon-11pm Mon-Thu & Sun, to midnight Fri & Sat; 🤝) Dating from the late 18th century, Llandudno's most atmospheric and oldest pub is a great place for a quiet pint of local ale or a hearty meal (£12 to £17) by the open fire on chilly days. It's a handy stop en route to or from the Great Orme.

Heartland Coffee Roasters
COFFEE

(☑ 01492-878757; www.facebook.com/HeartlandCoffeeUK; unit 6 Cwrt Roger Mostyn, Builder St; ☺ 10am-4pm Mon-Fri) Life's too short to drink bad coffee. Which is why this speciality coffee roaster on an industrial estate near the train station is an essential stop for genuine coffee lovers. Get bags of beans from locations as diverse as India and Sumatra, or have a cup of brew right there and then.

☆ Entertainment

Professor Codman's Punch & Judy Show
PUPPET THEATRE

(☑ 07900-555515; www.punchandjudy.com/codgal.htm; The Promenade; ☺ noon-4pm Sat & Sun year-round, daily school holidays Easter–mid-Sep) Queen Victoria herself watched this show, performed by the same family, with the same puppets, since 1860. Mr Punch's iconic red-and-white-striped booth sits near the entrance to the pier. If you're not familiar with the Punch and Judy tradition, you might be surprised by the violence and puppet-spouse abuse – but the kids don't seem to mind.

Venue Cymru PERFORMING ARTS
(☑box office 01492-872000; www.venuecymru.co.uk; The Promenade; ☉box office 10am-5.30pm Mon-Sat, plus 1hr before performances) With two auditoriums and a snooker arena, Venue Cymru is one of North Wales' leading event and performance venues. The line-up covers all bases, from big rock gigs to high-brow classical performances, big-name stand-ups, musicals and shows for children.

ⓘ Information

Great Orme Country Park Visitor Centre
(☑01492-874151; www.visitconwy.org.uk; Pyllau Rd, Great Orme; ☉10am-5.30pm Easter-Oct) The visitor centre on the summit of the Great Orme has 3D and interactive displays on the geology, flora and fauna of the area.

Llandudno Tourist Office (☑01492-577577; www.visitllandudno.org.uk; unit 26, Victoria Centre, Mostyn St; ☉9.30am-4.30pm Mon-Sat, 10.30am-4pm Sun) This tourist office has helpful staff, abundant information and an accommodation-booking service.

ⓘ Getting There & Around

Bus Local buses stop at the corner of Mostyn and Gloddaeth Sts. Bus routes include the half-hourly 5/5C to Caernarfon (1½ hours) via Bangor (one hour) and Conwy (22 minutes), and the thrice-daily X19 to Blaenau Ffestiniog (1¼ to 1½ hours) via Betws-y-Coed (50 minutes). Buses generally only run Monday to Saturday.

Bicycle Folks at **Busters Cycles** (☑07858 633874; https://family-cyclehire.online; Sunnyvale, Parsons Nose Lane, Kinmel Bay) rent out bicycles, delivered on request to Llandudno and other towns off the A5.

Train From the **train station** (Augusta St), frequent direct services head to/from Betws-y-Coed (£6.30, 50 minutes, seven daily), Blaenau Ffestiniog (£8.70, 1½ hours, six daily) and Chester (£19.40, 1¼ hours, five daily). For destinations such as Holyhead, London Euston, Birmingham New St and Manchester Piccadilly you'll need to change at Llandudno Junction (£2.90, 10 minutes, twice hourly) or Chester.

ISLE OF ANGLESEY (YNYS MÔN)

At 276 sq miles, the Isle of Anglesey is Wales' largest island. A stronghold of Welsh language and culture, it's largely pastoral and mostly flat, compared to neighbouring Snowdonia, with miles of inspiring coastline, secluded beaches and Wales' greatest concentration of ancient sites. Gastronomy features highly among Anglesey's attractions, with some of Wales' most creative dining found here.

More than 85 sq miles of Anglesey – including almost all of its coastline – has been designated an Area of Outstanding Natural Beauty; hiking (the island is encircled by the 125-mile Anglesey Coast Path), beachcombing and water sports are all key draws. Of the human-made landscape, the handsome Georgian town of Beaumaris is its most obviously appealing. The beaches of Trearddur Bay and Rhoscolyn also make fine bases if proximity to the sand is a must.

History

Taking over from Mesolithic hunters who arrived between 8000 and 4000 BC, small communities of farmers made the most of Anglesey's fertile land from around 2500 BC. The high concentration of monuments across the island – standing stones, burial chambers and circles – is testament to millennia of concentrated culture. The farming communities were supplanted by the Celts around 700 BC, and the island became Europe's most important Druid stronghold (p292). The Celts, in turn, were forced out by the Romans and, in AD 60, Anglesey was the last part of Wales to fall to their legions. When the Romans departed in the early 5th century, the mighty Welsh dynasty of the Princes of Gwynedd filled the power vacuum.

Given its outpost status and singular character, Anglesey has as fair a claim as any to being the Welsh heartland. One ancient name for the isle, bestowed by the prelate and historian Gerald of Wales in the 12th century, was Môn mam Cymru (Mother of Wales).

Menai Bridge

POP 3376

It's testimony to his genius that not only does engineer extraordinaire Thomas Telford have a large town in Shropshire named after him, this small town is named after one of his creations. The industrial age arrived in Anglesey in 1826 when Telford established the first permanent link to the mainland with his innovative 174m Menai

Suspension Bridge across the Menai Strait – the first bridge of its kind in the world. The central span is 30m high, allowing for the passage of tall ships. It was joined in 1850 by Robert Stephenson's Britannia Bridge, further south, which carried the newly laid railway. Impressive ironworks aside, Menai Bridge is also the unlikely gourmet capital of Anglesey.

◉ Sights & Activities

Thomas Telford Centre　　　MUSEUM
(☑01248-715046; www.menaibridges.co.uk; Mona Rd; adult/child £3/free; ◷10am-5pm Wed & Thu Apr-Oct) This small, volunteer-run museum is the best way to learn more about the feats of Victorian engineering that lie behind the iconic bridges connecting Anglesey with the mainland, and to explore the ecology of the Menai Strait. Friendly Menai Heritage volunteers regularly arrange talks, tours and family activities to show off some of their deserved local pride.

RibRide　　　BOATING
(☑0333-123 4303; www.ribride.co.uk; Water St; adult/child from £30/20) If you're dreaming of blasting along the waves in a hurricane of sea spray, these rigid inflatable boats (RIB) run several tours of the Menai Strait, from visits to Puffin Island and speedy blasts past Caernarfon Castle (p274) to Llanddwyn Island, to the Velocity experience, with the skipper pushing the boat right to the max.

🛏 Sleeping & Eating

★Château Rhianfa　　　BOUTIQUE HOTEL **£££**
(☑01248-713656; www.plasrhianfa.com; Beaumaris Rd, Glyngarth; d from £239, 6-person cottages £314; P 🔊) Those seeking to indulge their Prince Charming/fairy-tale-princess fantasies need look no further than this turreted Victorian mansion, styled after a French renaissance chateau. Chic and contemporary touches include round beds, free-standing baths, giant sleigh beds and sculpted gardens with views across the strait to Snowdonia. Daring pairings of local ingredients abound at the on-site restaurant.

Glyngarth is a little over a mile northeast of Menai Bridge's centre.

Dylan's　　　INTERNATIONAL **££**
(☑01248-716714; www.dylansrestaurant.co.uk; St George's Rd; mains £8-25; ◷noon-10pm; 🔊) Visible from Thomas Telford's famous suspension bridge, and itself overlooking the bird-filled shallows of the strait, this casual, much-awarded modern restaurant is Menai's most popular. Local seafood features heavily in dishes such as roasted lobster or linguini with seasonal mussels, and there are carnivore draws in the form of burgers, Welsh rump steak and braised lamb.

THE DRUIDS

The magical mystique that the ancient Druids enjoy today is assisted by a lack of evidence – coming from an oral culture, they naturally wrote down nothing about their beliefs. They were bards and diviners, the priest class of the Celtic religion, educators and healers as well as political advisors and so were vastly influential. The main sources of information about this spiritual aristocracy are Roman scholars, whose accounts are seen through an adversarial glass. The Romans are portrayed as a civilising force and the Celts and Druids as bloodthirsty and keen on human sacrifice (which did take place in sacred Druidic groves in isolated corners of Wales).

Resistance to the Romans was powered by Druidic influence in Britain. Anglesey was a major seat of Druidic learning because of its strategic placement between Wales, Ireland and France, with the island at the heart of Celtic sea traffic. According to the Roman historian Tacitus, when the Romans attacked Anglesey in AD 60, they were terrified by the resident wild women and holy fanatics who greeted them with howls and prayers, and the Romans found the altars there covered in the blood of prisoners. The conquerors set about destroying the Druids' shrines and sacred groves, and did all they could to impress their culture on the locals, but the result was inevitably a mix of new and old beliefs.

Druidism became a fashionable interest in the 18th century, and the Welsh poetic tradition is believed to stem from the Druids. In 1820 Edward Williams created Druidic ceremonies to be performed during the annual Eisteddfod, which accounts for many of the long beards and solemn ceremonies still in evidence at this festival of poetry and literature.

★ Sosban & the
Old Butchers
GASTRONOMY £££

(📞 01248-208131; www.sosbanandtheoldbutchers. com; Trinity House, 1 High St; 8-course tasting menu £125; ⊙ 7-11pm Wed-Sat) The Michelin-starred husband-and-wife chef team welcomes you inside the rustic slate dining room, still bearing vestiges of its days as an actual butcher shop. There is no menu. You will be eating eight boldly flavoured, contemporary dishes made from fresh North Wales ingredients of the day, such as lamb tail with smoked ricotta, or local mussels. Succinct wine menu. Book ahead.

❶ Getting There & Away

Menai Bridge is Anglesey's bus hub. Destinations include Holyhead (X4; 1¼ hours), Llanfair PG (X4; five minutes), Beaumaris (58; 22 minutes) and Bangor (4H, 42, 42A, X4; 12 minutes).

Southwest Anglesey

POP 6000

Stretching from a rather nondescript town with a very long name to Anglesey's water-sports capital of Rhosneigr, southwest Anglesey is a beguiling mix of ancient history, stately country houses, pastoral landscapes and sand dunes, punctuated by the odd gastronomic hotspot.

◎ Sights

★ Bryn Celli Ddu Burial
Chamber
ARCHAEOLOGICAL SITE

(Cadw; https://cadw.gov.wales/visit/places-to-visit/bryn-celli-ddu-burial-chamber; off A4080; ⊙ 10am-4pm) FREE There are neolithic burial mounds scattered all around Wales, but many have been completely stripped of their earthen covering by overenthusiastic archaeologists. What makes Bryn Celli Ddu fascinating is that it's relatively intact – you can enter the grass-covered barrow and pass into a stone-lined burial chamber, complete with original megalithic zigzag carvings, that was used as a communal grave 5000 years ago.

To find it, follow the signpost off the A4080 down a country lane.

Newborough Warren
NATURE RESERVE

(off A4080, Niwbwrch; seasonal entry £4; 🅿) From the tiny town of Newborough/Niwbwrch, follow the signs through the pine woods to Abermenai Point, a long, dune-backed, wild beach that borders the 240-hectare woods.

ART AT ANGLESEY'S HEART

The linchpin of Anglesey's visual-arts scene is **Oriel Ynys Môn** (📞 01248-724444; www.orielmon.org; B5111, Rhosmeirch, Llangefni; ⊙ 10am-4pm Wed-Sun; 🅿). The 'Anglesey Gallery' features temporary art exhibitions, a **History Gallery** exploring the island's past and role in the Roman invasion, licensed cafe **Blas Mwy**, and children's activity area the **Discovery Den**. But the main draw is the **Oriel Kyffin Williams**: exhibits change regularly but always feature some of the gallery's 400-plus works by Sir John 'Kyffin' Williams, a Llangefni boy and prolific artist whose portraits and landscapes provide a unique window into Welsh culture.

Park at the end, and then you can explore the woods and perhaps spot red squirrels or native Soay sheep, or else follow Newborough Beach to the tip of the peninsula, the 19th-century Twr Mawr lighthouse and the Twr Bach stone tower. Silvery dusks with Snowdonia views are bewitching.

Anglesey Sea Zoo
AQUARIUM

(📞 01248-430411; www.angleseyseazoo.co.uk; A4080, Brynsiencyn; adult/concession £8.25/7.25; ⊙ 10am-4.45pm Feb-Nov; 🅿 👶) 🍴 Signposted off the the A4080, this excellent aquarium introduces you to the denizens of the local waters, from lobster and cuckoo wrasse to tiny brine shrimp and Picasso-painting-like flatfish. Designers have re-created different environments, such as quayside and shipwrecks – tidal waves crash into the glass tank that simulates life in a tidal pool. A crowning touch is a life-sized model of a basking shark, the second-largest fish in the world. Conger eel or shark feedings are held daily.

Plas Newydd
HISTORIC BUILDING

(NT; 📞 01248-714795; www.nationaltrust.org.uk/plas-newydd-house-and-garden; A4080, Llanfairpwll; adult/child £12.50/5.80, garden only £8/4; ⊙ house 11am-4.30pm Mar-early Nov, garden 10.30am-5pm Mar-Oct, 11am-3pm Nov-Feb) Two miles southwest of Llanfair PG, the ancestral home of the marquesses of Anglesey, Plas Newydd (New House), is surrounded by tranquil gardens, with fine views across the Menai Strait to Snowdonia. The building has its origins in 1470, but most of today's Gothic manor took shape in the 18th century. Inside, the walls are hung with gilt-framed portraits of the Paget family ancestors (William Paget was secretary of state to Henry VIII), who owned the house until 1976.

Llanfair PG Train Station　　LANDMARK
(Holyhead Rd, Llanfair PG) The lacklustre small town with one of the world's longest, consonant-greedy names is an unlikely hotspot for visitors seeking photo opportunities on the train-station platform. The name (which means St Mary's Church in the Hollow of the White Hazel near a Rapid Whirlpool and the Church of St Tysilio near the Red Cave) was dreamed up in 1869 by a tailor from Menai Bridge to get tourists in. And it worked.

✖ Eating

★Moch a Môr　　MODERN WELSH ££
(☑01248-440077; www.themarramgrass.com; A4080, Newborough; mains £6.50-13; ☺8-11am & noon-9pm; ℗🛜) The alfresco pop-up incarnation of foodie magnet The Marram Grass is a simple concept. You idle in nooks beneath vine trellises and tuck into dishes made for sharing, from superlative hot dogs and truffle-speckled mac and cheese (with Welsh cheeses) to slow-cooked salt-marsh lamb and steamed Menai mussels. A succinct wine, craft-beer and cocktail menu seals the deal.

🛍 Shopping

★Tŷ Halen　　FOOD
(Halen Môn Saltcote; ☑01248-430871; www.halenmon.com; B4419; ☺11am-3.30pm) Used by Michelin-starred restaurants such as Fat Duck and Ynyshir, Halen Môn salt is known in the most exalted of foodie circles. Sourced directly from the Menai Strait's waters, it's sold in pure form and flavoured. Next door to Anglesey Sea Zoo (p293) the £1.25-million visitor centre explores the salt-making process and you can buy all 10 flavours at the shop.

Flavours include smoked, Tahitian vanilla, umami, chilli and garlic, The shop also sells other edibles, such as smoked water and salted caramel sauce, plus locally made ceramic dishes. There's an excellent, seasonal open-air cafe, too, that cooks up sumptuous lunches from local, organic ingredients; Saturday night is sourdough-pizza night.

ⓘ Getting There & Away

Bus The X4 bus heads between Llanfair PG and Holyhead (one hour), Llangefni (19 minutes), Menai Bridge (five minutes) and Bangor (18 minutes).

Car This part of Anglesey is tricky to cover with public transport, so having your own wheels makes it easier.

Train Normally, there are direct trains from Llanfair PG to Holyhead, Rhosneigr, Bangor, Conwy and Shrewsbury. At research time, they were suspended due to the Covid-19 pandemic.

Beaumaris (Biwmares)

POP 1249

Anglesey's most appealing town benefits from a winning combination of a waterfront location on the Menai Strait, with views of Snowdonia's mountains beyond, a formidable castle and an elegant collection of Georgian, Victorian and Edwardian buildings, housing a growing number of boutiques, galleries, smart hotels and chic eateries. Some of the houses are extremely old; look for the half-timbered house dating from 1400 – one of the oldest in Britain – on Castle St near the bottom of Church St.

The town's name dates back to the time of French-speaking Edward I, who built the castle. It's a corruption of *beau marais* (meaning 'beautiful marsh'), and was intended to attract English settlers. Historical buildings aside, Beaumaris is also the springboard for cruises to nearby Puffin Island, a bird sanctuary.

◎ Sights & Activities

★Beaumaris Castle　　CASTLE
(Cadw; www.cadw.gov.wales; Castle St; adult/child £6.50/3.90; ☺9.30am-5pm daily Mar-Jun, 10am-1pm & 2-5pm Mon-Wed, Sat & Sun Jul-Oct, shorter hours rest of year) Beyond a water-filled moat, Beaumaris Castle is the last and most technically perfect of the 'iron ring' of fortifications built by Edward I of England to consolidate his subjugation of Wales. Started in 1295, but never completed as fully designed, it enjoys World Heritage status. With its pleasing symmetry, water-filled moat, succession of four concentric 'walls within walls' and stout towers and gatehouse, it was originally connected to the sea from the moat, allowing for efficient delivery of supplies.

The walk along the top of part of the inner wall gives super views of the castle layout. Look out for the old privvies (drop toilets, marginally less unpleasant than the murder holes for those walking below) and the arrow slits in the wall for picking off invaders. The inner ward is rather empty, since the planned lavish palace never came to pass, but you can check out the compact chapel in the Chapel Tower after a stroll through internal passages in the walls.

From a defensive perspective, the castle was hit-and-miss. It was captured by Welsh forces under the command of Owain Glyndŵr in 1403, but taken back in 1405. During the English Civil War, the castle was loyal to Charles I and held out against the Parliamentarian troops for four years.

Old Court House Museum HISTORIC BUILDING
(Llys Biwmares; www.visitanglesey.co.uk; Castle St; adult/child £4/3; ⊙10.30am-5pm Sat-Thu Apr-Oct) The Beaumaris Court, opposite the castle, was an instrument of justice dispensed by the English between 1614 and 1971, with Welsh-speaking defendants at a distinct disadvantage as the proceedings were held in English – theft of cheese and a quarter of beef in 1768 incurred the penalty of being publicly whipped in four different towns, for example. An excellent free audio guide helps to paint the picture.

Beaumaris Gaol HISTORIC BUILDING
(www.visitanglesey.co.uk; Steeple Lane; adult/child £7/5; ⊙10am-5pm Apr-Oct, to 4pm Mar) This grim, stout-walled jail, opened in 1829 and largely unaltered since, was modern for its time, with toilets in every cell and a treadmill water pump. However, that's not enough to dispel the gloom of the windowless punishment cell, where condemned prisoners awaited their demise at the gibbet, or the stone-breaking yard where inmates were subjected to hard labour. Since it closed as a jail, it's been used as a children's clinic (cheery!) and a police station.

Penmon Priory CHURCH
(Cadw; www.cadw.gov.wales; B5109, Penmon; parking £3; ⊙10am-4pm; [P]) FREE Some 4 miles north of Beaumaris, Penmon provides a glimpse of Anglesey's long spiritual significance. An early Celtic monastery was established here in the 6th century by St Seiriol. Burnt down by the Danes in 971, its last relic is the basin of the holy well, tucked behind the current stone church. The earliest extant parts of that church include two 10th-century Celtic crosses, a font from around the turn of the 2nd millennium and some wonderful 12th-century Romanesque arches.

DON'T MISS

PUFFIN ISLAND SAFARIS

Home to noisy, pungent colonies of puffins, razorbills and guillemots, **Puffin Island/Ynys Seiriol** lies just off the eastern tip of Anglesey. You may not disembark on the island, but you can take a worthwhile wildlife cruise here with Seacoast Safaris from Beaumaris.

Ynys Seiriol is also the final resting place of St Seiriol, after whom the well at Penmon Priory is named, as well as a number of other saintly hermits who lived out their last days on the island.

Penmon Point VIEWPOINT
(B5109) Around 1 mile northeast of Penmon Priory, a starkly picturesque, narrow, winding road culminates in Anglesey's easternmost point, with terrific vistas of the Menai Strait, the lighthouse, Puffin Island and the Great Orme beyond the gun-metal waters. The car-parking charge at Penmon Priory includes access to the toll road; you can either park at the priory and walk, or else park at the point, near the cafe.

Seacoast Safaris BOATING
(✆07854 028393; www.seacoastsafaris.co.uk; Alma St, Pier House; ⊙Apr-Oct; 🚢) Off Anglesey's eastern point, the Special Protection Area of Puffin Island is alive with puffins, cormorants and kittiwakes, while seals, porpoises and dolphins call the waters around the 28-hectare island home. Seacoast's (weather-dependent) 90-minute boat trips cruise alongside the island (adut/child £15/10) or through Menai Strait; book at the kiosk at the entrance to the pier or by phone.

🛏 Sleeping

Kingsbridge CAMPGROUND £
(✆01248-490636; www.kingsbridgecaravanpark.co.uk; off B5109, Llanfaes; sites from £26; [P]🐾) 🌿 This well-equipped camping and caravanning site is also a haven for local wildlife and wildflowers, earning it 13 David Bellamy Conservation Awards. There are separate areas for families, and static caravans to rent by the week. It's located 2 miles north of Beaumaris.

★Bull HISTORIC HOTEL ££
(✆01248-810329; www.bullsheadinn.co.uk; Castle St; d inn/town house from £110/130, ste £166; 🛜)

These sister properties, the Bull and Townhouse, located across the road from each other, provide quite a contrast. Where the Bull – occupying an ancient coaching inn – is historic and retains original features, such as the heavy wooden beams (we love the suite with roll-top bath), the Townhouse is contemporary, high-tech and design driven. Breakfast is served at the inn.

Bishopsgate House
HOTEL ££

(☑ 01248-810302; www.bishopsgatehotel.co.uk; 54 Castle St; s/d from £60/74, f £144; P🕾🐾) The nine bedrooms in this fine, pale-green, Georgian town house are somewhat dated, and all very different: the deluxe rooms have jacuzzis and/or four-poster beds, while others have an antique sensibility or bold modern wallpaper. Expect a warm welcome, good breakfast and partial sea views.

🍴 Eating & Drinking

Red Boat Ice Cream Parlour
ICE CREAM £

(☑ 01248-810022; www.redboatgelato.com; 34 Castle St; scoop £2.60; ⊙10am-6pm; 🕾) This popular parlour whips up authentic Italian gelato in 35 different flavours, from the exotic (strawberry, mascarpone and balsamic vinegar) to the extremely Welsh (*bara brith*, a rich, fruit tea-loaf). It's so popular, in fact, that it's expanded and now offers breakfast, Dutch pancakes, pizza (£8 to £10) and other light meals.

★ Tredici Italian Kitchen
ITALIAN ££

(☑ 01248-811230; www.facebook.com/tredicikitchen; 13 Castle St; mains £14-16; ⊙6-9pm Mon-Wed, noon-9pm Thu, noon-3pm & 6-9pm Fri & Sat) Occupying an intimate 1st-floor dining room above a quality butcher and grocer, Tredici has brought a touch of the Mediterranean to Anglesey. While local produce is used where possible (Halen Môn sea salt perks up the fries, and the mussels are from the Menai Strait), the figs, mozzarella and other pizza toppings and calzone fillings are imported from sunnier climes.

Midland Tapas & Wine Bar
TAPAS ££

(☑ 01248-810429; https://themidlandtapas.com; 38 Castle St; tapas £4-7.50; ⊙noon-2.45pm & 6-9pm Thu, noon-2.45pm & 5.30-9pm Fri, 9-11.45am, noon-3.45pm & 5-9pm Sat, 10am-2.45pm & 6-9pm Sun; 🕾) One of two outlets (the other one being in Conwy), this sleek tapas bar puts a Welsh spin on Spanish classics. Platters of Spanish cheeses and charcuterie are present and correct, along with an admirably select wine list. But the highlights include spicy (Welsh) lamb meatballs, Anglesey pork belly and Menai Strait mussels. Grab some fellow bon vivants and go.

George & Dragon
PUB

(☑ 01248-810491; www.facebook.com/GeorgeAnd DragonHotelBeaumaris; Church St; ⊙11am-11pm; 🕾) For more than 600 years drinkers have been sipping their ales within these walls and beneath these low ceilings. Join this venerable throng, sip a cask or keg ale or one of the seasonal Robinson's Brewery craft beers, and while you're at it, keep an eye out for the horse brasses and 400-year-old wall paintings.

🛍 Shopping

Besides a weekly craft market and a scattering of gift shops, some of of Beaumaris' best souvenirs are found online. Check out the Little Chilli Shop (www.littlechillishop.com), an award-winning initiative by a local husband-and-wife team who grow and import all manner of chillies, and make hot sauces and chocolates with a punch of heat.

Beaumaris Artisan Market
ARTS & CRAFTS

(www.facebook.com/beaumarisartisanmarket; Cadnant St, David Hughes Community Centre; ⊙9am-5pm Sun) Taking place on Sundays just outside the community centre, these stalls showcase some of the best edibles from the area, as well as crafts, from ceramics to jewellery, by local artisans.

ℹ Information

Tourist Office
(☑ 01248-810040; www.beaumaris.com; Town Hall, Castle St; ⊙10am-2pm Mon-Fri) This information point is only staffed (by volunteers) for limited hours; at other times it's still accessible, and a handy spot to pick up brochures.

ℹ Getting There & Away

Bus Buses stop on Church St. Routes include a dozen-or-so 57 and 58 buses daily (fewer on Sunday) to Menai Bridge (18 minutes) and Bangor (35 to 45 minutes). Some 57 and 58 buses continue on to Penmon (10 minutes).

Car There's a large pay-and-display car park on the waterfront by the castle. If you're prepared to walk, there are often free parking spots on the Menai Bridge approach to town.

Moelfre

POP 610

The shipwreck magnet of Moelfre, an old herring-fishing port, is an attractive maritime village on the east coast. Besides the pretty crescent of white sand that is the Treath Lligwy beach, its main draw is its proximity to some of Anglesey's most impressive Neolithic sights.

◉ Sights

Gwylfan Moelfre Seawatch MUSEUM
(Seawatch Centre; ☑ 01248-410300; 2 Morannedd; ☺ 10.30am-4.30pm daily Easter-Oct, Sat & Sun rest of year) FREE Anglesey's treacherous east coast has claimed numerous ships over the centuries, perhaps most famously the *Royal Charter* in 1859, which took 460 lives and £360,000 of gold. This little centre is devoted to the brave souls of the Royal National Lifeboat Institute (RNLI), including Richard Evans (1905–2001), who rescued 281 people in his 49 years stationed here. His statue stands outside, as does a schedule of lifeboat launches.

Lligwy Burial Chamber ARCHAEOLOGICAL SITE
(Siambr Gladdu Lligwy; www.cadw.gov.wales; off A5025; ☺ 10am-4pm) FREE Sometime before 3000 BC the local people raised Lligwy's 25-tonne capstone into place, forming a stone chamber that they covered with an earthen mound. When the barrow was excavated in 1908, the bones of about 30 people were found buried within. To find it, look for the country lane marked 'Ancient Monument' near the roundabout on the approach to Moelfre. Park at the marked car park and walk back along the road; the chamber is on the right.

Din Lligwy RUINS
(Cadw; www.cadw.gov.wales; off A5025; ☺ 10am-4pm) FREE In the 4th century, during the relative stability of the lengthy Roman occupation, local farmers built a small fortified settlement here, consisting of stone buildings behind a large stone wall. All that remains are the foundations, but it's enough to give a good sense of the layout of the site. Nearby, across the fields, stand the photogenic remains of the 12th-century **Capel Lligwy**. Follow the country lane marked 'Ancient Monument' near the roundabout before Moelfre to find the car park.

🍴 Sleeping & Eating

Tyddyn Isaf Camping & Caravan Park CAMPGROUND £
(☑ 01248-410203; www.tyddynisaf.co.uk; Lligwy Bay, Dulas; sites from £36; 🐾) With sandy, undeveloped Lligwy Bay close at hand, this large, well-groomed campground is a repeat winner of the David Bellamy Conservation Award and makes a great base for family holidays. Facilities include a restaurant, bar and playground with a very cool lighthouse slide.

Ann's Pantry CAFE £
(☑ 01248-410386; www.annspantry.co.uk; mains £6-16; ☺ 10am-5pm Sun-Fri, to 9pm Sat; ⊕) With a pretty garden setting, a fine location overlooking Moelfre Beach, and exposed stone walls and nautical memorabilia on the inside, Ann's is a local favourite. The unpretentious menu includes filled sandwiches and ciabattas, homemade soup, grilled fish and burgers. On Saturday nights, Ann ups her game with beef stroganoff, salmon bake and more.

ⓘ Getting There & Away

Every 45 minutes or so, bus 62 heads to/from Amlwch (20 minutes), Benllech (six minutes), Menai Bridge (25 minutes) and Bangor (35 minutes).

Church Bay (Porth Swtan)

A tiny smidgeon of a village above a beautiful half-moon bay, Porth Swtan is one of the earliest settlements on Anglesey. Reachable via some picturesquely steep and narrow country lanes, it's both a foodie hotspot and a fine place to spend a warm day, sunbathing or shrimping in the rock pools.

◉ Sights

Swtan HOUSE
(☑ 01407-730186; https://swtan.cymru/home.html; Cyfeillion Swtan, Dilwyn; adult/child £4/1; ☺ noon-4pm Tue-Sun Easter-Sep) The last surviving thatched cottage on Anglesey, Swtan has been restored to provide a glimpse of life in the 19th century, with a central living and sleeping area abutted by the grain store, hen house and other outbuildings.

✖ Eating

Wavecrest Cafe
CAFE **£**

(📞 01407-730650; www.wavecrestcafe.co.uk; Rhydwyn; mains £5-10; ⊙10.30am-5pm Thu-Sun, daily summer holidays) This great little cafe is all about home-cooked food, prepared by friendly owner Penny. Unmissables include the fish pie and the melt-in-your-mouth pulled beef brisket in an artisan bun. If there's a few of you, enjoy a roast-meat platter on the picnic tables overlooking the sea, and don't leave without sampling the homemade ice cream.

Lobster Pot
SEAFOOD **£££**

(📞 01407-730241; http://thelobsterpotrestaurant. co.uk; Church Bay; mains £13-25; ⊙noon-2.30pm & 4.30-7pm Tue-Sat summer, shorter hours rest of year) Over 70 years old, this local institution is famous for its seafood. Its dedication to locavorism is admirable: the lamb, mussels, oysters and steak all come from Anglesey. Start with the oysters and progress to the lobster, grilled with garlic butter, or Thermidor, or buried under cairns of melted Welsh cheddar (lobster mornay). Great sea views from the outdoor tables.

❶ Getting There & Away

Bus The nearest buses stop a little over a mile away at Rhydwyn, but only once daily, so having your own wheels is pretty much essential. Bus 61 heads to Holyhead (25 minutes), Cemaes (12 minutes) and Amlwch (20 minutes).

Holyhead (Caergybi)

POP 11,864

In the heyday of the mail coaches, Holyhead (confusingly pronounced 'holly head') was the vital terminus of the London road and the main hub for onward boats to Ireland. The coming of the railway only increased the flow of people through town, but the recent increase in cheap flights has reduced the demand for ferries and Holyhead has fallen on hard times. Unless you're intending to catch a ferry to Ireland, Anglesey's largest town has little to detain you, though there are some lovely places to stay and eat at the nearby villages of Trearddur Bay and Rhoscolyn, 2 miles and around 5 miles south, respectively.

History

The area has a rich prehistoric and Roman past, visible in the impressive herringbone walls of the 4th-century fort from which the town takes its Welsh name, Caer Gybi. On the site of the fort stands St Cybi's Church, founded as a monastic settlement around 540.

◉ Sights

★South Stack Cliffs RSPB Reserve
WILDLIFE RESERVE

(📞 01407-762100; www.rspb.org.uk/wales; South Stack Rd; ⊙visitor centre 10am-5pm, cafe 10am-3pm; 🅿) **FREE** Two miles west of Holyhead, the sea vents its fury against the vertiginous South Stack Cliffs, an important Royal Society for the Protection of Birds (RSPB) reserve where up to 9000 seabirds nest. In May and June, guillemots, razorbills and 15 loved-up puffin couples congregate here, while choughs, fulmars, peregrine falcons and numerous other species may be spotted throughout the year. You can get information, hire binoculars and book guided walks at the visitor centre.

A steep, serpentine flight of steps leads down to the suspension bridge that crosses to the South Stack Lighthouse for tremendous cliff views. Numerous paths lead into the bracken-covered, hilly interior, climbing 219m **Holyhead Mountain** (Mynydd Twr) and skirting Neolithic stone circles. For a sheltered view, head to **Twr Ellin** (Ellin's Tower; April to September), a birdwatcher magnet equipped with binoculars, telescopes and a TV with a live feed from cameras on the cliffs.

Caer y Twr, one of Wales' most impressive Iron Age sites (open 10am to 4pm daily, admission free), is found at the blustery summit of Holyhead Mountain, but if you're not up for a 45-minute hike, there are also remains of Neolithic round houses a short stroll along a path that's opposite the car park.

South Stack Lighthouse
LIGHTHOUSE

(📞 01407-763900; www.trinityhouse.co.uk; South Stack Rd; adult/child £6/3; ⊙10am-4pm Easter-early Sep) The rocky islet of South Stack (Ynys Lawd) has a gloriously end-of-the-earth feel, with waves crashing around the base of the cliffs and guillemots and razorbills nesting overhead. The trail down to the rickety old bridge anchoring it to Holy Island is not for the faint-hearted, with 400 slippery steps and the promise of a steep return climb. South Stack is 3 miles west of Holyhead along South Stack Rd.

Holyhead

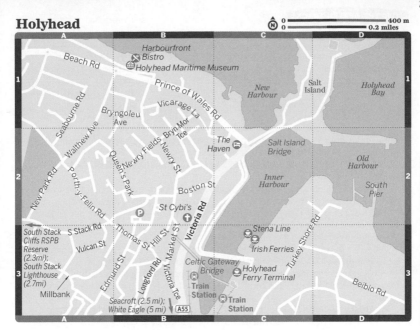

Admission includes a tour of the 28m-high lighthouse, built in 1809, reputedly haunted and still operating. The last lighthouse keeper departed in 1984, when operation became fully automated. It's now controlled from a remote planning centre in Harwich, Essex.

St Cybi's CHURCH
(www.holyheadparishchurches.co.uk/st-cybis-church-holyhead; Victoria Rd; ☉ hours vary) FREE St Cybi, the son of a 6th-century Cornish king, became a priest and eventually washed up in North Wales, where the King of Gwynedd gave him an old Roman naval fort in which to base a religious community. The Gothic church came much later, with the oldest parts built in the 13th century. Interesting medieval carvings peer out from the walls, while the light inside is softened by beautiful stained-glass windows from William Morris' workshop.

Holyhead Maritime Museum MUSEUM
(☎ 01407-769745; www.holyheadmaritimemuseum.co.uk; Newry Beach; adult/child £5/free; ☉ 10am-4pm Tue-Sun Easter-Oct; ℗♿) Small but lovingly restored, this little museum is housed in what is believed to be the oldest lifeboat house in Wales (c 1858). It makes for a family-friendly outing, with model ships, photographs and exhibits on Holyhead's maritime history from Roman times

onwards. Admire curiosities such as a mammoth's jawbone (unearthed in Holyhead Harbour in 1864) and the vintage hand-cranked diving pump, and catch the exhibition 'Holyhead at War' in the adjacent WWII air-raid shelter.

🛏 Sleeping & Eating

The Haven GUESTHOUSE £
(☎ 01407-760254; www.thehavenholyhead.com; Marine Sq; s/d from £40/50; ℗🛇🐾) About as close as you can get to the ferry, this welcoming guesthouse is run by Phil and Sian, who go out of their way to make you feel welcome. Rooms are spotless and snug, and it's worth spending an extra £10 on a sea-view room. Breakfast costs £5.

★ **Seacroft** B&B ££
(☎ 01407-860348; www.theseacroft.pub; Raven-spoint Rd, Trearddur Bay; s/d from £67/77; ℗🛇) There is much to love about this wonderful pub, situated at the southern end of Trearddur Bay's half-moon white-sand beach. Setting aside, there's half-a-dozen homely rooms upstairs, decked out in soothing neutral shades. Downstairs you can tuck into superlative versions of fish and chips, steak-and-ale pie and stacked burgers, washed down with award-winning cask ales.

ISLE OF ANGLESEY COASTAL PATH

Anglesey is a big draw for walkers thanks to the **Isle of Anglesey Coastal Path** (www.angleseycoastalpath.co.uk), a 130-mile route passing through a watery landscape of coastal heath, salt marsh, clifftops and beaches. It's well waymarked and not particularly gruelling, especially if you stick to the leisurely 12-day itinerary that's suggested, ranging from seven to 13 miles a day (strong walkers could easily slice off a few days), or alternatively tackle the stages as day hikes.

The official trailhead is at St Cybi's church in Holyhead, and though the path reaches a maximum altitude of just 219m, don't be fooled – its up-and-down nature means you'll be ascending over 4000m! Some of the stages, particularly the far-northern legs from Cemaes Bay to Church Bay, make for bracing strolls against a dramatic backdrop of wild, windswept scenery.

A great, introductory day walk from Beaumaris takes in the ancient monastic site of Penmon Priory (p295), Penmon Point (p295) with views across to Puffin Island, and Llanddona, a Blue Flag beach, for a refreshing dip. Arguably the most dramatic and scenic section runs from Treardddur Bay to Holyhead, passing picturesque coves and the sea-battered cliffs around the South Stack lighthouse.

Ordnance Survey (OS) Explorer Maps 262 (west coast) and 263 (east coast) are helpful, as is the *Isle of Anglesey Coastal Path – Official Guide* by Carl Rogers.

Public transport also shadows the route, so it's possible to skip stages (though you may miss out on the badge and certificate conferred on those who complete the entire circuit).

Anglesey Walking Holidays (☎01248-713611; www.angleseywalkingholidays.com; 3 Pen Rallt, Menai Bridge; per person from £375) offers self-guided walking and cycling packages, including accommodation, breakfast, luggage transfers and transport between trailheads.

White Eagle   GASTROPUB ££
(☎01407-860267; www.white-eagle.co.uk; Rhoscolyn; mains £12-18; ⊗kitchen noon-9pm, bar to 11pm; P♿☻) This busy gastropub, with a huge deck and gardens for kids to roam, is *the* place to eat and sample quality beers in this obscure southern corner of Holy Island. The seasonal menu (dry-aged steaks from Pwllheli, mussels from Menai Strait) reflects the pub's relationship with local farmers and producers, the portions are generously pub-sized and the service is friendly.

Harbourfront Bistro   INTERNATIONAL ££
(☎01407-763433; www.harbourfrontbistro.co.uk; Newry Beach; mains £12-16; ⊗noon-2.30pm Tue-Sun, 6-9pm Thu-Sat) For good food and sea views, this cosy little bistro adjoining the Maritime Museum (p299) is hard to beat. Sandwiches and baguettes are served alongside cooked lunches, along with coffee and pastries outside mealtimes. The deck is a relaxed spot to watch ships approaching the harbour on summer evenings.

ℹ Information

Holyhead doesn't have a tourist office, but some of the local stores stock brochures. The South Stack Cliffs RSPB Reserve visitor centre (p298) is a good source of advice about local walks.

ℹ Getting There & Away

Bus From the main local bus station, destinations include Bangor (route 4R/4B/X4; 1¾ hours, 14 daily Monday to Saturday) via Treardddur (15 minutes) and Menai Bridge (1½ hours); and Cemaes (61; 14 minutes, four daily Monday to Saturday).

Ferry When the weather's poor, it always pays to check with the ferry companies – **Irish Ferries** (☎0818 300 400; www.irishferries.com; foot passenger/motorcycle/car from £33/62/153) and **Stena Line** (☎08447 707 070; www.stenaline.co.uk; foot passenger/bicycle/car from £33/43/152) – before heading to the **ferry terminal** (www.holyheadport.com), as services are sometimes cancelled. Otherwise, each offers four daily services to Dublin.

Train From the **train station** (London Rd), trains head to/from Rhosneigr (£4.40, 10 minutes, 10 daily), Bangor (£9.50, 30 minutes, one to two hourly), Conwy (£15, one to 1¼ hours, 12 daily) and London Euston (£75, 3¾ hours, several daily).

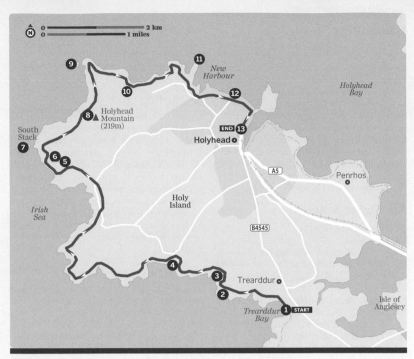

✦ Coastal Walk
Trearddur Bay to Holyhead

START TREARDDUR BEACH CAR PARK
END ST CYBI'S CHURCH
LENGTH 12 MILES; FIVE TO SIX HOURS

This walk takes in one of the most interesting sections of the Isle of Anglesey Coastal Path, circling the northern half of Holy Island. It's part of the Wales Coastal Path; look for the blue-and-yellow discs that point the way. To reach the start, catch bus 4 from Holyhead (10 minutes, hourly, Monday to Saturday).

Scallop-shaped ❶ **Trearddur Bay** has a sandy beach edged by rocks. Head right and continue along the path as it passes a succession of rocky coves. For the most part, the waymarked route hugs the road, but it does cut a few corners. At ❷ **Porth y Pwll**, a tiny bay with a scrap of sand, it leaves the road and rounds a headland before reaching the larger beach at ❸ **Porth y Post**.

The route then follows the road before heading to the cliffs and arching back to picturesque ❹ **Porth Dafarch**. From here the

path takes an amble along the cliffs before eventually coming back to the road, crossing it and continuing parallel to it. It then joins the narrow road heading to ❺ **Twr Ellin** (Ellin's Tower) and the ❻ **RSPB Visitor Centre** (p298). There's a cafe and toilet here, making it the perfect pit stop. If you're making good time and feeling energetic, stop to explore ❼ **South Stack Lighthouse** (p298), but beware: it's a very steep walk back up.

Pick up the track again for the most remote section of the walk, edging alongside ❽ **Holyhead Mountain** (219m) towards ❾ **North Stack**. Here the path loops back and passes ❿ **Breakwater Country Park** (another handy toilet and coffee stop) and then skirts the base of the ⓫ **breakwater** before reaching Holyhead. Walk along the promenade past the ⓬ **Maritime Museum** (p299) and then follow the road towards the port. Turn right onto Victoria Rd and follow it until you see the gate of ⓭ **St Cybi's** (p299) church on your right.

Rhosneigr

POP 840

The seaside village of Rhosneigr encompasses several bays, including a long, dune-backed, sandy beach – one of Anglesey's most beautiful. A popular resort in Edwardian times, but in decline since, Rhosneigr found a second wind (ahaha) in recent years and has reinvented itself as Anglesey's windsurfing and kitesurfing capital, with conditions most favourable on the north beach. Opportunistic surfers occasionally hit the waves here as well, particularly on the southern Broad Beach.

◉ Sights & Activities

★ Barclodiad y Gawres

Burial Mound   ARCHAEOLOGICAL SITE

(Cadw; https://cadw.gov.wales/visit/places-to-visit/barclodiad-y-gawres-burial-chamber; off A4080; ◷10am-4pm) FREE Sitting on a headland above the surfers' haven of Trecastle Bay, two miles south of Rhosneigr, Barclodiad y Gawres (the Giantess' Apronful) is Wales' largest neolithic tomb. When the original cross-shaped burial chamber of one of the most remarkable archaeological remains in the UK was excavated in the 1950s, archaeologists found five standing stones inside, decorated with spirals and zigzags similar to those found only inside the Bryn Celli Ddu (p293) mound and in Ireland's Boyne Valley.

Funsport   WATER SPORTS

(☑01407-810899; www.funsportonline.co.uk; 1 Beach Tce; ◷9am-5pm) Right by the beach at the bottom of town, this place rents out boards and wetsuits and provides a bragging venue with the Surf Cafe upstairs. It also offers taster courses in surfing (£20/35 for one/two hours), windsurfing (two hours £35 to £60) and kitesurfing (one hour £25 to £35).

✗ Eating

Oyster Catcher   BISTRO ££

(☑01407-812829; www.oystercatcheranglesey.co.uk; Maelog Lake, Rhosneigr; mains £14-20; ◷10am-11pm Mon-Sat, noon-8pm Sun; P) ✐ This striking, glass-fronted structure, backed by windswept sand dunes and with an upstairs open-air terrace overlooking the sand, serves hearty, well-prepared gastropub dishes to hungry walkers and surfers. Standout offerings include local oysters, steamed Menai mussels and the lobster roll.

❶ Getting There & Away

Anglesey Airport (☑01407-878056; Minffordd Rd) Flights to Cardiff with Eastern Airways (www.easternairways.com).

Bus Routes include 25 to Holyhead (35 minutes, three daily Monday to Saturday) and 45 to Llangefni (30 minutes, five daily Monday to Saturday).

Train From the **train station** (Station Rd), direct trains head to Holyhead (£4.40, 11 to 19 minutes, nine daily), Bangor (£6.70, 24 minutes, nine daily), Conwy (£14.80, 45 minutes to one hour) and Shrewsbury (£46.40, 2½ to three hours). Rhosneigr is a request stop, so inform the conductor that you wish to alight here.

Understand
Wales

History

Everywhere you go in Wales you'll see the nation's history written large. The landscape is littered with ancient burial mounds, standing stones, earthworks, rusting machinery, sculpted mountainsides, great mounds of slag, sturdy churches, dour chapels and evocative graveyards – and everywhere castles, castles and more castles. Travel through Wales with its history in mind and you'll find it easier to understand Welsh resentment and Welsh pride.

Early History

Little is known of Britain's earliest peoples, but by 3500 BCE the cromlechs, standing stones and stone circles that are evident throughout Britain today started to be raised. This is evidence of the presence of fairly large communities; for instance, it is estimated that it would have taken 200 people to raise the giant capstone at Tinkinswood, near Cardiff, into place.

It was much later, around 600 BCE, that the first wave of Celts arrived on Brtiain's shores and with them their poets and priests – the druids – who were revered as much for their knowledge as for their spiritual power. By the 3rd century BCE, they were the dominant force in Europe, with Celtic tribes ranging from Turkey to Ireland. The Celts had a defining role in Britain, making enormous technical and artistic advances and introducing a new social hierarchy, belief system and language. The British variant on the Celtic language became known as Brythonic, which later developed into modern Welsh.

The Romans

When Julius Caesar arrived in Britain in 55 BCE with 10,000 Roman legionnaires, the Celtic tribes who had occupied the island for over half a millennia put up a staunch resistance. In CE 43, the Romans returned with 40,000 men and proceeded to advance through Britain. Mona (Anglesey) was the centre of Druidic power and resistance to Rome. After the druids' last stand on Anglesey in CE 60, the Romans eventually took control of present-day Wales and England. They cemented their rule by building a series of military forts, the remains of which can still be seen

In a time renowned for its bloodshed, one Welsh ruler during the 12th century decided to make a different sort of statement. The gathering of musicians and bards at the fortress of Lord Rhys ap Gruffydd at Cardigan Castle over the winter of 1176 became the precursor of the modern eisteddfod, Wales' biggest cultural celebration to this day.

TIMELINE	250,000 BCE	600 BCE	CE 60
	Someone loses a tooth in a cave in Denbighshire, not realising what excitement it will cause a quarter of a million years later when it becomes the earliest evidence of a human presence in Wales.	The Celtic people begin to settle in Britain. It's unclear whether they displaced the indigenous people or whether the indigenous people adopted the Celtic culture and language.	The Druids' last stand on Anglesey unleashes the brute force of the Roman army, who set about destroying the island's sacred groves and shrines.

THE RED LADY

In 1823, the Reverend William Buckland discovered a human skeleton dyed with red ochre in a cave on the Gower coast. As he found jewellery buried along with the bones, Buckland assumed that the deceased must be a woman. Being a devout Christian, he believed she must date from the Roman era, as she could not be older than the biblical flood. The 'Red Lady', as the skeleton became known, was therefore a Roman prostitute or witch, according to Buckland.

Modern analysis shows that the Red Lady was actually a man – possibly a tribal chief – who died, aged around 21, some 33,000 years ago. Dating from before Britain was abandoned during the last ice age, his are the oldest human remains found in the UK to date, and represent the oldest known ritual burial in Western Europe. The Red Lady's peaceful seaside slumber is no more – he's now residing at Oxford University.

in Cardiff Castle, Caernarfon and, most impressively, at the 'city of the legion' Caerleon. In true Imperial fashion, they gradually Romanised the local population, while allowing them to maintain their own language, customs and gods – at least until Christianity became the official state religion in 391.

Wales Is Born

In the wake of the fall of the Western Roman Empire in the 5th century, various kingdoms arose across Britain and a new threat surfaced in the form of Germanic tribes such as the Saxons and the Angles. This era is shrouded in legend but it is quite possible that there was a figure such as King Arthur who briefly held the Saxon invaders at bay, inspiring romantic fables in the process.

Eventually, the Anglo-Saxons conquered most of present-day England, with native Brythonic-speakers holding on in remote places such as Wales and Cornwall. To this day, the Welsh word for the English is *Saeson* (Saxon); the English word for the Welsh derives from the old Anglo-Saxon word for foreigner. For their part, the Welsh started to refer to themselves as *cymry*, a word meaning 'fellow countrymen', and a separate Welsh identity was born – distinct for the first time from the rest of Britain.

Religion was a point of difference between the Christian Welsh and the pagan Saxons. In the 6th century religious communities were founded all over Wales. Many of these *llan* were associated with charismatic leaders, ushering in the so-called 'Age of Saints' and bequeathing Wales with a fair share of their current place names (Llandudno – St Tudno's community; Llandeilo – St Teilo's community etc). St David became a key figure, establishing his eponymous town as a centre of religion and learning.

383	c 410	5th century	6th century
Magnus Maximus, commander of Britain, becomes emperor of the Western Roman Empire. He enters Welsh mythology as Macsen Wledig, whose 'dream' inspires the architecture of Caernarfon Castle.	The Romans pull out of Britain and the empire starts to crumble. A number of disparate kingdoms emerge in Wales, including Morgannwg (Glamorgan), Gwent, Dyfed, Gwynedd and Powys.	The Saxons and other Germanic tribes arrive in Britain, eventually overrunning all of England. The Celtic Britons hold fast in the west where a separate Welsh identity starts to form.	Wales enters the 'Age of Saints'. Religious communities spring up all over the country, including the one founded in Pembrokeshire by Wales' patron saint, David.

During the 9th and 10th centuries savage coastal attacks in the south by Danish and Norse pirates forced the small kingdoms of Wales to co-operate. Rhodri Mawr (Rhodri the Great), a charismatic leader, managed to unite most of the kingdoms, only for them to be split among his sons.

His grandson, Hywel Dda (Hywel the Good), reunified the country and then went on to consolidate its laws, decreeing communal agricultural practices and affording women and children greater rights than other legal systems of the time.

Enter the Normans

When the Normans claimed England in 1066, William the Conqueror set up feudal barons, the Marcher Lords, along the Welsh border to secure his kingdom. Under sustained attack, the Welsh rulers were pushed back and it was not until Llywelyn ap Gruffydd (Llywelyn the Last) that a pan-Welsh leader again emerged. He adopted the title 'Prince of Wales' and by 1267 had forced England's Henry III to recognise him as such. But Llywelyn's triumph was short-lived and by 1277 he had lost much of what he had achieved.

Edward I fought to control the Welsh upstart and eventually killed both Llywelyn and his brother Dafydd. He then set up his 'Iron Ring' of castles to prevent further Welsh revolt. Of these, Caernarfon is the ultimate expression of military and royal authority, and it was here that his infant son, the future Edward II, was born. The younger Edward was later invested with the title Prince of Wales, a title bestowed, to this day, on the eldest son of the reigning monarch.

Curiously, against this troubled backdrop, Welsh storytelling and literature flourished. In 1176, Rhys ap Gruffydd (Lord Rhys), one of Wales' great leaders, convened the first bardic tournament – the original eisteddfod. The 13th-century Black Book of Carmarthen, the oldest surviving Welsh-language manuscript, also dates from this period and is today held at the National Library of Wales in Aberystwyth.

Owain Glyndŵr

Anti-English feeling was rife throughout Wales by 1400 and Owain ap Gruffydd (better known as Owain Glyndŵr), a descendant of the royal house of Powys, became the uprising's leader, declaring himself Prince of Wales and attacking neighbouring marcher lords.

Henry IV reacted harshly and passed a series of penal laws imposing severe restrictions on the Welsh. This only increased support for the rebellion and by 1404 Glyndŵr controlled most of Wales, capturing Harlech and Aberystwyth castles and summoning a parliament at Machynlleth and at Harlech. But Glyndŵr met his match in Prince Henry, son of Henry IV and hero of the Battle of Agincourt. After a series

A present-day reminder of the tensions between the Anglo-Saxons (in the form of the Kingdom of Mercia, under King Offa) and the Welsh is Offa's Dyke, the 8th-century fortification marking the boundary between the two. Offa's Dyke Path national trail traces this border, which still largely aligns with Wales' border today.

1066	1134	1176	13th century
The Normans invade England. By 1086, the Kingdom of Gwent has fallen and there are Norman castles in Chepstow, Monmouth and Caerleon, controlled by the powerful Marcher Lords.	Robert, the eldest son of William the Conqueror, dies in Cardiff Castle, where he had been imprisoned for many years by his brother, Henry I of England.	Rhys ap Gruffydd (Lord Rhys) convenes the first bardic tournament at Cardigan Castle, the original eisteddfod, as Welsh literature and storytelling flourish.	Llywelyn ap Gruffydd emerges as a unifying Welsh leader but is trounced by Edward I, who builds a ring of castles to suppress the Welsh uprising.

of defeats, Glyndŵr's allies deserted him and after 1406 he faded into myth-shrouded obscurity. Glyndŵr remains a great hero to the Welsh; he is memorialised in the Owain Glyndŵr Centre in Machynlleth, devoted to his life story, and the Glyndŵr's Way National Trail, a multiday walking track connecting places associated with him.

The Acts of Union

By the later part of the 15th century, the Welsh and English had learnt to coexist uneasily. With the Wars of the Roses raging, the Welsh cast their hopes on Harri Tudur (in English, Henry Tudor), viewing him as the prophesied ruler who would restore their fortunes. Born in Pembroke Castle, his claim to the English throne was through his Lancastrian mother, but his father was descended from a noble Welsh family from Anglesey. After years of exile in Brittany, Henry defeated Richard III in the Battle of Bosworth Field in 1485 and ascended the throne as Henry VII. This began the Tudor dynasty, which would reign until the death of Elizabeth I in 1603.

But it was Henry VIII who brought real change with the Tudor Acts of Union in 1536 and 1543 to establish English sovereignty over the country. Although the Welsh became equal citizens and were granted parliamentary representation for the first time, Welsh law was abolished and English was declared the official language of law and administration. The glory years of the Cistercian abbeys as centres of learning also came to an end when Henry VIII declared the independence of the Church of England in 1534 and dissolved the abbeys in 1536.

The effect of the Acts of Union was to make Wales a constituent part of England. Later, when Scotland and Ireland were brought into the fold to form the United Kingdom, Wales wasn't even represented on the Union Flag. Throughout the next two centuries, the Welsh gentry became increasingly Anglicised, while the majority of the ordinary people continued to speak Welsh.

The marcher lordships had a degree of autonomy from the English crown and maintained a separate legal status right up until the time of Henry VIII. Eventually the Marches came to cover much of the south and east of Wales and some of the neighbouring English counties.

The Reformation

Protestantism was initially slow to catch on in Wales and for many years places such as Monmouthshire and the Llŷn Peninsula had a determined Catholic underground. Under the reign of Elizabeth I, several Welsh priests were caught and executed; they're now recognised as saints by the Catholic Church. Acceptance of the Church of England was greatly assisted by the translation of the Bible into Welsh and the commencement of services in the native tongue.

In the 18th century, the Nonconformist Protestant churches – particularly the Methodists – started to make great inroads into the Welsh-speaking population, and eventually Wales became a land of

HISTORY THE ACTS OF UNION

1301	1400	1536 & 1543	1563
Edward I formally invests his son Edward with the title Prince of Wales, starting the tradition where the heir-apparent to the English throne is granted that title.	Welsh nationalist hero Owain Glyndŵr leads the Welsh in rebellion and is declared 'Prince of Wales' by his followers, but his rebellion is short-lived and victory fleeting.	The Tudor Acts of Union introduced by Henry VIII unite Wales and England, granting equal rights and parliamentary representation, but make English the main language.	Church services begin to be held in Welsh. Before then the Reformation had seen services move from one little-understood foreign language (Latin) to another (English). Protestantism starts to catch on.

chapels. Until very recently, the chapel was one of the defining symbols of Welsh life, with Sundays being bookended by lengthy services accompanied by hearty hymn-singing. Wherever you go in Wales, even in quite small villages, you'll see multiple chapels – although these days many are abandoned or have been converted into museums, apartments or even bars.

Romantic Wales

Towards the end of the 18th century the influence of the Romantic revival made the wild landscapes of Wales fashionable with genteel travellers. The works of landscape painters such as Richard Wilson did much to popularise the rugged mountains and ruined castles, and the rediscovery of Celtic and Druidic traditions fuelled a growing cultural revival and sense of Welsh identity.

Scholars were increasingly concerned about the need to preserve the culture and heritage of their country and efforts were made to collect and publish literature. Edward Williams (Iolo Morganwg to use his bardic name) went on to revive ancient bardic competitions and held the first 'modern' eisteddfod in Carmarthen in 1819.

Industrialisation & Unrest

The iron industry had been growing steadily across Wales since the mid-18th century with an explosion of ironworks around Merthyr Tydfil. Industrialists constructed roads, canals and tramways, changing the face of the valleys forever. Major engineering developments from this period include Thomas Telford's spectacular Pontcysyllte Aqueduct and his graceful suspension bridge at Conwy.

As the Industrial Revolution gathered pace, workers were increasingly dissatisfied with the appalling conditions and low rates of pay. Trade unions emerged and the first half of the 19th century was characterised by calls for a universal right to vote. In 1839, the Chartist Riots broke out in towns such as Newport when a petition of more than one million signatures was rejected by Westminster. Between 1839 and 1843, the Rebecca Riots broke out in the rural southwest. The name 'Rebecca' refers to a biblical verse: 'Rebecca...let thy seed possess the gate of those who hate them'. The 'Daughters of Rebecca' (men dressed in women's clothes) attacked the hated turnpike tollgates, which charged hefty tolls for those using the roads.

A quarter of a million people were employed in Wales' coal industry in the 1920s. Remnants of this heyday can be seen in World Heritage–listed Blaenavon and dozens of other communities in the valleys.

Reform & the Depression

By the second half of the 19th century, coal had superseded iron and the population of Wales exploded. In 1867, industrial workers and small tenant farmers were given the right to vote and the 1868 elections were

1642–49	1759–82	1865	1867
Major battles are fought at St Fagans and Pembroke during the English Civil War between the forces of King Charles I and the Parliamentarians led by Oliver Cromwell.	With the Industrial Revolution gripping the South Wales valleys, Dowlais and Merthyr Tydfil ironworks start production and Bethesda's slate quarry opens for business.	A Welsh colony is set up in Patagonia, Argentina. Welsh is the language of the courts, schools, chapels and newspapers until 1896.	Male industrial workers and small tenant farmers are given the right to vote. Suffrage for men is broadened over the following two decades.

a turning point for Wales. Henry Richard was elected as Liberal MP for Merthyr Tydfil, and brought ideas of land reform and native language to parliament for the first time.

The Secret Ballot Act of 1872 and the Reform Act of 1884 broadened suffrage and gave a voice to the rising tide of resentment over the hardships of the valleys and the payment of tithes (taxes) to the church. In 1900, Merthyr Tydfil returned James Keir Hardie as Wales' (and, along with Richard Bell in Derby, the UK's) first Labour MP.

National sentiment grew and education improved substantially. During WWI, Wales boomed and living standards rose as Welsh coal and agriculture fed the economy.

Between the world wars, the country suffered the results of economic depression and thousands were driven to emigrate in search of employment. The Labour Party weathered the storm and, as the 20th century progressed, became the dominant political force in Wales. In 1925, six young champions of Welsh nationalism founded Plaid Cenedlaethol Cymru (the Welsh Nationalist Party; later shortened to Plaid Cymru) in Pwllheli and began a campaign for self-government.

Postwar Wales & Industrial Decline

The postwar years were not kind to Wales. The coal industry went into steep decline, forcing the closure of mines and a bitter struggle as unemployment levels rose to twice the UK average. The Welsh language was suffering and national pride was at an all-time low.

The final blow came in 1957 when the North Wales village of Capel Celyn, near Bala, and the surrounding valley were flooded to provide water for the city of Liverpool, despite vigorous campaigning across Wales. There were too few Welsh MPs in the House of Commons to oppose the project and resentment still lingers over the issue, even today.

In 1847, the Education Commission published a damning report on education in Wales. It questioned Welsh morality and blamed the influences of religious nonconformity and the Welsh language for allegedly lax morals. The introduction of the 'Welsh Not', a ban on speaking Welsh in schools, created a tide of anger.

THE ABERFAN DISASTER

On 21 October 1966, Wales experienced one of its worst disasters. Heavy rain loosened an already dangerously unstable spoil heap above Aberfan, 4 miles south of Merthyr Tydfil, and sent a 500,000-tonne mudslide of liquefied coal slurry down onto the village. It wiped out a row of terraced houses and ploughed into Pantglas primary school. Most of the 144 killed were young children from the school.

Today, the A470 Cardiff–Merthyr Tydfil road cuts right through the spot where the spoil heap once stood. The site of the school has been turned into a memorial garden, while the village cemetery contains a long, double row of matching headstones, a mute and moving memorial to those who died.

1900	1916	1925	1939–45
James Keir Hardie, a Scotsman, becomes the first Labour MP to enter parliament after winning a seat in the Welsh mining town of Merthyr Tydfil.	With WWI in progress, David Lloyd George becomes prime minister, the only Welshman to have ever held the role. Welsh was his first language, English his second.	The Welsh Nationalist Party or Plaid Cenedlaethol Cymru (later Plaid Cymru) is formed and begins campaign for self-government.	WWII rages across Europe and much of Africa, Asia and the Pacific. Parts of Wales are bombed by the Germans, notably Swansea, Cardiff and the Rhondda Valley.

The 1960s became a decade of protest in Wales and Plaid Cymru gained ground. Welsh pop music began to flourish and Welsh publishing houses and record labels were set up. In 1962, Cymdeithas yr Iaith Gymraeg (the Welsh Language Society) was founded. Further electoral successes by Plaid Cymru in the 1970s started people thinking about a measure of Welsh self-government. In 1976, the Welsh Development Agency (WDA) was established to foster new business opportunities across Wales in the face of the decline in traditional industry.

Margaret Thatcher's Conservative Party initiated a sweeping campaign of privatisation during the 1980s, leading to severe cuts in the coal, manufacturing and steel industries. Agriculture, too, was in a state of disarray and unemployment began to soar. Welsh living standards lagged far behind the rest of Britain and, with the collapse of the UK Miners' Strike (1984–85), Welsh morale hit rock bottom. Many mines were subsequently shut down and whole communities destroyed. Some have since reopened purely as tourist attractions, notably Big Pit at Blaenavon and the Rhondda Heritage Park.

Something good did come out of the '80s, however, with the 1982 establishment of S4C (Sianel Pedwar Cymru), the Welsh-language TV

THE NEWPORT RISING

Chartism, a parliamentary reform movement that arose during the early years of Queen Victoria's reign, was particularly strong in Wales. It argued for a charter of reforms, most of which we would consider to be essential to democracy today: a vote for every man in a secret ballot (up until this time only male landowners could vote); no property requirement for Members of Parliament; equal-sized electorates; and payment for MPs (making it possible for poor men to serve).

On 4 November 1839, some 5000 men from the Usk, Ebbw and Rhymney Valleys converged on Newport, intent on taking control of the town and sparking off a national uprising in what would become the last mass armed rebellion against the authorities in Great Britain. The men tried to storm the Westgate Hotel on Commercial St, where several Chartists were being held. Police and infantrymen inside fired into the crowd, killing at least 20 people. Five men were subsequently imprisoned and three were sentenced to death (but were instead transported to Australia). The bodies of 10 rioters were surreptitiously recovered and buried secretly in the churchyard in unmarked graves.

The rising is remembered in several plaques and monuments around Newport, notably near the old Westgate Hotel (corner of Stow Hill and Commercial Streets), where the masonry is still bullet-scarred. Outside, among the hurrying shoppers, is an ensemble of determined bronze figures.

Property requirements for male voters weren't completely removed until 1918. Landless women had to wait another decade for the vote.

1955	1959	1962	1966
After a ballot of members of the Welsh local authorities, Cardiff is declared the first-ever Welsh capital, garnering three times as many votes as nearest contender, Caernarfon.	Wales adopts the red dragon on a white and green background as its official flag. Henry VII, the first Tudor king, used this banner at the Battle of Bosworth Field in 1485.	Cymdeithas yr Iaith Gymraeg (the Welsh Language Society) is founded to campaign for the legal statue for the language and for Welsh-speaking radio and TV.	A colliery spoil tip collapses on the village of Aberfan, near Merthyr Tydfil, killing 116 children and 28 adults. An enquiry blames the National Coal Board for extreme negligence.

channel. Support and enthusiasm for the Welsh language increased, night courses popped up all over the country, Welsh-speaking nurseries and schools opened, university courses were established and the number of Welsh speakers started to stabilise at around 20% of the population.

Devolution

The 1997 general election brought Tony Blair's 'New Labour' to power in the UK and the devolution process got off the ground once again. In September of that year, a referendum on the establishment of the Welsh Assembly scraped through by the narrowest of margins.

Lacking the powers granted to the Scottish Parliament, the Assembly was always going to have a hard time convincing the world, including Wales, of its merit. The unveiling of the new National Assembly building in Cardiff Bay and the passing of the Government of Wales Act in 2006, creating a new legislature and executive, gave the assembly more teeth, and helped the new seat of government to become part of the fabric of daily Welsh life.

A further referendum in 2011, asking whether the Assembly should be able to create laws in its own right, rather than having to have them rubber-stamped by the UK Parliament, passed with a much stronger affirmative vote. These law-making powers are still limited in scope, but include such important areas as housing, health, social welfare, tourism, culture and the Welsh language.

After Brexit & Covid-19

In June 2016, a slim majority of the British public voted in a referendum to leave the European Union (EU). While Scotland and Northern Ireland voted to stay by a comfortable margin, the Wales result was almost identical to England's, with 53% wanting to leave versus 47% to remain.

Before the vote, Wales' First Minister Carwyn Jones warned that the Welsh economy would 'tank' in the event of a British exit from the EU. Wales had been a net benefactor from EU funding, receiving an estimated £70 per head of population. As well as direct grants, it has benefited from farming subsidies. Indeed, the area that voted the most strongly to leave – the economically depressed Ebbw Vale in South Wales – had been one of the UK's biggest recipients of EU funds.

The anti-EU result reflected concerns about the threat of immigration on jobs and a distrust of European bureaucracy, as well as a general rejection of a status quo, which had failed to improve the lot of people living in Wales' more marginalised communities.

Interestingly, aside from cosmopolitan Cardiff, the counties voting with the highest majority to remain were two of the most strongly Welsh-speaking areas: Ceredigion and Gwynedd, which could well reflect

Between 2008 and 2010, one of Wales' biggest-ever archaeological digs was carried out on Holy Island, Anglesey. Discoveries included an early neolithic hall (c 3700 BCE), one of the biggest buildings ever uncovered from this time in Britain.

1984	1997	1999	2008
Margaret Thatcher's Conservative government announces the closure of 20 coal mines. The ensuing Miners' Strike ends in 1985 with the workers defeated. Further pit closures follow.	A referendum asking whether a Welsh Assembly should be formed narrowly passes. The 'yes' vote is strongest in the west (except Pembrokeshire); the majority of people in the border counties vote 'no'.	The first National Assembly for Wales is elected, with limited powers devolved from the UK Parliament. The Assembly is led by a coalition between the Welsh Labour Party and the Liberal Democrats.	Wales' last deep coal mine closes. The Tower Colliery in Hirwaun had been bought and operated successfully by a workers' collective since the National Coal Board had deemed it uneconomic in 1994.

DAVID LLOYD GEORGE (1863–1945)

David Lloyd George began his career as the champion of Welsh populist democracy and a critic of society and its institutions. A talented and witty orator, in 1890 he won his first seat as Liberal MP for Caernarfon Boroughs and, at 27, became the youngest member of the House of Commons.

As Chancellor of the Exchequer, he launched a broad but controversial agenda of social reform, including the introduction of old-age pensions, a 1909 budget that taxed the wealthy to fund services for the poor, and the 1911 National Insurance Act to provide health and unemployment insurance. Elected prime minister in 1916 after a divisive alliance with the Conservatives, Lloyd George went on to become an energetic war leader. He excelled at a time when strong leadership was needed, dismissing red tape and forcing his opinion when necessary.

Postwar industrial unrest and economic reconstruction dogged the country, however, and he eventually agreed to Irish independence to end civil war, a solution the Conservative alliance never forgave. Accusations of corruption, financial greed and the selling of honours began to ruin his reputation. Radicals, Welsh nationalists and campaigners for women's rights all felt betrayed. In 1922, the Conservatives staged a party revolt and broke up the shaky coalition. Lloyd George resigned immediately.

His popularity faded, the Liberal Party was in disarray, political allies had abandoned him, and both the Welsh and the British working class felt thoroughly deceived. Lloyd George's political career had reached a sad anticlimax.

He died in 1945 at Llanystumdwy, where there is now a small museum devoted to his life.

the fact that Wales has often throughout history felt closer to the continent than to England.

The 2020 Covid-19 pandemic saw further surfacing of a divide between Wales and England that was more than Dyke-wide. Under the terms of devolution, Wales (like Scotland) became responsible for dealing with issues such as health, and adopted a far more cautious approach to Covid-19 than England. Whilst some Welsh regions recorded some of the highest incidences of Covid-19 at many points, other regions such as Ceredigion had almost the lowest, yet blanket lockdowns were introduced, England-originating visitors turned back by police at the border, and one of Britain's best-known travel writers, Simon Calder, was bombarded with abuse when he suggested certain parts of Mid-Wales as a potential autumn break. What is already clear, though, is that measures to curb the spread of Covid-19 have severely impacted an economy where tourism, and mainly tourism from England, is hugely important.

2011	2016	2018	2020
A further referendum is held asking whether the Welsh Assembly should be able to make laws without the approval of the UK Parliament; 64% of the population vote 'yes'.	The UK holds a referendum regarding continuing its membership of the European Union. A slim majority (52% to 48%) votes to leave.	Welshman Geraint Thomas wins what is generally considered to be sport's very toughest individual test: the Tour de France.	In February, the first instance of Covid-19 coronavirus is recorded in Wales. In March, the UK heads into lockdown as the death toll rises.

Culture

Cultural debate in Wales coalesces on one theme: identity. What is the identity of Wales in the 21st century? What are the defining elements of Welsh culture? Historically, Wales struggled to overcome negative stereotypes about its lack of sophistication. But Welsh pride has been buoyed by the success of its pop and rock stars, actors and film-makers, writers and thinkers. To be Welsh today is a complex blend of historical association, ingrained defiance and Celtic spirit.

Rugby

The Kiwis come close, but we'd argue that there's nowhere more passionate about the game of rugby union than Wales. The national team punches well above its weight, and whenever they play, every pub in every village, town and city throughout the country packs out with enthusiastic red-clad fans. In the lead-up to the 2019 World Cup, Wales was ranked the top team in the world, although it eventually finished the competition in fourth place.

The big annual tournament is the Six Nations (p66) held in February and March between Wales, England, Scotland, Ireland, Italy and France. Wales has won three out of the last eight championships. Tickets for international matches are guaranteed to sell out, while success on the pitch has turned Wales' star players, such as Alun Wyn Jones and Leigh Halfpenny, into national sporting heroes.

Rugby union is equally well supported at club level, with four teams (Swansea's Ospreys, Newport's Dragons, Llanelli's Scarlets and the Cardiff Blues) representing Wales in the Pro12 competition. The rugby season takes place between September and Easter; for more information, check the Welsh Rugby Union website (www.wru.co.uk).

Music

Wales is known as 'the land of song'. According to a Welsh proverb, 'to be born Welsh is to be born with music in your blood and poetry in your soul'. There are references to the Celts as a musical race from as early as the 1st century BCE, when ancient scholars wrote of their legendary bards (poets who sing songs of eulogy and satire). Jump forward to the present day, and Britain's premium award for songwriting is named after a Welshman, composer and actor Ivor Novello (1893–1951).

Today the diversity of music in Wales is huge, yet united by a common factor – music remains at the heart of this nation. The Cory Band from the Rhondda Valley has won the European Brass Band Championships seven times. Child star Charlotte Church swapped her classical beginnings for perky pop before evolving into a more mature experimental sound. And the Welsh National Opera has continued to grow in stature since launching the career of opera singer Bryn Terfel, plucked from a North Wales sheep farm to become a national champion for the Welsh voice.

The Green Man Festival (www.greenman.net), held over four days in August near Crickhowell in Brecon Beacons National Park, has grown to be the biggest music festival in Wales, with a capacity of 25,000 people.

Folk

Traditional Welsh songs often tell stories in the form of complex verse, most commonly accompanied by the harp. Other traditional instruments include the *crwth* (an archaic string instrument played with a bow), the pibgorn (a reed pipe horn) and the Welsh bagpipes. The flame of traditional Welsh music is kept alight by both orthodox folk bands and emerging nu-folk artists. Catch a live session at local pubs, folk clubs or smaller festivals, and look out for bands such as 9Bach and Calan, which blend traditional and contemporary Welsh sounds with international influences. Welsh folk music even has a permanent home at Tŷ Siamas (National Centre for Welsh Folk Music) in Dolgellau. Events at the centre are an ideal way to keep abreast of new acts and influences.

Contemporary

Two of Wales' most beloved and successful musical artists rose to fame in the 1960s and are still hugely popular today: Cardiff's Dame Shirley Bassey and Pontypridd's Sir Tom Jones. Between them they have released five UK number one singles and four theme songs for James Bond movies.

Also coming to prominence at the end of the '60s was Carmarthenshire lad John Cale, firstly as an avant-garde multi-instrumentalist with hugely influential New York band, the Velvet Underground, and then as a prolific and consistently edgy solo artist. The late 1970s saw the ascendance of gravel-voiced Bonnie Tyler, who was joined at the top of the charts in the '80s by old-school rock-and-roller, Shakin' Stevens.

However, it was in the 1990s, at the tail end of the Britpop phenomenon, that the success of a cluster of Welsh indie rock groups became worthy of a pop-cultural designation all of its own: Cool Cymru. Bands such as Manic Street Preachers, Catatonia, Stereophonics, Super Furry Animals (who recorded in both English and Welsh) and comic rappers Goldie Lookin Chain changed the staid image of Wales as a nation of melodious harpists and male voice choirs forever. The Manics and Stereophonics are still going strong, while their contemporary Gruff Rhys,

---

THE EISTEDDFOD

Nothing encapsulates Welsh culture like the eisteddfod (literally a gathering or session). Infused with a sense of Celtic history and drawing heavily on the bardic tradition of verbal storytelling, this uniquely Welsh celebration is the descendant of ancient tournaments in which poets and musicians competed for a seat of honour in the households of noblemen. The first recorded tournament dates from 1176, but the tradition slowly waned following the Tudor Acts of Union in the mid-16th century. In the late 18th century, Edward Williams (better known by his bardic name of Iolo Morganwg) reinvented the eisteddfod as a modern Welsh festival.

Today the **National Eisteddfod of Wales** (Eisteddfod Genedlaethol Cymru; ☑08454-090900; www.eisteddfod.cymru; ☺Aug) is one of Europe's largest cultural events and a barometer of contemporary Welsh culture, with aspiring bands and emerging artists often making their debut there. The whole event takes place in Welsh, but there's loads of help on hand for non-Welsh speakers. The festival is held during the first week of August, alternately in North and South Wales. The **Urdd Eisteddfod** (☑0345-257 1613; www.urdd.cymru; ☺May/Jun), the youth version of the event, is held over five days from the end of May.

Another event to watch out for is the International Musical Eisteddfod (p234), which is held in Llangollen each July. Acts from over 40 countries compete with folk tunes, choral harmony and recitals. Competitions take place daily and famous names take to the stage for gala concerts every night.

MALE VOICE CHOIRS

Born out of the Temperance Movement in the mid-19th century, the m
meibion) became an institution in the coal-mining towns of the south
the collapse of the former mining communities, the choirs struggled
and some allowed women to join their ranks.

They have enjoyed a renaissance of late, with younger people sign
local choir to flex their vocal chords. In 2008, Only Men Aloud!, a Ca
part-timers, beat stiff competition to win BBC TV reality show, *Last Choir Standing*.

Local choirs still practise in the back rooms of pubs, rugby clubs and church halls each
week. Most are happy to have visitors sit in on rehearsals.

lead singer with the Super Furry Animals, has pursued an acclaimed
solo career.

Bangor-born Duffy started her career singing in Welsh but exploded
onto the charts in 2008 with English-language *Rockferry,* which went on
to win a Grammy for best pop vocal album. Her 2010 follow-up album
was nowhere near as successful, and she's now all but retired from the
music industry.

Today the Welsh music scene may not be as hyped as it once was, but
its true substance has come to the fore with an important network of
artists, labels and agencies. Look out for Welsh-language indie artists
Gwenno and Adwaith, alternative rockers Future of the Left and The Joy
Formidable, singer-songwriter Cate le Bon, indie popsters Los Campesi-
nos! and heavy metallers Bullet for My Valentine.

Cinema & TV

Blessed with striking scenery and a seemingly endless supply of excellent actors – from Richard Burton to Michael Sheen – Welsh landscapes
and faces have been gracing the silver screen since the earliest days of
cinema. Famously it was a film set in Wales, *How Green Was My Valley,*
which beat *Citizen Kane* to a Best Picture and Best Director Oscar in
1941. Other Welsh Academy Award winners include actors Hugh Griffith
(1912–1980), Ray Milland (1907–1986), Sir Anthony Hopkins, Catherine
Zeta-Jones and Christian Bale.

Like *How Green Was My Valley,* many of the best Welsh films have
explored the lives of working-class communities. Bedwas-born director
Karl Francis based *Above Us the Earth* (1977) on the true story of a colliery closure, featuring an amateur cast in real valley locations. Another
cult success was a low-budget documentary about life in a Mid-Wales
village, *Sleep Furiously* (2008), described as an elegy for the landscape
and population of Trefeurig, Ceredigion. The film was directed by Gide-
on Koppel, who himself was brought up in Trefeurig – where his family
sought refuge from Nazi Germany.

Welsh director Justin Kerrigan has enjoyed considerable commercial
success with a series of films including Cardiff-based *Human Traffic*
(1999), a story of drug-fuelled hedonistic youth that captured the late-
'90s zeitgeist. Another exploration of urban decline, this time set in
Swansea, *Twin Town* (1997) launched the career of Rhys Ifans.

Of the 21st-century crop, one of the most notable is *The Edge of Love*
(2008), a biopic about the life and loves of Dylan Thomas, featuring Matthew Rhys in the role of Thomas. The Bafta-nominated comedy-drama
Submarine (2010), set in Swansea, was critically acclaimed and enjoyed
a highly successful global release. Even more successful was *Pride* (2014),
an uplifting true story about an unlikely alliance between gay rights ac-
tivists and striking South Wales miners in the 1980s.

For more
information about
Welsh film, visit
the website of
Fflim Cymru
Wales (www.
ffilmcymruwales.
com). The BAFTA
Cymru awards
(www.bafta.org/
wales) celebrate
the work of Welsh
actors, directors
and crews.

The Welsh-language TV channel S4C has been instrumental in supporting emerging talent and promoting Welsh culture to the outside world. A fantastic success story for S4C was the Welsh-language docudrama *Solomon a Gaenor,* nominated for an Oscar for Best Foreign Language Film in 1999. Another S4C production *Eldra,* a coming-of-age tale about a young Romany girl growing up in a slate-quarrying community in North Wales, won the 2003 Spirit of Moondance award at the Sundance Film Festival.

S4C and BBC Cymru Wales have also provided a springboard for small-screen success, challenging preconceptions and fuelling independent production. One of their most ambitious coproductions was the moody police detective drama which screened in Welsh on S4C as *Y Gwyll* and in English on the BBC as *Hinterland.*

BBC Cymru Wales' golden run of productions has included the reboot of *Doctor Who,* its spin-off *Torchwood* (both filmed mainly in Cardiff), supernatural drama *Being Human,* and the much-loved sitcom *Gavin & Stacey* (the latter two were partly set in Barry).

Theatre

The leading English-language professional theatre company in Wales is the Clwyd Theatr Cymru (p230), based in Mold in northeast Wales and attracting top-name performers such as Sir Anthony Hopkins. Cardiff's acclaimed Sherman Theatre (p75) produces a wide range of productions each year, including theatre for young people and inventive adaptations of classic dramas. The highly acclaimed **Music Theatre Wales** (www.musictheatre.wales), a pioneering force in contemporary opera, has a growing international reputation.

Perhaps the most ambitious theatre event ever held in Wales was a 72-hour live production by the National Theatre Wales and Michael Sheen, held over Easter weekend in 2011. *The Passion in Port Talbot* was a hard-hitting, multi-location play loosely based on Christ's Passion, which included a 'last supper' of beer and sandwiches at a local social club.

For more, visit the website of the Arts Council of Wales (www.arts.wales).

Literature

Wales has an incredibly rich literary history, with storytelling firmly embedded in the national psyche. The Welsh language is also a defining characteristic, its lyrical nature and descriptive quality heavily influencing the style of Welsh writers. Caradoc Evans' (1883–1945) controversial collection of short stories, *My People,* was one of the first works of fiction to bring Welsh literature to a worldwide audience. Its publication in 1915 saw a move away from established nostalgic themes and instead exposed a darker side of Welsh life.

Welsh literature matured in the 1930s, with home-grown heroes taking on working-class life and developing more realistic, socially rooted works. Among the leading figures were Kate Roberts (1891–1985), who explored the experiences of a slate-quarrying family in rural Wales with *Traed Mewn Cyffion* (Feet in Chains), published in 1936. The following year, poet and painter David Jones (1895–1974) produced his epic of war, *In Parenthesis.* Perhaps the most famous of these works, due in large part to its Academy-award-winning movie adaptation, was the 1939 novel *How Green Was My Valley* (1939) by Richard Llewellyn (1906–1983), set in a coal-mining community.

In an international sense, however, it is the bad-boy genius of Welsh poetry, Dylan Thomas (1914–53), who is Wales' most notable export. He is best known for his comic play for voices, *Under Milk Wood* (first broadcast in 1954, the year after his death), describing a day in the life of an

...ious Hollywood stars, including Charlie Chaplin, Christian Bale and Catherine Zeta-Jones, first trod the boards at regional theatres in Wales. The highest-profile performances are found at the Wales Millennium Centre in Cardiff Bay, while the city's Chapter arts centre is an important venue for fringe events.

Dylan Thomas' reputation for hard drinking almost overshadows the impact of his literary works, but he is acclaimed for writing half a dozen of the greatest poems in the English language, including such timeless works as *Fern Hill* and *Do Not Go Gentle into That Good Night.*

THE POETRY OF RS THOMAS

One of Wales' most passionate and most reclusive modern writers, the priest-turned-poet RS Thomas (1913–2000), was an outspoken critic of the so-called Welsh 'cultural suicide' and a staunch supporter of unpopular causes. Nominated for the Nobel Prize in Literature in 1996, his uncompromising work has a pure, sparse style, which he used to explore his profound spirituality and the natural world.

RS Thomas was also more politically controversial than any other Welsh writer, becoming the Welsh conscience and campaigning fervently on behalf of indigenous language and culture. In the late 1980s and early 1990s, he was at the centre of a highly public row when he praised the arsonists who firebombed English-owned holiday homes in Wales.

You can follow sites closely associated with Thomas around the Llŷn Peninsula, including the Aberdaron church where he was the vicar from 1967 to 1978.

insular Welsh community. You can visit his grave and boathouse home in Laugharne.

The elegant *On the Black Hill* (1982), by Bruce Chatwin (1940–89), also evokes the joys and hardships of small-town life, exploring Welsh spirit and cross-border antipathy through the lives of torpid twin-brother farmers.

Poetry

The loss of the referendum for devolution in March 1979 was a cathartic moment for modern Welsh literature. It sparked a flood of political and engaged writing and poetry, most notably the left-wing historian Gwyn Alf Williams' re-evaluation of Welsh history in his masterpiece *When Was Wales?*

This renaissance of Welsh poetry among a younger generation of poets, such as Menna Elfyn, Myrddin ap Dafydd, Ifor ap Glyn and Iwan Llwyd, took poetry out of the chapel, study and lecture room to be performed in pubs, clubs and cloisters. This led to a series of poetry tours, making Welsh-language poetry once again a popular medium of protest and performance. Recent years have also seen an increasing crossover between Welsh and English poetry and literature, with poets and musicians, such as Twm Morys and Gwyneth Glyn, establishing new audiences with their blend of words and music.

Literary Events

Laugharne Weekend, April

Hay Festival, late May

National Eisteddfod, August

Dylan Thomas Festival, late October

Myths & Legends

Considering Wales' lyrical language, complex history, fairy-tale landscape and wealth of mysterious ancient sites, it's hardly surprising that Welsh culture is rich in legend and mythology. Embellished by generations of storytellers, musicians and poets, these tales of supernatural strength, magic, grotesque beasts and heroic adventurers offer an insight into ancient Celtic beliefs.

King Arthur

King Arthur has inspired more legends and folk tales, and given his name to more features of the landscape in Wales, than any other figure. He is mentioned in the oldest surviving Welsh manuscripts but his true identity remains unknown. Depicted variously as a giant with superhuman strength, a dwarf king who rode a goat and a Celtic god, it is most likely he was a 5th- or 6th-century cavalry leader who led early Britons against Saxon invaders. By the 9th century, Arthur was famous as a fighter throughout the British Isles and in the centuries that followed, other writers – most recently and perhaps most famously the Victorian poet Alfred Lord Tennyson – climbed on the bandwagon, weaving in love

CULTURE CASTLES & OTHER ARCHITECTURE

> **WALES IN WORDS**
> ....
> **How Green Was My Valley** (Richard Llewellyn; 1939) Spellbinding account of life in a South Wales coal-mining community.
>
> **Portrait of the Artist as a Young Dog** (Dylan Thomas; 1940) Short-story collection capturing lovely-ugly Swansea and evoking the stoic spirit of early-20th-century South Wales.
>
> **The Mabinogion** (Penguin Classics; 1976) Classic collection of folk tales.
>
> **On the Black Hill** (Bruce Chatwin; 1982) An engrossing look at 20th-century rural life in the borderlands, as experienced by an eccentric pair of twin brothers.
>
> **Wales: Epic Views of a Small Country** (Jan Morris; 1998) A love letter to Wales celebrating the origins of its culture.
>
> **Neighbours from Hell** (Mike Parker; 2007) Informed look at Anglo-Welsh rivalry.

stories, Christian symbolism and medieval pageantry to create the romance that surrounds Arthur today.

Merlin the Magician

This great Welsh wizard is most likely modelled upon Myrddin Emrys (Ambrosius), a 6th-century holy man who became famous for his prophecies. It was probably Geoffrey of Monmouth who changed Myrddin's name to Merlin and presented him as the wise, wizardly advisor to Arthur's father, King Uther Pendragon. One of Merlin's seminal acts was to disguise Uther as Duke Gorlois, allowing him to spend the night with the duke's wife, Ygerna, who duly conceived Arthur. Merlin also predicted that Uther's true heir would draw a sword from a stone and acquired the sword Excalibur from a Lady of the Lake. Merlin's own end appears to have come courtesy of this same lady when she trapped the wizard in a cave on Bryn Myrddin (Merlin's Hill), east of Carmarthenshire, where wind-carried groans and clanking chains are part of local lore even today.

The Red Dragon

One of the first mythical beasts in British heraldry, the red dragon (*y ddraig goch*) is a powerful symbol in ancient legends. It was apparently used on the banners of British soldiers on their way to Rome in the 4th century, and was then adopted by Welsh kings in the 5th century to demonstrate their authority after the Roman withdrawal. Cadwaladr, the 7th-century king of Gwynedd, used it for his standard in battle, forever associating the symbol with Wales. In the 14th century, Welsh archers used the red dragon as their emblem, and Owain Glyndŵr used it as a standard in his revolt against the English crown. A century later, Harri Tudur (in English, Henry Tudor) combined the red dragon with the heraldic colours of his Welsh family (the green and white of the house of Tudor), and used it as his standard at the Battle of Bosworth, where he became King Henry VII of England. It was only in 1959 that Henry VII's banner was adopted as the official flag of Wales.

Few of Wales' ancient myths and legends were written down and consequently many were lost. *The Mabinogion* (Tales of Hero's Youth), a translation of two remarkable 14th-century folk-tale compendiums, remains the key source of Welsh legends.

Castles & Other Architecture

Castles are Wales' most famous historical and architectural attraction and the country is covered with them – the 'magnificent badge of our subjection', as 18th-century writer Thomas Pennant put it. They are a living-history statement on Wales' past and a symbol of its complex social heritage. The most impressive castles are those built by Edward I in North Wales. Among them, Caernarfon Castle (p274), built between 1283 and 1330, has retained all of its original strength and beauty. Harlech

Castle (p244) is a great example of a perfectly concentric castle, whereby one line of defence is enclosed by another. Conwy Castle (p281) is considered to be one of the greatest fortresses of medieval Europe, and the medieval city walls are among the most complete in the world.

Apart from castles, Welsh architecture is most commonly associated with the country's industrial heritage and its contemporary, post-millennium transformation. Among the former, Blaenavon's ironworks, quarries and workers' houses received Unesco World Heritage status at the turn of the millennium. The town was joined on the Unesco World Heritage list in 2009 by the Thomas Telford–designed Pontcysyllte Aqueduct (p232) in Llangollen.

For a taste of modern architecture, Richard Rogers' Senedd (p62), the National Assembly debating chamber in Cardiff Bay, is an elegant mix of slate and Welsh oak, while its neighbour, the Wales Millennium Centre (p62), has a striking design of stacked Welsh slate topped with a bronzed-steel shell. Also worth a look in Cardiff is the award-winning, purpose-built facility for the Royal Welsh College of Music & Drama (p75) on the edge of Bute Park.

Visual Arts

Founding Royal Academy member Richard Wilson (1714–1782) celebrated the romantic essence of the ruined castles and craggy peaks of North Wales in his vivid canvasses. When the French Revolution effectively closed Europe to British artists, many followed his lead (most notably JMW Turner) and Wales emerged as a fashionable destination for landscape painters.

Two of the most significant Welsh artists at the turn of the 20th century were Pembrokeshire siblings Gwen John (1876–1939) and Augustus John (1878–1961). Ceri Richards (1903–71), heavily influenced by Matisse, followed a little later. All are well represented at the National Museum Cardiff (p55) and the Glynn Vivian Art Gallery (p130) in Swansea, alongside notable contemporary artists such as Shani Rhys James.

Sir John 'Kyffin' Williams (1918–2006), whose trademark was thickly layered oil on canvas, also found inspiration in the Welsh landscape. His work is collected at the Oriel Ynys Môn (p293) in Llangefni, Anglesey.

Wales' leading international art prize is the Artes Mundi (Arts of the World) award. The prize brings together outstanding artists from around the world who stimulate thinking about the human condition and humanity. Its aim is to give a platform to contemporary artists who are established in their own countries but have received little critical recognition in the UK. The £40,000 award, the UK's biggest arts prize, is awarded on a biannual basis. The shortlisted entrants are displayed at the National Museum Cardiff.

Many heritage sites in Wales are administered by either the National Trust or by Cadw, the division within the National Assembly government charged with the protection, conservation and promotion of the historic environment.

The Welsh Table

Over the past couple of decades, a quiet revolution has been taking place in the better kitchens of Wales. Although Welsh cuisine has traditionally been simple and humble, it has always been blessed by access to some of the UK's best fresh produce, quality seafood and distinctive herds of beef and lamb. With a new generation of young chefs bringing an innovative, modern take to traditional Welsh recipes, the food scene is buzzing.

Welsh Specialities

Historically, Welsh cuisine was based on what could be grown locally and cheaply. Food was functional and needed to satisfy the needs of labourers on the farm or workers down the mine. It was hearty and wholesome but not exactly haute cuisine.

Above Traditional Welsh *cawl*

The most traditional Welsh dish remains *cawl,* the hearty, one-pot soupy stew of bacon, lamb, cabbage, swede and potato. It's one of those

DON'T MISS EXPERIENCES
....

Farmers markets Sniff out local producers at the likes of Cardiff's Riverside Market (p71) for the pick of organic produce and tasty snacks.

Welsh cakes Best straight off the griddle, like those sold at Swansea Market (p134) and Cardiff Market (p76).

Culinary stars Wales now boasts six Michelin-starred eateries; book ahead for world-class fine dining with a Welsh slant.

Full Welsh breakfast The best place to try cockles and laverbread is over breakfast at a traditional Welsh B&B.

warm, cosy dishes that you long for when you're walking in the hills. Equally comforting are faggots, meatballs made from offal and offcuts (usually bits of bacon, pig's liver, heart, belly and, sometimes, testicles), served with mashed potatoes and peas and drowned in gravy.

Another famous favourite is Welsh rarebit, a kind of cheese on toast, generously drizzled with a secret ingredient tasting suspiciously like beer. For breakfast, there's nothing more Welsh than laverbread. It's not actually bread at all, but a surprisingly delicious concoction of boiled seaweed mixed with oatmeal and served with bacon or cockles.

Traditional staples feature prominently in contemporary Welsh cooking. Fancy versions of *cawl*, faggots, rarebit and laverbread abound, and menus showcase Welsh lamb (particularly the strongly flavoured meat originating from the Gower salt marshes) and Welsh black beef. On the coast, look out for *sewin* (wild sea trout), Penclawdd cockles, Porthgain crab and lobster, and Conwy mussels.

Local cheeses also feature prominently, either added to dishes or served on their own. The most famous three are the hard, crumbly Caerphilly, the brie-like Perl Wen and the creamy blue Perl Las. Two notable, award-winning producers are Carmarthenshire's organic cheesery, Caws Cenarth (p151), and the Blaenavon Cheddar Company (p124), where handmade cheeses are matured down the mineshaft of the Big Pit National Coal Museum.

For something sweet, try Welsh cakes, small, scone-like sweets laced with sugar and raisins and cooked on the griddle, or *bara brith*, a traditional heavy fruit loaf served with tea.

Where to Eat

Pubs remain the most convenient and affordable option with most serving food between noon and 2pm, and 5pm and 9pm. They can be hit-and-miss, but mostly you'll get a perfectly reasonable meal. An increasing number of places are championing local produce and bringing the concept of the gastropub to Wales. The trend for talented chefs to abandon their urban stomping grounds, wind down a peg or two and get closer to their ingredients is making waves in rural Wales and could turn your quick pit-stop lunch into a long, lingering affair.

In larger towns and cities you'll find switched-on bistros and restaurants serving anything from decent to superbly inspired food. Cardiff has an excellent range of ethnic restaurants, with an especially good selection of Indian establishments. In rural areas, an increasingly popular extension of the restaurant business is the concept of the restaurant with rooms, whereby fine dining and a cosy bed are generally only a staircase apart. Most of these places combine gourmet food with a small number of lovingly decorated rooms.

For most restaurants you'll need to book ahead, particularly on weekends, and a 10% tip is customary for good service but not obligatory. In

Local Treats
....
Bara brith
....
Cawl
....
Faggots
....
Laverbread
....
Perl Las
....
Sewin
....
Welsh cakes

Welsh cakes

smaller towns, the only food available on a Sunday may be the popular roast dinner served at pubs and hotel restaurants.

There are plenty of cafes in Wales but very few to satisfy serious coffee lovers – although this is slowly changing and there are now some great places scattered about. Most can be relied upon for at least a decent cup of tea and an old-fashioned bacon sandwich, dripping in brown sauce. Practically every eating place, including pubs, offers at least one token vegetarian dish, though don't expect it to always be inspired.

Local Brews & Drams

First Catch Your Peacock (1996) by Bobby Freeman is a classic guide to Welsh food, combining proven recipes with cultural and social history.

A new generation of local microbreweries is busy crafting tasty real ales, lagers and ciders, supplying local bars and selling to specialist stores. Among the names to look out for is Aberdare's Grey Trees Brewery (www.greytrees brewery.com); in 2019 its Afghan pale ale was the runner-up in CAMRA's Champion Beer of Britain award. Tiny Rebel took the top spot in 2015 for Cwtch, its Welsh red ale; try it at the brewery on the industrial outskirts of Newport, or at its city-centre bars in Newport and Cardiff (p73).

The North Wales town of Porthmadog, located on the fringes of Snowdonia National Park, is home to the Purple Moose (p262) brewery, one of Wales' most successful microbreweries, supplying pubs from Anglesey to Harlech. Its Snowdonia Ale and Dark Side of the Moose have both been award winners. Similarly, the Gower Brewery (www.gowerbrewery.com) is well represented in pubs throughout its namesake peninsula.

Welsh whisky is also enjoying a renaissance with the Penderyn Distillery (p108), located in the southern reaches of Brecon Beacons National Park and boasting an impressive visitors' centre. Also worth seeking out is Pembroke Dock's Barti Rum (www.bartirum.wales), named after a Pembrokeshire pirate, which produces an unusual spiced rum flavoured with laver seaweed.

The Natural Environment

Few countries are as densely packed with conservation sites as Wales, and the natural environment here is rigorously protected with more than one-fifth of the country falling within a national park. The craggy peaks, rugged coastlines and patchwork fields have long rebuffed settlement and harbour numerous historic, cultural and economic treasures. Thankfully, the National Assembly has now enshrined sustainable development into the statute books, hopefully paving the way for preservation of the nation's diverse landscapes.

Geology

The country's geology, more than anything else, has helped shape the destiny of Wales. The slate mountains of Snowdonia and the rich deposits of coal in the southern valleys altered the face of Wales, attracting

Above Atlantic grey seal

hordes of workers and fuelling the Industrial Revolution. Jump back 2000 years and the Romans were mining gold from Dolaucothi, while 2000 years before that, copper was being mined from Llandudno's Great Orme.

Since the 17th century, geologists have pondered the mysteries of Wales' rippled rocks, puzzling fossils and ice-moulded valleys. In contrast with Wales' relatively young evolutionary age of just 200 million years, some of the world's oldest rocks lie exposed at Pembrokeshire's St Davids Head.

Two of Unesco's Global Geoparks, protected sites of international geological significance, are found in Wales: Fforest Fawr, in the western half of Brecon Beacons National Park, and GeoMôn, in Anglesey.

Fauna

Atlantic grey seals headline the fascinating coastal wildlife, with their fluffy white pups peppering Pembrokeshire's shores in late September and early October. One of only two semi-resident bottlenose dolphin populations in Europe can also be found in Cardigan Bay.

Twitchers, meanwhile, head for Pembrokeshire's offshore islands, a seabird haven from April to mid-August. Grassholm Island has among the world's largest gannet colonies, with 39,000 pairs nesting there during breeding season (April to September). Colonies of guillemots, razorbills, storm petrels, kittiwakes and puffins crowd the rock faces of Skomer, Middleholm and Skokholm Islands, along with 50% of the world's Manx shearwater population.

In North Wales, numbers of hen harriers and Welsh black grouse are increasing, and otters are re-establishing themselves along the River Teifi and in the border area of northern Powys. Also making a comeback are pine martens and polecats, both of which had, until recently, only survived in isolated pockets of the country. There are plans, too, to reintroduce beavers to Mid-Wales' Dyfi Valley.

Flora

Following years of industrialisation, just 14% of the Welsh countryside remains covered by woodland, characterised mostly by non-native Sitka spruce, a fast-growing crop shirked by most wildlife. In many areas, erosion caused by cultivation and overgrazing has prevented native species from rooting and reseeding, although native ash is thriving on the Gower Peninsula and in the Brecon Beacons. Several types of orchid grow in its shade, together with common dog violets, from March to May.

Away from grazing animals, alpine plants breed in mountainous regions, although hikers and climbers can cause irreparable damage to purple saxifrage and moss campion nestling between the rocks on higher

For an impression of how the oak forests of the Welsh landscape once looked, visit one of the sites managed by Natural Resources Wales, such as the Coed y Brenin Forest Park near Dolgellau.

RED KITE COUNTRY

Doggedly fighting its way back from the verge of extinction, the majestic red kite (*Milvus milvus*) is now a familiar sight in Mid-Wales. This aerobatic bird with its 2m-long wingspan was once common across the UK and was even afforded royal protection in the Middle Ages. However, in the 16th century it was declared a vermin and mercilessly hunted to near extinction.

The red kites partly owe their reprieve to a 100-year-long campaign in the Tywi and Cothi Valleys of Mid-Wales. Today, 1000-plus pairs of red kites navigate the Welsh sky.

If you want to see these magnificent creatures up close, head to one of the feeding stations such as Gigrin Farm (p211), near Rhayader, or Llanddeusant (p108) in Brecon Beacons National Park.

Red kites

slopes. Rare cotton grass sprouts from inland bogs and soggy peat lands in midsummer, among bog pimpernel and thriving myrtle. Meanwhile butterwort, one of Britain's few insectivorous plants, traps insects in wet grassland at Cwm Cadlan near Penderyn, in Brecon Beacons National Park.

Protected Species

Animals once on the endangered list, such as bottlenose dolphins, minke whales and lesser horseshoe bats are no longer officially endangered per se, but it's still estimated that one in six of all species are nevertheless endangered, including plants, fungi and invertebrates such as the jewel-like Snowdon beetle.

A vestige of the last ice age, the Snowdon lily has survived on the mountain's slopes for over 10,000 years, yet warmer climates and overgrazing have drastically reduced its numbers. Also on the critical list are the distinctive shrub Ley's whitebeam, which flowers in late May and early June in the Taff Valley, and the fen orchid, rare throughout Europe, protected in the Kenfig National Nature Reserve near Port Talbot.

New Environmental Challenges

When it comes to environmental issues, Wales is hugely ambitious. The environmental focus is perhaps sharper in Wales because the crucial tourism industry is so closely associated with the country's natural environment. Dogged in this endeavour, the National Assembly received independence from the rest of the UK on environmental legislation.

The 'One Wales: One Planet' manifesto lays down challenges to be achieved by 2025, among them a minimum 80% reduction in carbon-based energy reliance and an electricity supply derived entirely from renewable sources. Bolstering its ambition to eliminate waste

The enthusiasm for sustainable lifestyles in Wales can be traced back to St David himself, who taught his followers the importance of living in harmony with nature. He was a committed vegetarian.

ALTERNATIVE ENERGY

Innocuous though they may seem, land-based wind turbines have become one of the most contentious, divisive issues in rural Wales. Nobody disputes the need for sustainable energy and few object to community-based schemes that bring much-needed income to small towns and villages. However, the visual impact of commercial schemes and their irregular output has sparked protest. Although the focus has turned to offshore wind farms and tidal power as viable alternatives, the battle continues with every new planning application.

More recently, controversy has surrounded the proposal to open a new nuclear power plant on Anglesey. The previous nuclear plant, Wylfa, ceased operation in 2015, but Wylfa Newydd could become one of the first of a new generation of nuclear power stations planned across the UK. Locals are fiercely opposed; however as of November 2020, money seems to be the project's main hindrance: the proposed plant's builders have pulled out.

production by 2050, Wales already recycles and composts more than 45% of its rubbish.

Although agri-environment schemes such as 'Glastir' remunerate farmers who adopt environmentally sensitive practices and incorporate tree-planting programs aimed at dramatically expanding woodland, the comprehensive 2013 State of Nature study warned that wildlife in Wales was at a crisis point with one in 10 species facing extinction. Farming practices were blamed for loss of habitat, as were woodland management policies for not placing enough emphasis on biodiversity. Upland wading birds like curlews and lapwings, and wildflowers, butterflies and woodland plants are, say conservation groups, likely to be most adversely affected.

Critics also maintain that government policies are not always in line with sustainable development indicators. In 2012, test drilling for shale gas was approved, a decision that could have had major implications for the Welsh environment. Campaigners warned of catastrophic consequences if companies were allowed to use fracking (a controversial extraction technique that blasts water, sand and chemicals through rock at extreme pressures) to release gas in the abandoned mines of South Wales. In 2015, the Welsh Assembly imposed a moratorium on the practice and in 2018 announced that they would not support or renew fracking licences for petroleum companies.

Survival Guide

Directory A–Z

Accessible Travel

For many travellers with a disability, Wales is a strange mix of user-friendliness and unfriendliness. It is worth noting the following:

➡ New buildings, such as large new hotels and tourist attractions, are wheelchair-accessible.

➡ Older accommodations have been converted from hard-to-adapt older buildings, meaning disability-friendly accommodation can be at a premium and that travellers with mobility problems may pay more for accommodation than their able-bodied fellows.

➡ Newer buses sometimes have steps that lower for easier access, as do trains. It pays to check before setting out.

➡ Tourist offices, tourist attractions and public buildings like supermarkets reserve parking spaces for people with disabilities near the entrance.

➡ Most tourist offices in Wales are wheelchair accessible, have counter sections at wheelchair height and provide information on accessibility in their particular area.

➡ Many ticket offices and banks are fitted with hearing loops to assist the hearing impaired.

➡ **Cadw** (☑0300 025 6000; www.cadw.gov.wales) allows wheelchair users, the visually impaired and their companions free entry to monuments under its auspices.

➡ **Shopmobility** (☑07541-858162; www.nfsuk.org) is a UK-wide scheme under which wheelchairs and electric scooters are available in some towns at central points for access to shopping areas.

➡ Download Lonely Planet's free Accessible Travel guide from http://lptravel.to/AccessibleTravel.

Useful resources:

➡ Visit Wales (www.visitwales.com/explore/accessible-wales) publishes useful information on accessibility online.

➡ **Disability Rights UK** (☑0330 995 0400; www.disabilityrightsuk.org) publishes *Holidays in the British Isles*, an annually-updated guide to accessible accommodation in the UK and Ireland.

➡ **Disability Wales** (☑029-2088 7325; www.disabilitywales.org) the national association of disability groups in Wales; a good source of information.

Customs Regulations

➡ Goods brought in and out of countries within the EU incur no additional taxes provided duty has been paid somewhere within the EU and the goods are strictly for personal consumption only. Duty-free shopping is available only if you're leaving the EU. After leaving the EU in 2020, changes are expected to these arrangements

➡ Travellers arriving in the UK from other EU countries can bring in up to 800 cigarettes, 400 cigarillos, 200 cigars, 1kg of tobacco, 10L of spirits, 20L of fortified wine, 90L of wine and 110L of beer, provided the goods are for personal use only.

➡ For travellers arriving from outside the EU, the duty-free allowance for adults is a maximum of 200 cigarettes *or* 100 cigarillos *or* 50 cigars *or* 250g of tobacco; 4L of still table wine; 16L of beer; 1L of spirits *or* 2L of fortified/sparkling wine; and £390 worth of all other goods (including gifts and souvenirs). Anything over this limit must be declared to customs officers. People under 17 years do not get the alcohol and tobacco allowances.

➡ For details of restricted goods and quarantine regulations, refer to the HM Revenue & Customs section of www.gov.uk.

Discount Cards

It's worth noting the following handy discount cards or discount opportunities:

Climate

Llandudno

Aberstwyth

Cardiff

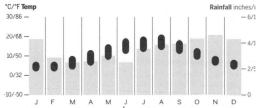

Cadw (www.cadw.gov.wales) Manages many historic monuments, often ancient/ruined ones, country-wide). One-year membership costs £48 for individuals, £74 for couples and £81 for a family (two adults plus all children under 16 years) and gets free entry to all sites.

National Trust (www.national trust.org.uk) Manages many heritage properties such as country estates and gardens, plus areas of countryside, nation-wide). One-year membership costs £63 for individuals, £105 for a couple and £111 for a family (two adults plus up to five children under 18). As well as free entry into NT properties, membership allows free parking at the many trust-owned car parks, particularly those on the Pembrokeshire/Gower coasts.

Membership of one, or both, of the above trusts is well worth considering, especially if you're going to be in Wales a while. Both organisations care for hundreds of spectacular sites and you only need visit five or six with a membership card to see savings. Join by post or phone, or online.

National Union of Students (NUS) cards/16–25 Railcards (www.16-25railcard.co.uk) Discounted entrance to many attractions across Wales.

Senior Coachcard (www.nationalexpress.com/en/offers/coachcards/senior; annual fee £12.50) Travellers aged 60-plus receive 30% off standard National Express bus fares.

Senior Railcard (www.senior-railcard.co.uk; annual fee £30) Get 30% off most rail fares.

Many attractions have lower admission prices for those aged over 60; it's always worth asking even if it's not posted. If you plan to do lots of travelling by bus or train, there are some good-value travel passes too: ask when you board.

Electricity

Type G
230V/50Hz

Health

Visiting Wales doesn't pose any particular health concerns for the international traveller, and no specific vaccinations are required. Tap water is safe to drink in Wales.

Availability & Cost of Health Care

The National Health Service (NHS) provides free treatment for residents across the UK, including Wales.

The European Health Insurance Card (EHIC) will not be valid for the majority of EU residents when visiting Wales as of the beginning of 2021. You should ensure you have appropriate travel insurance before coming to Wales if you want to make use of NHS facilities.

Insurance

However you're travelling, take out a comprehensive travel insurance policy that covers you for medical expenses, luggage theft or loss, and cancellation of (or delays in) your travel arrangements.

Paying for your flight tickets with a credit card often provides limited travel-accident insurance (ie it covers accidental death, loss of limbs or permanent total disablement). However, this should not be relied upon instead of a full travel insurance policy.

Worldwide travel insurance is available at www. lonelyplanet.com/travel -insurance. You can buy, extend and claim online anytime.

Internet Access

Most accommodation providers and indeed cafes, bars, restaurants and tourist attractions now offer free wi-fi internet access to guests. Some trains and coach services also have free wi-fi, although the connectivity is not as good.

Legal Matters

If you are a victim of petty crime, head to the nearest police station to file a crime report; you will need this for your insurance claim. Take some identification with you, such as a passport.

Police have powers to detain anyone suspected of having committed an offence punishable by imprisonment (including drug offences) for up to six hours. They can search you, take photographs and fingerprints, and question you. Not giving your correct name and address is an offence, but you are not obliged to answer any other questions.

After six hours, the police must either formally charge you or let you go. If you are detained and/or arrested, you have the right to inform a lawyer and one other person.

Possession of a small amount of cannabis is an offence punishable by a fine, but possession of a larger amount of cannabis, or any amount of harder drugs, is much more serious, with a sentence of up to 14 years in prison. Police have the right to search anyone they suspect of possessing drugs.

Drivers may not exceed a blood alcohol level of 80mg/100mL (35mg on the breath). Traffic offences (illegal parking, speeding etc) often incur a fine, which you're usually given 30 to 60 days to pay. Speeding incurs a minimum £100 fine and three penalty points if you hold a UK driving licence.

LGBTIQ+ Travellers

In general, Wales is tolerant of homosexuality but the macho image of the rugby-playing Welshmen still prevails in some smaller communities – although the public 'coming out' of Welsh rugby hardman Gareth Thomas has challenged even that bastion of blokedom.

Cardiff has the only significant gay scene and even that is quite small. Wales' biggest LGBT bash is **Pride Cymru** (www.pridecymru.co.uk; ⊙late Aug), held in Cardiff.

For more information try:

Diva (www.divamag.co.uk) British lesbian magazine.

Gay Times (www.gaytimes. co.uk) Longstanding gay magazine.

Pink UK (www.pinkuk.com) UK-wide gay and lesbian resource.

Switchboard (☎0300 330 0630; www.switchboard.lgbt; ⊙10am-11pm) London-based LGBT helpline.

Maps

You can pick up a decent detailed road map, such as the *Philip's Navigator Wales Cymru* or the *AA Road Atlas*

Great Britain and Ireland, at almost any motorway service station you stop at on the way through Wales.

Walkers and cyclists should have a good, detailed map before setting off on any trip.

Most tourist offices and local bookshops stock maps produced by the UK's national mapping agency, the Ordnance Survey (www. ordnancesurvey.co.uk), which cover all its regions, including the useful 1:50,000 Landranger series and extremely detailed 1:25,000 Explorer series. Maps can be ordered online at the OS website or purchased from tourist offices, national park offices and bookshops.

Money

ATMs & Eftpos

Nearly all banks in Wales have ATMs linked to international systems such as Cirrus, Maestro or Visa. However, an increasing number of ATMs, especially those in small shops and at service stations, will charge for withdrawal (£1.50-plus). It's best to seek a regular ATM at a bank that offers free withdrawals.

Credit & Debit Cards

Visa and MasterCard are widely accepted in Wales (American Express and Diners Club less so), although some smaller businesses and B&Bs may prefer payment in cash. If your credit card is lost or stolen, contact the relevant provider.

Currency

The currency in Wales is the pound sterling (£). Wales has the same major banks as elsewhere in the UK. There are 1p, 2p, 5p, 10p, 20p, 50p, £1 and £2 coins and £5, £10, £20 and £50 notes.

Money Changers

Most banks and larger post offices change foreign currency; US dollars and euros are currently easiest to change.

Taxes & Refunds

Value-added tax (VAT) is a 20% sales tax levied on most goods and services and is included in advertised prices. Travellers living outside the UK can claim the tax back by presenting the (unused) goods and a completed VAT 407 form (obtained from many retailers) as they leave the country.

Tipping

There is no obligation to tip in Wales, even if a 'service charge' has been automatically added to your bill (although this is uncommon).

Restaurants, cafes and bars with table service Up to 10% for good service. If you order at the bar or counter, you're not expected to tip.

Taxis It's not common practice to tip unless the driver has gone out of their way to help you.

Opening Hours

Business hours are generally 9am to 5.30pm Monday to Friday. The following hours usually apply:

Banks 9.30am–5pm Monday to Friday, 9.30am–1pm Saturday (main branches)

Post offices 9am–5pm Monday to Friday, 9am–12.30pm Saturday

Shops 9am–5.30pm or 6pm Monday to Saturday, sometimes also 11am–4pm Sunday

Cafes 9am–5pm Monday to Saturday, sometimes 11am–4pm Sunday

Restaurants noon–2pm & 6–10pm, often closed Sunday evenings and all day Monday

Pubs and bars 11am/noon–11pm (10pm during Covid-19)

Late-licence bars, that would normally stay open until 2am or later, were also closing at 10pm during Covid-19.

Some businesses in small country towns still have a weekly early closing day – it's different in each region. From November to Easter many tourist sights and associated businesses close entirely.

Post

The Royal Mail service (www.royalmail.com) is generally very reliable. There's a handy branch finder on www.post-office.co.uk.

Mail sent within the UK can go either 1st or 2nd class. First-class mail is faster (normally next-day delivery) and more expensive (76p for a letter up to 100g) than 2nd-class mail (65p); rates depend on the size/weight of what you're sending.

International services start at £1.45 for a postcard to anywhere in the world.

Public Holidays

If New Year's Day, Christmas Day or Boxing Day falls on a weekend, the following Monday is usually treated as a public holiday instead.

Most businesses and banks close on official public holidays. Most larger attractions stay open for all but Christmas Day, when virtually everything – attractions, shops, banks, offices – closes (although some pubs open at lunchtime). There's usually no public transport on Christmas Day or Boxing Day.

New Year's Day 1 January

Good Friday March/April

Easter Monday March/April

May Day First Monday in May

Spring Bank Holiday Last Monday in May

Summer Bank Holiday Last Monday in August

Christmas Day 25 December

Boxing Day 26 December

Safe Travel

Wales is a pretty safe place, but use your common sense. The country was hit by Covid-19, along with other parts of the UK, with relative seriousness. In this regard, take all precautions that you would in your own country and be respectful of any lasting rules in place as a result of the pandemic.

Never assume that it will be warm and dry, even in summer, especially in mountainous areas. Mist can drop suddenly, leaving you dangerously chilled and disoriented. Never venture onto the heights without checking the Met Office (www.metoffice.gov.uk) mountain forecast and without being sensibly equipped with good waterproof gear, a compass and a map. Always ensure someone knows where you're heading.

Telephone

The UK uses the GSM 900/1800 mobile phone network, which is the standard for most of the world but isn't compatible with the GSM 1900 network commonly used in the Americas. Most modern mobile devices can function on both networks; check before you leave home.

The EU had largely dispensed with roaming charges for member states, although just as the charges stopped, Brexit happened. From January 1 2021, even EU travellers can no longer be guaranteed to avoid roaming charges, although key operators O2, Vodafone, Three and EE have said they have no plans to implement charges. For other travellers, international roaming rates can be prohibitively high. You may find it cheaper to get a UK number. This is easily done: buy a SIM card (from £6 to £10, including credit) and stick it in your phone. Your phone may be 'locked' by your home network, however, in which case you'll have to either get it unlocked or purchase a pay-as-you-go phone along with your SIM card (around £50).

To dial a UK number from overseas, dial your country's international access code, then ⏩44 (the country code for the UK), then the local number *without* the initial 0. To call internationally from the UK, dial ⏩00 and then the country code.

Toilets

UK toilets are of the plain, sit-down variety. Public toilets can be a hit-and-miss affair, but are almost always equipped with toilet paper and usually soap. In urban areas, public toilets are generally clean but there may be a small fee (20p to 50p) to use them. Toilets at motorway service stations are regularly maintained and free.

For a more luxurious loo off-the-beaten-track, you can always stop at a local cafe or pub to use the facilities. Etiquette says you should at least buy a drink while you're there.

Tourist Information

Where tourist offices are still open (there's normally one per region), you'll find them excellent. They're usually well-stocked with free maps and brochures and often also sell books on Welsh culture and local sights, maps and even local art. Staff speak English, often Welsh, and sometimes have a basic grasp of other major European languages. The national parks also have their own tourist offices.

Visit Wales (⏩0333 006 3001; www.visitwales.co.uk; ⏰9am-5pm Mon-Fri) The department for tourism within the Welsh Assembly. Its contact centre is your first port of call for information on visiting Wales.

Visit Britain (www.visitbritain.com) Run by the UK's official tourist board and has in-depth coverage of the entire island.

Visas

➡ If you're a citizen of one of the European Economic Area nations or of Switzerland, you don't need a visa to enter Britain for stays of up to six months.

➡ Citizens of Australia, Canada, New Zealand, Malaysia, Japan, Israel, Brazil, Argentina, the USA and several other countries do not require a visa to stay for up to six months as a tourist, but are prohibited from working.

➡ Visitors from most other countries will need to apply for a Standard Visitor visa (£95).

➡ Visa regulations are always subject to change, especially during the period of Britain's departure from the EU, so check with your local British embassy, high commission or consulate before leaving home. For more information, visit www.gov.uk.

Volunteering

For volunteering opportunities within Wales, refer to the websites of Volunteering Wales (www.volunteering-wales.net) and the Wales Council for Voluntary Action (www.wcva.org.uk).

Women Travellers

Women travellers shouldn't encounter any particular problems in Wales, though it's worth keeping your wits about you and taking the usual precautions for your safety in Cardiff, Swansea, Newport and Merthyr Tydfil, especially at night.

Work

➡ As the UK and therefore Wales left the EU in January 2021, the ease with which residents from the European Economic Area can work in the UK has been affected, with most now likely to need to apply for a visa in advance, if they want employment. The UK visa-checking resource (www.gov.uk/check-uk-visa) clarifies what those coming to the UK to visit, study or work will need.

➡ Commonwealth citizens with a UK-born parent may have a 'right of abode' (including to work) in the UK.

➡ Commonwealth citizens with a UK-born grandparent could qualify for a UK Ancestry visa, allowing them to work full-time for up to five years in the UK.

➡ The Tier 5 (Youth Mobility Scheme) visa allows citizens of certain countries (Australia, Canada, Japan, Monaco, New Zealand, Hong Kong, South Korea, Taiwan), as well as British nationals (overseas), and British overseas citizens, aged 18 to 30 and with £1890 in savings, to work for up to two years in the UK.

Transport

GETTING THERE & AWAY

Aside from ferries from Ireland and a small range of international flights to Cardiff airport, visitors to Wales arrive by train, car or coach from neighbouring England. Flights, cars and tours can be booked online at lonelyplanet.com/bookings.

Entering the Country

The UK strictly controls its borders and will not hesitate to deny entry to travellers lacking the correct visas or other appropriate documentation.

Air

Although Cardiff has an international airport, most overseas visitors fly into London. Five international airports service the UK's capital but Heathrow is by far the biggest, serving most of the world's major airlines. It is also the closest to Wales. Other options include Manchester, which is handy for North Wales, and Bristol and Birmingham, both close to the Welsh border.

Many of the airlines directly servicing Wales are budget operators, which means you might get a good deal if you're coming from one of the handful of destinations that they fly from.

Airports & Airlines

Cardiff Airport (☑01446-711111; www.cardiff-airport.com; Rhoose, CF62 3BD) is 12 miles southwest of Cardiff, past Barry. Aside from summer-only services and charters, these are the airlines flying into Cardiff and the destinations they serve:

Eastern Airways (www.easternairways.com) Belfast, Anglesey, Teeside

KLM (www.klm.com) Amsterdam

Loganair (www.loganair.co.uk) Edinburgh, Glasgow

Ryanair (www.ryanair.com) Málaga, Faro

TUI Airways (www.tui.co.uk) Operates March to October only; Alicante, Gran Canaria, Lanzarote, Málaga, Tenerife, Rhodes, Antalya, Paphos, Dubrovnik, Corfu

Vueling (www.vueling.com) Alicante, Málaga, Palma de Mallorca

Land

The entire eastern edge of Wales shares a land border with England and aside from the odd 'Welcome to...' sign, you'd barely notice you were crossing between the two.

Bus

Buses between England and Wales are generally slower and cheaper but not any more flexible than trains.

Local buses zip across the border from Gloucester, Hereford and Ludlow. Routes do not always increase with distance. Less popular routes often cost more.

National Express (☑0871 781 8181; www.nationalexpress.com) operates services to Wales' major cities and tourist towns from some major English cities.

Megabus (☑0900 1600 900; http://uk.megabus.com) offers one-way fares from London to Cardiff (via Newport) from as little as £14.

Car & Motorcycle

From London, getting to Wales is a simple matter of heading west on the M4 motorway (which passes Heathrow airport) and sitting on it until you cross the impressive bridge over the River Severn.

The toll that was the bane of many a traveller for years has now been abolished, so entrance into Wales is free (hooray!) There's a second bridge a little further north on the M48 leading to Chepstow.

Train

Trains in the UK are privatised and expensive, and the fare structure is bewildering. In general, the cheapest tickets are those bought well in advance. Timetables and fares are available from www.thetrainline.com.

All rail connections from Continental Europe to Wales pass through the Channel Tunnel to London. The high-speed passenger service **Eurostar** (☎0343 218 6186; www.eurostar.com) links London St Pancras International with Paris or Brussels. Book early to secure the best fares. Cheaper rail connections can be had by crossing the Channel by ferry.

Fast train services run to Cardiff from London Paddington, Bristol and Birmingham. Direct trains from London Paddington also stop in Newport and Swansea (change in Swansea for points further west). Trains from London Euston head directly all the way to Llandudno Junction, Bangor and Holyhead in the far north.

From Manchester, there are trains to Llandudno Junction and Abergavenny. Frequent services shunt across the border between Gloucester and Chepstow.

For trains within, originating in and predominantly journeying in Wales, Transport for Wales (www.tfwrail. wales) is the main operator.

Main lines heading through the centre of Wales include the following:

Cambrian Line (www.thecambrianline.co.uk) Birmingham to Aberystwyth through Shrewsbury, Welshpool, Newtown and Machynlleth.

Heart of Wales Line (www. heart-of-wales.co.uk) A scenic route through the heart of Mid-Wales from Shrewsbury to Swansea via Knighton, Llandrindod Wells, Llanwrtyd Wells, Llandovery and Llandeilo.

Sea

Ferries from Ireland operate from Dublin to Holyhead (1¾ to 3½ hours) and from Rosslare to Pembroke Dock (four hours) and Fishguard (3½ hours). The main ferry companies are **Irish Ferries** (☎08717 300 400; www. irishferries.com) and **Stena Line** (☎0344 770 7070; www. stenaline.co.uk).

Fares vary considerably depending on the season, day, time and length of stay. Typical one-way fares start at £32 for a foot passenger and £118 for a car and driver. Bikes can be transported for £10. Keep an eye out for promotional fares that can reduce the cost considerably.

Ferries to England

There's a wide array of ferry services to England from Continental Europe, including:

➡ Netherlands to Hull and Newcastle

➡ Belgium to Hull

➡ Spain to Portsmouth

➡ France to Dover, Newhaven, Portsmouth, Poole and Plymouth.

For details, check out www. directferries.co.uk or www. ferrybooker.com. All of these port towns are linked into the train network, allowing you to get to Wales with two or three connecting trains.

GETTING AROUND

When people talk of the north–south divide in Wales, it's not just about language –

part of it is physical. The barrier created by the Cambrian Mountains, Brecon Beacons and Snowdonia means that it's often quicker to duck in and out of England to get between north and south Wales. The same is true by train: there's a network of lines that slowly zigzag their way through the country but the faster train connections head through Bristol and Birmingham. That said, both roads and rail lines are extremely scenic. In Wales that old adage about the journey outweighing the destination is aptly demonstrated.

Wales is one of those places where Brits come to get back to nature, so it's extremely well set up for walkers and cyclists. With a flexible schedule and a modicum of patience, it's quite possible to explore the country by public transport. However, it's worth considering hiring a car for at least part of your trip, especially if you're on a limited time schedule and you're not averse to losing yourself in the sort of narrow country lanes that require pulling over when a car approaches from the other direction.

Buses are often the cheapest way to get around but you'll generally get to places quicker by train. For information on services, your best bet is the local tourist office where you'll be able to pick up maps and timetables. For up-to-date information and a journey planner covering public transport throughout Wales, visit **Traveline Cymru** (☎0800 464 0000; www.traveline.cymru).

MAJOR BUS CONNECTIONS

FROM	TO	COST (£)	TIME (HR)
London	Cardiff	from 14	3½
London	Swansea	from 16	5
London	Tenby	from 22	6¾
London	Aberystwyth	from 7	7

MAJOR TRAIN CONNECTIONS

FROM	TO	COST (£)	TIME (HR)
London Paddington	Cardiff	from 27	2
London Paddington	Swansea	from 37	3
London Euston	Bangor	72	3¾
London Euston	Holyhead	75	4
Gloucester	Chepstow	11	½
Birmingham	Machynlleth	25	2¼
Birmingham	Aberystwyth	33	3
Manchester	Abergavenny	65	2½

Air

The only useful internal flights are the Eastern Airways (www.easternairways.com) services between Cardiff and Anglesey.

Bicycle

Rural Wales is an amazing place for cycling: traffic on back roads is limited, and there are loads of multi-use trails and long-distance cycling routes as part of Sustrans' National Cycle Network (www.sustrans.org.uk). Wales' terrain, though, veering between the hilly and the mountainous for the most part, and without too much in the way of perfect cycling weather, make long-distance pedalling best suited to experienced tourers.

In the larger towns and cities, there are few bike lanes and the usual problems with inconsiderate motorists. Bike theft can also be a major problem in urban areas.

Bikes can be taken on most trains, although there is limited space for them. On most services it's worth making a reservation for your bike at least 24 hours in advance; there is a small charge for this on some routes.

Transport for Wales (https://tfwrail.wales), which operates most rail services in Wales, publishes a guide called *Cycling by Train*,

downloadable from the website.

Hire

Most sizeable or tourist towns in Wales have at least one shop where you can hire bikes from £14 to £28 per day for a tourer and £25 to £50 for a full-suspension mountain bike. Many hire outfits will require you to make a deposit of about £50 for a tourer and up to £100 for a top-of-the-line mean machine.

Boat

Aside from tourist boats to the offshore islands, there are no ferry services between ports in Wales.

Bus

Wales' bus services are operated by dozens of private companies but you'll find centralised information on routes and timetables with **Traveline Cymru** (☏0800 464 0000; www.traveline.cymru). Buses are mostly reasonably priced and efficient,

---

RAIL & SAIL

A little-known option for travelling between the UK and Ireland, SailRail is an absolute bargain. The combined train and ferry service connects all UK and Irish train stations, and by comparison to airlines' restrictive fare rules, it's incredibly flexible. You can make changes to your booking, get a partial refund for some types of unused tickets and you can even rock up to a train station and buy your ticket on the day. And the best bit? Tickets cost from just £33 one way, children aged five to 15 pay half-price and under fives go free (but must have a reservation for the ferry). It's worth checking the main rail routes before booking to avoid unnecessary connections.

Check the following websites for details:

➜ Transport for Wales (https://tfwrail.wales/ticket-types/sailrail)

➜ Irish Ferries (www.irishferries.com/uk-en/special-offers-from-britain-to-ireland/rail-sail)

➜ Stena Lina (www.stenaline.co.uk/ferries-to-ireland/rail-sail)

TRAVEL PASSES

If you're planning a whirlwind tour of Wales by public transport, you might like to consider an Explore Wales pass (https://tfwrail.wales; adult/child £99/49.50). It allows free travel in Wales and adjacent areas of England on all rail routes and many bus routes. The pass allows unlimited bus travel plus four days of train travel within an eight-day period. Cheaper passes (£69/34.50) are available if you're only wanting to visit South Wales or North and Mid-Wales. Passes can be bought at most staffed train stations and rail-accredited travel agencies in Wales.

although services are limited or non-existent in rural areas and even the better-served destinations can still have much reduced weekend services (many routes don't run at all on Sundays). Generally you'll need to hail the bus with an outstretched arm and pay the driver on board. Some buses, particularly in the cities, don't give change, so it pays to carry coins.

Coaches are mainly run by **National Express** (☎0871 781 8181; www.nationalexpress. com), and for these you'll need to book and pay in advance.

Long-distance bus services are thin on the ground. Following are the principal cross-regional routes, most of which operate daily:

T1C Cardiff, Swansea, Carmarthen, Aberaeron, Aberystwyth

T2 Aberystwyth, Machynlleth, Dolgellau, Caernarfon, Bangor

T3 Wrexham, Llangollen, Bala, Dolgellau, Barmouth

T4 Cardiff, Merthyr Tydfil, Brecon, Llandrindod Wells, Newtown

T5 Haverfordwest, Fishguard, Cardigan, New Quay, Aberaeron, Aberystwyth

Bus Passes

Apart from the combined bus-and-rail Explore Wales passes, there are lots of regional and local one-day and one-week passes, but many are only worthwhile if you're planning to do a lot of trav-elling. You can usually buy tickets from the bus driver.

Southeast Wales Network Rider For travel on First Cymru bus routes across Cardiff and Southeast Wales (including Monmouthshire and the South Wales Valleys). Seven-day tickets adult/child £27/18.

Red Rover Valid for one day on buses 1 to 99 in Gwynedd and the Isle of Anglesey in northwest Wales (adult/child £6.80/3.40). You can buy these tickets from the driver; for full details ask at a tourist office.

If you are planning to travel throughout the UK, National Express has a variety of passes and discount cards, including options for senior travellers. More information is available at www.national-express.com.

Car & Motorcycle

If you want to see the more remote regions of Wales or to cram in as much as possible in a short time, travelling by car or motorcycle is the easiest way to go.

Getting around North or South Wales is easy, but elsewhere roads are considerably slower, especially in the mountains and through Mid-Wales. To get from the northeast to the southeast, it's quickest to go via England. Rural roads are often single-track affairs with passing places only at intervals, and they can be treacherous in winter. In built-up areas be sure to check the parking restrictions as traffic wardens and wheel clampers can be merciless.

Wales can be a dream for motorcyclists, with quiet, good-quality, winding roads and beautiful scenery. Just make sure your wet-weather gear is up to scratch.

If you're bringing your own vehicle from abroad, make sure you check that your insurance will cover you in the UK; third-party insurance is a minimum requirement. If you're renting a car, check the fine print – policies can vary widely and the cheapest hire rates often include a hefty excess (for which you are liable in the event of an accident).

Automobile Associations

The main motoring organisations – such as the **Automobile Association** (AA; ☎0800 887 766, 0344 209 0754; www.theaa.com), the **Environmental Transport Association** (ETA; ☎0333 000 1234; www.eta.co.uk) and the **Royal Automobile Club** (RAC; ☎0330 159 1111; www.rac.co.uk) – provide services such as 24-hour breakdown assistance, maps and touring information. Others, such as the **Auto-Cycle Union** (☎01788-566400; www.acu.org.uk) and **British Motorcyclists Federation** (☎01162-795112; www.bmf.co.uk), are more like clubs.

Hire

Hire cars can be expensive in the UK but you'll usually get a better rate by booking online in advance. To hire a car, drivers must usually be between 25 and 65 years of age – outside these limits, special conditions or insurance requirements may apply. You will also need a credit card to make an advance booking and act as a deposit.

For a compact car, expect to pay in the region of £130 a week (including insurance etc). Most cars are manual;

automatic cars are available but they're generally more expensive to hire. If you need a baby chair or booster seat, specify this at the time of booking.

Hire-car companies include the following:

Alamo (☑0800 028 2390; www.alamo.co.uk)

Avis (☑0808 284 0014; www.avis.co.uk)

Budget (☑0808 284 4444; www.budget.co.uk)

Europcar (☑0871 384 9900; www.europcar.co.uk)

Hertz (☑in Cardiff 029-2022 4548, in London 0207-365 4199; www.hertz.co.uk)

Road Rules

A copy of the Highway Code can be bought in most bookshops or read online at www.gov.uk/highway-code.

The most basic rules:

➡ Drive on the left, overtake to the right.

➡ When entering a roundabout, give way to the right.

➡ Safety belts must be worn by the driver and all passengers.

➡ Motorcyclists and their passengers must wear helmets.

➡ The legal alcohol limit is 80mg of alcohol per 100ml of blood or 35mg on the breath.

➡ It is illegal to use a mobile phone while driving a car unless you have a hands-free kit installed.

➡ On a single-track lane where two vehicles are oncoming, etiquette dictates that the vehicle arriving at a passing place first waits there (not always adhered to!).

Taxi

You'll usually find a taxi rank outside the train station in bigger towns. In smaller places, the best place to find the local taxi phone number is in the local pub.

Train

Like in the rest of the UK, the Welsh rail network has been privatised. **National Rail** (☑03457 48 49 50; www.nationalrail.co.uk) provides centralised timetable information for all train operators in the UK, and allows you to buy tickets online using a credit card. You can also buy tickets online through www.thetrainline.com.

In Wales, most of the services are operated by Transport for Wales (https://tfwrail.wales), although the **Great Western Railway** (☑0345 700 0125; www.gwr.com) operates the London Paddington–Newport–Cardiff–Swansea route and **Avanti West Coast Trains** (☑0345 528 0253; www.avantiwestcoast.co.uk) has the London Euston–Chester–Llandudno Junction–Bangor–Holyhead route.

Classes & Costs

There are two classes of rail travel in the UK: 1st class and 'standard' class. First class costs about 50% more than standard and simply isn't worth the extra money. Also, during the Covid-19

Train Routes

0   50 km
0   25 miles

Liverpool Bay

Holyhead Bay
Holyhead
Colwyn Bay
Prestatyn
Llandudno Junction
Rhyl
Dee Estuary
Llanfair PG
Conwy
Abergele
Flint
Bangor
Queensferry
Caernarfon Bay
Betws-y-Coed
Brymbo
Wrexham
Porthmadog
Blaenau Ffestiniog
Rhosllanerchrugog
Criccieth
Ruabon
Pwllheli
Llanfair
Harlech
ENGLAND
Dyffryn Ardudwy
Barmouth
Llanfair
Fairbourne
Caereinion
Welshpool
Tywyn
Montgomery
Aberdovey
Machynlleth
Carno
Cardigan Bay
Newtown
Aberystwyth
Devil's Bridge
Knighton
Llandrindod Wells
WALES
Cilmery
Llanwrtyd Wells
Fishguard Harbour
Llandovery
Carmarthen
Llandeilo
Merthyr
Tydfil
Abergavenny
Haverfordwest
Narberth
St Clears
Glyn Neath
Rhymney
Pontypool
Milford Haven
Saundersfoot
Pontarddulais
Blackwood
Usk
Pembroke Dock
Burry Port
Hengoed
Cwmbran
Caerleon
Chepstow
Tenby
Llanelli
Neath
Pembroke
Swansea
Trealaw
Porth
Newport
Caldicot
Port Talbot
Llantrisant
Caerphilly
St Mellons
Bridgend
St Fagans
CARDIFF
Llandaff
Bristol Channel
Barry

pandemic, First Class had largely been temporarily suspended to make social distancing easier.

You can roll up to a station and buy a standard single (one-way) or return ticket, but this is often the most expensive way to go. Each train company sets its own fares and has its own discounts, and passengers can only use tickets on services operated by the company that issued the ticket.

You might find that the same journey will have a different fare depending on whether you buy it at the station, over the phone or online. The fare system is so bizarre that in some cases two singles are cheaper than a return ticket, and even a one-way journey can be cheaper if you split it into two (ie if you're going from A to C, it can be cheaper to buy a single from A to B, and another single from B to C; go

figure). You can check your options at www.splityourticket.co.uk.

The least expensive fares have advance-purchase and minimum-stay requirements, as well as limited availability. Children under five years travel free; those aged between five and 15 pay half-price for most tickets. When travelling with children, it is almost always worth buying a Family & Friends Railcard (www.familyandfriends-rail-card.co.uk).

Main fare classifications:

→ **Advance** Has limited availability so must be booked well in advance; can only be used on the specific trains booked.

→ **Anytime** Buy any time, travel any time.

→ **Off-peak** Buy any time, travel outside peak hours.

Railcards

Railcards are valid for one year and entitle the holder to discounts of up to 30% on most rail (and some ferry) fares in the UK. You can buy a railcard at most train stations or at www.railcard.co.uk, but it must be delivered to a UK address and takes several days to arrive. Railcards are accepted by all train companies.

→ **16–25 Railcard** (£30; www.16-25railcard.co.uk) For those aged 16 to 25 years, or a full-time UK student of any age.

→ **Two Together Railcard** (£30; www.twotogether -railcard.co.uk) For two people travelling together, aged 16 or over.

→ **Disabled Persons Railcard** (£20; www. disabledpersons-railcard. co.uk) Applies to its holder and one person accompanying them.

→ **Family & Friends Railcard** (£30; www.familyandfriends -railcard.co.uk) Allows discounts for up to four adults travelling together (only one needs to hold a card and you'll need one child in tow), and a 60% discount on children's fares.

→ **Senior Railcard** (£30; www.senior-railcard.co.uk) For anyone aged 60 or over.

Train Passes

BritRail passes (available only to non-Brits and bought overseas) are not cost effec-tive for a holiday in Wales. More useful are the passes offered by the main train operator, Transport for Wales (https://tfwrail.wales) which include the following:

→ **Explore Wales Pass** All Transport for Wales trains, valid for any four days of travel within an eight-day period (adult/child £99/45).

→ **Explore North Wales and Mid-Wales/ Explore South Wales** All Transport for Wales services within either of these two regions, with the same criteria as the Explore Wales pass (adult/child £69/34.50).

→ **Explore West Wales** All Transport for Wales services from Carmarthen to southwest Wales (day pass adult/child £13.50/6.70). Other day passes include the Ffestiniog Round Robin (£44/22) and Heart of Wales Circular (£41/20.50).

Language

You can get by almost anywhere in Wales these days without speaking Welsh. Nevertheless, anyone who's serious about getting to grips with Welsh culture will find it fun trying to speak basic Welsh.

The Welsh language belongs to the Celtic branch of the Indo-European language family. It's closely related to Breton and Cornish, and more distantly to Irish, Scottish and Manx. It's estimated there are over 700,000 Welsh speakers in Wales.

Pronunciation

All letters in Welsh are pronounced and the stress is usually on the second-last syllable. Letters are pronounced as in English, except for those listed below. If you read our coloured pronunciation guides as if they were English, you will be understood.

Note that vowels can be long or short. Those marked with a circumflex (eg ê) are long; those with a grave accent (eg è) short.

a	short as in 'map'; long as in 'farm'
e	short as in 'pen'; long as in 'there'
i	short as in 'bit'; long as in 'sleep'
o	short as in 'box'; long as in 'bore'
u	as i (short and long)
w	short as the 'oo' in 'book'; long as the 'oo' in 'spook'
y	as i (short or long); sometimes as the 'a' in 'about', especially in one-syllable words such as y, yr, fy, dy and yn

WANT MORE?

For in-depth language information and handy phrases, check out Lonely Planet's *British Language & Culture*. You'll find it at **shop.lonelyplanet.com**, or you can buy Lonely Planet's iPhone phrasebooks at the Apple App Store.

In words of one syllable, vowels followed by two consonants are short – eg *corff* (body). If a one-syllable word ends in *p, t, c, m* or *ng*, the vowel is short – eg *llong* (ship). If it ends in *b, d, g, f, dd, ff, th, ch* or *s*, the vowel is long – eg *bad* (boat) – as is any vowel at the end of a one-syllable word, eg *pla* (plague). In words of more than one syllable, all unstressed vowels are short, eg *caria-don* (lovers). Stressed vowels can be long or short and in general follow the rules for one-syllable words. Welsh also has several vowel sound combinations:

ae/ai/au	as the 'y' in 'my'
aw	as the 'ow' in 'cow'
ei/eu/ey	as the 'ay' in 'day'
ew	as a short 'e' followed by 'oo'
iw/uw/yw	as the 'ew' in 'few'
oe/oi	as 'oy' in 'boy'
ow	as the 'ow' in 'tow'
wy	as 'uey' (as in 'chop suey') or as the 'wi' in 'wing' (especially after g)

The combinations *ch, dd, ff, ng, ll, ph, rh* and *th* count as single consonants.

c	always as 'k'
ch	as the 'ch' in the Scottish *loch*
dd	as the 'th' in 'this'
ff	as the 'f' in 'fork'
g	always as the 'g' in 'garden'
ng	as the 'ng' in 'sing'
ll	as 'hl' (put the tongue in the position for 'l' and breathe out)
ph	as 'f'
r	rolled
rh	pronounced as 'hr'
s	always as in 'so'
si	as the 'sh' in 'shop'
th	always as the 'th' in 'thin'

BASICS

Hello.
Sut mae.   sit mai

Good morning.
Bore da.   *bo·re* dah

Good afternoon.
Prynhawn da.   *pruhn·*hown dah

Good evening.
Noswaith dda.   *nos·*waith thah

Good night.
Nos da.   nohs dah

See you (later).
Wela i chi (wedyn).   *we·*lah ee khee (*we·*din)

Goodbye.
Hwyl fawr.   hueyl vowr

Please.
Os gwelwch in dda.   os *gwe·*lookh uhn thah

Thank you (very much).
Diolch (in fawr iawn).   dee·*olkh* (uhn vowr yown)

You're welcome.
Croeso.   kroy·soh

Excuse me.
Esgusodwch fi.   es·gi·so·dookh vee

Sorry./Forgive me.
Mae'n ddrwg gyda fi.   main throog *guh·*da vee

Don't mention it.
Peidiwch â sôn.   *pay·*dyookh ah sohn

May I?
Ga i?   gah ee

Do you mind?
Oes ots gyda chi?   oys ots *gi·*da khee

How are you?
Sut ydych chi?   sit *uh·*deekh khee

(Very) well.
(Da) iawn.   (dah) yown

What's your name?
Beth yw eich enw chi?   beth yu uhkh e·noo khee

My name is ...
Fy enw i yw ...   vuh e·noo ee yu ...

Where are you from?
O ble ydych chi'n dod?   oh ble *uh·*deekh kheen dohd

I'm from ...
Dw i'n dod o ...   doo een dohd oh ...

I don't understand.
Dw i ddim in deall.   doo ee thim uhn *deh·*ahl

How do you say ...?
Sut mae dweud ...?   sit mai dwayd ...

What's this called in Welsh?
Beth yw hwn yn Gymraeg?   beth yu hoon uhn *guhm·*raig

I don't know.
Wn i ddim.   oon ee dhim

Yes & No

How you say 'yes' and 'no' in Welsh depends on the verb used in the question. So, rather than simply 'yes', you might answer 'I do' *(Ydw)* or 'It is' *(Ydy).* Here are just a few examples:

Yes./No.	*Ie./Nage.*	yeh/*nah·*geh

(general use when the question doesn't start with a verb)

I do./I am.	*Ydw.*	uh·*doo*
I don't./ I'm not.	*Nac ydw.*	nak uh·*doo*
It is.	*Ydy.*	uh·*dee*
It isn't.	*Nac ydy.*	nak uh·*dee*
There is.	*Oes.*	oys
There isn't.	*Nac oes.*	nak oys

EATING & DRINKING

Are you serving food?
Ydych chi'n gweini bwyd?   uh·deekh kheen *gway·*nee bweed

A table for ..., please.
Bwrdd i ... os gwelwch yn dda.   boordh ee ... os *gwe·*lookh uhn thah

Can I see the menu, please?
Ga i weld y fwydlen, os gwelwch yn dda?   gah ee weld uh *voo·*eed·len os *gwe·*lookh uhn thah

What's the special of the day?
Beth yw pryd arbennig y dydd?   beth yu preed ar·*be·*nig uh deeth

Can I have ...?
Ga i ...?   gah ee ...

The bill, please.
Y bil, os gwelwch yn dda.   uh bil os *gwe·*lookh uhn thah

Cheers!
Iechyd Da!   ye·khid dah

I'd like a (half) pint of ...	*Ga i (hanner o) beint o ...*	gah ee (ha·ner oh) baynt oh ...
bitter	*chwerw*	khwe·roo
cider	*seidr*	say·duhr
lager	*lager*	lah·guhr

TIME, DATES & NUMBERS

minute	*munud*	mi·nid
hour	*awr*	owr
week	*wythnos*	oo·ith·nos
month	*mis*	mees
today	*heddiw*	hedh·yoo
tomorrow	*yfory*	uh·voh·ree

PLACE NAMES

Welsh place names are often based on words that describe a landmark or a feature of the countryside.

bach	bahkh	small
bro	broh	vale
bryn	brin	hill
caer	kair	fort
capel	ka·pl	chapel
carreg	kar·eg	stone
clwn	kloon	meadow
coed	koyd	wood/forest
cwm	koom	valley
dinas	dee·nas	hill fortress
eglwys	eglueys	church
fach	vahkh	small
fawr	vowr	big
ffordd	forth	road
glan	glahn	shore
glyn	glin	valley
isa	issa	lower
llan	hlan	church/enclosure
llyn	hlin	lake
maes	mais	field
mawr	mowr	big
mynydd	muhneeth	mountain
nant	nahnt	valley/stream
ogof	o·gov	cave
pen	pen	head/top/end
plas	plahs	hall/mansion
pont	pont	bridge
rhos	hros	moor/marsh
twr	toor	tower
tŷ	tee	house
uchaf	ikhav	upper
ynys	uh·nis	island/holm

Monday	Dydd Llun	deeth hleen
Tuesday	Dydd Mawrth	deeth mowrrth
Wednesday	Dydd Mercher	deeth merr·kherr
Thursday	Dydd Iau	deeth yigh
Friday	Dydd Gwener	deeth gwe·ner
Saturday	Dydd Sadwrn	deeth sa·doorn
Sunday	Dydd Sul	deeth seel

January	Ionawr	yo·nowr
February	Chwefror	khwev·rohr
March	Mawrth	mowrth
April	Ebrill	ehb·rihl
May	Mai	mai
June	Mehefin	me·he·vin
July	Gorffennaf	gor·fe·nahv
August	Awst	owst
September	Medi	me·dee
October	Hydref	huhd·rev
November	Tachwedd	tahkh·weth
December	Rhagfyr	hrag·vir

0	dim	dim
1	un	een
2	dau (m)	dy
	dwy (f)	duey
3	tri (m)	tree
	tair (f)	tair
4	pedwar (m)	ped·wahr
	pedair (f)	ped·air
5	pump	pimp
6	chwech	khwekh
7	saith	saith
8	wyth	ueyth
9	naw	now
10	deg	dehg

GLOSSARY

AONB – Area of Outstanding Natural Beauty
aber – confluence of water bodies; river mouth
ap – prefix in a Welsh name meaning 'son of' (Welsh)

bridleway – path that can be used by walkers, horse riders and cyclists
byway – secondary or side road

Cadw – Welsh historic monuments agency (Welsh)
castell – castle (Welsh)
coasteering – making your way around the coastline by rock climbing, gully scrambling, caving, wave riding and cliff jumping
Cool Cymru – rise of Welsh bands during the mid- to late 1990s
cromlech – burial chamber (Welsh)
Cymraeg – Welsh language (Welsh)
Cymru – Wales (Welsh)

dolmen – chambered tomb

eisteddfod – literally a gathering or session; festival in which competitions are held in music, poetry, drama and the fine arts; plural eisteddfodau (Welsh)

Gymraeg – Welsh language (Welsh)

hiraeth – sense of longing for the green, green grass of home (Welsh)

Landsker Line – boundary between Welsh-speaking and English-speaking areas in south-west Wales

Mabinogion – key source of Welsh folk legends
menhir – standing stone
merthyr – martyr (Welsh)
mynydd – mountain (Welsh)

National Assembly – National (Welsh) Assembly; devolved regional government of Wales, in power since 1999
newydd – new (Welsh)
NT – National Trust

ogham – ancient Celtic script
oriel – gallery (Welsh)
OS – Ordnance Survey

Plaid Cymru – Party of Wales; originally Plaid Cenedlaethol Cymru (Welsh Nationalist Party)

RSPB – Royal Society for the Protection of Birds

S4C – Sianel Pedwar Cymru; national Welsh-language TV broadcaster
SSSI – Site of Special Scientific Interest
Sustrans – sustainable transport charity encouraging people to walk, cycle and use public transport

towpath – path running beside a river or canal
tre – town (Welsh)

urdd – youth (Welsh)

way – long-distance trail

y, yr – the, of the (Welsh)
YHA – Youth Hostel Association

Behind the Scenes

SEND US YOUR FEEDBACK

We love to hear from travelers – your comments keep us on our toes and help make our books better. Our well-traveled team reads every word on what you loved or loathed about this book. Although we cannot reply individually to your submissions, we always guarantee that your feedback goes straight to the appropriate authors, in time for the next edition. Each person who sends us information is thanked in the next edition – the most useful submissions are rewarded with a selection of digital PDF chapters.

Visit **lonelyplanet.com/contact** to submit your updates and suggestions or to ask for help. Our award-winning website also features inspirational travel stories, news and discussions.

Note: We may edit, reproduce and incorporate your comments in Lonely Planet products such as guidebooks, websites and digital products, so let us know if you don't want your comments reproduced or your name acknowledged. For a copy of our privacy policy visit lonelyplanet.com/legal.

OUR READERS

Many thanks to the travelers who used the last edition and wrote to us with helpful hints, useful advice and interesting anecdotes: William Chant, Roger Evans, David Griffiths, Mike Hall, Kathy Hanley, Martin Lee, Andrew Moncrieff, Meirion Powell, Matthew Williams, Rod Wilson

WRITER THANKS

Kerry Walker

Wales is my adopted home and I am deeply indebted to many of its wonderful locals and tourism professionals for making this guide what it is. A special *diolch* goes to Pat Edgar (Visit Pembrokeshire) and Paula Ellis for their insights and assistance. Big thanks also to my partner (and fellow author) Luke for his support and shared love of Wales, and my beautiful baby daughter, Eira ('Snow'), for helping me to see the country through fresh new eyes.

Peter Dragicevich

I flew to Wales to commence on-the-road research for this book in early March 2020, just as the shadow of COVID-19 was starting to spread around the globe. Two weeks later, with borders slamming shut and the airlines in disarray, my trusty long-term travel agent managed to get me on a flight home to New Zealand. My thanks and thoughts are with David Inglis, and all the wonderful travel professionals who have lost their jobs due to this pandemic.

Anna Kaminski

I'd like to thank Sandie for entrusting me with my favourite part of Wales and everyone else who's helped me along the way. In particular: Mike and Jane in Penmaenmawr, Dolgun Uchaf owners in Dolgellau, Ceri and James in Conwy, Alys and John in Caernarfon, the Caerwylan Hotel staff in Criccieth, the Go Below! folks, Bryn Eltyd Eco Guest House in Blaenau Ffestiniog, Joe Brown staff for trekking advice in Llanberis, and Jan Morris for the memorable meeting in Llanystumdwy.

Luke Waterson

From castellated Chepstow in the Southeast to ruggedly countrified Corris on the cusp of Snowdonia, a wonderfully array of individuals stepped up to help me this edition: much appreciated, given this got researched amidst a global pandemic! Thanks especially to Gemma Simmons and Jane Cook (Cardiff), Angharad and Carey Hill (Swansea) and the guys at the George Borrow Hotel in Ponterwyd: lifesavers and cold beer providers! A big *diolch* to the other writers too: not least my traveller-truelove Kerry.

ACKNOWLEDGEMENTS

Climate map data adapted from Peel MC, Finlayson BL & McMahon TA (2007) 'Updated World Map of the Köppen-Geiger Climate Classification', *Hydrology and Earth System Sciences*, 11, 1633–44.

Cover photograph: Snowdon Mountain Railway, Mount Snowdon; Rixpix/Getty Images ©

THIS BOOK

This 7th edition of Lonely Planet's *Wales* guidebook was researched and written by Kerry Walker, Peter Dragicevich, Anna Kaminski and Luke Waterson. This guidebook was produced by the following:

Senior Product Editor Sandie Kestell

Product Editor Joel Cotterell

Book Designer Gwen Cotter

Assisting Editors Andrew Bain, Nigel Chin, Andrea Dobbin, Sasha Drew, Carly Hall, Victoria Harrison, Trent Holden, Kellie Langdon, Kate Morgan, Gabrielle Stefanos, Brana Vladisavljevic

Cartographer Mark Griffiths

Cover Researcher Fergal Condon

Thanks to Karen Henderson, Genna Patterson, James Smart

Index

Map Legend

Sights
- Beach
- Bird Sanctuary
- Buddhist
- Castle/Palace
- Christian
- Confucian
- Hindu
- Islamic
- Jain
- Jewish
- Monument
- Museum/Gallery/Historic Building
- Ruin
- Shinto
- Sikh
- Taoist
- Winery/Vineyard
- Zoo/Wildlife Sanctuary
- Other Sight

Activities, Courses & Tours
- Bodysurfing
- Diving
- Canoeing/Kayaking
- Course/Tour
- Sento Hot Baths/Onsen
- Skiing
- Snorkelling
- Surfing
- Swimming/Pool
- Walking
- Windsurfing
- Other Activity

Sleeping
- Sleeping
- Camping
- Hut/Shelter

Eating
- Eating

Drinking & Nightlife
- Drinking & Nightlife
- Cafe

Entertainment
- Entertainment

Shopping
- Shopping

Information
- Bank
- Embassy/Consulate
- Hospital/Medical
- Internet
- Police
- Post Office
- Telephone
- Toilet
- Tourist Information
- Other Information

Geographic
- Beach
- Gate
- Hut/Shelter
- Lighthouse
- Lookout
- Mountain/Volcano
- Oasis
- Park
- Pass
- Picnic Area
- Waterfall

Population
- Capital (National)
- Capital (State/Province)
- City/Large Town
- Town/Village

Transport
- Airport
- Border crossing
- Bus
- Cable car/Funicular
- Cycling
- Ferry
- Metro station
- Monorail
- Parking
- Petrol station
- S-Bahn/Subway station
- Taxi
- T-bane/Tunnelbana station
- Train station/Railway
- Tram
- U-Bahn/Underground station
- Other Transport

Routes
- Tollway
- Freeway
- Primary
- Secondary
- Tertiary
- Lane
- Unsealed road
- Road under construction
- Plaza/Mall
- Steps
- Tunnel
- Pedestrian overpass
- Walking Tour
- Walking Tour detour
- Path/Walking Trail

Boundaries
- International
- State/Province
- Disputed
- Regional/Suburb
- Marine Park
- Cliff
- Wall

Hydrography
- River, Creek
- Intermittent River
- Canal
- Water
- Dry/Salt/Intermittent Lake
- Reef

Areas
- Airport/Runway
- Beach/Desert
- Cemetery (Christian)
- Cemetery (Other)
- Glacier
- Mudflat
- Park/Forest
- Sight (Building)
- Sportsground
- Swamp/Mangrove

Note: Not all symbols displayed above appear on the maps in this book

OUR STORY

A beat-up old car, a few dollars in the pocket and a sense of adventure. In 1972 that's all Tony and Maureen Wheeler needed for the trip of a lifetime – across Europe and Asia overland to Australia. It took several months, and at the end – broke but inspired – they sat at their kitchen table writing and stapling together their first travel guide, *Across Asia on the Cheap*. Within a week they'd sold 1500 copies. Lonely Planet was born.

Today, Lonely Planet has offices in the US, Ireland and China, with a network of over 2000 contributors in every corner of the globe. We share Tony's belief that 'a great guidebook should do three things: inform, educate and amuse'.

OUR WRITERS

Kerry Walker

Brecon Beacons & Southeast Wales, St Davids & Pembrokeshire Kerry is an award-winning travel writer, photographer and Lonely Planet author, specialising in Central and Southern Europe. Based in Wales, she has authored/co-authored more than a dozen Lonely Planet titles. An adventure addict, she loves mountains, cold places and true wilderness.

Kerry also wrote the Plan Your Trip chapters.

Peter Dragicevich

Cardiff, Mid-Wales After a successful career in niche newspaper and magazine publishing, both in his native New Zealand and in Australia, Peter finally gave into Kiwi wanderlust, giving up staff jobs to chase his diverse roots around much of Europe. Over the last 15 years he's written over 100 books for Lonely Planet on an oddly disparate collection of countries, all of which he's come to love. He once again calls Auckland, New Zealand his home – although his current nomadic existence means he's often elsewhere.

Peter also contributed to the Understand chapters.

Anna Kaminski

Snowdonia & the Llŷn, Anglesey & the North Coast Originally from the Soviet Union, Anna grew up in Cambridge, UK. She graduated from the University of Warwick with a degree in Comparative American Studies, a background in the history, culture and literature of the Americas and the Caribbean, and an enduring love of Latin America. Her restless wanderings led her to settle briefly in Oaxaca and Bangkok and her flirtation with criminal law saw her volunteering as a lawyer's assistant in the courts, ghettos and prisons of Kingson, Jamaica. Anna has contributed to almost 30 Lonely Planet titles. When not on the road, Anna calls London home.

Luke Waterson

Cardiff; Brecon Beacons & Southeast Wales; Swansea, Gower & Carmarthenshire; Mid-Wales Luke became addicted at an early age to exploring out-of-the-way places, and writing about them. He's now authored/contributed to more than 60 Lonely Planet titles, mainly on far-flung destinations. Luke lives in Wales with fellow travel writer Kerry Walker, writes novels and co-writes offbeat Wales travel site Undiscovered Wales (https://undiscovered-wales.co.uk).

Luke also wrote the Survival Guide and contributed to the Understand chapters.

Published by Lonely Planet Global Limited
CRN 554153
7th edition – August 2021
ISBN 978 1 78701 367 4
© Lonely Planet 2021   Photographs © as indicated 2021
10 9 8 7 6 5 4 3
Printed in Singapore

Although the authors and Lonely Planet have taken all reasonable care in preparing this book, we make no warranty about the accuracy or completeness of its content and, to the maximum extent permitted, disclaim all liability arising from its use.